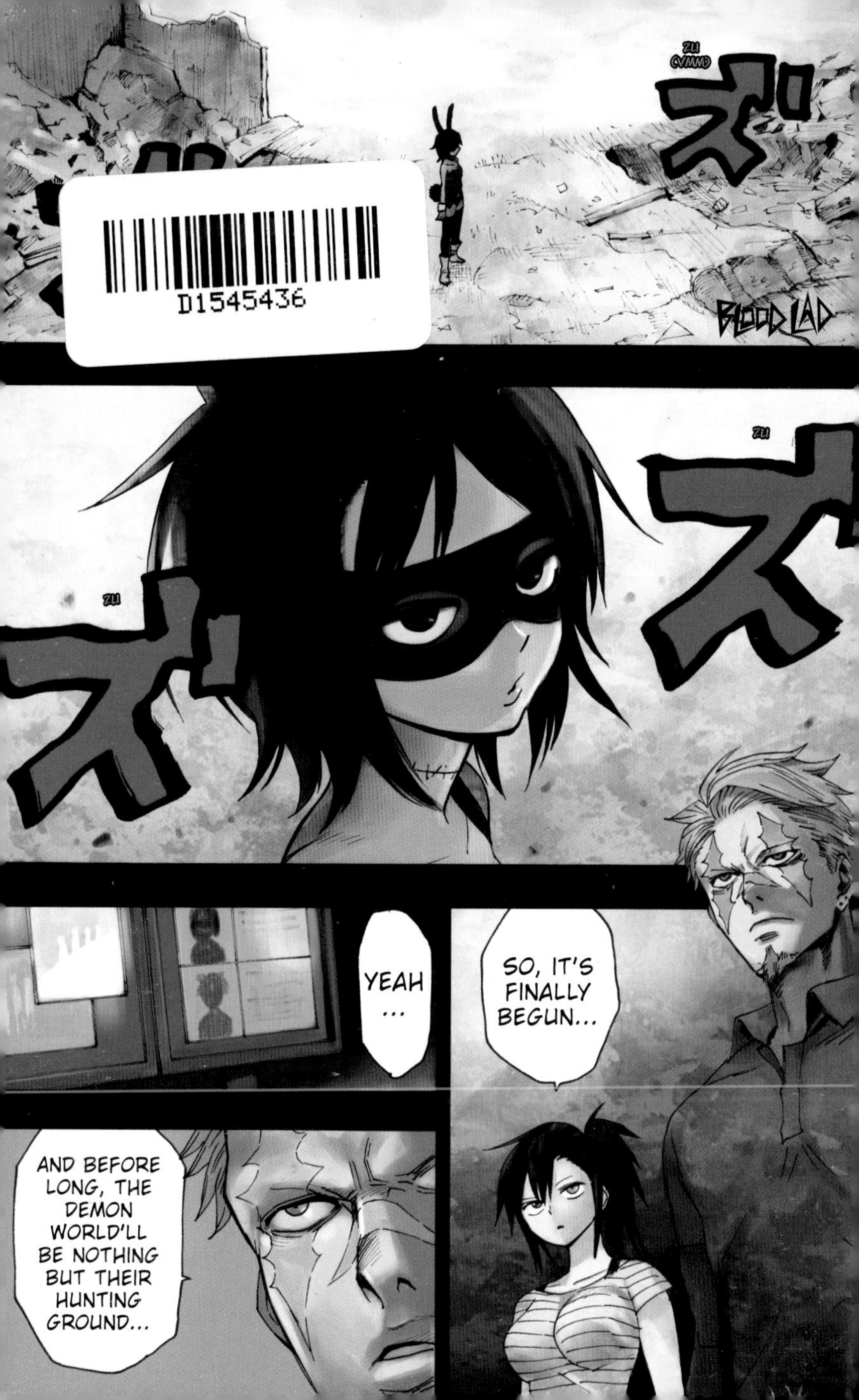
ZU (VMMM)
BLOOD LAD
ZU
ZU
SO, IT'S FINALLY BEGUN...
YEAH ...
AND BEFORE LONG, THE DEMON WORLD'LL BE NOTHING BUT THEIR HUNTING GROUND...

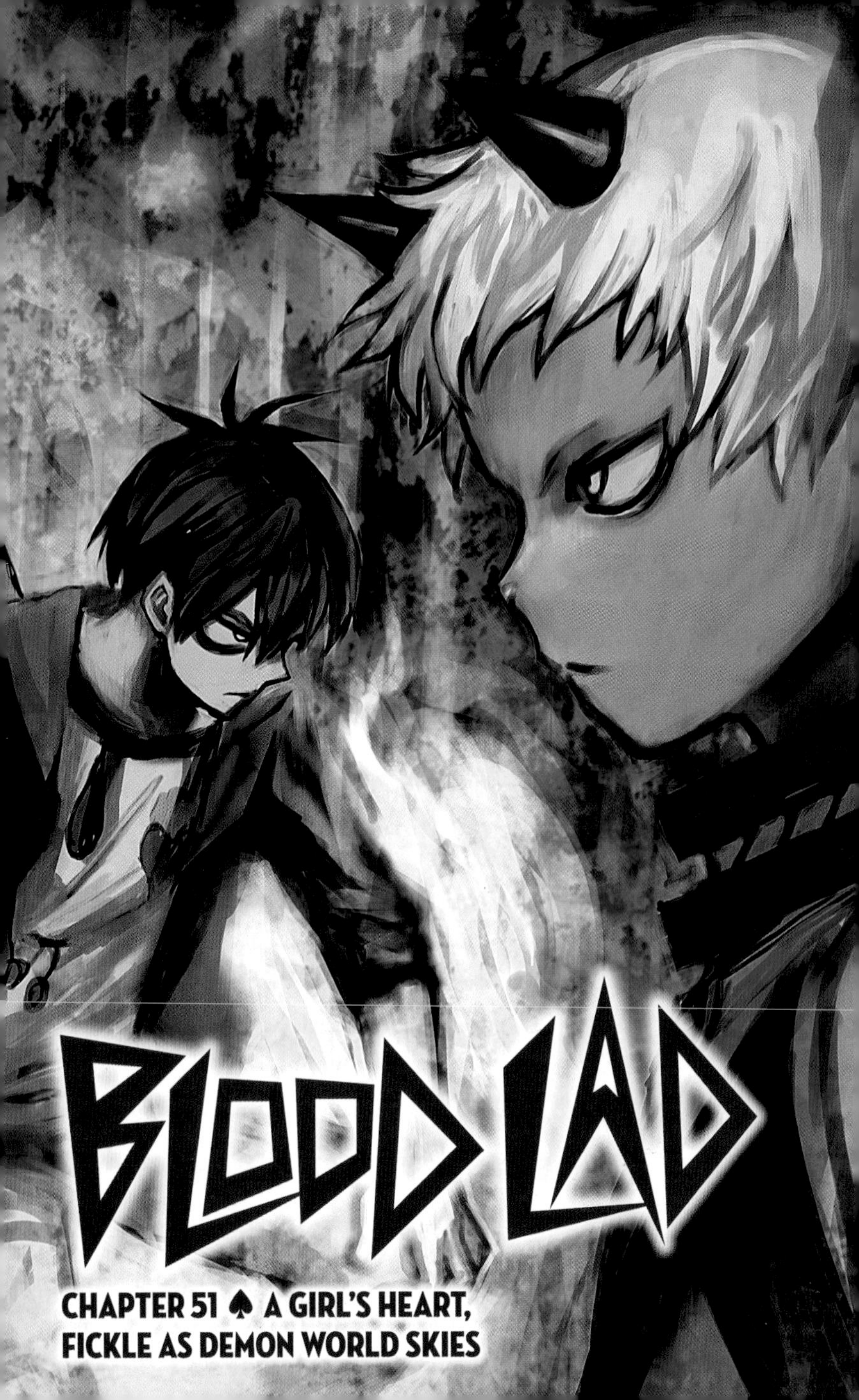
BLOOD LAD
CHAPTER 51 ♠ A GIRL'S HEART, FICKLE AS DEMON WORLD SKIES

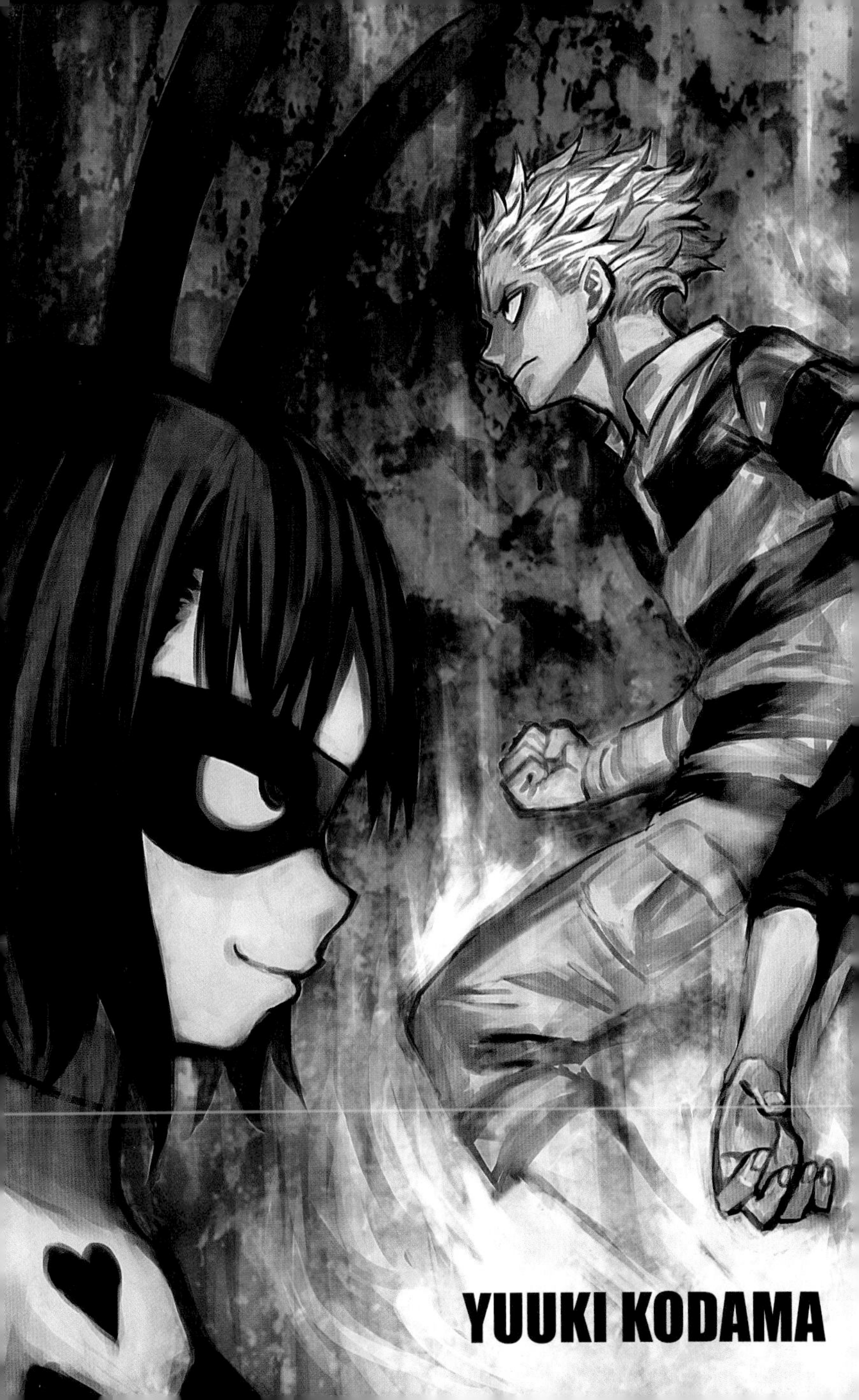
YUUKI KODAMA

CONTENTS

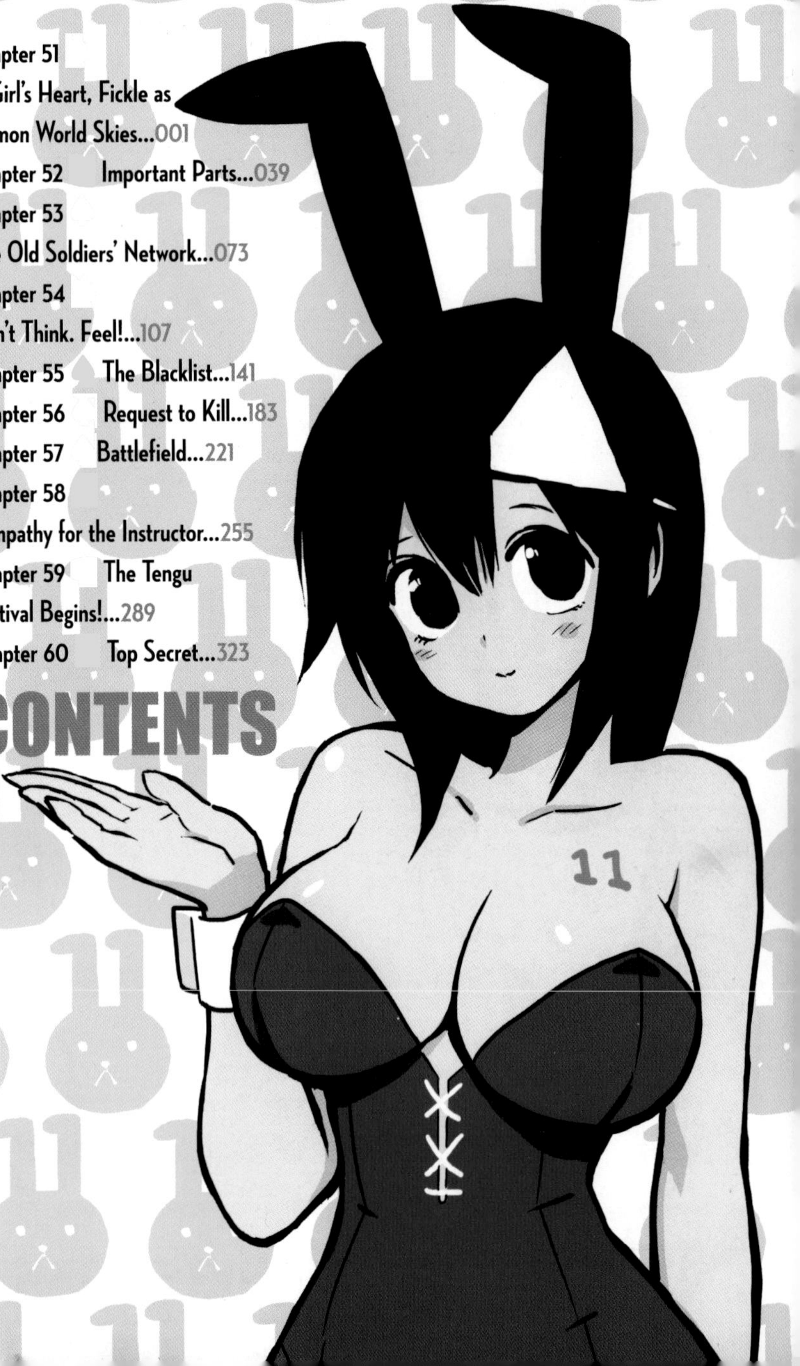
11

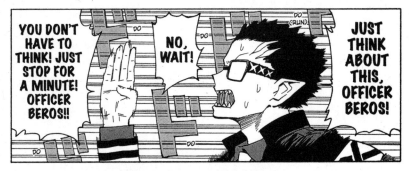

JUST THINK ABOUT THIS, OFFICER BEROS!
DO (RUN)
NO, WAIT!
YOU DON'T HAVE TO THINK! JUST STOP FOR A MINUTE! OFFICER BEROS!!
I SAID YOU DON'T HAVE TO COME ALONG...
...CAPTAIN!!
I'M GONNA FIND THAT BASS...
...MYSELF!
OKAY, I GET IT, BUT WHERE EXACTLY ARE YOU GOING!?
JUST GOIN' WITH THE FLOW!
WILL YOU JUST STOP!?
Ring ring ...
ring ring ...
CRAP...

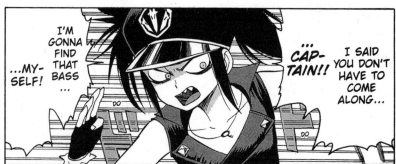

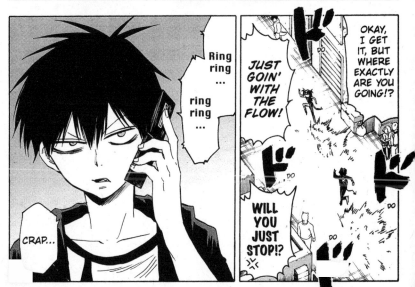

BOX: ANIMAL SNACKS

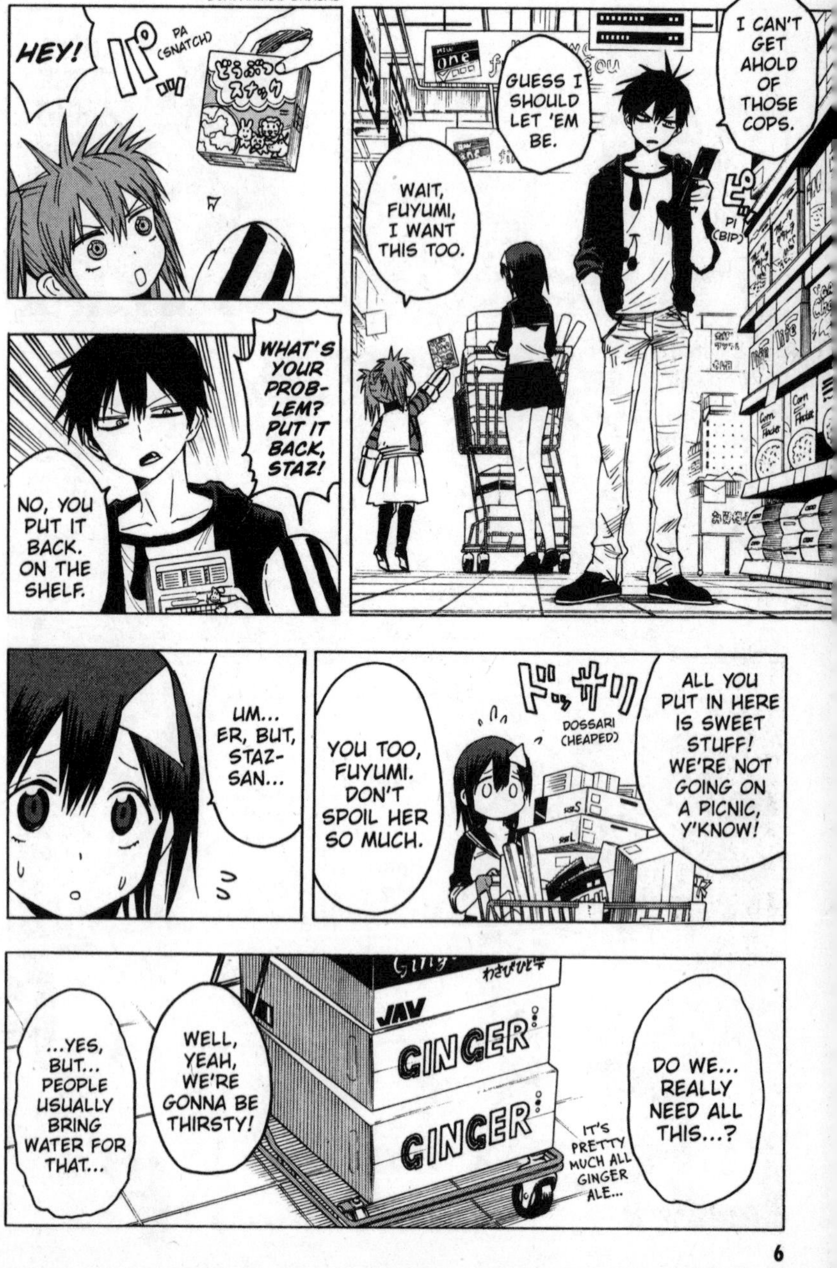
I CAN'T GET AHOLD OF THOSE COPS.
GUESS I SHOULD LET 'EM BE.
PI (BIP)
WAIT, FUYUMI, I WANT THIS TOO.
PA (SNATCH)
HEY!
WHAT'S YOUR PROB-LEM? PUT IT BACK, STAZ!
NO, YOU PUT IT BACK. ON THE SHELF.
ALL YOU PUT IN HERE IS SWEET STUFF! WE'RE NOT GOING ON A PICNIC, Y'KNOW!
DOSSARI (HEAPED)
YOU TOO, FUYUMI. DON'T SPOIL HER SO MUCH.
UM... ER, BUT, STAZ-SAN...
DO WE... REALLY NEED ALL THIS...?
IT'S PRETTY MUCH ALL GINGER ALE...
WELL, YEAH, WE'RE GONNA BE THIRSTY!
...YES, BUT... PEOPLE USUALLY BRING WATER FOR THAT...

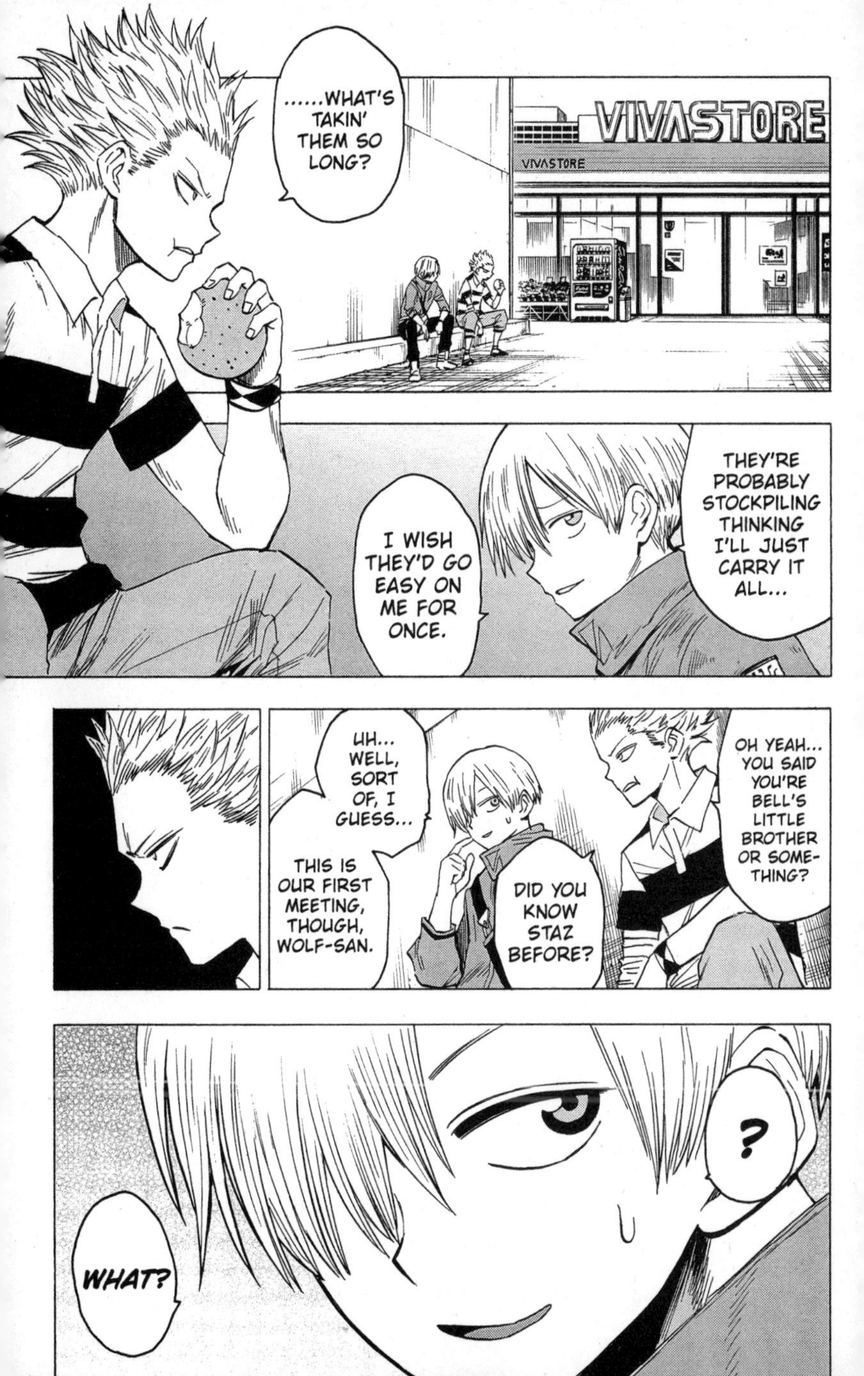
VIVASTORE
VIVASTORE
......WHAT'S TAKIN' THEM SO LONG?
THEY'RE PROBABLY STOCKPILING THINKING I'LL JUST CARRY IT ALL...
I WISH THEY'D GO EASY ON ME FOR ONCE.
OH YEAH... YOU SAID YOU'RE BELL'S LITTLE BROTHER OR SOME-THING?
UH... WELL, SORT OF, I GUESS...
THIS IS OUR FIRST MEETING, THOUGH, WOLF-SAN.
DID YOU KNOW STAZ BEFORE?
?
WHAT?

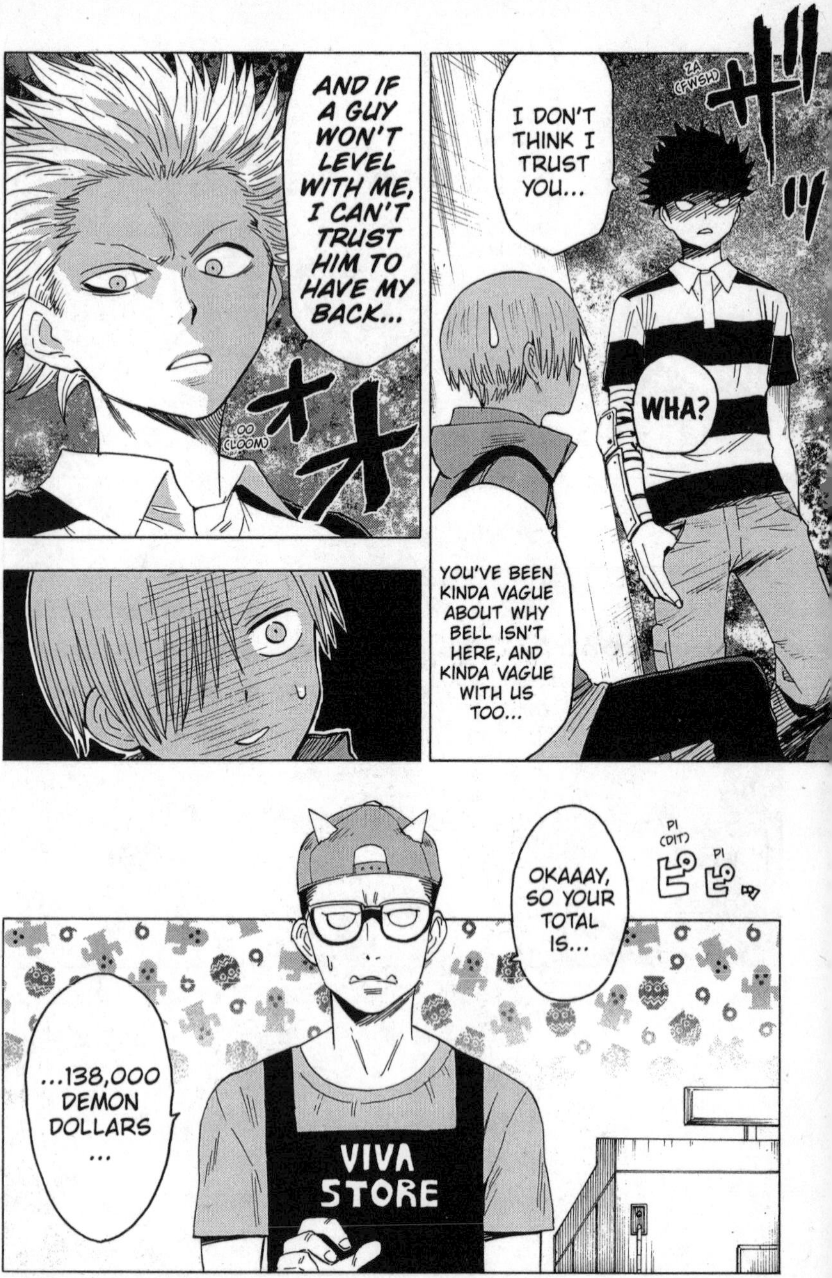
ZA (FWSH)
I DON'T THINK I TRUST YOU...
WHA?
YOU'VE BEEN KINDA VAGUE ABOUT WHY BELL ISN'T HERE, AND KINDA VAGUE WITH US TOO...
AND IF A GUY WON'T LEVEL WITH ME, I CAN'T TRUST HIM TO HAVE MY BACK...
OO (LOOM)
PI (DIT) PI
OKAAAY, SO YOUR TOTAL IS...
...138,000 DEMON DOLLARS...
VIVA STORE

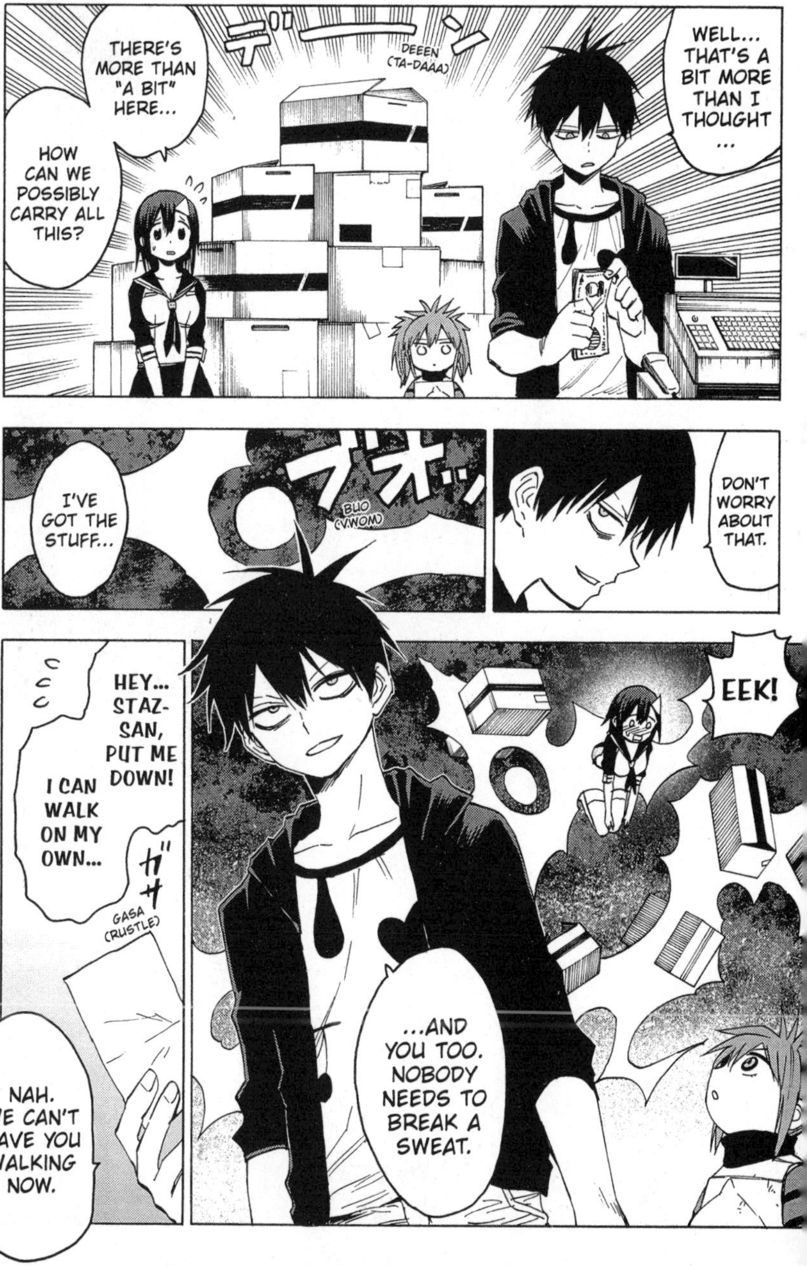
WELL... THAT'S A BIT MORE THAN I THOUGHT...
デーーーン
DEEEN (TA-DAAA)
THERE'S MORE THAN "A BIT" HERE...
HOW CAN WE POSSIBLY CARRY ALL THIS?
DON'T WORRY ABOUT THAT.
I'VE GOT THE STUFF...
ブオッ
BUO (V.WOM)
EEK!
...AND YOU TOO. NOBODY NEEDS TO BREAK A SWEAT.
HEY... STAZ-SAN, PUT ME DOWN!
I CAN WALK ON MY OWN...
ガサ
GASA (RUSTLE)
NAH. WE CAN'T HAVE YOU WALKING NOW.

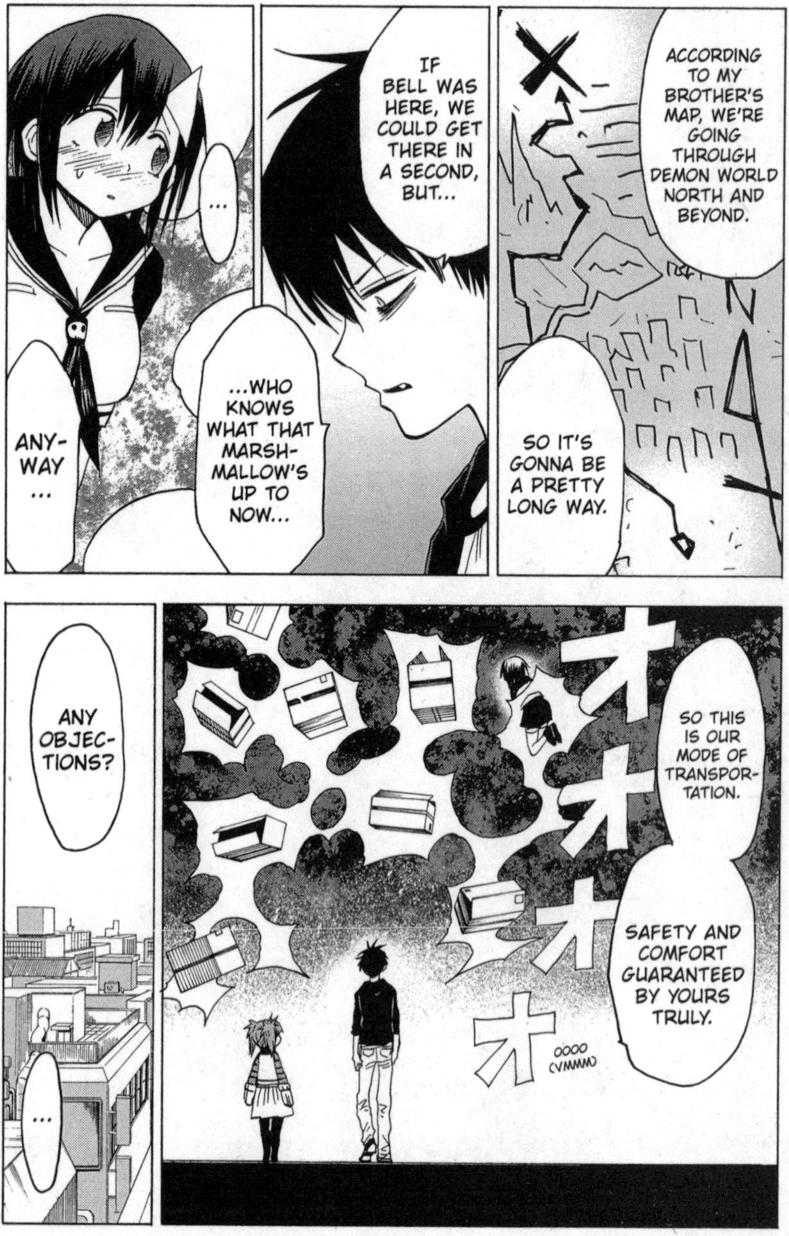
ACCORDING TO MY BROTHER'S MAP, WE'RE GOING THROUGH DEMON WORLD NORTH AND BEYOND.
SO IT'S GONNA BE A PRETTY LONG WAY.
IF BELL WAS HERE, WE COULD GET THERE IN A SECOND, BUT...
...WHO KNOWS WHAT THAT MARSH-MALLOW'S UP TO NOW...
...
ANY-WAY ...
SO THIS IS OUR MODE OF TRANSPOR-TATION.
SAFETY AND COMFORT GUARANTEED BY YOURS TRULY.
OOOO (VMMM)
ANY OBJEC-TIONS?
...

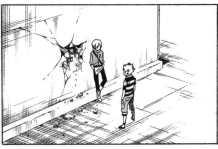

ARE YOU ...
...SERI-OUSLY FOR REAL...?
DON'T TELL ANY-ONE.
WOLF...I TOLD YOU BECAUSE I TRUST YOU.
AND IT'S NOT LIKE YOU HAVE NOTHING TO DO WITH IT.
SO CAN YOU TRUST ME A LITTLE MORE NOW?
......
YEAH... SORRY, I WAS WRONG...
NO, IT'S FINE...... DON'T WORRY ABOUT IT...
HEY, KIDS.
DADDY'S HOME.

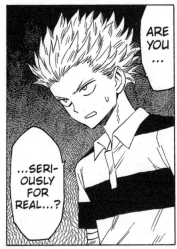

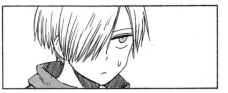

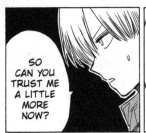

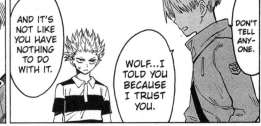

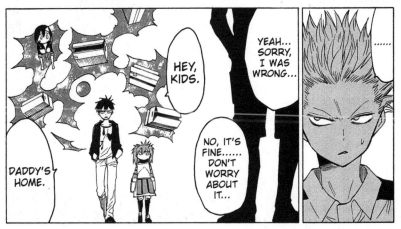

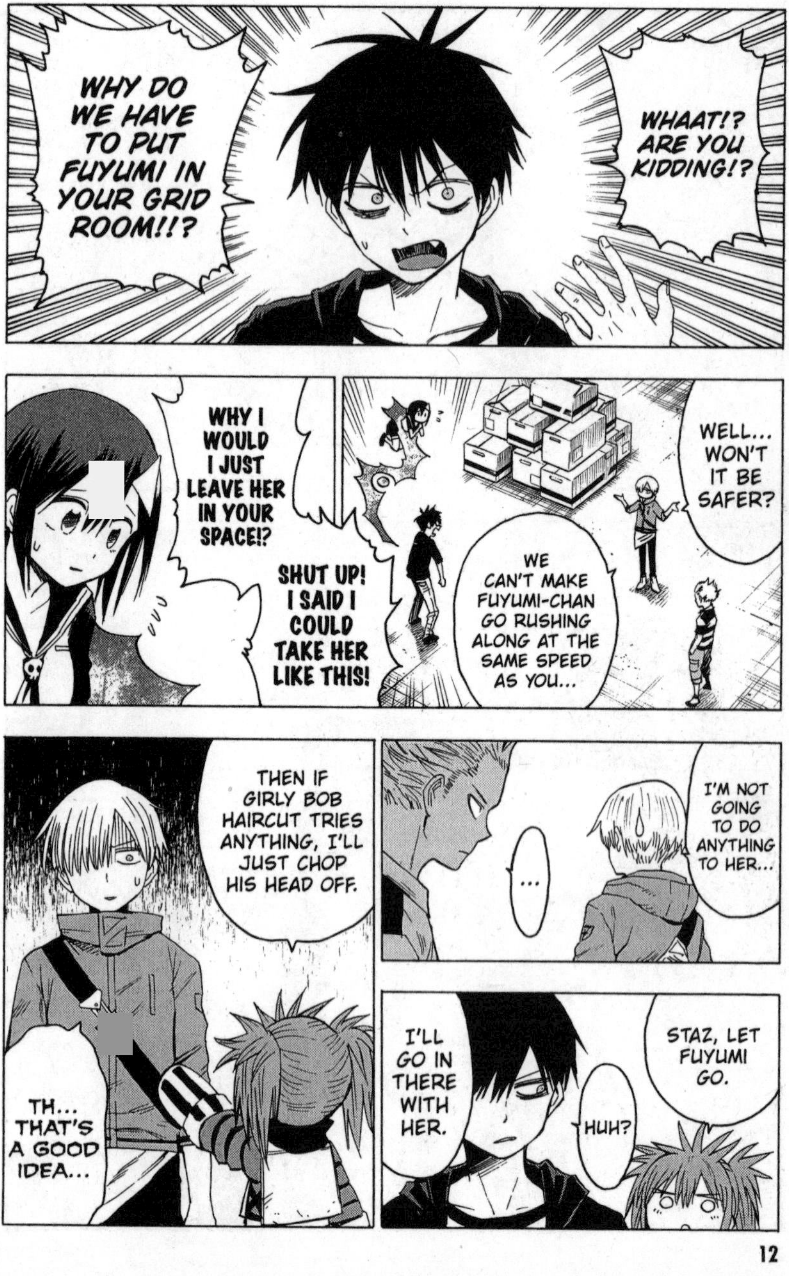
WHAAT!? ARE YOU KIDDING!?
WHY DO WE HAVE TO PUT FUYUMI IN YOUR GRID ROOM!!?
WELL... WON'T IT BE SAFER?
WE CAN'T MAKE FUYUMI-CHAN GO RUSHING ALONG AT THE SAME SPEED AS YOU...
SHUT UP! I SAID I COULD TAKE HER LIKE THIS!
WHY I WOULD I JUST LEAVE HER IN YOUR SPACE!?
I'M NOT GOING TO DO ANYTHING TO HER...
...
STAZ, LET FUYUMI GO.
HUH?
I'LL GO IN THERE WITH HER.
THEN IF GIRLY BOB HAIRCUT TRIES ANYTHING, I'LL JUST CHOP HIS HEAD OFF.
TH... THAT'S A GOOD IDEA...

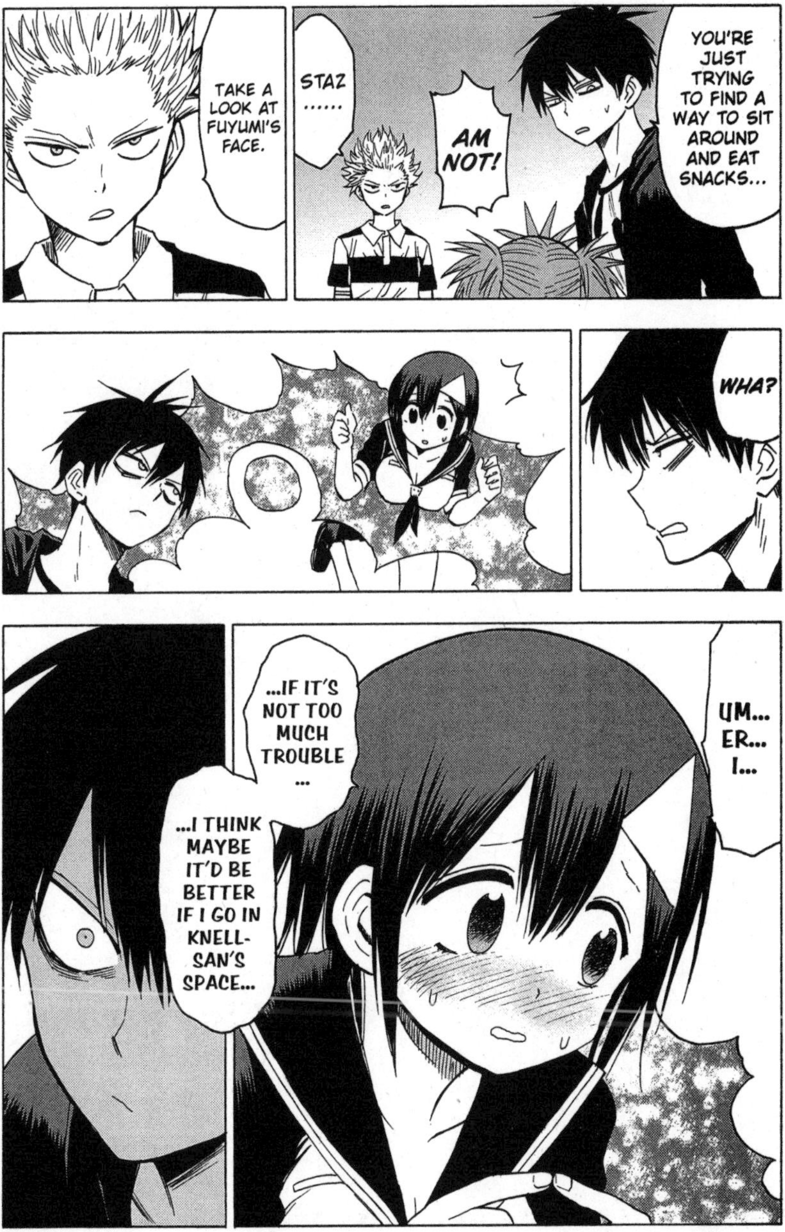
YOU'RE JUST TRYING TO FIND A WAY TO SIT AROUND AND EAT SNACKS...
AM NOT!
STAZ ......
TAKE A LOOK AT FUYUMI'S FACE.
WHA?
UM... ER... I...
...IF IT'S NOT TOO MUCH TROUBLE ...
...I THINK MAYBE IT'D BE BETTER IF I GO IN KNELL-SAN'S SPACE...

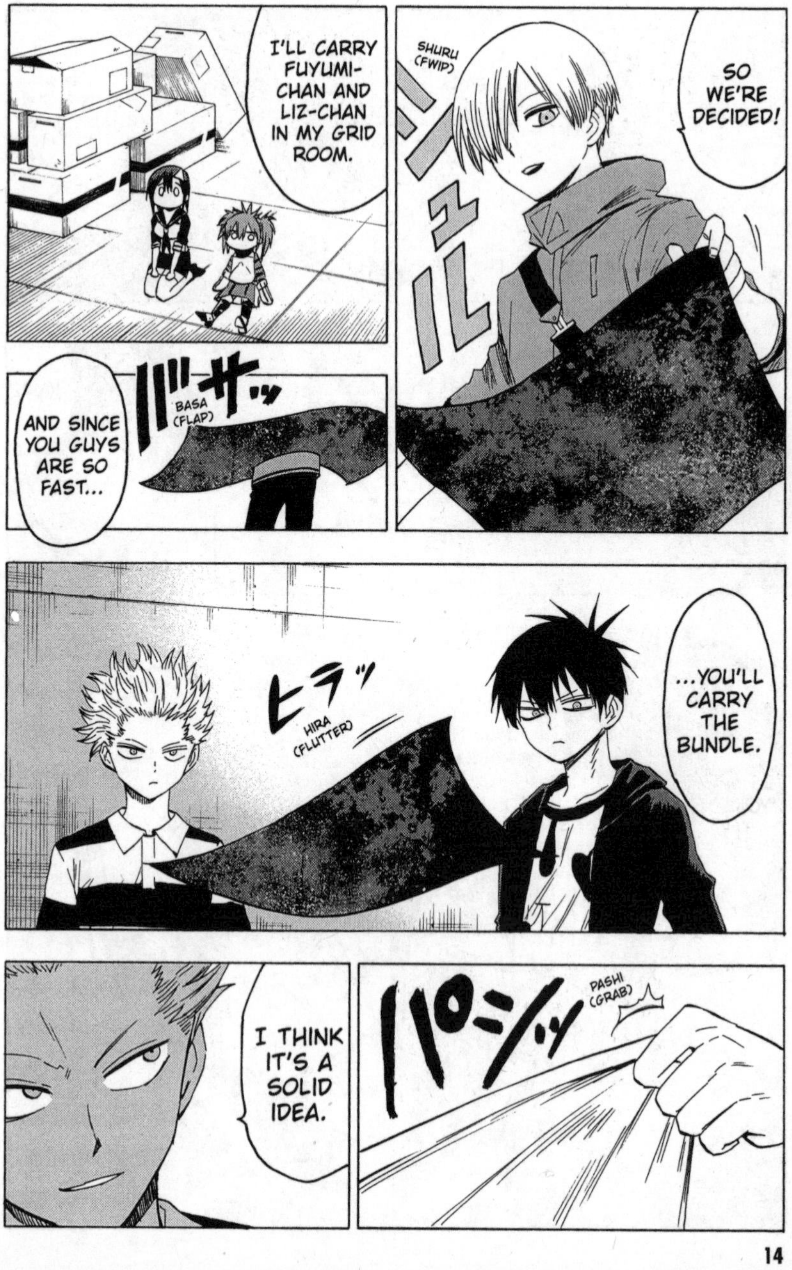
SHURU (FWIP)
SO WE'RE DECIDED!
I'LL CARRY FUYUMI-CHAN AND LIZ-CHAN IN MY GRID ROOM.
BASA (FLAP)
AND SINCE YOU GUYS ARE SO FAST...
HIRA (FLUTTER)
...YOU'LL CARRY THE BUNDLE.
PASHI (GRAB)
I THINK IT'S A SOLID IDEA.

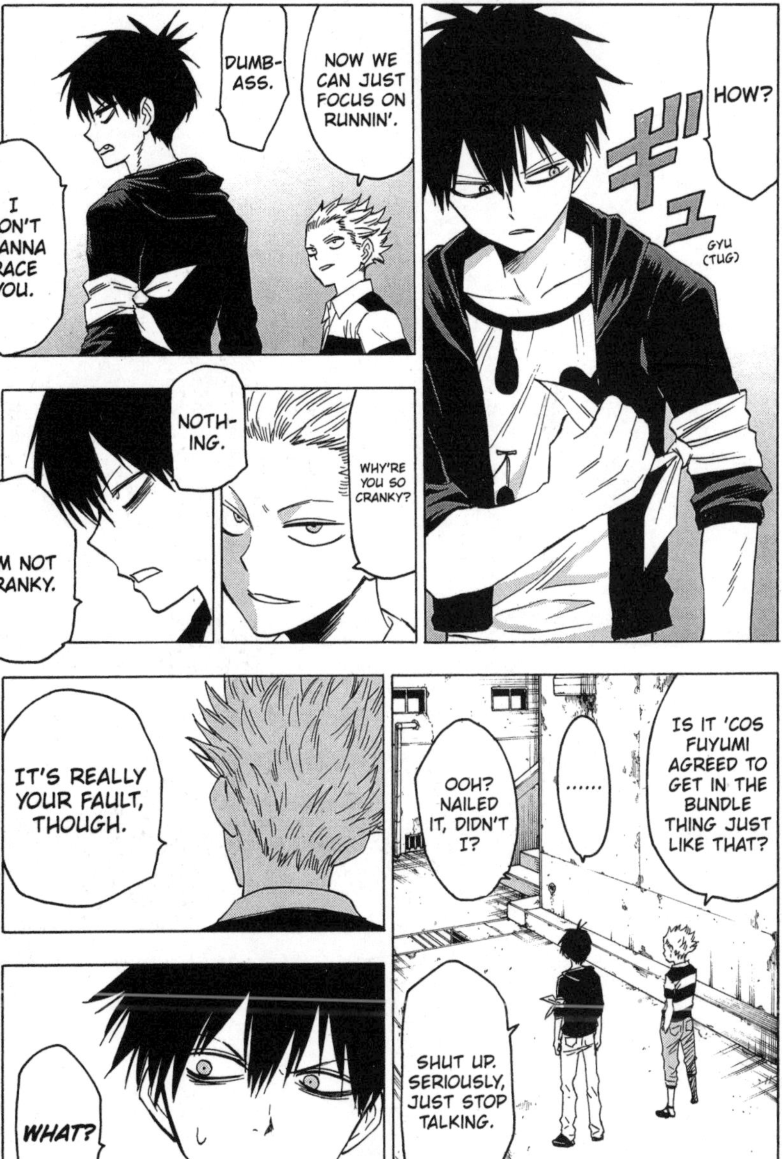
HOW?
ギュ
GYU (TUG)
NOW WE CAN JUST FOCUS ON RUNNIN'.
DUMB-ASS.
I DON'T WANNA RACE YOU.
WHY'RE YOU SO CRANKY?
NOTH-ING.
I'M NOT CRANKY.
IS IT 'COS FUYUMI AGREED TO GET IN THE BUNDLE THING JUST LIKE THAT?
......
OOH? NAILED IT, DIDN'T I?
SHUT UP. SERIOUSLY, JUST STOP TALKING.
IT'S REALLY YOUR FAULT, THOUGH.
WHAT?

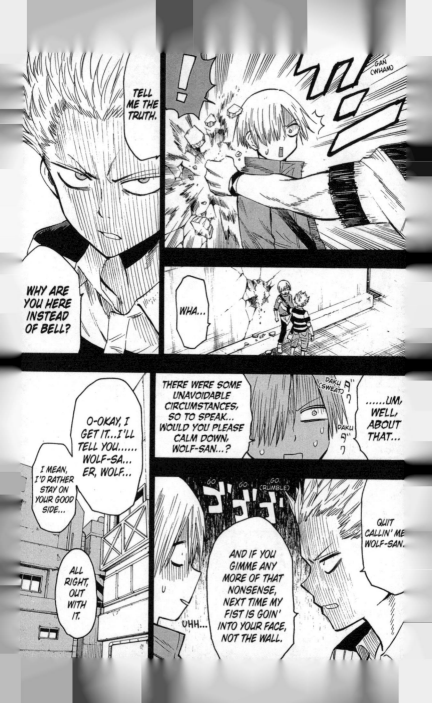

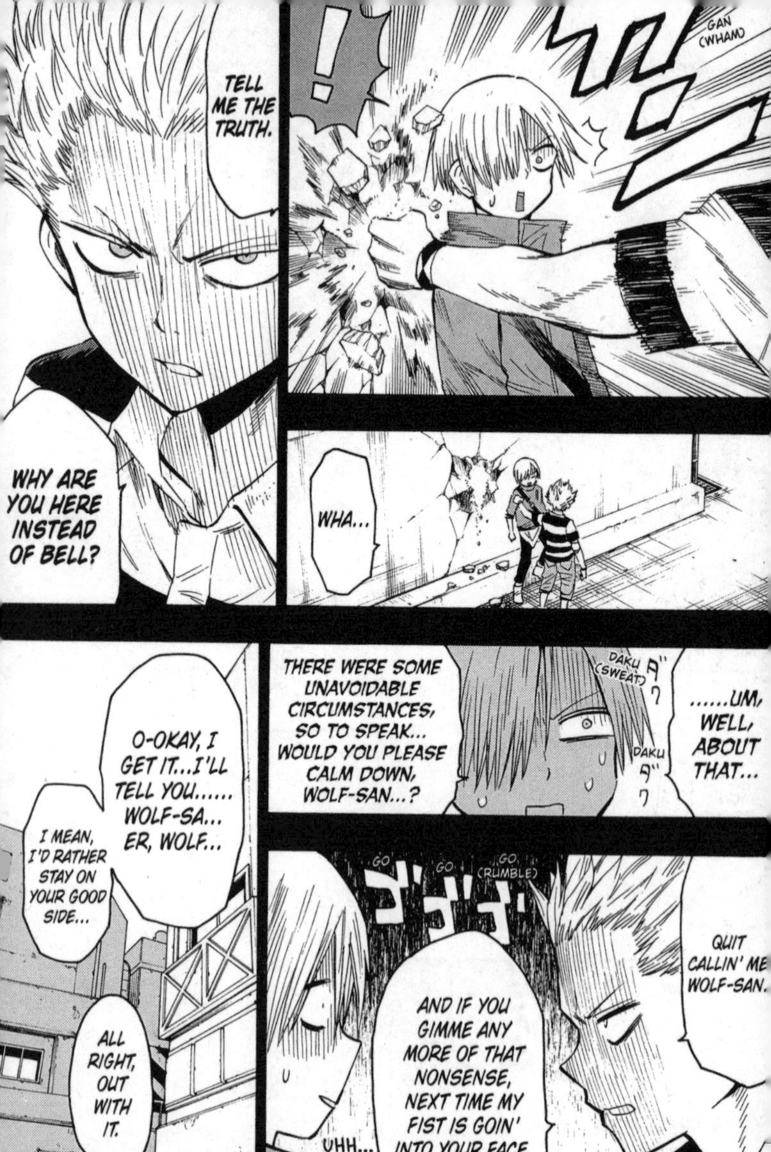
GAN (WHAM)
!
WHA...
TELL ME THE TRUTH.
WHY ARE YOU HERE INSTEAD OF BELL?
......UM, WELL, ABOUT THAT...
DAKU (SWEAT)
ダク
DAKU
ダク
THERE WERE SOME UNAVOIDABLE CIRCUMSTANCES, SO TO SPEAK... WOULD YOU PLEASE CALM DOWN, WOLF-SAN...?
QUIT CALLIN' ME WOLF-SAN.
GO GO GO (RUMBLE)
ゴゴゴ
AND IF YOU GIMME ANY MORE OF THAT NONSENSE, NEXT TIME MY FIST IS GOIN' INTO YOUR FACE, NOT THE WALL.
UHH...
O-OKAY, I GET IT...I'LL TELL YOU...... WOLF-SA... ER, WOLF...
I MEAN, I'D RATHER STAY ON YOUR GOOD SIDE...
ALL RIGHT, OUT WITH IT.

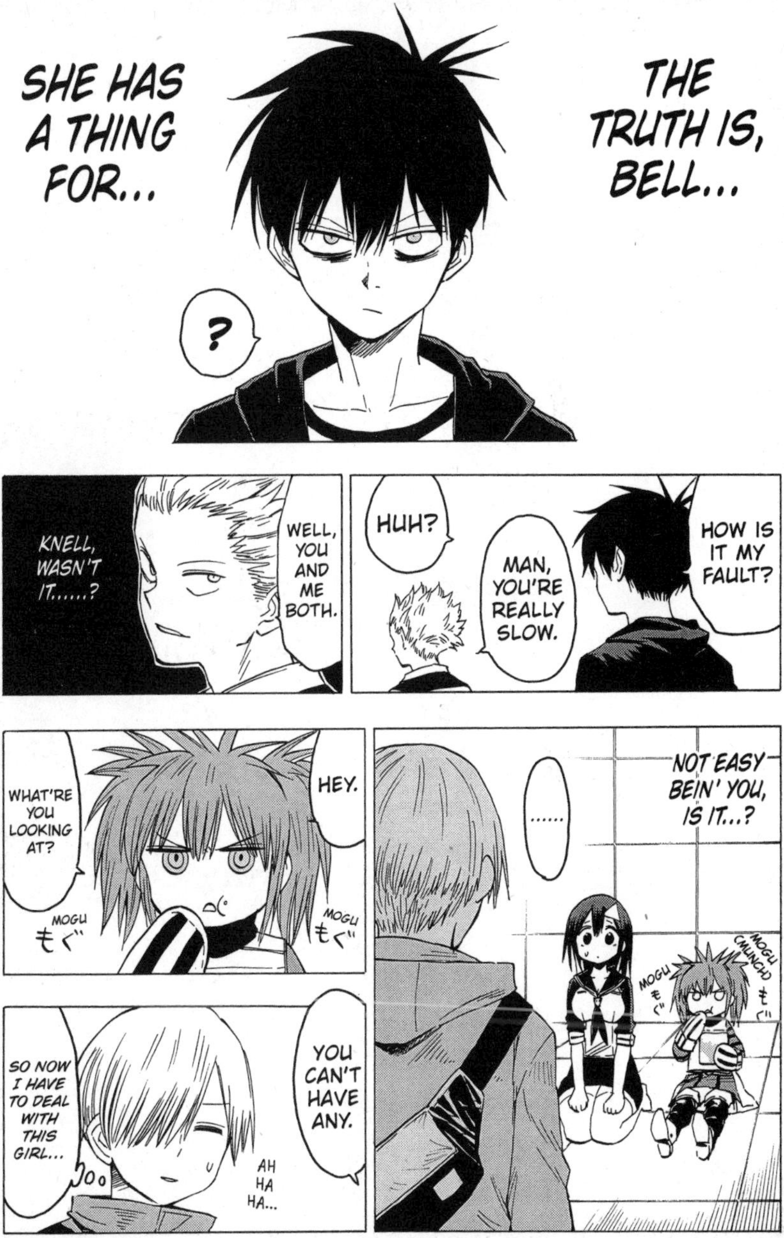
THE TRUTH IS, BELL...
SHE HAS A THING FOR...
?
HOW IS IT MY FAULT?
MAN, YOU'RE REALLY SLOW.
HUH?
WELL, YOU AND ME BOTH.
KNELL, WASN'T IT......?
NOT EASY BEIN' YOU, IS IT...?
......
MOGU (MUNCH) もぐ
MOGU もぐ
HEY.
WHAT'RE YOU LOOKING AT?
MOGU もぐ
MOGU もぐ
YOU CAN'T HAVE ANY.
AH HA HA...
SO NOW I HAVE TO DEAL WITH THIS GIRL...

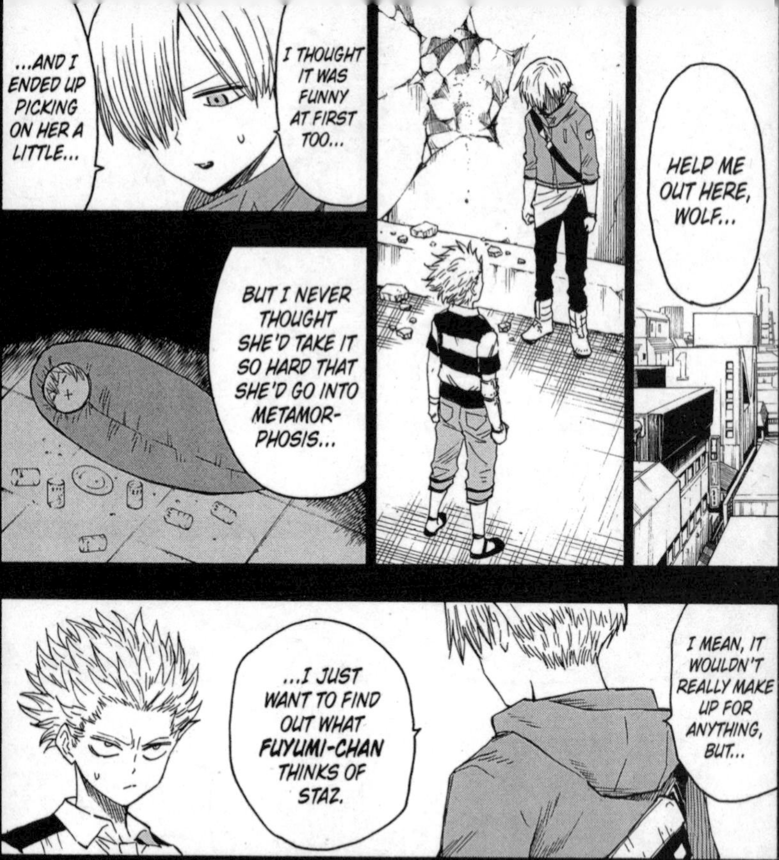
HELP ME OUT HERE, WOLF...
I THOUGHT IT WAS FUNNY AT FIRST TOO...
...AND I ENDED UP PICKING ON HER A LITTLE...
BUT I NEVER THOUGHT SHE'D TAKE IT SO HARD THAT SHE'D GO INTO METAMOR-PHOSIS...
I MEAN, IT WOULDN'T REALLY MAKE UP FOR ANYTHING, BUT...
...I JUST WANT TO FIND OUT WHAT FUYUMI-CHAN THINKS OF STAZ.
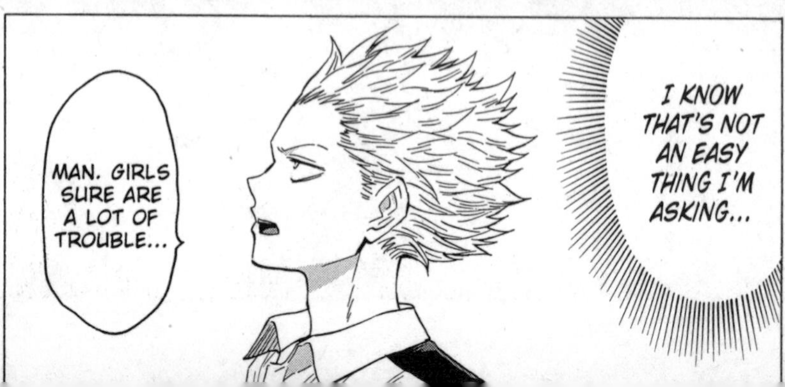
I KNOW THAT'S NOT AN EASY THING I'M ASKING...
MAN. GIRLS SURE ARE A LOT OF TROUBLE...

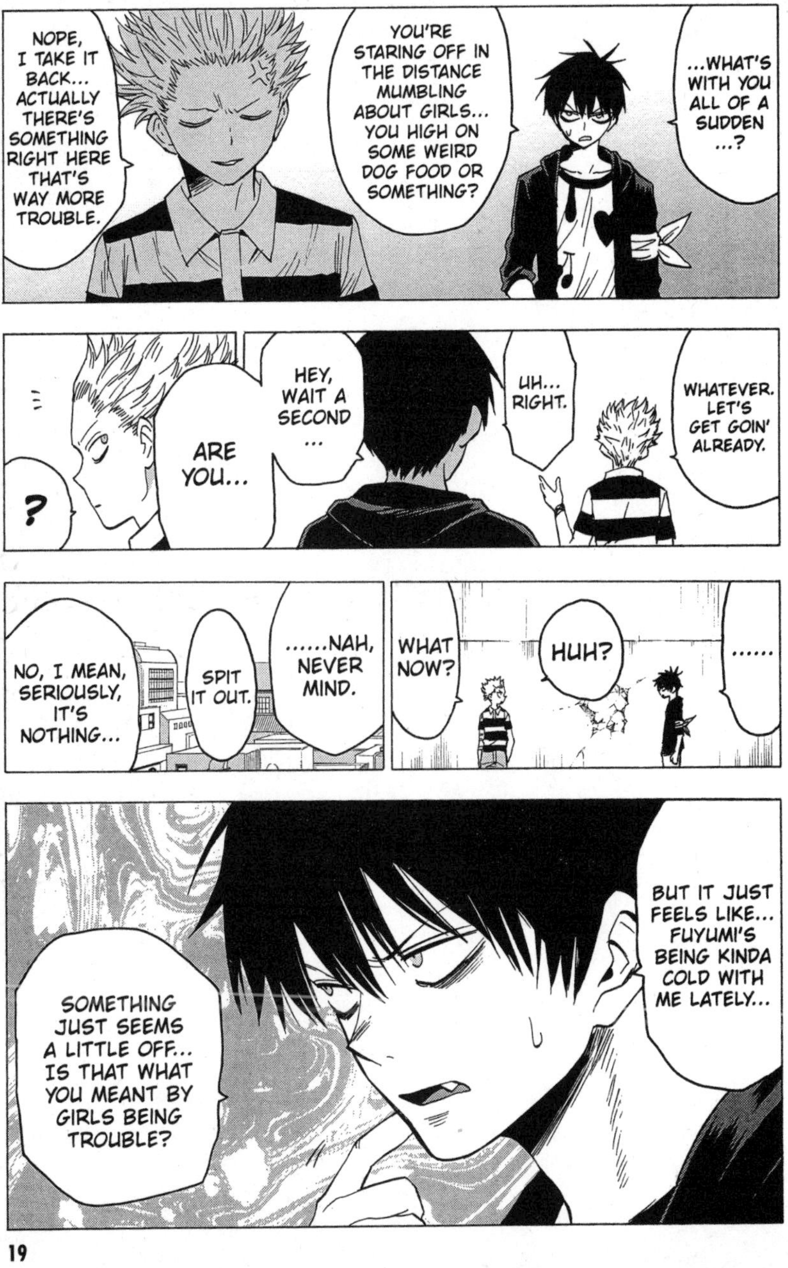
...WHAT'S WITH YOU ALL OF A SUDDEN ...?
YOU'RE STARING OFF IN THE DISTANCE MUMBLING ABOUT GIRLS... YOU HIGH ON SOME WEIRD DOG FOOD OR SOMETHING?
NOPE, I TAKE IT BACK... ACTUALLY THERE'S SOMETHING RIGHT HERE THAT'S WAY MORE TROUBLE.
WHATEVER. LET'S GET GOIN' ALREADY.
UH... RIGHT.
HEY, WAIT A SECOND ...
ARE YOU...
?
......
HUH?
WHAT NOW?
......NAH, NEVER MIND.
SPIT IT OUT.
NO, I MEAN, SERIOUSLY, IT'S NOTHING...
BUT IT JUST FEELS LIKE... FUYUMI'S BEING KINDA COLD WITH ME LATELY...
SOMETHING JUST SEEMS A LITTLE OFF... IS THAT WHAT YOU MEANT BY GIRLS BEING TROUBLE?

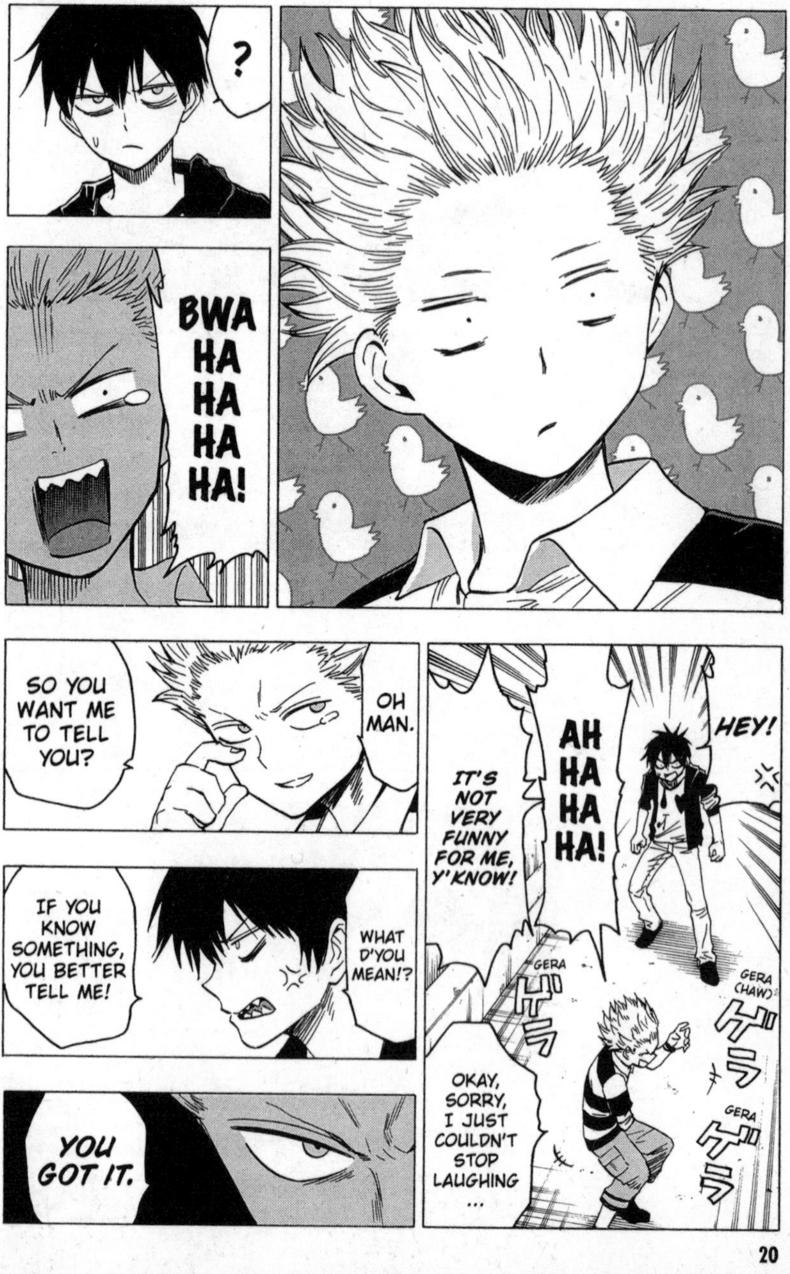
?
BWA HA HA HA HA HA!
HEY!
AH HA HA HA HA!
IT'S NOT VERY FUNNY FOR ME, Y'KNOW!
GERA (HAW)
ゲラ
GERA
ゲラ
GERA
ゲラ
OKAY, SORRY, I JUST COULDN'T STOP LAUGHING ...
OH MAN.
SO YOU WANT ME TO TELL YOU?
WHAT D'YOU MEAN!?
IF YOU KNOW SOMETHING, YOU BETTER TELL ME!
YOU GOT IT.

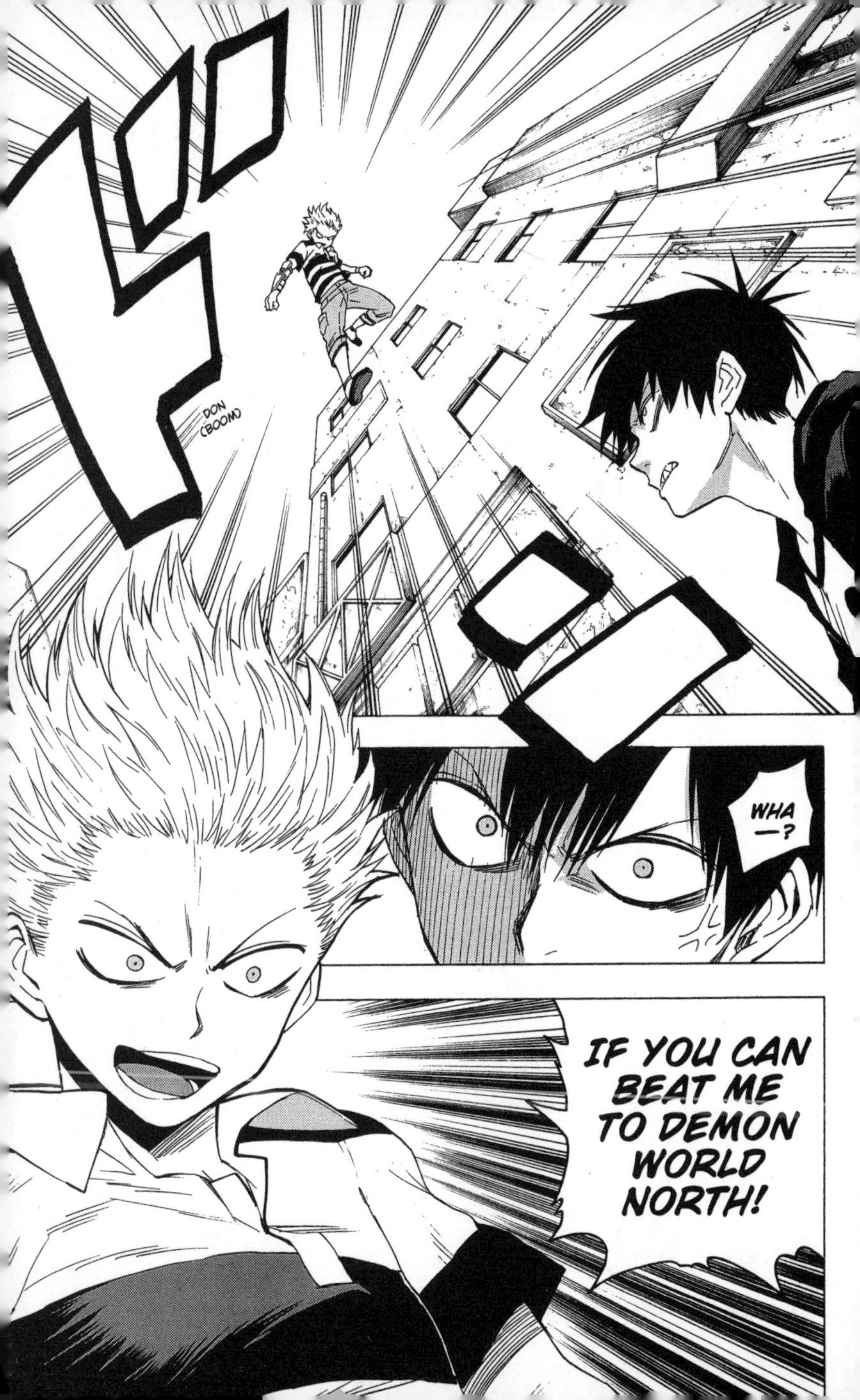
DON
(BOOM)
WHA—?
IF YOU CAN BEAT ME TO DEMON WORLD NORTH!

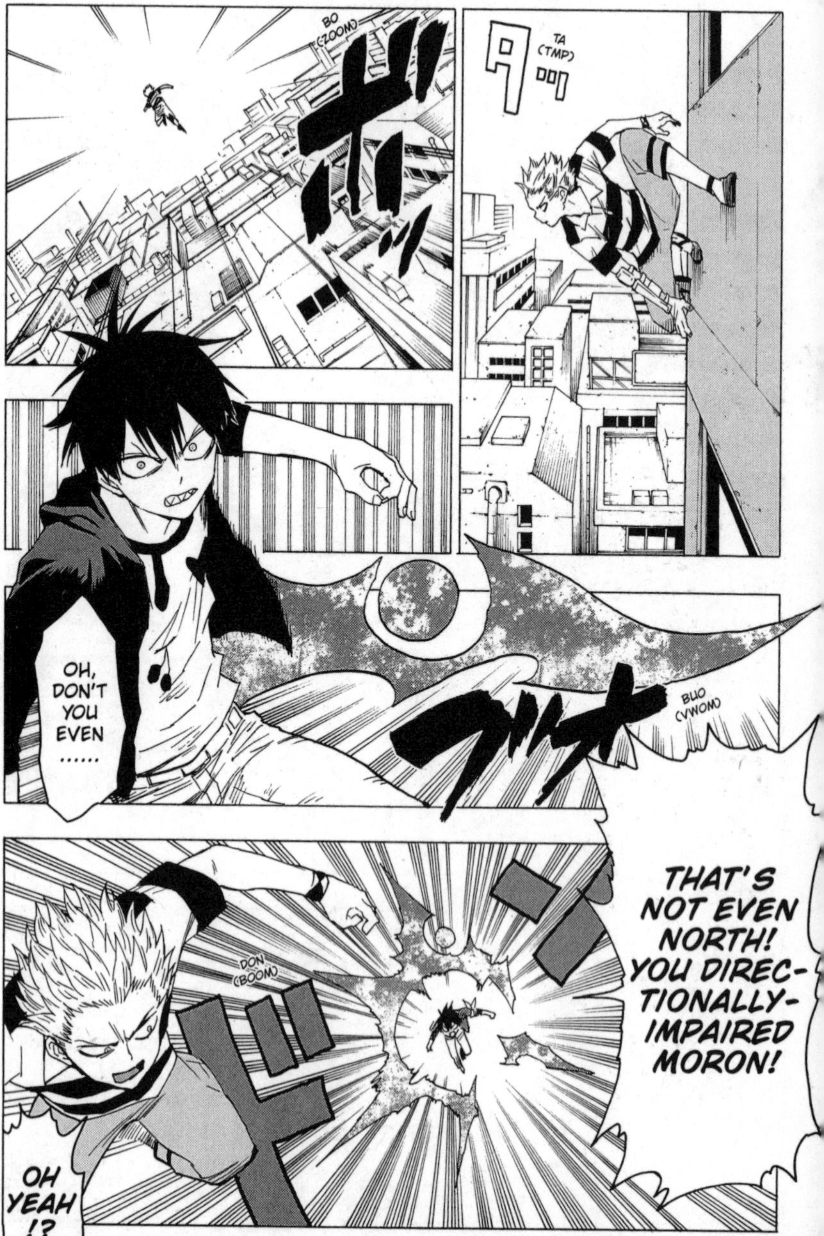
TA
(TMP)
BO
(ZOOM)
OH, DON'T YOU EVEN ......
BUO
(VWOM)
THAT'S NOT EVEN NORTH! YOU DIRECTIONALLY-IMPAIRED MORON!
DON
(BOOM)
OH YEAH !?

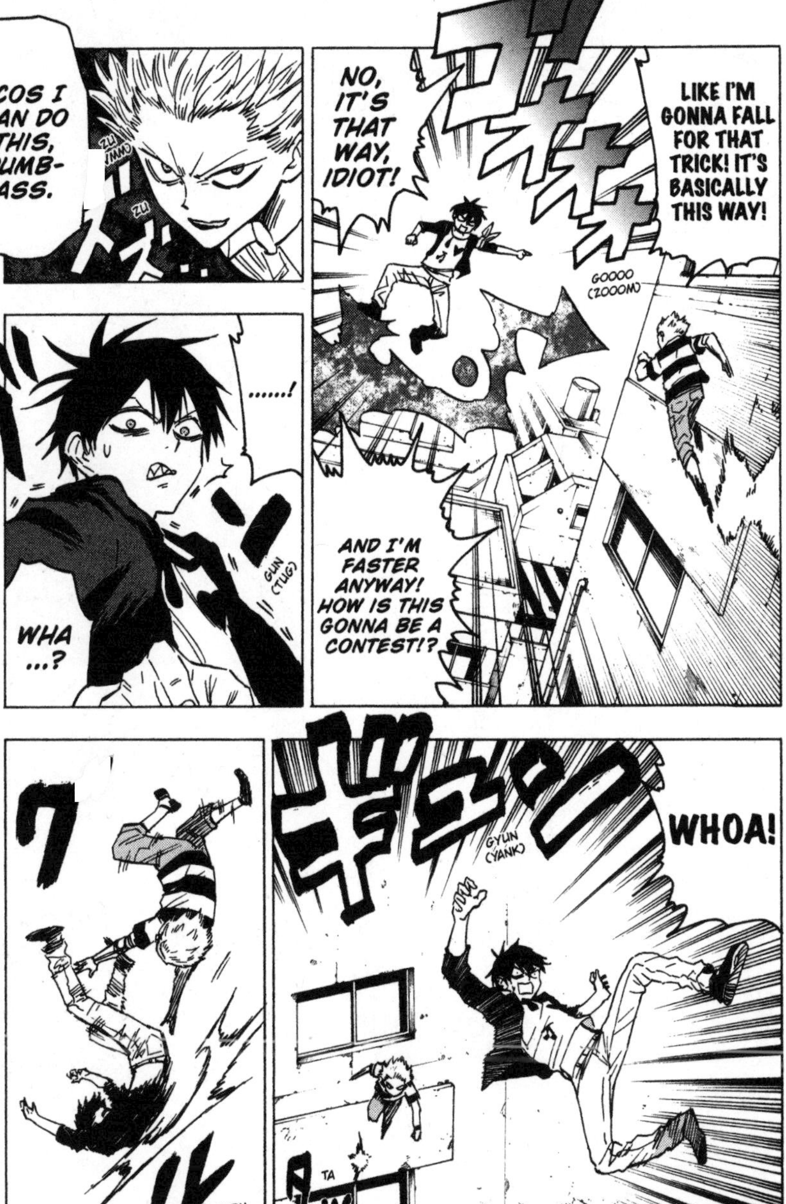
LIKE I'M GONNA FALL FOR THAT TRICK! IT'S BASICALLY THIS WAY!
NO, IT'S THAT WAY, IDIOT!
GOOOO (ZOOOM)
AND I'M FASTER ANYWAY! HOW IS THIS GONNA BE A CONTEST!?
'COS I CAN DO THIS, DUMB-ASS.
ZU
ZU
......!
GUN (TUG)
WHA ...?
WHOA!
GYUN (YANK)
TA
GURU (FLIP)

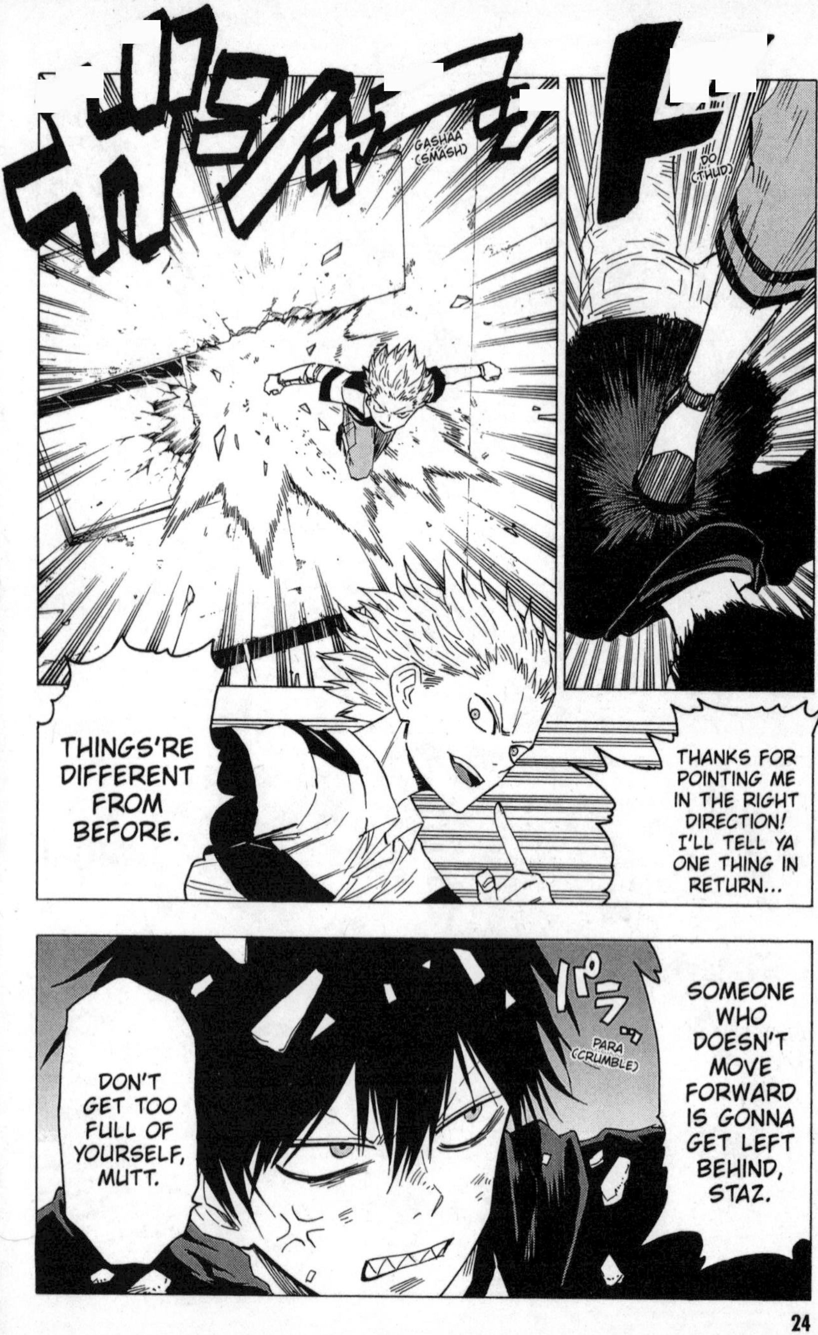
DO
(THUD)
GASHAA
(SMASH)
THANKS FOR POINTING ME IN THE RIGHT DIRECTION! I'LL TELL YA ONE THING IN RETURN...
THINGS'RE DIFFERENT FROM BEFORE.
SOMEONE WHO DOESN'T MOVE FORWARD IS GONNA GET LEFT BEHIND, STAZ.
PARA
(CRUMBLE)
DON'T GET TOO FULL OF YOURSELF, MUTT.

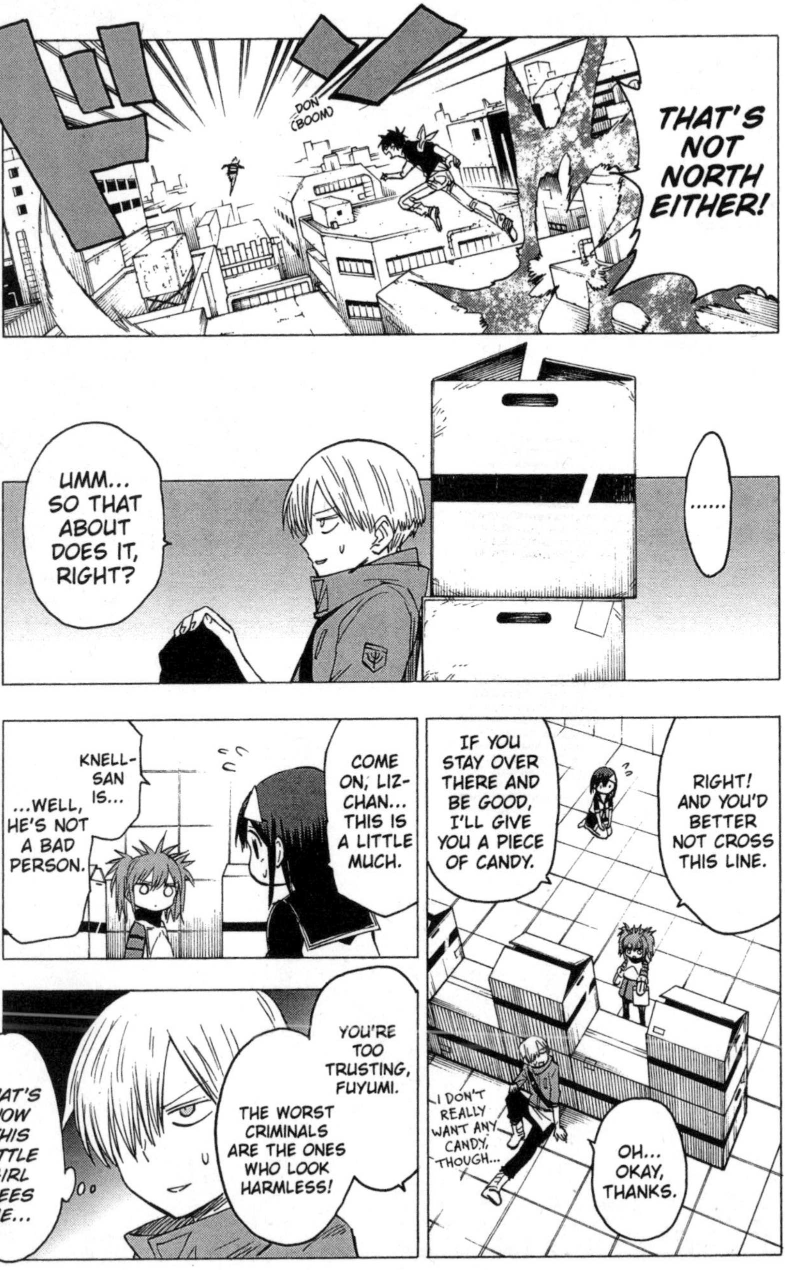
THAT'S NOT NORTH EITHER!
DON (BOOM)
......
UMM... SO THAT ABOUT DOES IT, RIGHT?
RIGHT! AND YOU'D BETTER NOT CROSS THIS LINE.
IF YOU STAY OVER THERE AND BE GOOD, I'LL GIVE YOU A PIECE OF CANDY.
OH... OKAY, THANKS.
I DON'T REALLY WANT ANY CANDY, THOUGH...
COME ON, LIZ-CHAN... THIS IS A LITTLE MUCH.
KNELL-SAN IS...
...WELL, HE'S NOT A BAD PERSON.
YOU'RE TOO TRUSTING, FUYUMI.
THE WORST CRIMINALS ARE THE ONES WHO LOOK HARMLESS!
THAT'S HOW THIS LITTLE GIRL SEES ME...

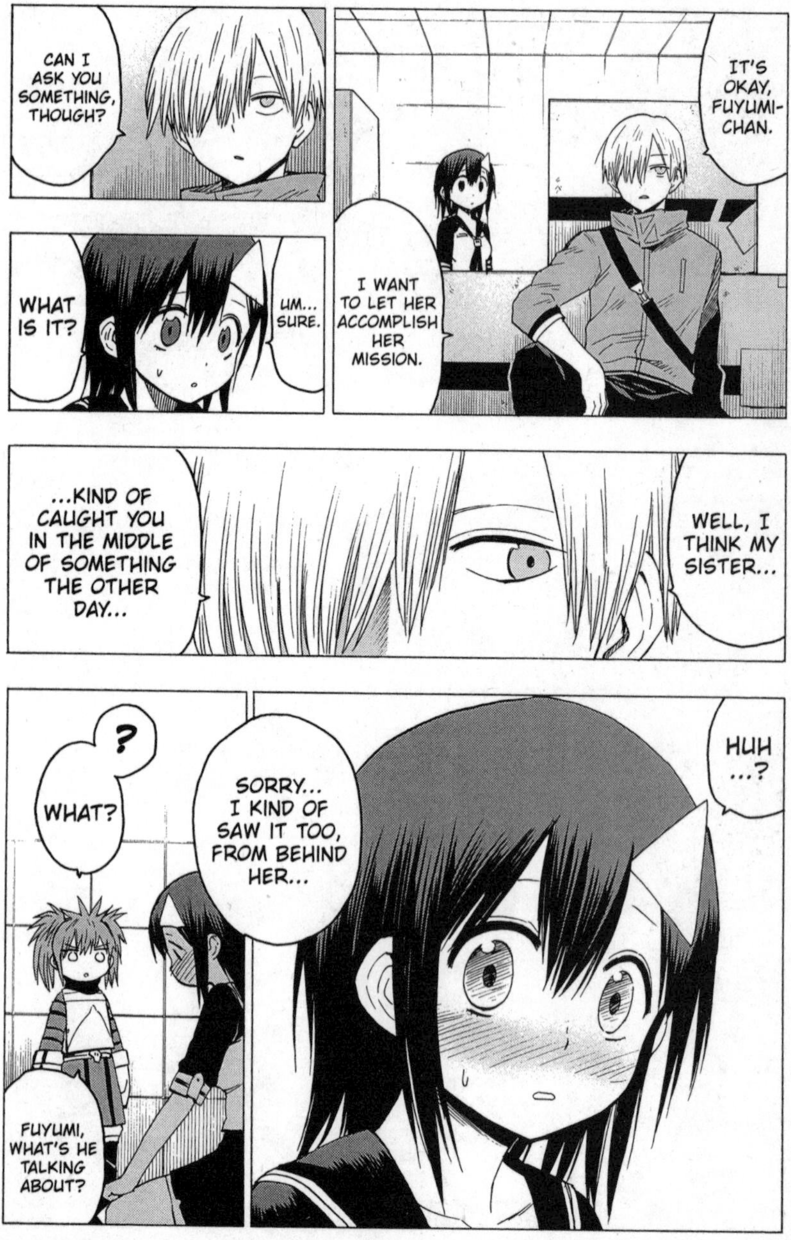
IT'S OKAY, FUYUMI-CHAN.
I WANT TO LET HER ACCOMPLISH HER MISSION.
CAN I ASK YOU SOMETHING, THOUGH?
UM... SURE.
WHAT IS IT?
WELL, I THINK MY SISTER...
...KIND OF CAUGHT YOU IN THE MIDDLE OF SOMETHING THE OTHER DAY...
HUH ...?
SORRY... I KIND OF SAW IT TOO, FROM BEHIND HER...
?
WHAT?
FUYUMI, WHAT'S HE TALKING ABOUT?

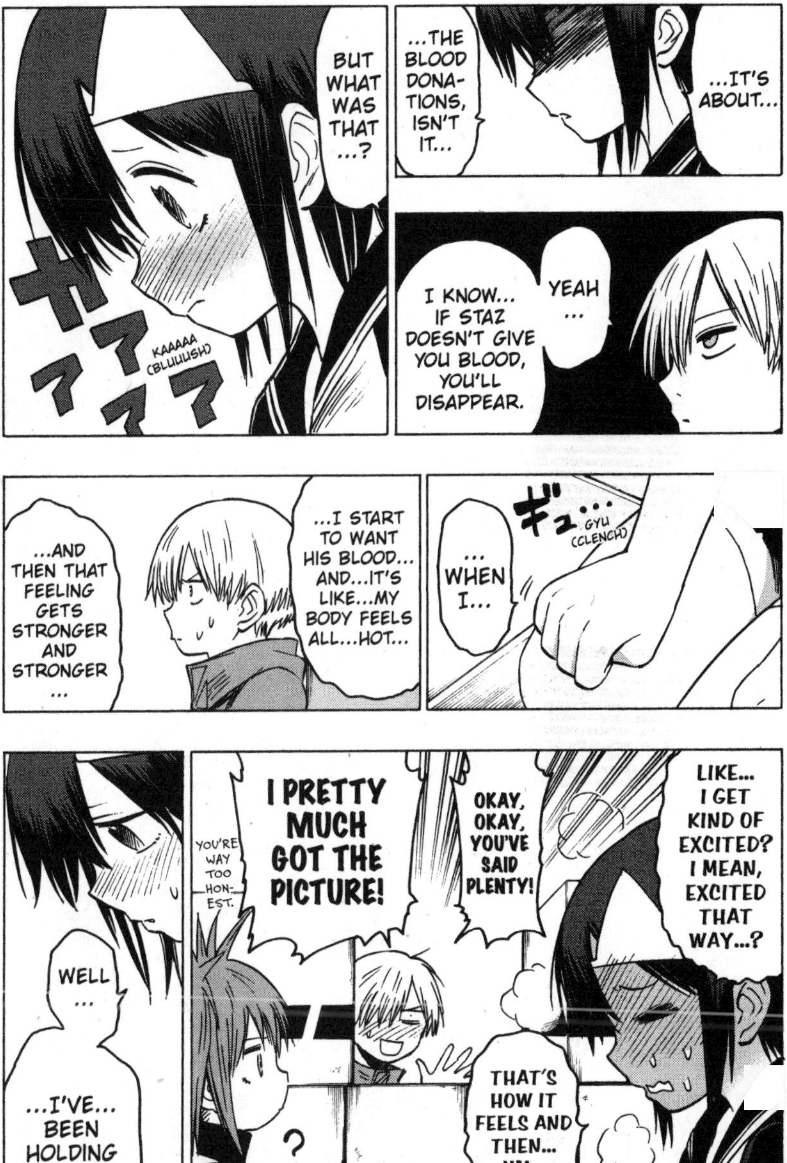
...IT'S ABOUT...
...THE BLOOD DONATIONS, ISN'T IT...
YEAH...
I KNOW... IF STAZ DOESN'T GIVE YOU BLOOD, YOU'LL DISAPPEAR.
BUT WHAT WAS THAT...?
KAAAAA (BLUUUSH)
GYU (CLENCH)
...WHEN I...
...I START TO WANT HIS BLOOD... AND...IT'S LIKE...MY BODY FEELS ALL...HOT...
...AND THEN THAT FEELING GETS STRONGER AND STRONGER...
LIKE... I GET KIND OF EXCITED? I MEAN, EXCITED THAT WAY...?
OKAY, OKAY, YOU'VE SAID PLENTY!
I PRETTY MUCH GOT THE PICTURE!
YOU'RE WAY TOO HON-EST.
THAT'S HOW IT FEELS AND THEN... UM...
?
WELL...
...I'VE... BEEN HOLDING IT IN.

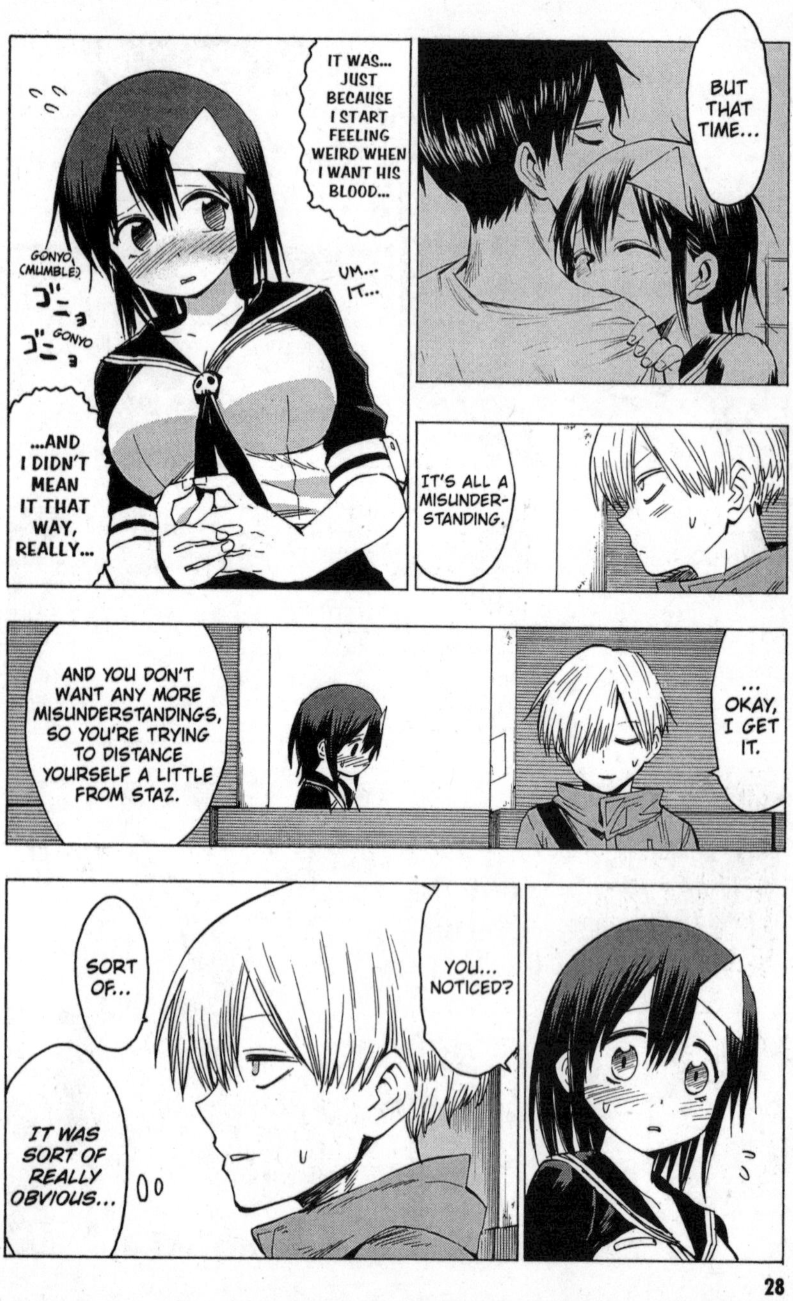
BUT THAT TIME...
IT'S ALL A MISUNDERSTANDING.
IT WAS... JUST BECAUSE I START FEELING WEIRD WHEN I WANT HIS BLOOD...
UM... IT...
GONYO (MUMBLE)
ゴニョ
GONYO
ゴニョ
...AND I DIDN'T MEAN IT THAT WAY, REALLY...
...OKAY, I GET IT.
AND YOU DON'T WANT ANY MORE MISUNDERSTANDINGS, SO YOU'RE TRYING TO DISTANCE YOURSELF A LITTLE FROM STAZ.
YOU... NOTICED?
SORT OF...
IT WAS SORT OF REALLY OBVIOUS...

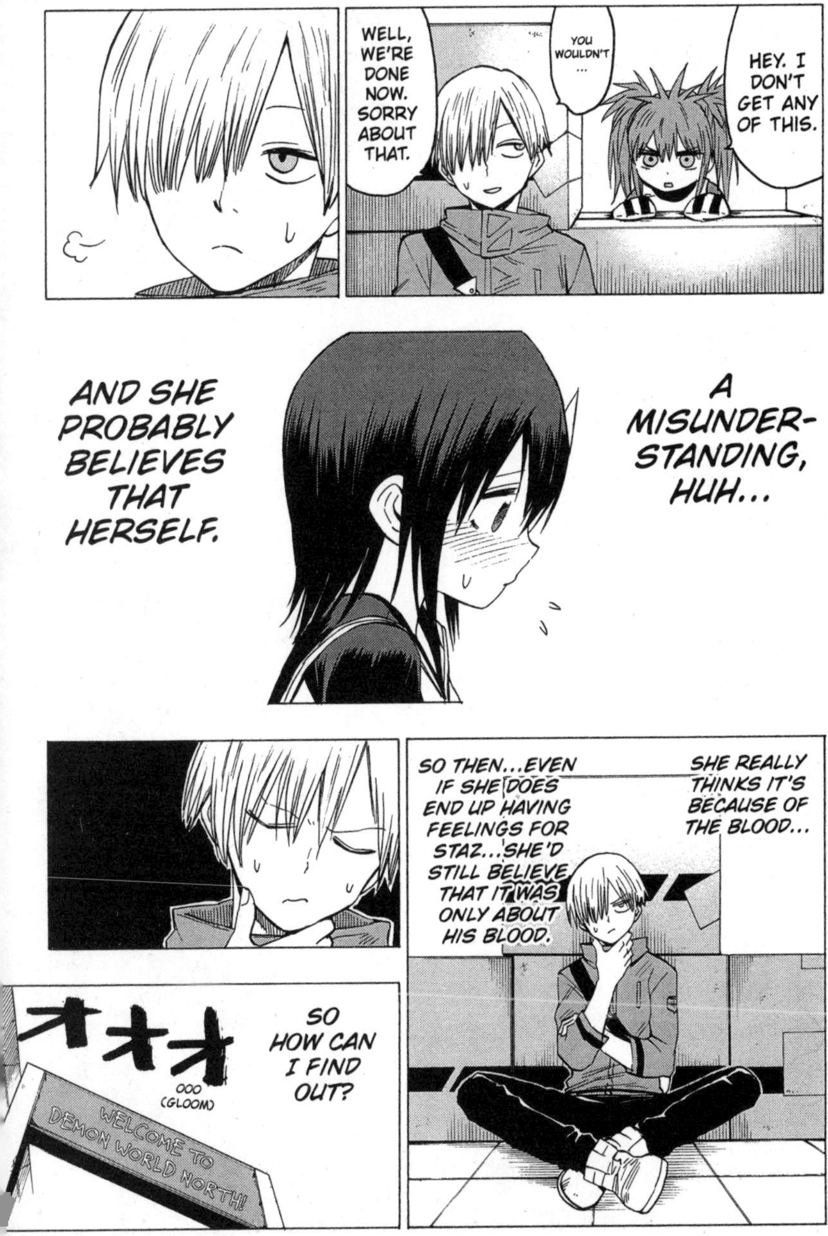
HEY. I DON'T GET ANY OF THIS.
YOU WOULDN'T ...
WELL, WE'RE DONE NOW. SORRY ABOUT THAT.
A MISUNDERSTANDING, HUH...
AND SHE PROBABLY BELIEVES THAT HERSELF.
SHE REALLY THINKS IT'S BECAUSE OF THE BLOOD...
SO THEN...EVEN IF SHE DOES END UP HAVING FEELINGS FOR STAZ...SHE'D STILL BELIEVE THAT IT WAS ONLY ABOUT HIS BLOOD.
SO HOW CAN I FIND OUT?
オオオ
OOO (GLOOM)
WELCOME TO DEMON WORLD NORTH!

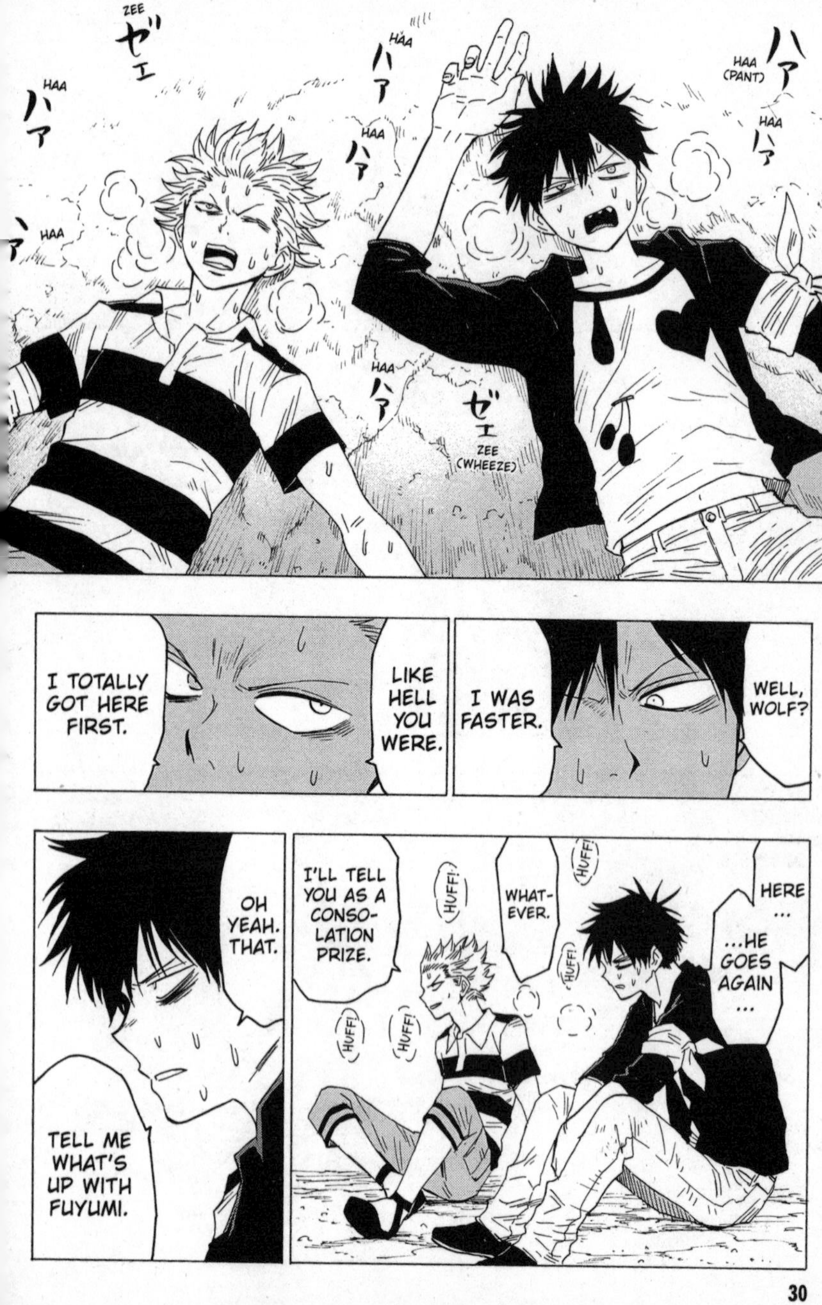
ハア
HAA (PANT)
ハァ
HAA
ハア
HÄA
ハァ
HAA
ゼエ
ZEE
ハア
HAA
ハア
HAA
ゼェ
ZEE (WHEEZE)
ハァ
HAA
WELL, WOLF?
I WAS FASTER.
LIKE HELL YOU WERE.
I TOTALLY GOT HERE FIRST.
HERE...
...HE GOES AGAIN...
HUFF!
WHAT-EVER.
HUFF!
HUFF!
I'LL TELL YOU AS A CONSO-LATION PRIZE.
HUFF!
HUFF!
OH YEAH. THAT.
TELL ME WHAT'S UP WITH FUYUMI.

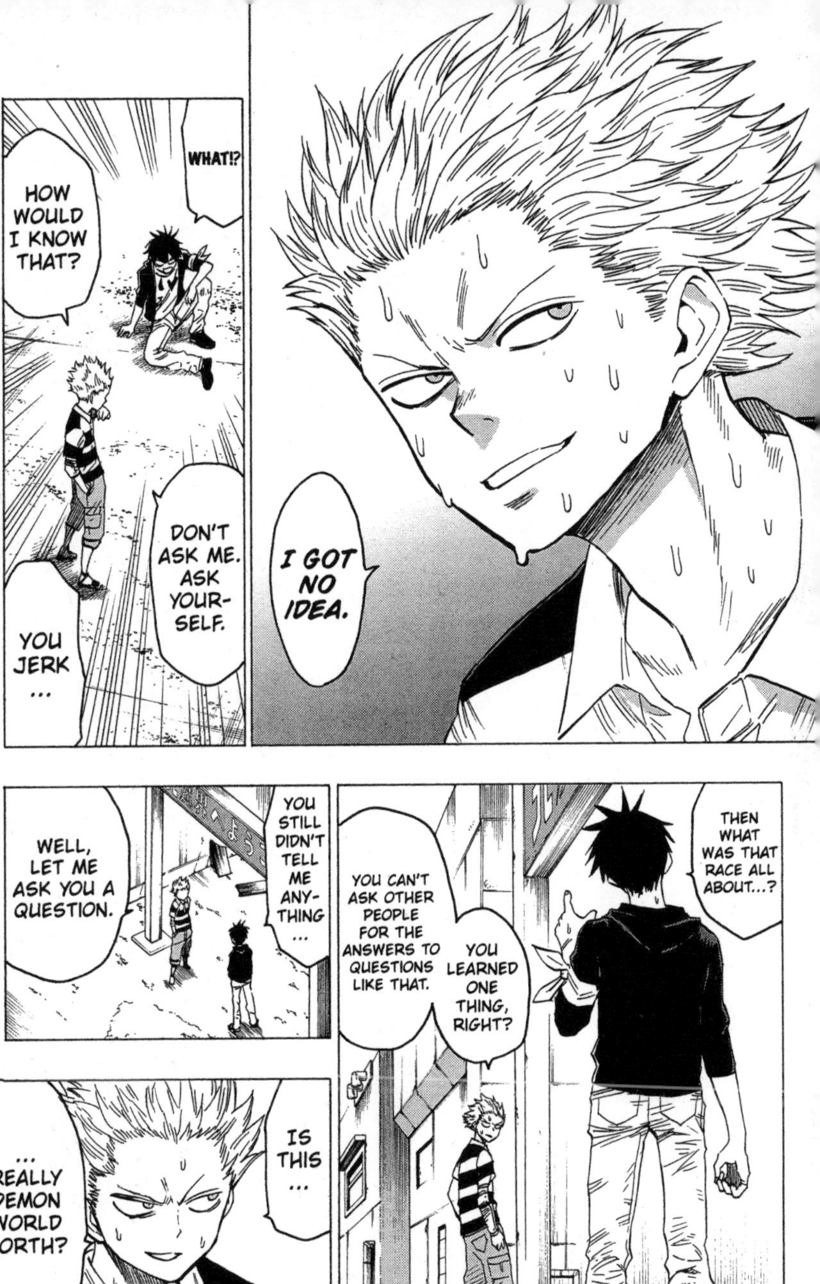
I GOT NO IDEA.
WHAT!?
HOW WOULD I KNOW THAT?
DON'T ASK ME. ASK YOURSELF.
YOU JERK...
THEN WHAT WAS THAT RACE ALL ABOUT...?
YOU CAN'T ASK OTHER PEOPLE FOR THE ANSWERS TO QUESTIONS LIKE THAT.
YOU LEARNED ONE THING, RIGHT?
YOU STILL DIDN'T TELL ME ANYTHING...
WELL, LET ME ASK YOU A QUESTION.
IS THIS...
...REALLY DEMON WORLD NORTH?

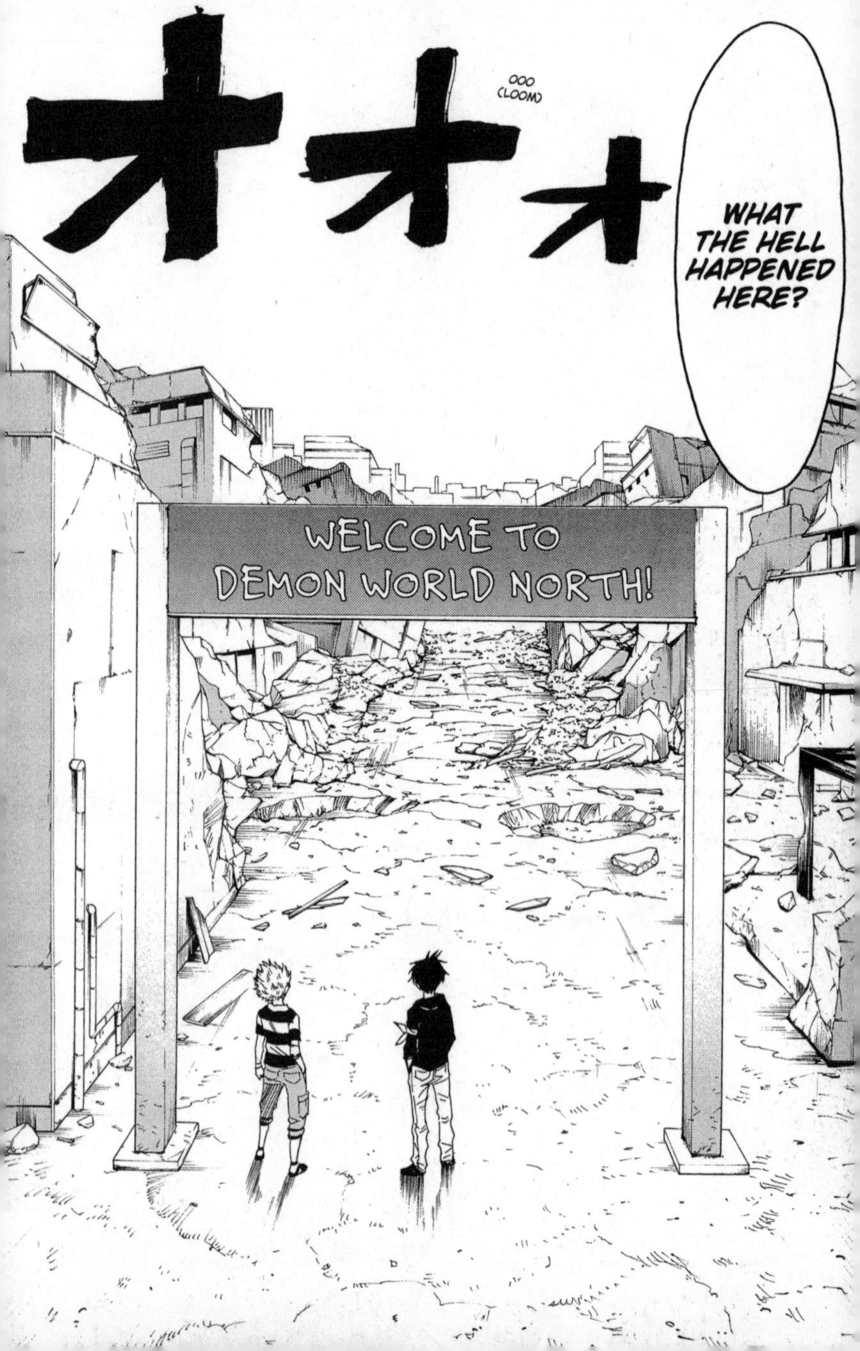
WHAT THE HELL HAPPENED HERE?
オオォ
OOO (LOOM)
WELCOME TO DEMON WORLD NORTH!

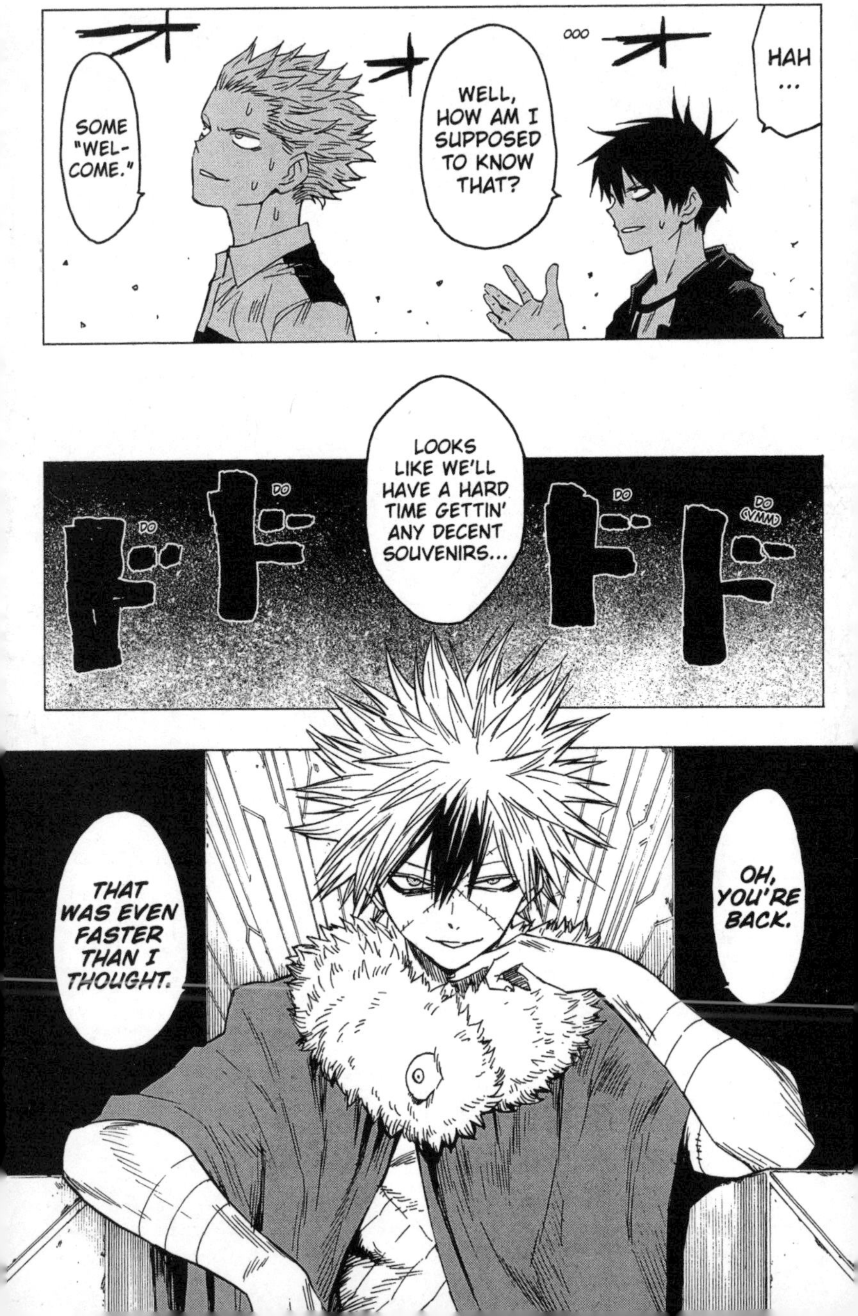
HAH ...
ooo
WELL, HOW AM I SUPPOSED TO KNOW THAT?
SOME "WEL-COME."
DO (VMM)
DO
LOOKS LIKE WE'LL HAVE A HARD TIME GETTIN' ANY DECENT SOUVENIRS...
DO
DO
OH, YOU'RE BACK.
THAT WAS EVEN FASTER THAN I THOUGHT.

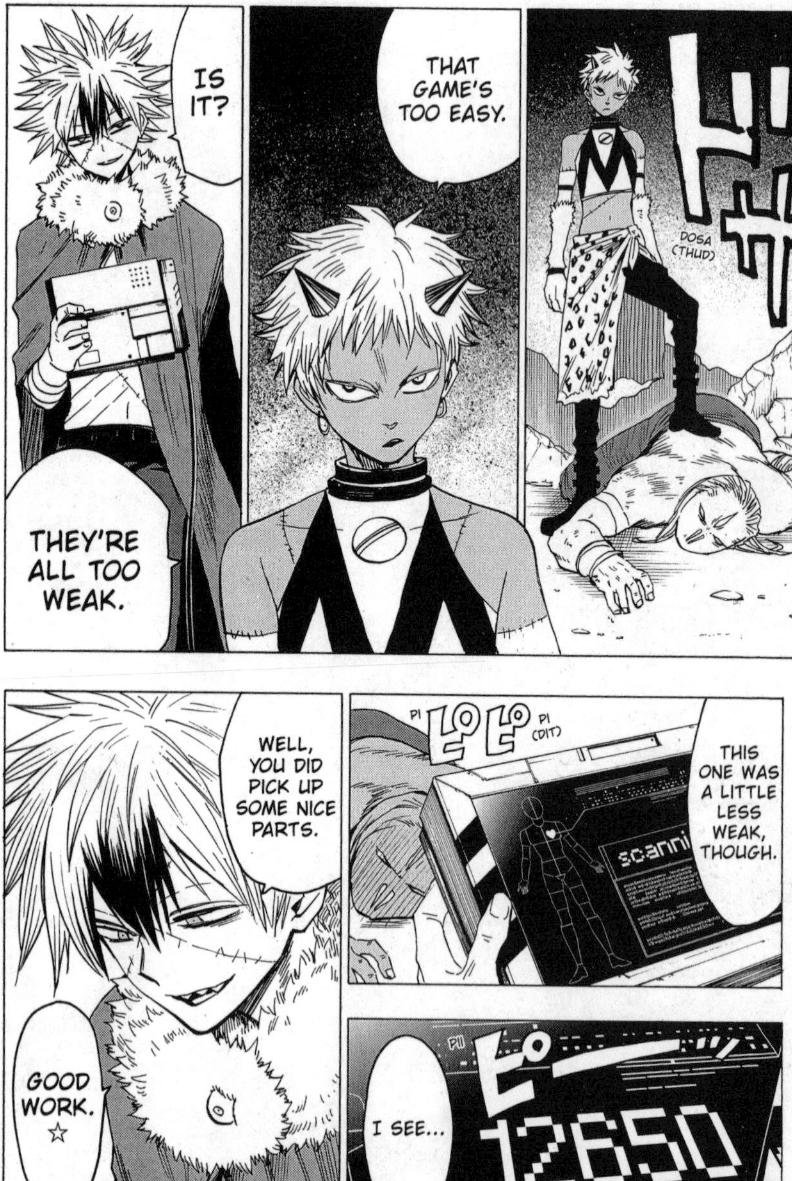
DOSA
(THUD)
THAT GAME'S TOO EASY.
IS IT?
THEY'RE ALL TOO WEAK.
PI PI
(DIT)
THIS ONE WAS A LITTLE LESS WEAK, THOUGH.
scanni
PII
I SEE...
12650
WELL, YOU DID PICK UP SOME NICE PARTS.
GOOD WORK. ☆

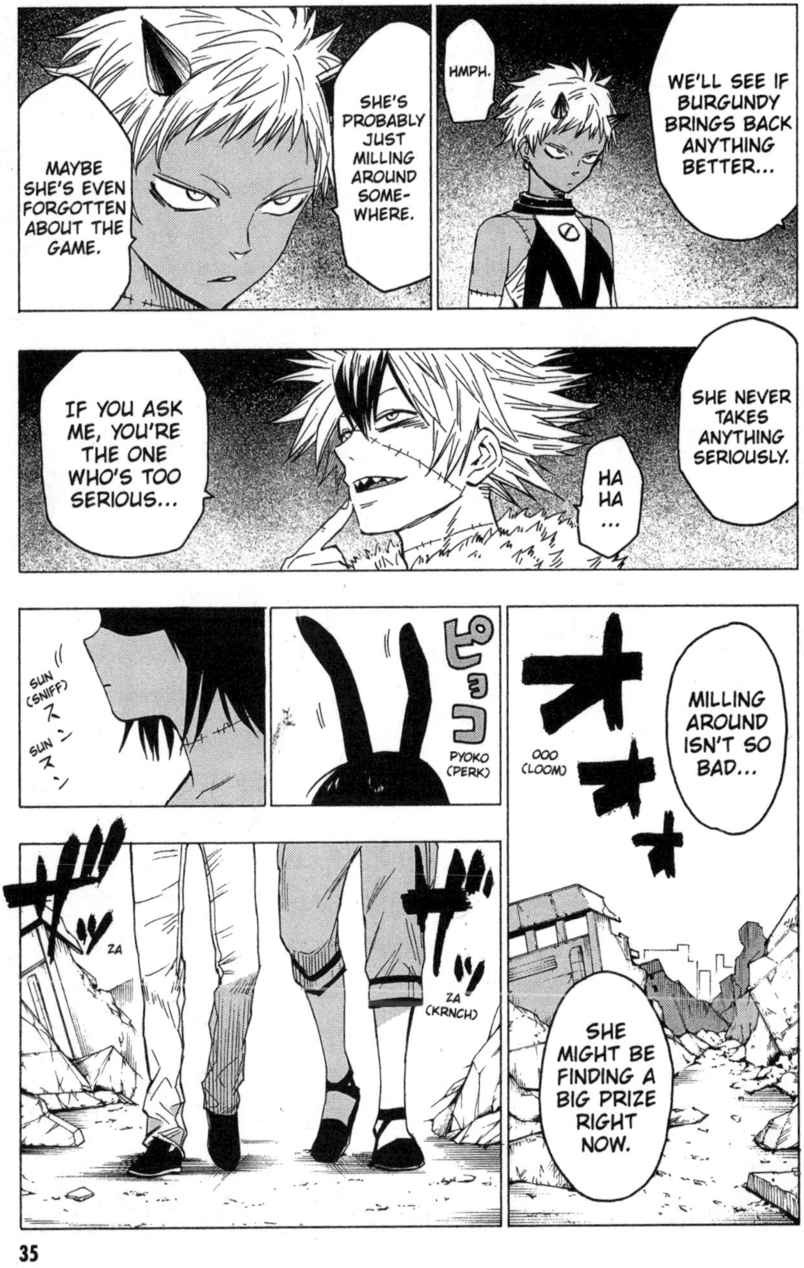
WE'LL SEE IF BURGUNDY BRINGS BACK ANYTHING BETTER...
HMPH.
SHE'S PROBABLY JUST MILLING AROUND SOME-WHERE.
MAYBE SHE'S EVEN FORGOTTEN ABOUT THE GAME.
SHE NEVER TAKES ANYTHING SERIOUSLY.
HA HA ...
IF YOU ASK ME, YOU'RE THE ONE WHO'S TOO SERIOUS...
MILLING AROUND ISN'T SO BAD...
オォォ
OOO (LOOM)
SHE MIGHT BE FINDING A BIG PRIZE RIGHT NOW.
ピョコ
PYOKO (PERK)
スンスン
SUN (SNIFF) SUN
ザッ
ZA (KRNCH)
ザッ
ZA

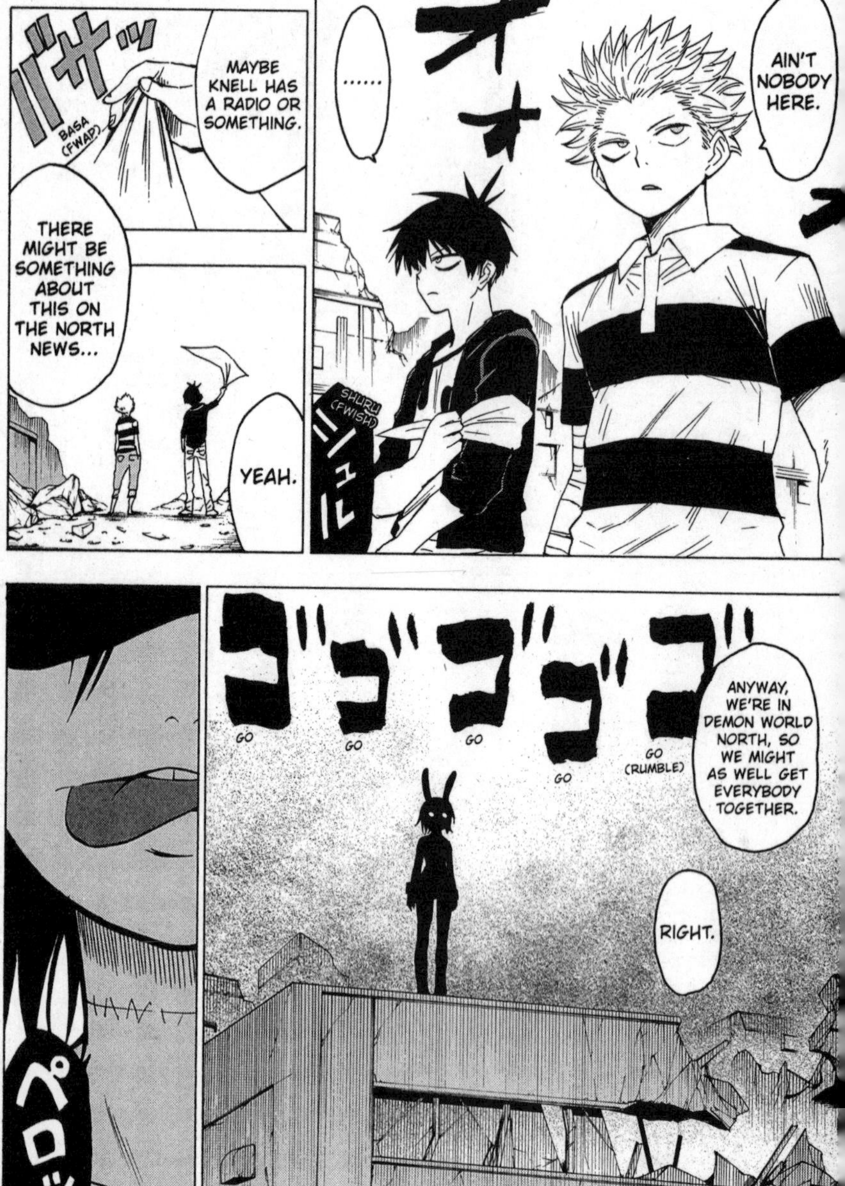
OOO
(LOOM)
AIN'T NOBODY HERE.
......
SHURU
(FWISH)
BASA
(FWAP)
MAYBE KNELL HAS A RADIO OR SOMETHING.
THERE MIGHT BE SOMETHING ABOUT THIS ON THE NORTH NEWS...
YEAH.
GO
GO
GO
GO
GO
(RUMBLE)
ANYWAY, WE'RE IN DEMON WORLD NORTH, SO WE MIGHT AS WELL GET EVERYBODY TOGETHER.
RIGHT.
PERO
(LICK)

♠ To Be Continued ♠

ANIMAL SNACKS

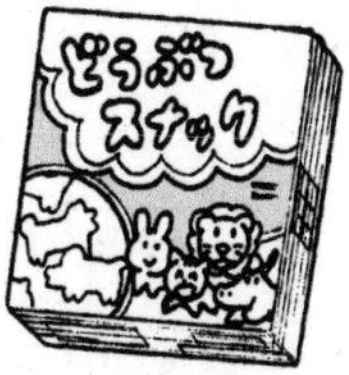
どうぶつ
スナック

CUTE LITTLE COOKIES IN ANIMAL SHAPES. YOU CAN HAVE THEM IF YOU'RE GOOD.

BLOOD LAD

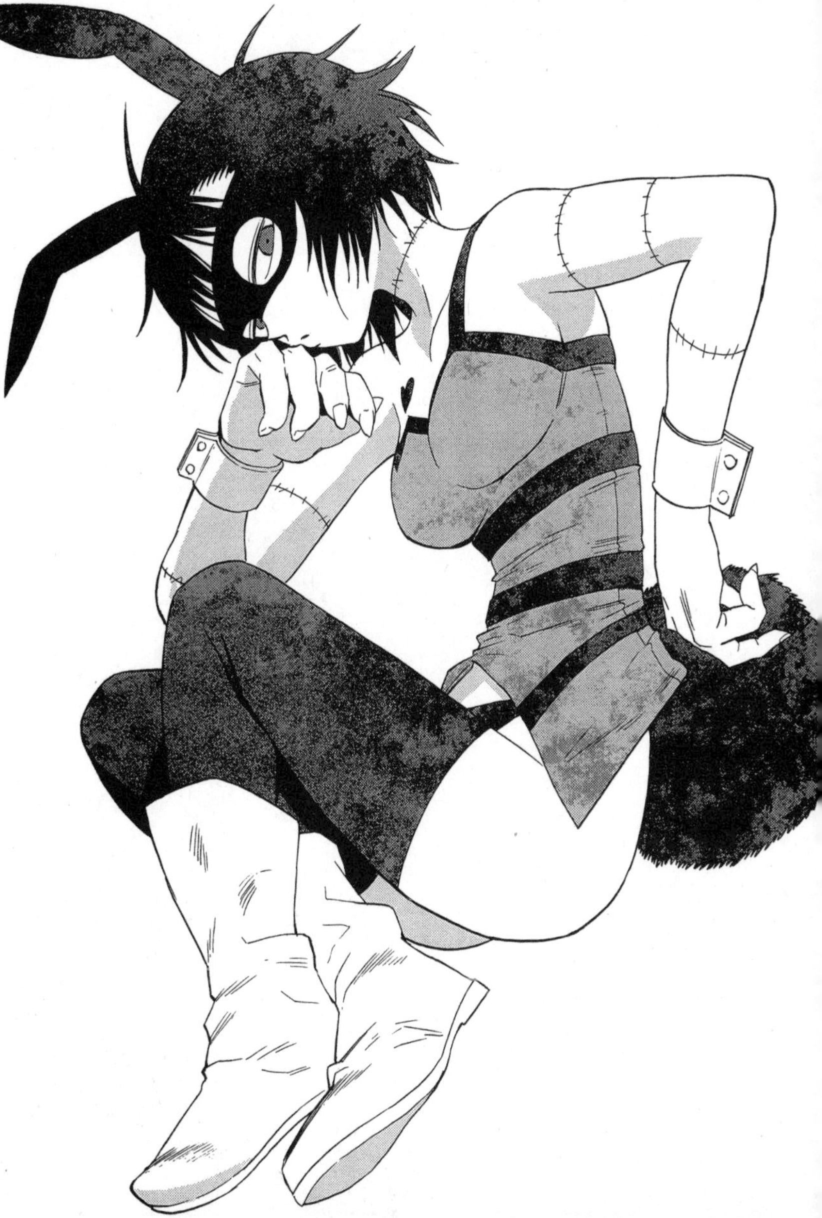

CHAPTER 52 ♠ IMPORTANT PARTS

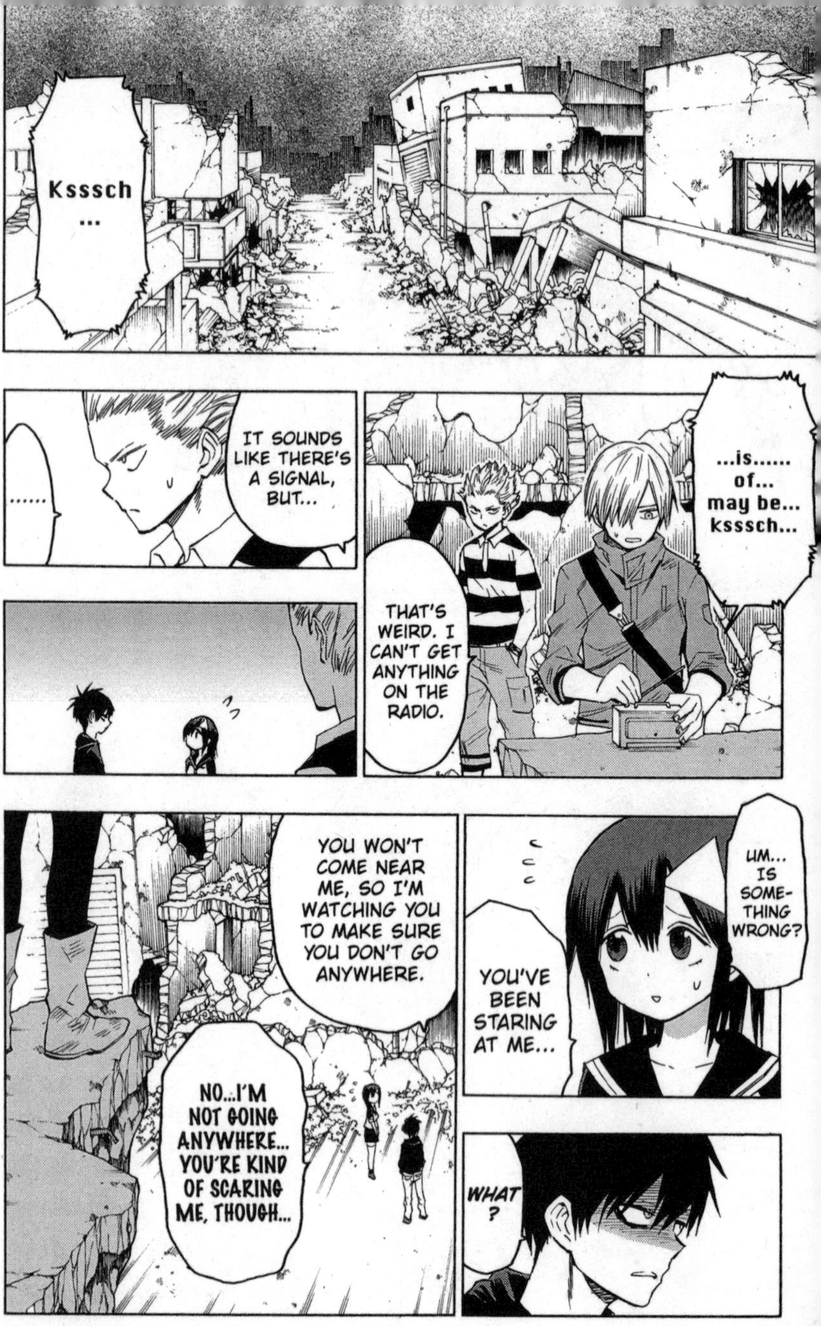
Ksssch
...
...is......
of...
may be...
ksssch...
THAT'S WEIRD. I CAN'T GET ANYTHING ON THE RADIO.
IT SOUNDS LIKE THERE'S A SIGNAL, BUT...
......
UM... IS SOME-THING WRONG?
YOU'VE BEEN STARING AT ME...
WHAT?
YOU WON'T COME NEAR ME, SO I'M WATCHING YOU TO MAKE SURE YOU DON'T GO ANYWHERE.
NO...I'M NOT GOING ANYWHERE... YOU'RE KIND OF SCARING ME, THOUGH...

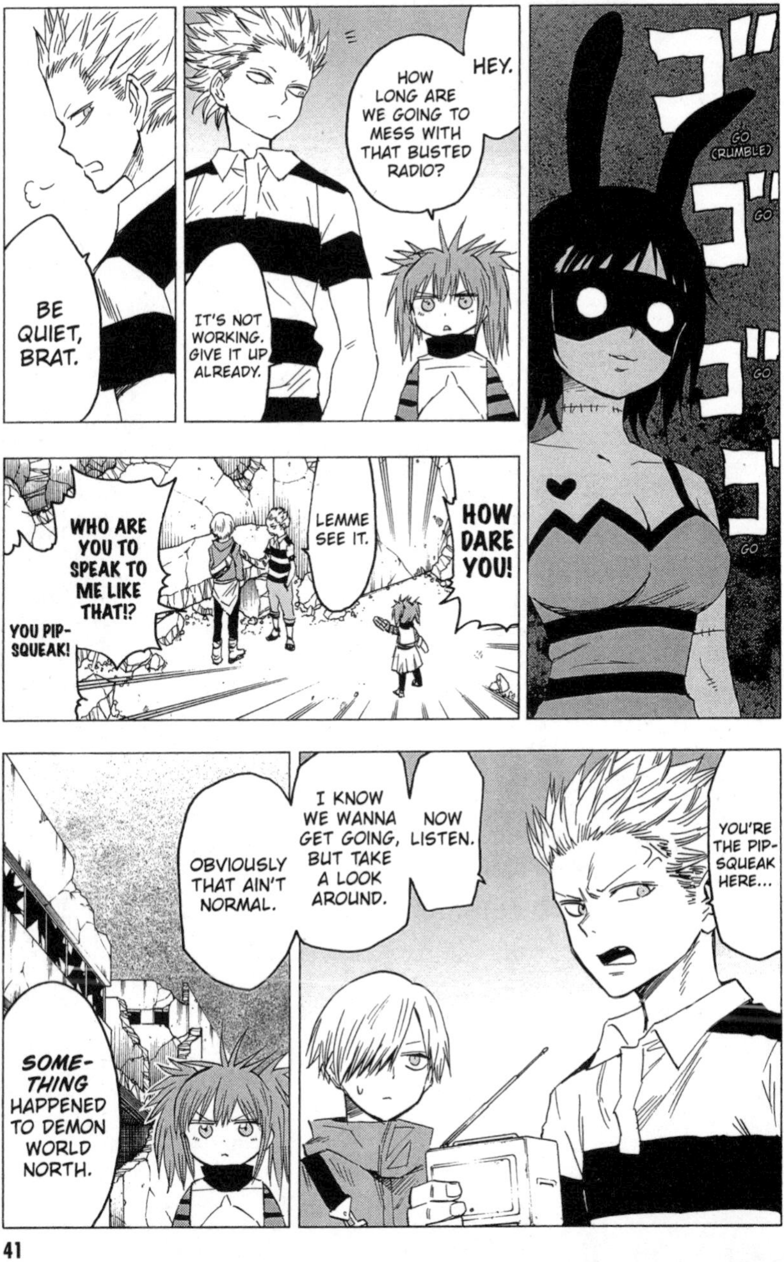

GO (RUMBLE)
GO
GO
GO
HEY.
HOW LONG ARE WE GOING TO MESS WITH THAT BUSTED RADIO?
IT'S NOT WORKING. GIVE IT UP ALREADY.
BE QUIET, BRAT.
HOW DARE YOU!
LEMME SEE IT.
WHO ARE YOU TO SPEAK TO ME LIKE THAT!?
YOU PIP-SQUEAK!
YOU'RE THE PIP-SQUEAK HERE...
NOW LISTEN.
I KNOW WE WANNA GET GOING, BUT TAKE A LOOK AROUND.
OBVIOUSLY THAT AIN'T NORMAL.
SOMETHING HAPPENED TO DEMON WORLD NORTH.

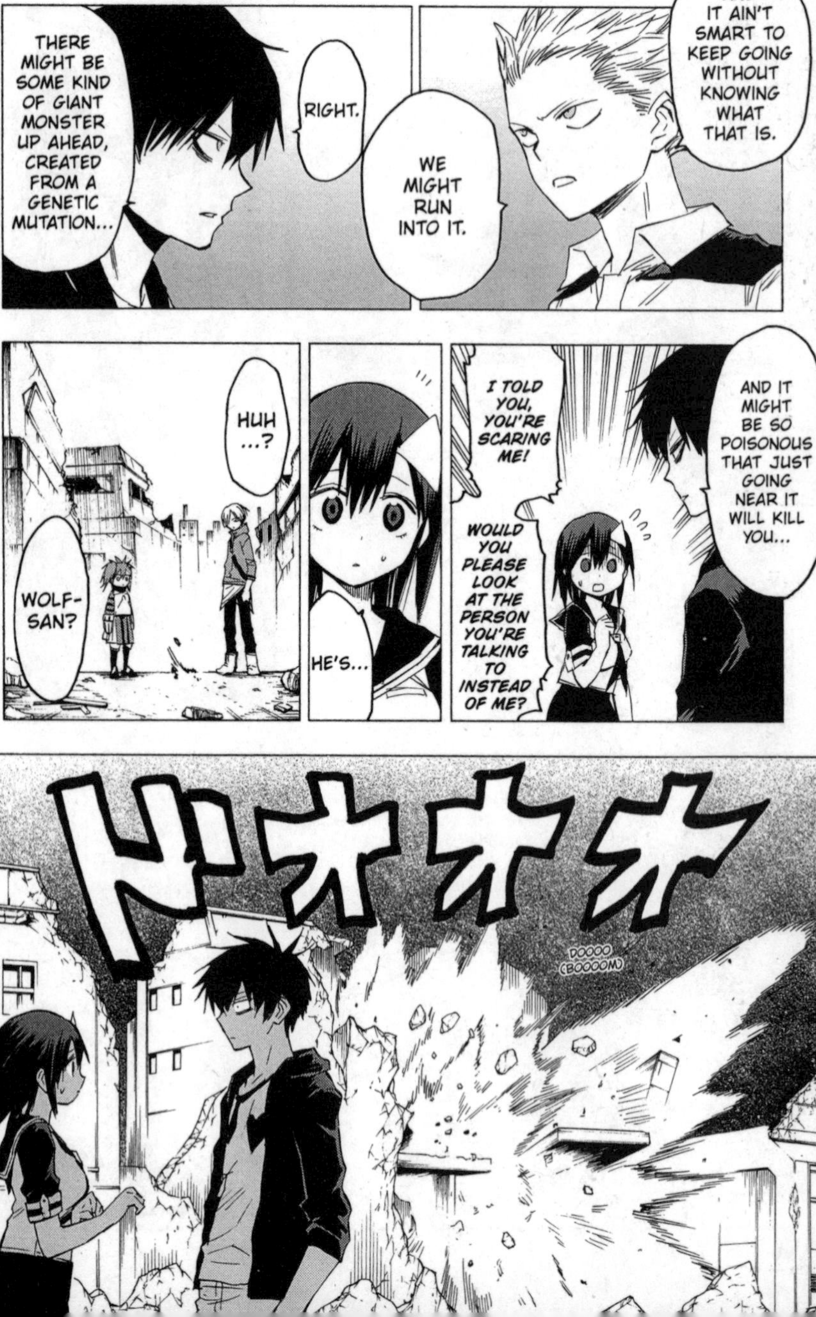
AND IT AIN'T SMART TO KEEP GOING WITHOUT KNOWING WHAT THAT IS.
WE MIGHT RUN INTO IT.
RIGHT.
THERE MIGHT BE SOME KIND OF GIANT MONSTER UP AHEAD, CREATED FROM A GENETIC MUTATION...
AND IT MIGHT BE SO POISONOUS THAT JUST GOING NEAR IT WILL KILL YOU...
I TOLD YOU, YOU'RE SCARING ME!
WOULD YOU PLEASE LOOK AT THE PERSON YOU'RE TALKING TO INSTEAD OF ME?
HE'S...
HUH ...?
WOLF-SAN?
ドオオオ
DOOOO (BOOOOM)

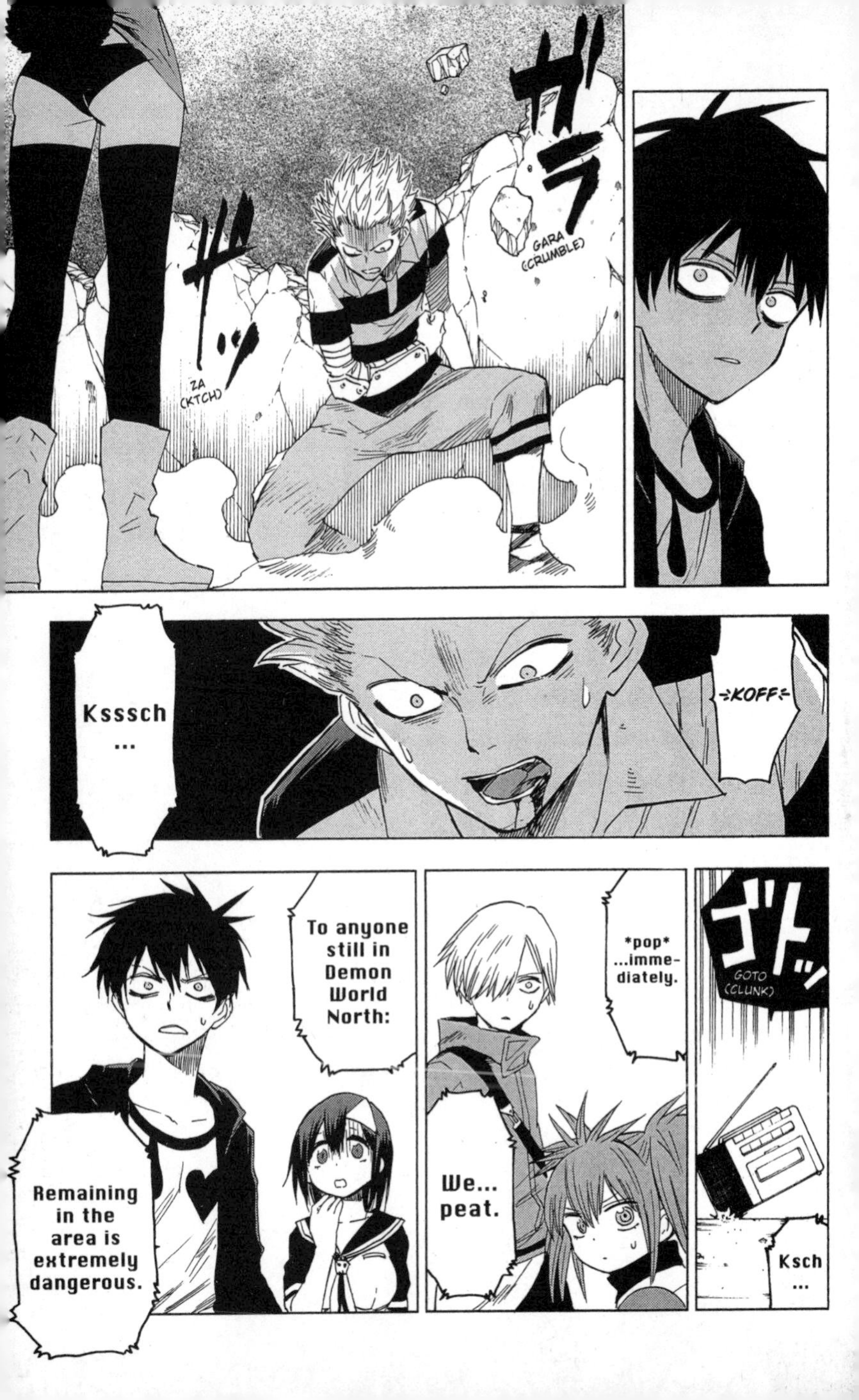
GARA (CRUMBLE)
ZA (KTCH)
KOFF
Ksssch ...
GOTO (CLUNK)
Ksch ...
pop ...imme-diately.
We... peat.
To anyone still in Demon World North:
Remaining in the area is extremely dangerous.

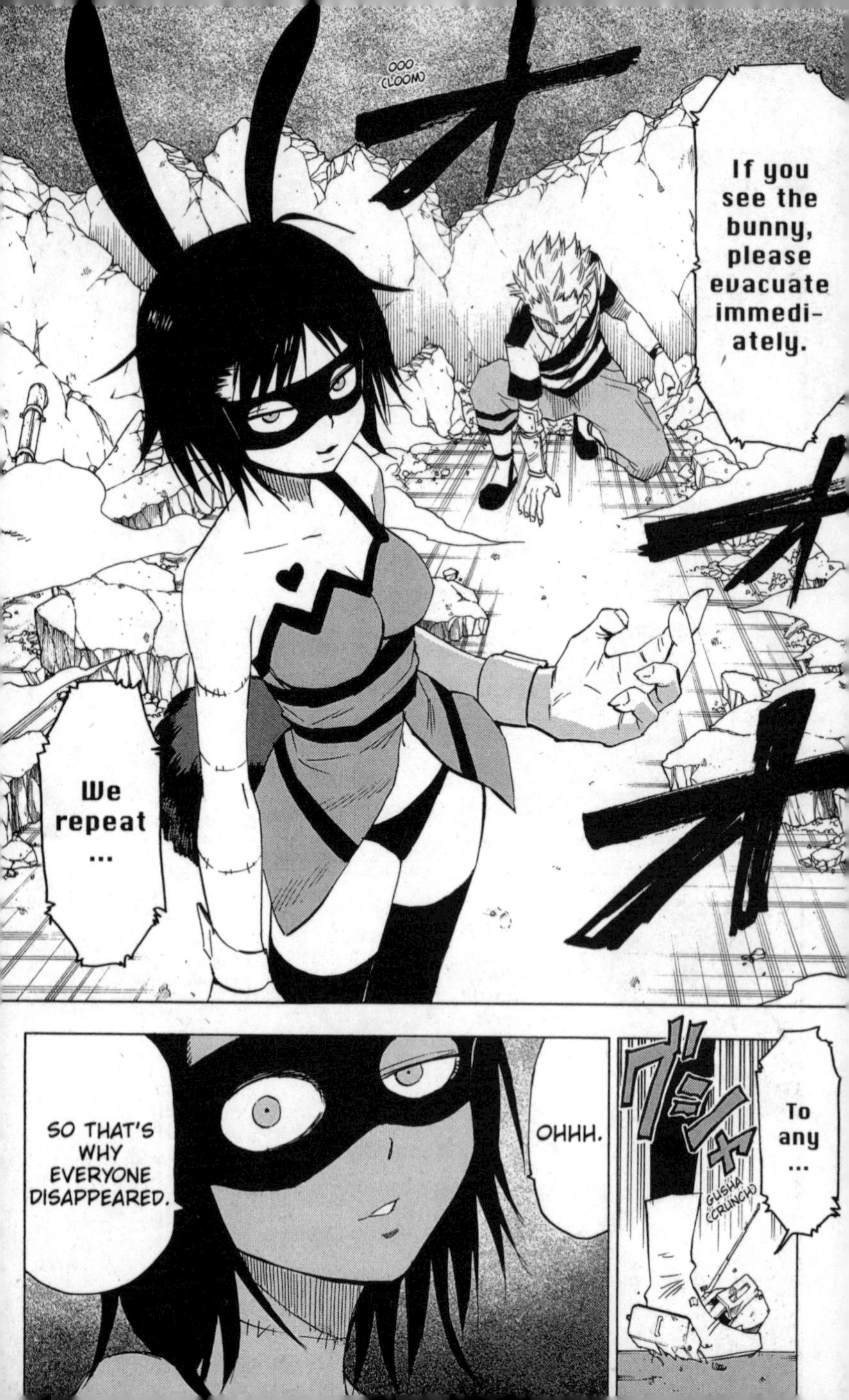
ooo
(LOOM)
If you see the bunny, please evacuate immediately.
We repeat ...
To any ...
GUSHA
(CRUNCH)
OHHH.
SO THAT'S WHY EVERYONE DISAPPEARED.

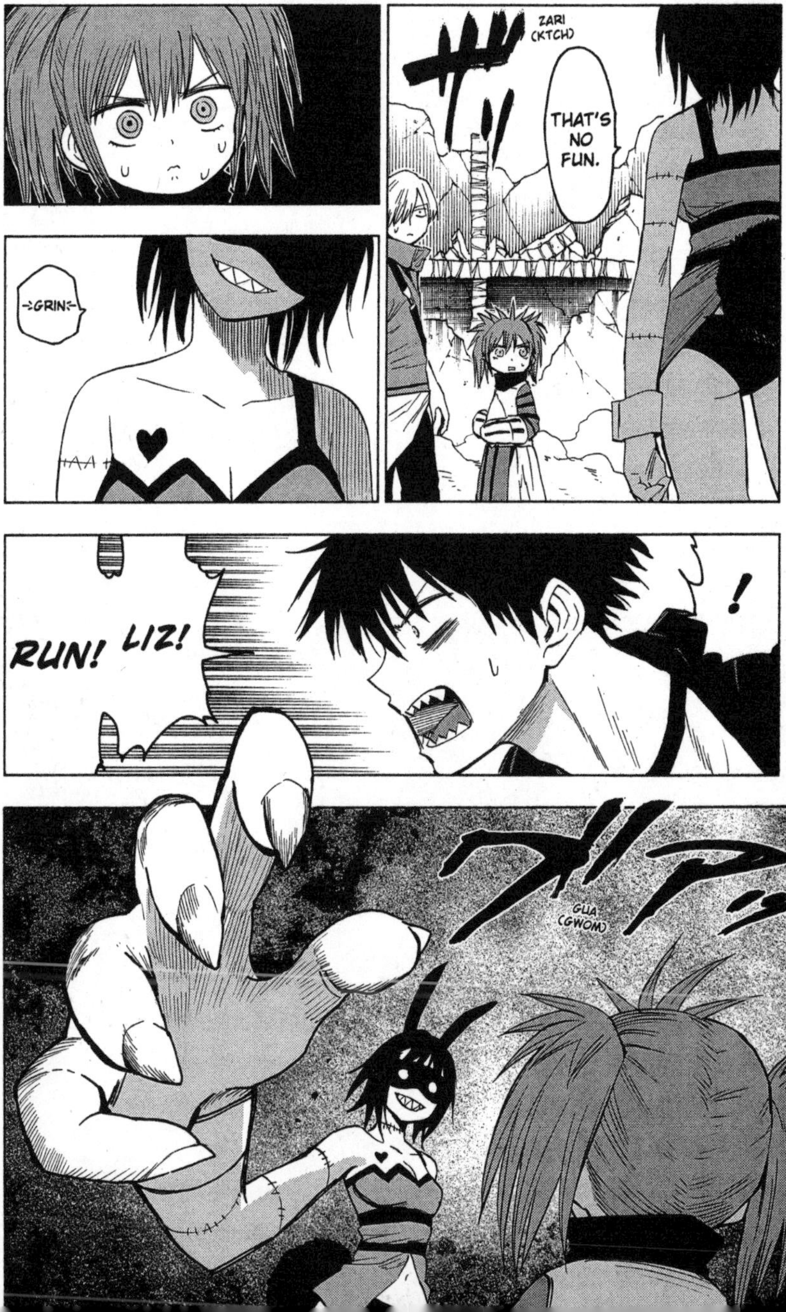
ZARI (KTCH)
THAT'S NO FUN.
-GRIN-
!
LIZ!
RUN!
GUA (GWOM)

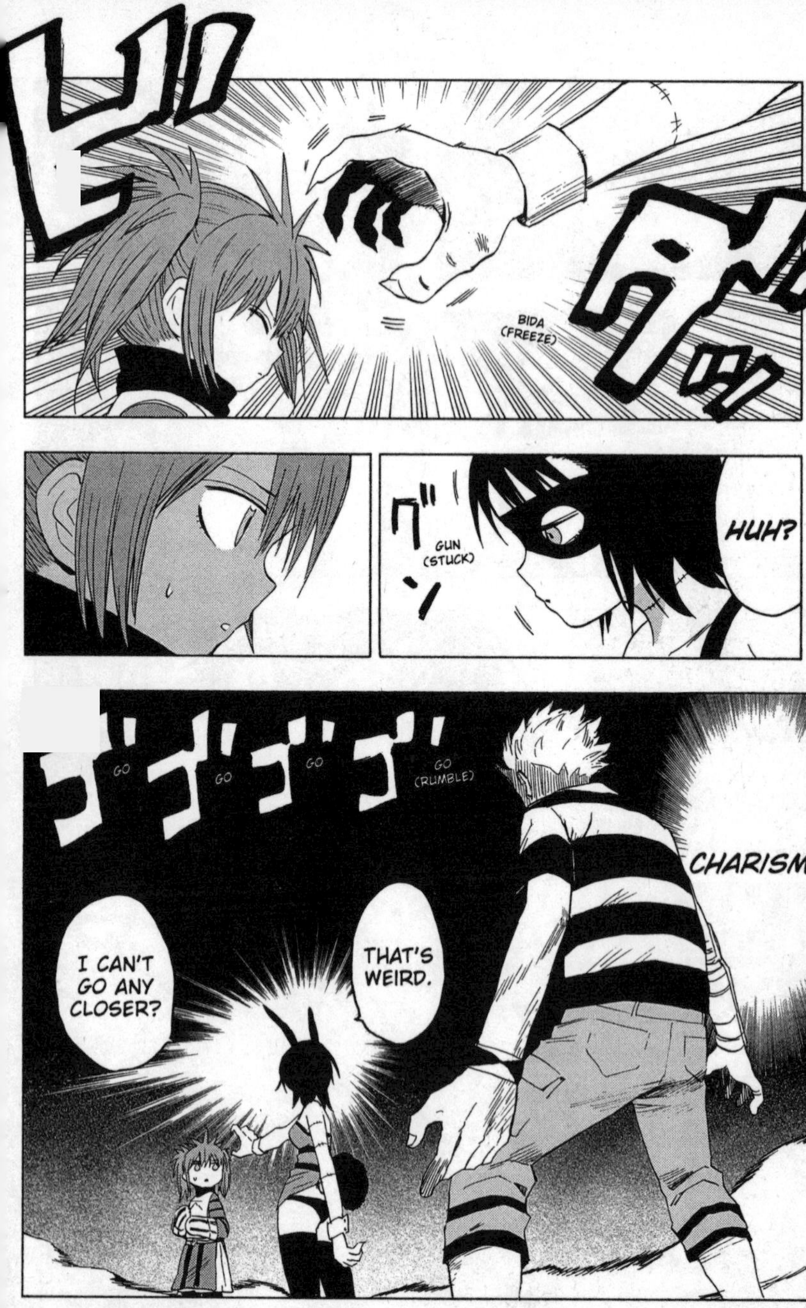
BIDA
(FREEZE)
HUH?
GUN
(STUCK)
CHARISMA.
GO GO GO GO
(RUMBLE)
THAT'S WEIRD.
I CAN'T GO ANY CLOSER?

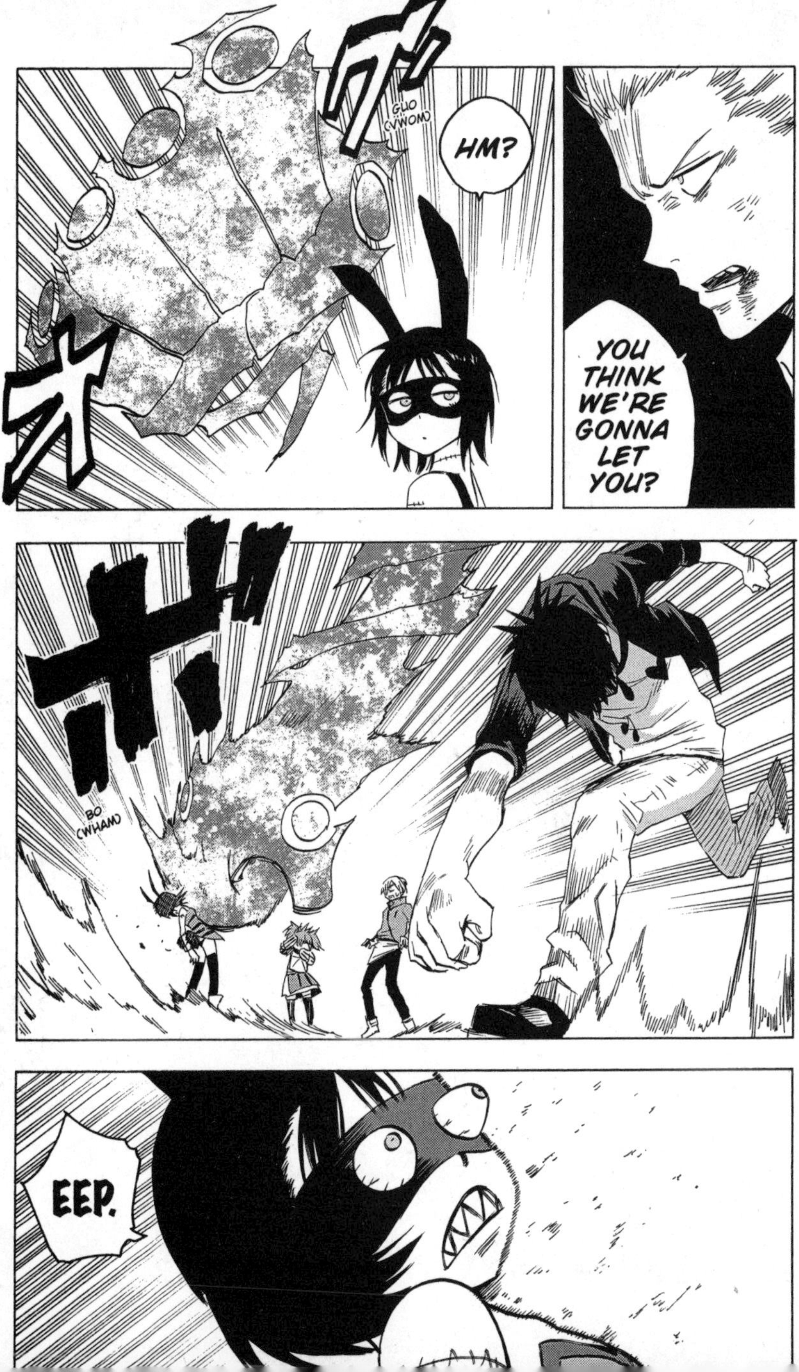
YOU THINK WE'RE GONNA LET YOU?
GUO (VWOM)
HM?
BO (WHAM)
EEP.

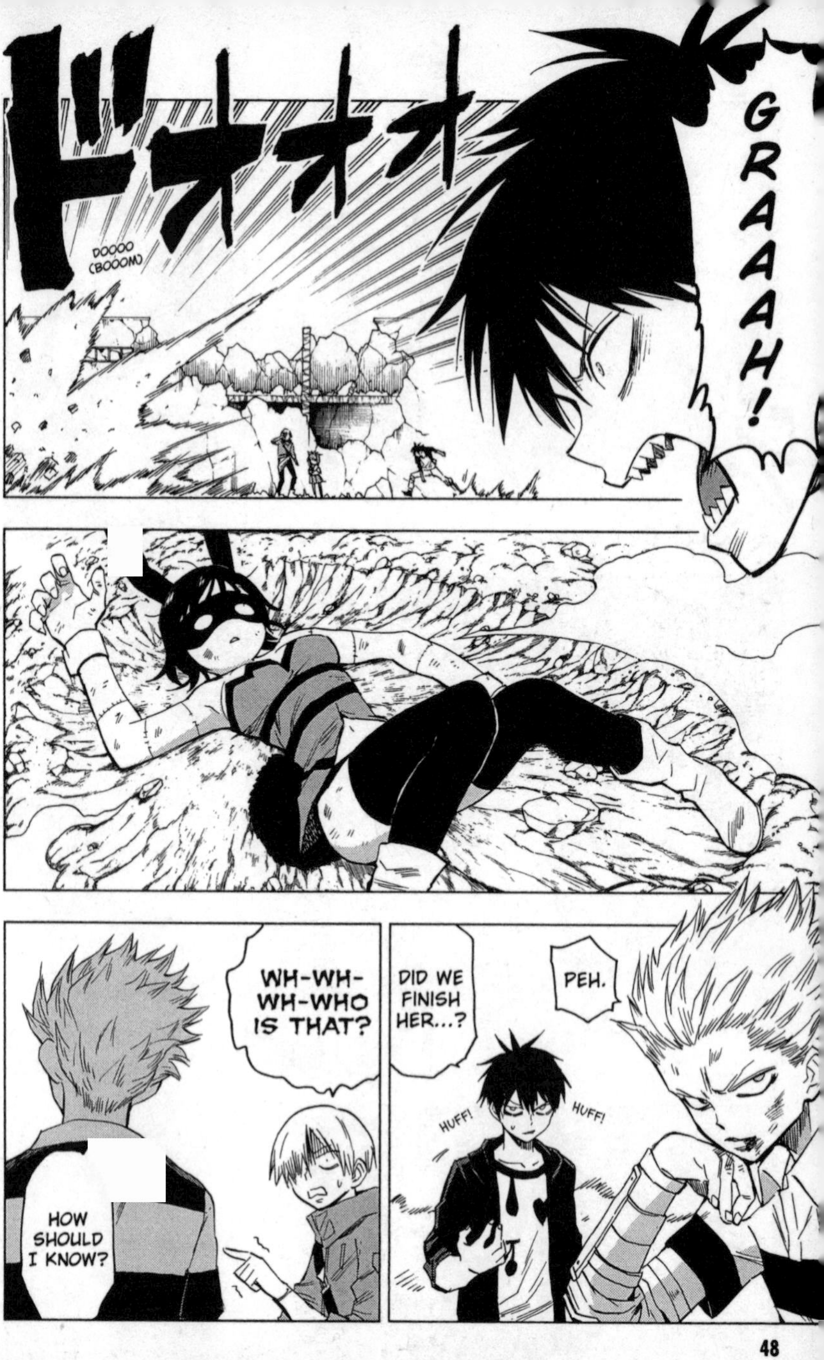
GRAAAAH!
ドオオオ
DOOOO (BOOOM)
PEH.
DID WE FINISH HER...?
HUFF!
HUFF!
WH-WH-WH-WHO IS THAT?
HOW SHOULD I KNOW?

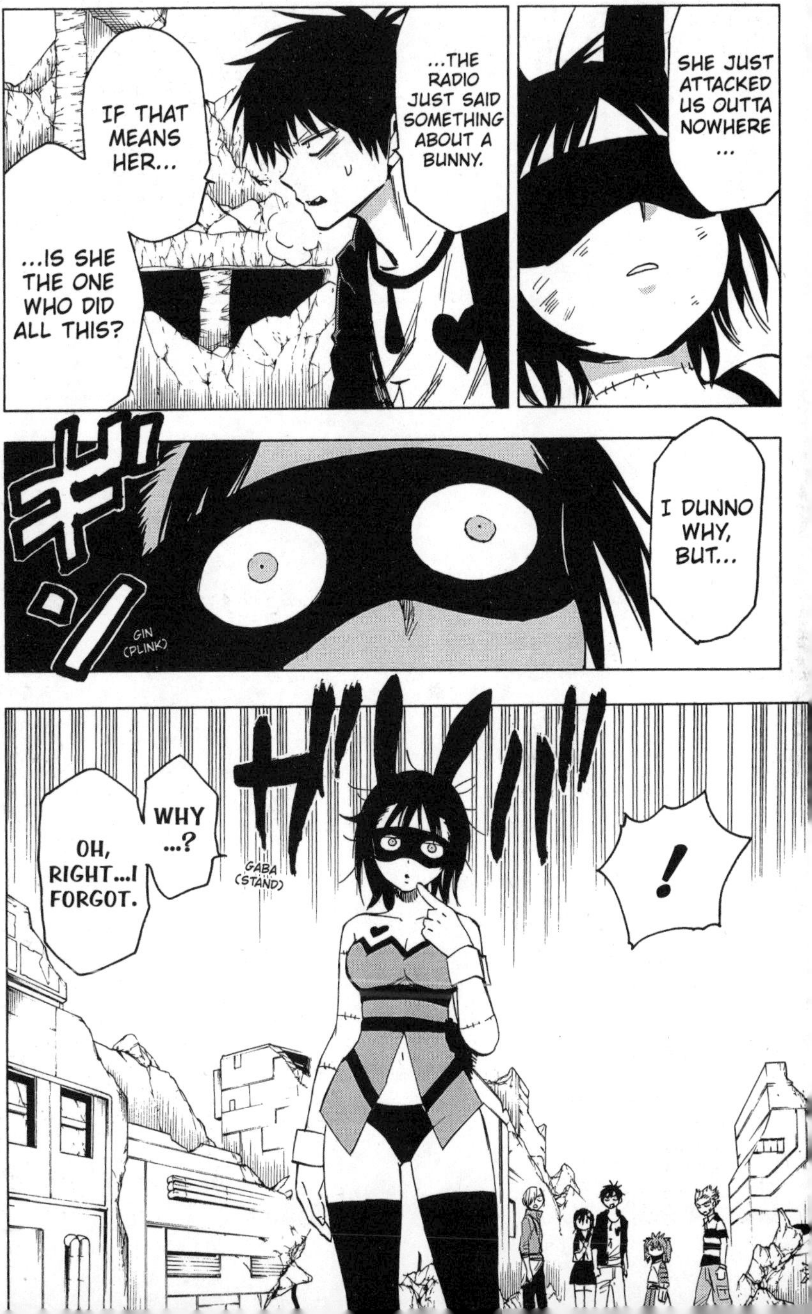
SHE JUST ATTACKED US OUTTA NOWHERE...
...THE RADIO JUST SAID SOMETHING ABOUT A BUNNY.
IF THAT MEANS HER...
...IS SHE THE ONE WHO DID ALL THIS?
I DUNNO WHY, BUT...
GIN (PLINK)
!
GABA (STAND)
WHY...?
OH, RIGHT...I FORGOT.

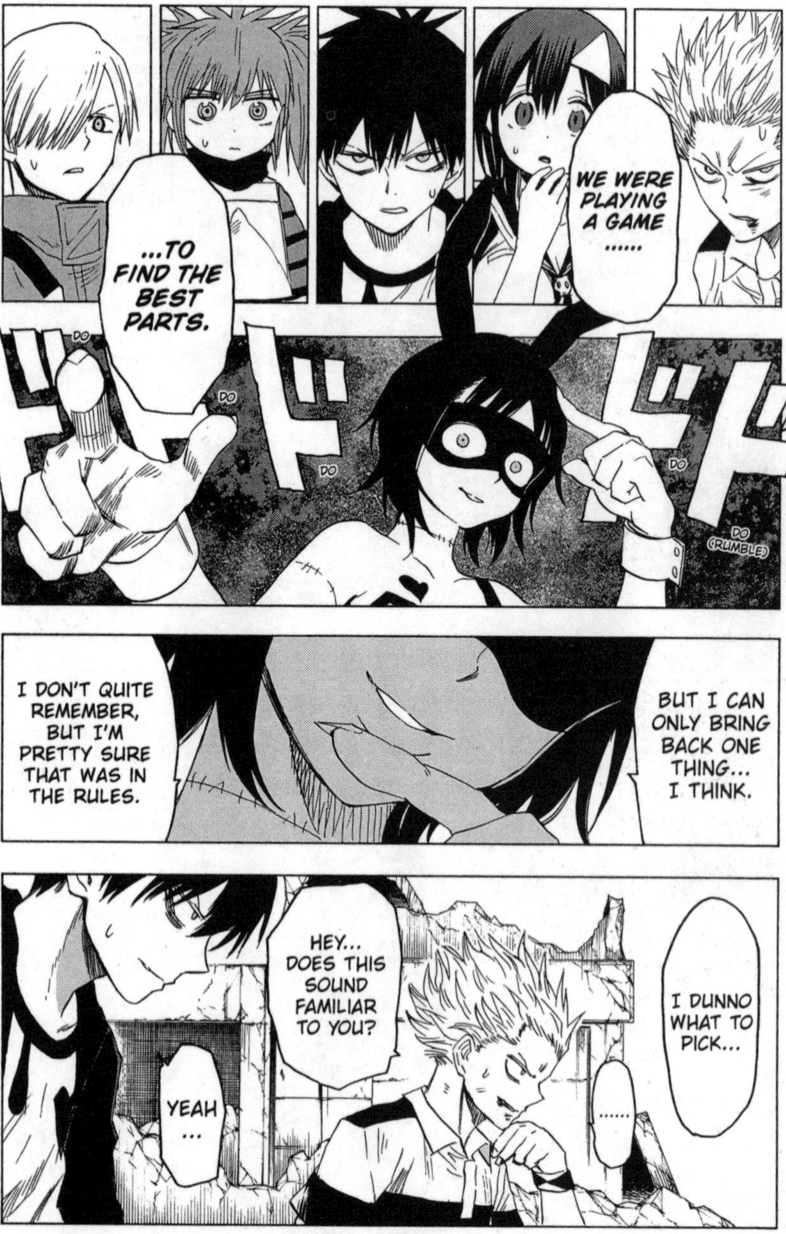
WE WERE PLAYING A GAME ......
...TO FIND THE BEST PARTS.
DO
DO
DO
DO
DO (RUMBLE)
BUT I CAN ONLY BRING BACK ONE THING... I THINK.
I DON'T QUITE REMEMBER, BUT I'M PRETTY SURE THAT WAS IN THE RULES.
I DUNNO WHAT TO PICK...
......
HEY... DOES THIS SOUND FAMILIAR TO YOU?
YEAH ...

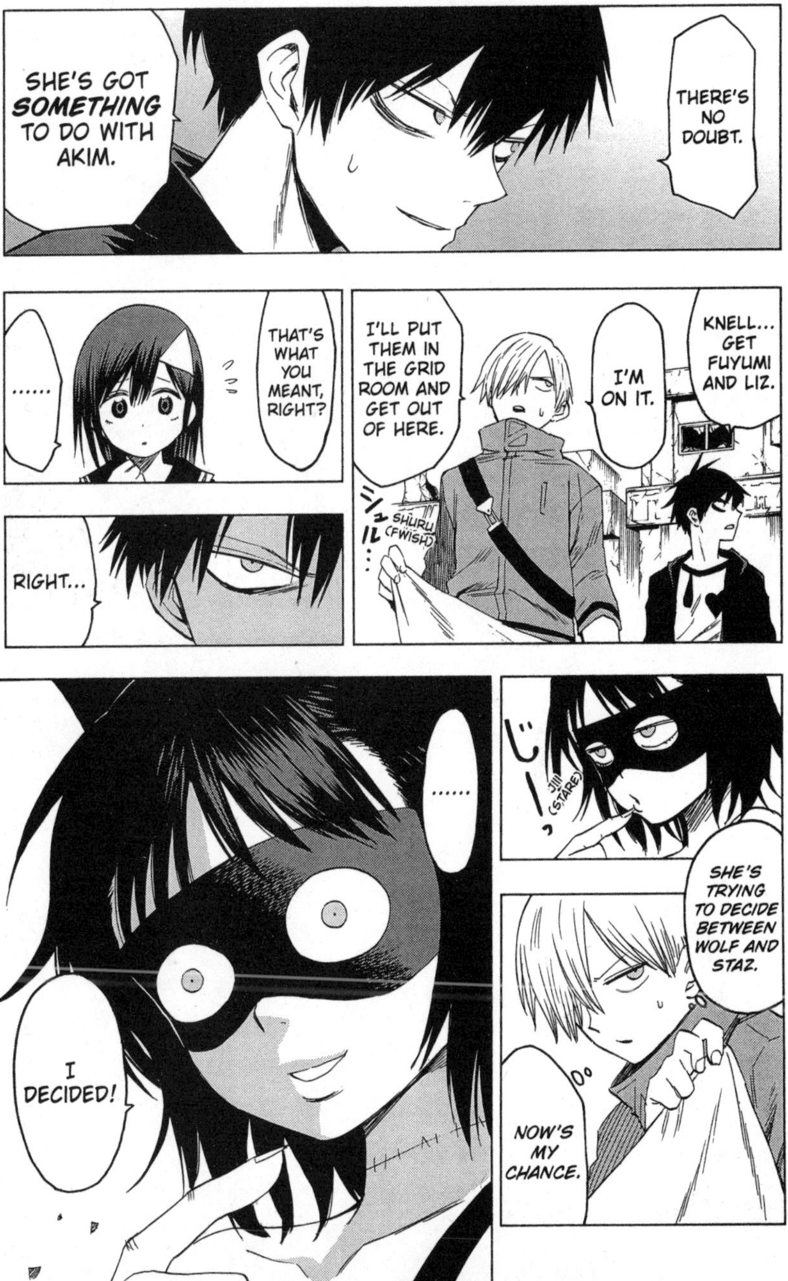
THERE'S NO DOUBT.
SHE'S GOT *SOMETHING* TO DO WITH AKIM.
KNELL... GET FUYUMI AND LIZ.
I'M ON IT.
I'LL PUT THEM IN THE GRID ROOM AND GET OUT OF HERE.
シュル… SHURU (FWISH)
THAT'S WHAT YOU MEANT, RIGHT?
......
RIGHT...
じーっ JIII (STARE)
SHE'S TRYING TO DECIDE BETWEEN WOLF AND STAZ.
NOW'S MY CHANCE.
......
I DECIDED!

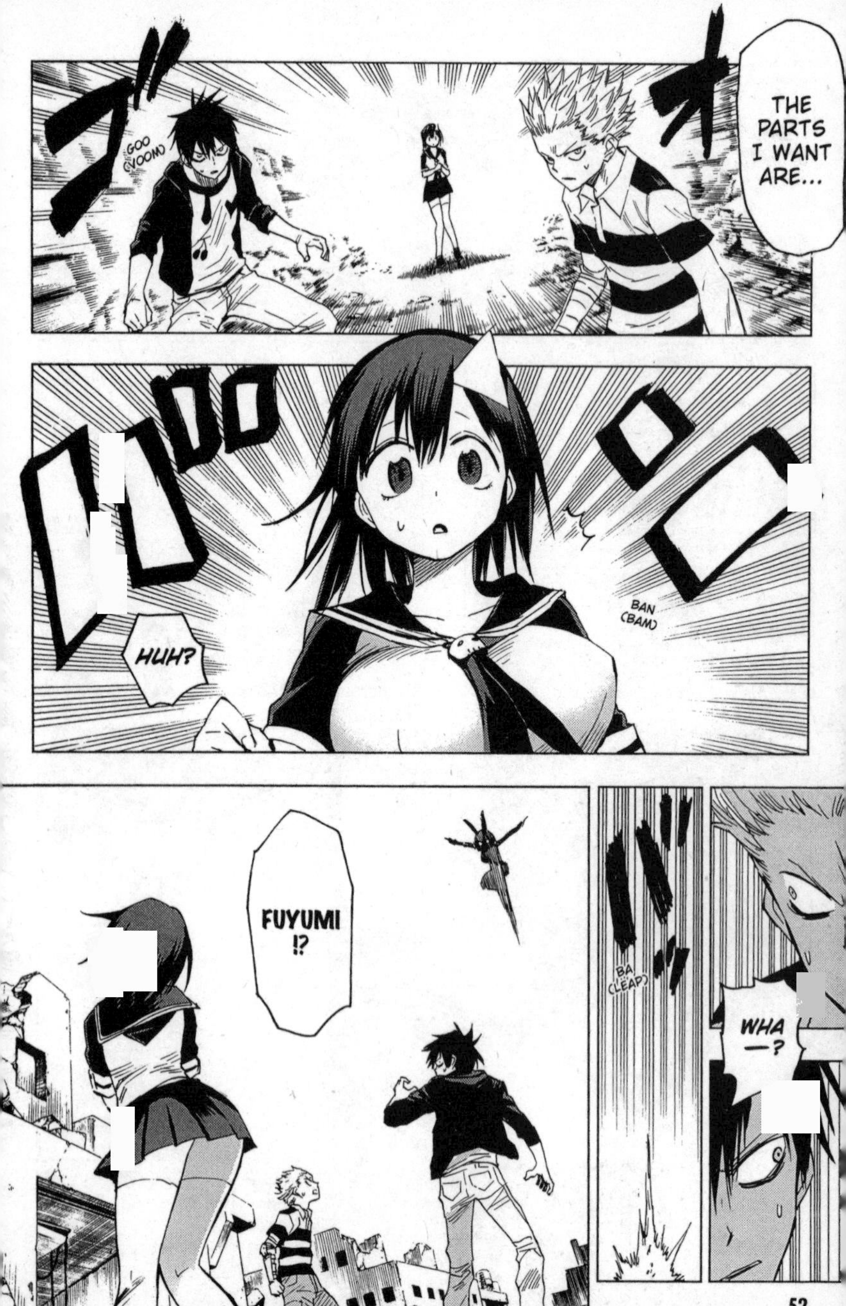
THE PARTS I WANT ARE...
GOO (VOOM)
BAN (BAM)
HUH?
WHA—?
BA (LEAP)
FUYUMI !?

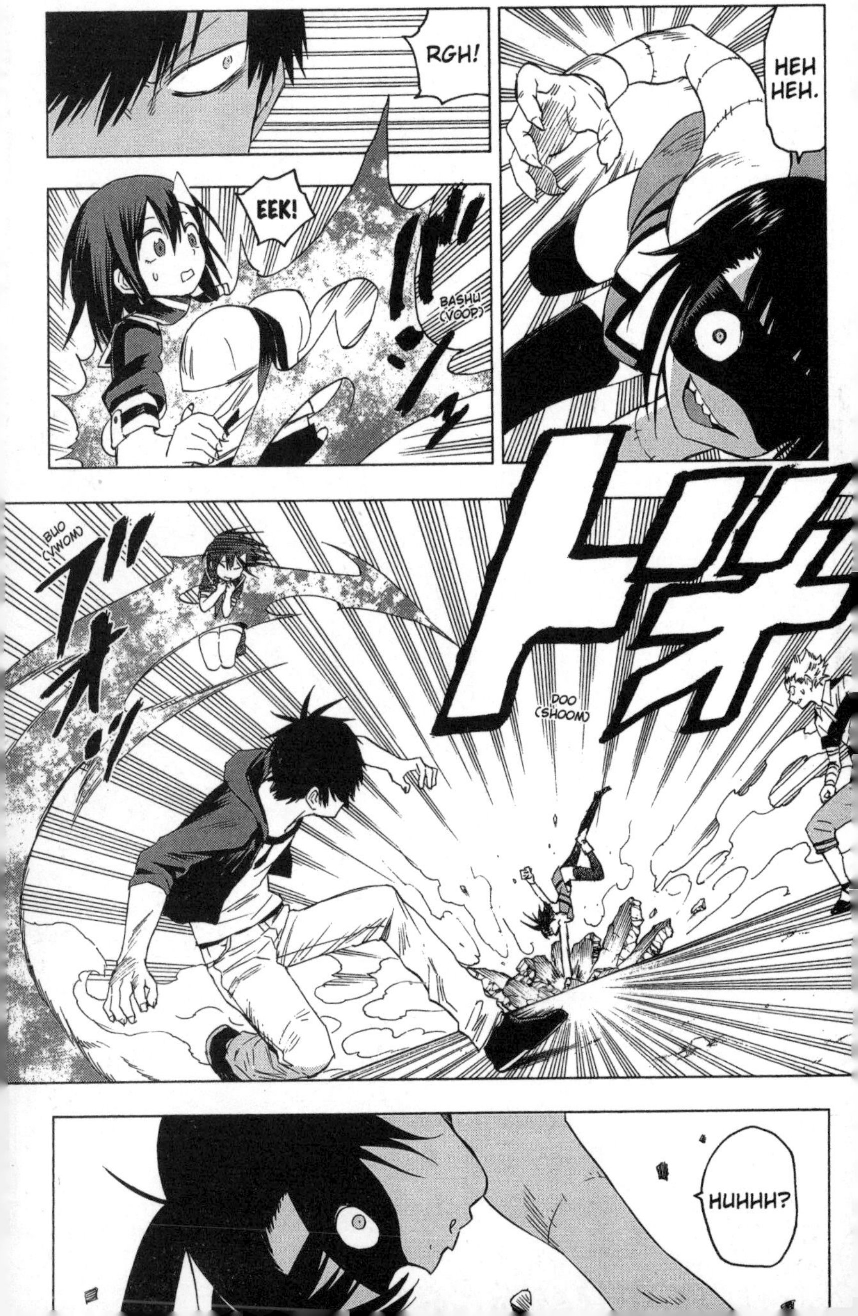
HEH HEH.
RGH!
EEK!
BASHU (VOOP)
DOO (SHOOM)
BUO (VWOM)
HUHHH?

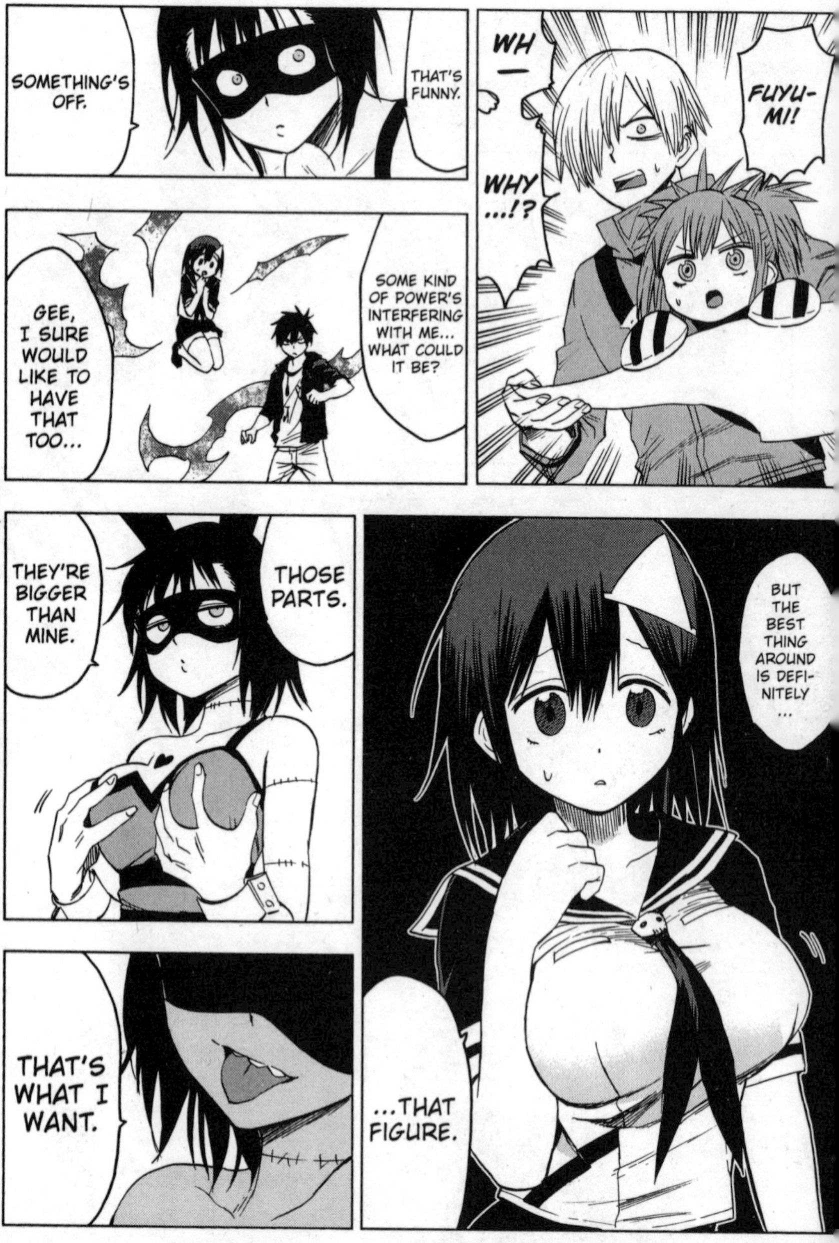
FUYU-MI!
WH—
WHY...!?
THAT'S FUNNY.
SOMETHING'S OFF.
SOME KIND OF POWER'S INTERFERING WITH ME... WHAT COULD IT BE?
GEE, I SURE WOULD LIKE TO HAVE THAT TOO...
BUT THE BEST THING AROUND IS DEFINITELY...
...THAT FIGURE.
THOSE PARTS.
THEY'RE BIGGER THAN MINE.
THAT'S WHAT I WANT.

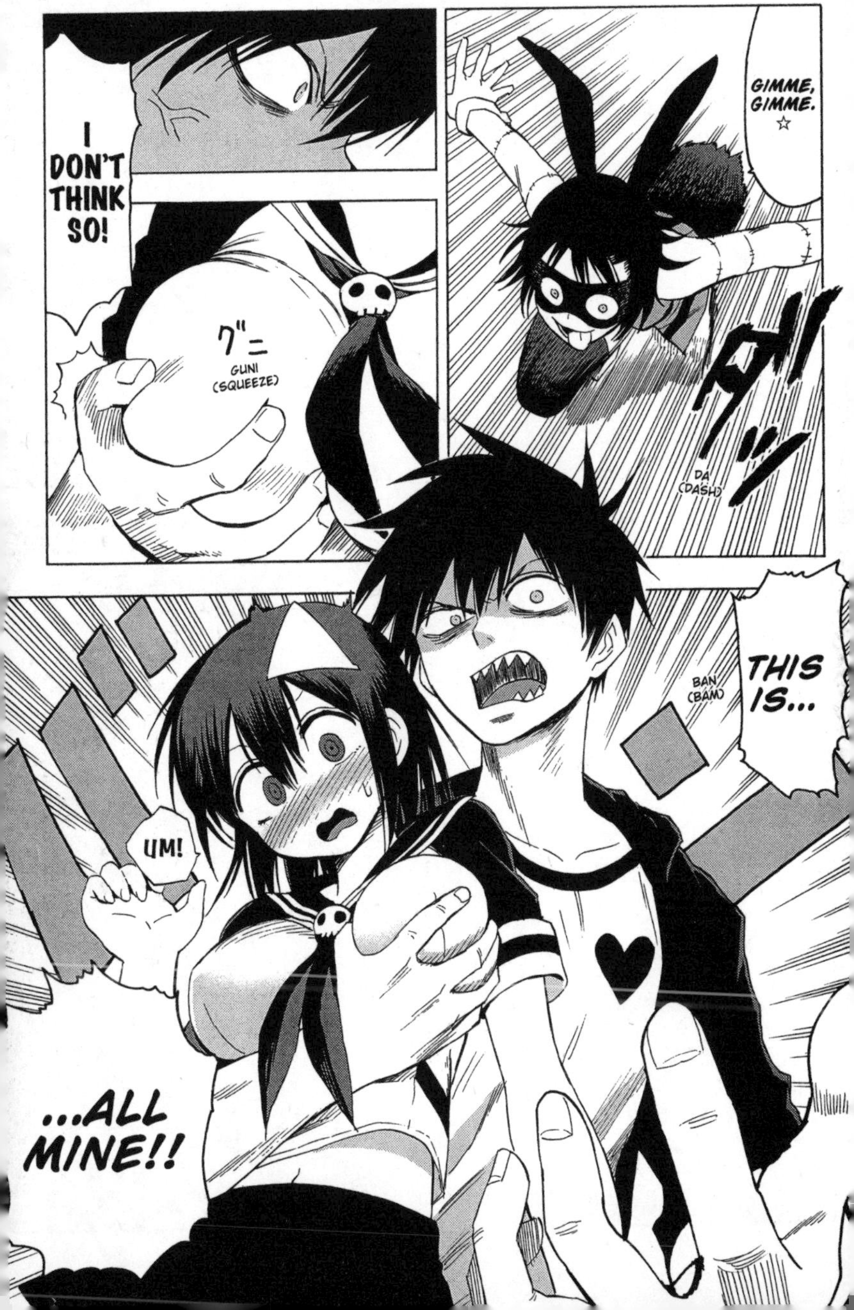
GIMME, GIMME. ☆
ダッ
DA (DASH)
I DON'T THINK SO!
グニ
GUNI (SQUEEZE)
THIS IS...
BAN (BAM)
UM!
...ALL MINE!!

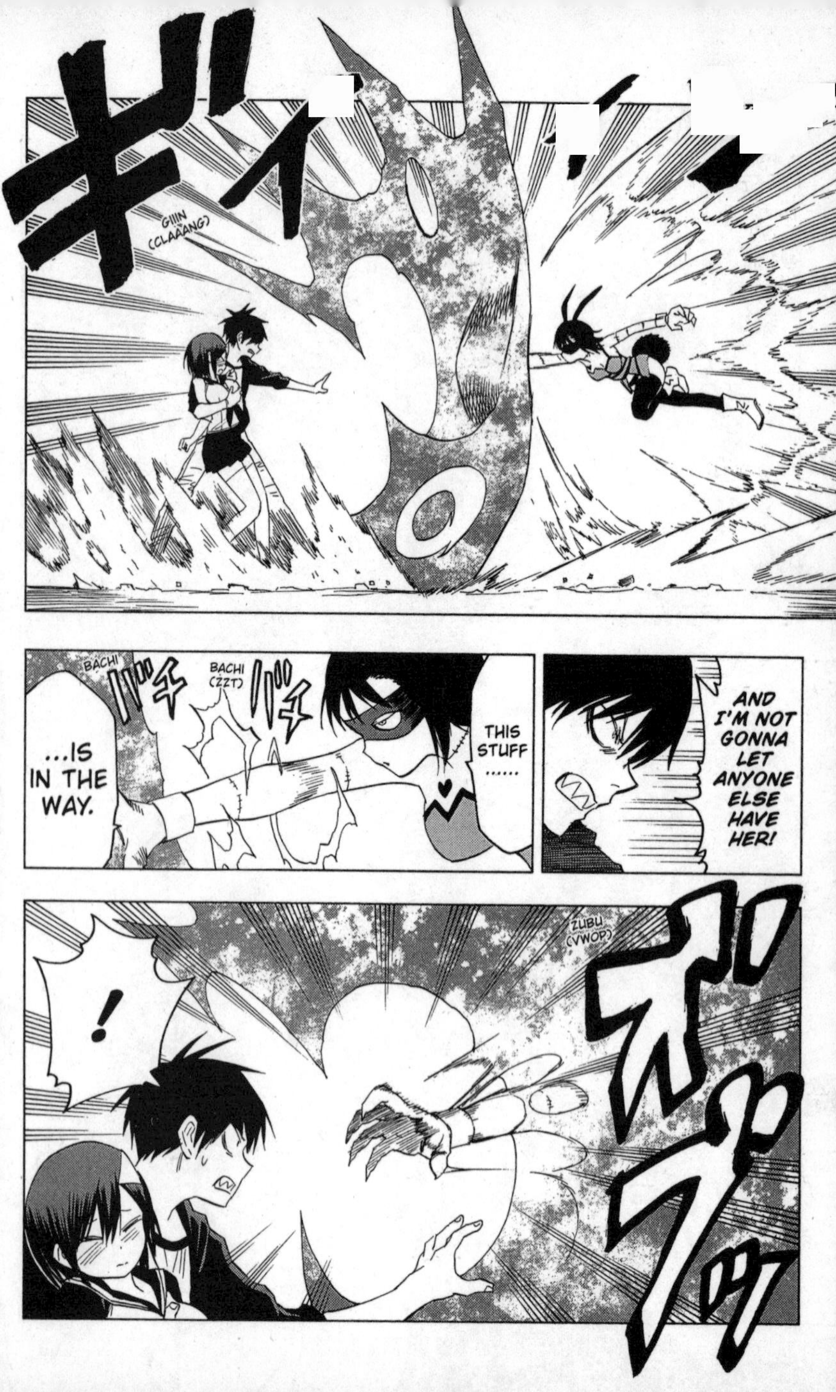
GIIIN (CLAAANG)
AND I'M NOT GONNA LET ANYONE ELSE HAVE HER!
BACHI (ZZT)
BACHI
THIS STUFF......
...IS IN THE WAY.
ZUBU (VWOP)
!

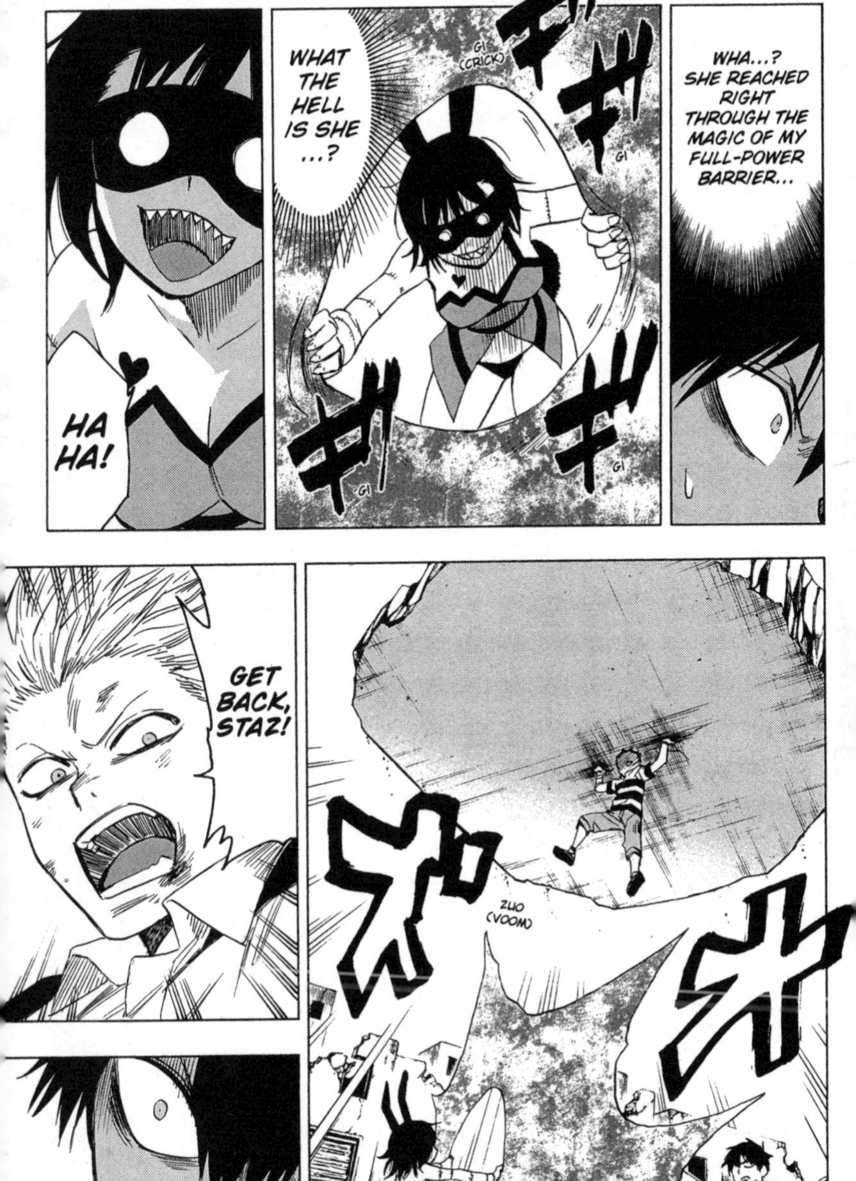
WHA...? SHE REACHED RIGHT THROUGH THE MAGIC OF MY FULL-POWER BARRIER...
GI (CRICK)
WHAT THE HELL IS SHE ...?
GI
GI
GI
HA HA!
ZUO (VOOM)
GET BACK, STAZ!

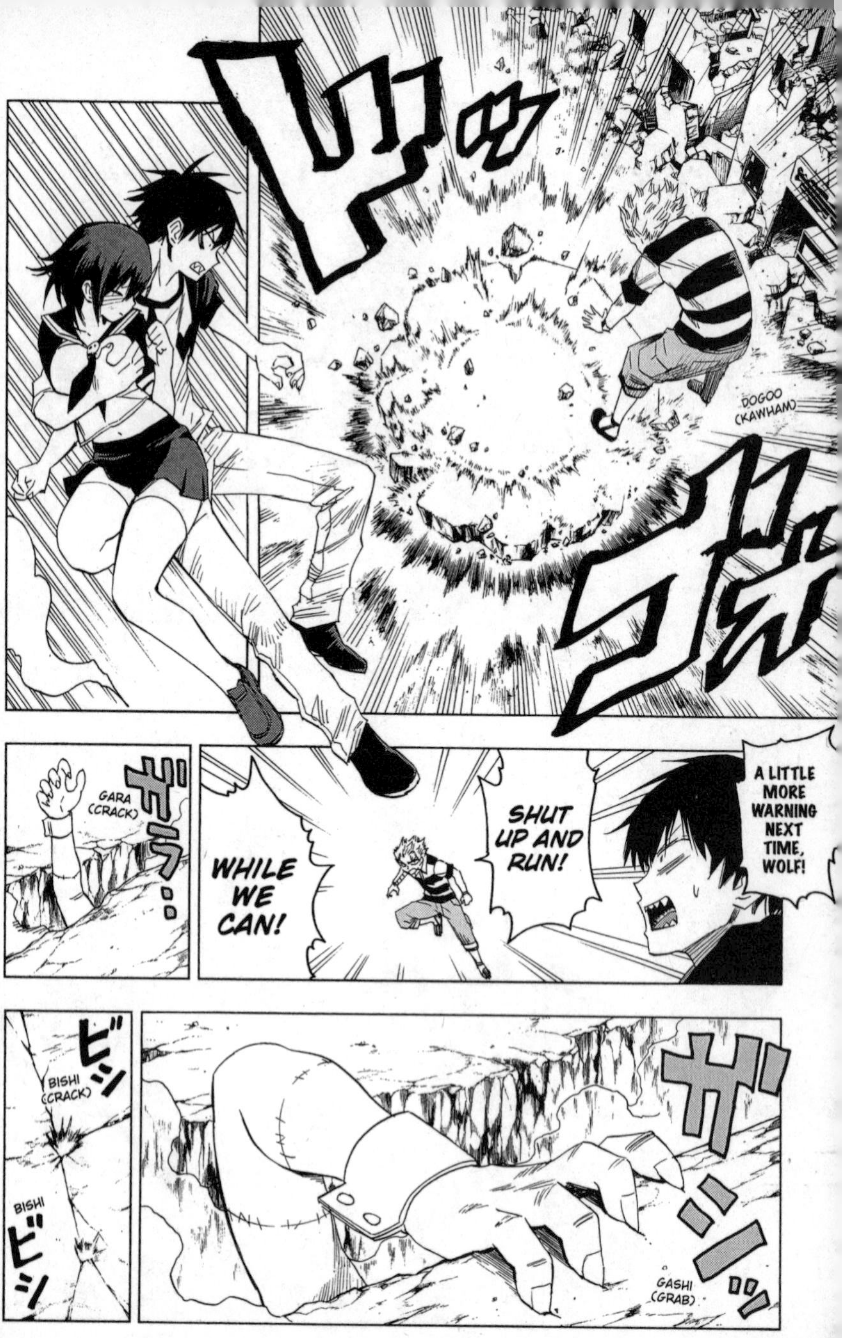
DOGOO
(KAWHAM)
A LITTLE MORE WARNING NEXT TIME, WOLF!
SHUT UP AND RUN!
WHILE WE CAN!
GARA
(CRACK)
GASHI
(GRAB)
BISHI
(CRACK)
BISHI

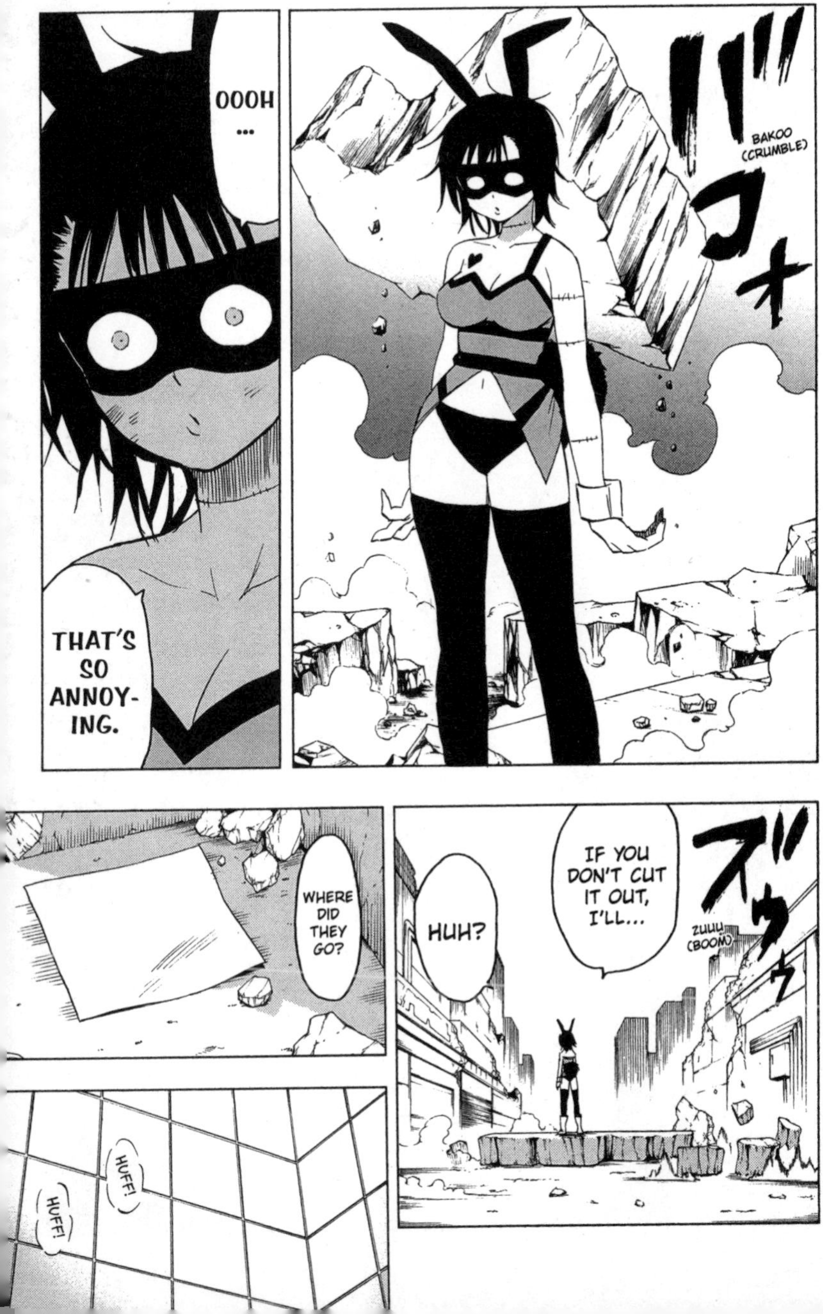
BAKOO (CRUMBLE)
OOOH ...
THAT'S SO ANNOY-ING.
ZUUU (BOOM)
IF YOU DON'T CUT IT OUT, I'LL...
HUH?
WHERE DID THEY GO?
HUFF!
HUFF!

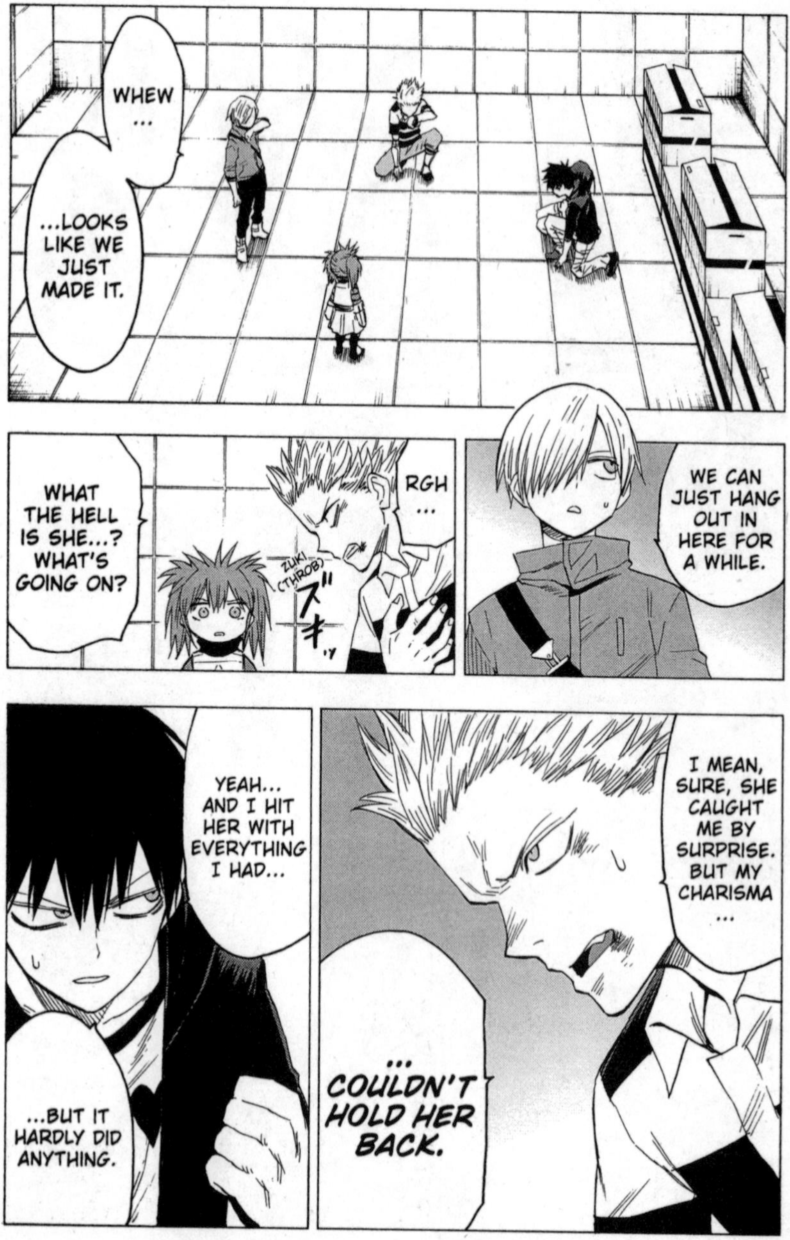
WHEW
...
...LOOKS LIKE WE JUST MADE IT.
WE CAN JUST HANG OUT IN HERE FOR A WHILE.
RGH
...
ZUKI (THROB)
ズキッ
WHAT THE HELL IS SHE...? WHAT'S GOING ON?
I MEAN, SURE, SHE CAUGHT ME BY SURPRISE. BUT MY CHARISMA
...
...
COULDN'T HOLD HER BACK.
YEAH... AND I HIT HER WITH EVERYTHING I HAD...
...BUT IT HARDLY DID ANYTHING.

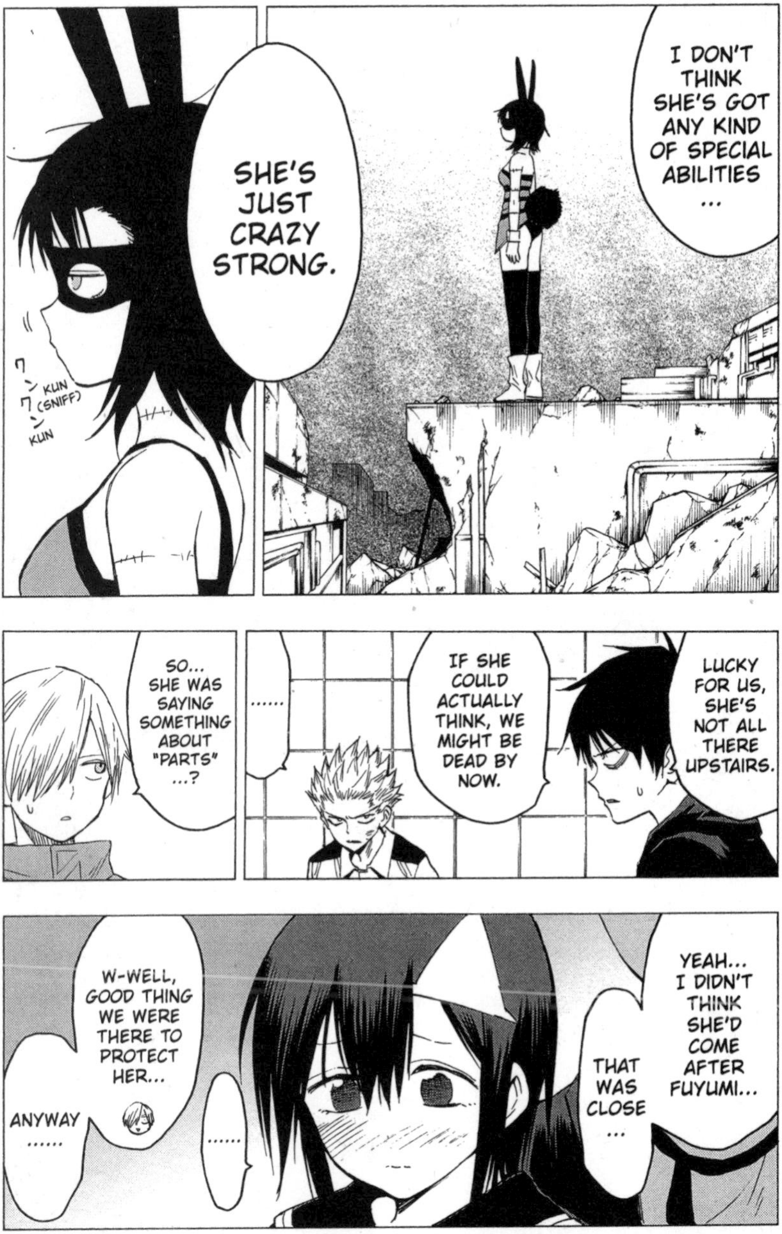
I DON'T THINK SHE'S GOT ANY KIND OF SPECIAL ABILITIES...
SHE'S JUST CRAZY STRONG.
KUN (SNIFF) KUN
LUCKY FOR US, SHE'S NOT ALL THERE UPSTAIRS.
IF SHE COULD ACTUALLY THINK, WE MIGHT BE DEAD BY NOW.
......
SO... SHE WAS SAYING SOMETHING ABOUT "PARTS"...?
YEAH... I DIDN'T THINK SHE'D COME AFTER FUYUMI...
THAT WAS CLOSE...
W-WELL, GOOD THING WE WERE THERE TO PROTECT HER...
......
ANYWAY......

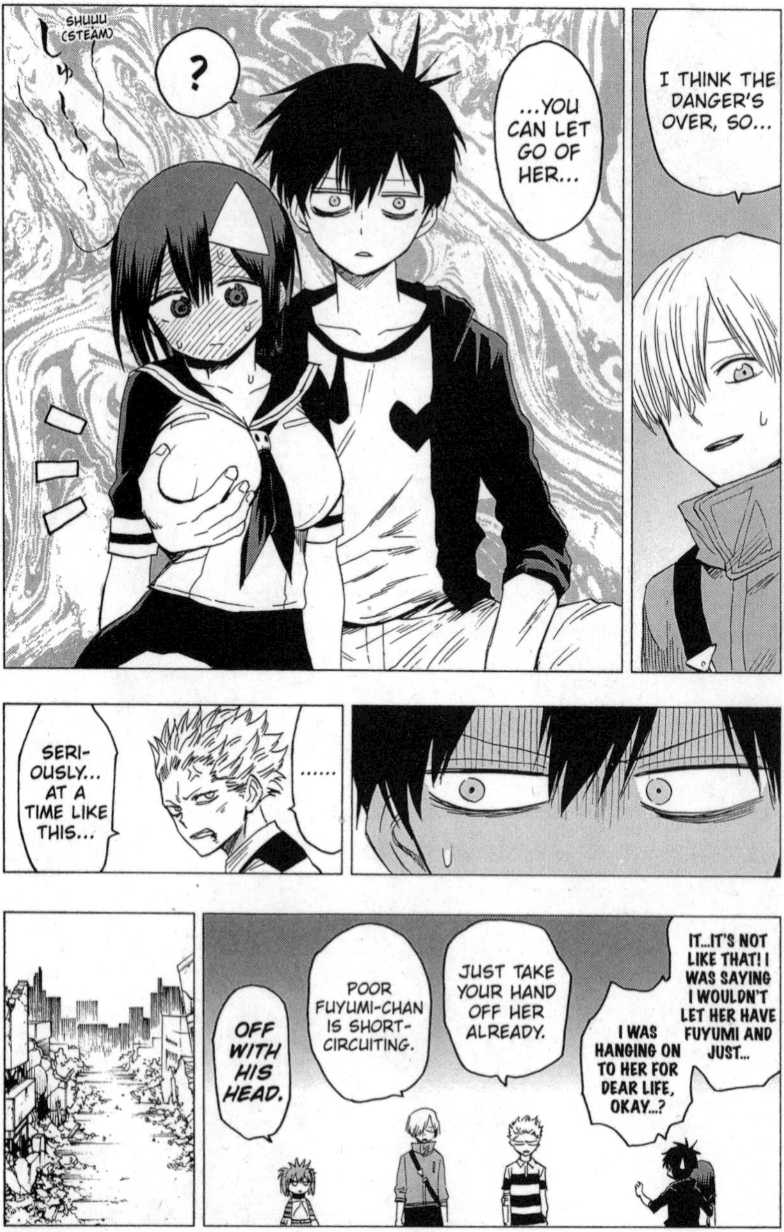
I THINK THE DANGER'S OVER, SO...
...YOU CAN LET GO OF HER...
?
SHUUU (STEAM)
......
SERIOUSLY... AT A TIME LIKE THIS...
IT...IT'S NOT LIKE THAT! I WAS SAYING I WOULDN'T LET HER HAVE FUYUMI AND JUST...
I WAS HANGING ON TO HER FOR DEAR LIFE, OKAY...?
JUST TAKE YOUR HAND OFF HER ALREADY.
POOR FUYUMI-CHAN IS SHORT-CIRCUITING.
OFF WITH HIS HEAD.

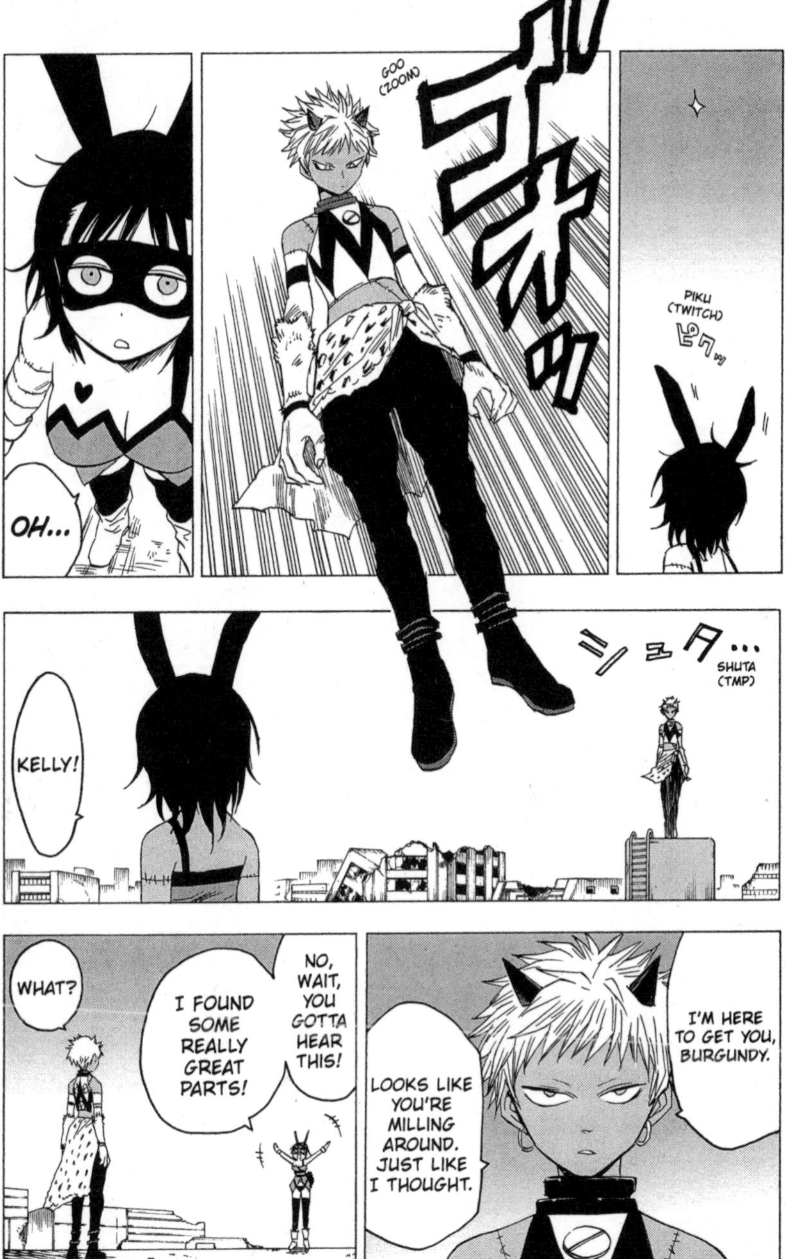
PIKU (TWITCH)
ピクッ
GOO (ZOOM)
OH...
シュタ…
SHUTA (TMP)
KELLY!
I'M HERE TO GET YOU, BURGUNDY.
LOOKS LIKE YOU'RE MILLING AROUND. JUST LIKE I THOUGHT.
NO, WAIT, YOU GOTTA HEAR THIS!
I FOUND SOME REALLY GREAT PARTS!
WHAT?

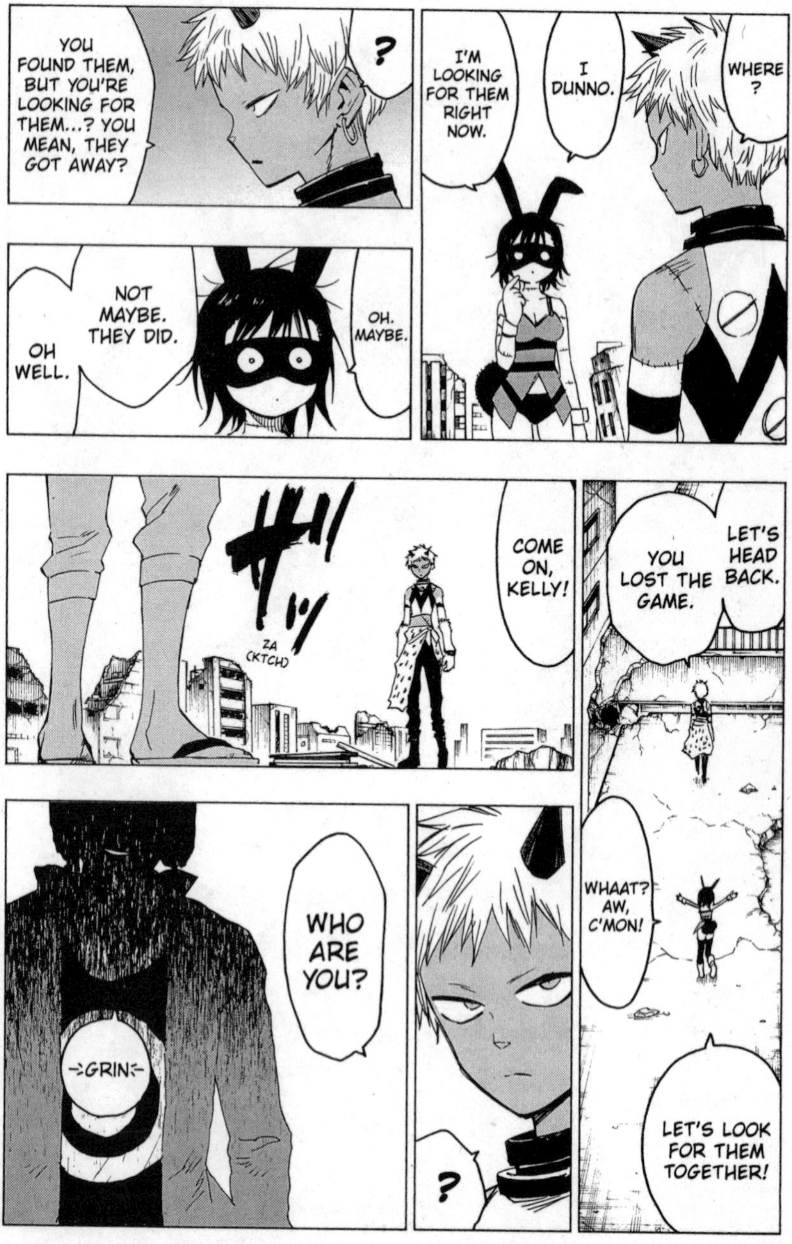
WHERE ?
I DUNNO.
I'M LOOKING FOR THEM RIGHT NOW.
?
YOU FOUND THEM, BUT YOU'RE LOOKING FOR THEM...? YOU MEAN, THEY GOT AWAY?
OH. MAYBE.
NOT MAYBE. THEY DID.
OH WELL.
LET'S HEAD BACK.
YOU LOST THE GAME.
WHAAT? AW, C'MON!
LET'S LOOK FOR THEM TOGETHER!
COME ON, KELLY!
ZA (KTCH)
?
WHO ARE YOU?
GRIN

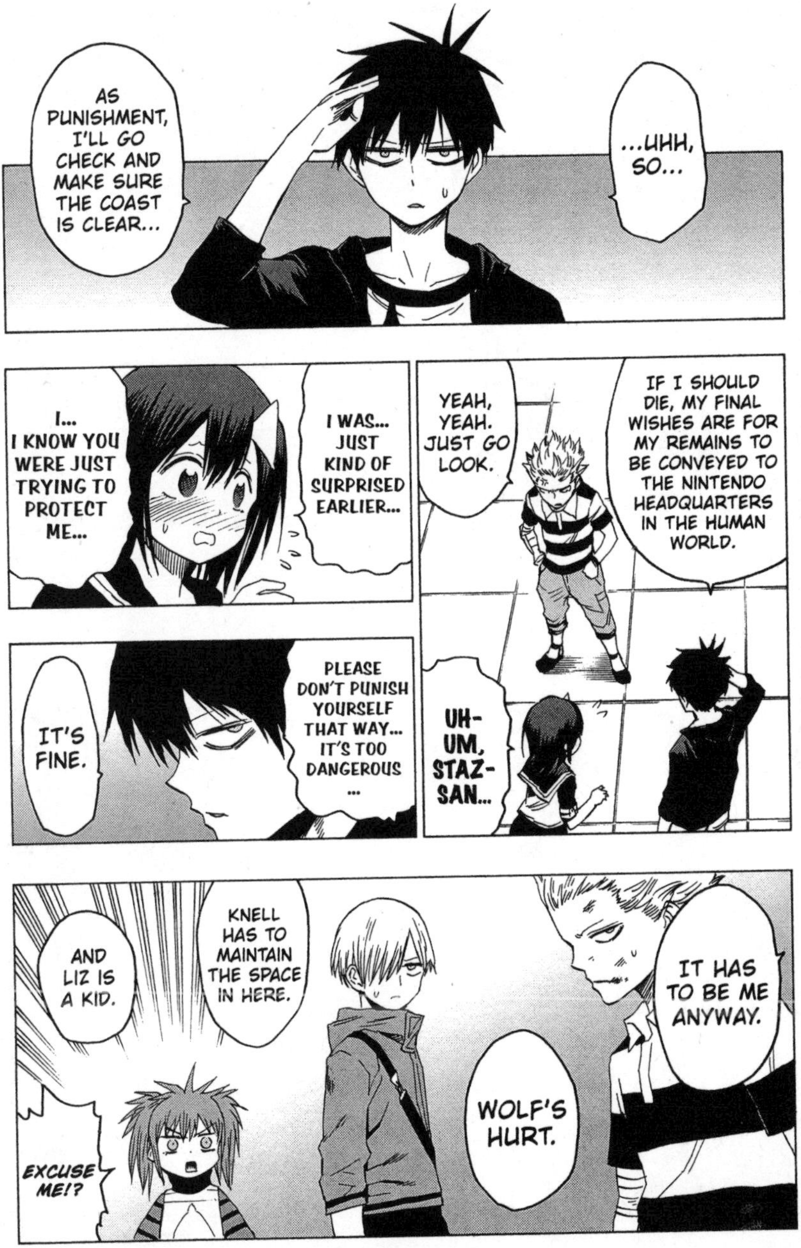
...UHH, SO...
AS PUNISHMENT, I'LL GO CHECK AND MAKE SURE THE COAST IS CLEAR...
IF I SHOULD DIE, MY FINAL WISHES ARE FOR MY REMAINS TO BE CONVEYED TO THE NINTENDO HEADQUARTERS IN THE HUMAN WORLD.
YEAH, YEAH. JUST GO LOOK.
UH-UM, STAZ-SAN...
I WAS... JUST KIND OF SURPRISED EARLIER...
I... I KNOW YOU WERE JUST TRYING TO PROTECT ME...
PLEASE DON'T PUNISH YOURSELF THAT WAY... IT'S TOO DANGEROUS ...
IT'S FINE.
IT HAS TO BE ME ANYWAY.
WOLF'S HURT.
KNELL HAS TO MAINTAIN THE SPACE IN HERE.
AND LIZ IS A KID.
EXCUSE ME!?

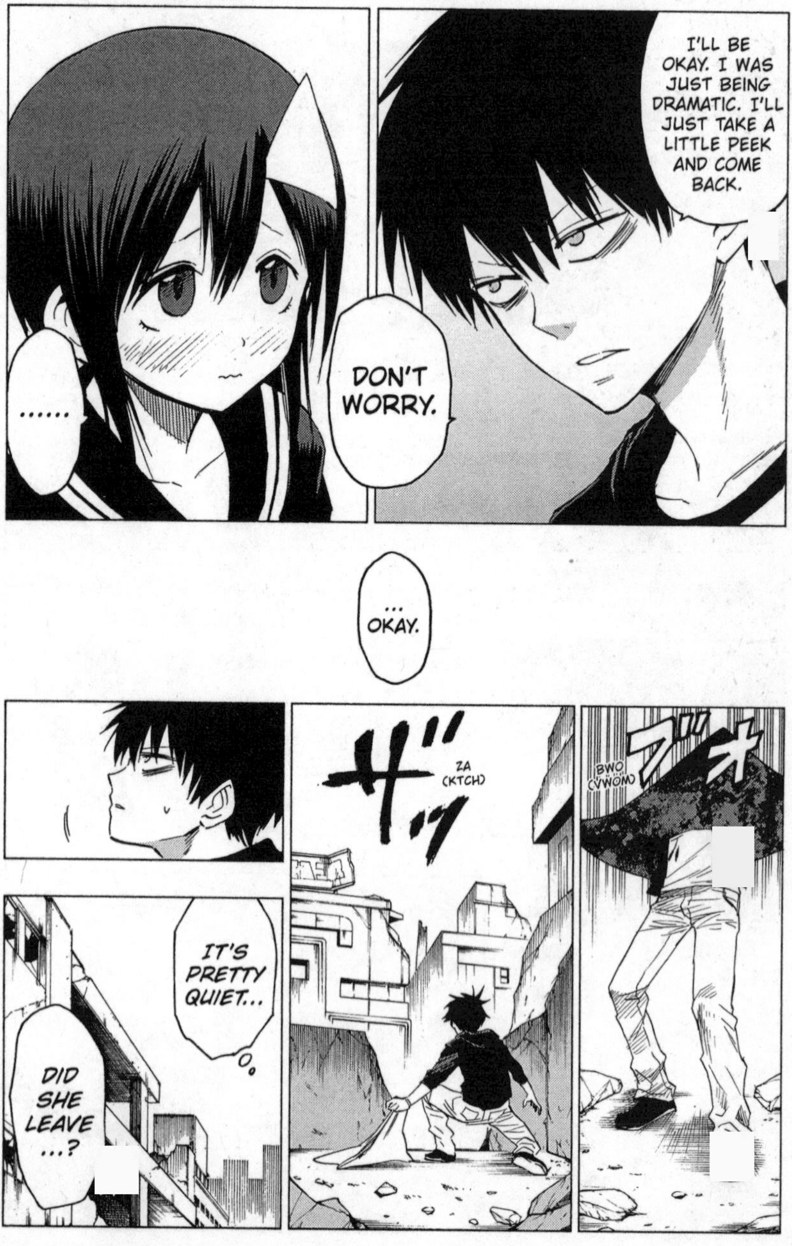
I'LL BE OKAY. I WAS JUST BEING DRAMATIC. I'LL JUST TAKE A LITTLE PEEK AND COME BACK.
DON'T WORRY.
......
... OKAY.
BWO (VWOM)
ZA (KTCH)
IT'S PRETTY QUIET...
DID SHE LEAVE ...?

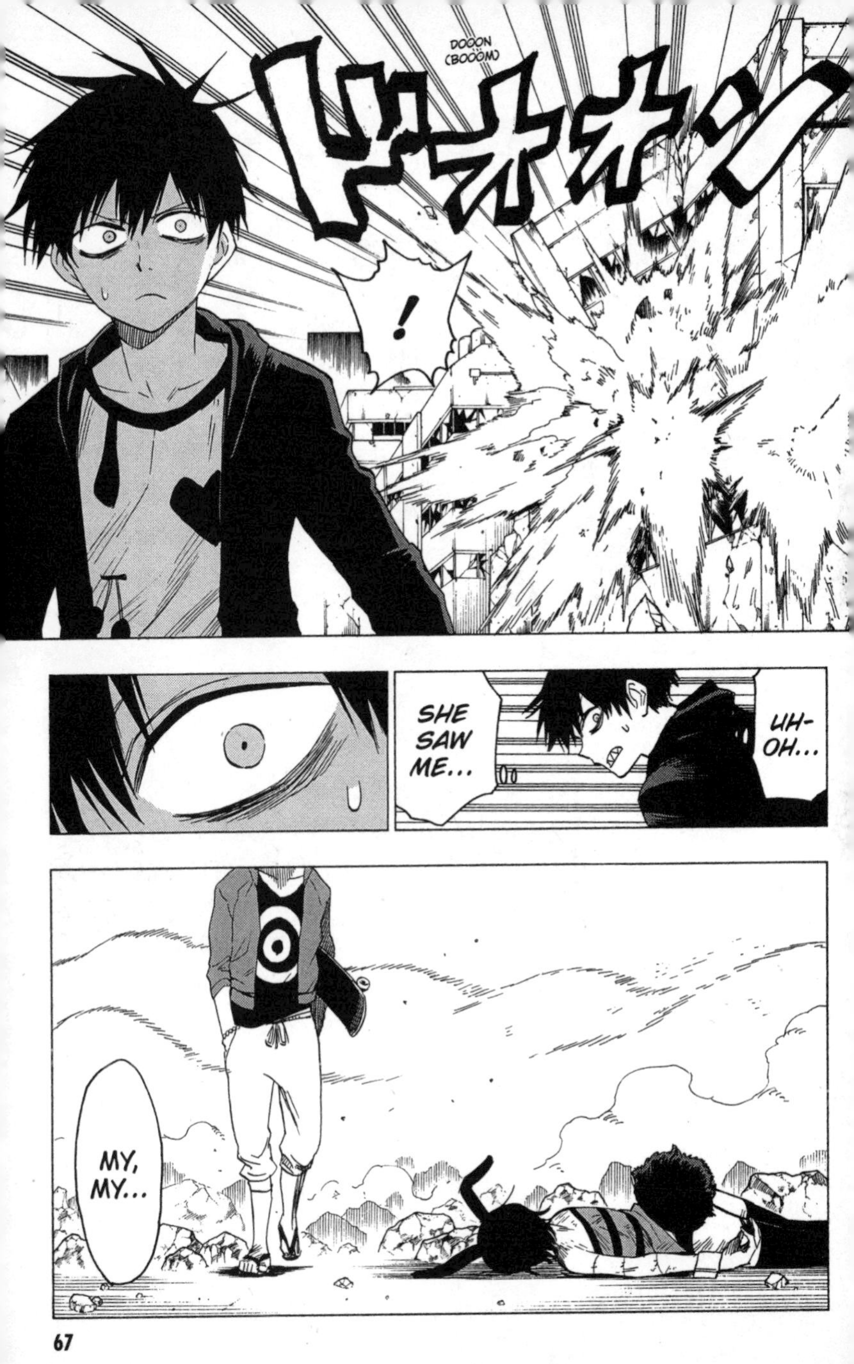
DOOON
(BOÖÖM)
!
UH-OH...
SHE SAW ME...
MY, MY...

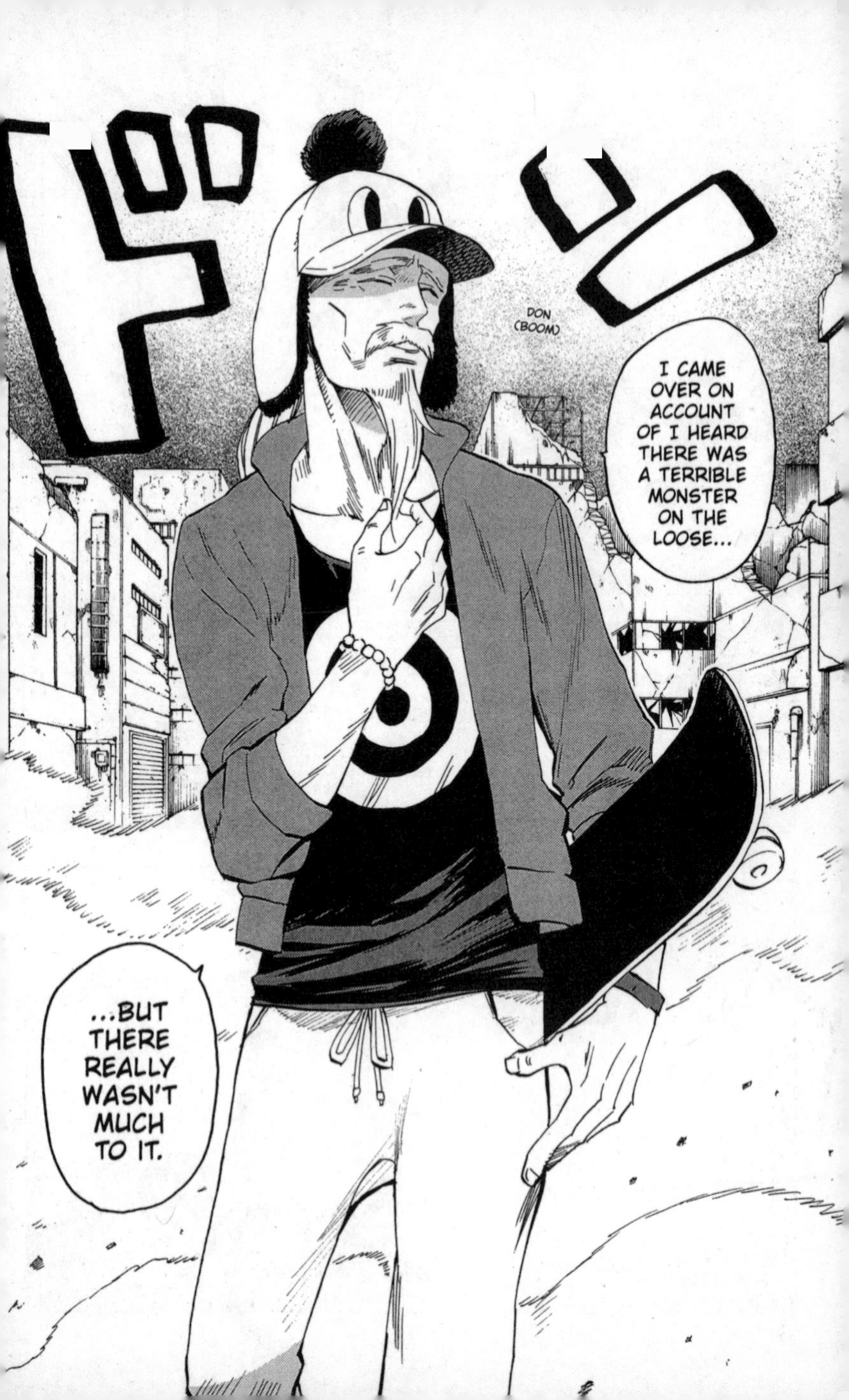
DON
(BOOM)
I CAME OVER ON ACCOUNT OF I HEARD THERE WAS A TERRIBLE MONSTER ON THE LOOSE...
...BUT THERE REALLY WASN'T MUCH TO IT.

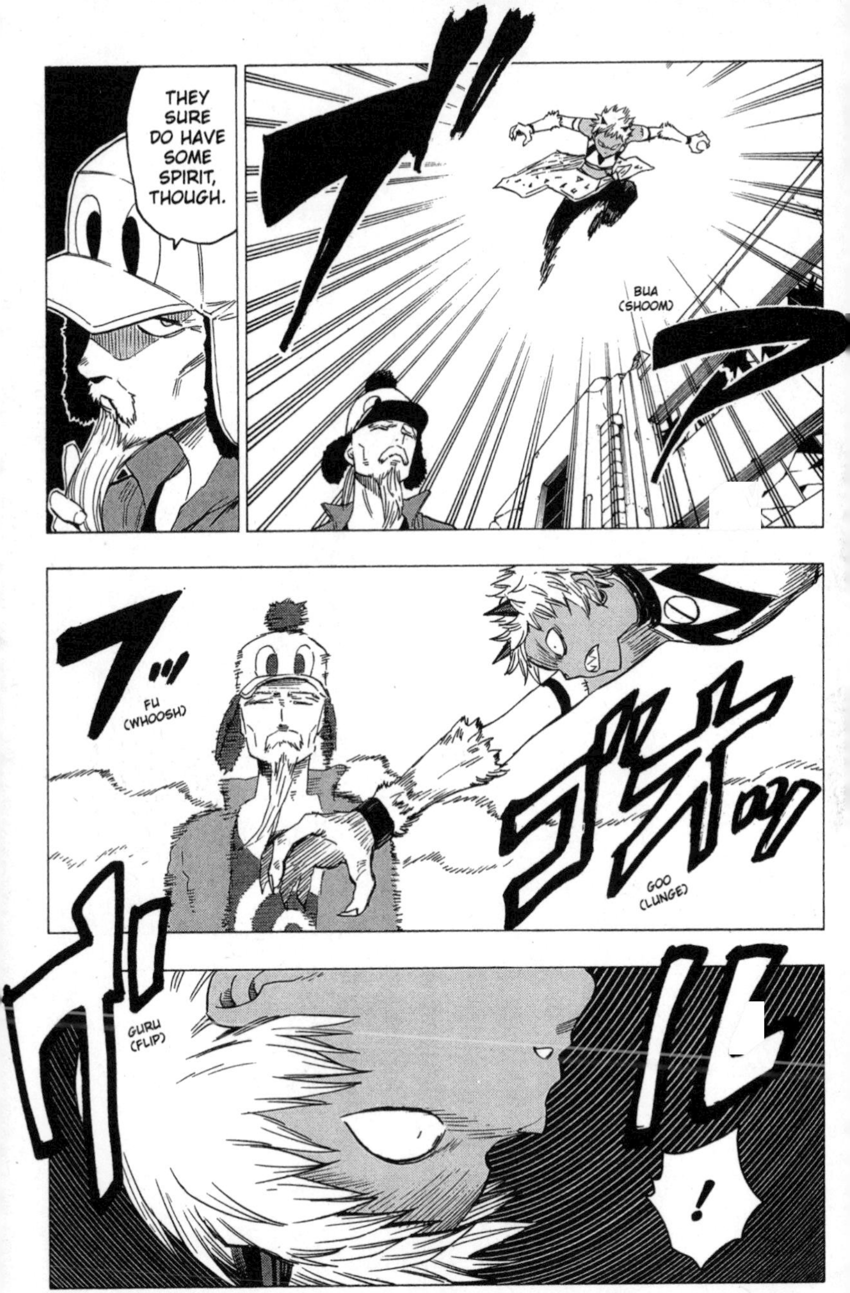
BUA (SHOOM)
THEY SURE DO HAVE SOME SPIRIT, THOUGH.
GOO (LUNGE)
FU (WHOOSH)
!
GURU (FLIP)

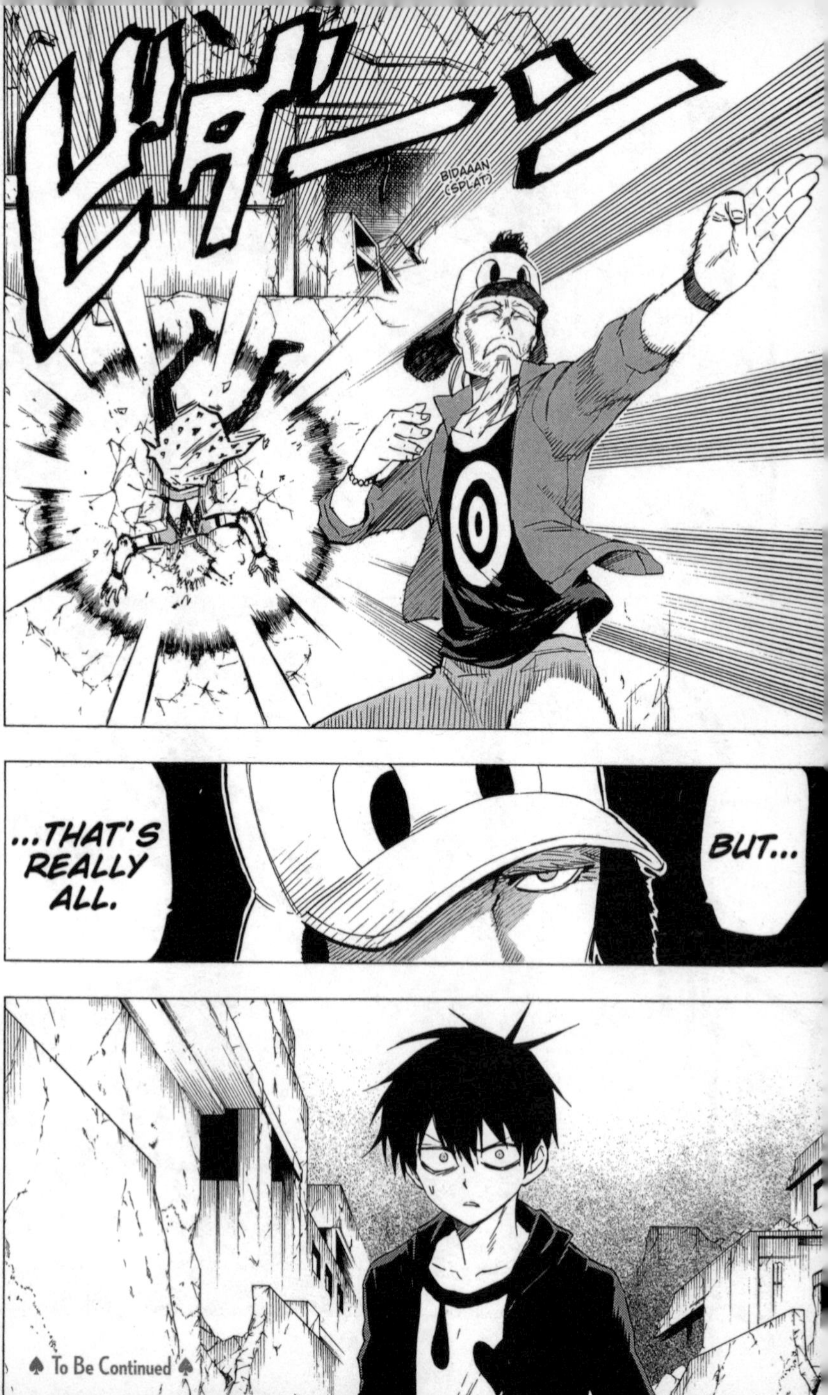
BIDAAAN
(SPLAT)
BUT...
...THAT'S REALLY ALL.
To Be Continued

THE BEST PARTS

EFFECTIVE IN
INTIMIDATING ONE'S
OPPONENT, THESE ARE
ALSO THOUGHT TO HAVE
HIGH SHOCK ABSORPTION
PROPERTIES.

BLOOD LAD

CHAPTER 53 ♠ THE OLD SOLDIERS' NETWORK

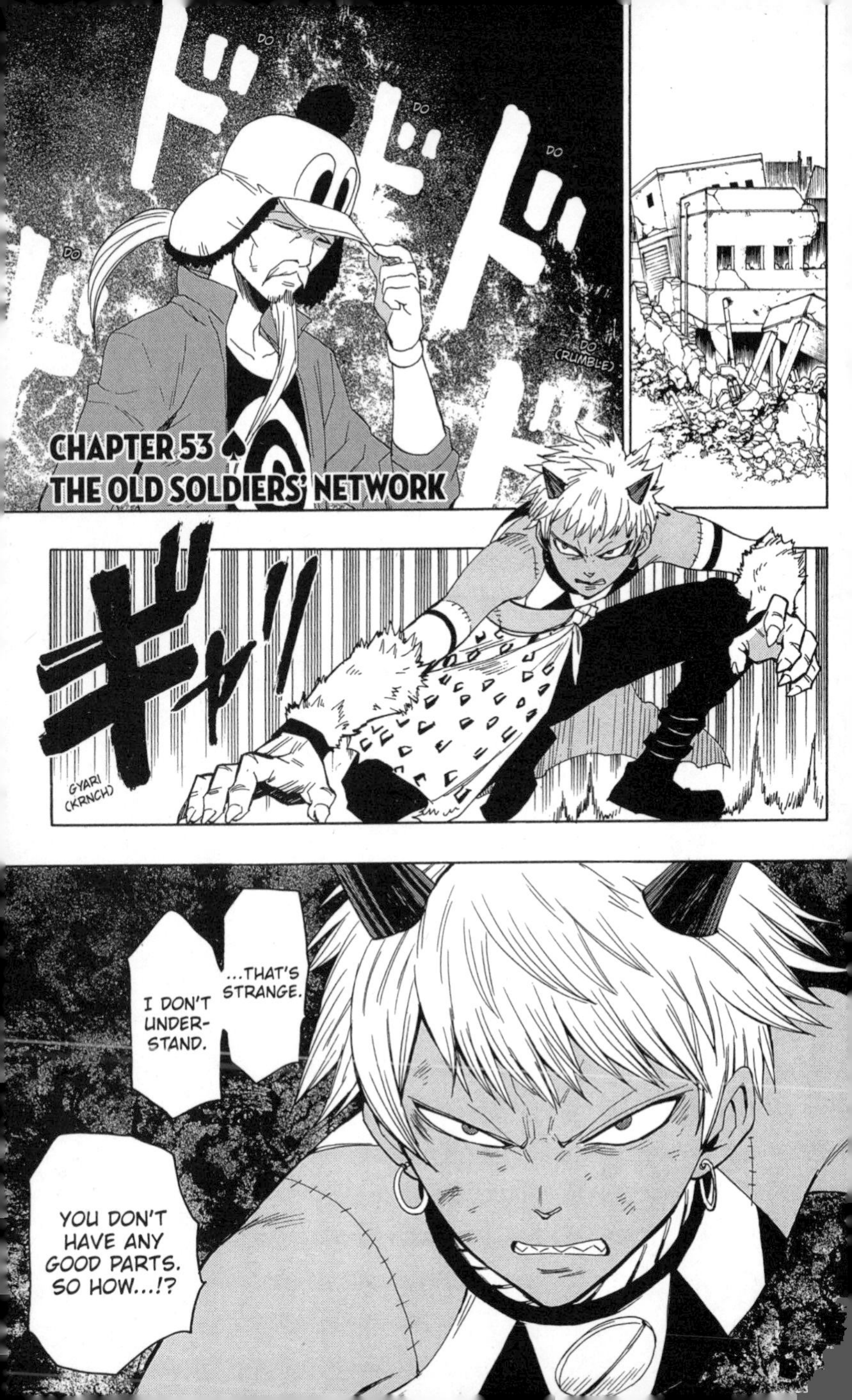
DO
(RUMBLE)
DO
DO
DO
DO
GYARI
(KRNCH)
...THAT'S STRANGE.
I DON'T UNDER-STAND.
YOU DON'T HAVE ANY GOOD PARTS. SO HOW...!?

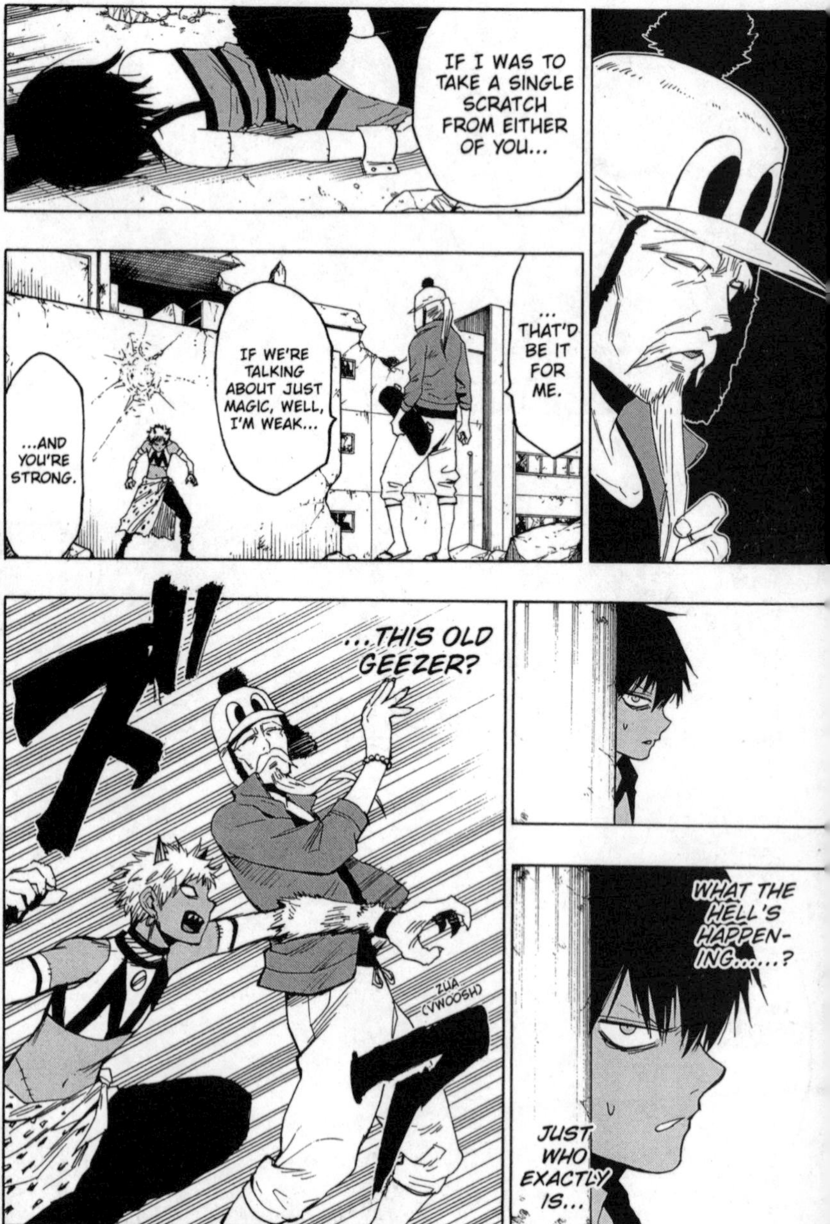
IF I WAS TO TAKE A SINGLE SCRATCH FROM EITHER OF YOU...
...THAT'D BE IT FOR ME.
IF WE'RE TALKING ABOUT JUST MAGIC, WELL, I'M WEAK...
...AND YOU'RE STRONG.
WHAT THE HELL'S HAPPEN-ING......?
JUST WHO EXACTLY IS...
...THIS OLD GEEZER?
ZUA (VWOOSH)

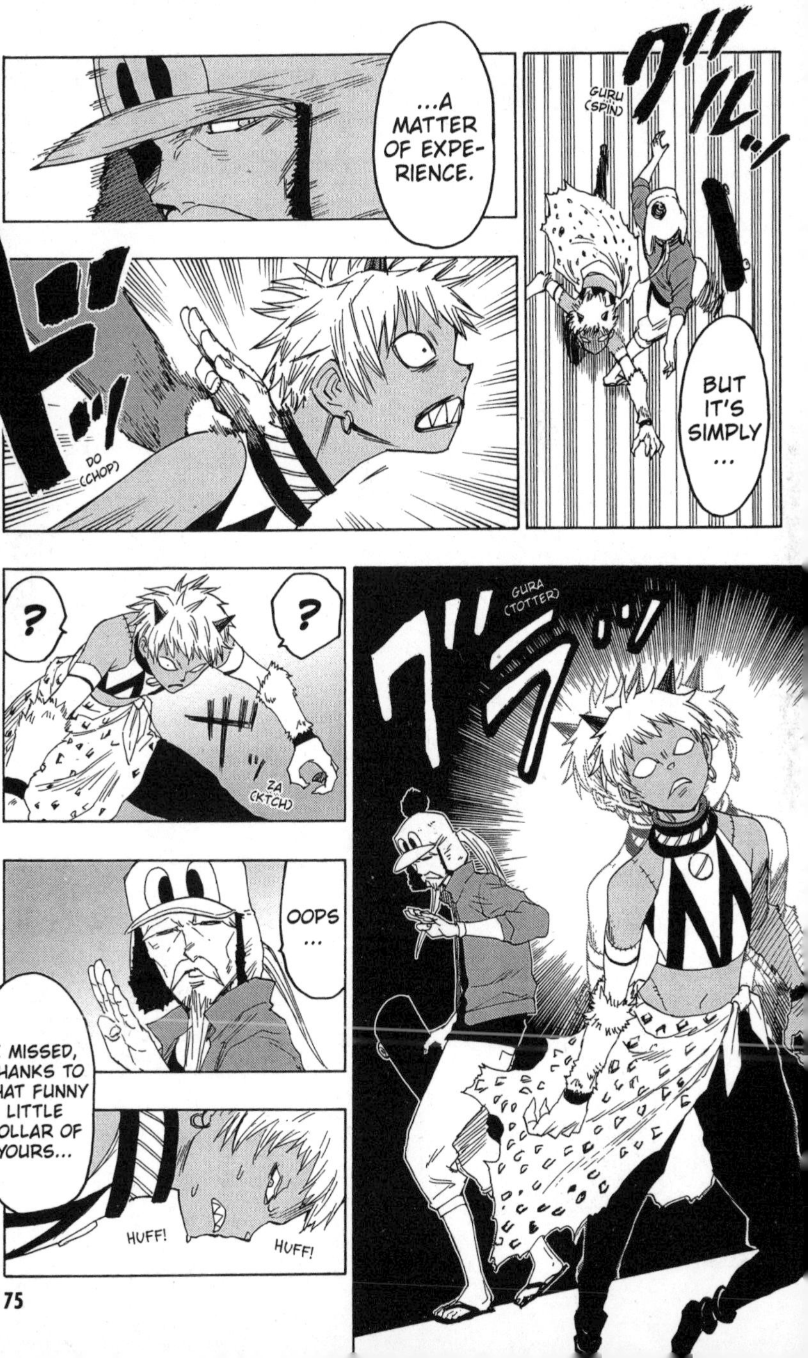
GURU (SPIN)
BUT IT'S SIMPLY ...
...A MATTER OF EXPE-RIENCE.
DO (CHOP)
GURA (TOTTER)
?
?
ZA (KTCH)
OOPS ...
I MISSED, THANKS TO THAT FUNNY LITTLE COLLAR OF YOURS...
HUFF!
HUFF!

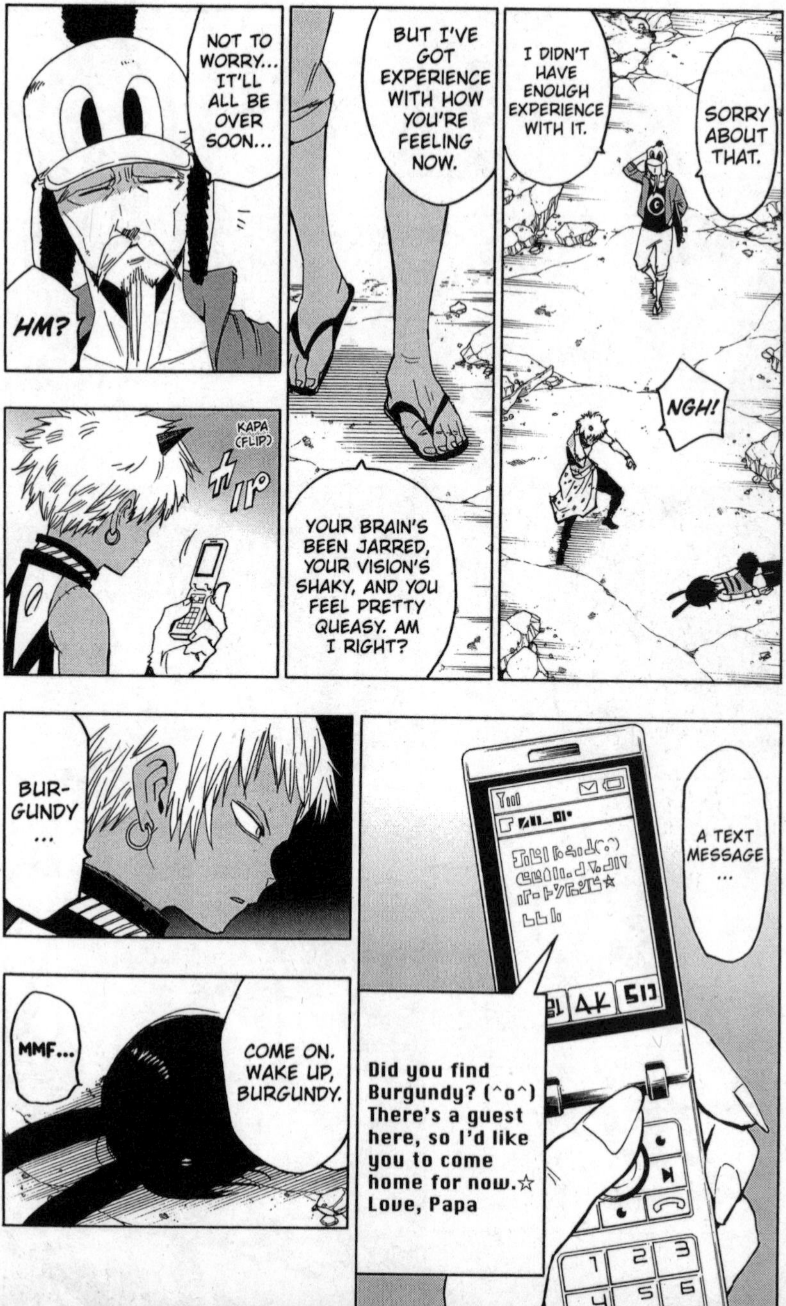

SORRY ABOUT THAT.
I DIDN'T HAVE ENOUGH EXPERIENCE WITH IT.
NGH!
BUT I'VE GOT EXPERIENCE WITH HOW YOU'RE FEELING NOW.
YOUR BRAIN'S BEEN JARRED, YOUR VISION'S SHAKY, AND YOU FEEL PRETTY QUEASY. AM I RIGHT?
NOT TO WORRY... IT'LL ALL BE OVER SOON...
HM?
KAPA (FLIP)
A TEXT MESSAGE ...
Did you find Burgundy? (^o^) There's a guest here, so I'd like you to come home for now.☆ Love, Papa
BUR-GUNDY ...
COME ON. WAKE UP, BURGUNDY.
MMF...

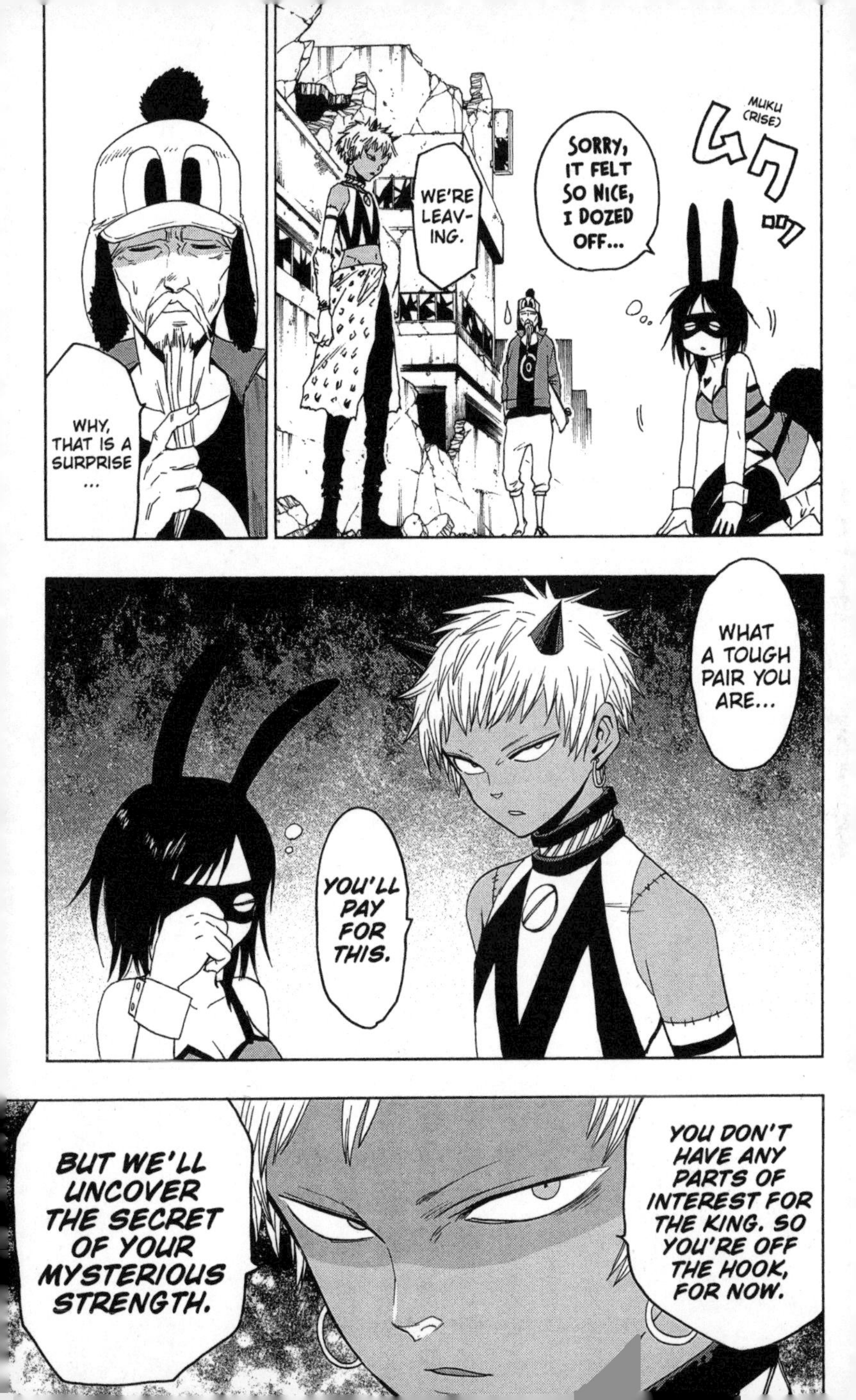

MUKU (RISE)
ムク
SORRY, IT FELT SO NICE, I DOZED OFF...
WE'RE LEAV-ING.
WHY, THAT IS A SURPRISE...
WHAT A TOUGH PAIR YOU ARE...
YOU'LL PAY FOR THIS.
YOU DON'T HAVE ANY PARTS OF INTEREST FOR THE KING. SO YOU'RE OFF THE HOOK, FOR NOW.
BUT WE'LL UNCOVER THE SECRET OF YOUR MYSTERIOUS STRENGTH.

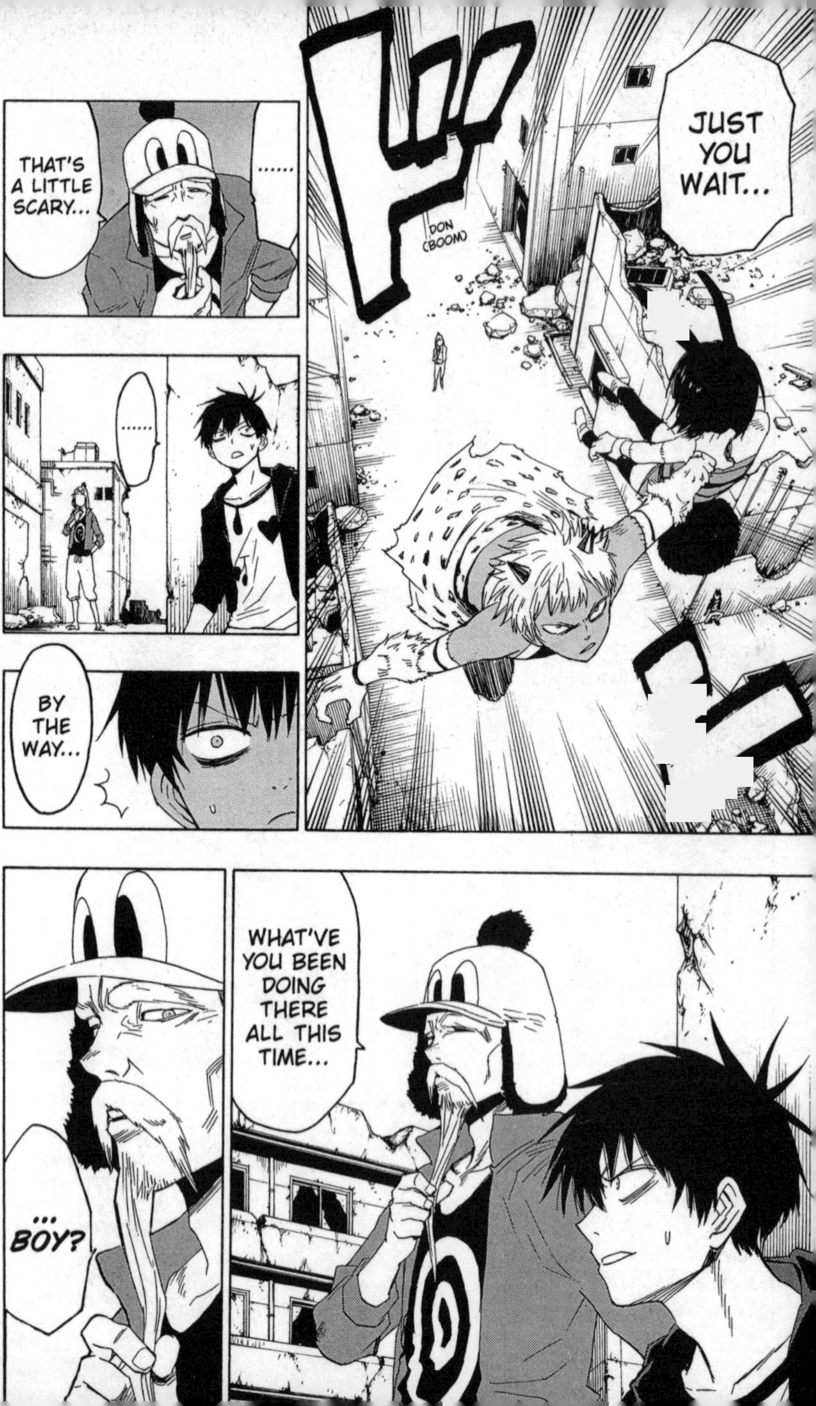
JUST YOU WAIT...
DON (BOOM)
......
THAT'S A LITTLE SCARY...
......
BY THE WAY...
WHAT'VE YOU BEEN DOING THERE ALL THIS TIME...
...BOY?

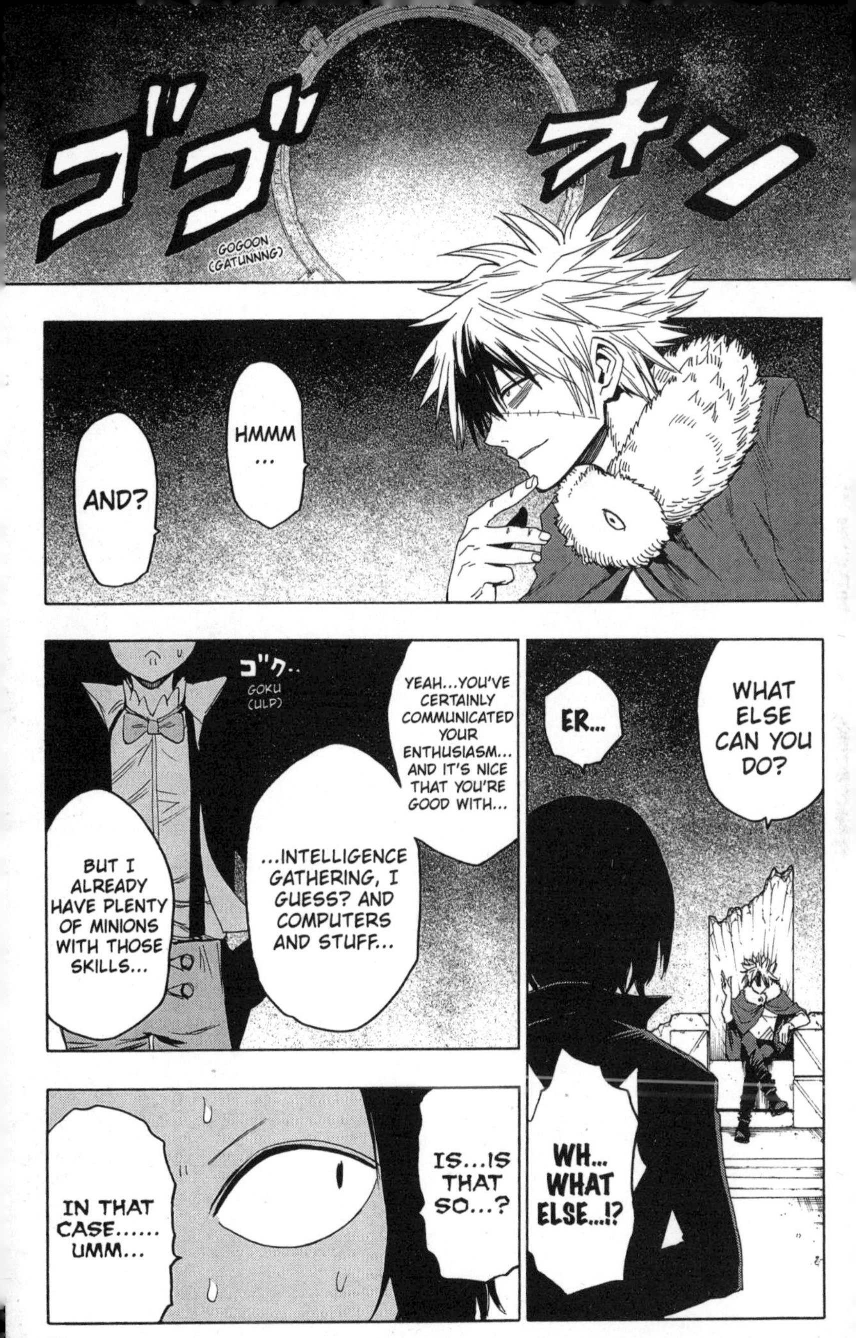
ゴゴオン
GOGOON (GATUNNNG)
HMMM...
AND?
WHAT ELSE CAN YOU DO?
ER...
YEAH...YOU'VE CERTAINLY COMMUNICATED YOUR ENTHUSIASM... AND IT'S NICE THAT YOU'RE GOOD WITH...
ゴク..
GOKU (ULP)
...INTELLIGENCE GATHERING, I GUESS? AND COMPUTERS AND STUFF...
BUT I ALREADY HAVE PLENTY OF MINIONS WITH THOSE SKILLS...
WH... WHAT ELSE...!?
IS...IS THAT SO...?
IN THAT CASE...... UMM...

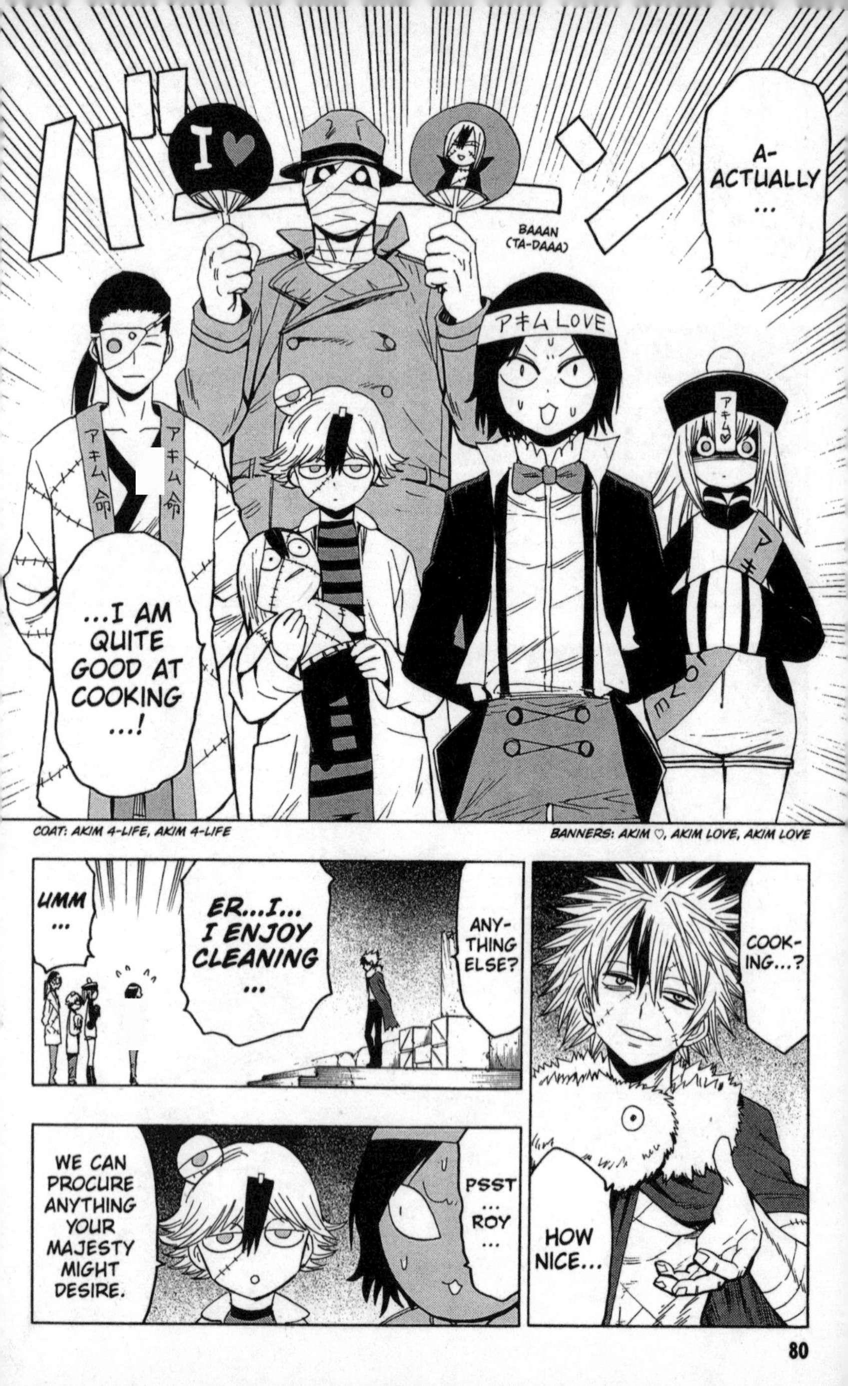
A-ACTUALLY...
BAAAN (TA-DAAA)
アキム LOVE
...I AM QUITE GOOD AT COOKING...!
COOK-ING...?
HOW NICE...
ANY-THING ELSE?
ER...I... I ENJOY CLEANING...
UMM...
PSST... ROY...
WE CAN PROCURE ANYTHING YOUR MAJESTY MIGHT DESIRE.

BANNERS: AKIM ♡, AKIM LOVE, AKIM LOVE

COAT: AKIM 4-LIFE, AKIM 4-LIFE

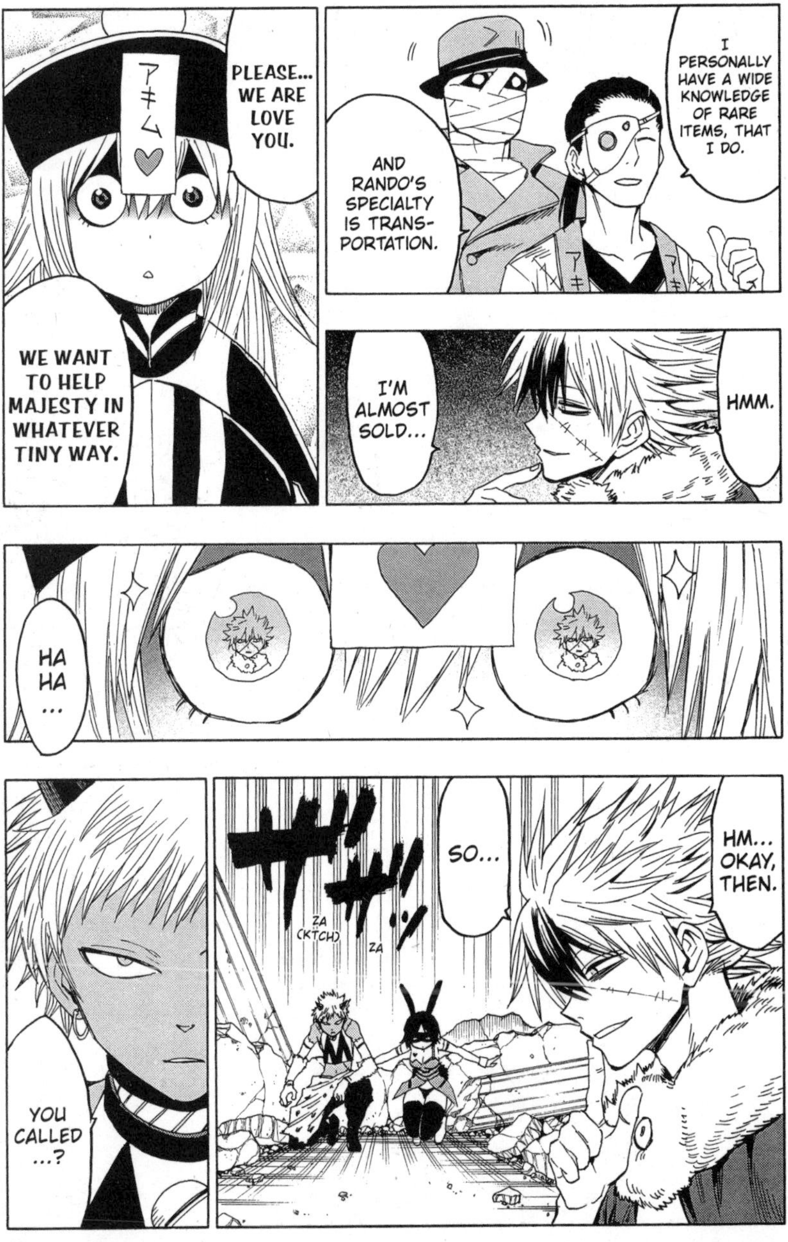

I PERSONALLY HAVE A WIDE KNOWLEDGE OF RARE ITEMS, THAT I DO.
AND RANDO'S SPECIALTY IS TRANS-PORTATION.
HMM.
I'M ALMOST SOLD...
PLEASE... WE ARE LOVE YOU.
アキム
WE WANT TO HELP MAJESTY IN WHATEVER TINY WAY.
HA HA ...
HM... OKAY, THEN.
SO...
ZA (KTCH) ZA
YOU CALLED ...?

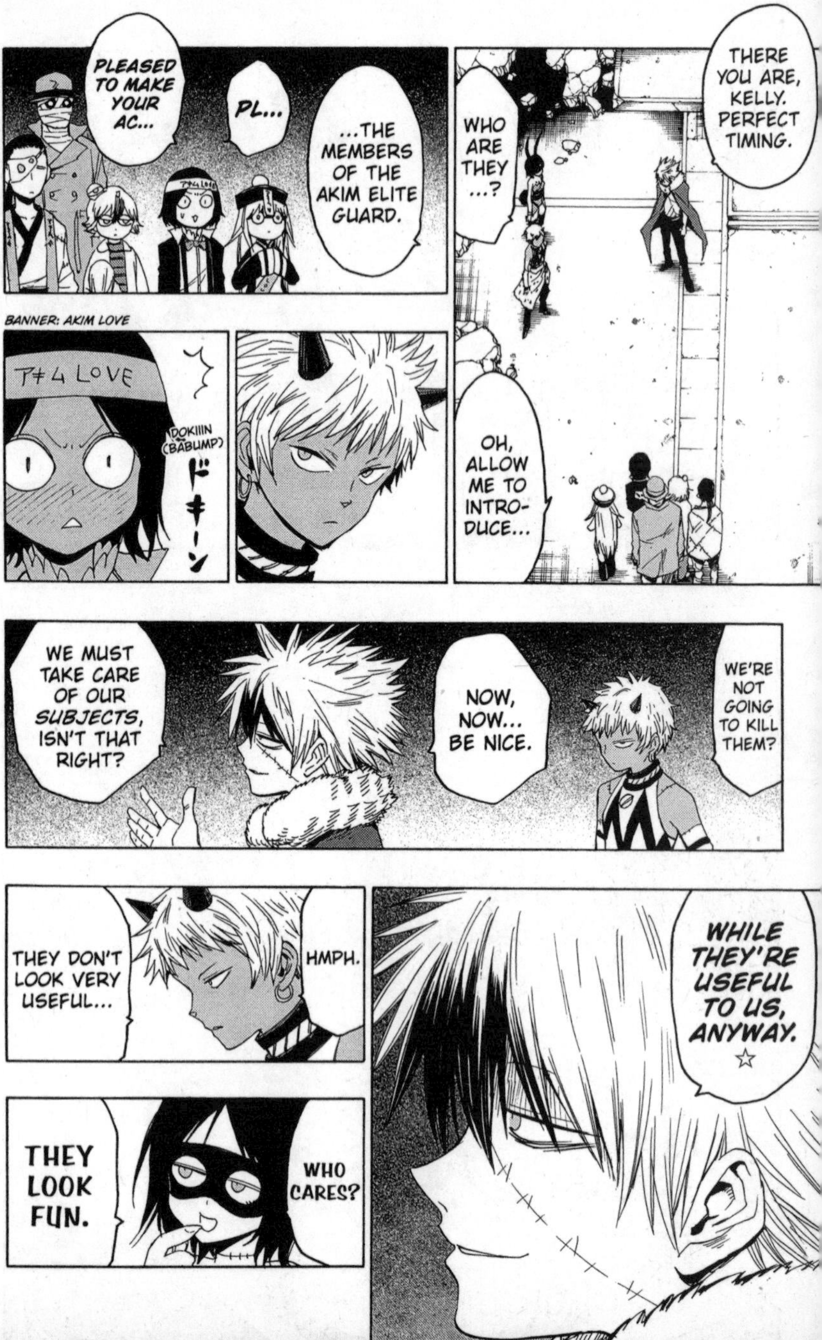
THERE YOU ARE, KELLY. PERFECT TIMING.
WHO ARE THEY ...?
OH, ALLOW ME TO INTRODUCE...
...THE MEMBERS OF THE AKIM ELITE GUARD.
PL...
PLEASED TO MAKE YOUR AC...
BANNER: AKIM LOVE
DOKIIIN (BABUMP)
ドキーン
アキム LOVE
WE'RE NOT GOING TO KILL THEM?
NOW, NOW... BE NICE.
WE MUST TAKE CARE OF OUR SUBJECTS, ISN'T THAT RIGHT?
WHILE THEY'RE USEFUL TO US, ANYWAY. ☆
HMPH.
THEY DON'T LOOK VERY USEFUL...
WHO CARES?
THEY LOOK FUN.

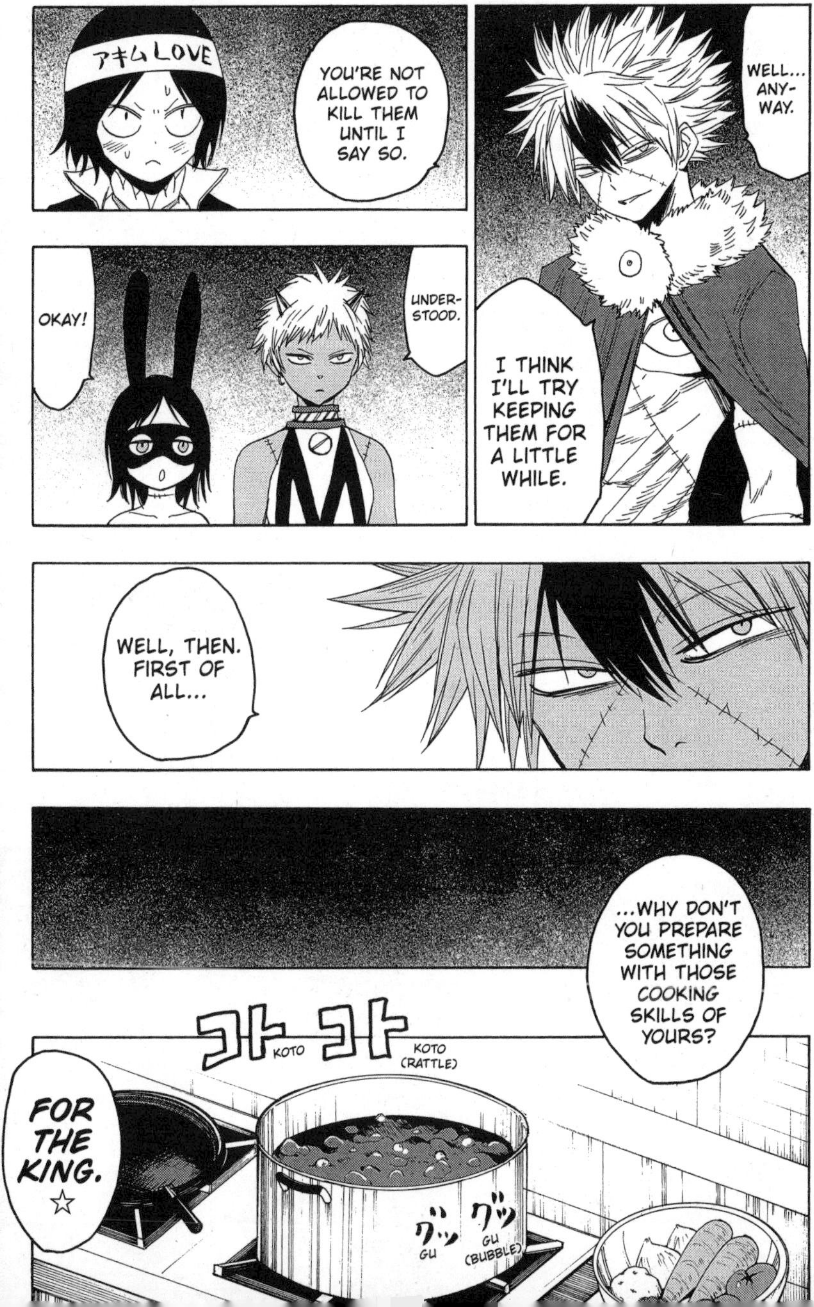
WELL... ANY-WAY.
I THINK I'LL TRY KEEPING THEM FOR A LITTLE WHILE.
アキムLOVE
YOU'RE NOT ALLOWED TO KILL THEM UNTIL I SAY SO.
UNDER-STOOD.
OKAY!
WELL, THEN. FIRST OF ALL...
...WHY DON'T YOU PREPARE SOMETHING WITH THOSE COOKING SKILLS OF YOURS?
コト KOTO
コト KOTO (RATTLE)
FOR THE KING. ☆
グツ GU
グツ GU (BUBBLE)

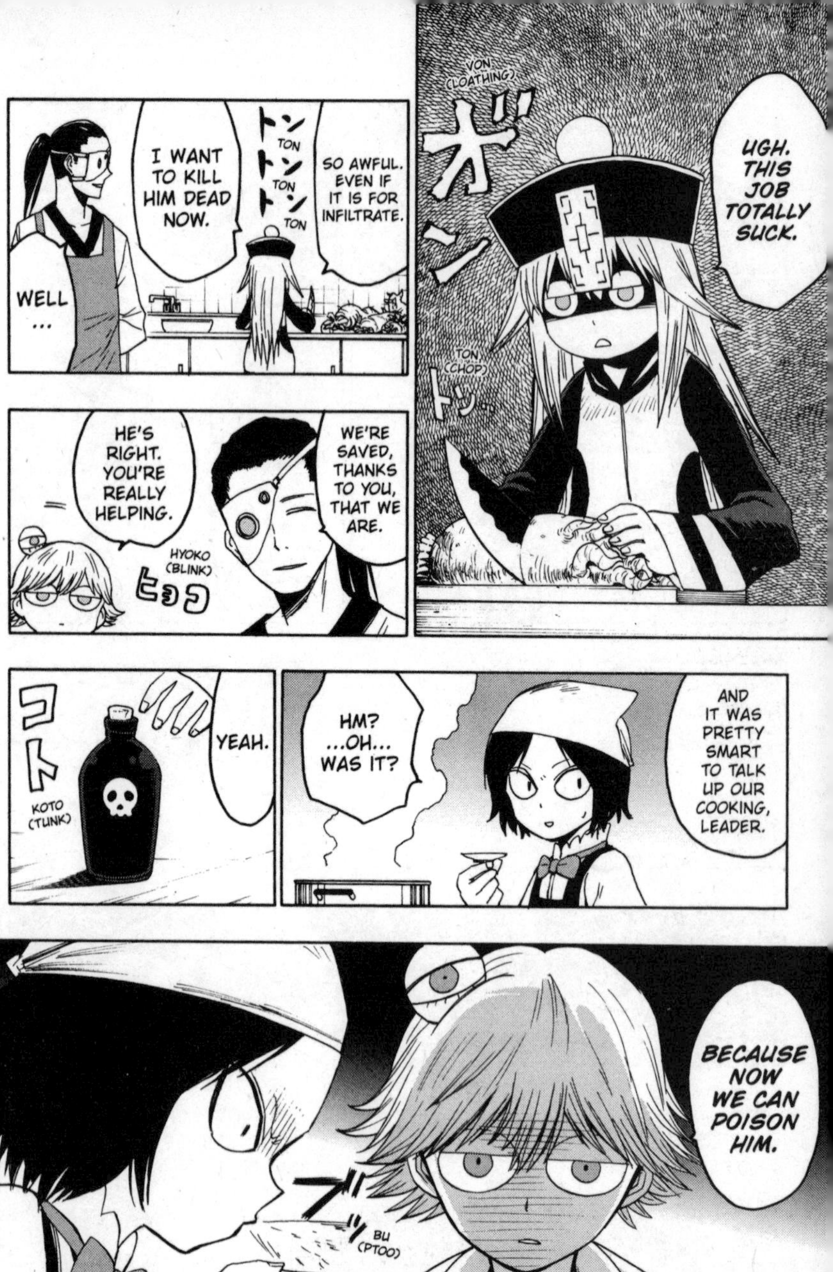
UGH. THIS JOB TOTALLY SUCK.
VON (LOATHING)
TON (CHOP)
SO AWFUL. EVEN IF IT IS FOR INFILTRATE.
TON TON TON
I WANT TO KILL HIM DEAD NOW.
WELL...
WE'RE SAVED, THANKS TO YOU, THAT WE ARE.
HE'S RIGHT. YOU'RE REALLY HELPING.
HYOKO (BLINK)
AND IT WAS PRETTY SMART TO TALK UP OUR COOKING, LEADER.
HM? ...OH... WAS IT?
YEAH.
KOTO (TUNK)
BECAUSE NOW WE CAN POISON HIM.
BU (PTOO)

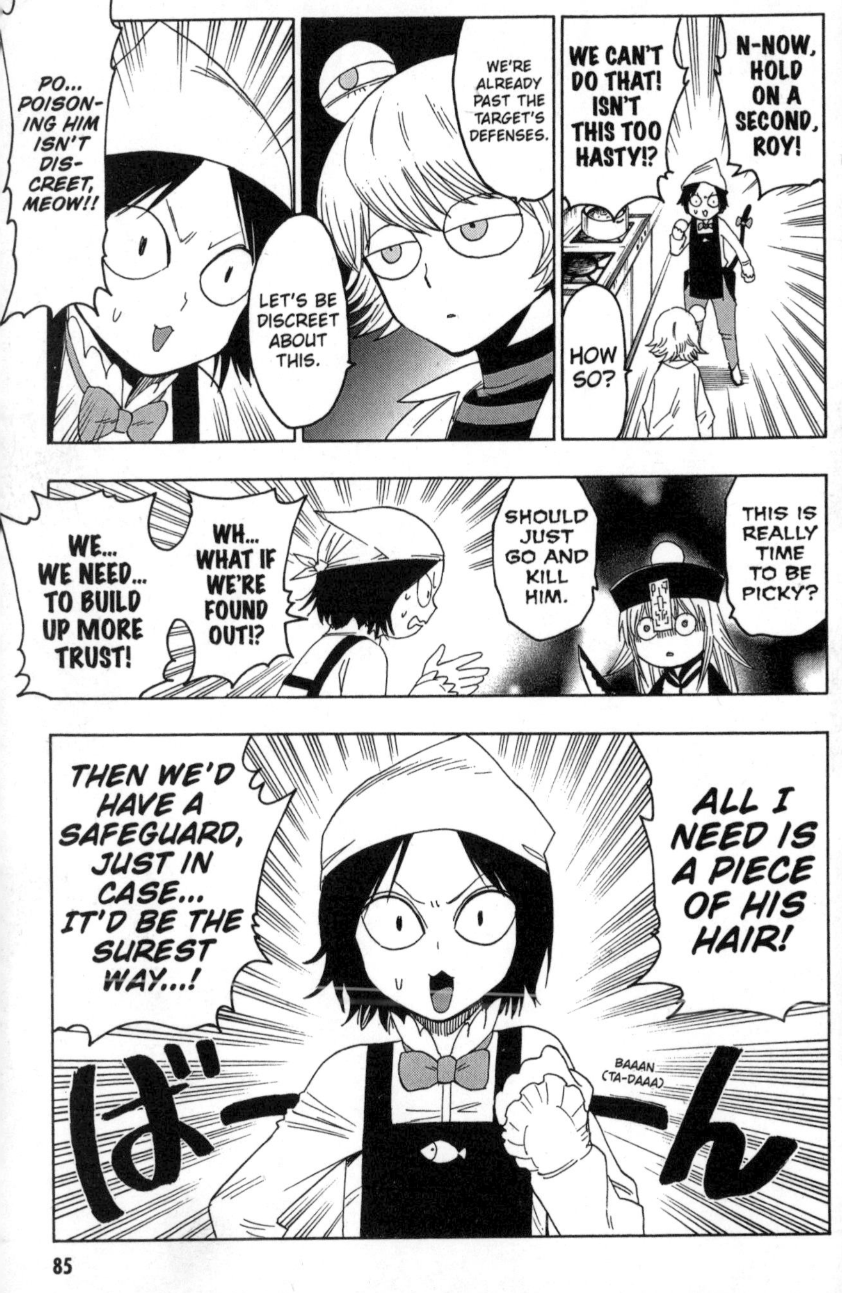
N-NOW, HOLD ON A SECOND, ROY!
WE CAN'T DO THAT! ISN'T THIS TOO HASTY!?
HOW SO?
WE'RE ALREADY PAST THE TARGET'S DEFENSES.
LET'S BE DISCREET ABOUT THIS.
PO... POISON-ING HIM ISN'T DIS-CREET, MEOW!!
THIS IS REALLY TIME TO BE PICKY?
SHOULD JUST GO AND KILL HIM.
WH... WHAT IF WE'RE FOUND OUT!?
WE... WE NEED... TO BUILD UP MORE TRUST!
ALL I NEED IS A PIECE OF HIS HAIR!
THEN WE'D HAVE A SAFEGUARD, JUST IN CASE... IT'D BE THE SUREST WAY...!
ばーん
BAAAN (TA-DAAA)

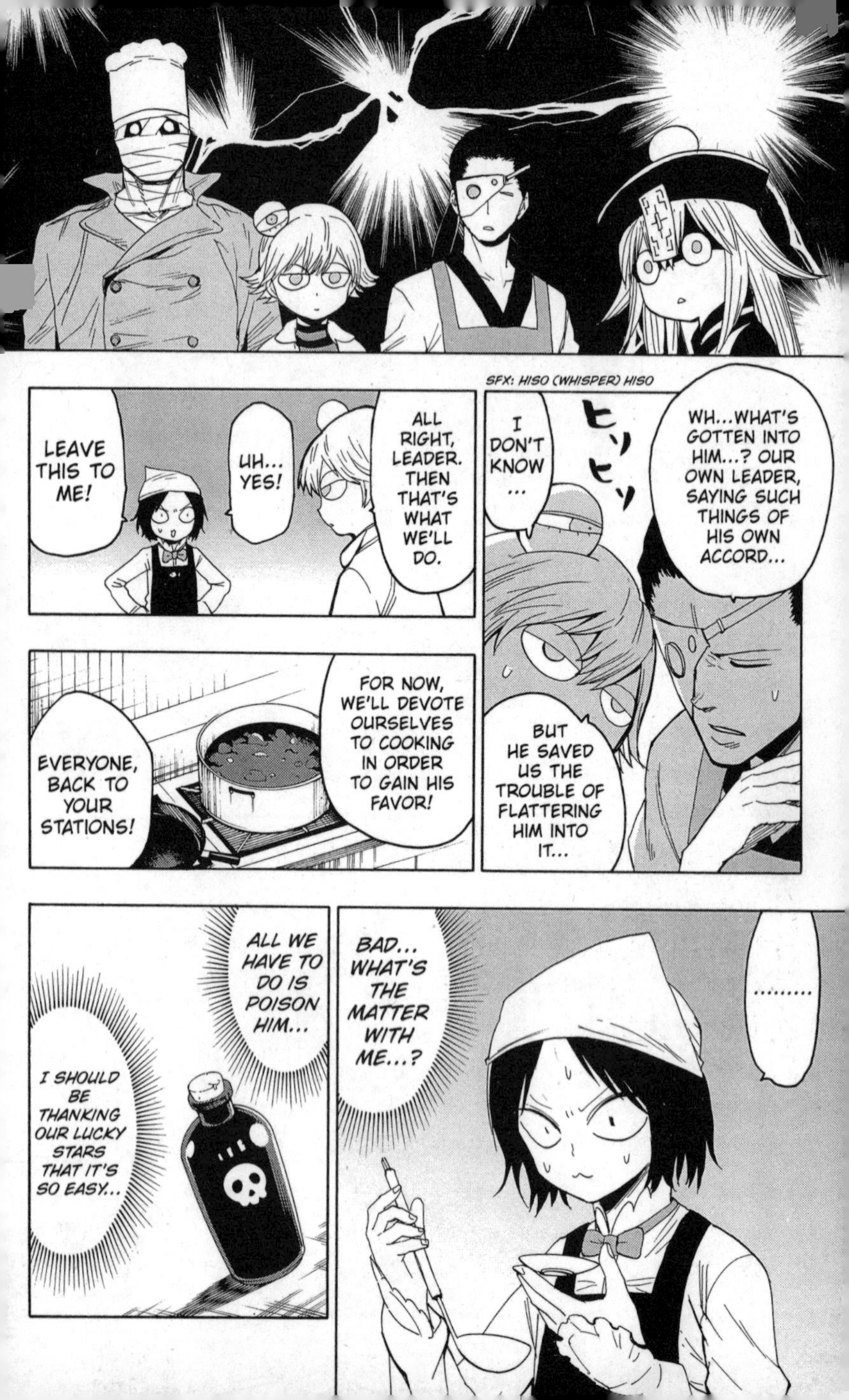
SFX: HISO (WHISPER) HISO
WH...WHAT'S GOTTEN INTO HIM...? OUR OWN LEADER, SAYING SUCH THINGS OF HIS OWN ACCORD...
ヒソヒソ
I DON'T KNOW...
BUT HE SAVED US THE TROUBLE OF FLATTERING HIM INTO IT...
ALL RIGHT, LEADER. THEN THAT'S WHAT WE'LL DO.
UH... YES!
LEAVE THIS TO ME!
FOR NOW, WE'LL DEVOTE OURSELVES TO COOKING IN ORDER TO GAIN HIS FAVOR!
EVERYONE, BACK TO YOUR STATIONS!
....
BAD... WHAT'S THE MATTER WITH ME...?
ALL WE HAVE TO DO IS POISON HIM...
I SHOULD BE THANKING OUR LUCKY STARS THAT IT'S SO EASY...

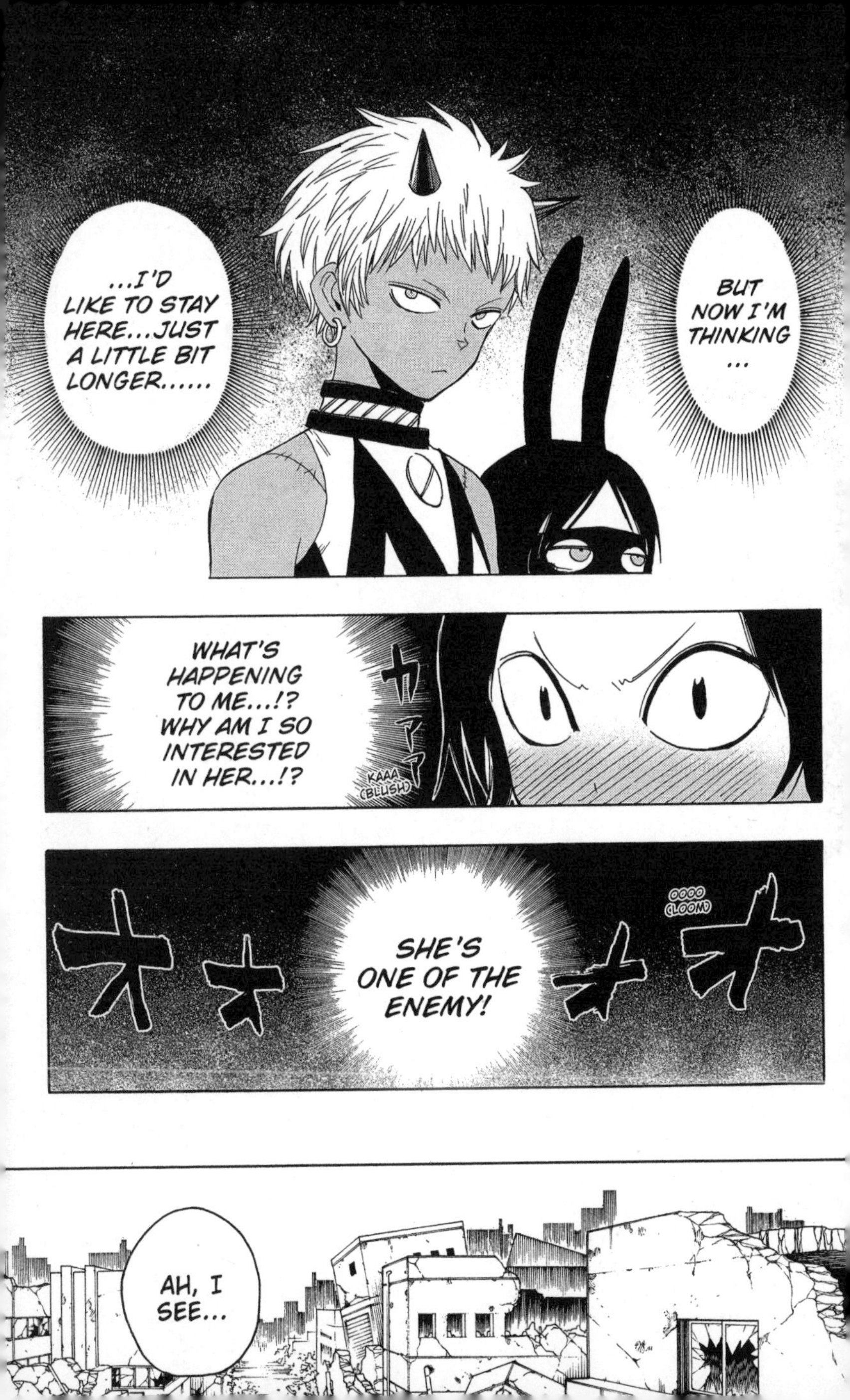
BUT NOW I'M THINKING ...
...I'D LIKE TO STAY HERE...JUST A LITTLE BIT LONGER......
カァァ
KAAA (BLUSH)
WHAT'S HAPPENING TO ME...!? WHY AM I SO INTERESTED IN HER...!?
オォォォ
OOOO (GLOOM)
SHE'S ONE OF THE ENEMY!
AH, I SEE...

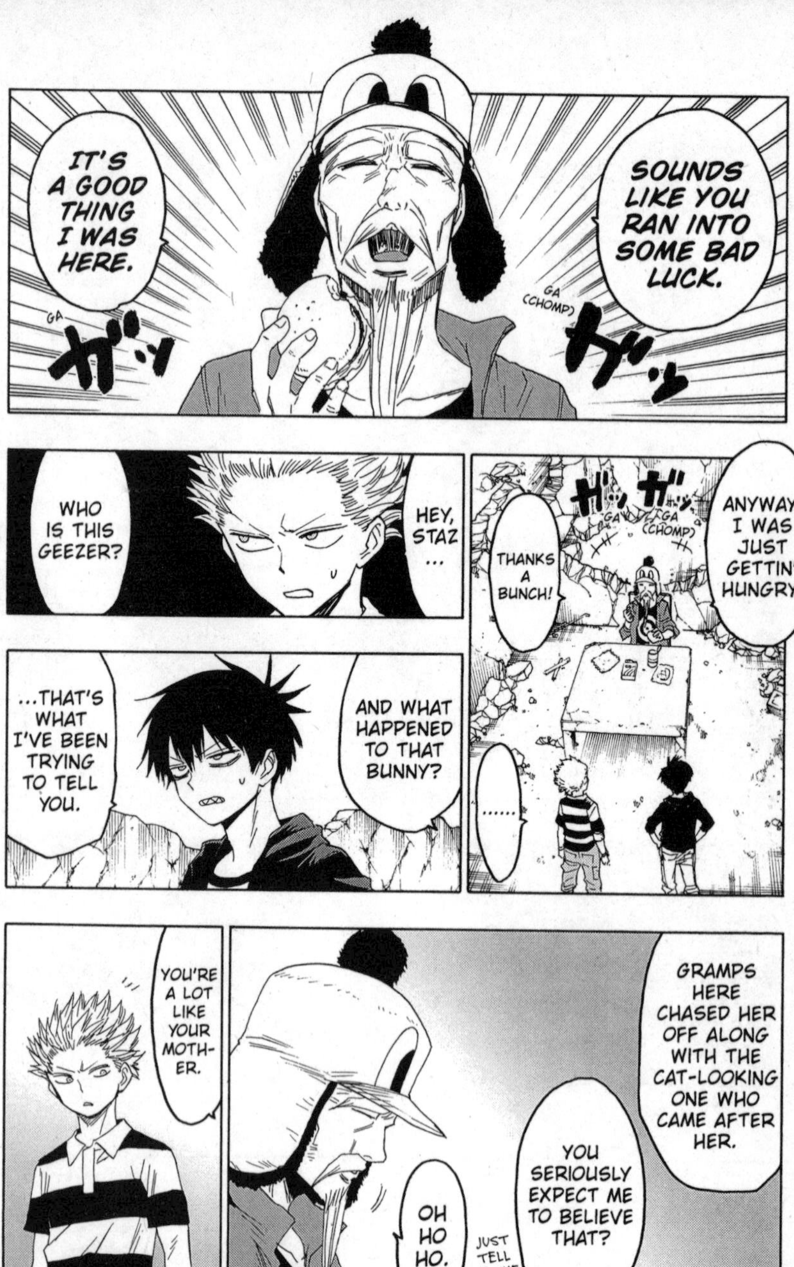
SOUNDS LIKE YOU RAN INTO SOME BAD LUCK.
GA (CHOMP)
IT'S A GOOD THING I WAS HERE.
GA
ANYWAY, I WAS JUST GETTIN' HUNGRY.
GA (CHOMP)
GA
THANKS A BUNCH!
......
HEY, STAZ ...
WHO IS THIS GEEZER?
AND WHAT HAPPENED TO THAT BUNNY?
...THAT'S WHAT I'VE BEEN TRYING TO TELL YOU.
GRAMPS HERE CHASED HER OFF ALONG WITH THE CAT-LOOKING ONE WHO CAME AFTER HER.
YOU SERIOUSLY EXPECT ME TO BELIEVE THAT?
JUST TELL ME THE TRUTH.
OH HO HO.
YOU'RE A LOT LIKE YOUR MOTHER.

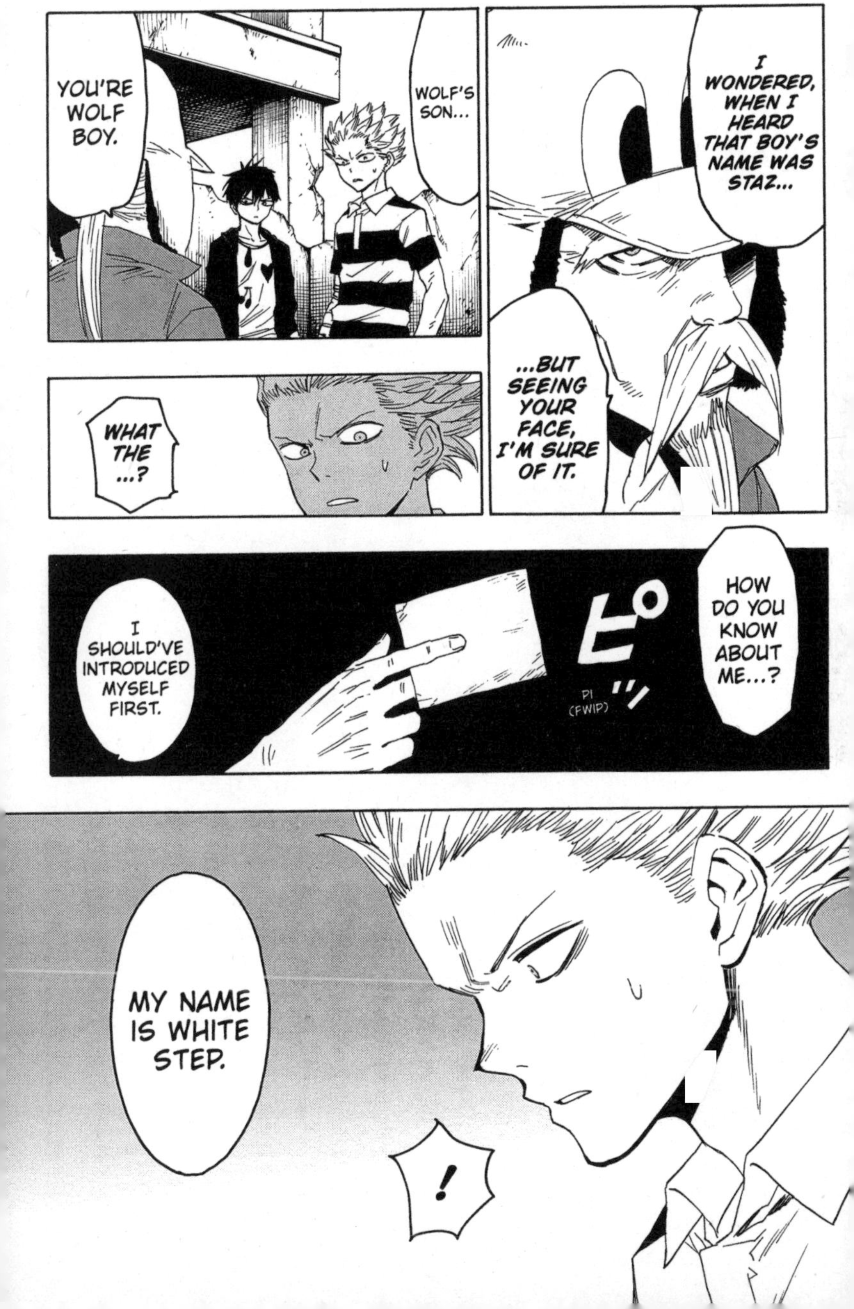
I WONDERED, WHEN I HEARD THAT BOY'S NAME WAS STAZ...
...BUT SEEING YOUR FACE, I'M SURE OF IT.
WOLF'S SON...
YOU'RE WOLF BOY.
WHAT THE ...?
HOW DO YOU KNOW ABOUT ME...?
ピッ
PI (FWIP)
I SHOULD'VE INTRODUCED MYSELF FIRST.
MY NAME IS WHITE STEP.
!

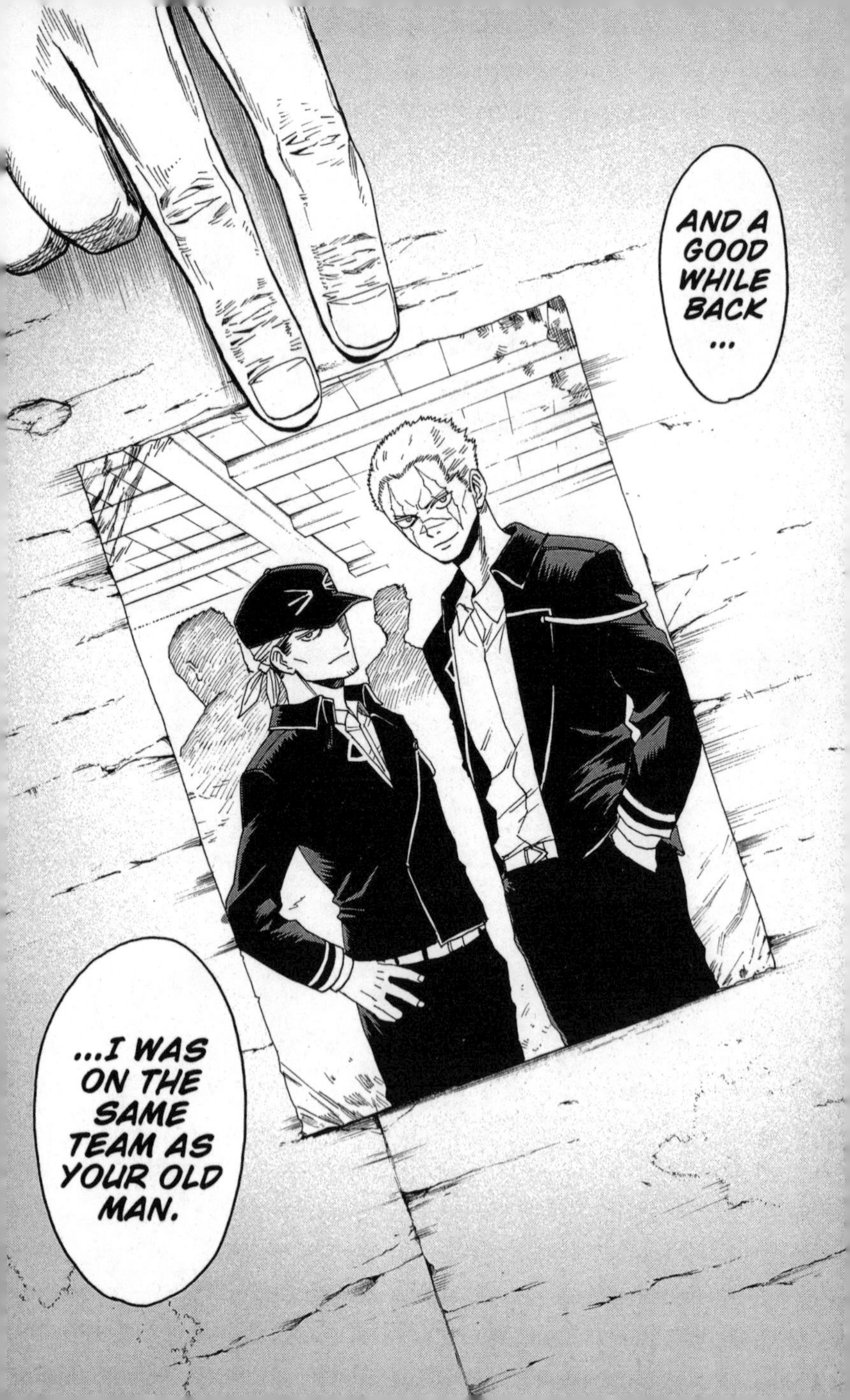
AND A GOOD WHILE BACK ...
...I WAS ON THE SAME TEAM AS YOUR OLD MAN.

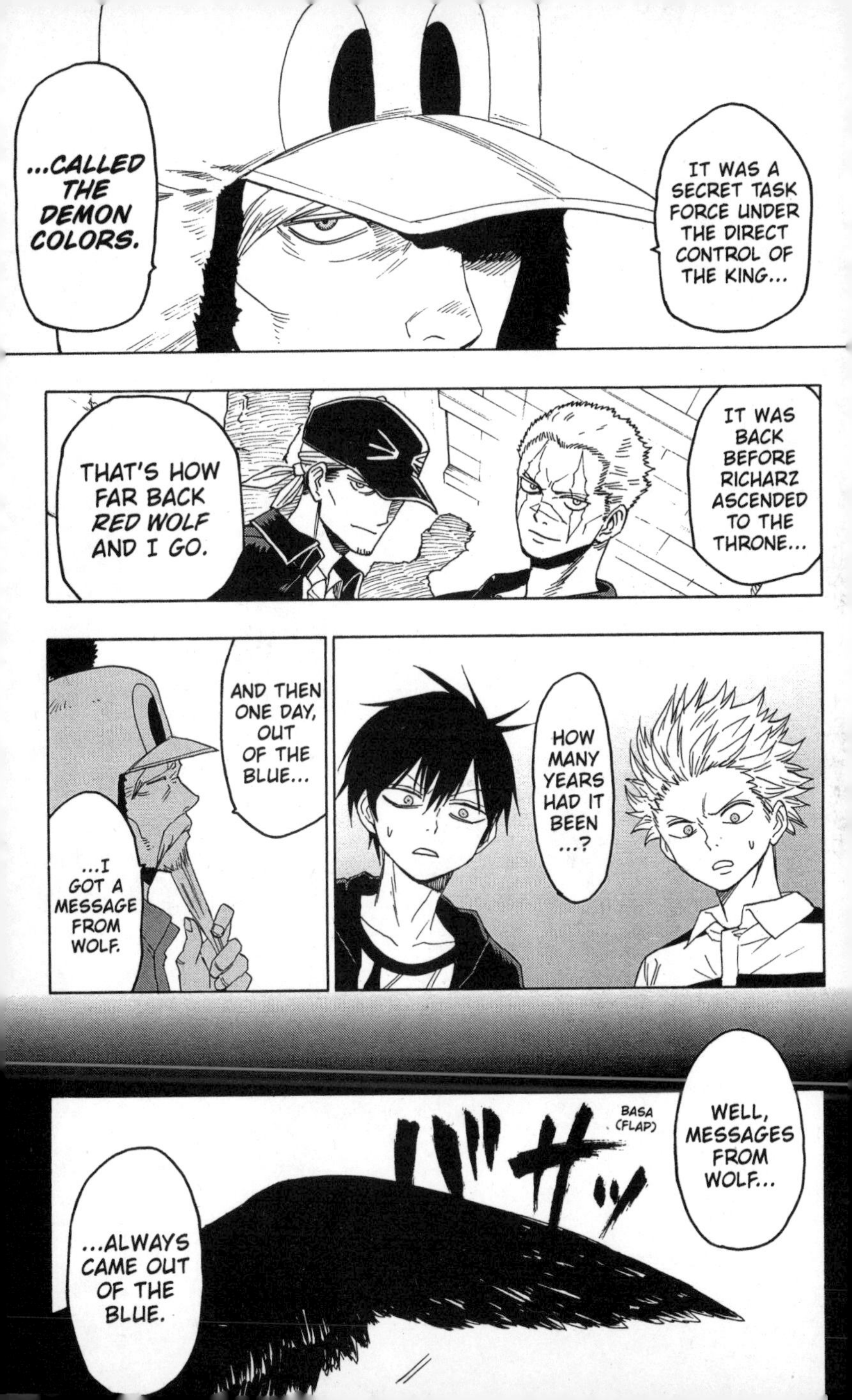
IT WAS A SECRET TASK FORCE UNDER THE DIRECT CONTROL OF THE KING...
...CALLED THE DEMON COLORS.
IT WAS BACK BEFORE RICHARZ ASCENDED TO THE THRONE...
THAT'S HOW FAR BACK *RED WOLF* AND I GO.
HOW MANY YEARS HAD IT BEEN ...?
AND THEN ONE DAY, OUT OF THE BLUE...
...I GOT A MESSAGE FROM WOLF.
WELL, MESSAGES FROM WOLF...
バサッ
BASA (FLAP)
...ALWAYS CAME OUT OF THE BLUE.

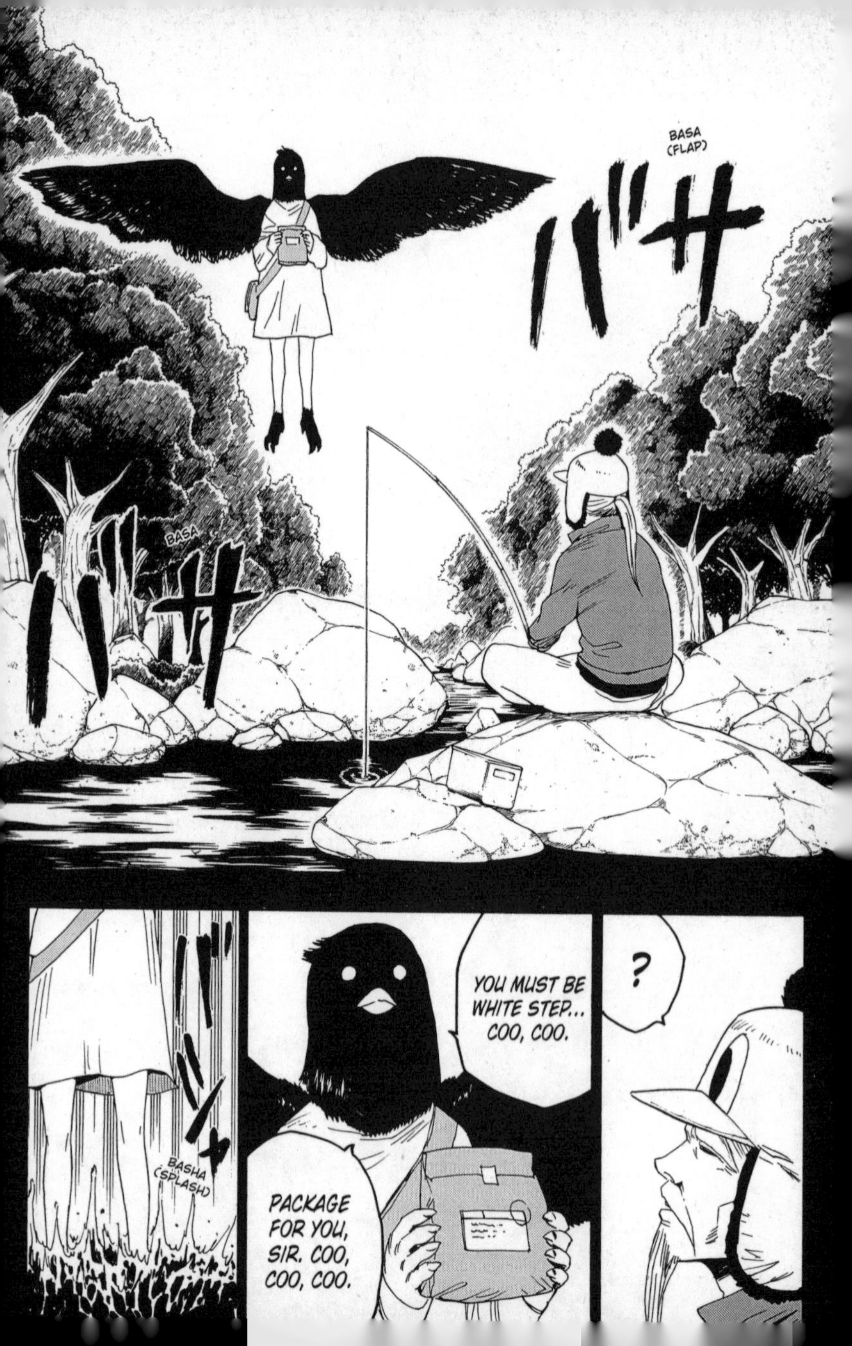
BASA
(FLAP)
BASA
?
YOU MUST BE WHITE STEP... COO, COO.
PACKAGE FOR YOU, SIR. COO, COO, COO.
BASHA
(SPLASH)

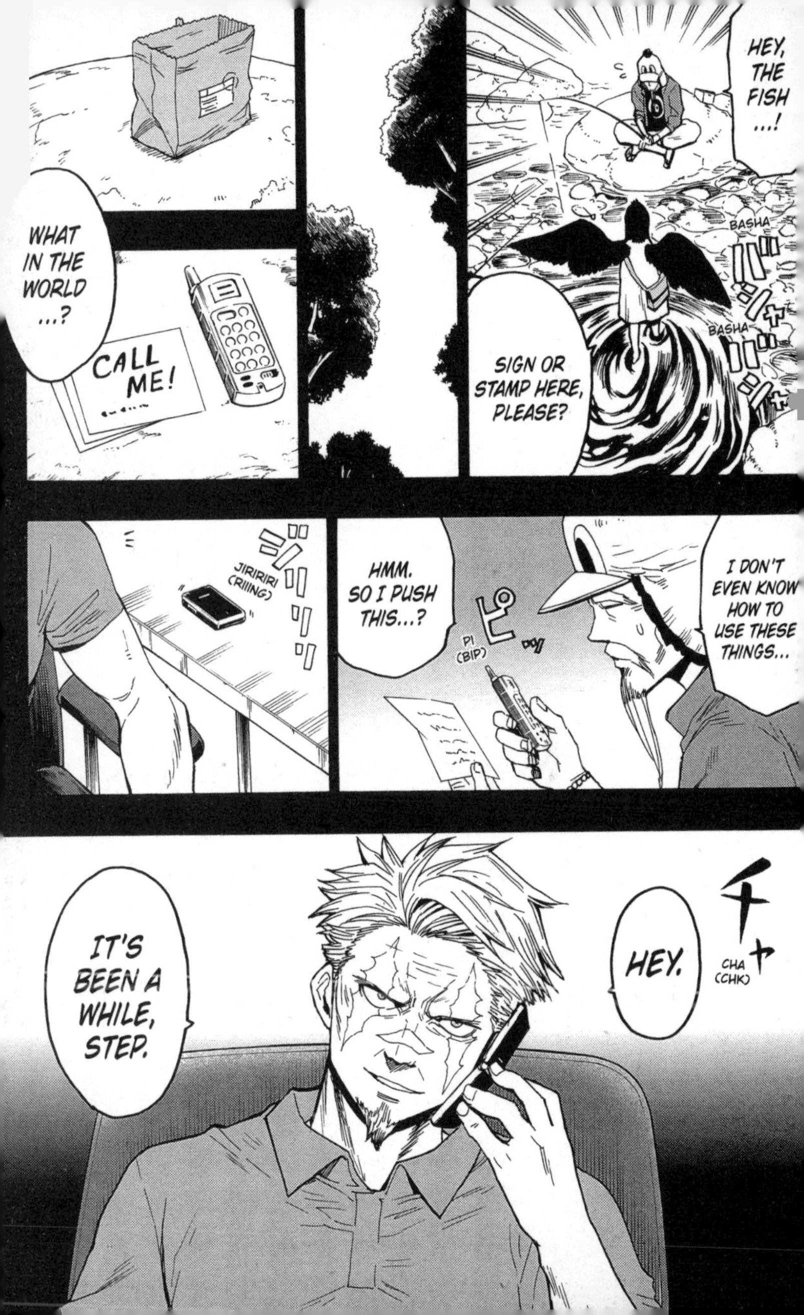
HEY, THE FISH ...!
BASHA
BASHA
SIGN OR STAMP HERE, PLEASE?
WHAT IN THE WORLD ...?
CALL ME!
I DON'T EVEN KNOW HOW TO USE THESE THINGS...
HMM. SO I PUSH THIS...?
PI (BIP)
JIRIRIRI (RIIING)
CHA (CHK)
HEY.
IT'S BEEN A WHILE, STEP.

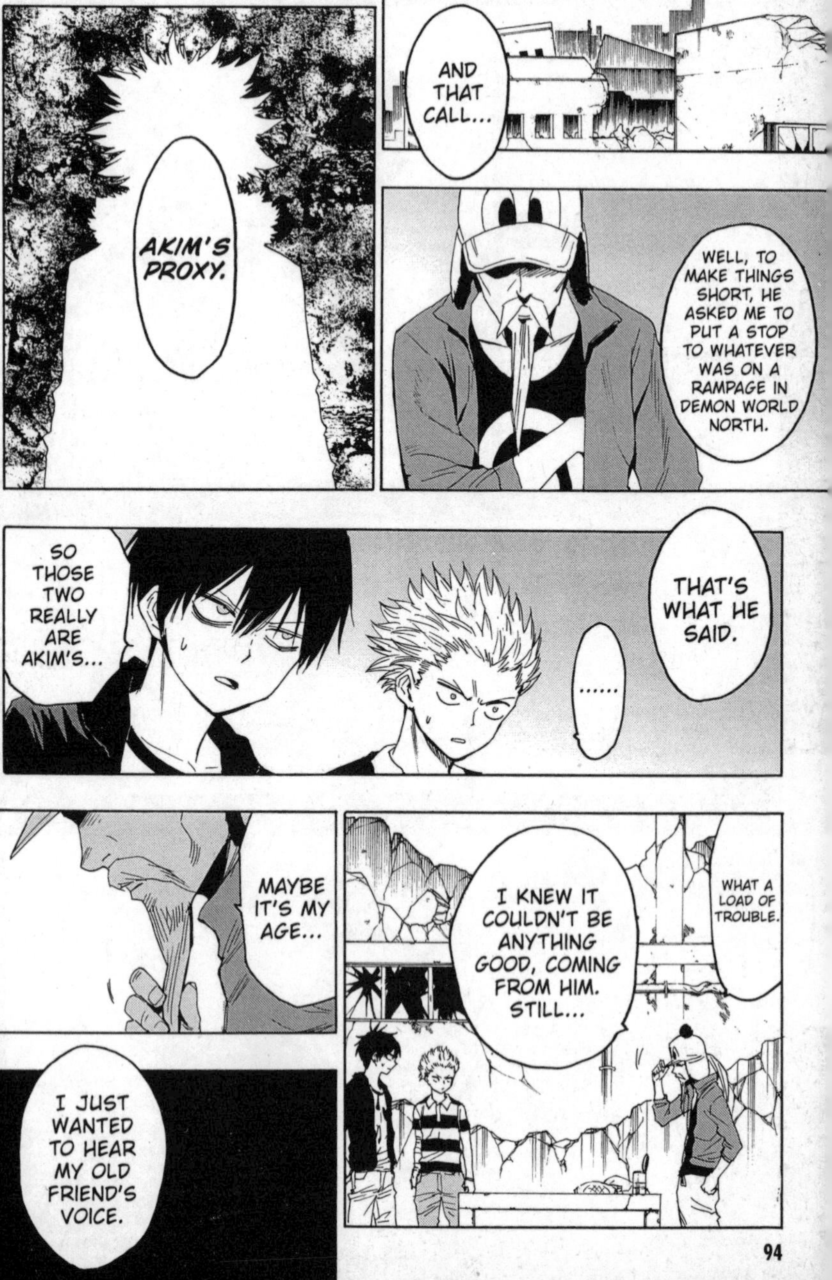
AND THAT CALL...
WELL, TO MAKE THINGS SHORT, HE ASKED ME TO PUT A STOP TO WHATEVER WAS ON A RAMPAGE IN DEMON WORLD NORTH.
AKIM'S PROXY.
THAT'S WHAT HE SAID.
......
SO THOSE TWO REALLY ARE AKIM'S...
WHAT A LOAD OF TROUBLE.
I KNEW IT COULDN'T BE ANYTHING GOOD, COMING FROM HIM. STILL...
MAYBE IT'S MY AGE...
I JUST WANTED TO HEAR MY OLD FRIEND'S VOICE.

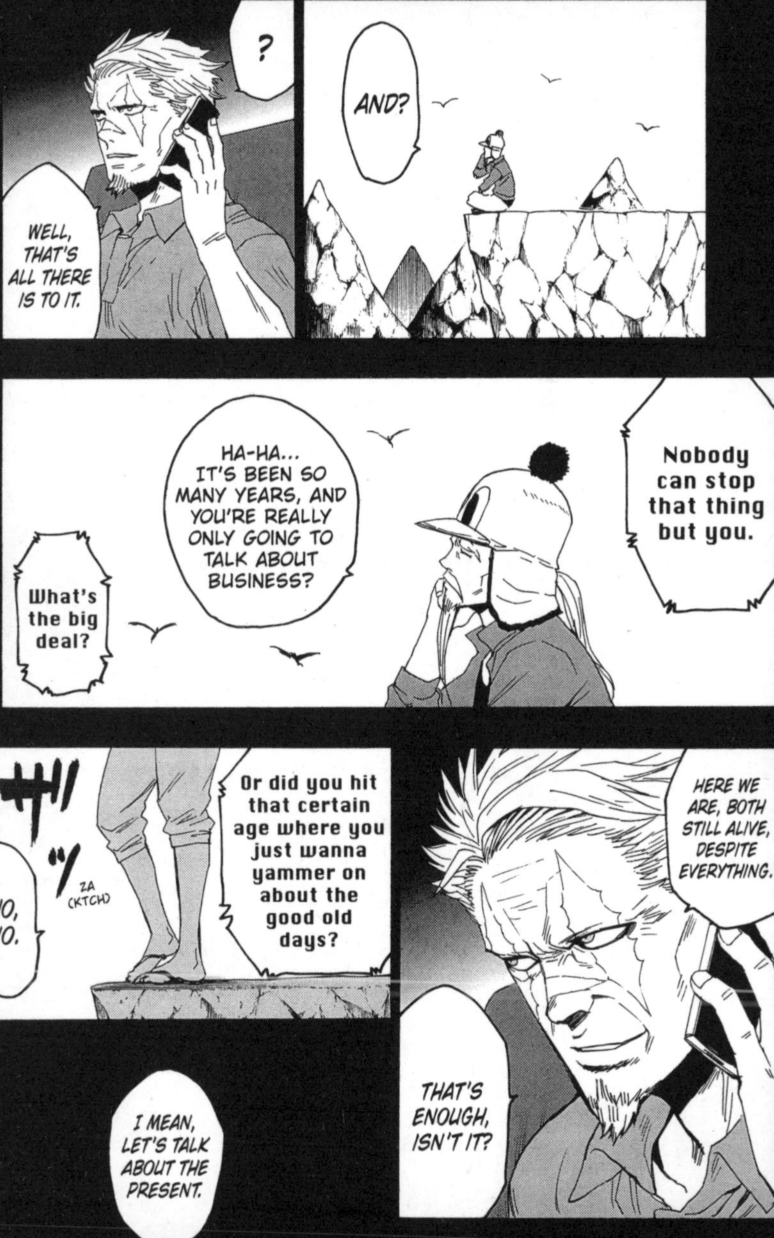
AND?
?
WELL, THAT'S ALL THERE IS TO IT.
Nobody can stop that thing but you.
HA-HA... IT'S BEEN SO MANY YEARS, AND YOU'RE REALLY ONLY GOING TO TALK ABOUT BUSINESS?
What's the big deal?
HERE WE ARE, BOTH STILL ALIVE, DESPITE EVERYTHING.
THAT'S ENOUGH, ISN'T IT?
Or did you hit that certain age where you just wanna yammer on about the good old days?
ZA (KTCH)
NO, NO.
I MEAN, LET'S TALK ABOUT THE PRESENT.

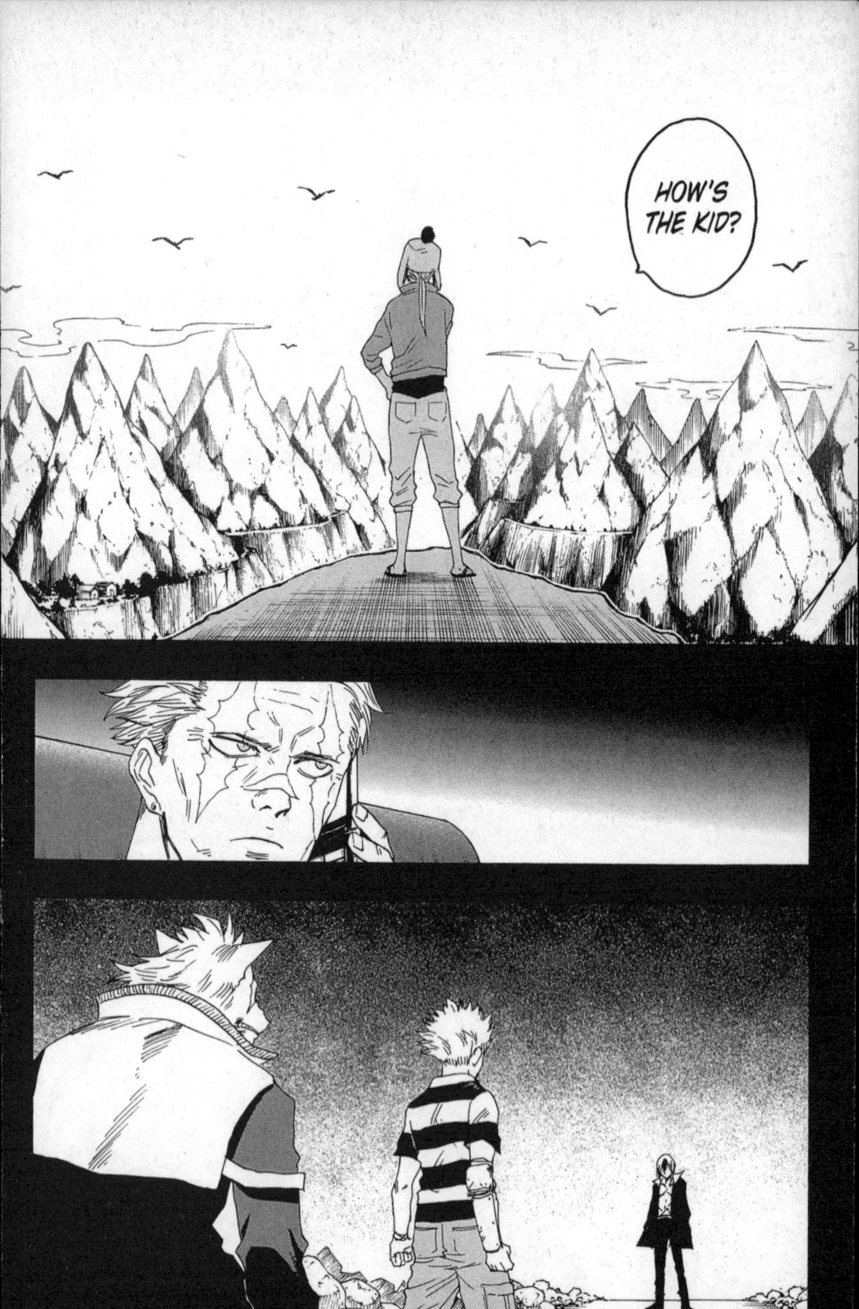
HOW'S THE KID?

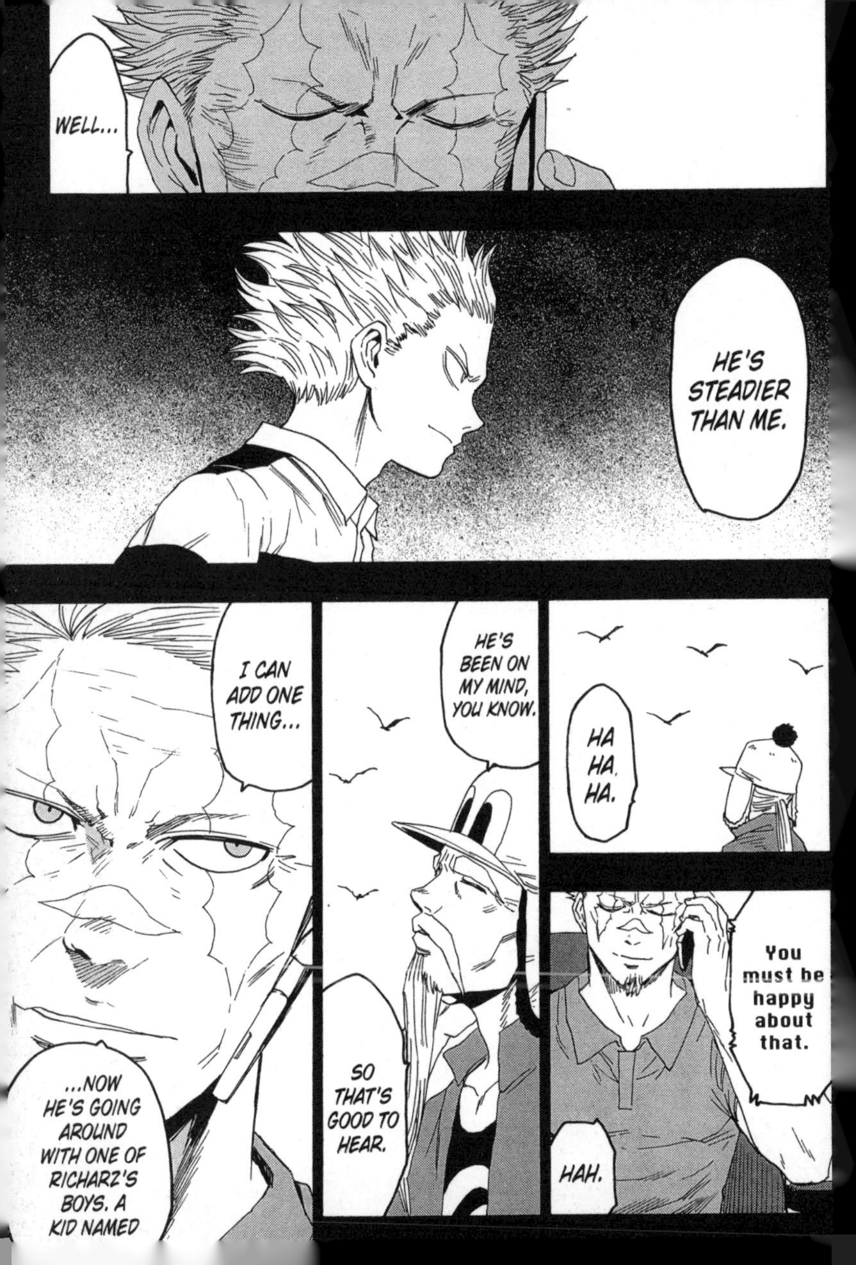
WELL...
HE'S STEADIER THAN ME.
HA HA. HA.
You must be happy about that.
HAH.
HE'S BEEN ON MY MIND, YOU KNOW.
SO THAT'S GOOD TO HEAR.
I CAN ADD ONE THING...
...NOW HE'S GOING AROUND WITH ONE OF RICHARZ'S BOYS. A KID NAMED

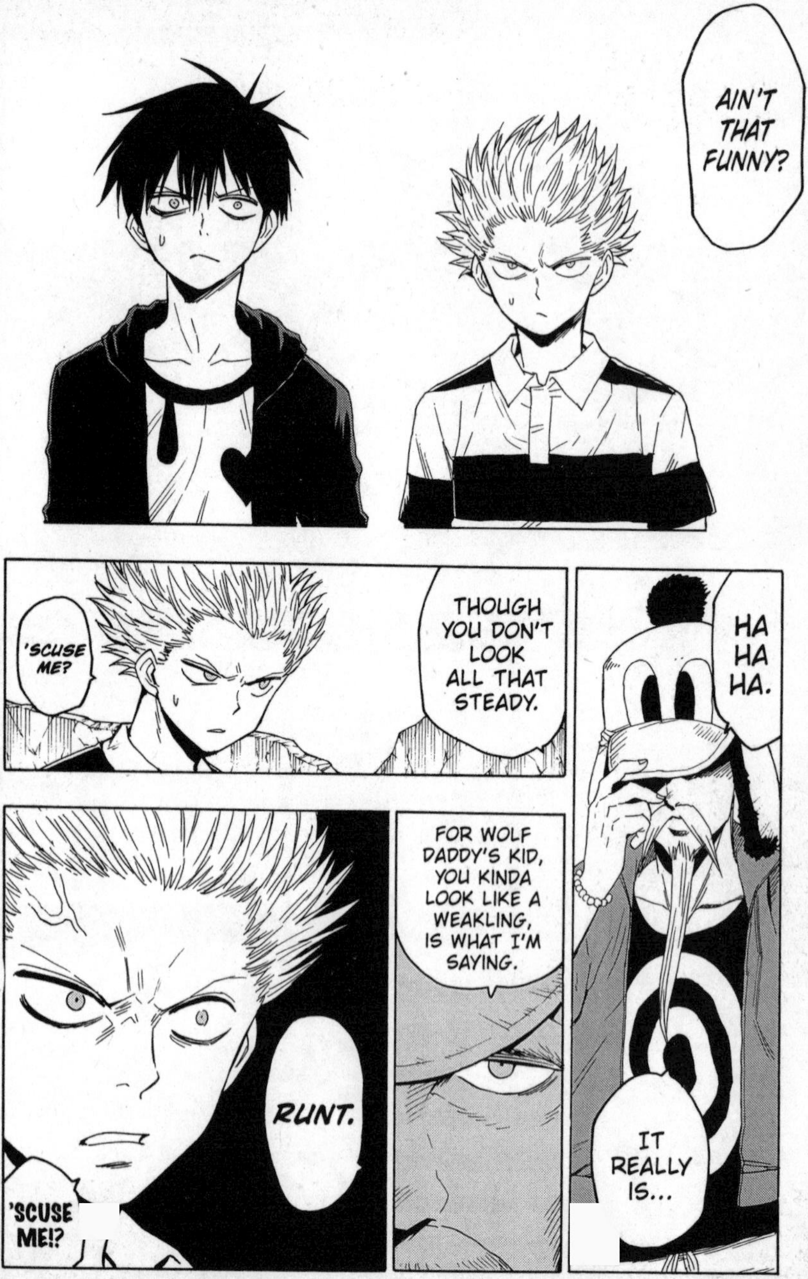
AIN'T THAT FUNNY?
HA HA HA.
IT REALLY IS...
THOUGH YOU DON'T LOOK ALL THAT STEADY.
'SCUSE ME?
FOR WOLF DADDY'S KID, YOU KINDA LOOK LIKE A WEAKLING, IS WHAT I'M SAYING.
RUNT.
'SCUSE ME!?

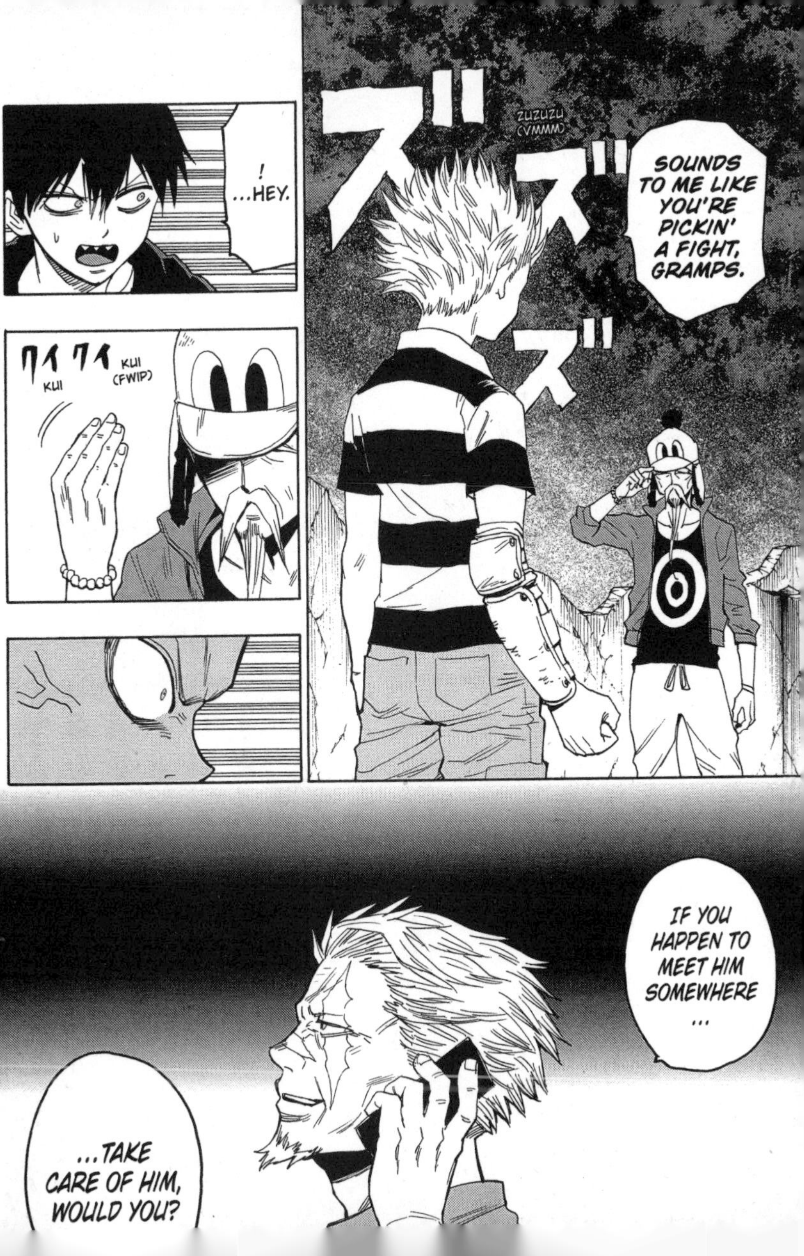
ズズズ
ZUZUZU (VMMM)
SOUNDS TO ME LIKE YOU'RE PICKIN' A FIGHT, GRAMPS.
! ...HEY.
クイ クイ
KUI KUI (FWIP)
IF YOU HAPPEN TO MEET HIM SOMEWHERE...
...TAKE CARE OF HIM, WOULD YOU?

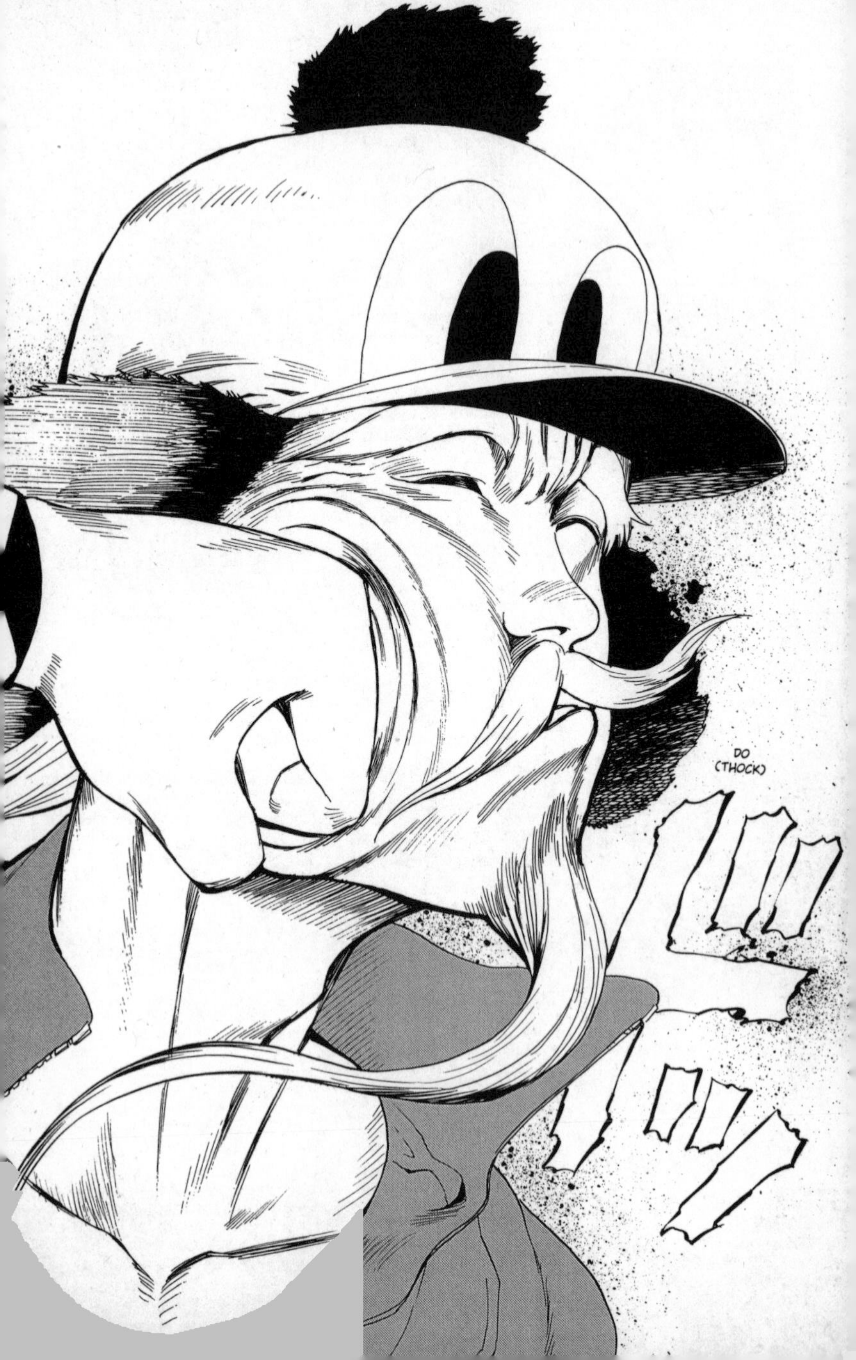
DO
(THOCK)

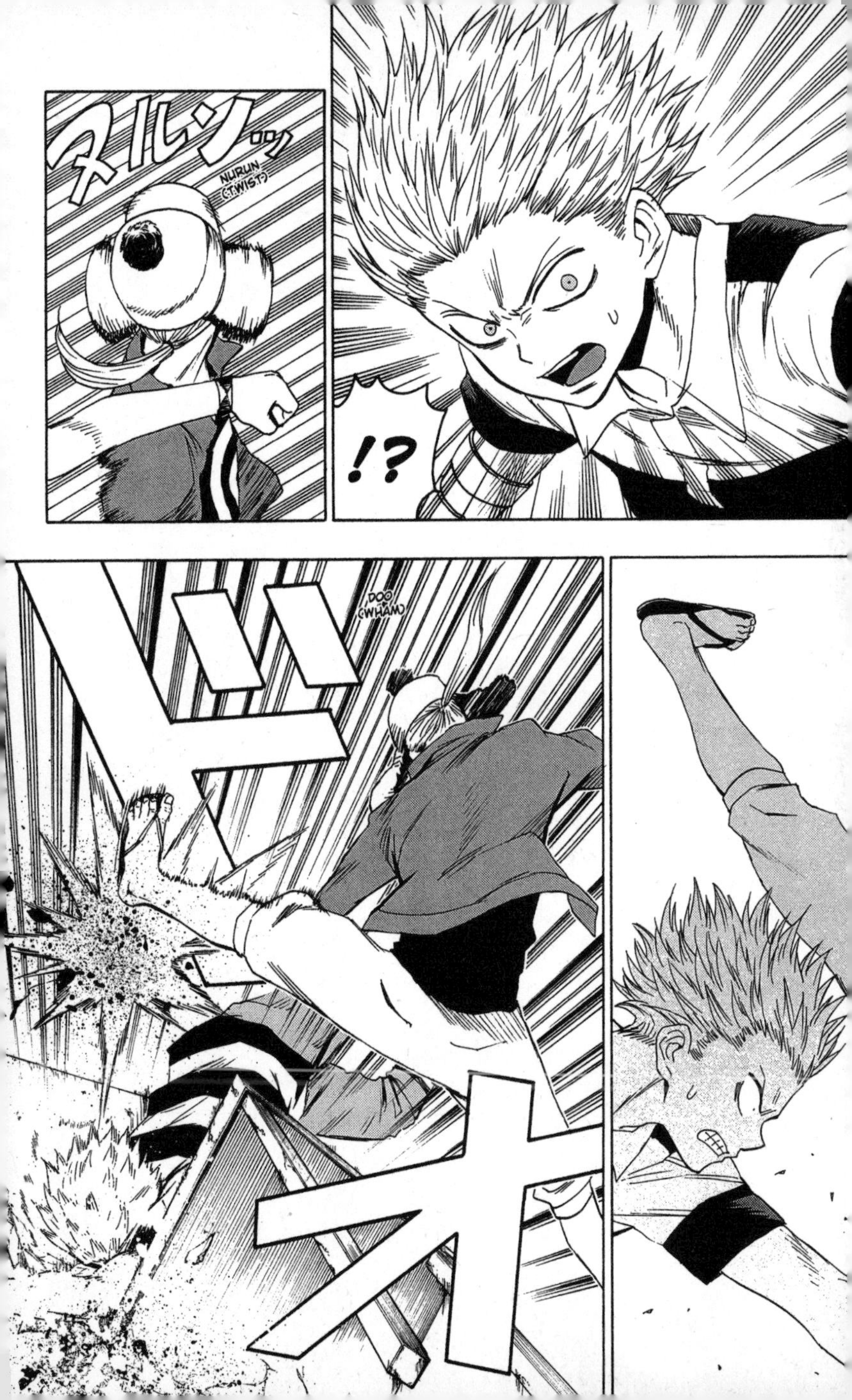
!?
ヌルンッ
NURUN
(TWIST)
ドォ
DOO
(WHAM)

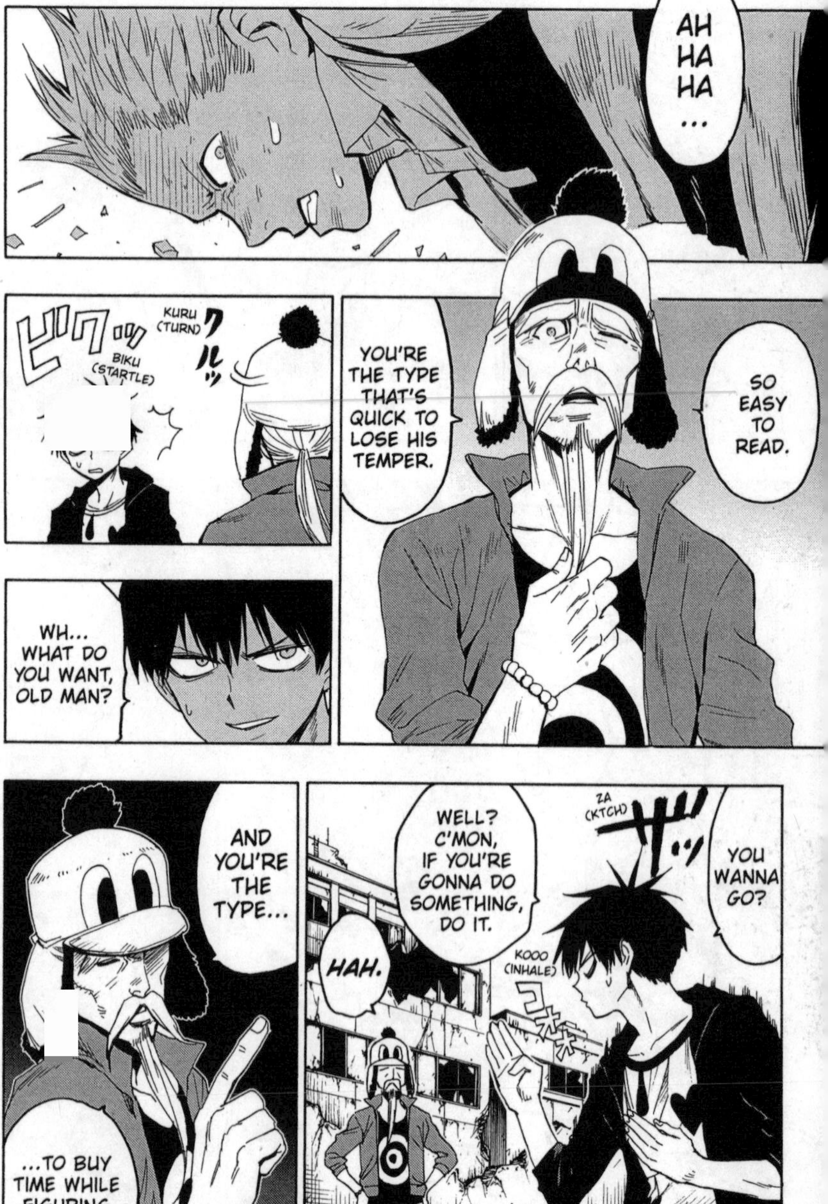
AH HA HA ...
SO EASY TO READ.
YOU'RE THE TYPE THAT'S QUICK TO LOSE HIS TEMPER.
KURU (TURN)
BIKU (STARTLE)
WH... WHAT DO YOU WANT, OLD MAN?
YOU WANNA GO?
ZA (KTCH)
WELL? C'MON, IF YOU'RE GONNA DO SOMETHING, DO IT.
KOOO (INHALE)
HAH.
AND YOU'RE THE TYPE...
...TO BUY TIME WHILE FIGURING OUT HOW TO ESCAPE.

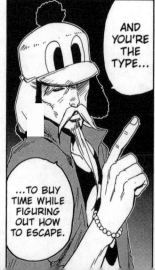

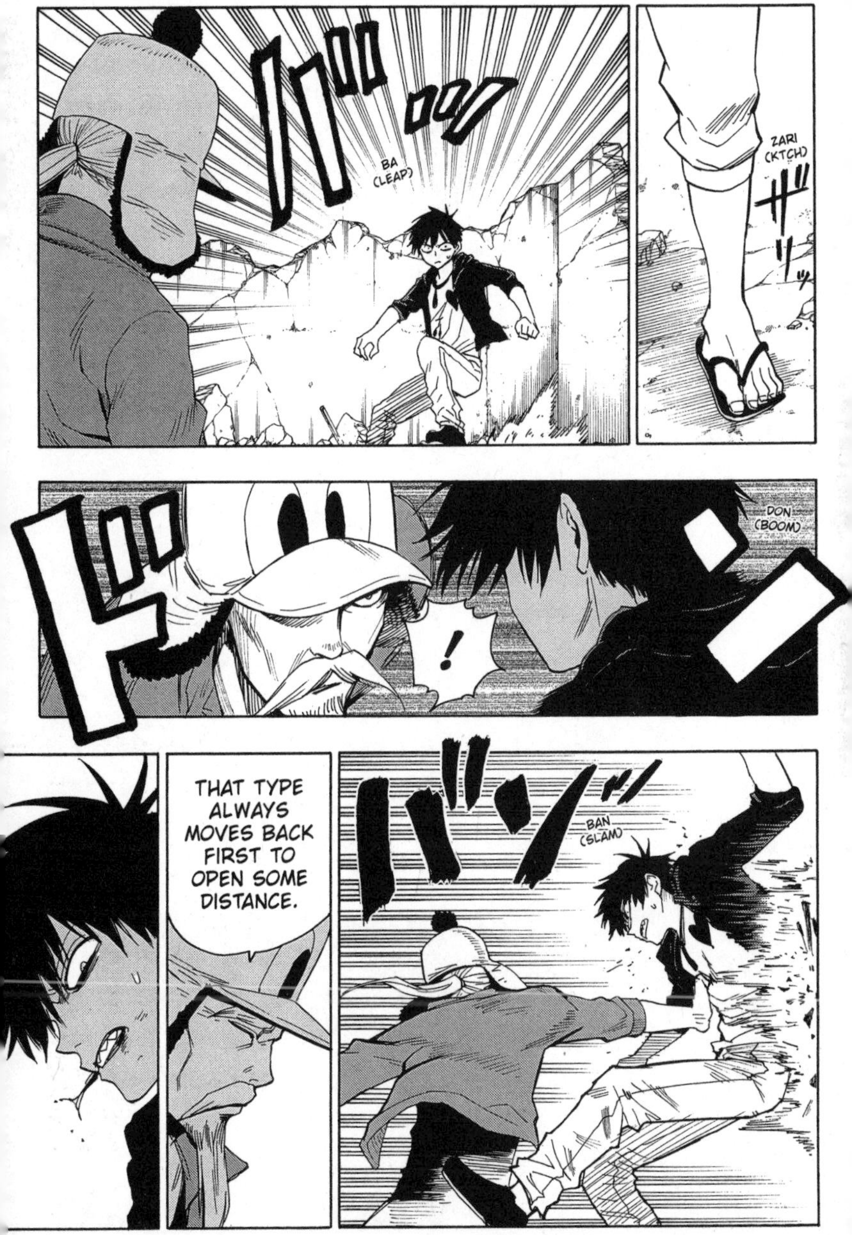
ZARI (KTCH)
BA (LEAP)
DON (BOOM)
!
BAN (SLAM)
THAT TYPE ALWAYS MOVES BACK FIRST TO OPEN SOME DISTANCE.

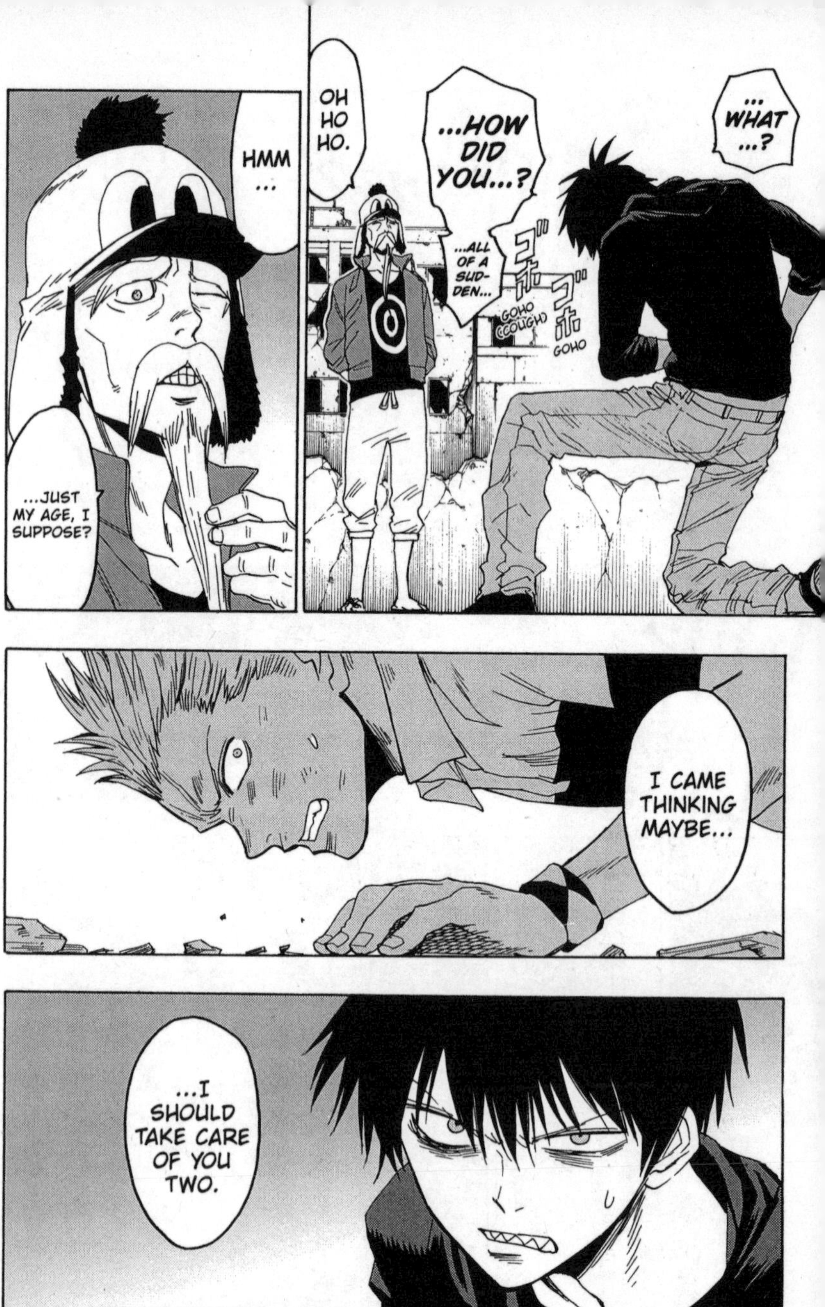
...WHAT...?
...HOW DID YOU...?
...ALL OF A SUDDEN...
ゴホ
GOHO (COUGH)
ゴホ
GOHO
OH HO HO.
HMM...
...JUST MY AGE, I SUPPOSE?
I CAME THINKING MAYBE...
...I SHOULD TAKE CARE OF YOU TWO.

♠ To Be Continued ♠

THE POISON

100% PURE, UNDILUTED POISON. IT HAS AN INCREDIBLY HARSH TASTE. HOWEVER, IT'S SAID THAT BY THE TIME YOU CAN TASTE IT, YOU'RE ALREADY DEAD.

BLOOD LAD

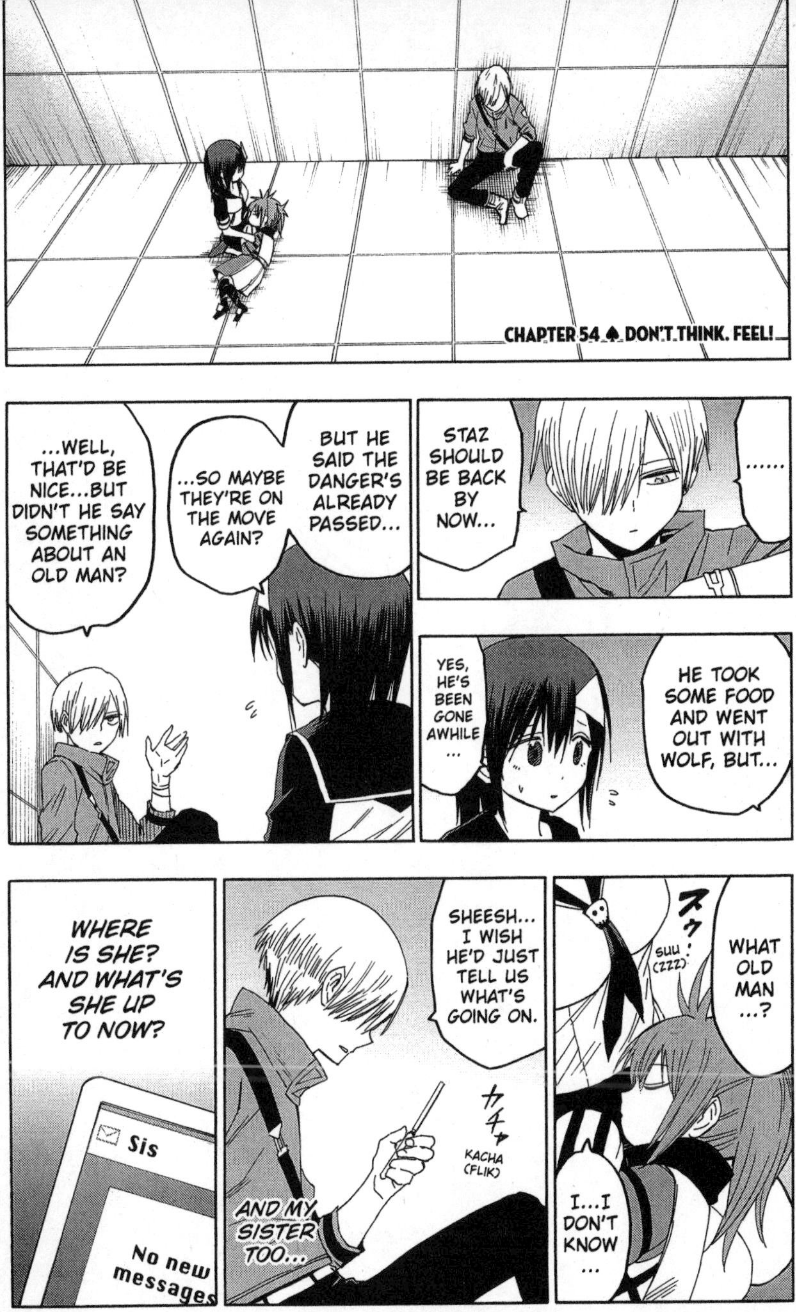
CHAPTER 54 ♠ DON'T THINK. FEEL!
......
STAZ SHOULD BE BACK BY NOW...
HE TOOK SOME FOOD AND WENT OUT WITH WOLF, BUT...
YES, HE'S BEEN GONE AWHILE...
BUT HE SAID THE DANGER'S ALREADY PASSED...
...SO MAYBE THEY'RE ON THE MOVE AGAIN?
...WELL, THAT'D BE NICE...BUT DIDN'T HE SAY SOMETHING ABOUT AN OLD MAN?
WHAT OLD MAN...?
スゥ
SUU (ZZZ)
I...I DON'T KNOW...
SHEESH... I WISH HE'D JUST TELL US WHAT'S GOING ON.
カチャ
KACHA (FLIK)
AND MY SISTER TOO...
WHERE IS SHE? AND WHAT'S SHE UP TO NOW?
Sis
No new messages

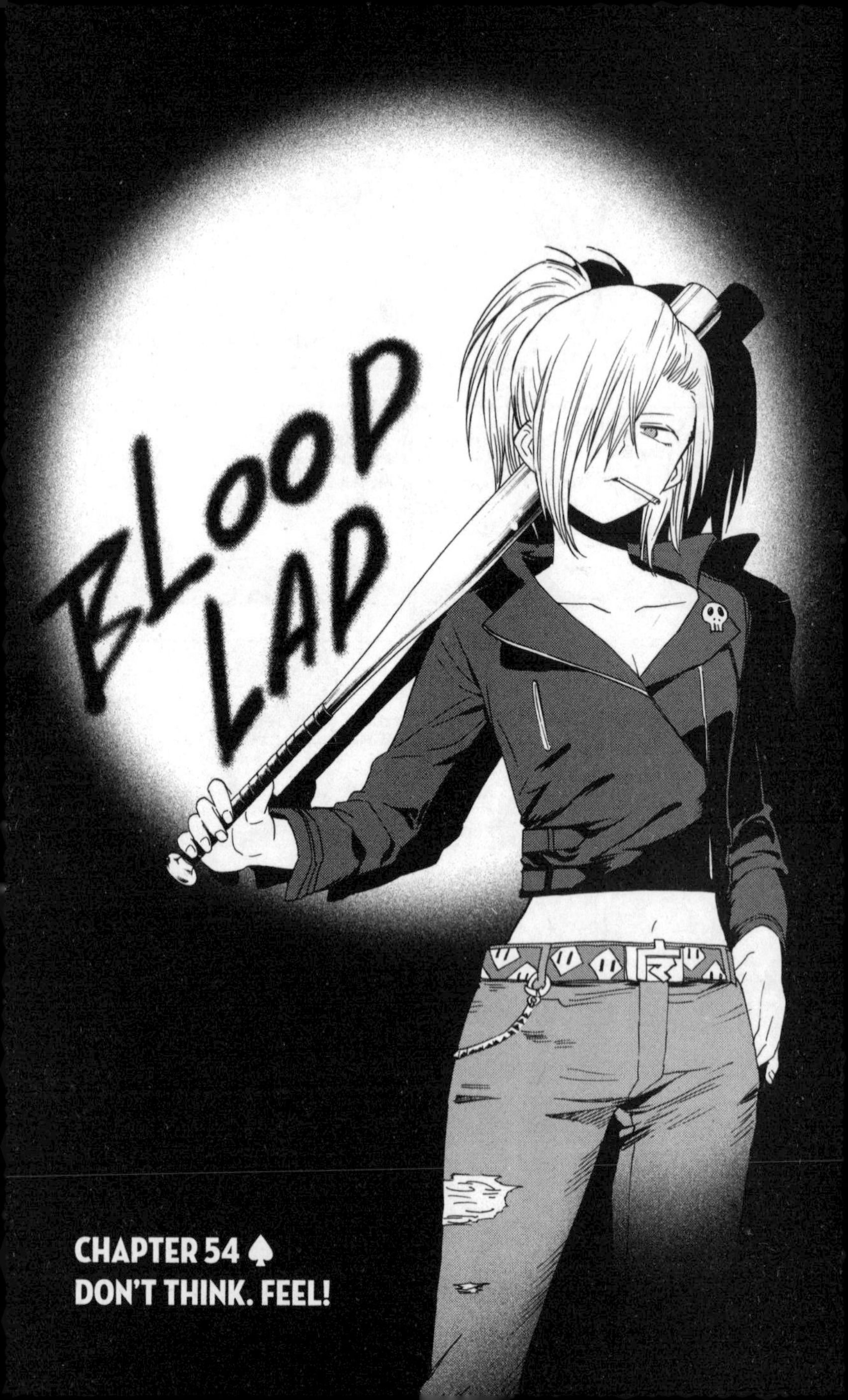
BLOOD LAD
CHAPTER 54 ♠
DON'T THINK. FEEL!

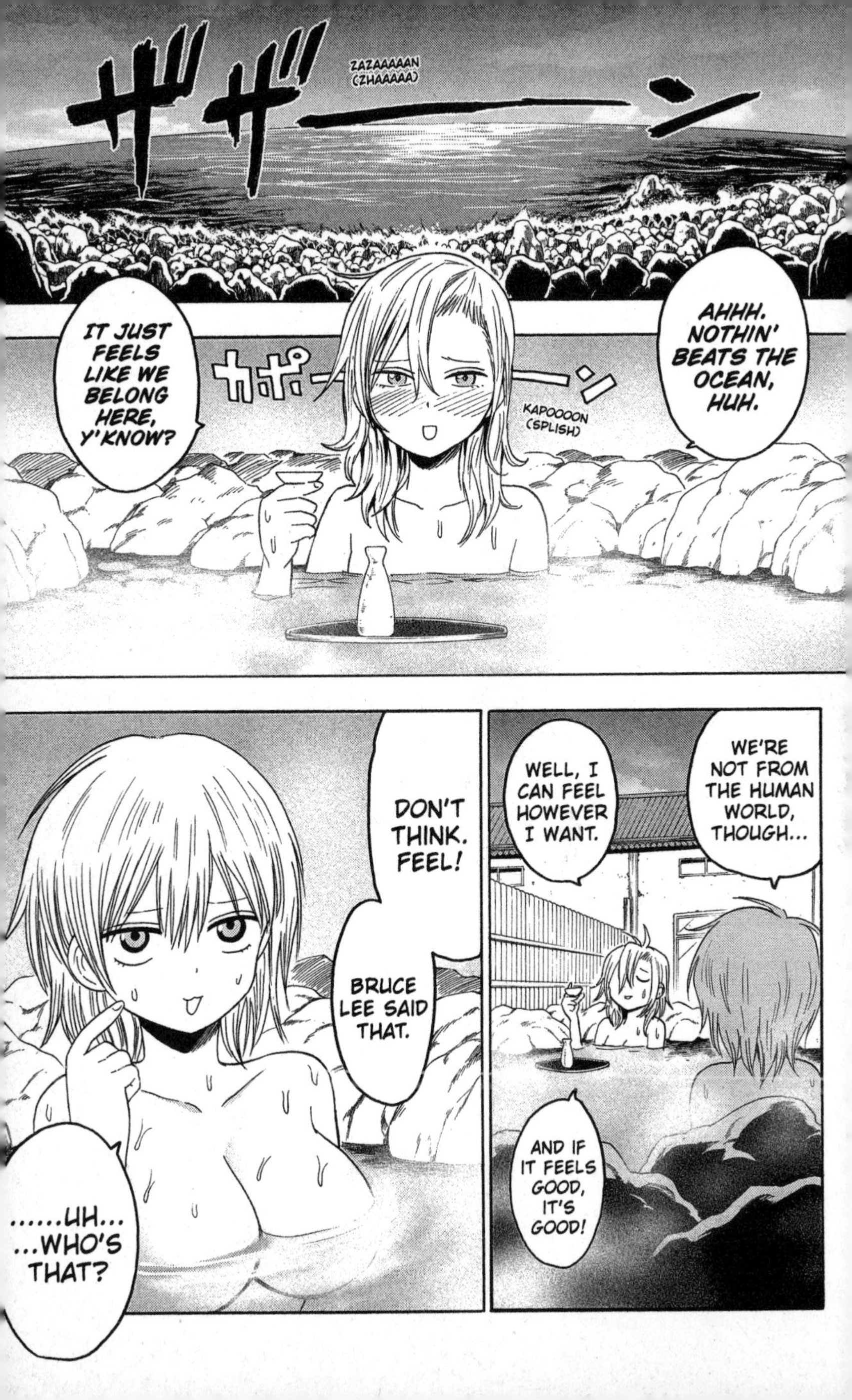
ZAZAAAAAN
(ZHAAAAAA)
AHHH. NOTHIN' BEATS THE OCEAN, HUH.
KAPOOOON
(SPLISH)
IT JUST FEELS LIKE WE BELONG HERE, Y'KNOW?
WE'RE NOT FROM THE HUMAN WORLD, THOUGH...
WELL, I CAN FEEL HOWEVER I WANT.
AND IF IT FEELS GOOD, IT'S GOOD!
DON'T THINK. FEEL!
BRUCE LEE SAID THAT.
......UH... ...WHO'S THAT?

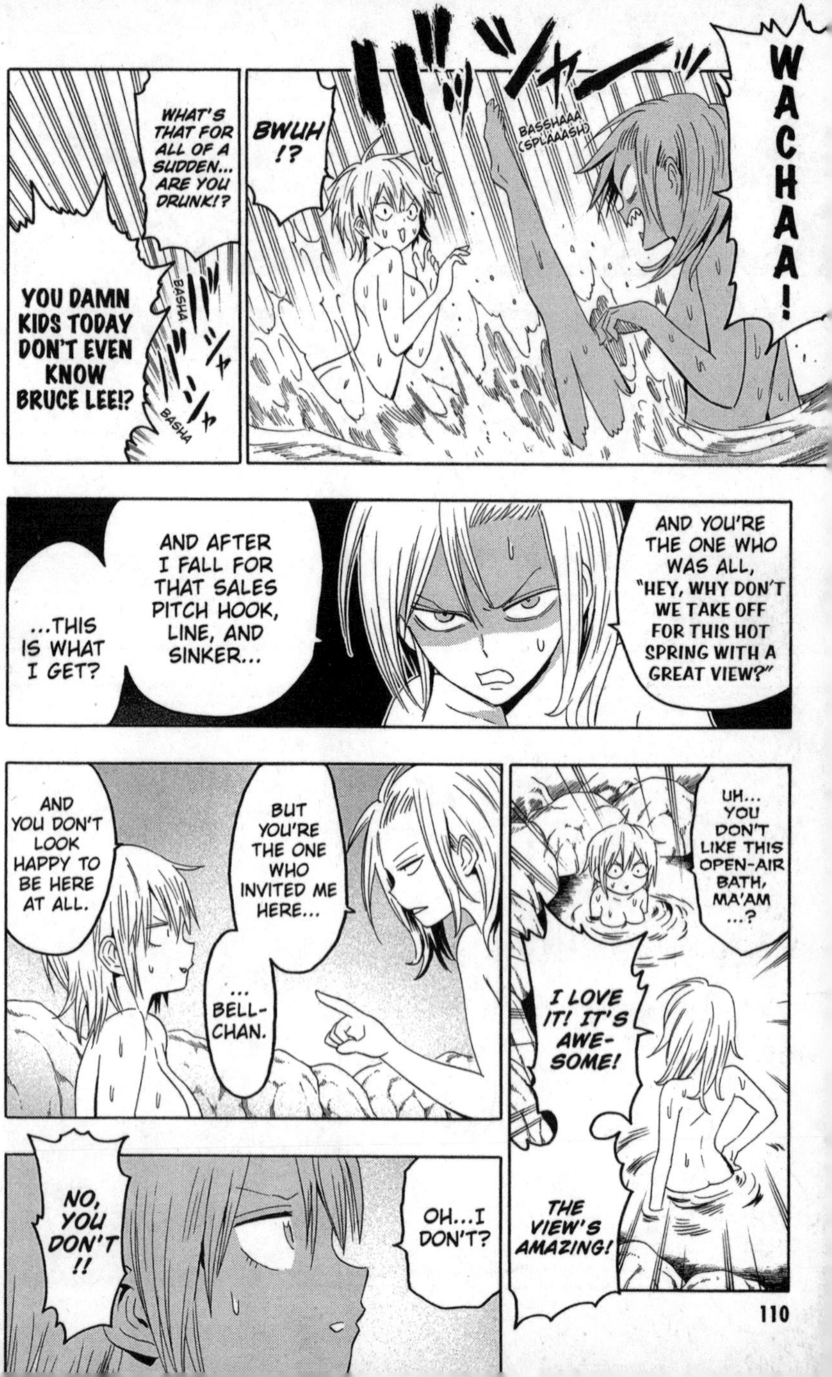
WACHAA!
BASSHAAA (SPLAAASH)
BWUH !?
BASHA
WHAT'S THAT FOR ALL OF A SUDDEN... ARE YOU DRUNK!?
YOU DAMN KIDS TODAY DON'T EVEN KNOW BRUCE LEE!?
BASHA
AND YOU'RE THE ONE WHO WAS ALL, "HEY, WHY DON'T WE TAKE OFF FOR THIS HOT SPRING WITH A GREAT VIEW?"
AND AFTER I FALL FOR THAT SALES PITCH HOOK, LINE, AND SINKER...
...THIS IS WHAT I GET?
UH... YOU DON'T LIKE THIS OPEN-AIR BATH, MA'AM ...?
I LOVE IT! IT'S AWESOME!
THE VIEW'S AMAZING!
BUT YOU'RE THE ONE WHO INVITED ME HERE...
... BELL-CHAN.
AND YOU DON'T LOOK HAPPY TO BE HERE AT ALL.
OH...I DON'T?
NO, YOU DON'T !!

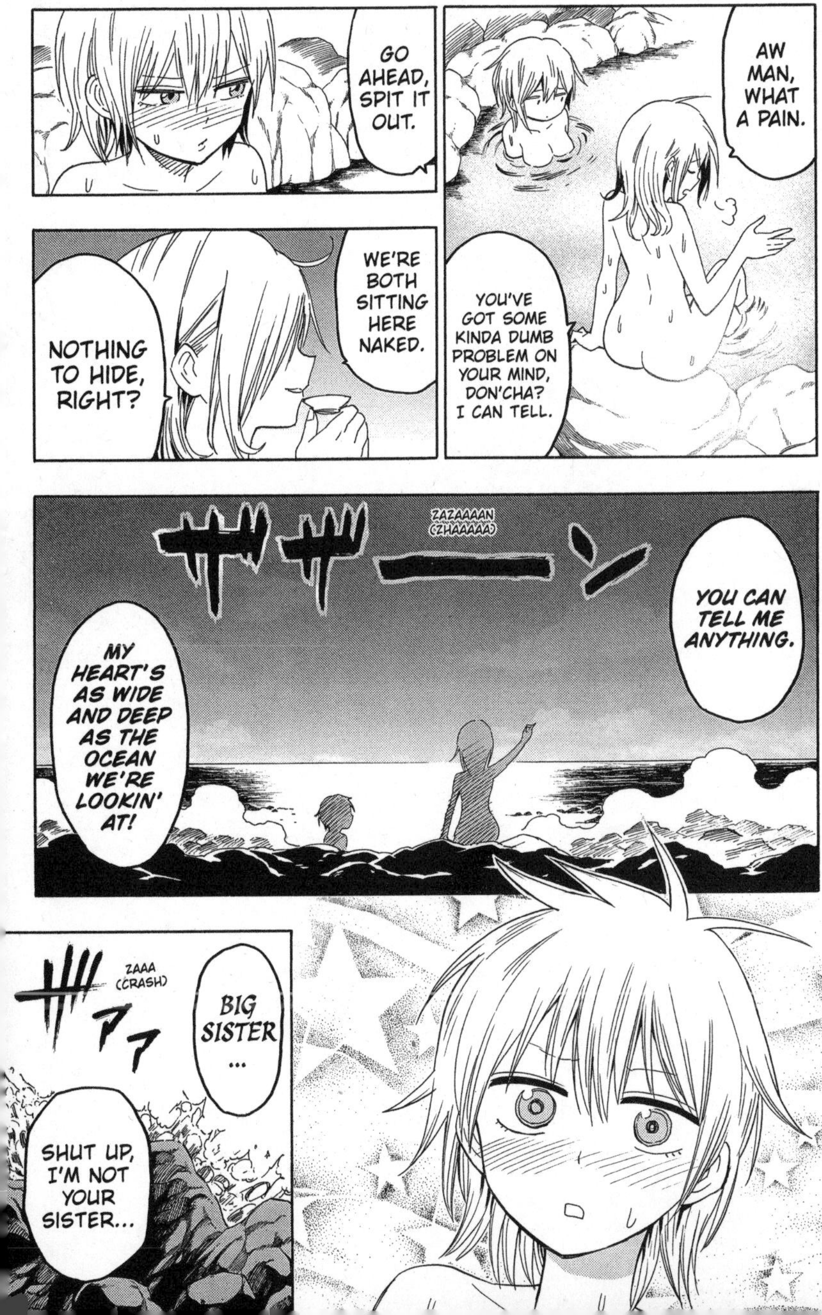
AW MAN, WHAT A PAIN.
YOU'VE GOT SOME KINDA DUMB PROBLEM ON YOUR MIND, DON'CHA? I CAN TELL.
GO AHEAD, SPIT IT OUT.
WE'RE BOTH SITTING HERE NAKED.
NOTHING TO HIDE, RIGHT?
ZAZAAAAN (ZHAAAAA)
YOU CAN TELL ME ANYTHING.
MY HEART'S AS WIDE AND DEEP AS THE OCEAN WE'RE LOOKIN' AT!
BIG SISTER...
ZAAA (CRASH)
SHUT UP, I'M NOT YOUR SISTER...

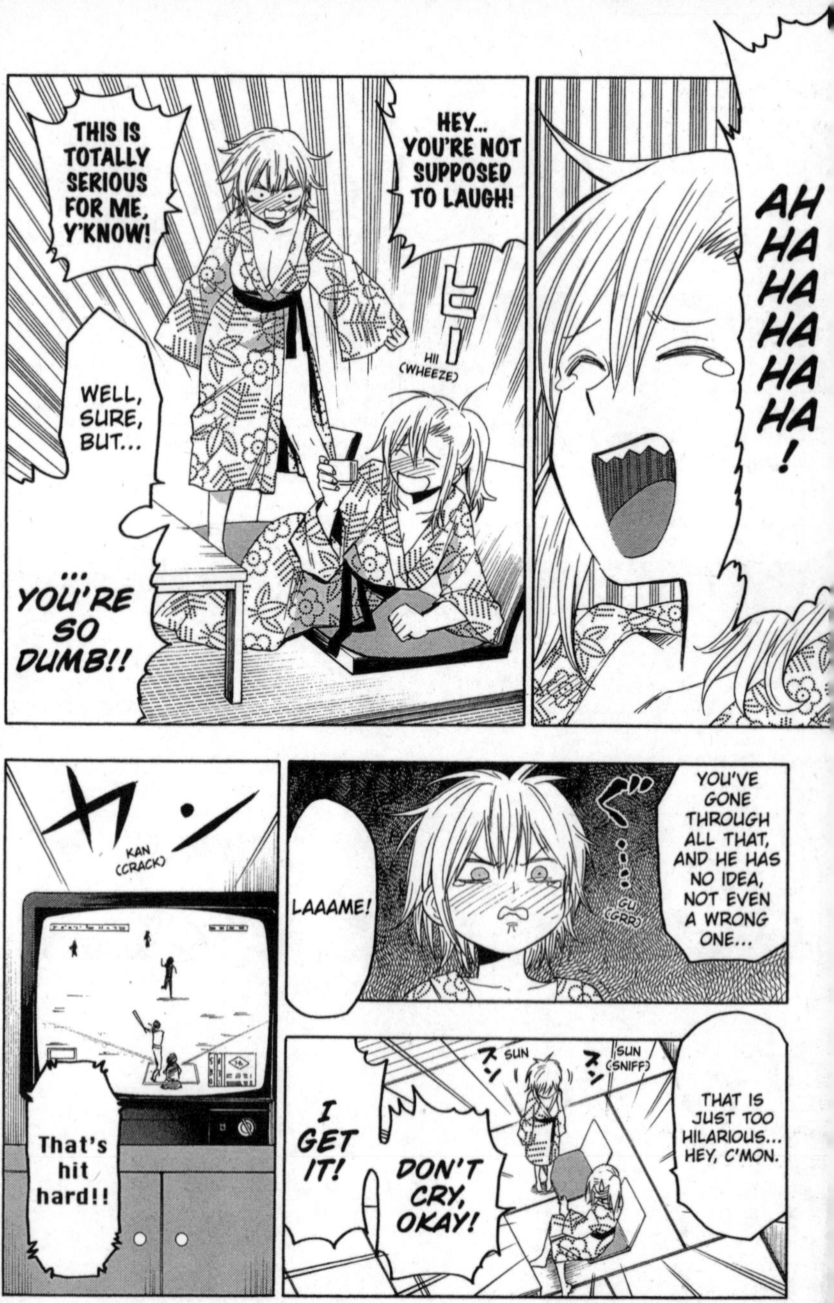
AH HA HA HA HA HA!
HEY... YOU'RE NOT SUPPOSED TO LAUGH!
ヒー
HII (WHEEZE)
THIS IS TOTALLY SERIOUS FOR ME, Y'KNOW!
WELL, SURE, BUT...
...YOU'RE SO DUMB!!
YOU'VE GONE THROUGH ALL THAT, AND HE HAS NO IDEA, NOT EVEN A WRONG ONE...
ぐ...
GU (GRR)
LAAAME!
THAT IS JUST TOO HILARIOUS... HEY, C'MON.
ズン
SUN (SNIFF)
ズン
SUN
DON'T CRY, OKAY!
I GET IT!
カン
KAN (CRACK)
That's hit hard!!

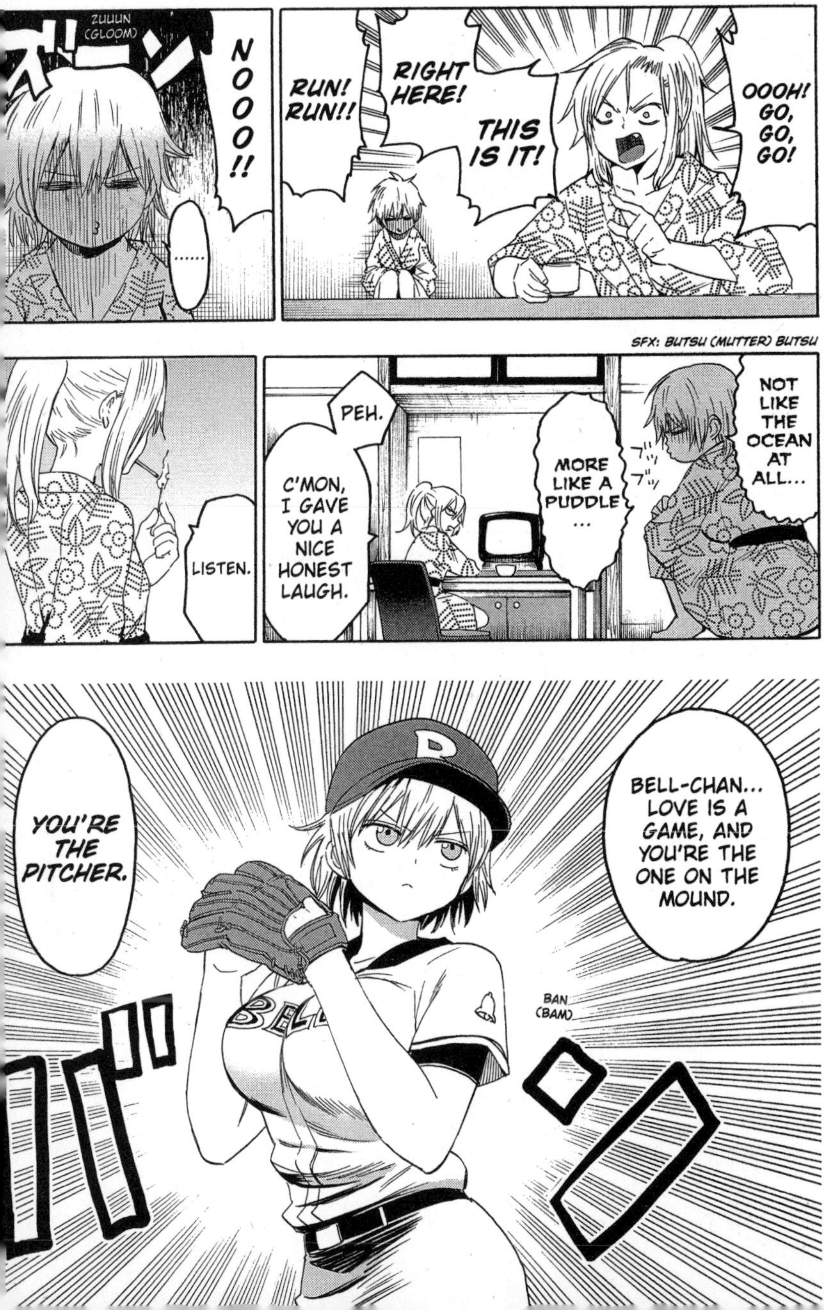
OOOH! GO, GO, GO!
THIS IS IT!
RIGHT HERE!
RUN! RUN!!
NOOOO!!
ZUUUN (GLOOM)
......
SFX: BUTSU (MUTTER) BUTSU
NOT LIKE THE OCEAN AT ALL...
MORE LIKE A PUDDLE ...
PEH.
C'MON, I GAVE YOU A NICE HONEST LAUGH.
LISTEN.
BELL-CHAN... LOVE IS A GAME, AND YOU'RE THE ONE ON THE MOUND.
BAN (BAM)
YOU'RE THE PITCHER.

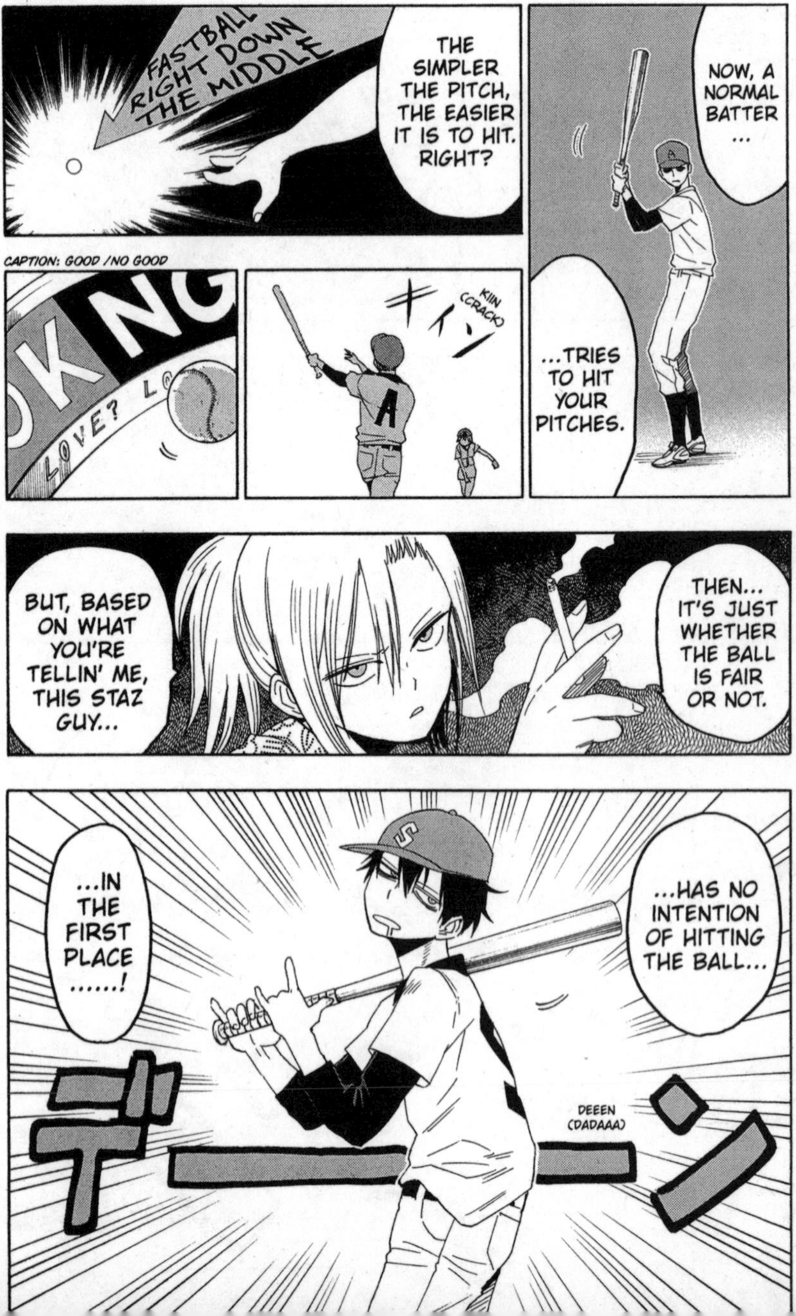
NOW, A NORMAL BATTER ...
...TRIES TO HIT YOUR PITCHES.
FASTBALL RIGHT DOWN THE MIDDLE
THE SIMPLER THE PITCH, THE EASIER IT IS TO HIT. RIGHT?
KIIN (CRACK)
CAPTION: GOOD /NO GOOD
OK NG
LOVE? LO
THEN... IT'S JUST WHETHER THE BALL IS FAIR OR NOT.
BUT, BASED ON WHAT YOU'RE TELLIN' ME, THIS STAZ GUY...
...HAS NO INTENTION OF HITTING THE BALL...
...IN THE FIRST PLACE......!
DEEEN (DADAAA)

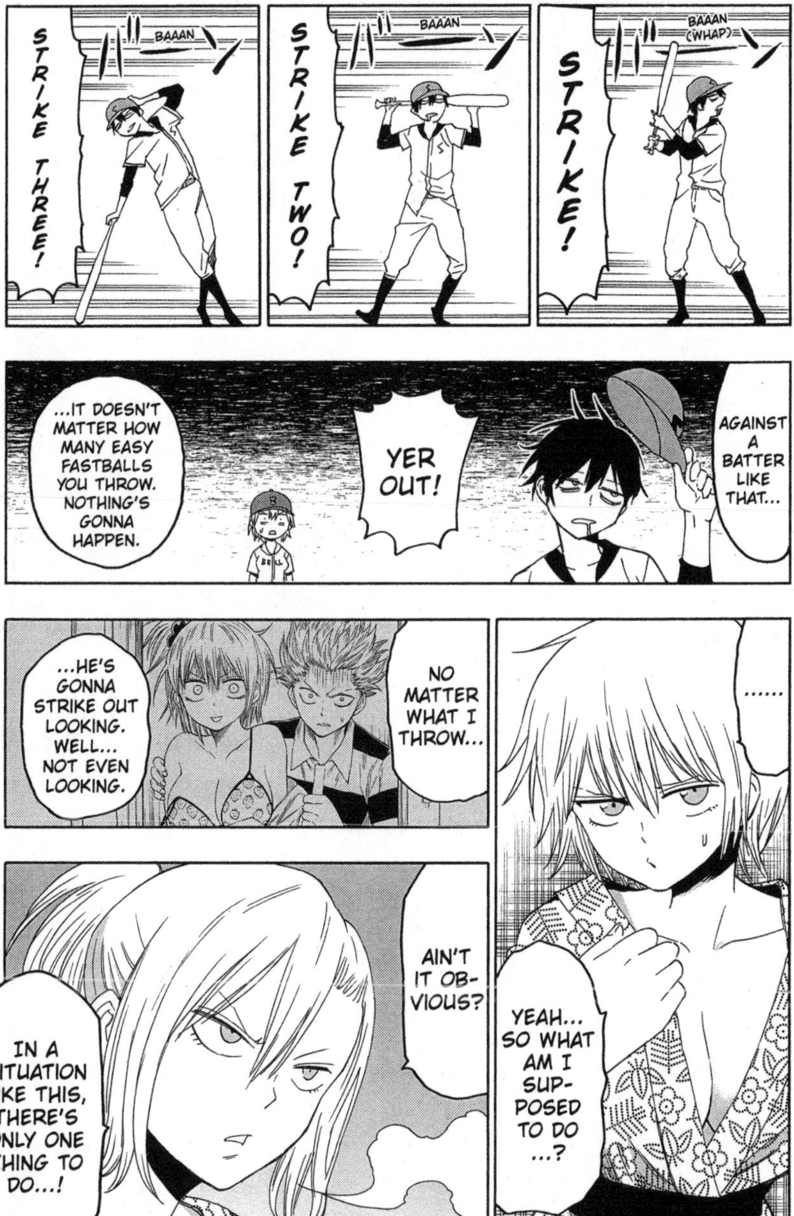
BAAAN (WHAP)
STRIKE!
BAAAN
STRIKE TWO!
BAAAN
STRIKE THREE!
AGAINST A BATTER LIKE THAT...
YER OUT!
...IT DOESN'T MATTER HOW MANY EASY FASTBALLS YOU THROW. NOTHING'S GONNA HAPPEN.
......
YEAH... SO WHAT AM I SUP-POSED TO DO ...?
NO MATTER WHAT I THROW...
...HE'S GONNA STRIKE OUT LOOKING. WELL... NOT EVEN LOOKING.
AIN'T IT OB-VIOUS?
IN A SITUATION LIKE THIS, THERE'S ONLY ONE THING TO DO...!

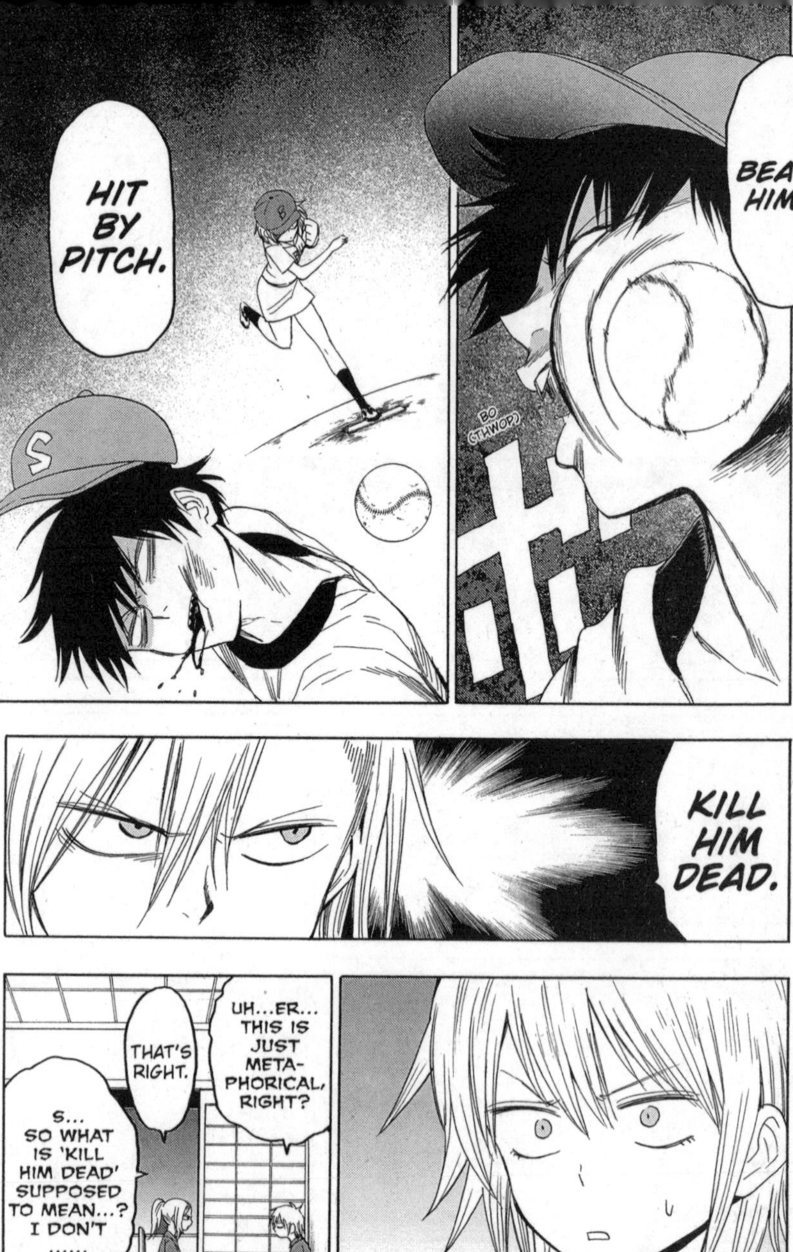
BEAN HIM.
BO (THWOP)
HIT BY PITCH.
KILL HIM DEAD.
UH...ER... THIS IS JUST META-PHORICAL, RIGHT?
THAT'S RIGHT.
S... SO WHAT IS 'KILL HIM DEAD' SUPPOSED TO MEAN...? I DON'T ......

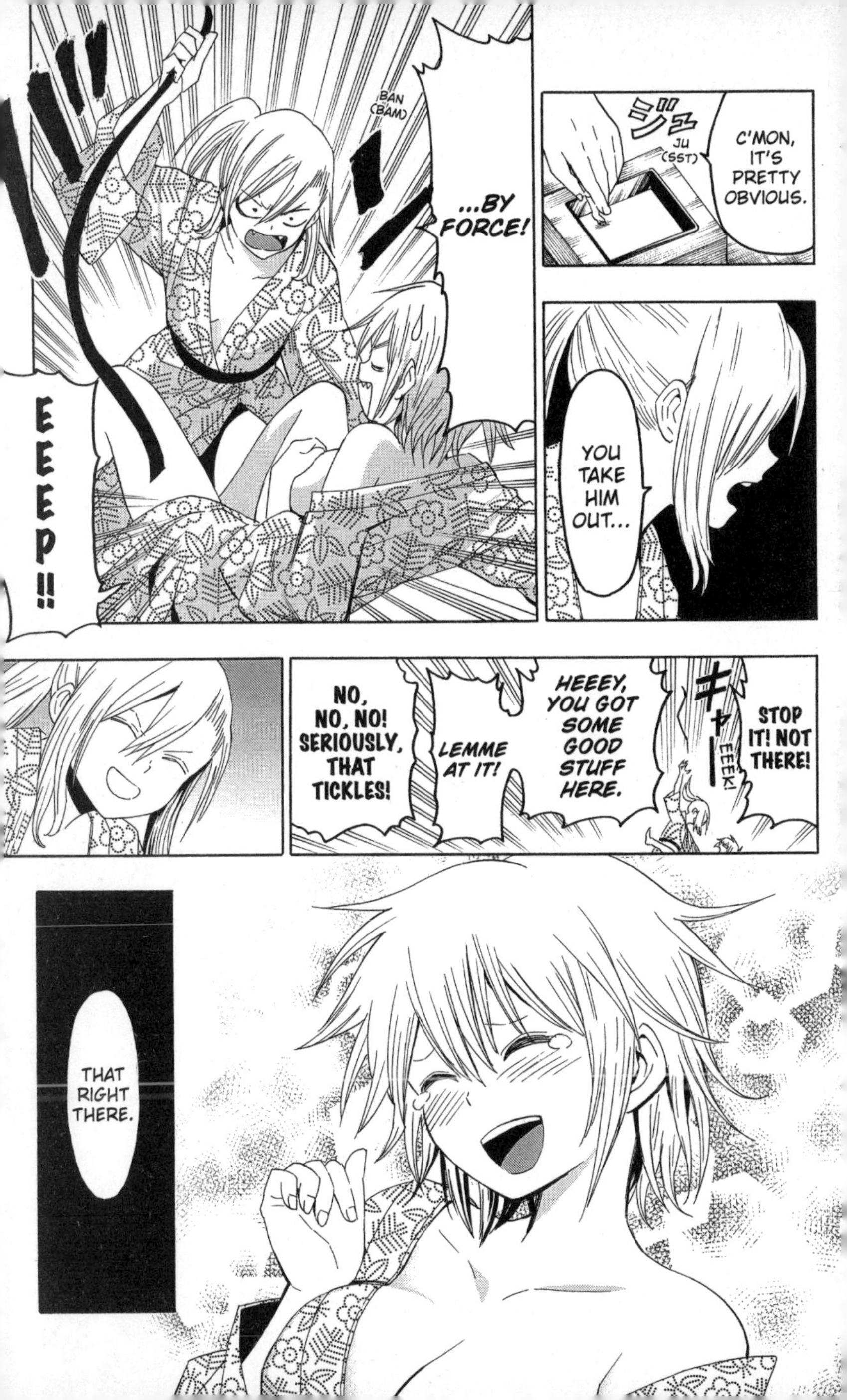
ジュ
JU (SST)
C'MON, IT'S PRETTY OBVIOUS.
YOU TAKE HIM OUT...
...BY FORCE!
BAN (BAM)
EEEP!!
STOP IT! NOT THERE!
キャー
EEEK!
HEEEY, YOU GOT SOME GOOD STUFF HERE.
LEMME AT IT!
NO, NO, NO! SERIOUSLY, THAT TICKLES!
THAT RIGHT THERE.

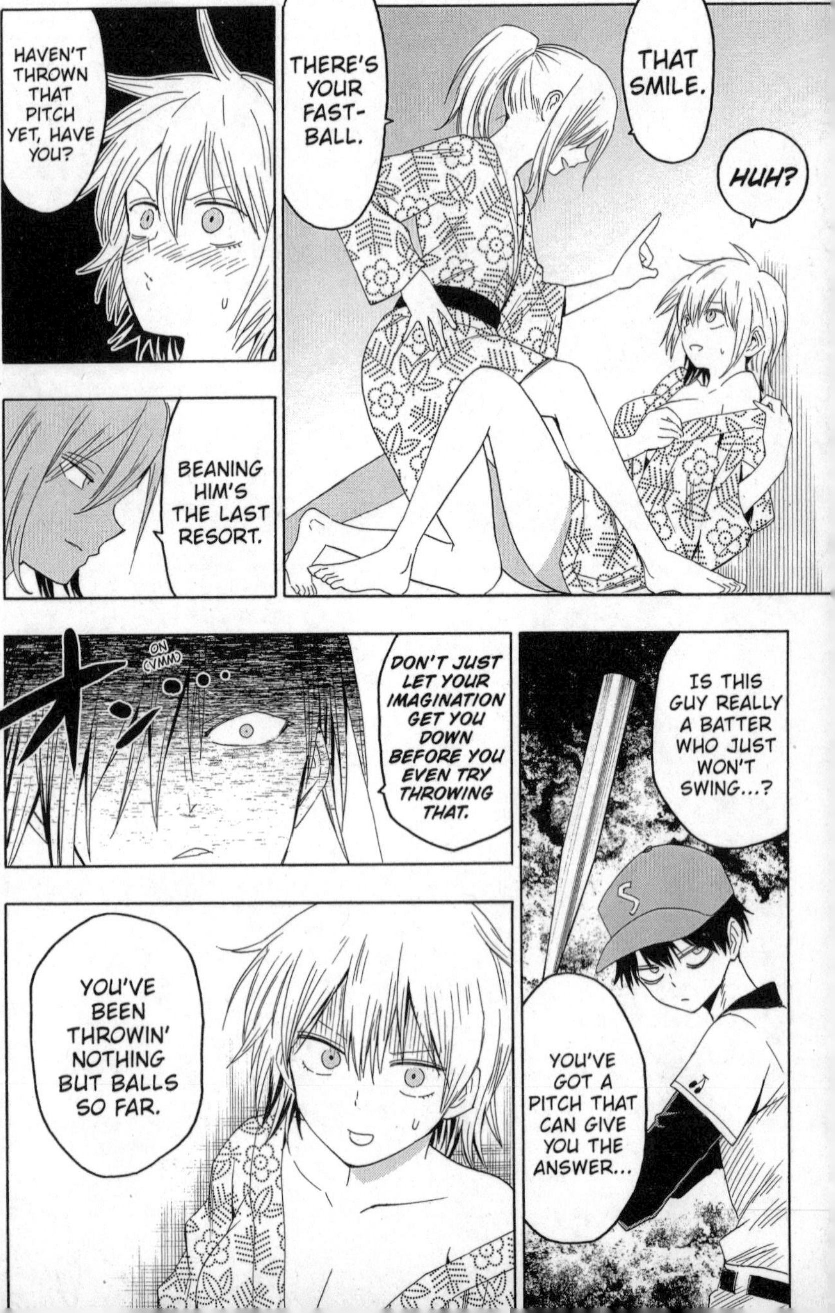
THAT SMILE.
HUH?
THERE'S YOUR FAST-BALL.
HAVEN'T THROWN THAT PITCH YET, HAVE YOU?
BEANING HIM'S THE LAST RESORT.
IS THIS GUY REALLY A BATTER WHO JUST WON'T SWING...?
YOU'VE GOT A PITCH THAT CAN GIVE YOU THE ANSWER...
DON'T JUST LET YOUR IMAGINATION GET YOU DOWN BEFORE YOU EVEN TRY THROWING THAT.
ON (VMM)
YOU'VE BEEN THROWIN' NOTHING BUT BALLS SO FAR.

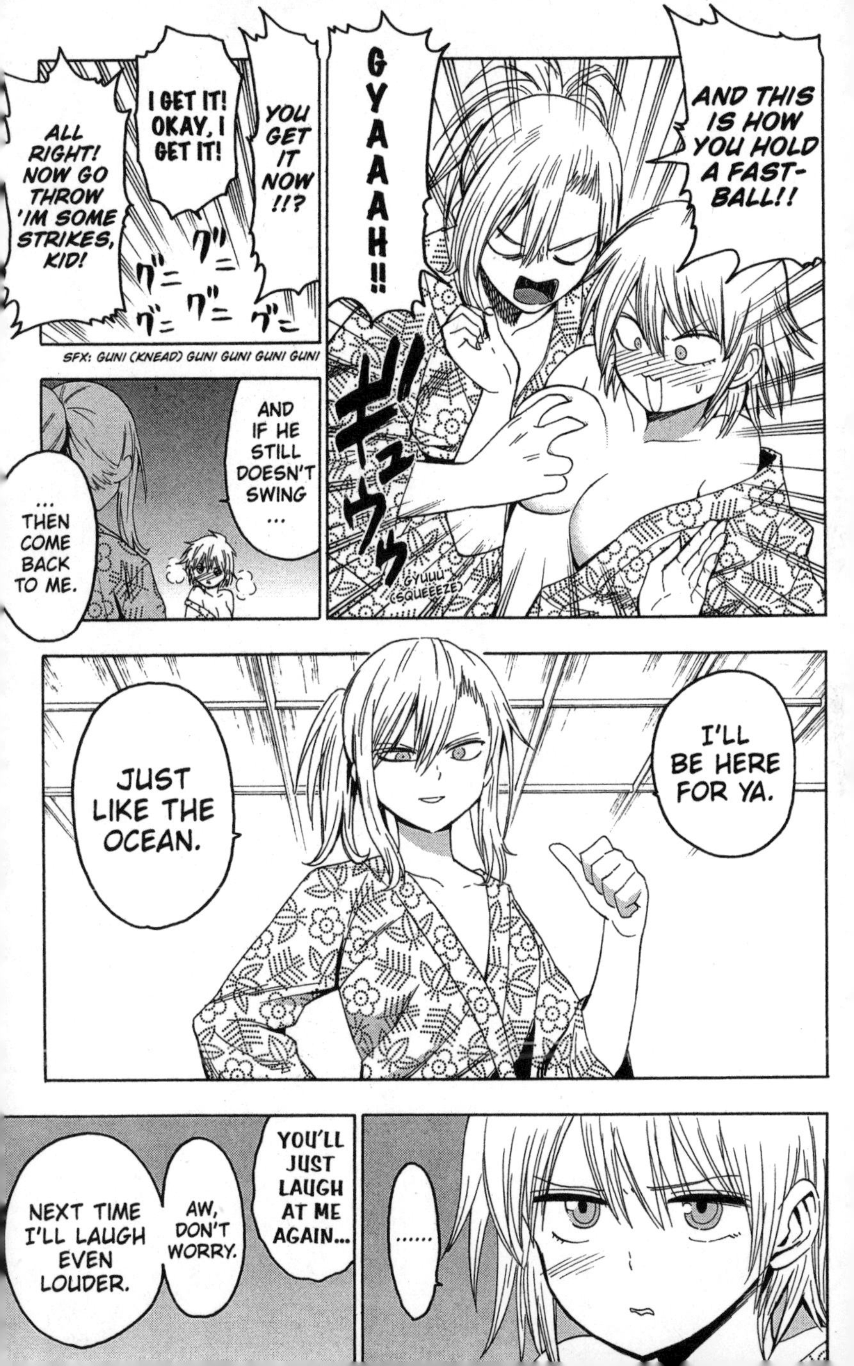
AND THIS IS HOW YOU HOLD A FAST-BALL!!
GYAAAAH!!
GYUUU (SQUEEEZE)
YOU GET IT NOW!!?
I GET IT! OKAY, I GET IT!
ALL RIGHT! NOW GO THROW 'IM SOME STRIKES, KID!
SFX: GUNI (KNEAD) GUNI GUNI GUNI GUNI
AND IF HE STILL DOESN'T SWING...
...THEN COME BACK TO ME.
I'LL BE HERE FOR YA.
JUST LIKE THE OCEAN.
......
YOU'LL JUST LAUGH AT ME AGAIN...
AW, DON'T WORRY.
NEXT TIME I'LL LAUGH EVEN LOUDER.

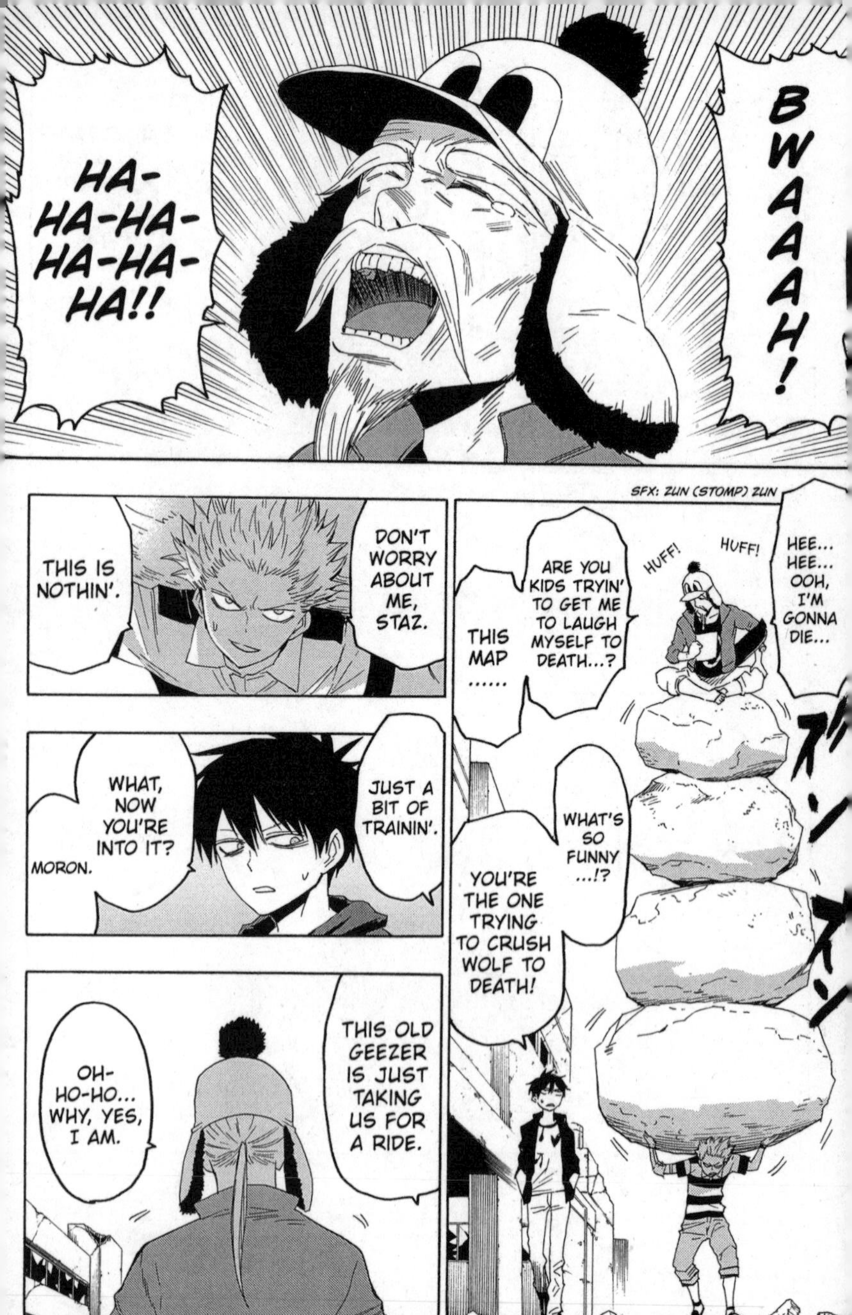
BWAAAAH!
HA-HA-HA-HA-HA-HA-HA!!
SFX: ZUN (STOMP) ZUN
HEE... HEE... OOH, I'M GONNA DIE...
HUFF! HUFF!
ARE YOU KIDS TRYIN' TO GET ME TO LAUGH MYSELF TO DEATH...?
THIS MAP......
WHAT'S SO FUNNY...!?
YOU'RE THE ONE TRYING TO CRUSH WOLF TO DEATH!
DON'T WORRY ABOUT ME, STAZ.
THIS IS NOTHIN'.
JUST A BIT OF TRAININ'.
WHAT, NOW YOU'RE INTO IT?
MORON.
THIS OLD GEEZER IS JUST TAKING US FOR A RIDE.
OH-HO-HO... WHY, YES, I AM.

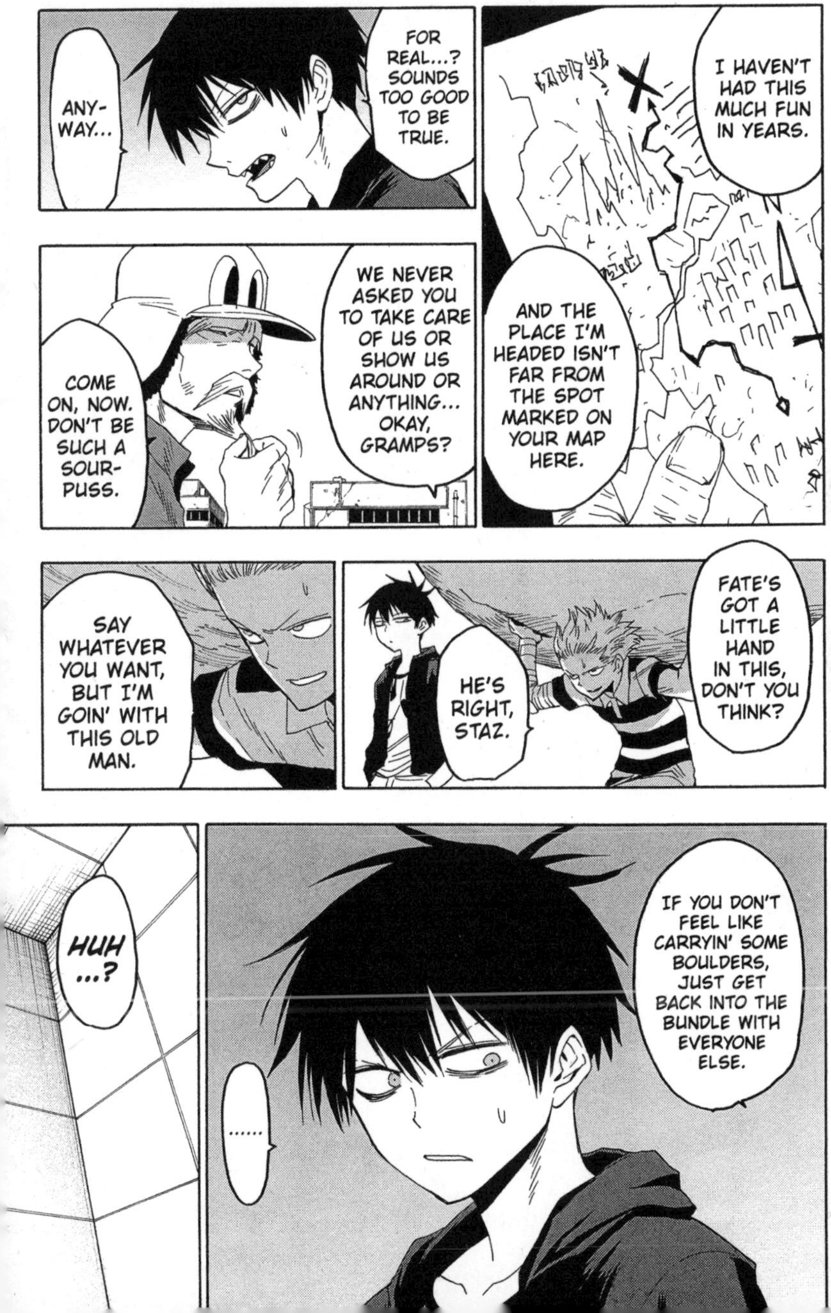
I HAVEN'T HAD THIS MUCH FUN IN YEARS.
AND THE PLACE I'M HEADED ISN'T FAR FROM THE SPOT MARKED ON YOUR MAP HERE.
FOR REAL...? SOUNDS TOO GOOD TO BE TRUE.
ANY-WAY...
WE NEVER ASKED YOU TO TAKE CARE OF US OR SHOW US AROUND OR ANYTHING... OKAY, GRAMPS?
COME ON, NOW. DON'T BE SUCH A SOUR-PUSS.
FATE'S GOT A LITTLE HAND IN THIS, DON'T YOU THINK?
HE'S RIGHT, STAZ.
SAY WHATEVER YOU WANT, BUT I'M GOIN' WITH THIS OLD MAN.
IF YOU DON'T FEEL LIKE CARRYIN' SOME BOULDERS, JUST GET BACK INTO THE BUNDLE WITH EVERYONE ELSE.
......
HUH...?

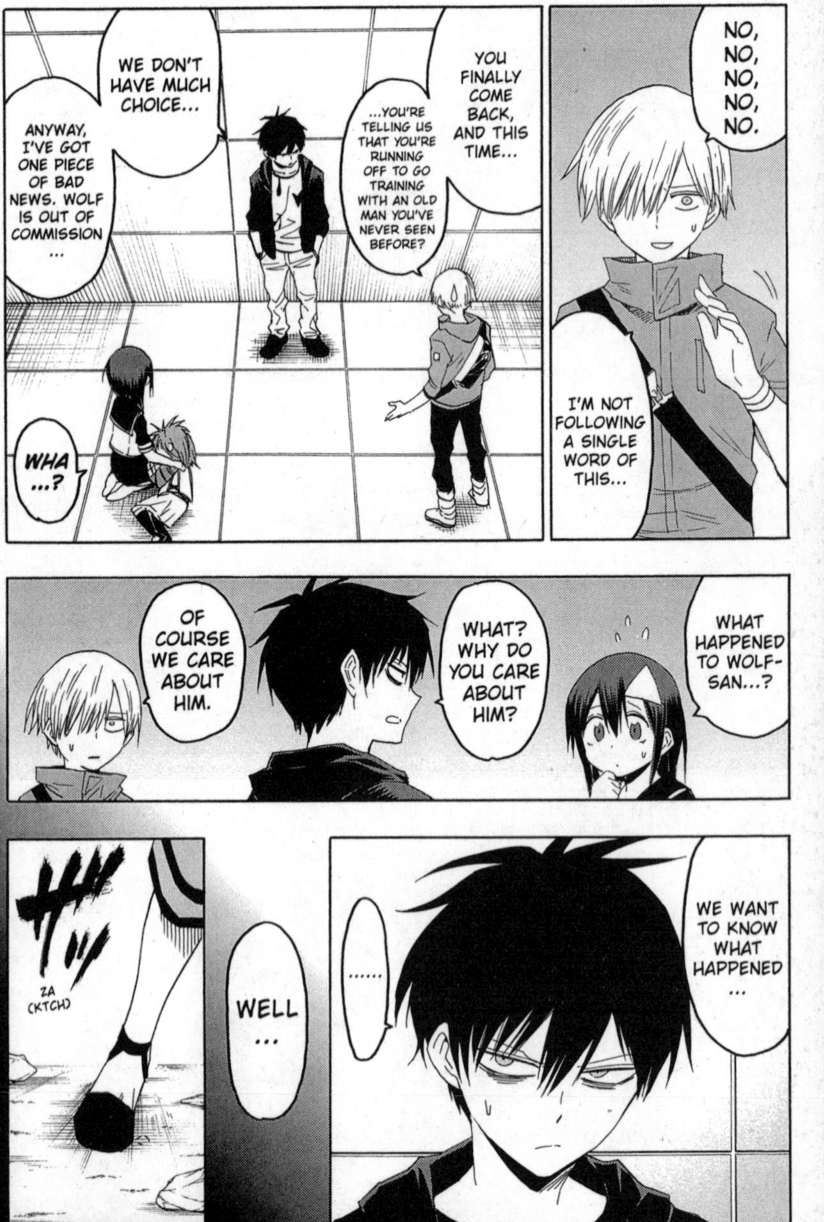
NO, NO, NO, NO, NO.
I'M NOT FOLLOWING A SINGLE WORD OF THIS...
YOU FINALLY COME BACK, AND THIS TIME...
...YOU'RE TELLING US THAT YOU'RE RUNNING OFF TO GO TRAINING WITH AN OLD MAN YOU'VE NEVER SEEN BEFORE?
WE DON'T HAVE MUCH CHOICE...
ANYWAY, I'VE GOT ONE PIECE OF BAD NEWS. WOLF IS OUT OF COMMISSION...
WHA...?
WHAT HAPPENED TO WOLF-SAN...?
WHAT? WHY DO YOU CARE ABOUT HIM?
OF COURSE WE CARE ABOUT HIM.
WE WANT TO KNOW WHAT HAPPENED...
......
WELL...
ZA (KTCH)

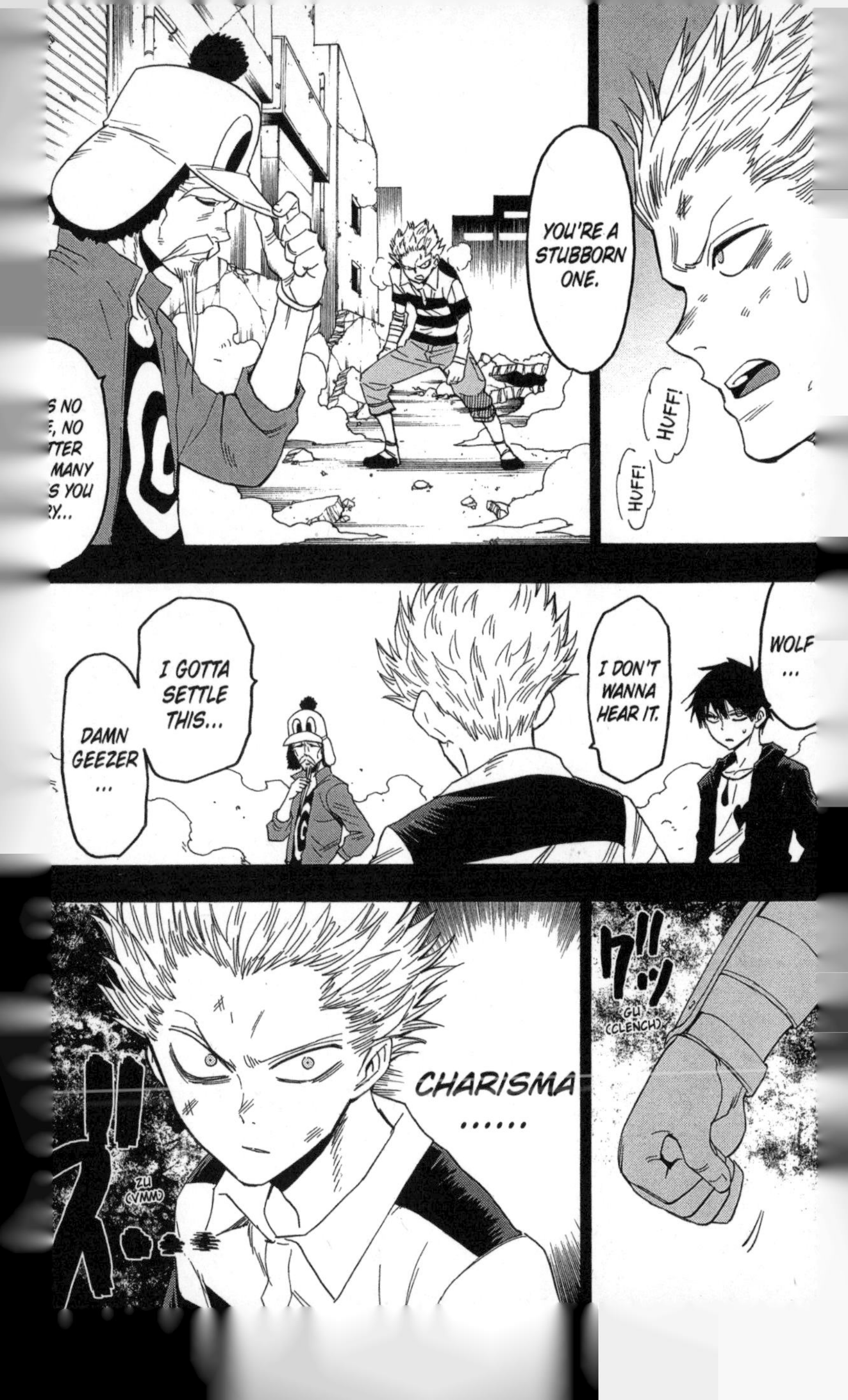
YOU'RE A STUBBORN ONE.
HUFF!
HUFF!
S NO
E, NO
TTER
MANY
S YOU
RY...
WOLF ...
I DON'T WANNA HEAR IT.
I GOTTA SETTLE THIS...
DAMN GEEZER ...
GU (CLENCH)
CHARISMA ......
ZU (VMM)

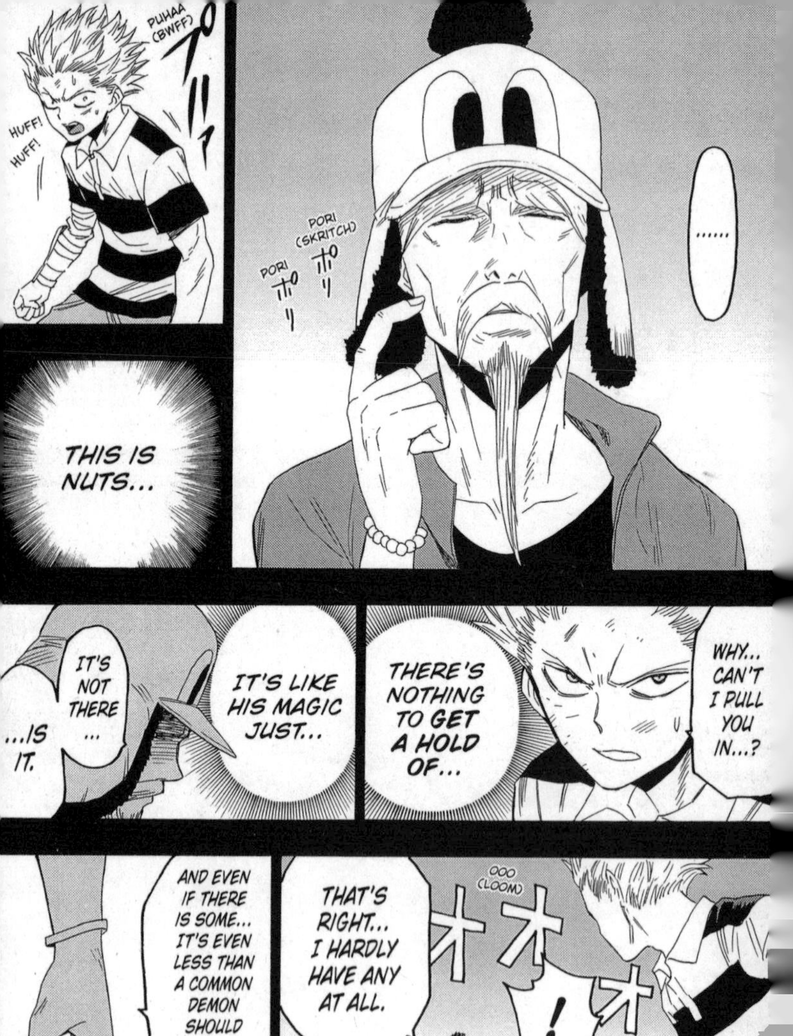
......
PORI (SKRITCH)
PORI
PUHAA (BWFF)
HUFF! HUFF!
THIS IS NUTS...
WHY... CAN'T I PULL YOU IN...?
THERE'S NOTHING TO GET A HOLD OF...
IT'S LIKE HIS MAGIC JUST...
IT'S NOT THERE ...
...IS IT.
OOO (LOOM)
!
THAT'S RIGHT... I HARDLY HAVE ANY AT ALL.
AND EVEN IF THERE IS SOME... IT'S EVEN LESS THAN A COMMON DEMON SHOULD HAVE... ISN'T IT?
KOKI (CRICK)

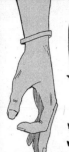

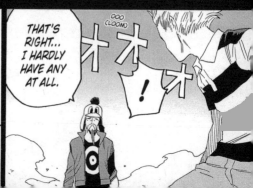

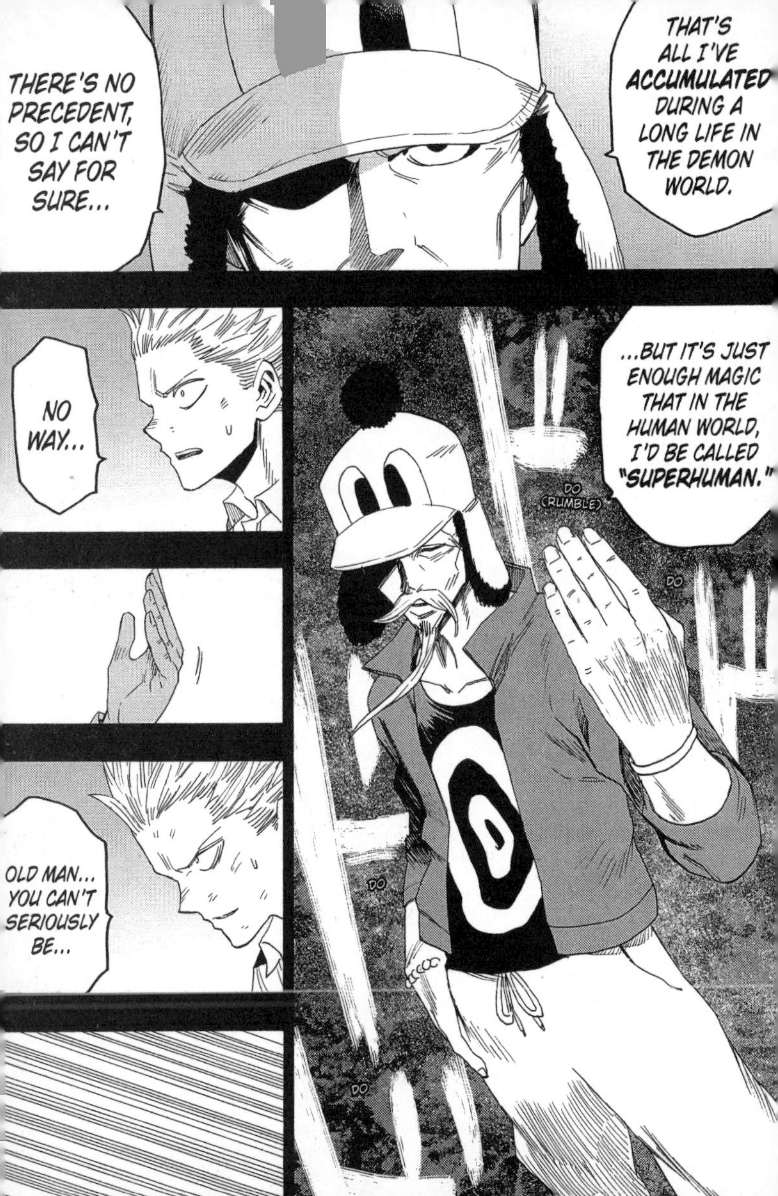
THAT'S ALL I'VE **ACCUMULATED** DURING A LONG LIFE IN THE DEMON WORLD.
THERE'S NO PRECEDENT, SO I CAN'T SAY FOR SURE...
...BUT IT'S JUST ENOUGH MAGIC THAT IN THE HUMAN WORLD, I'D BE CALLED **"SUPERHUMAN."**
DO (RUMBLE)
DO
DO
DO
NO WAY...
OLD MAN... YOU CAN'T SERIOUSLY BE...

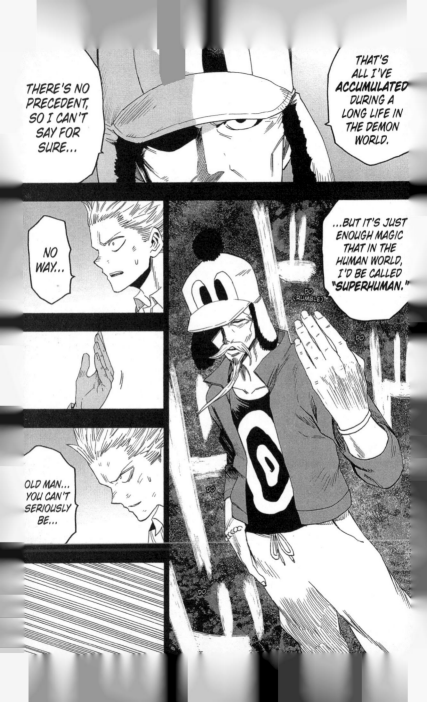

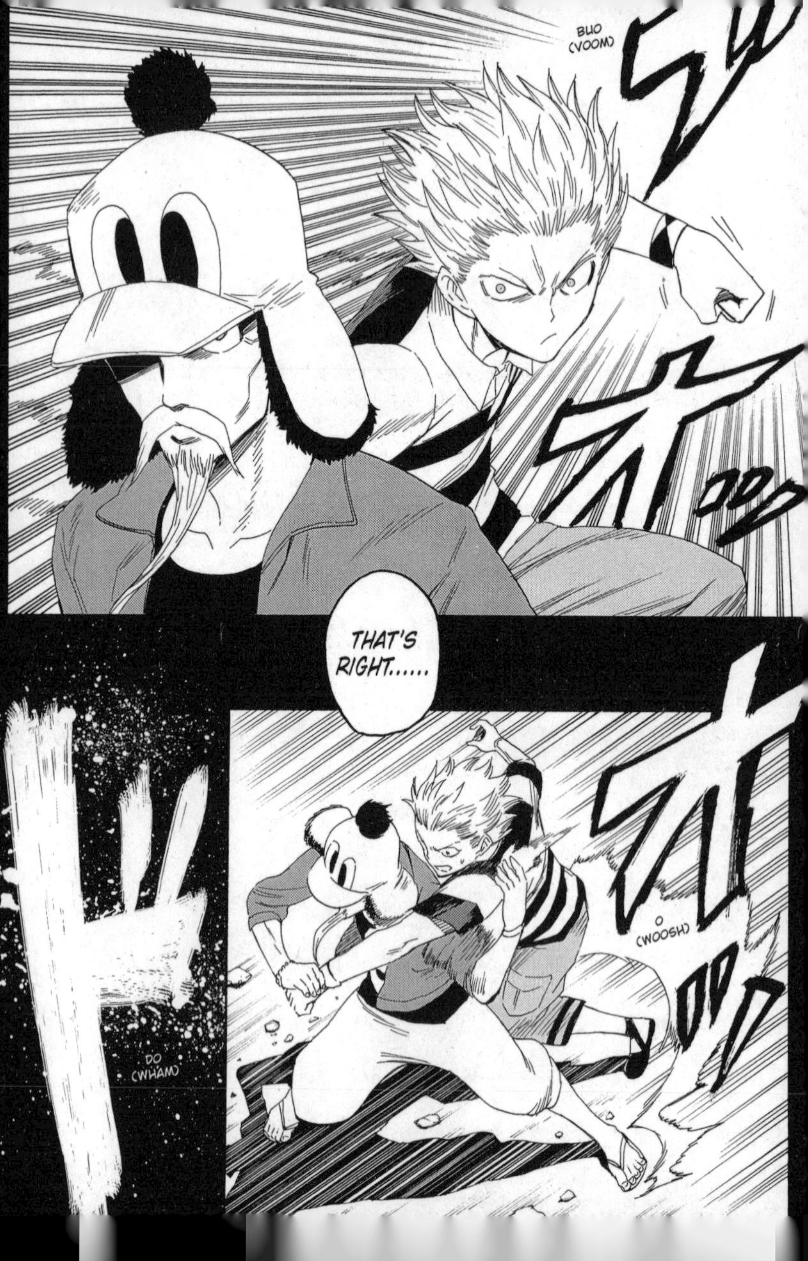
BUO
(VOOM)
THAT'S RIGHT......
O
(WOOSH)
DO
(WHAM)

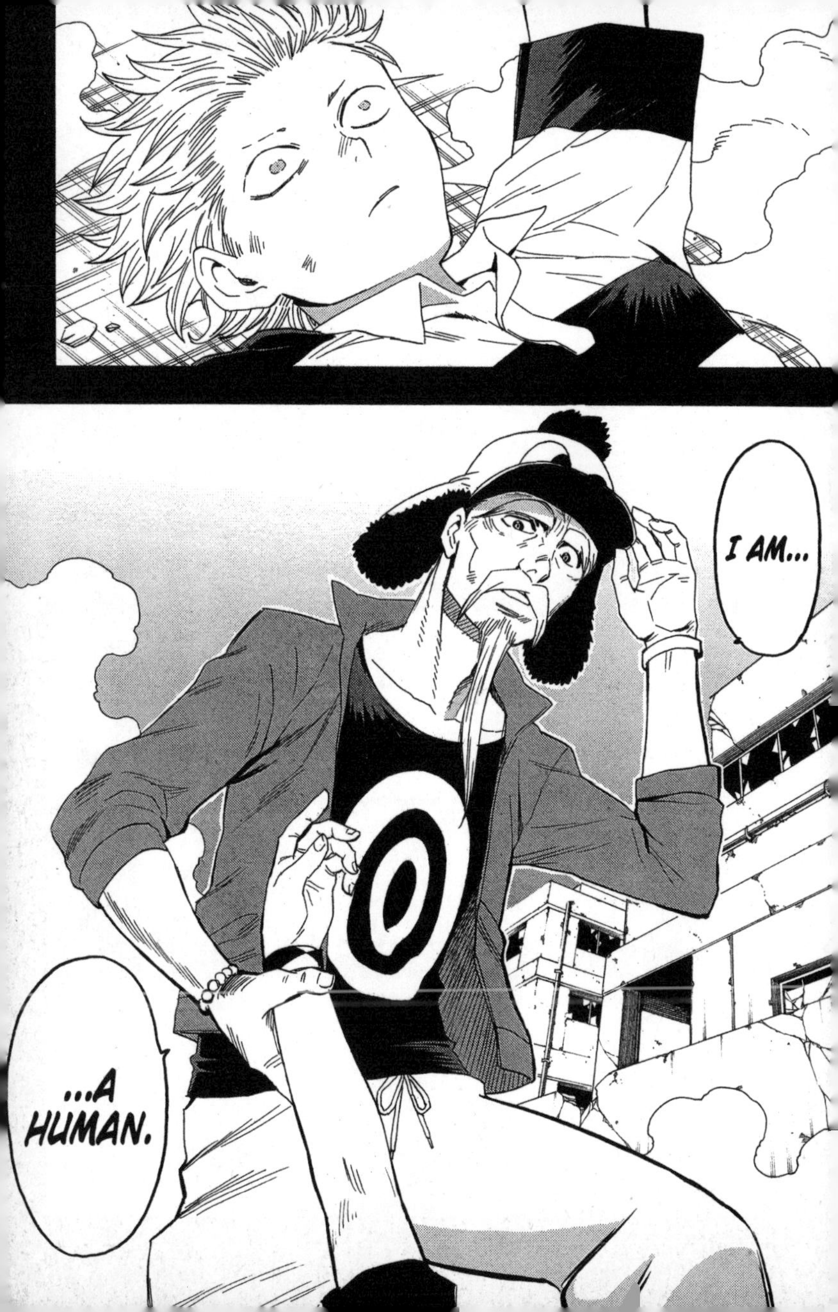
I AM...
...A HUMAN.

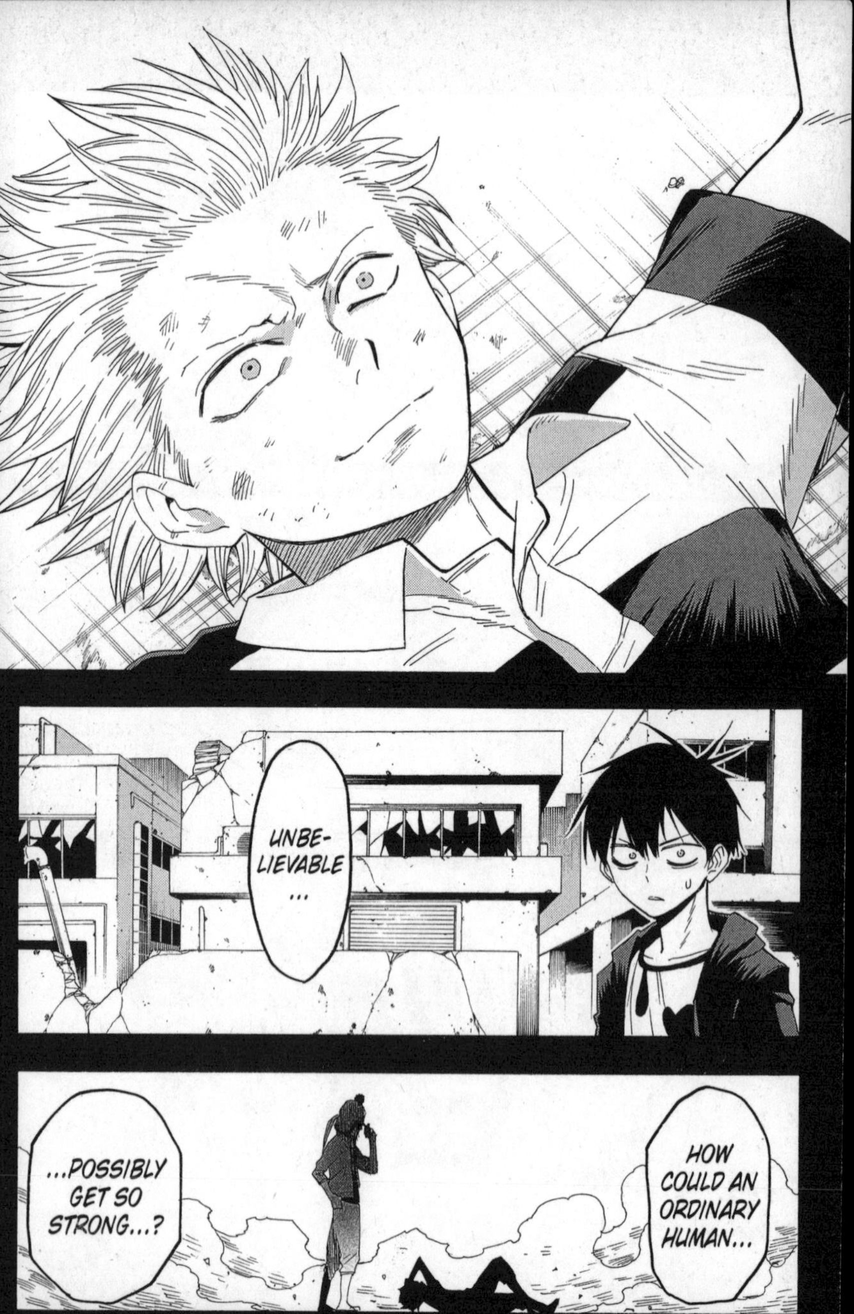
UNBE-
LIEVABLE
...
HOW COULD AN ORDINARY HUMAN...
...POSSIBLY GET SO STRONG...?

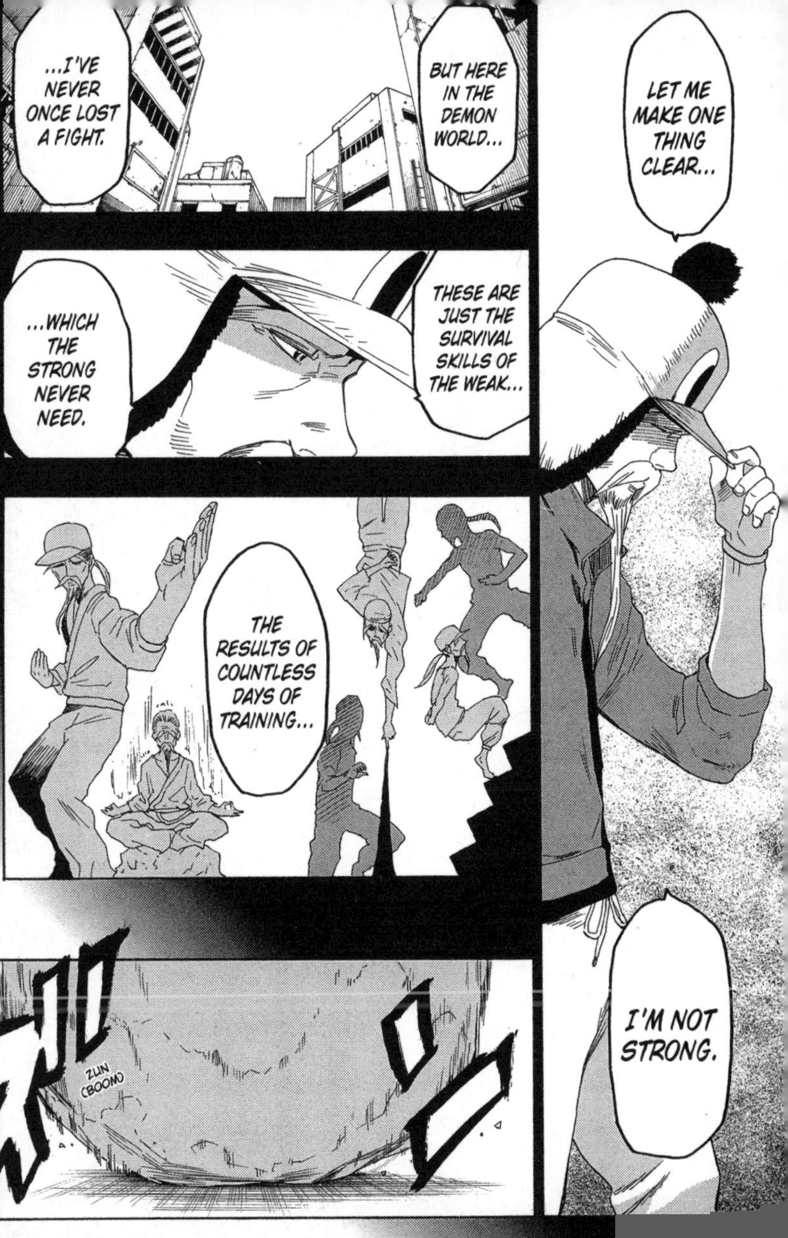
LET ME MAKE ONE THING CLEAR...
I'M NOT STRONG.
BUT HERE IN THE DEMON WORLD...
...I'VE NEVER ONCE LOST A FIGHT.
THESE ARE JUST THE SURVIVAL SKILLS OF THE WEAK...
...WHICH THE STRONG NEVER NEED.
THE RESULTS OF COUNTLESS DAYS OF TRAINING...
ZUN (BOOM)

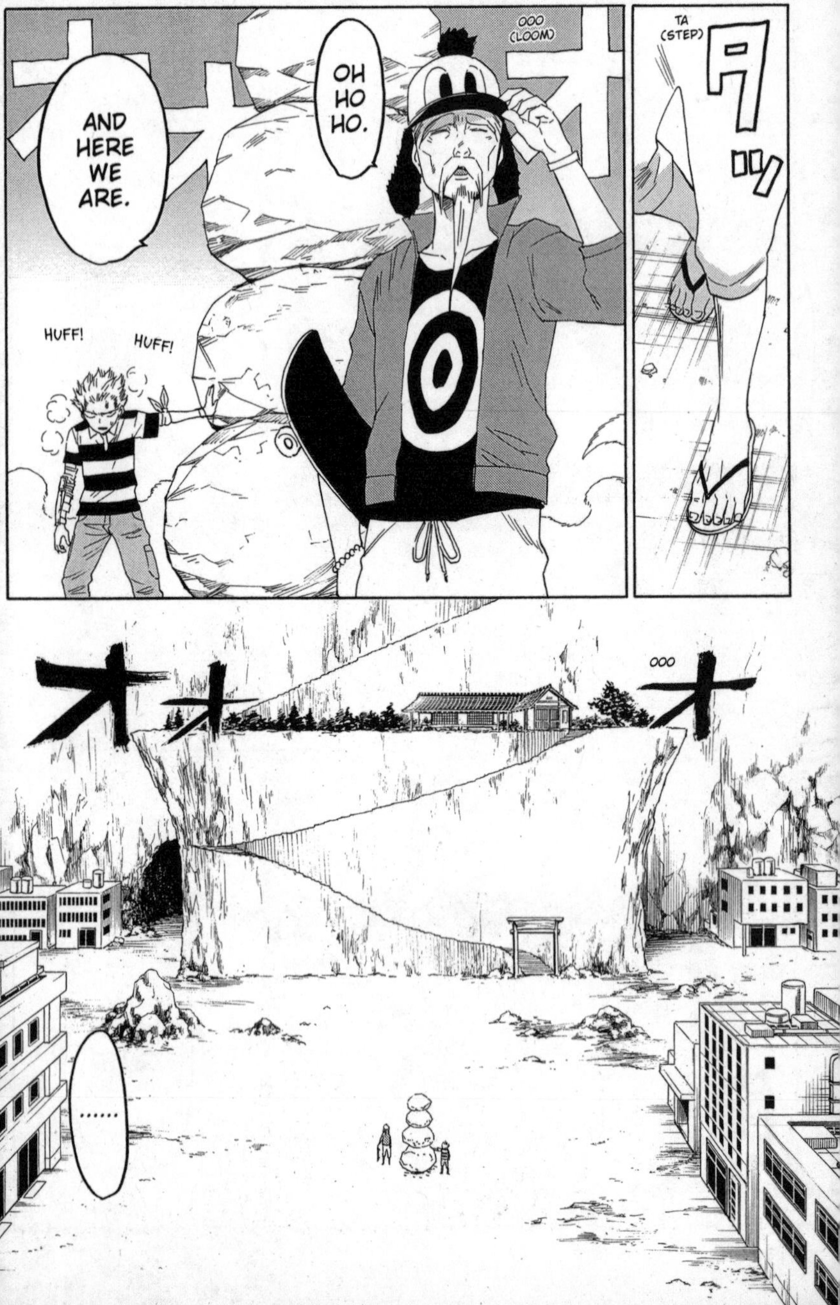

タッ
TA (STEP)
オオオ
OOO (LOOM)
OH HO HO.
AND HERE WE ARE.
HUFF!
HUFF!
オオオ
OOO
......

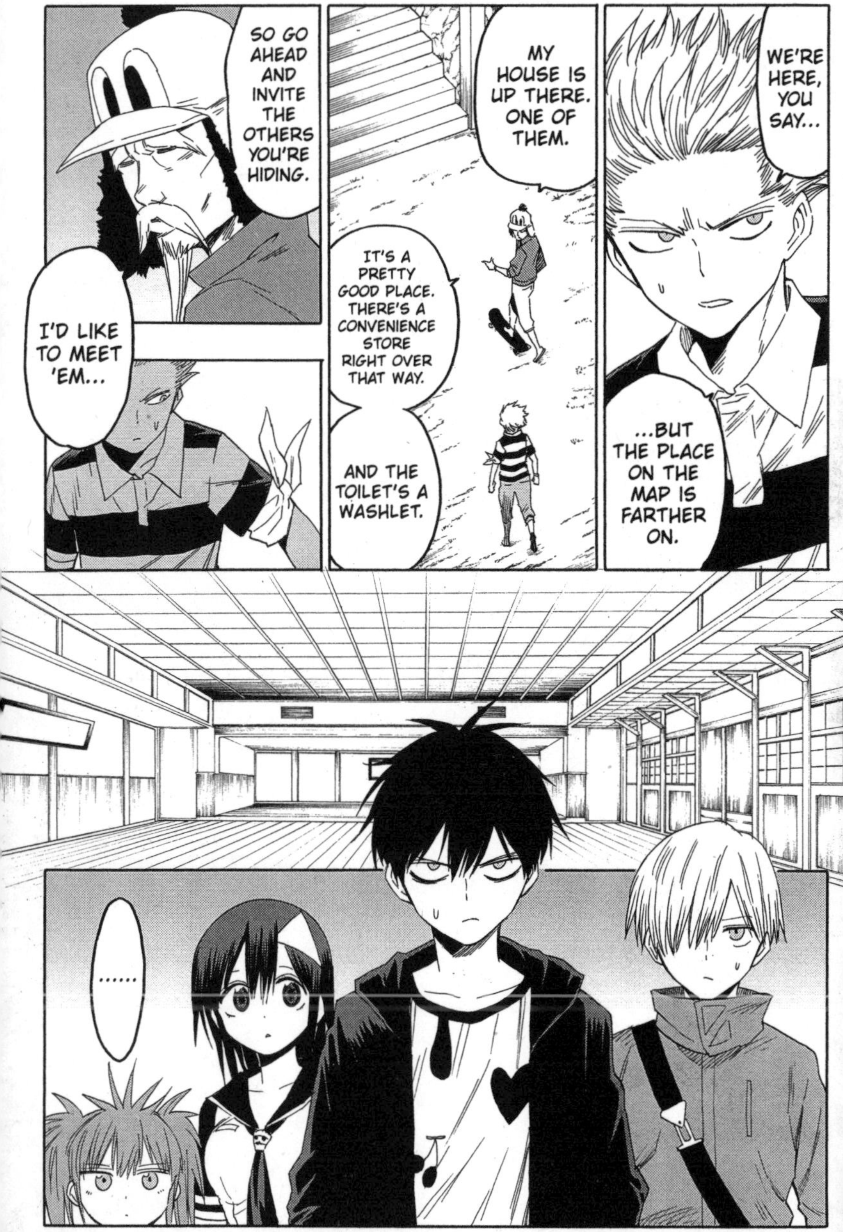
WE'RE HERE, YOU SAY...
...BUT THE PLACE ON THE MAP IS FARTHER ON.
MY HOUSE IS UP THERE. ONE OF THEM.
IT'S A PRETTY GOOD PLACE. THERE'S A CONVENIENCE STORE RIGHT OVER THAT WAY.
AND THE TOILET'S A WASHLET.
SO GO AHEAD AND INVITE THE OTHERS YOU'RE HIDING.
I'D LIKE TO MEET 'EM...
......

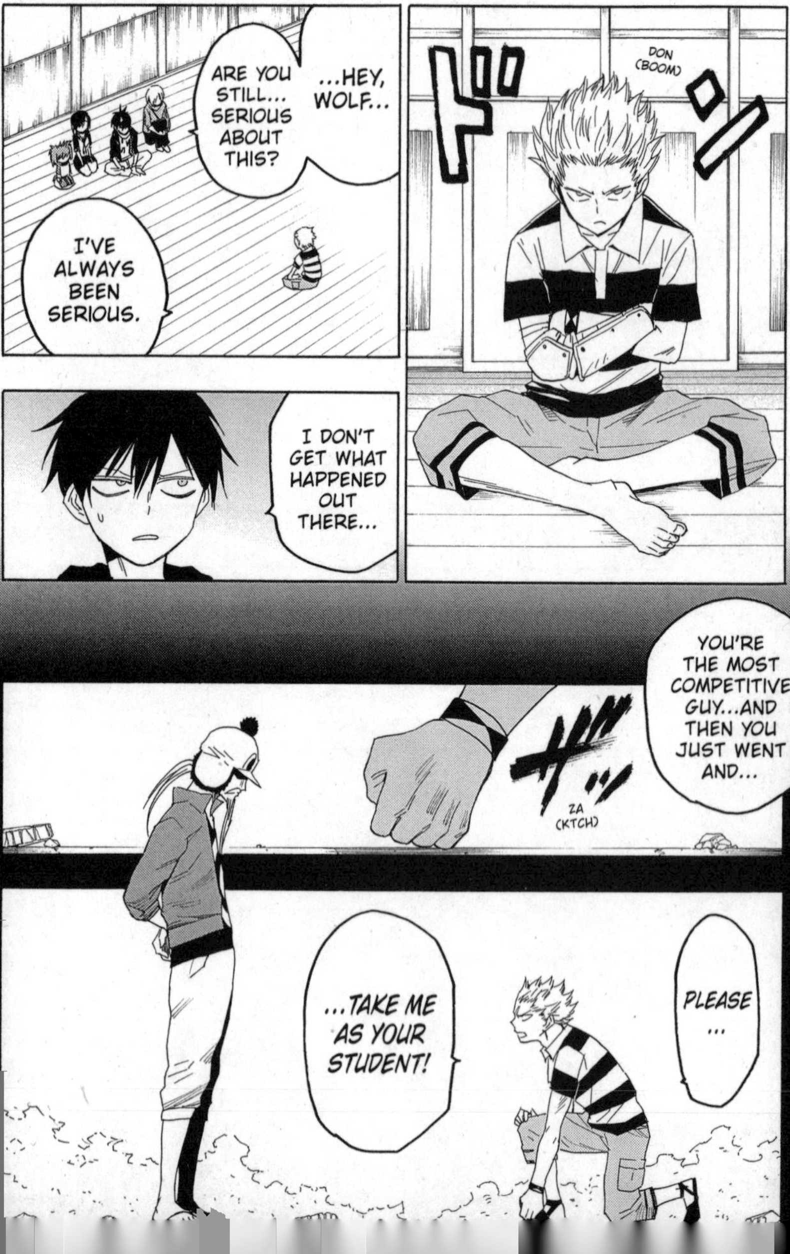
DON (BOOM)
...HEY, WOLF...
ARE YOU STILL... SERIOUS ABOUT THIS?
I'VE ALWAYS BEEN SERIOUS.
I DON'T GET WHAT HAPPENED OUT THERE...
YOU'RE THE MOST COMPETITIVE GUY...AND THEN YOU JUST WENT AND...
ZA (KTCH)
PLEASE ...
...TAKE ME AS YOUR STUDENT!

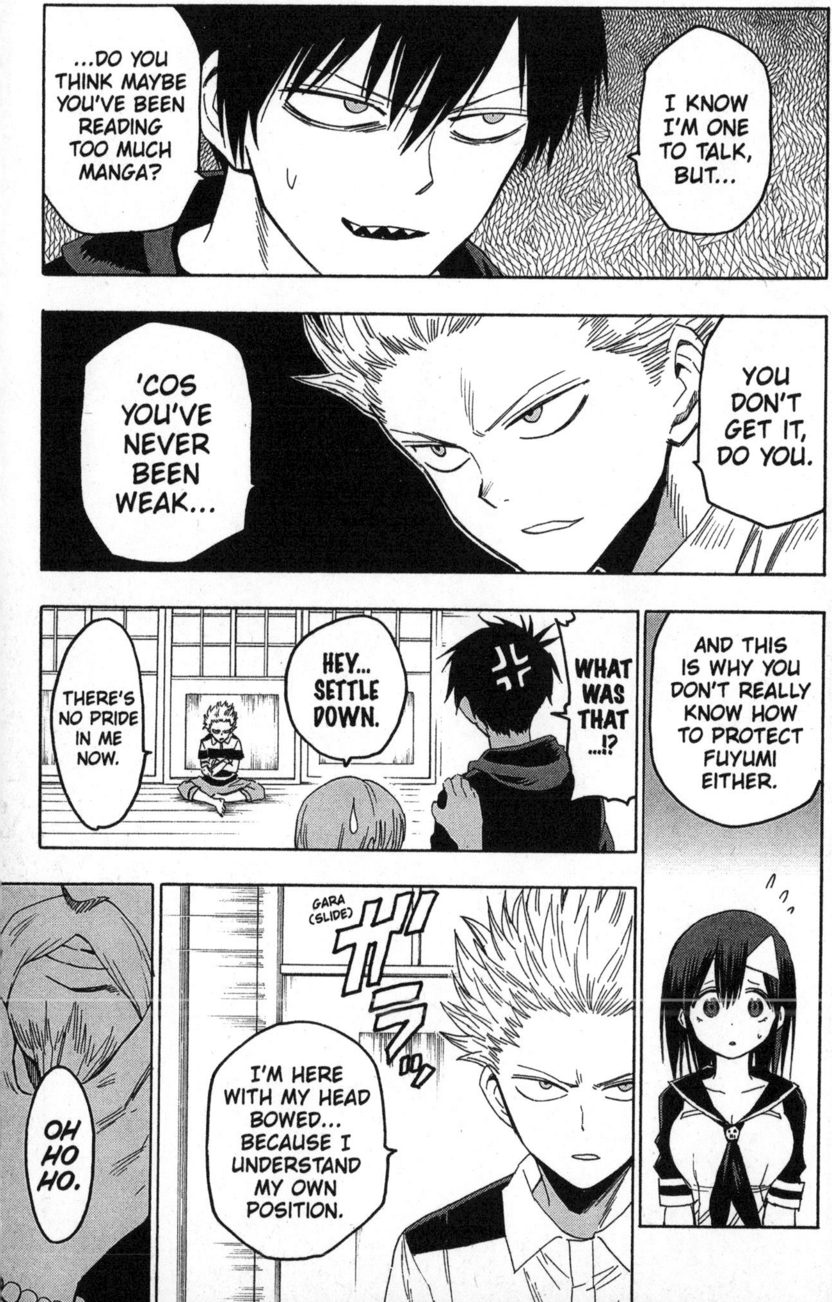
I KNOW I'M ONE TO TALK, BUT...
...DO YOU THINK MAYBE YOU'VE BEEN READING TOO MUCH MANGA?
YOU DON'T GET IT, DO YOU.
'COS YOU'VE NEVER BEEN WEAK...
AND THIS IS WHY YOU DON'T REALLY KNOW HOW TO PROTECT FUYUMI EITHER.
WHAT WAS THAT ...!?
HEY... SETTLE DOWN.
THERE'S NO PRIDE IN ME NOW.
GARA (SLIDE)
I'M HERE WITH MY HEAD BOWED... BECAUSE I UNDERSTAND MY OWN POSITION.
OH HO HO.

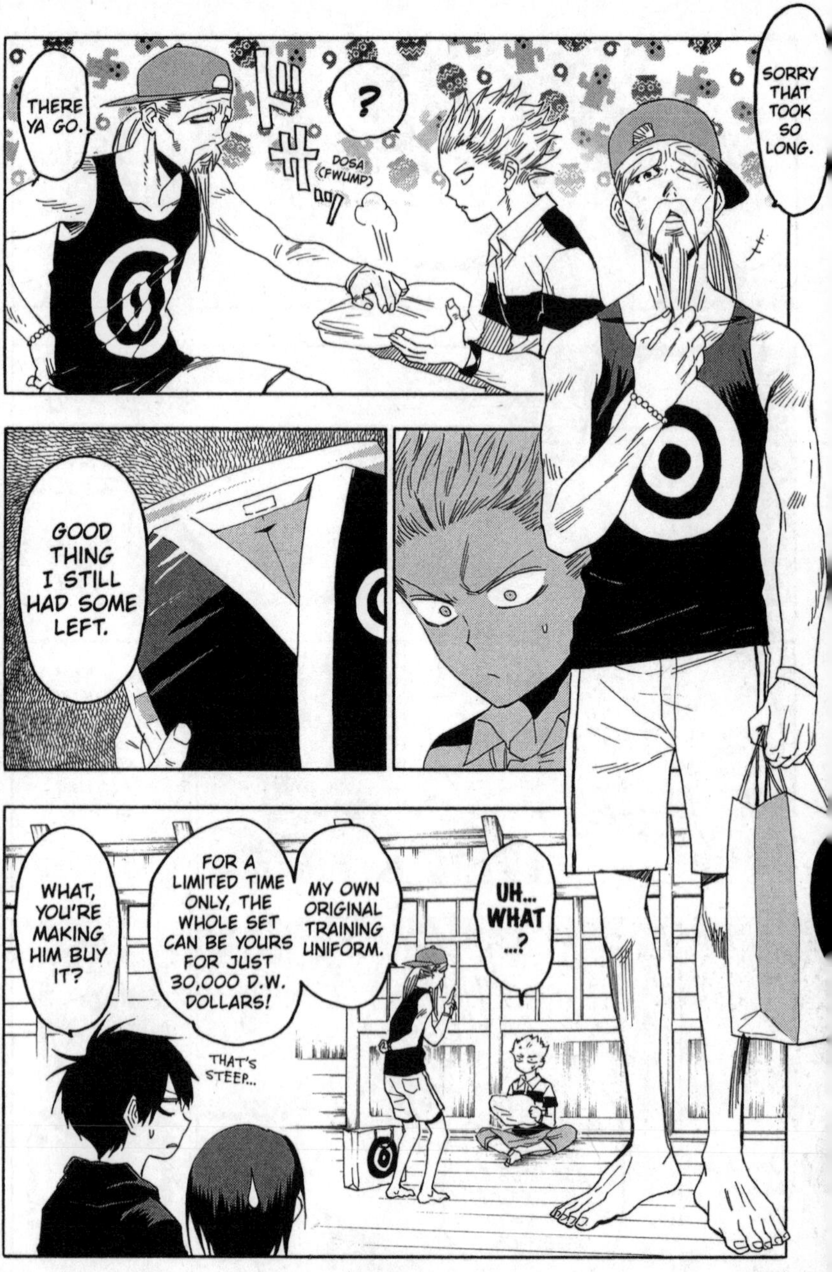
SORRY THAT TOOK SO LONG.
?
DOSA (FWUMP)
THERE YA GO.
GOOD THING I STILL HAD SOME LEFT.
UH... WHAT ...?
MY OWN ORIGINAL TRAINING UNIFORM.
FOR A LIMITED TIME ONLY, THE WHOLE SET CAN BE YOURS FOR JUST 30,000 D.W. DOLLARS!
WHAT, YOU'RE MAKING HIM BUY IT?
THAT'S STEEP...

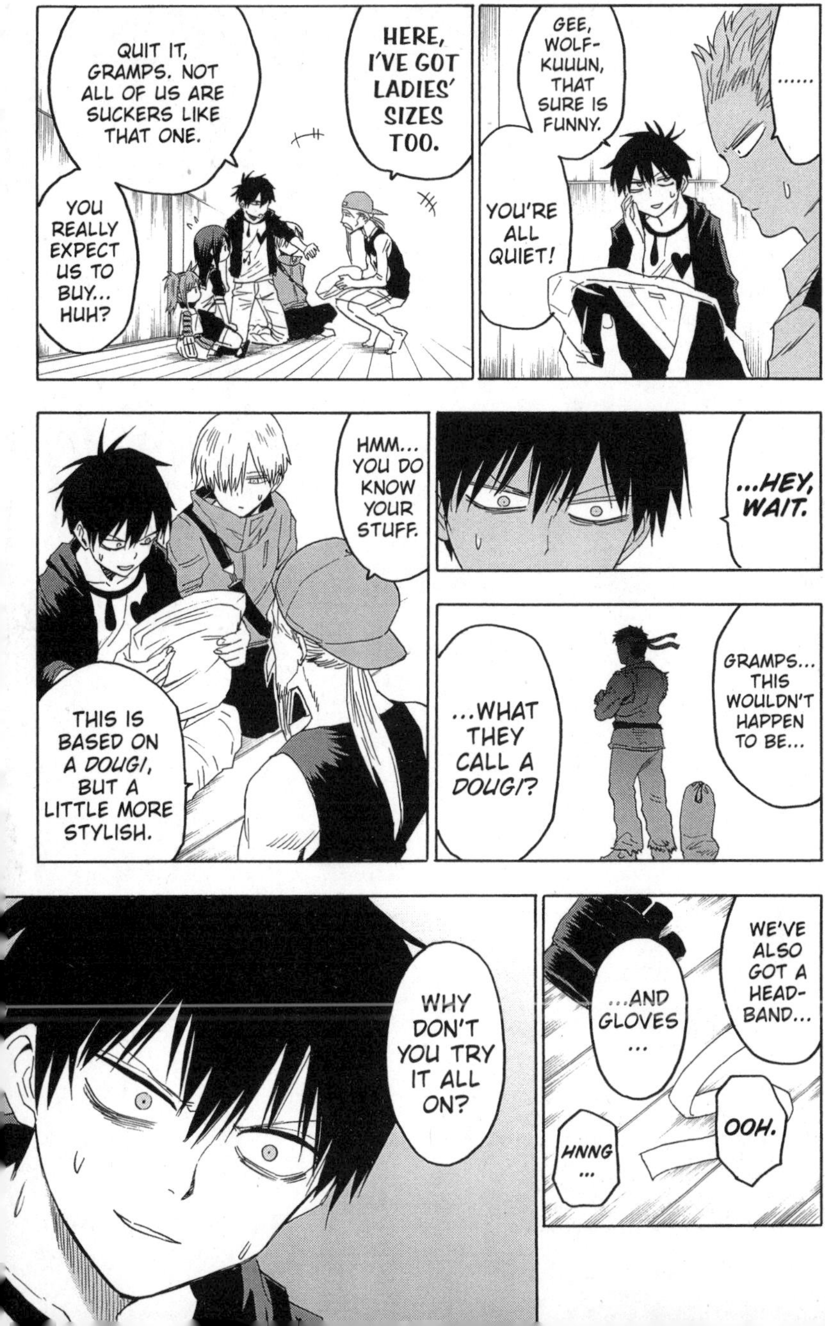
GEE, WOLF-KUUUN, THAT SURE IS FUNNY.
......
YOU'RE ALL QUIET!
HERE, I'VE GOT LADIES' SIZES TOO.
QUIT IT, GRAMPS. NOT ALL OF US ARE SUCKERS LIKE THAT ONE.
YOU REALLY EXPECT US TO BUY... HUH?
...HEY, WAIT.
GRAMPS... THIS WOULDN'T HAPPEN TO BE...
...WHAT THEY CALL A *DOUGI*?
HMM... YOU DO KNOW YOUR STUFF.
THIS IS BASED ON A *DOUGI*, BUT A LITTLE MORE STYLISH.
WE'VE ALSO GOT A HEAD-BAND...
...AND GLOVES...
OOH.
HNNG...
WHY DON'T YOU TRY IT ALL ON?

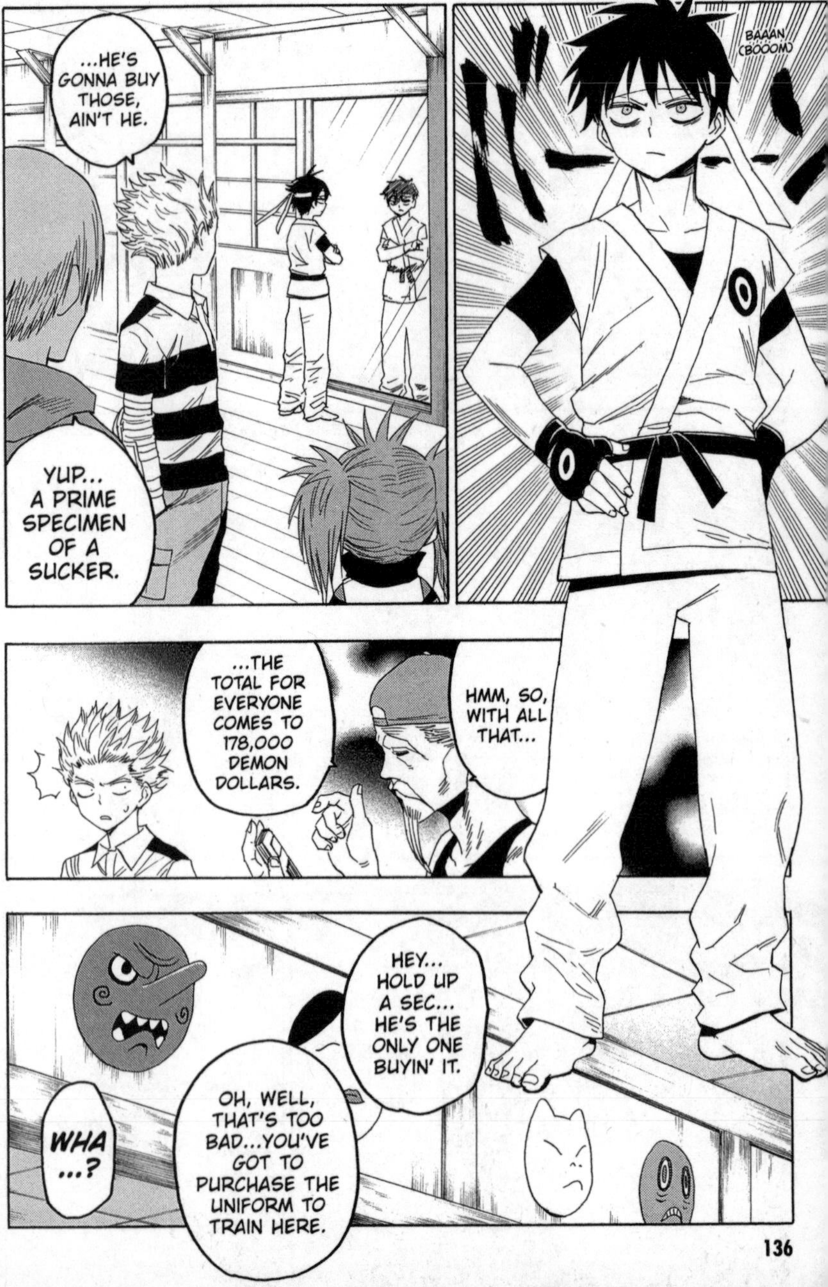
BAAAN (BOOOM)
...HE'S GONNA BUY THOSE, AIN'T HE.
YUP... A PRIME SPECIMEN OF A SUCKER.
HMM, SO, WITH ALL THAT...
...THE TOTAL FOR EVERYONE COMES TO 178,000 DEMON DOLLARS.
HEY... HOLD UP A SEC... HE'S THE ONLY ONE BUYIN' IT.
OH, WELL, THAT'S TOO BAD...YOU'VE GOT TO PURCHASE THE UNIFORM TO TRAIN HERE.
WHA ...?

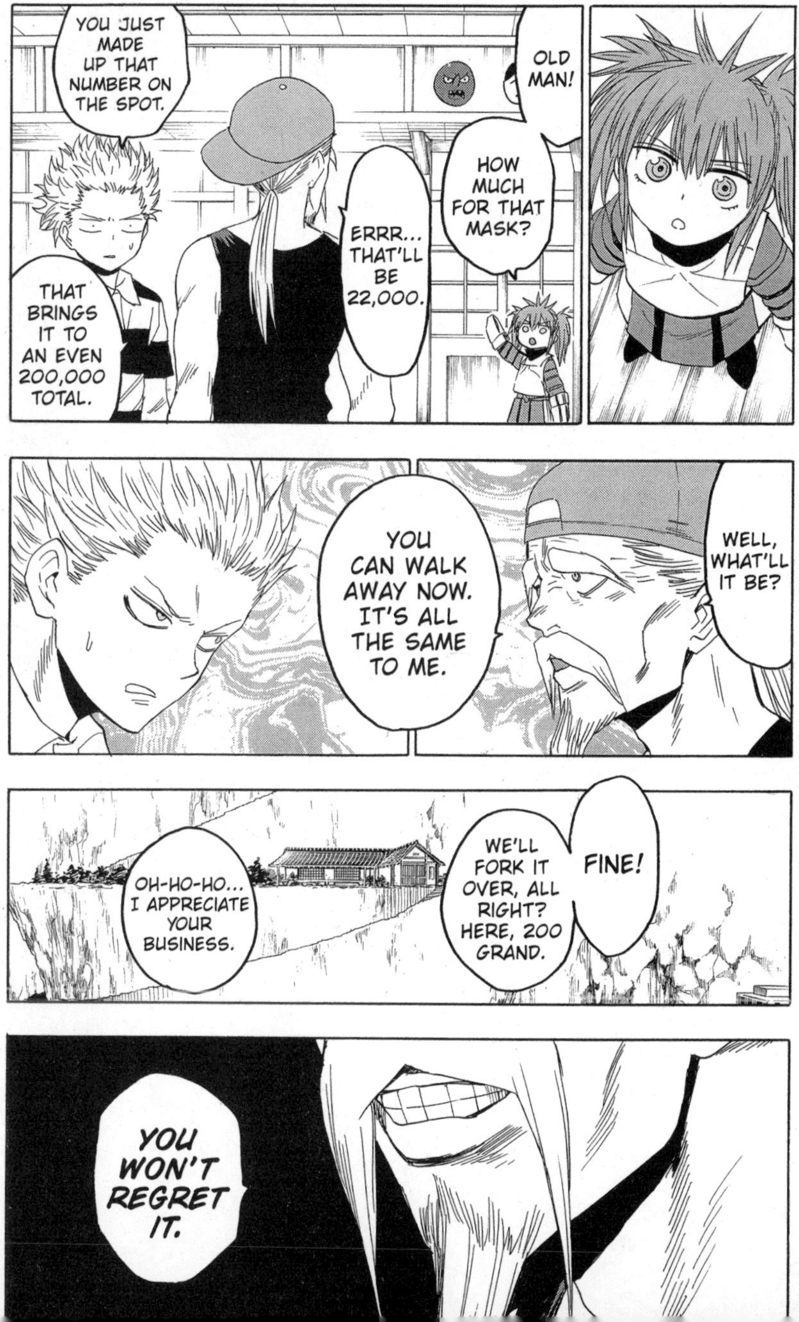
OLD MAN!
HOW MUCH FOR THAT MASK?
ERRR... THAT'LL BE 22,000.
THAT BRINGS IT TO AN EVEN 200,000 TOTAL.
YOU JUST MADE UP THAT NUMBER ON THE SPOT.
WELL, WHAT'LL IT BE?
YOU CAN WALK AWAY NOW. IT'S ALL THE SAME TO ME.
FINE!
WE'LL FORK IT OVER, ALL RIGHT? HERE, 200 GRAND.
OH-HO-HO... I APPRECIATE YOUR BUSINESS.
YOU WON'T REGRET IT.

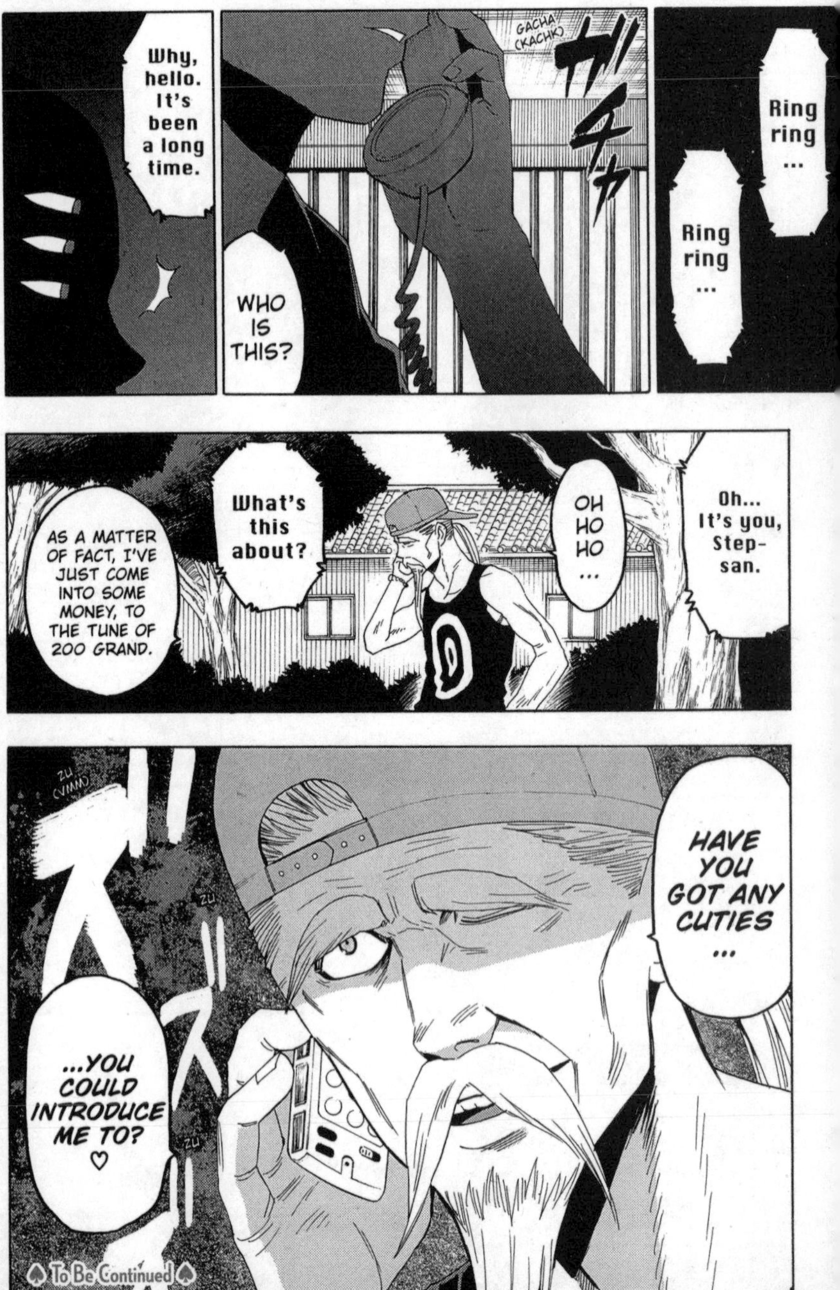
Ring ring ...
Ring ring ...
GACHA (KACHK)
WHO IS THIS?
Why, hello. It's been a long time.
Oh... It's you, Step-san.
OH HO HO ...
What's this about?
AS A MATTER OF FACT, I'VE JUST COME INTO SOME MONEY, TO THE TUNE OF 200 GRAND.
ZU (VMM)
HAVE YOU GOT ANY CUTIES ...
...YOU COULD INTRODUCE ME TO? ♡
ZU
ZU
To Be Continued

DOUGI

A MYSTERIOUS SET OF CLOTHING THAT FOCUSES THE WEARER'S FEELINGS. NO MATTER WHAT SORT OF RIDICULOUS THING YOU'RE TOLD TO DO, WEARING THESE YOU'LL SAY, "BRING IT ON!"

BLOOD LAD

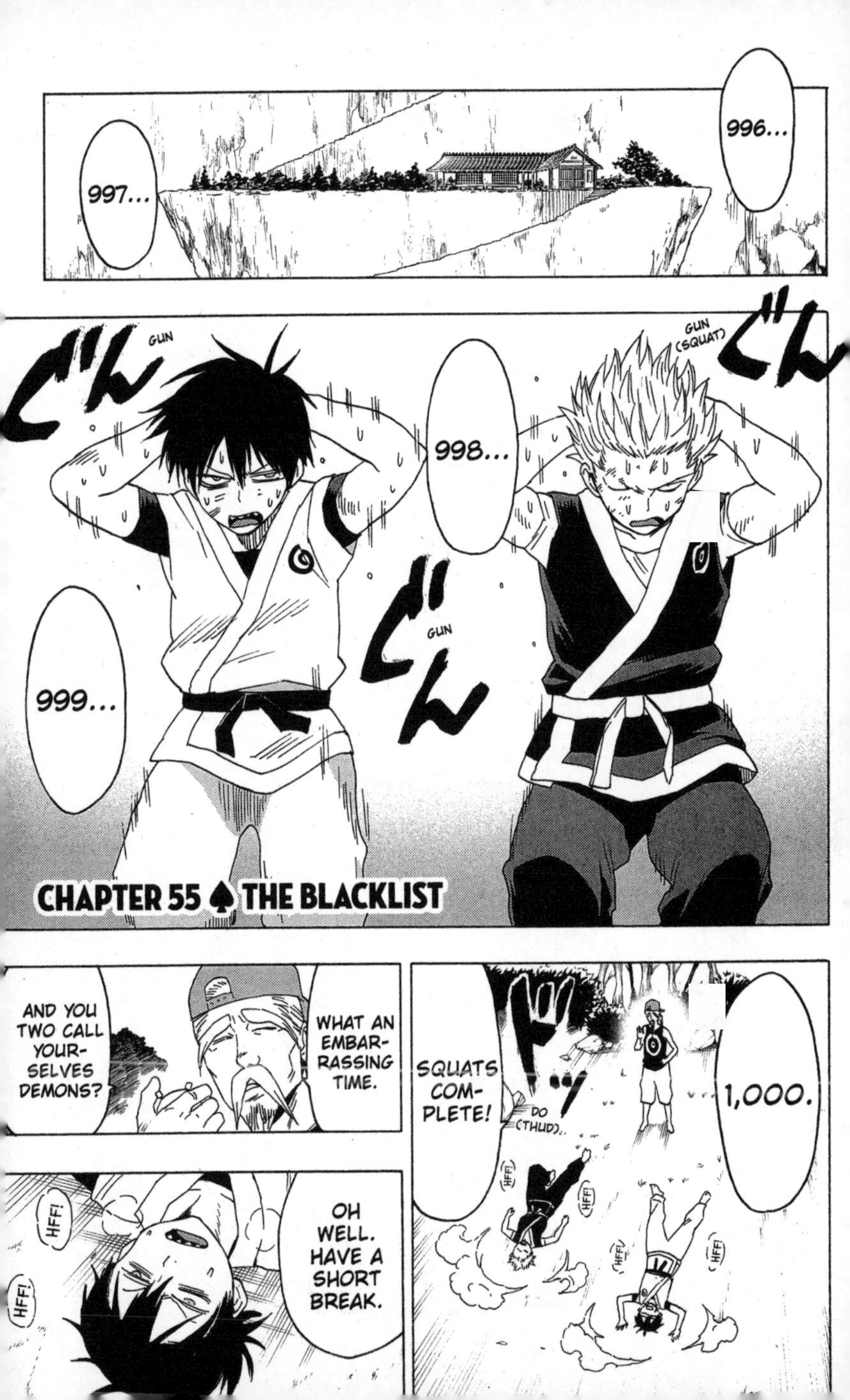

996...
997...
GUN (SQUAT)
998...
GUN
GUN
999...
CHAPTER 55 ♠ THE BLACKLIST
1,000.
SQUATS COMPLETE!
DO (THUD)
HFF!
HFF!
HFF!
HFF!
WHAT AN EMBARRASSING TIME.
AND YOU TWO CALL YOURSELVES DEMONS?
OH WELL. HAVE A SHORT BREAK.
HFF!
HFF!

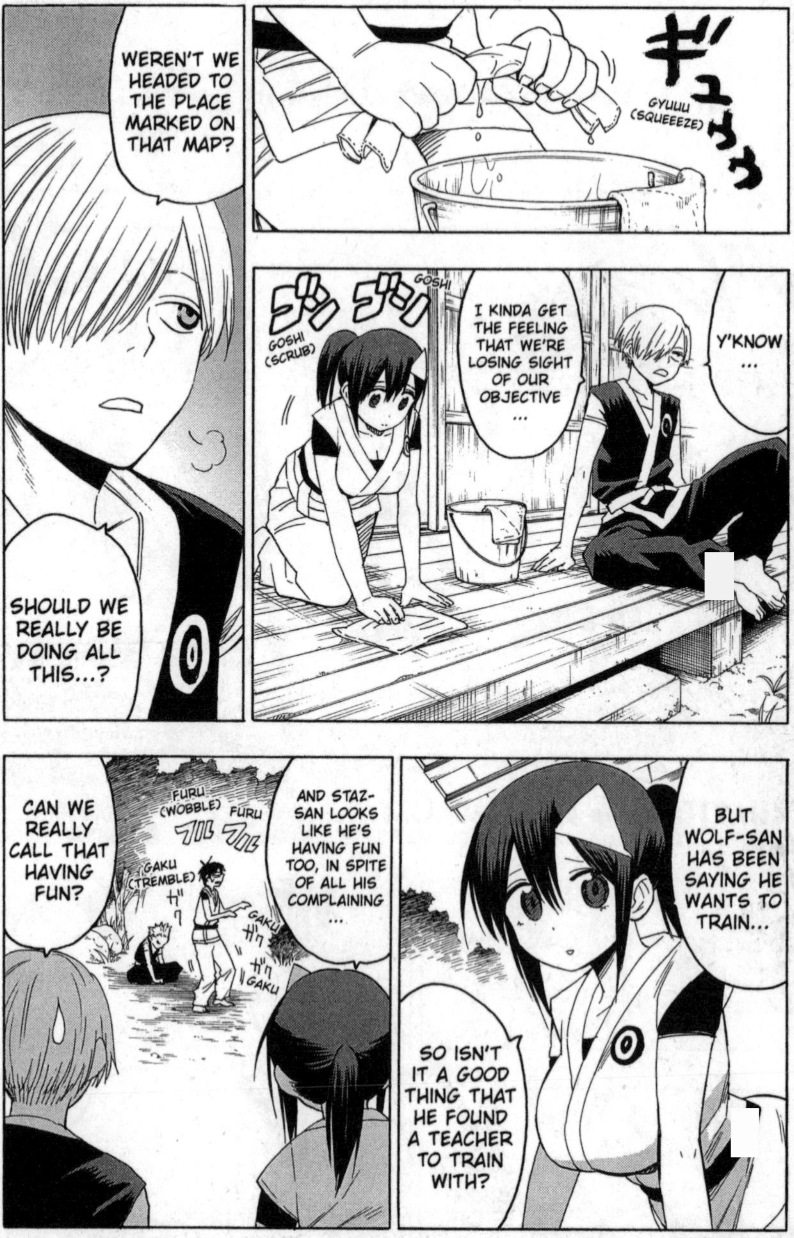
GYUUU (SQUEEEZE)
Y'KNOW ...
I KINDA GET THE FEELING THAT WE'RE LOSING SIGHT OF OUR OBJECTIVE ...
GOSHI
GOSHI (SCRUB)
WEREN'T WE HEADED TO THE PLACE MARKED ON THAT MAP?
SHOULD WE REALLY BE DOING ALL THIS...?
BUT WOLF-SAN HAS BEEN SAYING HE WANTS TO TRAIN...
SO ISN'T IT A GOOD THING THAT HE FOUND A TEACHER TO TRAIN WITH?
AND STAZ-SAN LOOKS LIKE HE'S HAVING FUN TOO, IN SPITE OF ALL HIS COMPLAINING ...
FURU (WOBBLE) FURU
GAKU (TREMBLE)
GAKU
GAKU
CAN WE REALLY CALL THAT HAVING FUN?

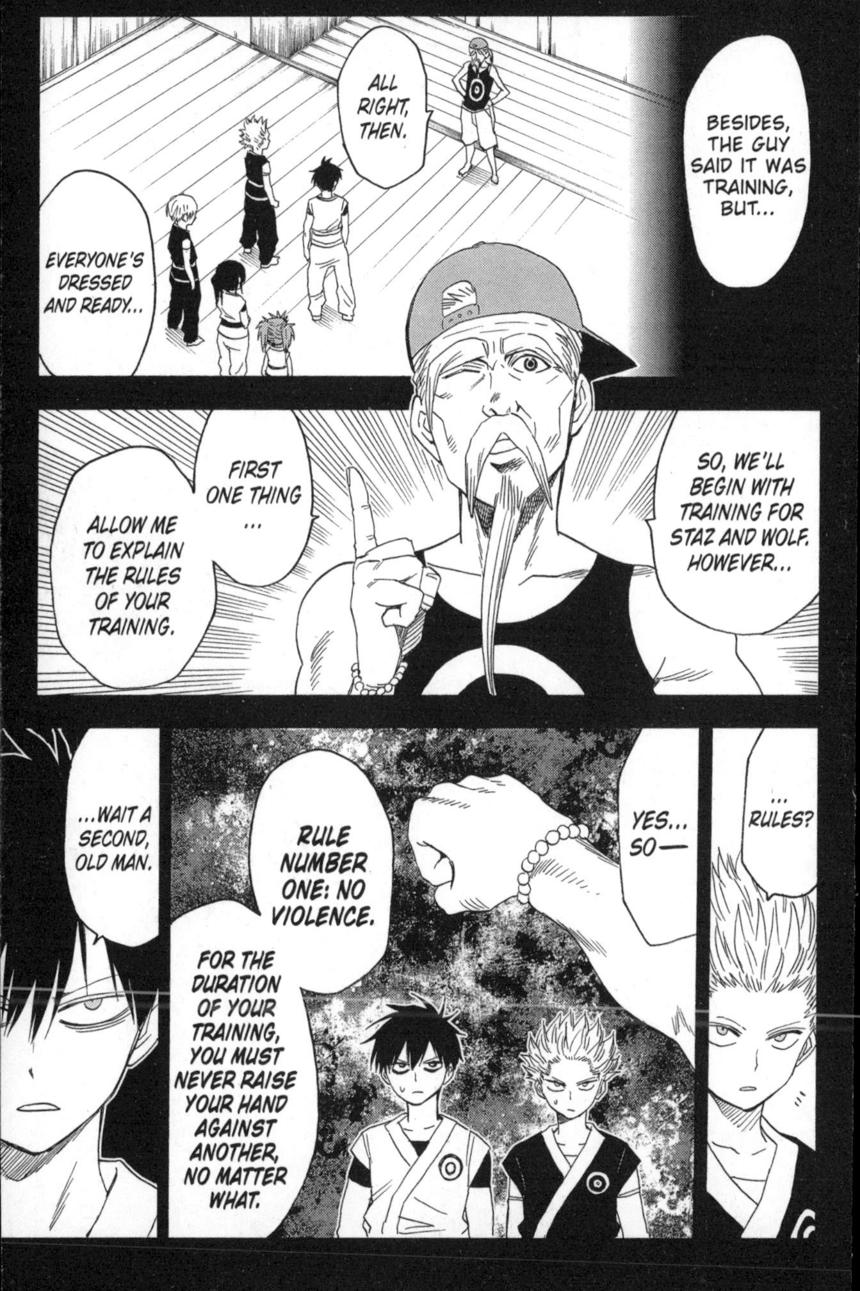
BESIDES, THE GUY SAID IT WAS TRAINING, BUT...
ALL RIGHT, THEN.
EVERYONE'S DRESSED AND READY...
SO, WE'LL BEGIN WITH TRAINING FOR STAZ AND WOLF. HOWEVER...
FIRST ONE THING ...
ALLOW ME TO EXPLAIN THE RULES OF YOUR TRAINING.
... RULES?
YES... SO—
RULE NUMBER ONE: NO VIOLENCE.
FOR THE DURATION OF YOUR TRAINING, YOU MUST NEVER RAISE YOUR HAND AGAINST ANOTHER, NO MATTER WHAT.
...WAIT A SECOND, OLD MAN.

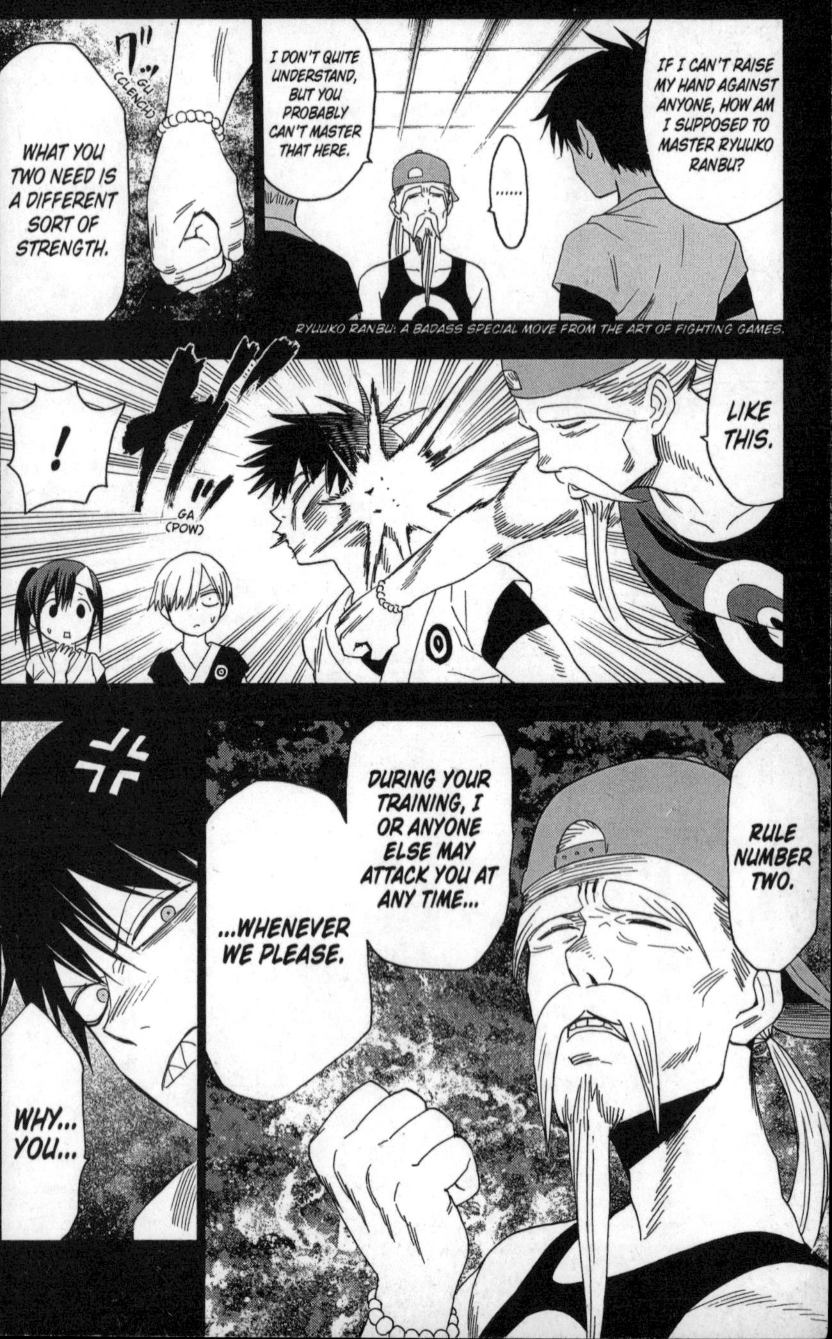
IF I CAN'T RAISE MY HAND AGAINST ANYONE, HOW AM I SUPPOSED TO MASTER RYUUKO RANBU?
......
I DON'T QUITE UNDERSTAND, BUT YOU PROBABLY CAN'T MASTER THAT HERE.
GU (CLENCH)
WHAT YOU TWO NEED IS A DIFFERENT SORT OF STRENGTH.
RYUUKO RANBU: A BADASS SPECIAL MOVE FROM THE ART OF FIGHTING GAMES.
LIKE THIS.
GA (POW)
!
RULE NUMBER TWO.
DURING YOUR TRAINING, I OR ANYONE ELSE MAY ATTACK YOU AT ANY TIME...
...WHENEVER WE PLEASE.
WHY... YOU...

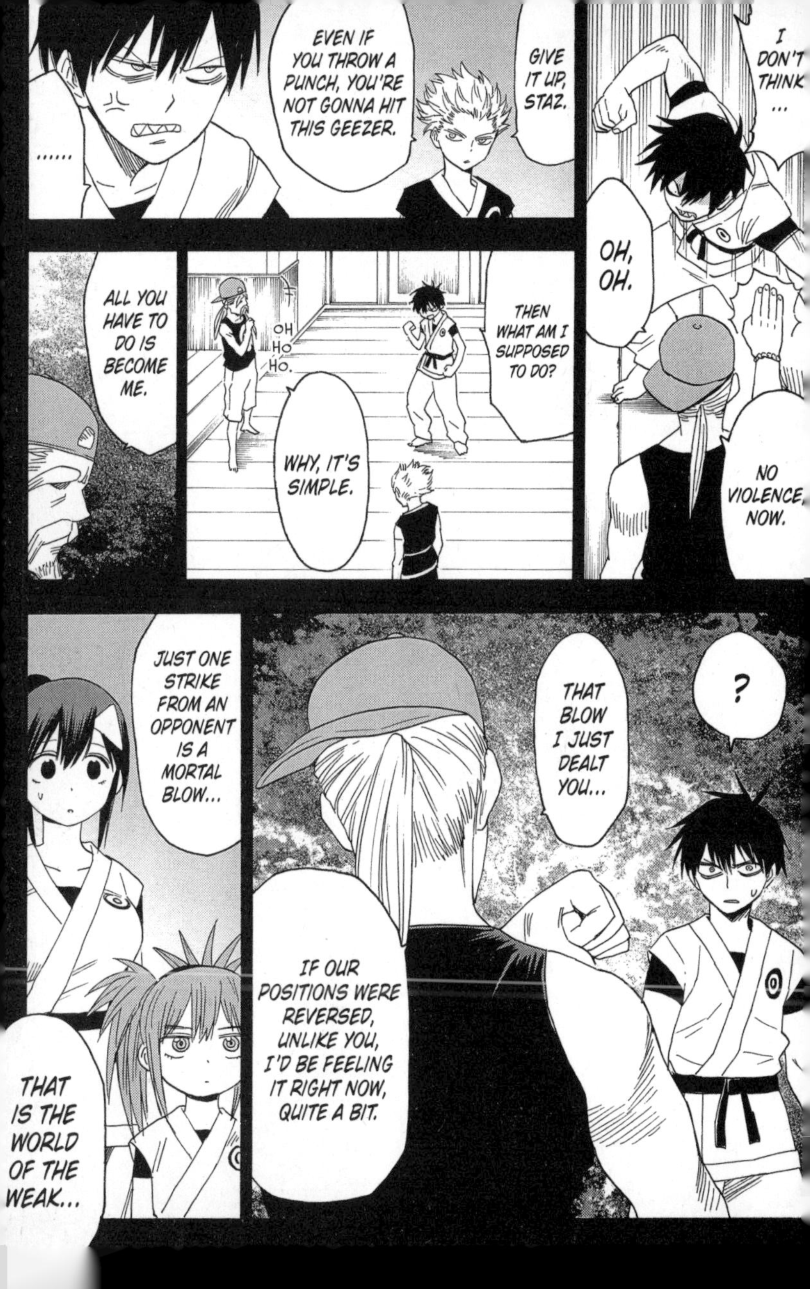
I DON'T THINK ...
OH, OH.
NO VIOLENCE, NOW.
GIVE IT UP, STAZ.
EVEN IF YOU THROW A PUNCH, YOU'RE NOT GONNA HIT THIS GEEZER.
......
THEN WHAT AM I SUPPOSED TO DO?
OH HO HO.
WHY, IT'S SIMPLE.
ALL YOU HAVE TO DO IS BECOME ME.
?
THAT BLOW I JUST DEALT YOU...
IF OUR POSITIONS WERE REVERSED, UNLIKE YOU, I'D BE FEELING IT RIGHT NOW, QUITE A BIT.
JUST ONE STRIKE FROM AN OPPONENT IS A MORTAL BLOW...
THAT IS THE WORLD OF THE WEAK...

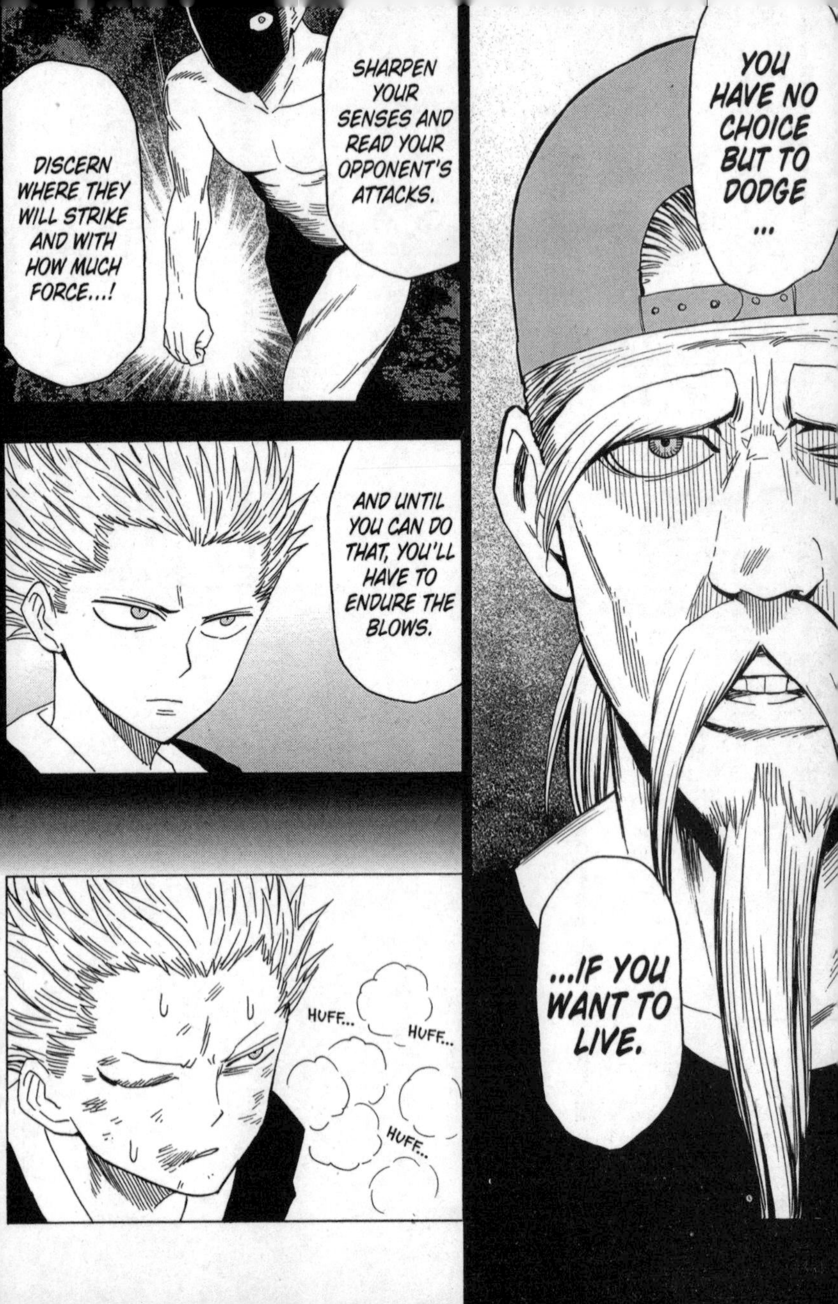
YOU HAVE NO CHOICE BUT TO DODGE ...
...IF YOU WANT TO LIVE.
SHARPEN YOUR SENSES AND READ YOUR OPPONENT'S ATTACKS.
DISCERN WHERE THEY WILL STRIKE AND WITH HOW MUCH FORCE...!
AND UNTIL YOU CAN DO THAT, YOU'LL HAVE TO ENDURE THE BLOWS.
HUFF...
HUFF...
HUFF...

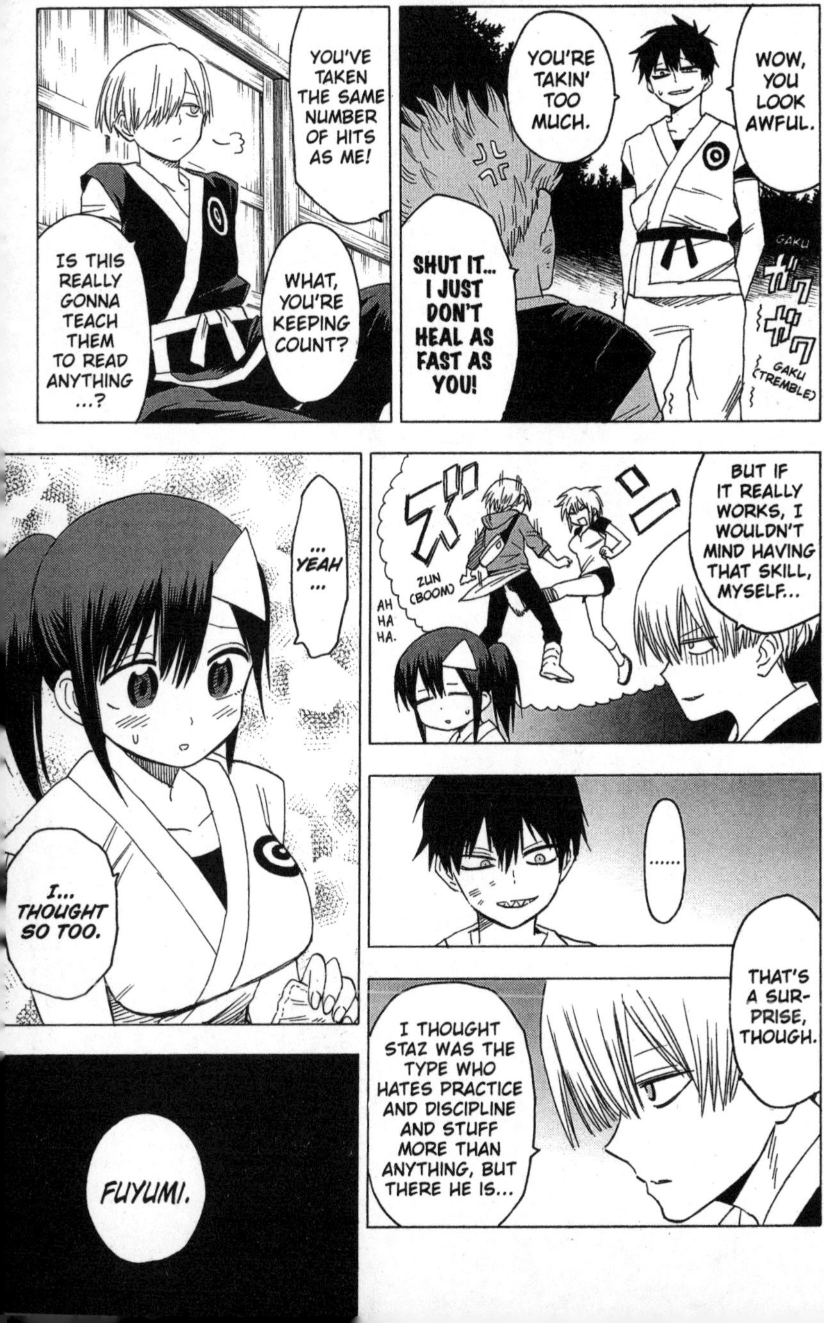
WOW, YOU LOOK AWFUL.
GAKU GAKU (TREMBLE)
YOU'RE TAKIN' TOO MUCH.
SHUT IT... I JUST DON'T HEAL AS FAST AS YOU!
YOU'VE TAKEN THE SAME NUMBER OF HITS AS ME!
WHAT, YOU'RE KEEPING COUNT?
IS THIS REALLY GONNA TEACH THEM TO READ ANYTHING...?
BUT IF IT REALLY WORKS, I WOULDN'T MIND HAVING THAT SKILL, MYSELF...
ZUN (BOOM)
AH HA HA.
......
THAT'S A SURPRISE, THOUGH.
I THOUGHT STAZ WAS THE TYPE WHO HATES PRACTICE AND DISCIPLINE AND STUFF MORE THAN ANYTHING, BUT THERE HE IS...
...YEAH...
I... THOUGHT SO TOO.
FUYUMI.

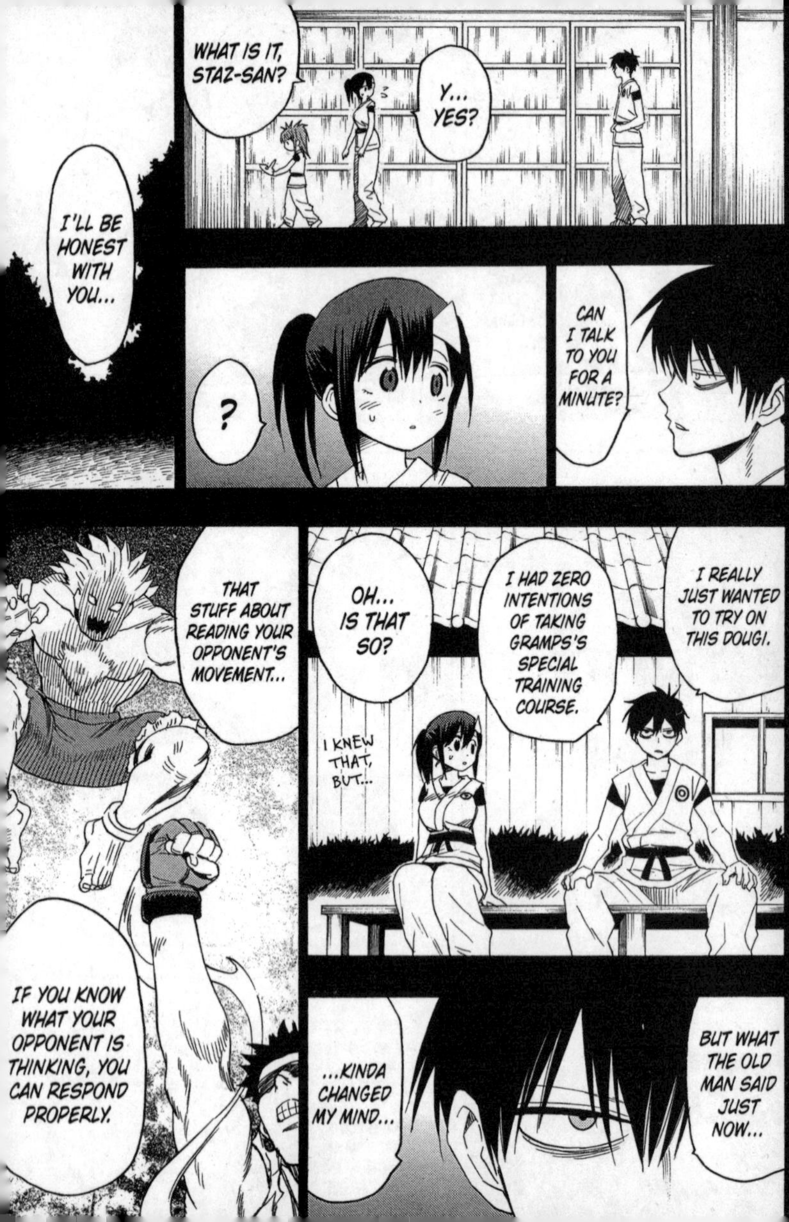
Y... YES?
WHAT IS IT, STAZ-SAN?
CAN I TALK TO YOU FOR A MINUTE?
?
I'LL BE HONEST WITH YOU...
I REALLY JUST WANTED TO TRY ON THIS DOUGI.
I HAD ZERO INTENTIONS OF TAKING GRAMPS'S SPECIAL TRAINING COURSE.
OH... IS THAT SO?
I KNEW THAT, BUT...
BUT WHAT THE OLD MAN SAID JUST NOW...
...KINDA CHANGED MY MIND...
THAT STUFF ABOUT READING YOUR OPPONENT'S MOVEMENT...
IF YOU KNOW WHAT YOUR OPPONENT IS THINKING, YOU CAN RESPOND PROPERLY.

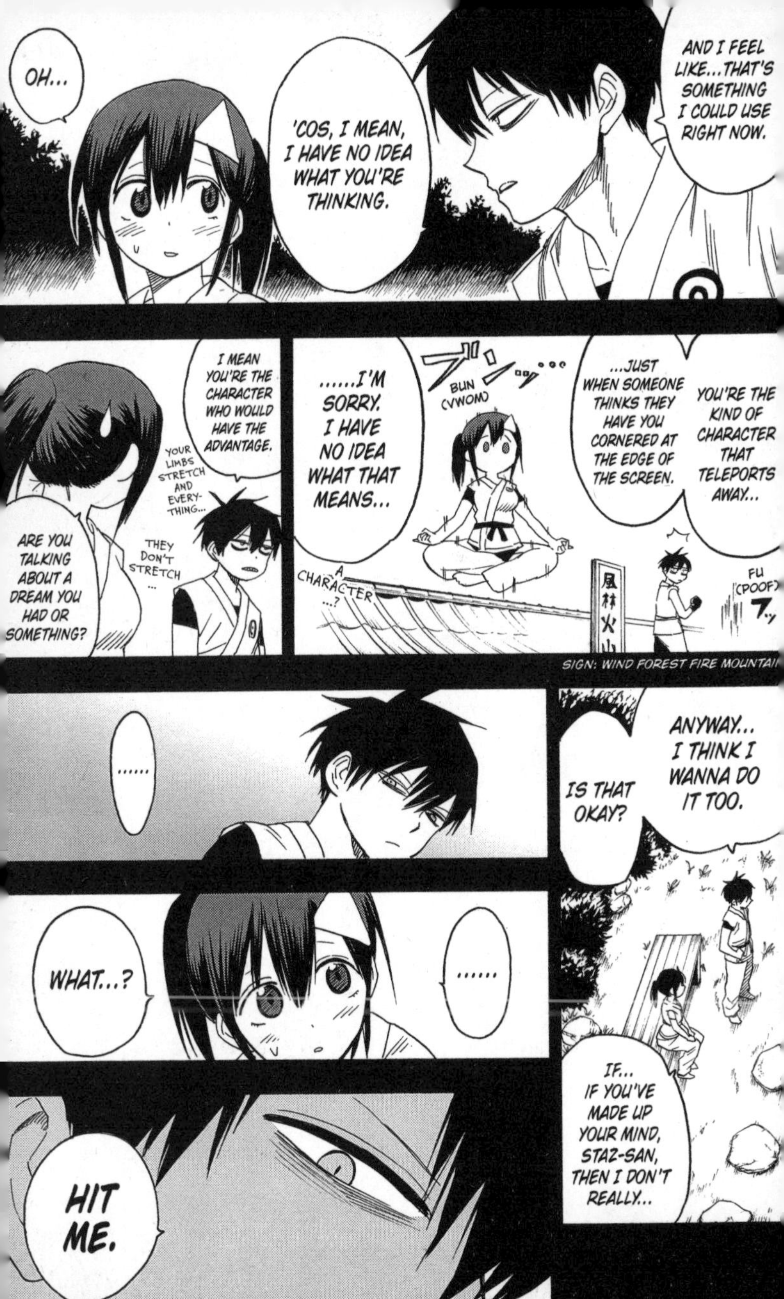
AND I FEEL LIKE...THAT'S SOMETHING I COULD USE RIGHT NOW.
'COS, I MEAN, I HAVE NO IDEA WHAT YOU'RE THINKING.
OH...
YOU'RE THE KIND OF CHARACTER THAT TELEPORTS AWAY...
...JUST WHEN SOMEONE THINKS THEY HAVE YOU CORNERED AT THE EDGE OF THE SCREEN.
BUN (VWOM)
......I'M SORRY. I HAVE NO IDEA WHAT THAT MEANS...
FU (POOF)
A CHARACTER ...?
I MEAN YOU'RE THE CHARACTER WHO WOULD HAVE THE ADVANTAGE.
YOUR LIMBS STRETCH AND EVERY-THING...
ARE YOU TALKING ABOUT A DREAM YOU HAD OR SOMETHING?
THEY DON'T STRETCH...
SIGN: WIND FOREST FIRE MOUNTAI
ANYWAY... I THINK I WANNA DO IT TOO.
IS THAT OKAY?
IF... IF YOU'VE MADE UP YOUR MIND, STAZ-SAN, THEN I DON'T REALLY...
......
......
WHAT...?
HIT ME.

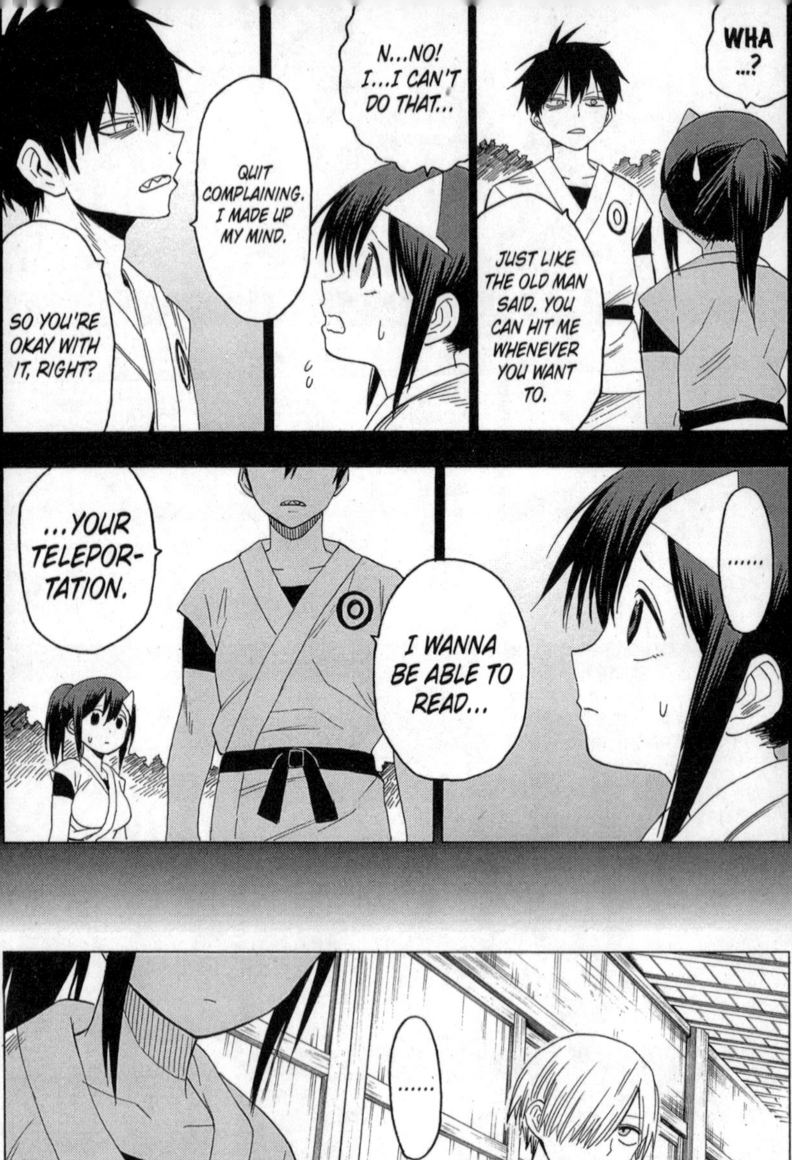
WHA ...?
JUST LIKE THE OLD MAN SAID. YOU CAN HIT ME WHENEVER YOU WANT TO.
N...NO! I...I CAN'T DO THAT...
QUIT COMPLAINING. I MADE UP MY MIND.
SO YOU'RE OKAY WITH IT, RIGHT?
......
I WANNA BE ABLE TO READ...
...YOUR TELEPOR-TATION.
......

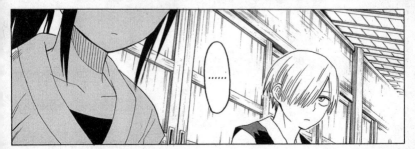

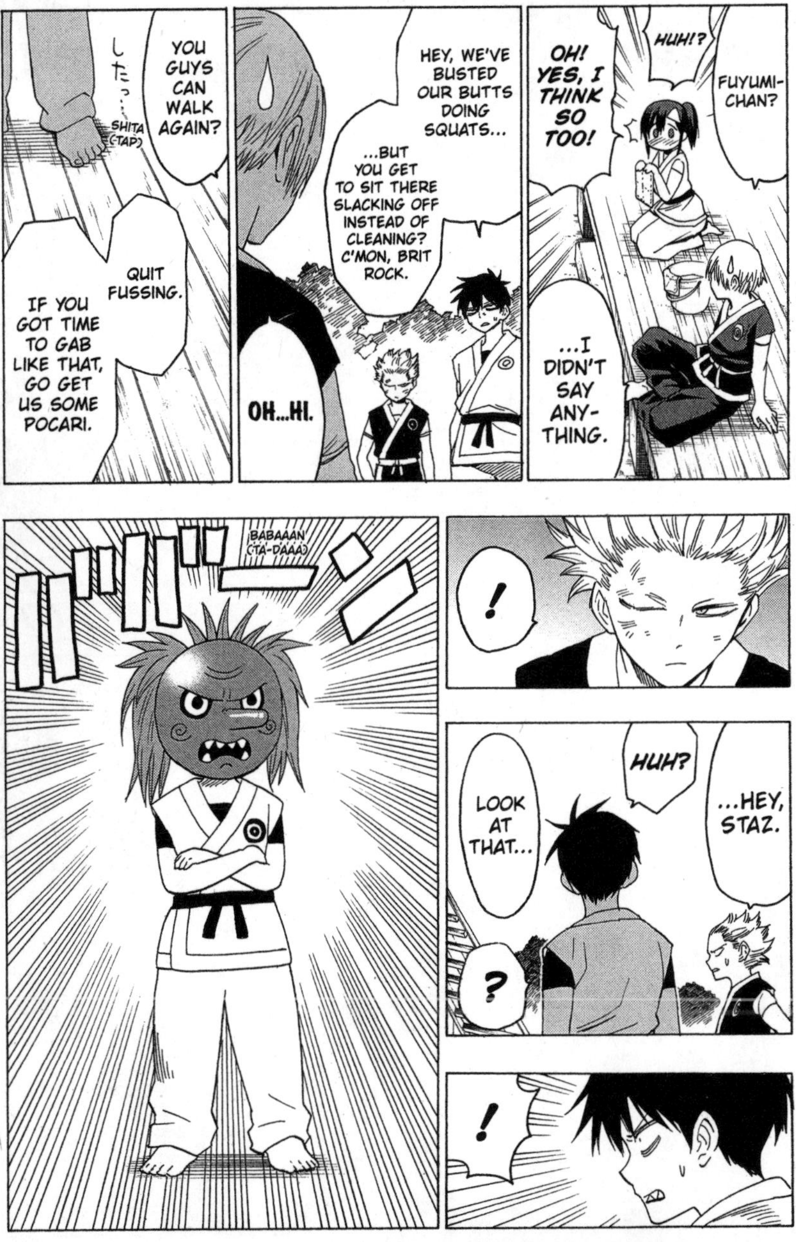
FUYUMI-CHAN?
HUH!?
OH! YES, I THINK SO TOO!
...I DIDN'T SAY ANYTHING.
HEY, WE'VE BUSTED OUR BUTTS DOING SQUATS...
...BUT YOU GET TO SIT THERE SLACKING OFF INSTEAD OF CLEANING? C'MON, BRIT ROCK.
OH...HI.
YOU GUYS CAN WALK AGAIN?
したっ
SHITA (TAP)
QUIT FUSSING.
IF YOU GOT TIME TO GAB LIKE THAT, GO GET US SOME POCARI.
!
...HEY, STAZ.
HUH?
LOOK AT THAT...
?
!
BABAAAN (TA-DAAA)

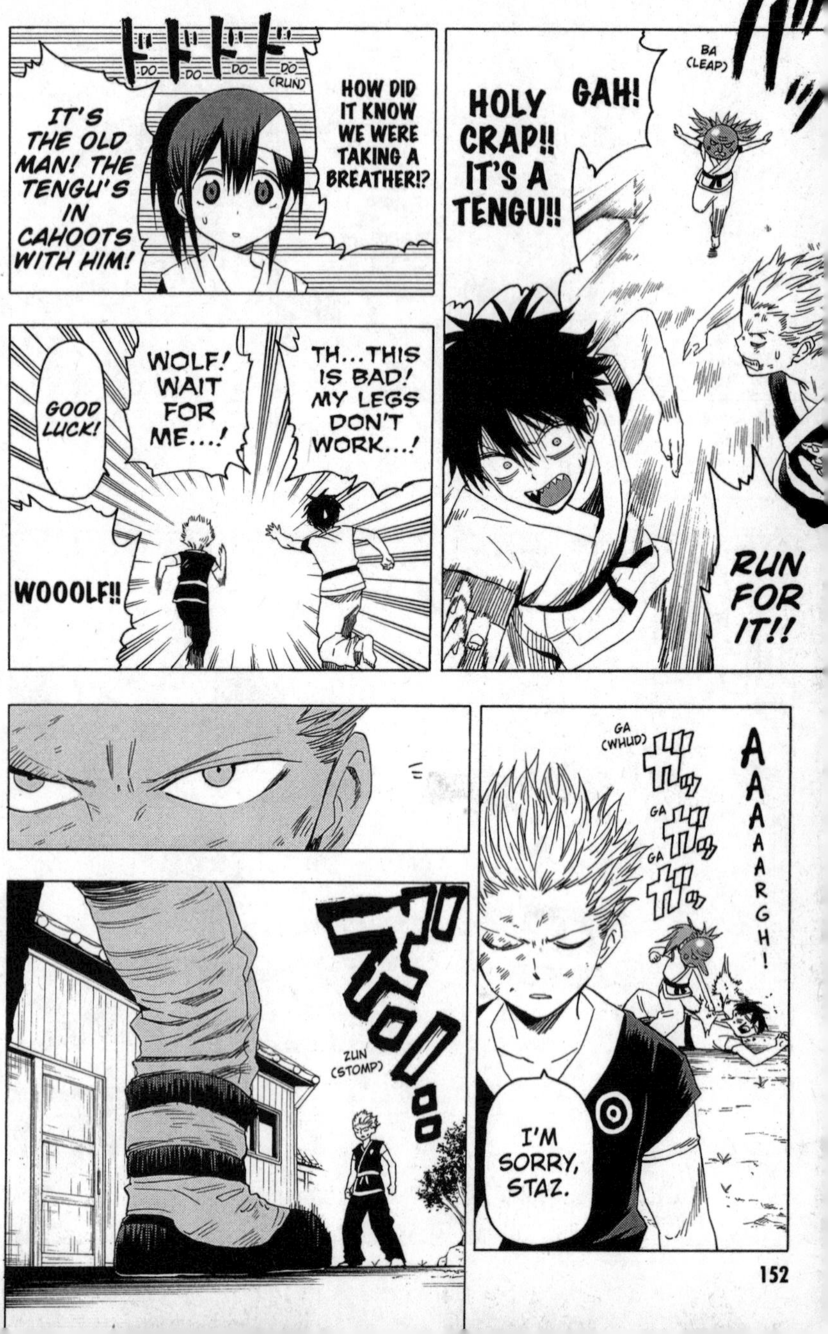
BA (LEAP)
GAH!
HOLY CRAP!! IT'S A TENGU!!
RUN FOR IT!!
DO DO DO DO (RUN)
HOW DID IT KNOW WE WERE TAKING A BREATHER!?
IT'S THE OLD MAN! THE TENGU'S IN CAHOOTS WITH HIM!
TH...THIS IS BAD! MY LEGS DON'T WORK...!
WOLF! WAIT FOR ME...!
GOOD LUCK!
WOOOLF!!
GA (WHUD) GA GA
AAAAAARGH!
I'M SORRY, STAZ.
ZUN (STOMP)

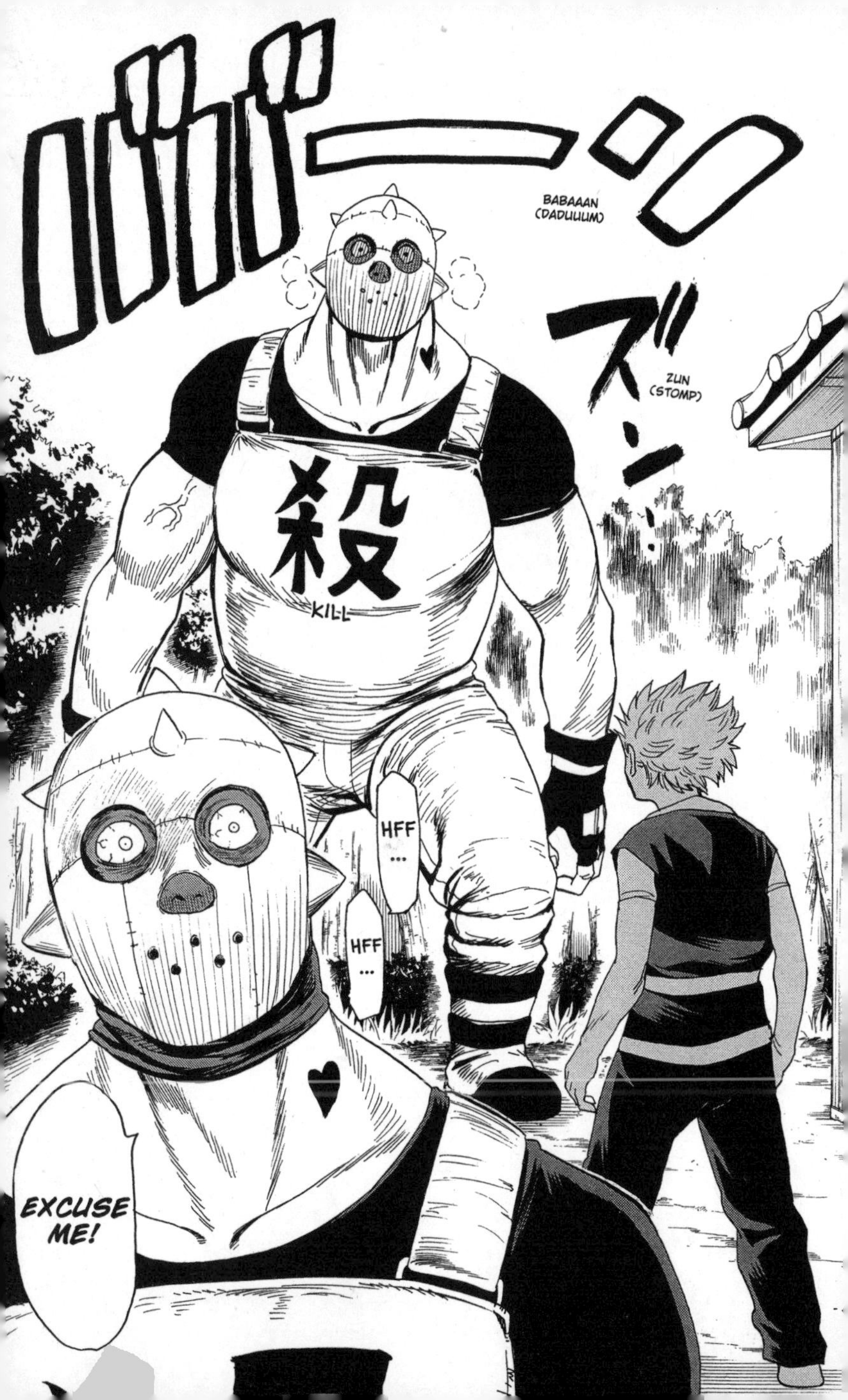
BABAAAN
(DADUUUM)
ZUN
(STOMP)
殺
KILL
HFF ...
HFF ...
EXCUSE ME!

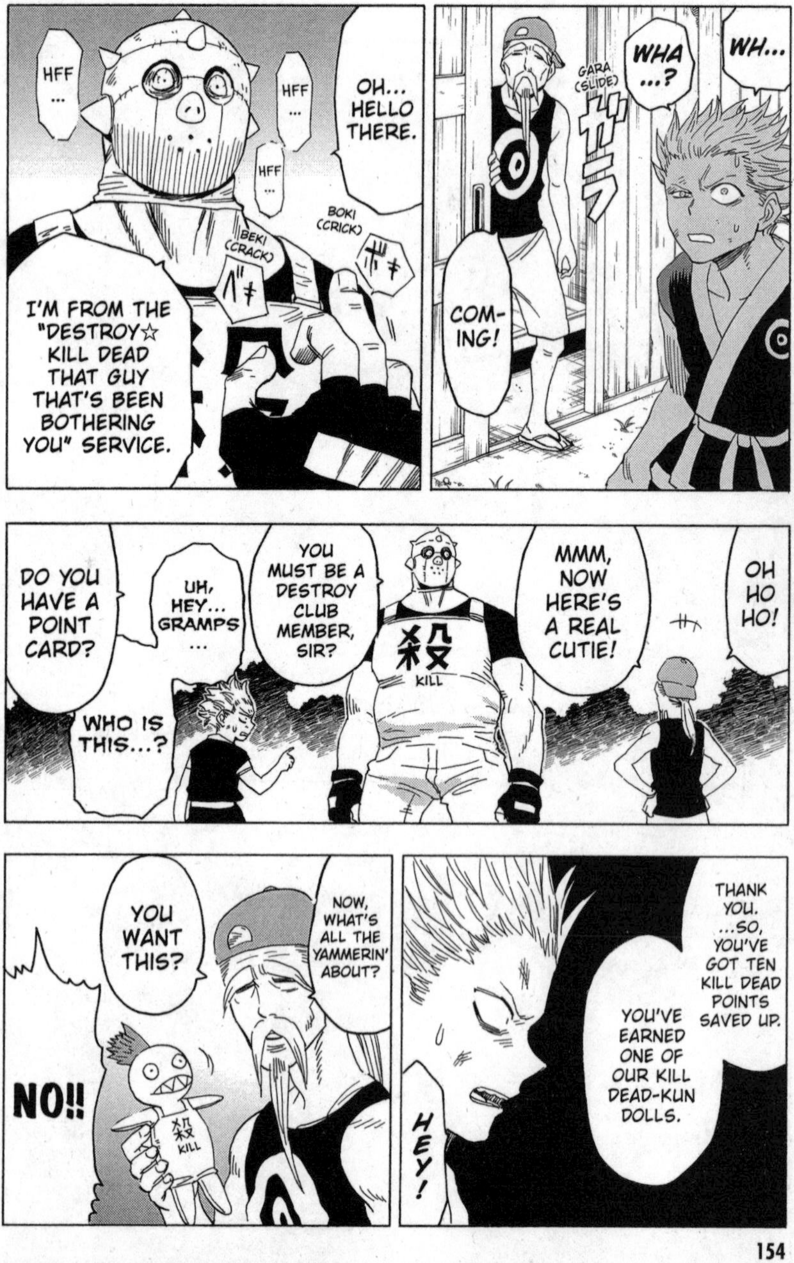
WH...
WHA ...?
GARA (SLIDE)
COM- ING!
OH... HELLO THERE.
HFF ...
HFF ...
HFF ...
BOKI (CRICK)
BEKI (CRACK)
I'M FROM THE "DESTROY☆ KILL DEAD THAT GUY THAT'S BEEN BOTHERING YOU" SERVICE.
OH HO HO!
MMM, NOW HERE'S A REAL CUTIE!
YOU MUST BE A DESTROY CLUB MEMBER, SIR?
KILL
UH, HEY... GRAMPS ...
DO YOU HAVE A POINT CARD?
WHO IS THIS...?
THANK YOU. ...SO, YOU'VE GOT TEN KILL DEAD POINTS SAVED UP.
YOU'VE EARNED ONE OF OUR KILL DEAD-KUN DOLLS.
HEY!
NOW, WHAT'S ALL THE YAMMERIN' ABOUT?
YOU WANT THIS?
KILL
NO!!

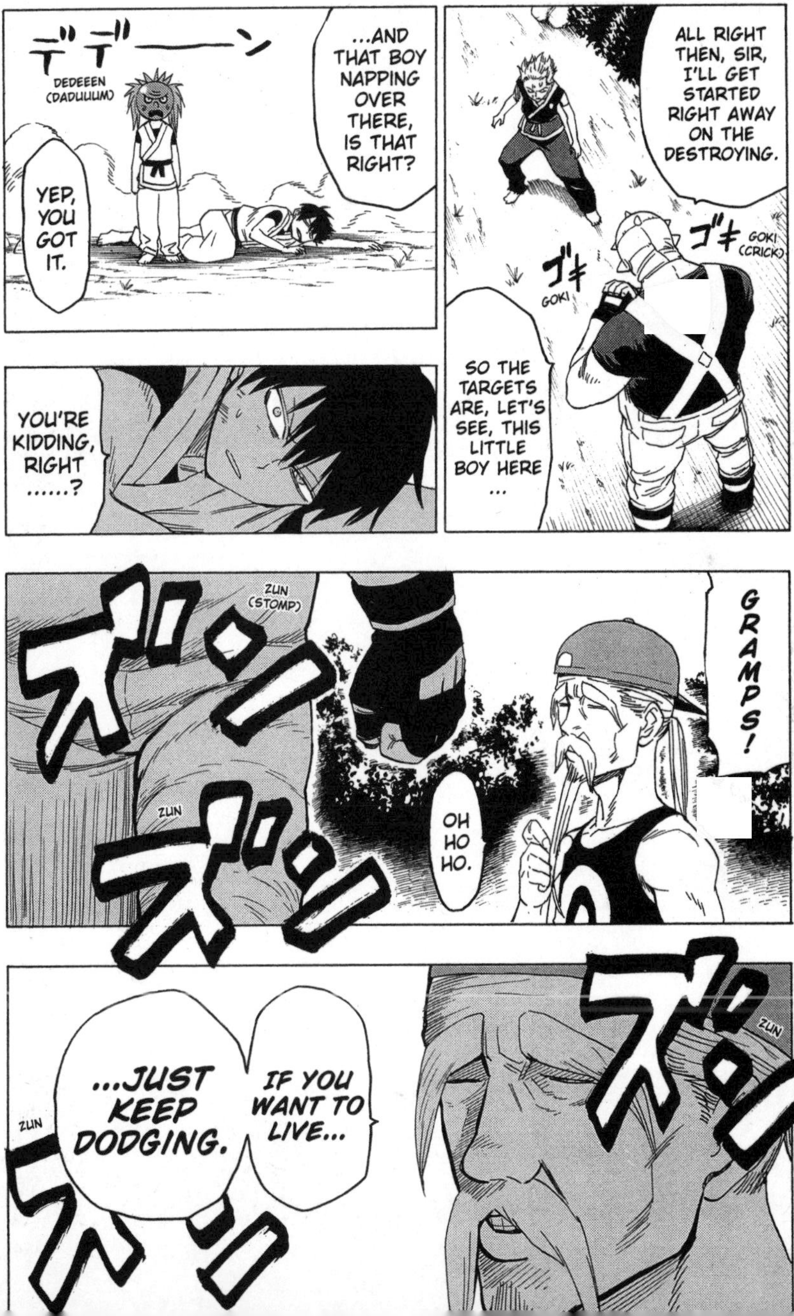
ALL RIGHT THEN, SIR, I'LL GET STARTED RIGHT AWAY ON THE DESTROYING.
GOKI (CRICK)
GOKI
SO THE TARGETS ARE, LET'S SEE, THIS LITTLE BOY HERE ...
...AND THAT BOY NAPPING OVER THERE, IS THAT RIGHT?
DEDEEEN (DADUUUM)
YEP, YOU GOT IT.
YOU'RE KIDDING, RIGHT ......?
GRAMPS!
OH HO HO.
ZUN (STOMP)
ZUN
ZUN
IF YOU WANT TO LIVE...
...JUST KEEP DODGING.
ZUN

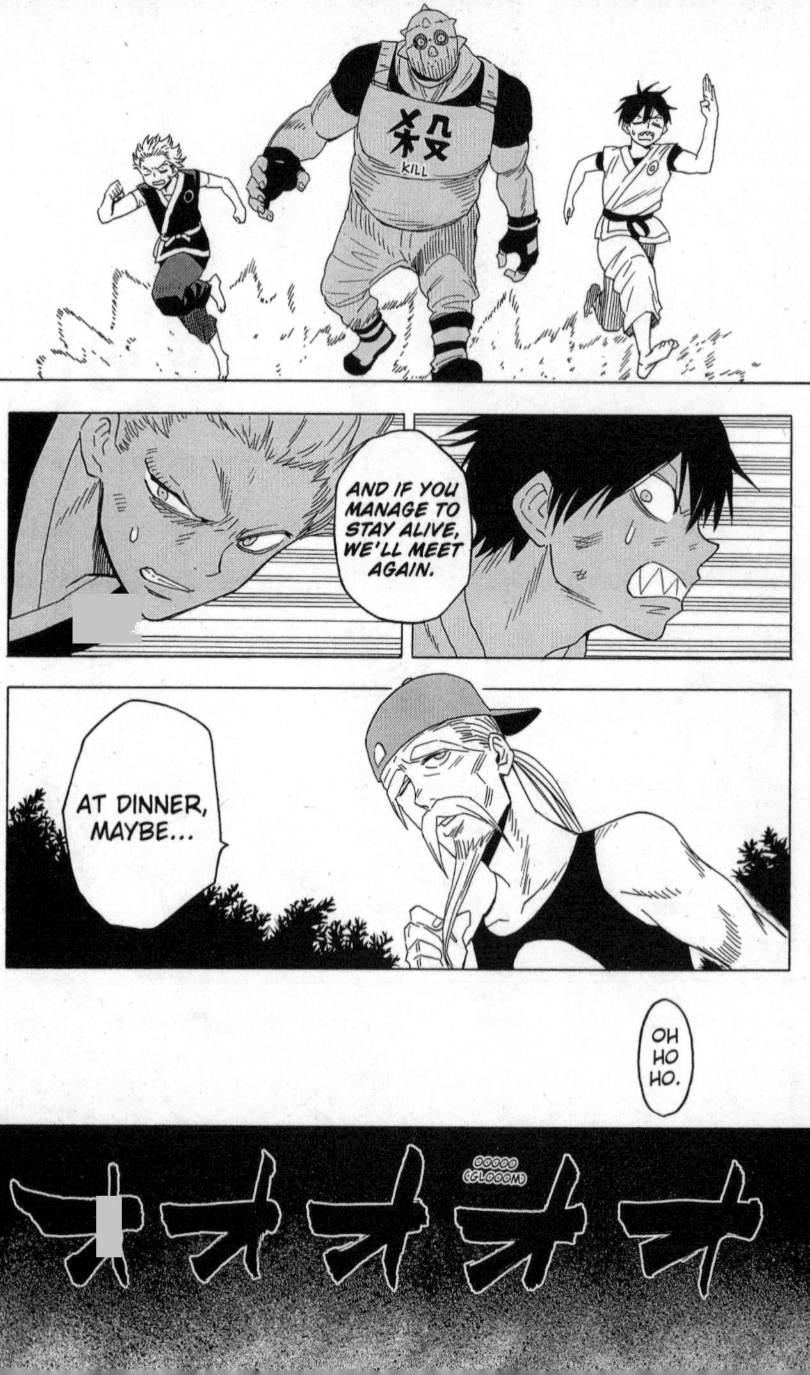
殺
KILL
AND IF YOU MANAGE TO STAY ALIVE, WE'LL MEET AGAIN.
AT DINNER, MAYBE...
OH HO HO.
オオオオオ
OOOOO (GLOOOM)

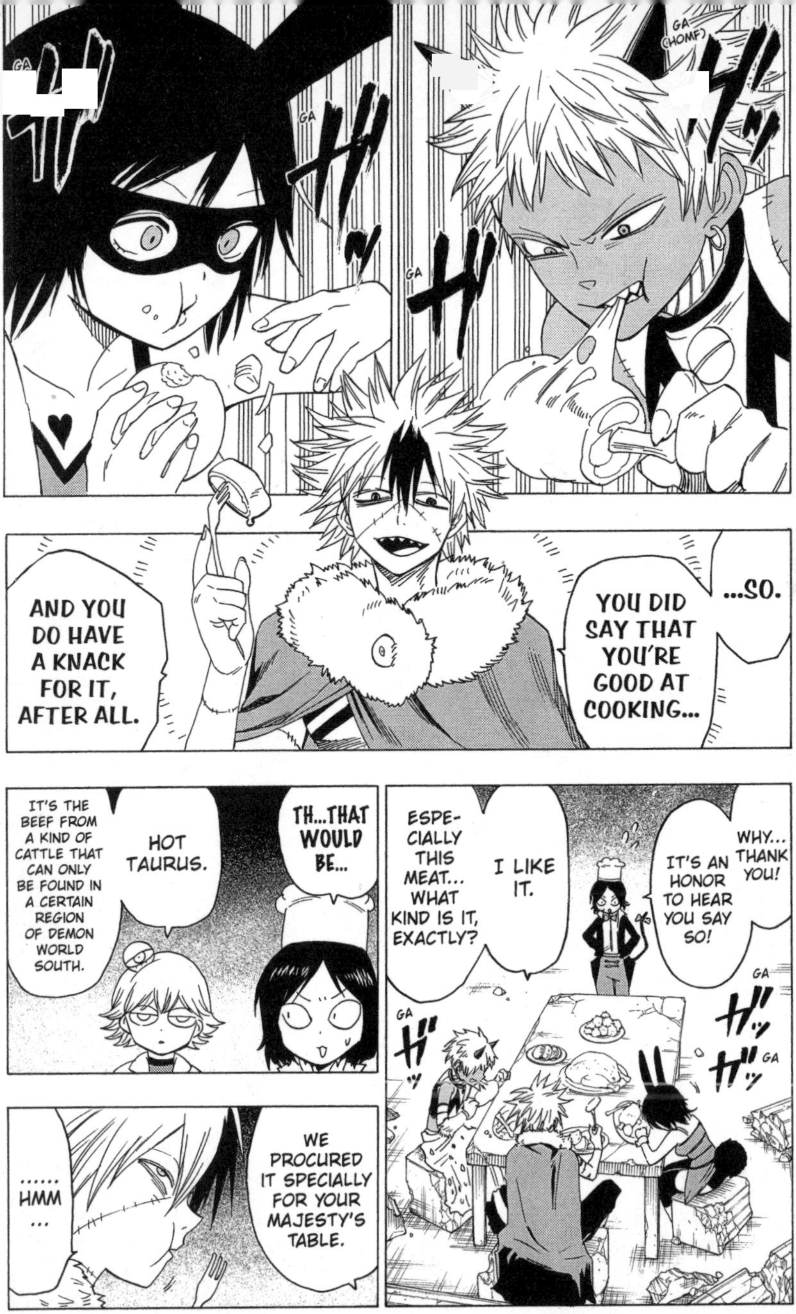
GA (HOMF)
GA
GA
GA
...SO.
YOU DID SAY THAT YOU'RE GOOD AT COOKING...
AND YOU DO HAVE A KNACK FOR IT, AFTER ALL.
WHY... THANK YOU!
IT'S AN HONOR TO HEAR YOU SAY SO!
I LIKE IT.
ESPE-CIALLY THIS MEAT... WHAT KIND IS IT, EXACTLY?
GA
GA
GA
TH...THAT WOULD BE...
HOT TAURUS.
IT'S THE BEEF FROM A KIND OF CATTLE THAT CAN ONLY BE FOUND IN A CERTAIN REGION OF DEMON WORLD SOUTH.
WE PROCURED IT SPECIALLY FOR YOUR MAJESTY'S TABLE.
......HMM...

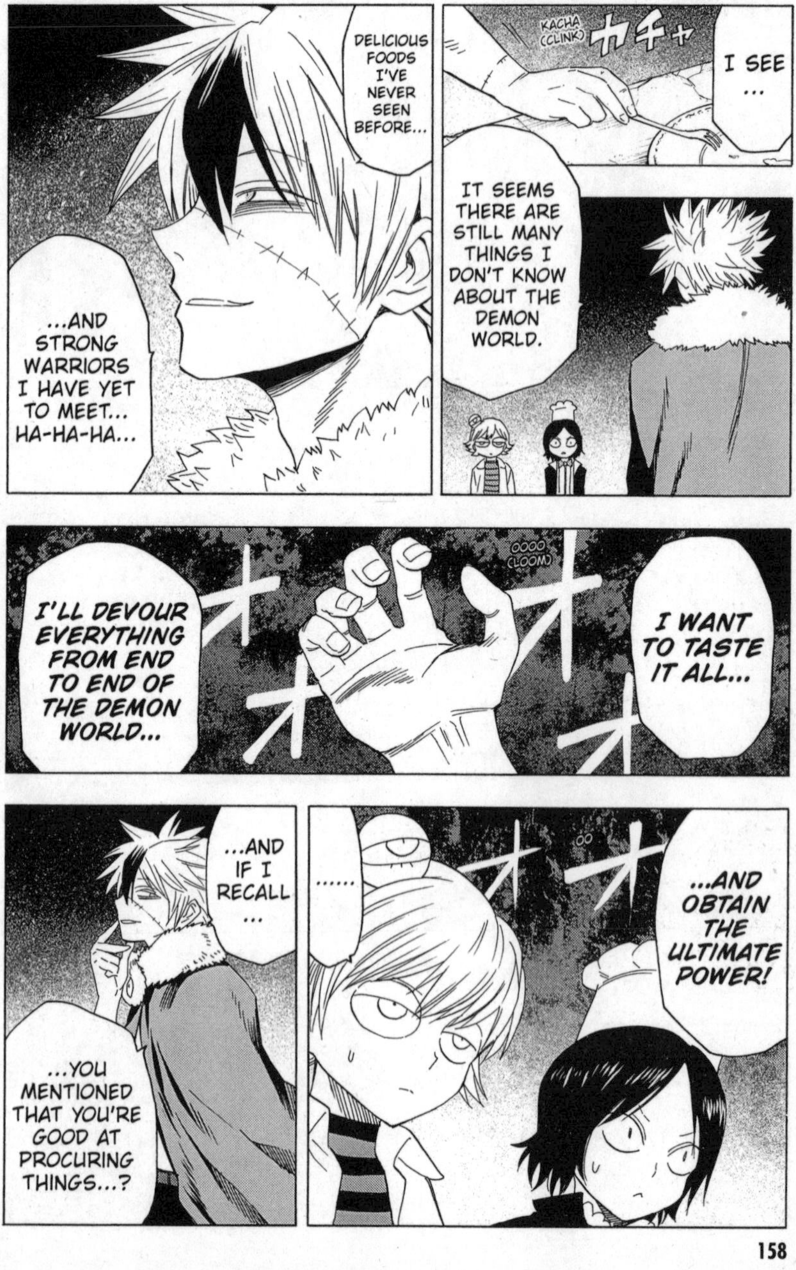
KACHA (CLINK)
I SEE ...
IT SEEMS THERE ARE STILL MANY THINGS I DON'T KNOW ABOUT THE DEMON WORLD.
DELICIOUS FOODS I'VE NEVER SEEN BEFORE...
...AND STRONG WARRIORS I HAVE YET TO MEET... HA-HA-HA...
OOOO (LOOM)
I WANT TO TASTE IT ALL...
I'LL DEVOUR EVERYTHING FROM END TO END OF THE DEMON WORLD...
...AND OBTAIN THE ULTIMATE POWER!
OO
......
...AND IF I RECALL ...
...YOU MENTIONED THAT YOU'RE GOOD AT PROCURING THINGS...?

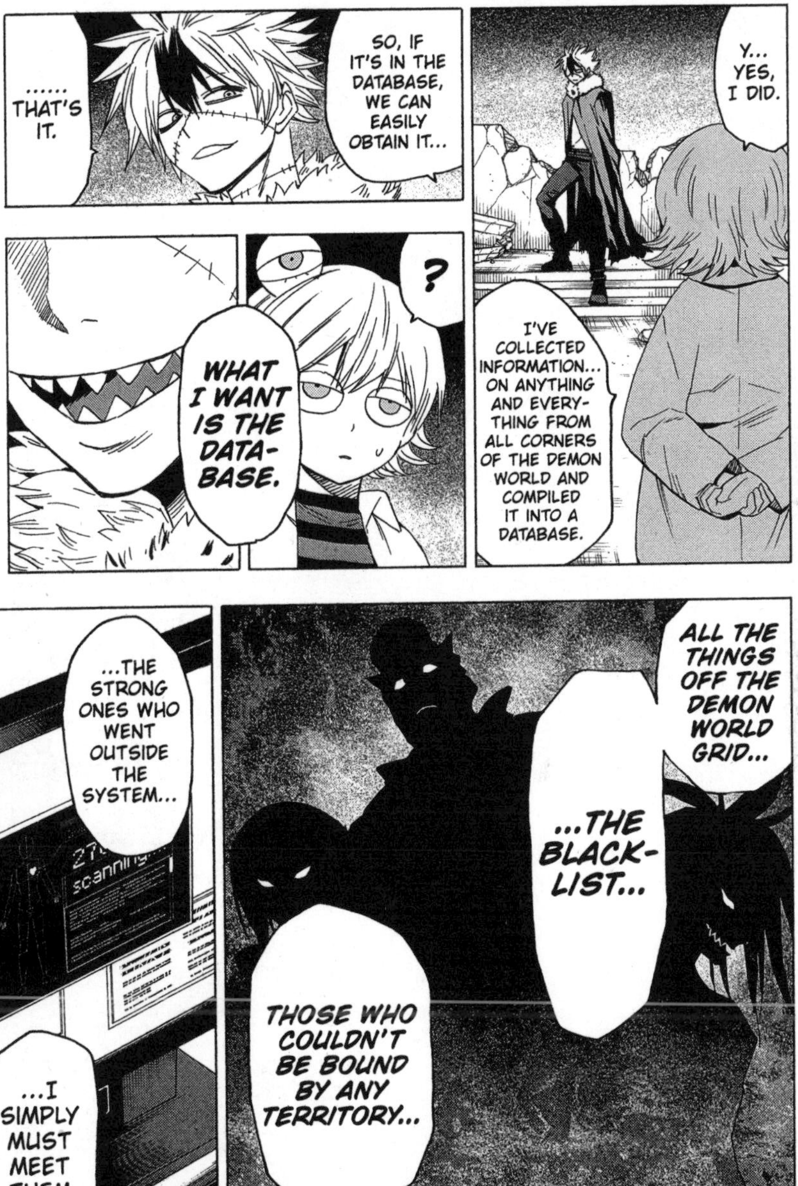
Y... YES, I DID.
I'VE COLLECTED INFORMATION... ON ANYTHING AND EVERYTHING FROM ALL CORNERS OF THE DEMON WORLD AND COMPILED IT INTO A DATABASE.
SO, IF IT'S IN THE DATABASE, WE CAN EASILY OBTAIN IT...
...... THAT'S IT.
?
WHAT I WANT IS THE DATABASE.
ALL THE THINGS OFF THE DEMON WORLD GRID...
...THE BLACKLIST...
THOSE WHO COULDN'T BE BOUND BY ANY TERRITORY...
...THE STRONG ONES WHO WENT OUTSIDE THE SYSTEM...
...I SIMPLY MUST MEET THEM ALL...

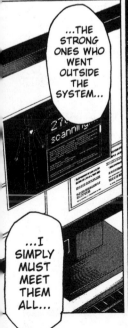

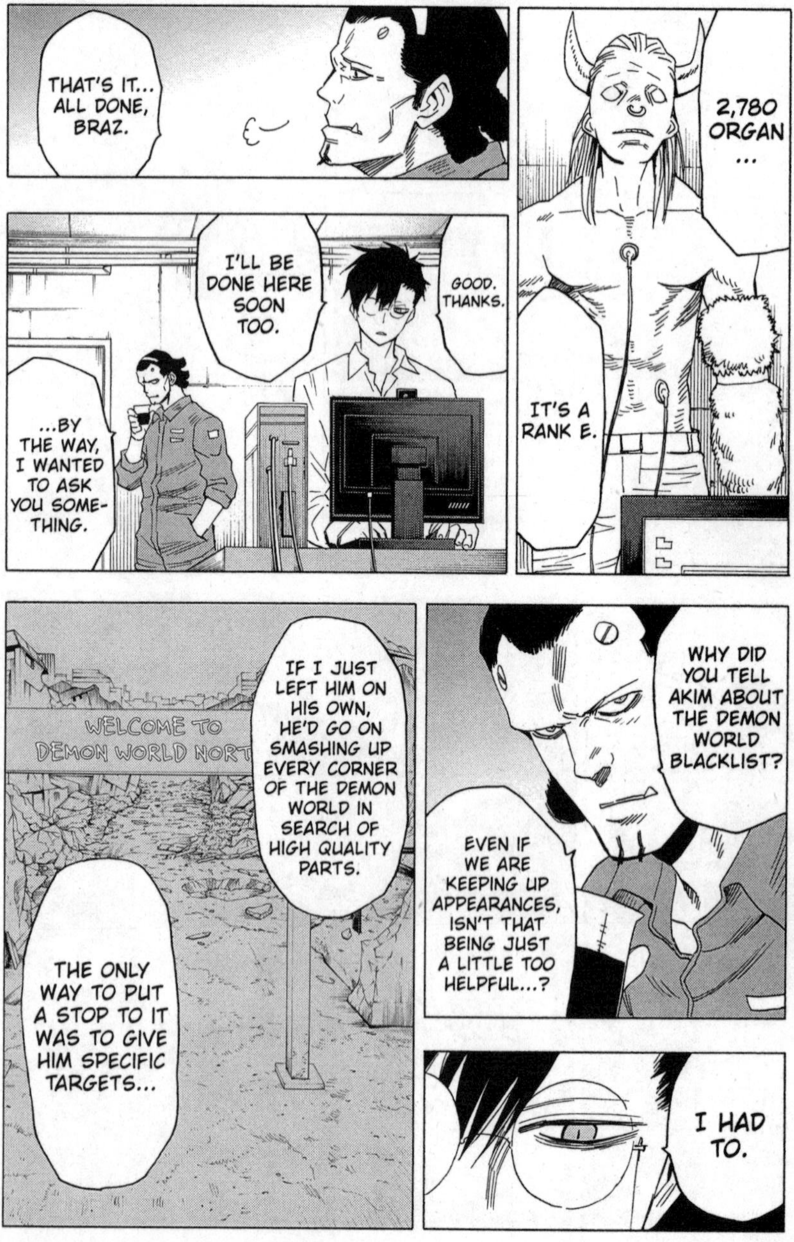
2,780 ORGAN ...
IT'S A RANK E.
THAT'S IT... ALL DONE, BRAZ.
I'LL BE DONE HERE SOON TOO.
GOOD. THANKS.
...BY THE WAY, I WANTED TO ASK YOU SOME-THING.
WHY DID YOU TELL AKIM ABOUT THE DEMON WORLD BLACKLIST?
EVEN IF WE ARE KEEPING UP APPEARANCES, ISN'T THAT BEING JUST A LITTLE TOO HELPFUL...?
I HAD TO.
WELCOME TO DEMON WORLD NORT
IF I JUST LEFT HIM ON HIS OWN, HE'D GO ON SMASHING UP EVERY CORNER OF THE DEMON WORLD IN SEARCH OF HIGH QUALITY PARTS.
THE ONLY WAY TO PUT A STOP TO IT WAS TO GIVE HIM SPECIFIC TARGETS...

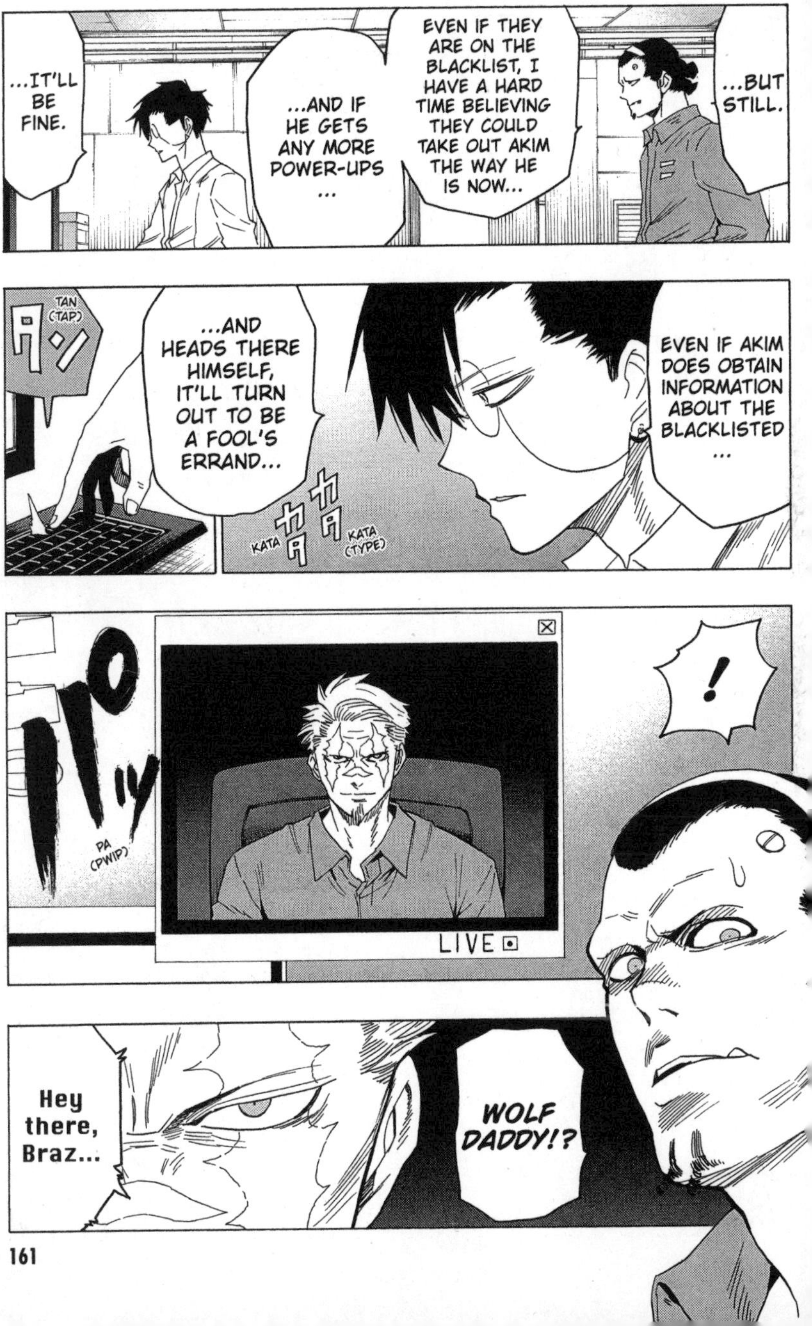
...BUT STILL.
EVEN IF THEY ARE ON THE BLACKLIST, I HAVE A HARD TIME BELIEVING THEY COULD TAKE OUT AKIM THE WAY HE IS NOW...
...AND IF HE GETS ANY MORE POWER-UPS ...
...IT'LL BE FINE.
EVEN IF AKIM DOES OBTAIN INFORMATION ABOUT THE BLACKLISTED ...
KATA KATA (TYPE)
...AND HEADS THERE HIMSELF, IT'LL TURN OUT TO BE A FOOL'S ERRAND...
TAN (TAP)
!
LIVE
PA (PWIP)
WOLF DADDY!?
Hey there, Braz...

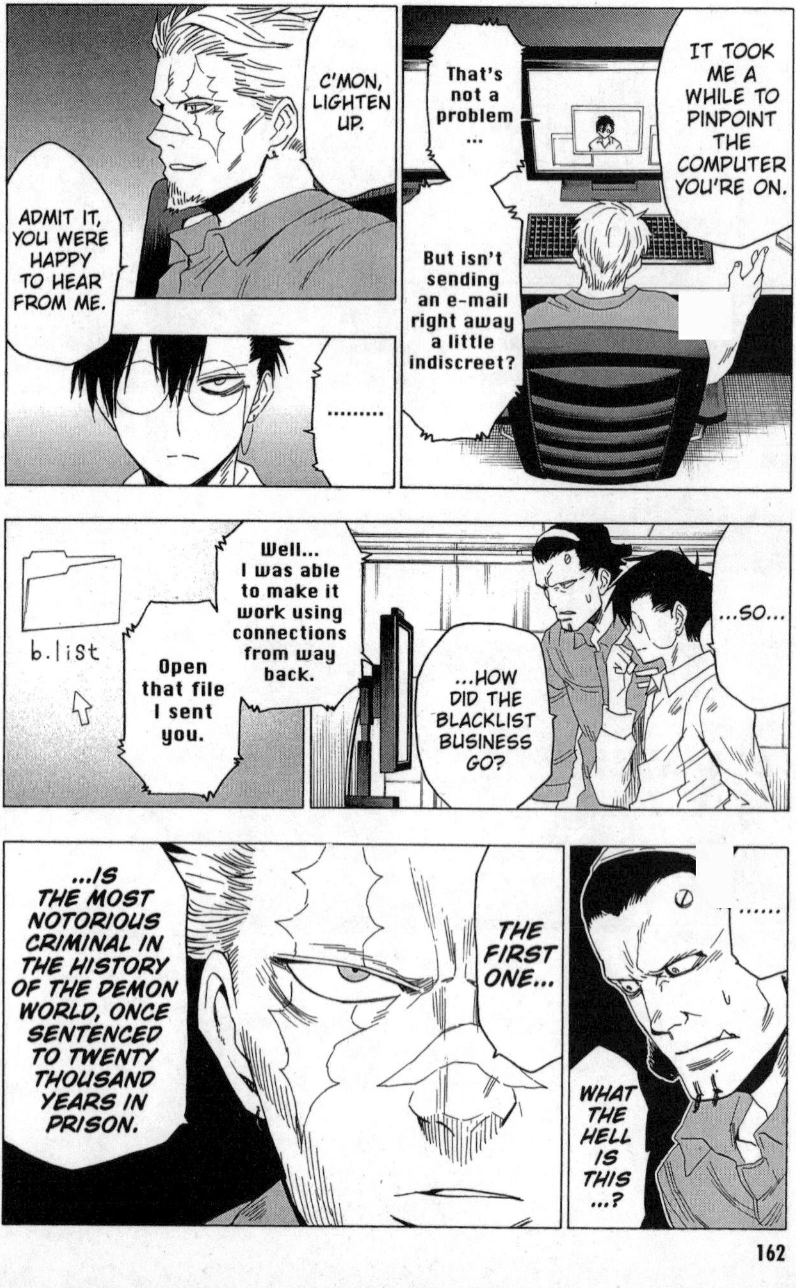

IT TOOK ME A WHILE TO PINPOINT THE COMPUTER YOU'RE ON.
That's not a problem...
But isn't sending an e-mail right away a little indiscreet?
C'MON, LIGHTEN UP.
ADMIT IT, YOU WERE HAPPY TO HEAR FROM ME.
....
...SO...
...HOW DID THE BLACKLIST BUSINESS GO?
Well... I was able to make it work using connections from way back.
Open that file I sent you.
b.list
......
WHAT THE HELL IS THIS ...?
THE FIRST ONE...
...IS THE MOST NOTORIOUS CRIMINAL IN THE HISTORY OF THE DEMON WORLD, ONCE SENTENCED TO TWENTY THOUSAND YEARS IN PRISON.

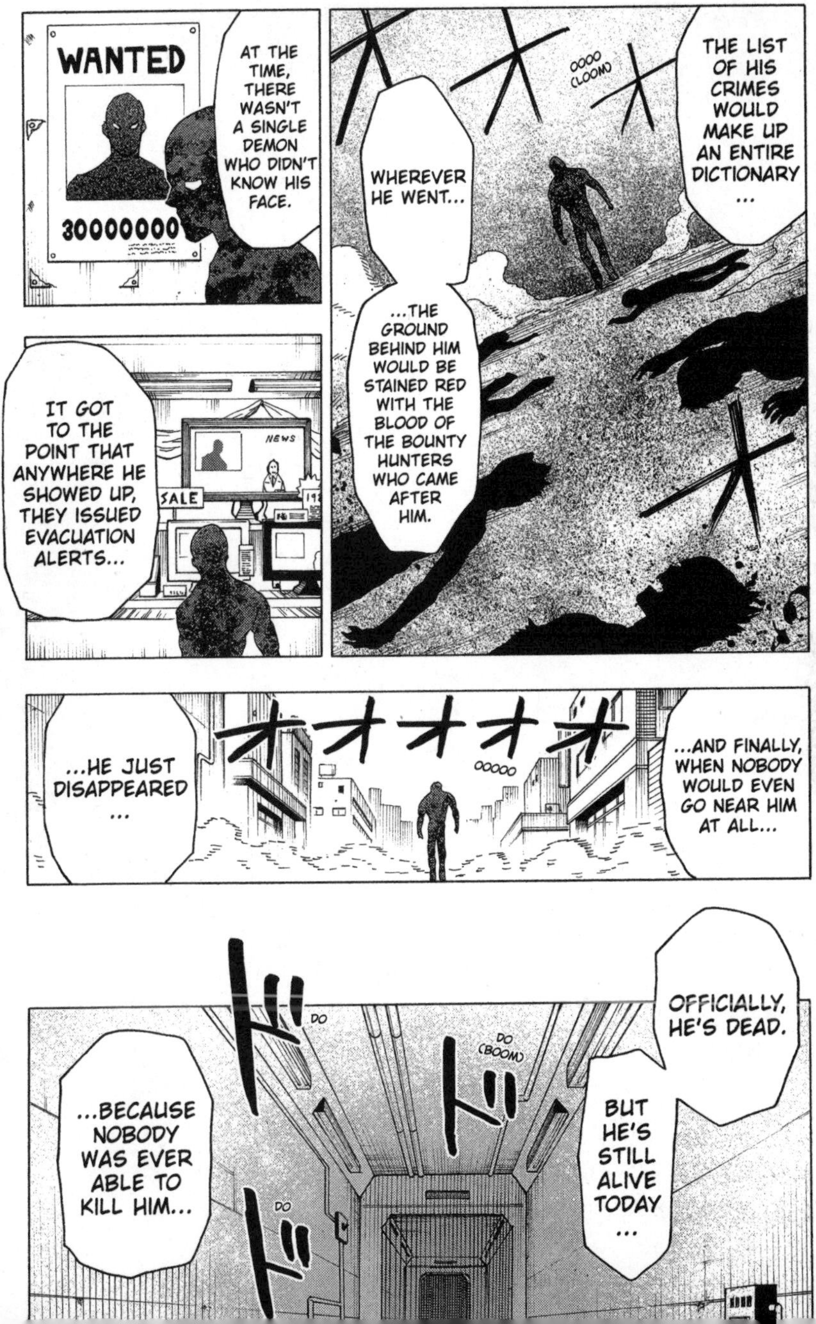
THE LIST OF HIS CRIMES WOULD MAKE UP AN ENTIRE DICTIONARY...
OOOO (LOOM)
WHEREVER HE WENT...
...THE GROUND BEHIND HIM WOULD BE STAINED RED WITH THE BLOOD OF THE BOUNTY HUNTERS WHO CAME AFTER HIM.
WANTED
30000000
AT THE TIME, THERE WASN'T A SINGLE DEMON WHO DIDN'T KNOW HIS FACE.
NEWS
SALE
IT GOT TO THE POINT THAT ANYWHERE HE SHOWED UP, THEY ISSUED EVACUATION ALERTS...
...AND FINALLY, WHEN NOBODY WOULD EVEN GO NEAR HIM AT ALL...
OOOOO
...HE JUST DISAPPEARED...
OFFICIALLY, HE'S DEAD.
BUT HE'S STILL ALIVE TODAY...
DO (BOOM)
DO
DO
...BECAUSE NOBODY WAS EVER ABLE TO KILL HIM...

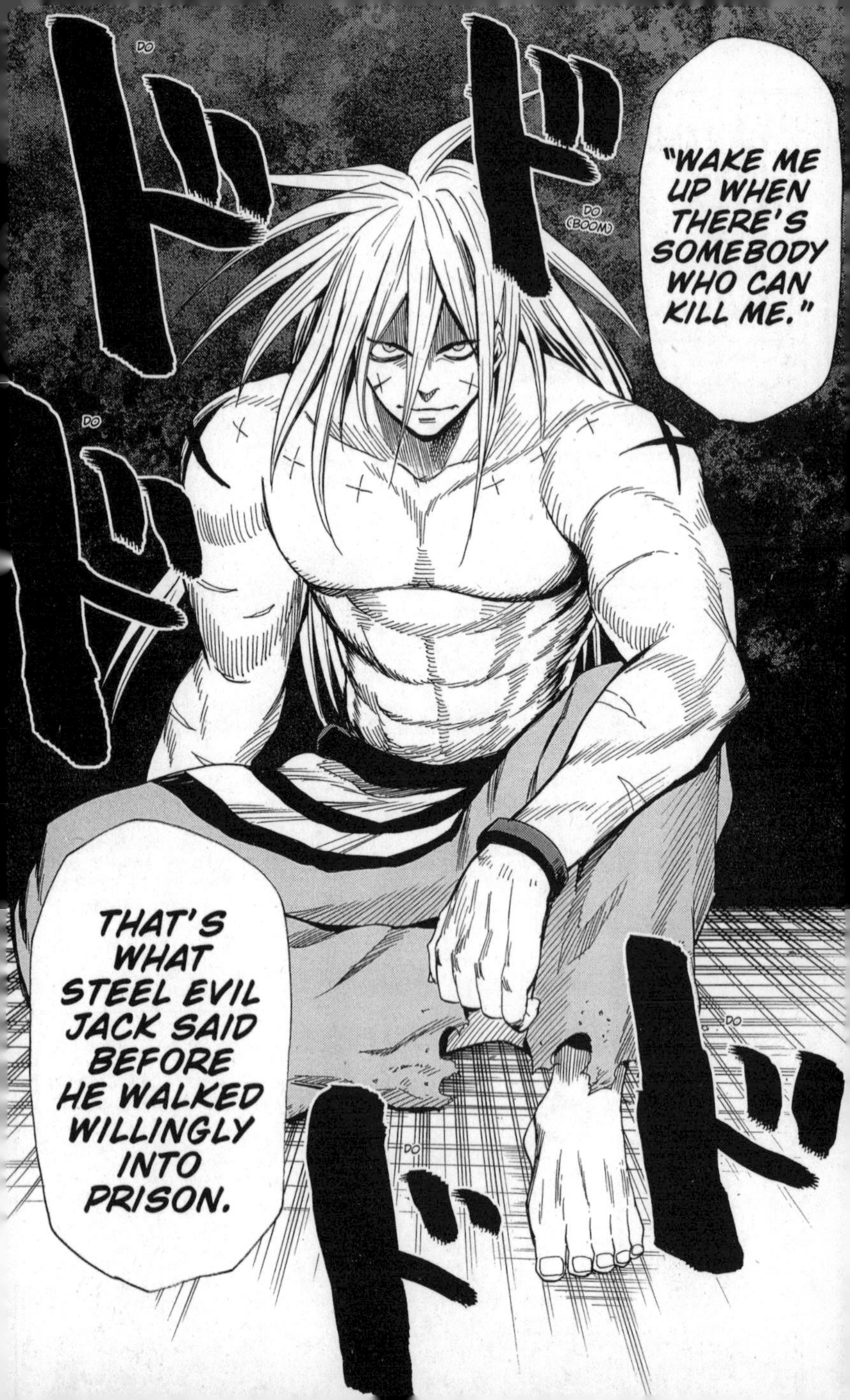
"WAKE ME UP WHEN THERE'S SOMEBODY WHO CAN KILL ME."
DO (BOOM)
DO
DO
DO
DO
THAT'S WHAT STEEL EVIL JACK SAID BEFORE HE WALKED WILLINGLY INTO PRISON.

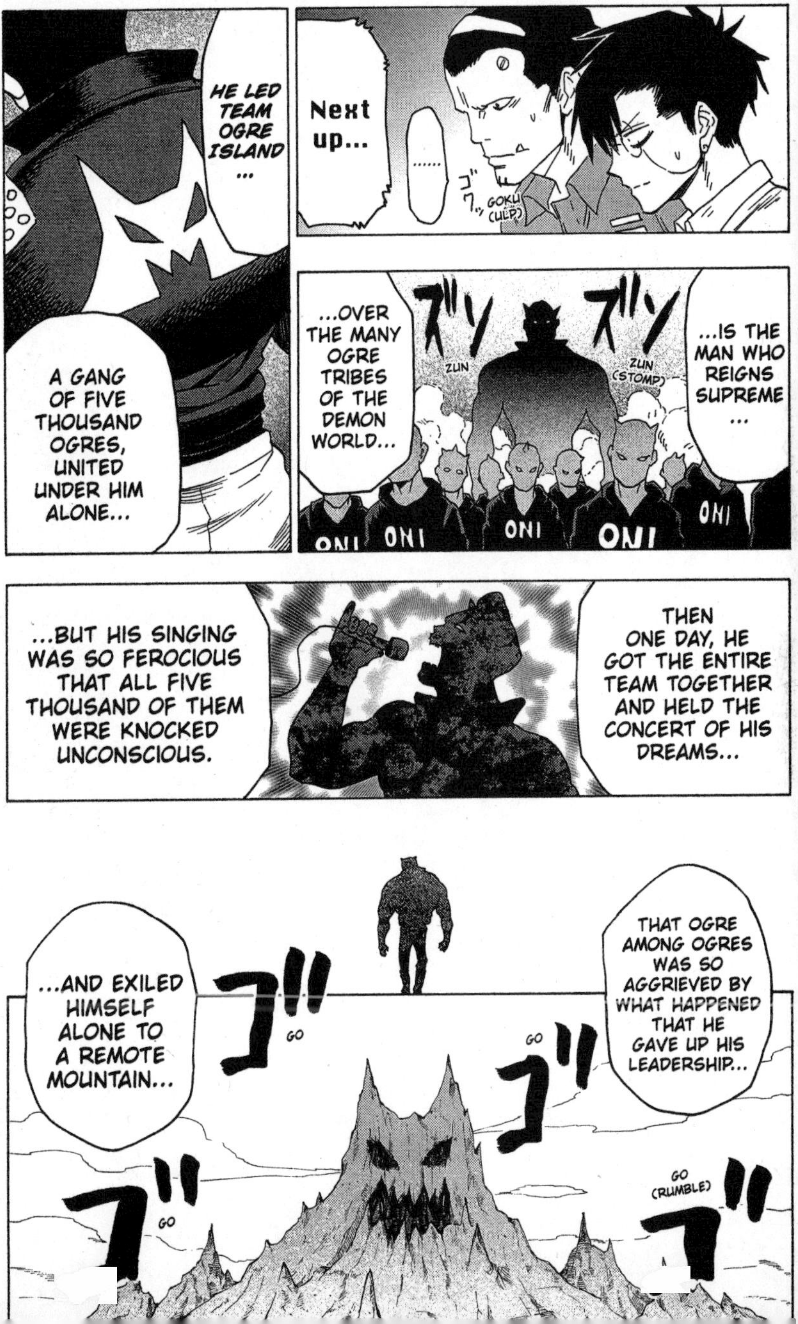
Next up...
......
GOKU (ULP)
...IS THE MAN WHO REIGNS SUPREME...
ZUN (STOMP)
ZUN
...OVER THE MANY OGRE TRIBES OF THE DEMON WORLD...
ONI
ONI
ONI
ONI
ONI
HE LED TEAM OGRE ISLAND...
A GANG OF FIVE THOUSAND OGRES, UNITED UNDER HIM ALONE...
THEN ONE DAY, HE GOT THE ENTIRE TEAM TOGETHER AND HELD THE CONCERT OF HIS DREAMS...
...BUT HIS SINGING WAS SO FEROCIOUS THAT ALL FIVE THOUSAND OF THEM WERE KNOCKED UNCONSCIOUS.
THAT OGRE AMONG OGRES WAS SO AGGRIEVED BY WHAT HAPPENED THAT HE GAVE UP HIS LEADERSHIP...
GO
GO (RUMBLE)
...AND EXILED HIMSELF ALONE TO A REMOTE MOUNTAIN...
GO
GO

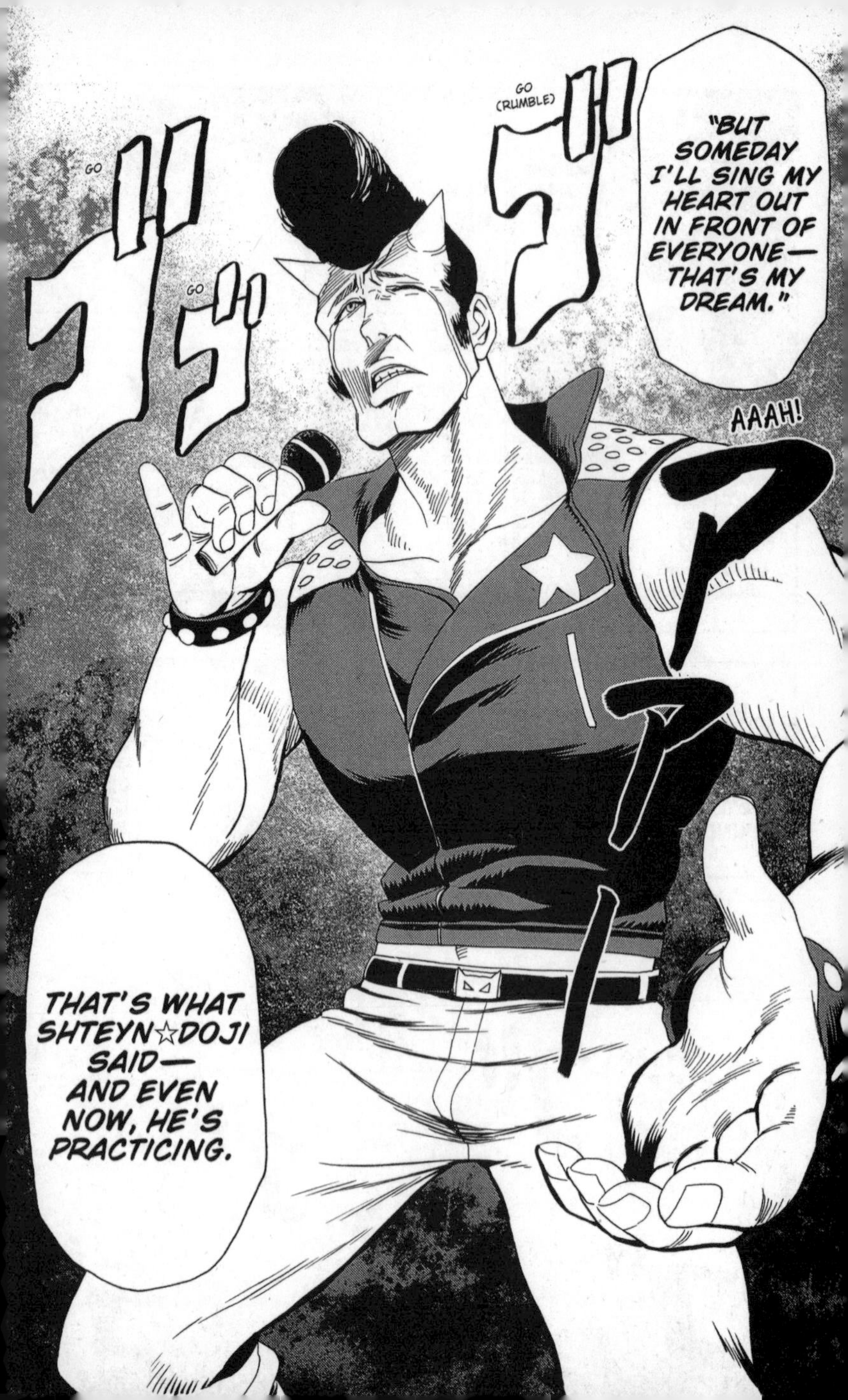
"BUT SOMEDAY I'LL SING MY HEART OUT IN FRONT OF EVERYONE— THAT'S MY DREAM."
GO (RUMBLE)
GO
GO
AAAH!
THAT'S WHAT SHTEYN☆DOJI SAID— AND EVEN NOW, HE'S PRACTICING.

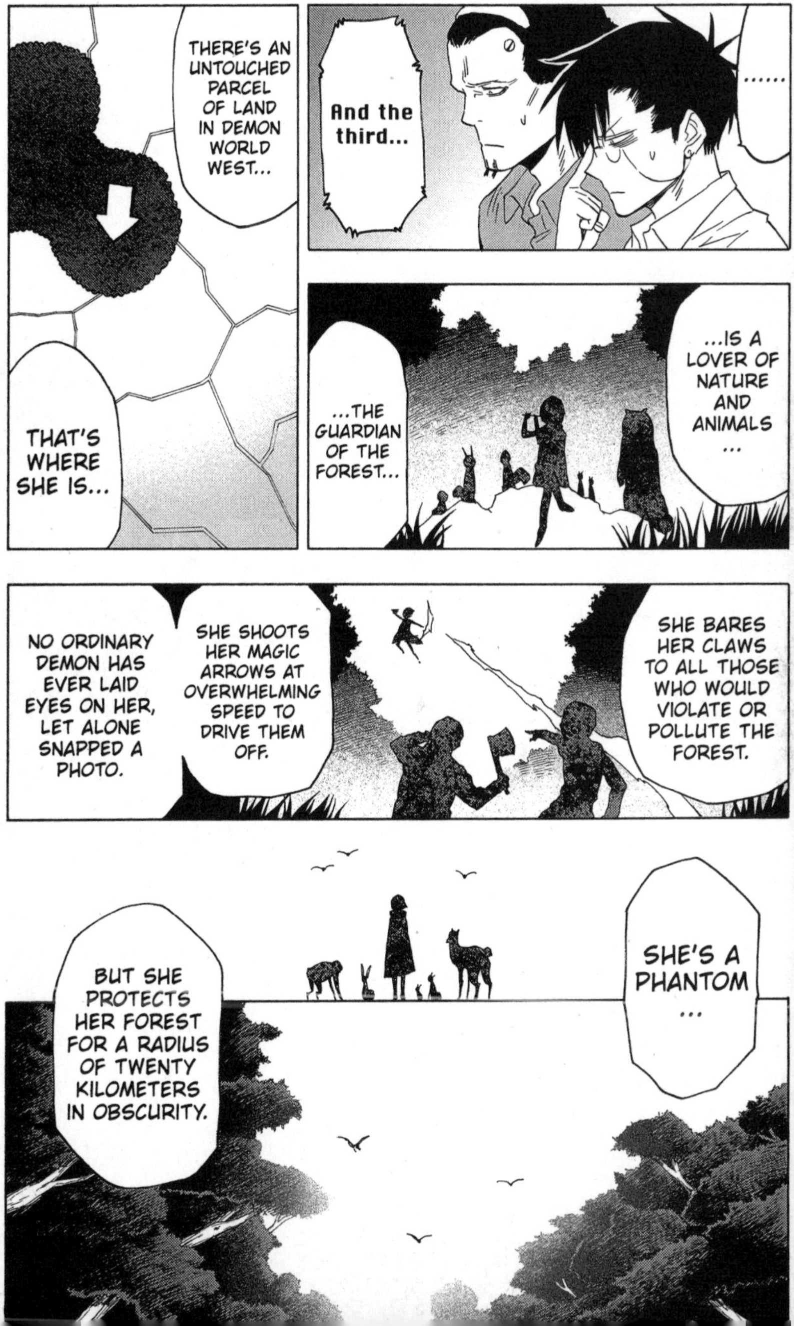
......
And the third...
...THE GUARDIAN OF THE FOREST...
...IS A LOVER OF NATURE AND ANIMALS...
THERE'S AN UNTOUCHED PARCEL OF LAND IN DEMON WORLD WEST...
THAT'S WHERE SHE IS...
SHE BARES HER CLAWS TO ALL THOSE WHO WOULD VIOLATE OR POLLUTE THE FOREST.
SHE SHOOTS HER MAGIC ARROWS AT OVERWHELMING SPEED TO DRIVE THEM OFF.
NO ORDINARY DEMON HAS EVER LAID EYES ON HER, LET ALONE SNAPPED A PHOTO.
SHE'S A PHANTOM...
BUT SHE PROTECTS HER FOREST FOR A RADIUS OF TWENTY KILOMETERS IN OBSCURITY.

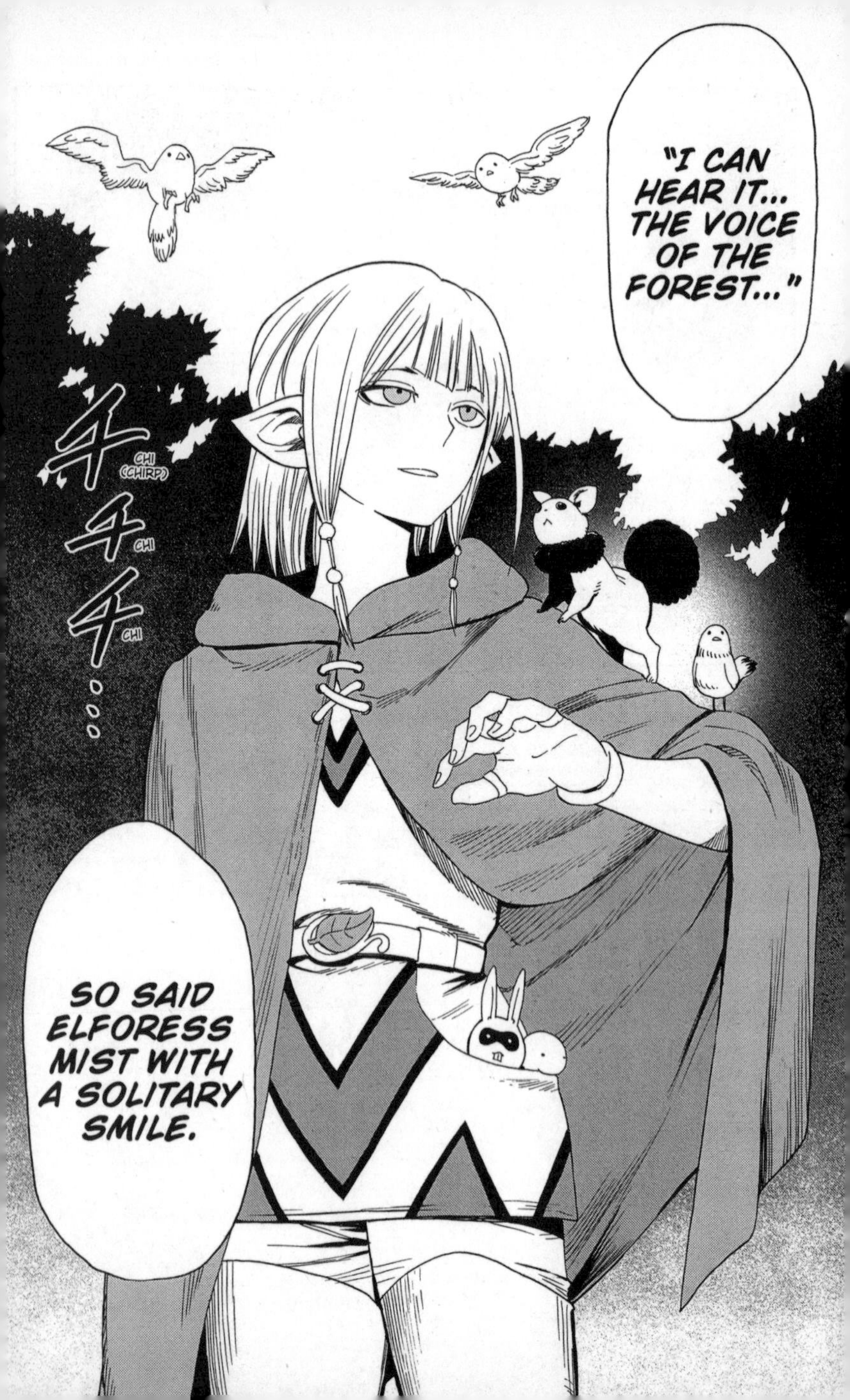
"I CAN HEAR IT... THE VOICE OF THE FOREST..."
CHI (CHIRP)
CHI
CHI
SO SAID ELFORESS MIST WITH A SOLITARY SMILE.

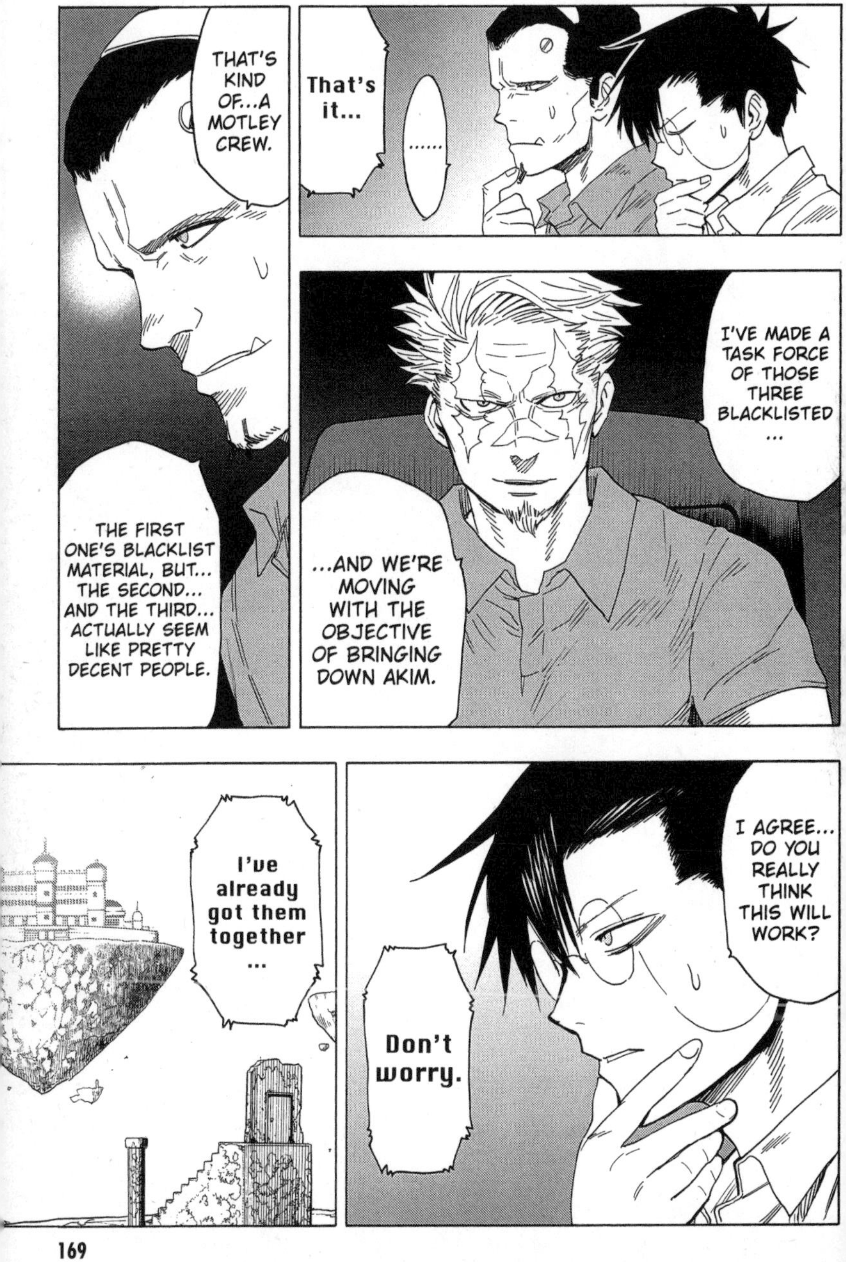
......
That's it...
I'VE MADE A TASK FORCE OF THOSE THREE BLACKLISTED ...
...AND WE'RE MOVING WITH THE OBJECTIVE OF BRINGING DOWN AKIM.
THAT'S KIND OF...A MOTLEY CREW.
THE FIRST ONE'S BLACKLIST MATERIAL, BUT... THE SECOND... AND THE THIRD... ACTUALLY SEEM LIKE PRETTY DECENT PEOPLE.
I AGREE... DO YOU REALLY THINK THIS WILL WORK?
Don't worry.
I've already got them together ...

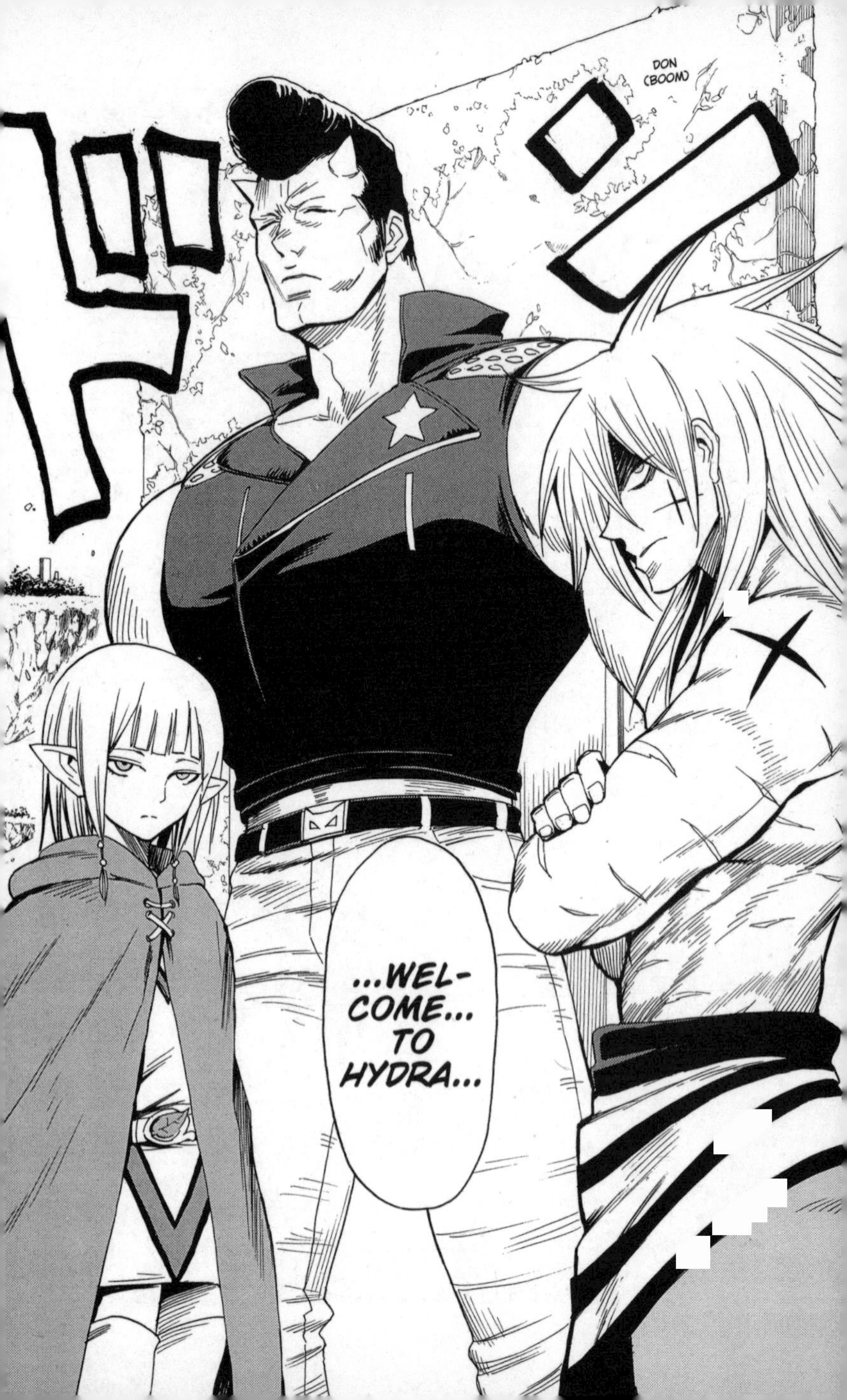
DON (BOOM)
...WEL-COME... TO HYDRA...

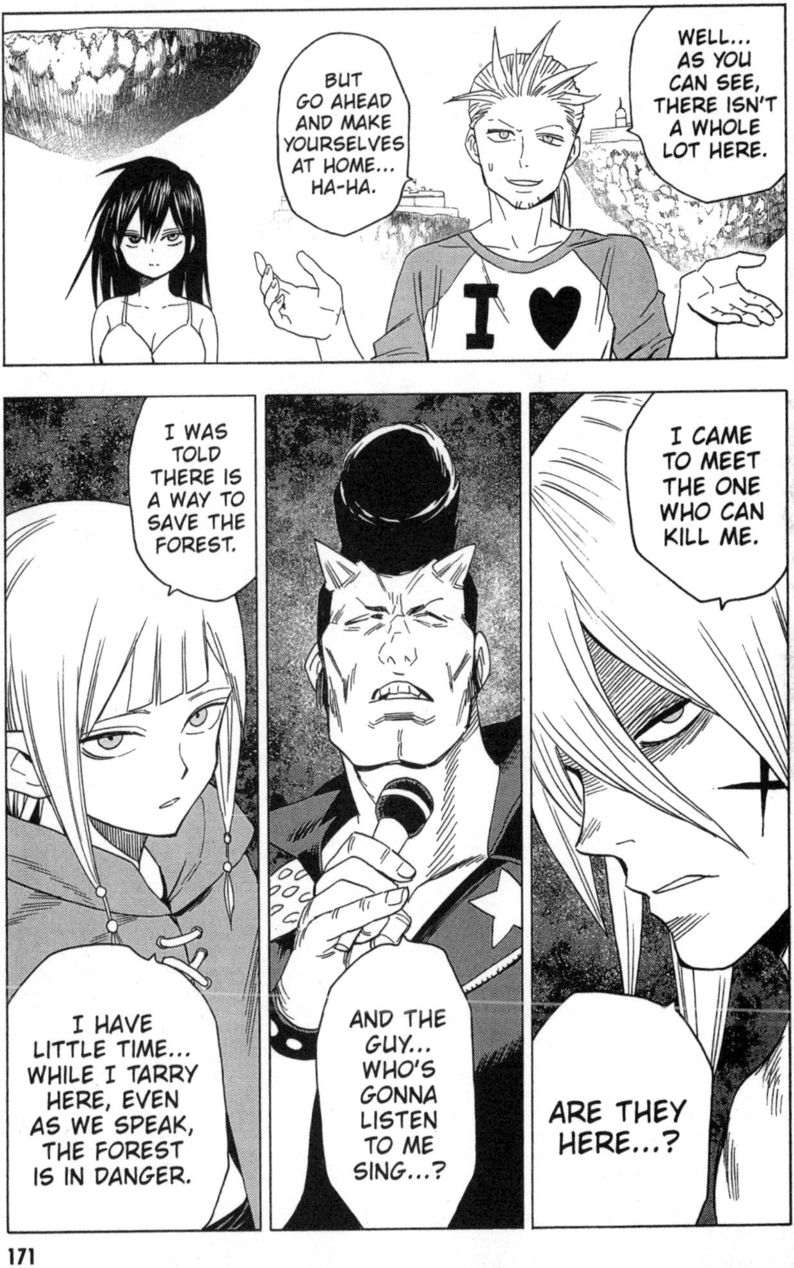
WELL... AS YOU CAN SEE, THERE ISN'T A WHOLE LOT HERE.
BUT GO AHEAD AND MAKE YOURSELVES AT HOME... HA-HA.
I CAME TO MEET THE ONE WHO CAN KILL ME.
ARE THEY HERE...?
AND THE GUY... WHO'S GONNA LISTEN TO ME SING...?
I WAS TOLD THERE IS A WAY TO SAVE THE FOREST.
I HAVE LITTLE TIME... WHILE I TARRY HERE, EVEN AS WE SPEAK, THE FOREST IS IN DANGER.

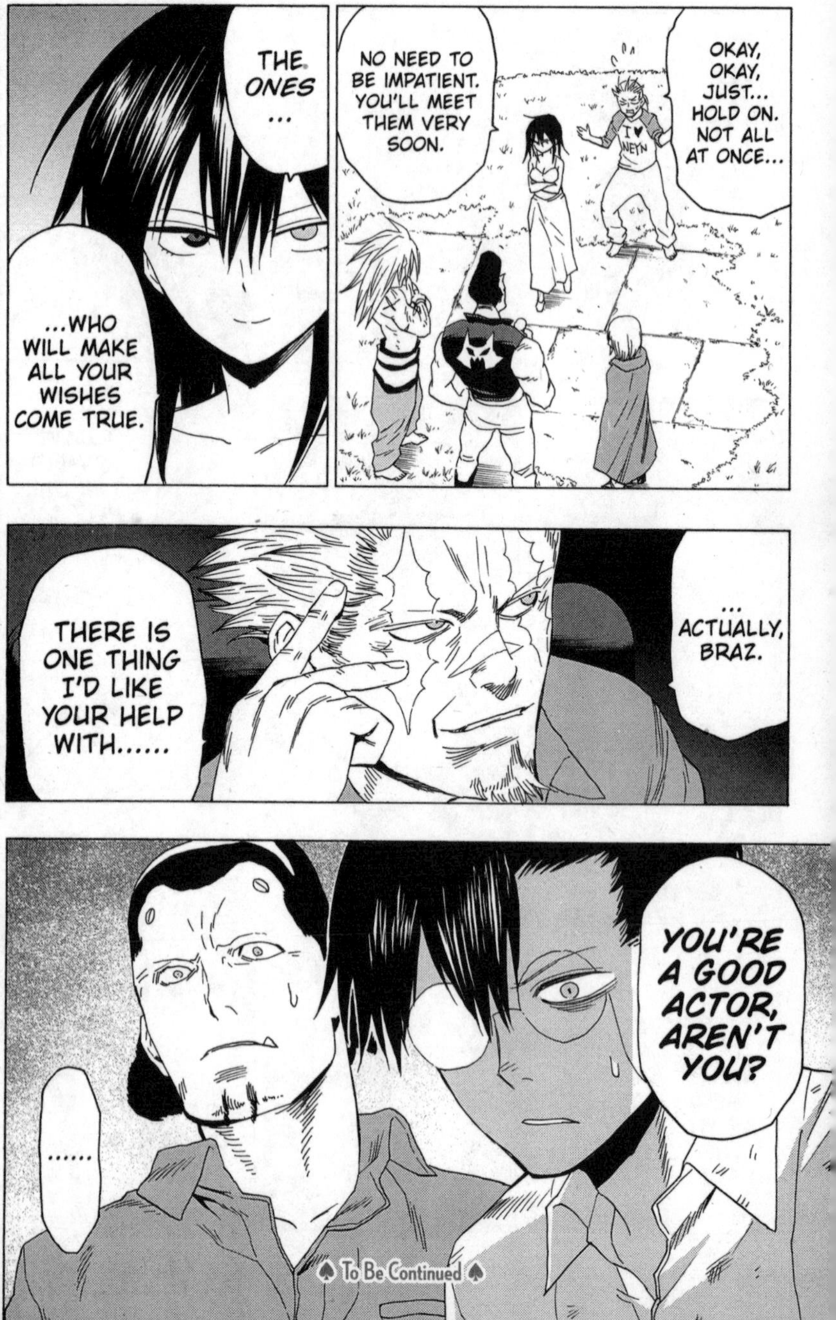
OKAY, OKAY, JUST... HOLD ON. NOT ALL AT ONCE...
NO NEED TO BE IMPATIENT. YOU'LL MEET THEM VERY SOON.
I ♥ NEYN
THE ONES ...
...WHO WILL MAKE ALL YOUR WISHES COME TRUE.
... ACTUALLY, BRAZ.
THERE IS ONE THING I'D LIKE YOUR HELP WITH......
YOU'RE A GOOD ACTOR, AREN'T YOU?
......
To Be Continued

UNIDENTIFIED TENGU

A MYSTERIOUS TENGU
THAT SUDDENLY
APPEARED. ITS TRUE
IDENTITY IS HIDDEN.
IF IT FINDS YOU,
IT'LL BEAT YOU UP.

BLOOD LAD

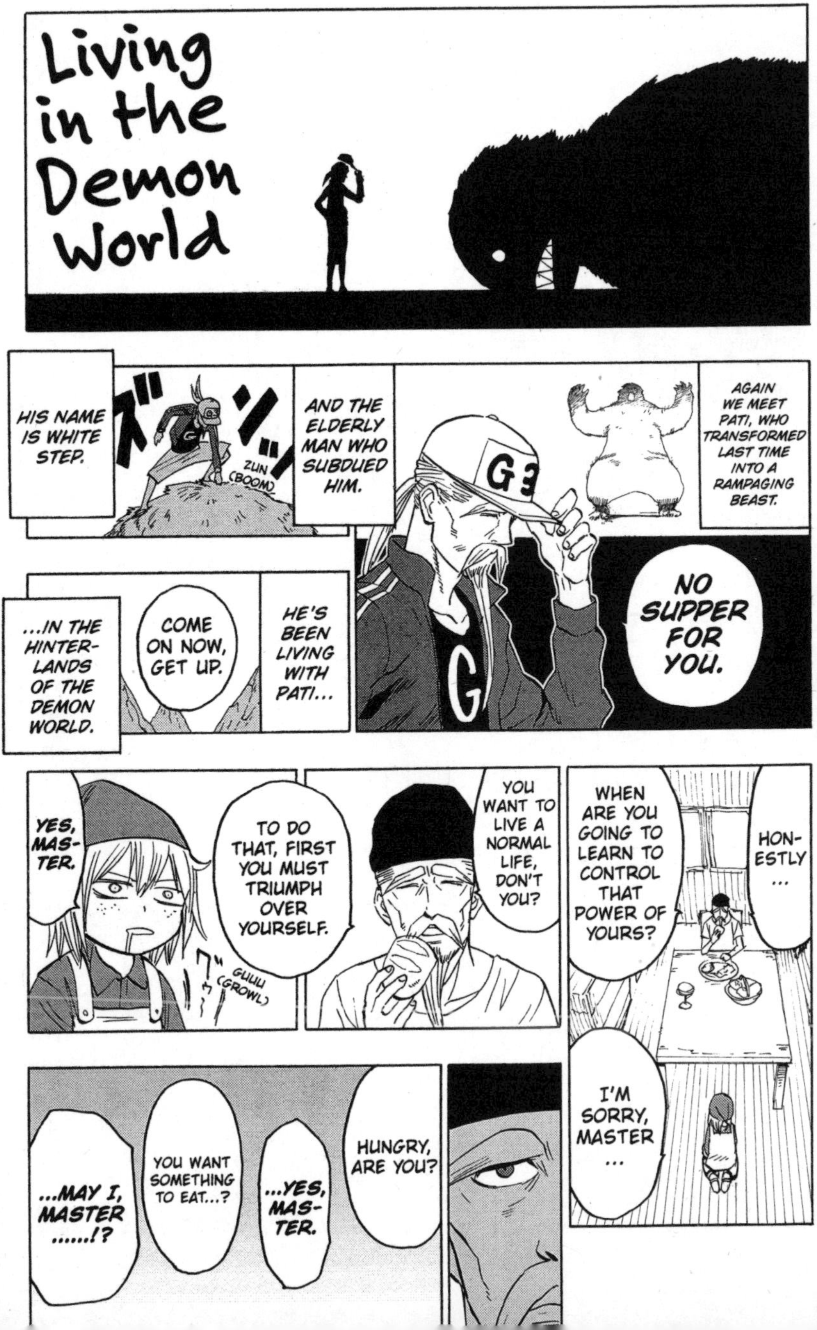

Living in the Demon World
AGAIN WE MEET PATI, WHO TRANSFORMED LAST TIME INTO A RAMPAGING BEAST.
AND THE ELDERLY MAN WHO SUBDUED HIM.
NO SUPPER FOR YOU.
HIS NAME IS WHITE STEP.
ズン
ZUN (BOOM)
HE'S BEEN LIVING WITH PATI...
COME ON NOW, GET UP.
...IN THE HINTER-LANDS OF THE DEMON WORLD.
HON-ESTLY...
WHEN ARE YOU GOING TO LEARN TO CONTROL THAT POWER OF YOURS?
I'M SORRY, MASTER...
YOU WANT TO LIVE A NORMAL LIFE, DON'T YOU?
TO DO THAT, FIRST YOU MUST TRIUMPH OVER YOURSELF.
YES, MAS-TER.
GUUU (GROWL)
HUNGRY, ARE YOU?
...YES, MAS-TER.
YOU WANT SOMETHING TO EAT...?
...MAY I, MASTER ......!?

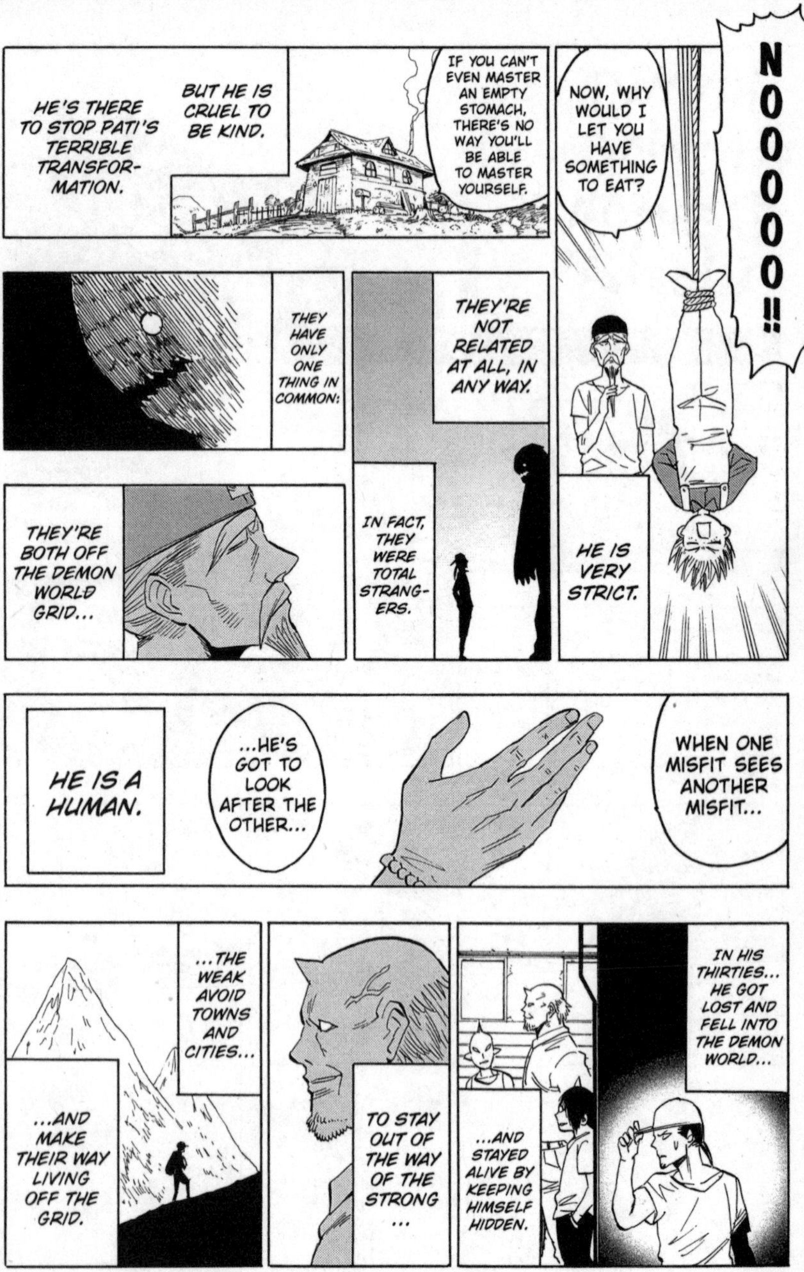
NOW, WHY WOULD I LET YOU HAVE SOMETHING TO EAT?
NOOOOOO!!
HE IS VERY STRICT.
IF YOU CAN'T EVEN MASTER AN EMPTY STOMACH, THERE'S NO WAY YOU'LL BE ABLE TO MASTER YOURSELF.
BUT HE IS CRUEL TO BE KIND.
HE'S THERE TO STOP PATI'S TERRIBLE TRANSFORMATION.
THEY'RE NOT RELATED AT ALL, IN ANY WAY.
IN FACT, THEY WERE TOTAL STRANGERS.
THEY HAVE ONLY ONE THING IN COMMON:
THEY'RE BOTH OFF THE DEMON WORLD GRID...
WHEN ONE MISFIT SEES ANOTHER MISFIT...
...HE'S GOT TO LOOK AFTER THE OTHER...
HE IS A HUMAN.
IN HIS THIRTIES... HE GOT LOST AND FELL INTO THE DEMON WORLD...
...AND STAYED ALIVE BY KEEPING HIMSELF HIDDEN.
TO STAY OUT OF THE WAY OF THE STRONG...
...THE WEAK AVOID TOWNS AND CITIES...
...AND MAKE THEIR WAY LIVING OFF THE GRID.

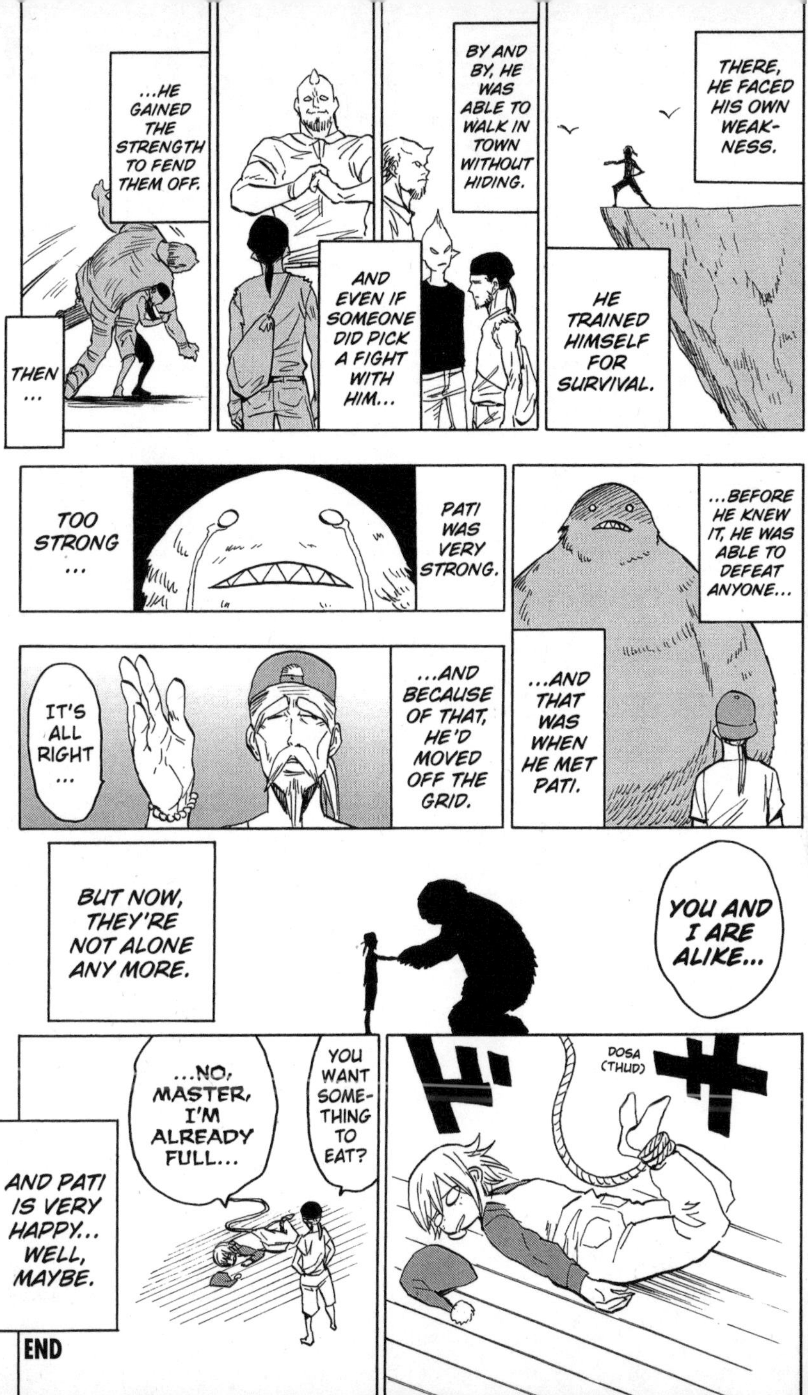
THERE, HE FACED HIS OWN WEAKNESS.
HE TRAINED HIMSELF FOR SURVIVAL.
BY AND BY, HE WAS ABLE TO WALK IN TOWN WITHOUT HIDING.
AND EVEN IF SOMEONE DID PICK A FIGHT WITH HIM...
...HE GAINED THE STRENGTH TO FEND THEM OFF.
THEN ...
...BEFORE HE KNEW IT, HE WAS ABLE TO DEFEAT ANYONE...
...AND THAT WAS WHEN HE MET PATI.
PATI WAS VERY STRONG.
TOO STRONG ...
...AND BECAUSE OF THAT, HE'D MOVED OFF THE GRID.
IT'S ALL RIGHT ...
YOU AND I ARE ALIKE...
BUT NOW, THEY'RE NOT ALONE ANY MORE.
DOSA (THUD)
YOU WANT SOMETHING TO EAT?
...NO, MASTER, I'M ALREADY FULL...
AND PATI IS VERY HAPPY... WELL, MAYBE.
END

BLOOD LAD 11

These images appeared under the jacket of the original edition of *Blood Lad*!

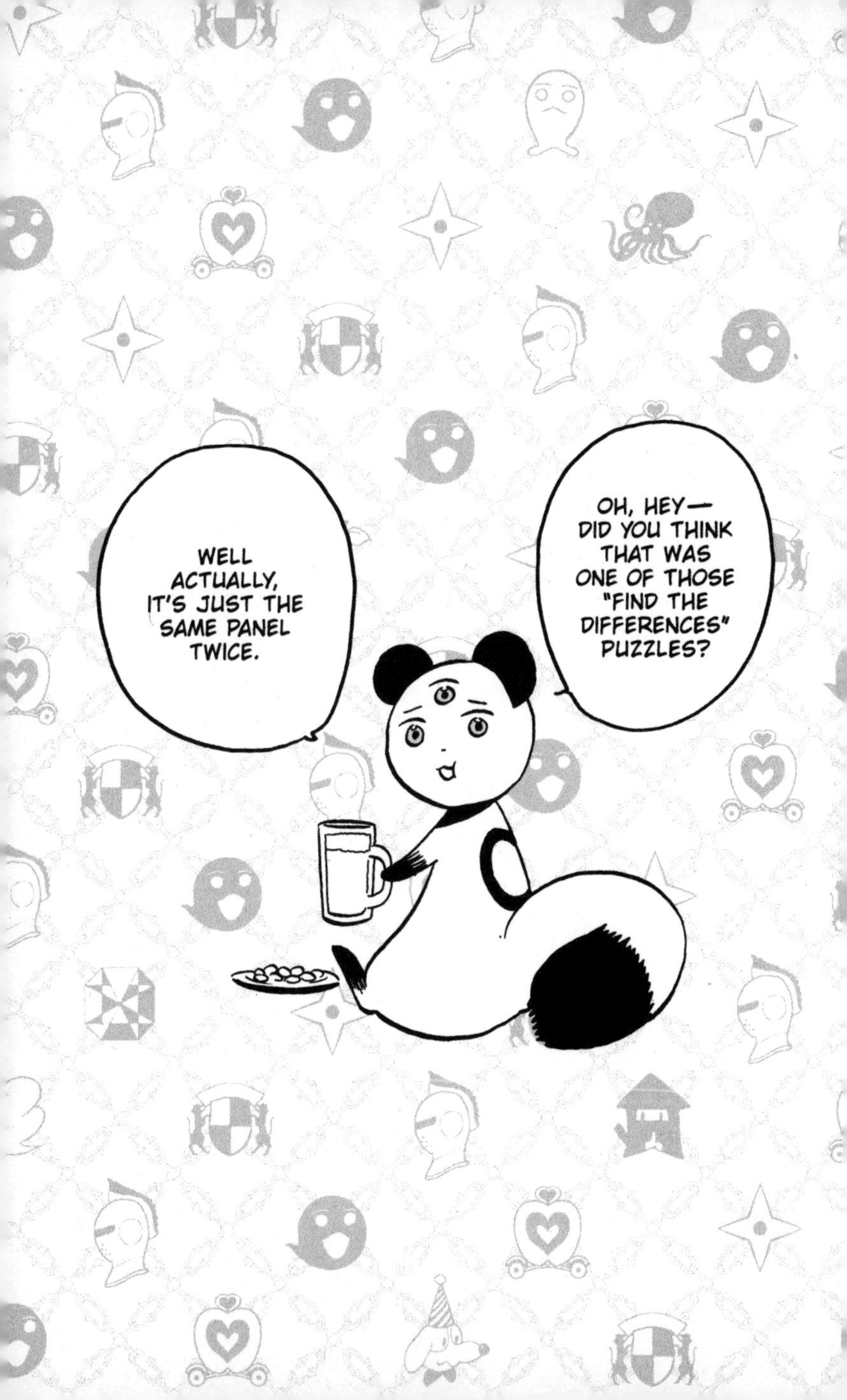
OH, HEY— DID YOU THINK THAT WAS ONE OF THOSE "FIND THE DIFFERENCES" PUZZLES?
WELL ACTUALLY, IT'S JUST THE SAME PANEL TWICE.

BLOOD LAD

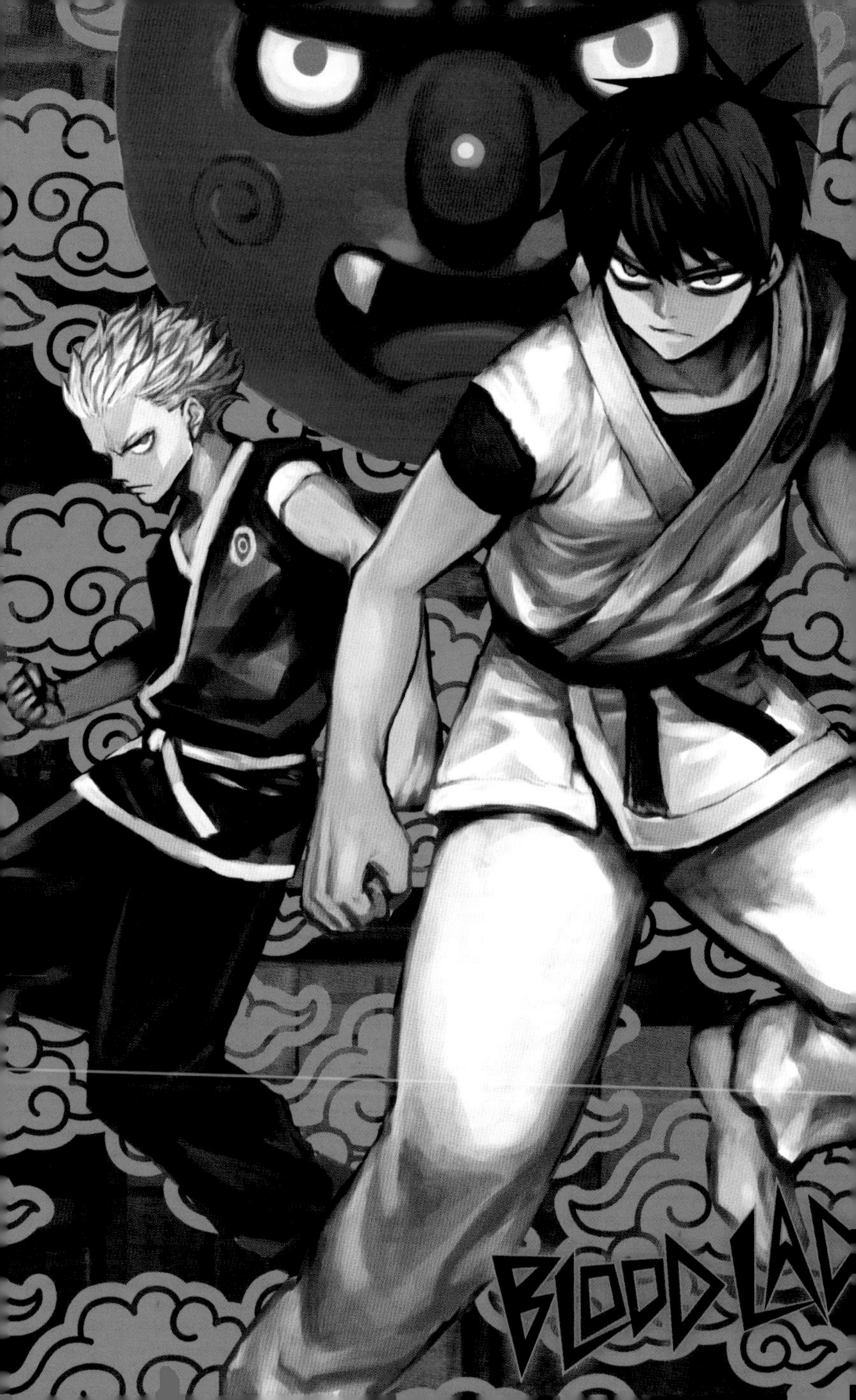
BLOOD LAD

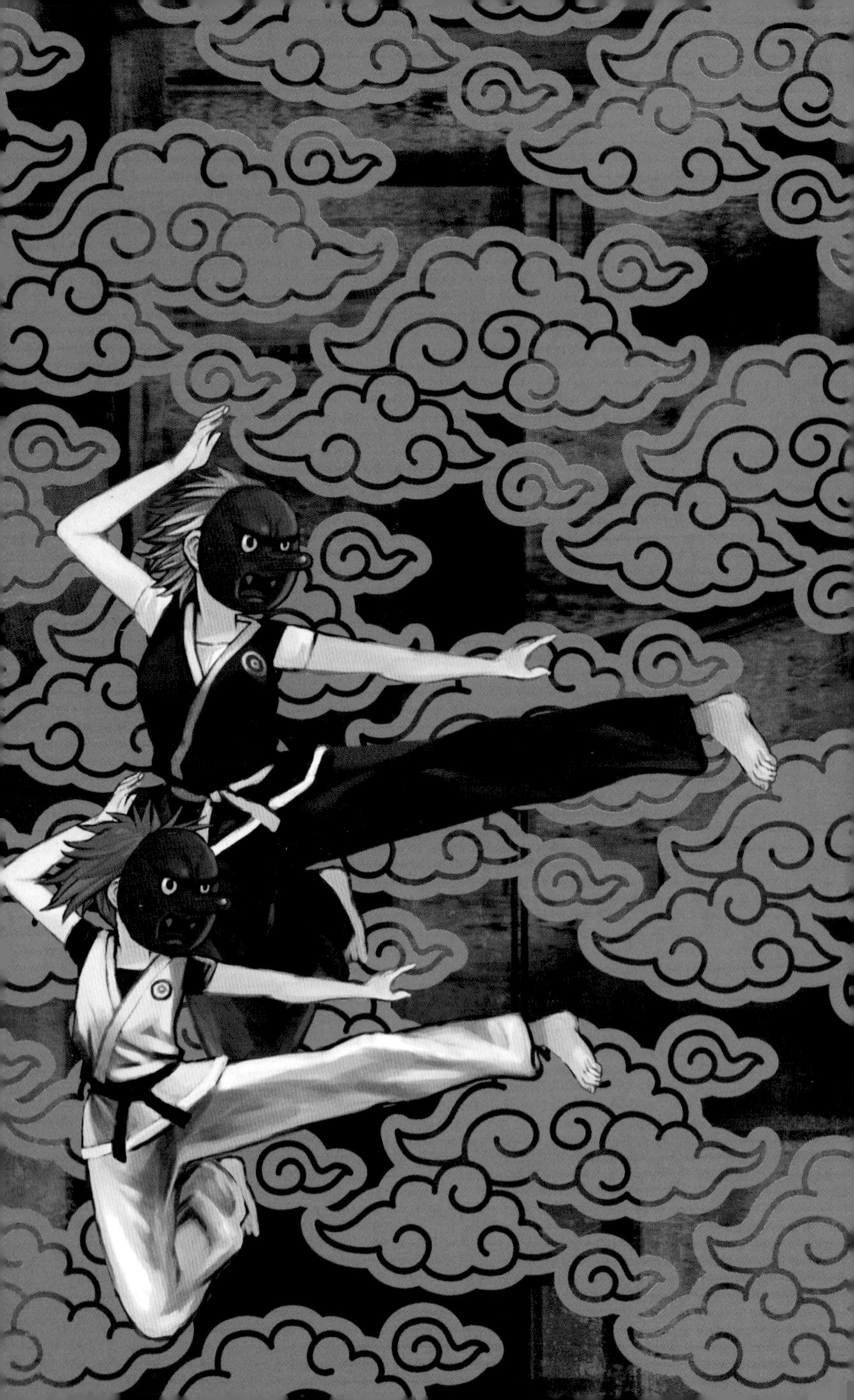

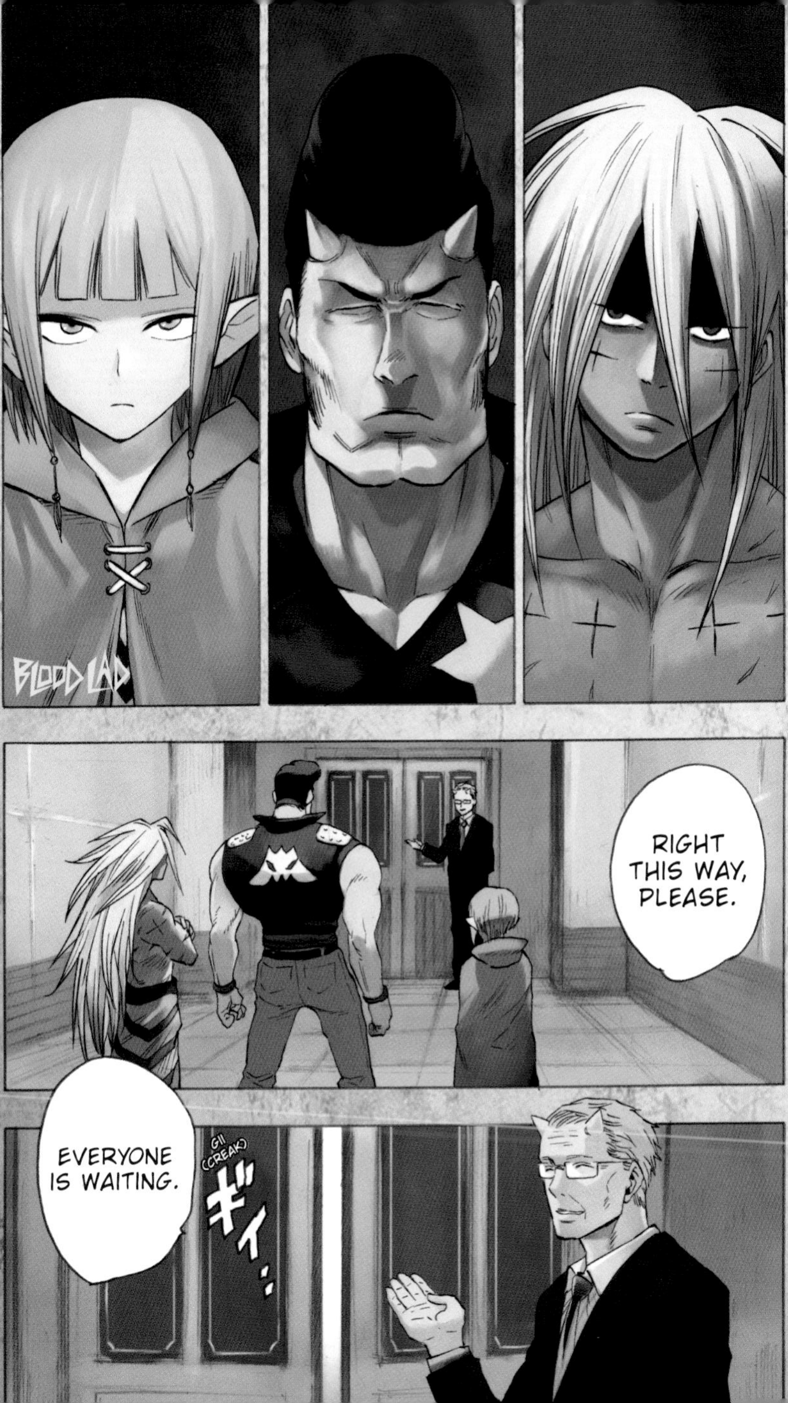
BLOOD LAD
RIGHT THIS WAY, PLEASE.
EVERYONE IS WAITING.
ギイ…
GII (CREAK)

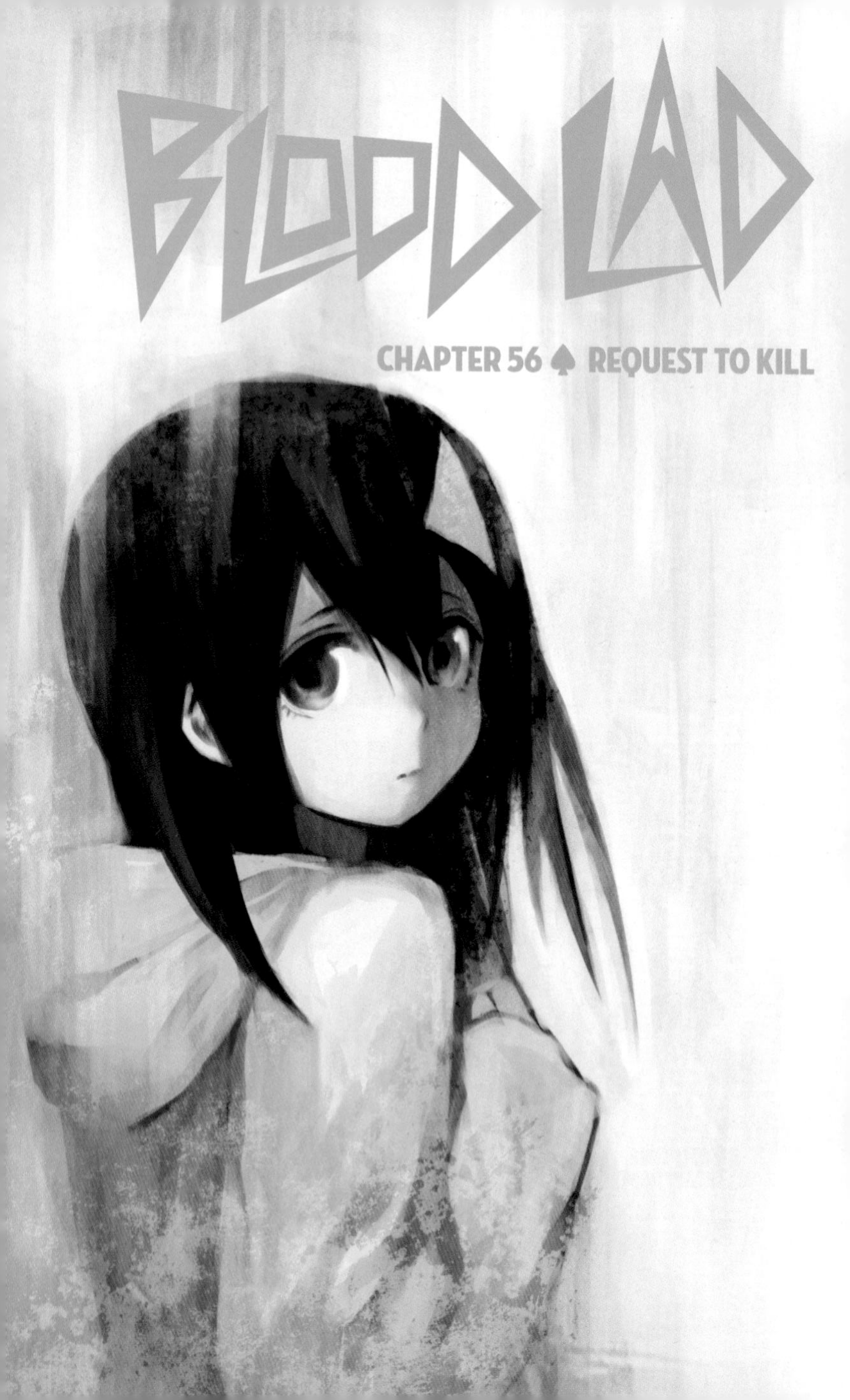
BLOOD LAD
CHAPTER 56 ♠ REQUEST TO KILL

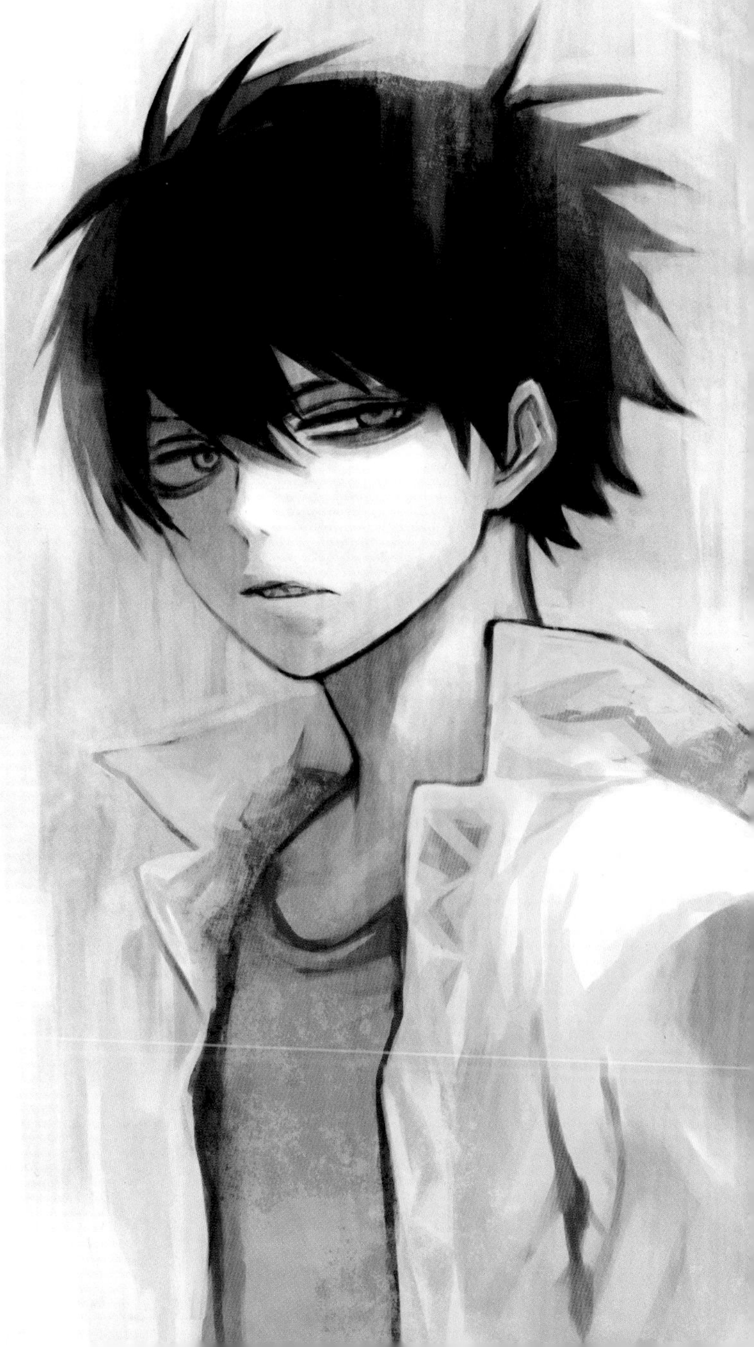

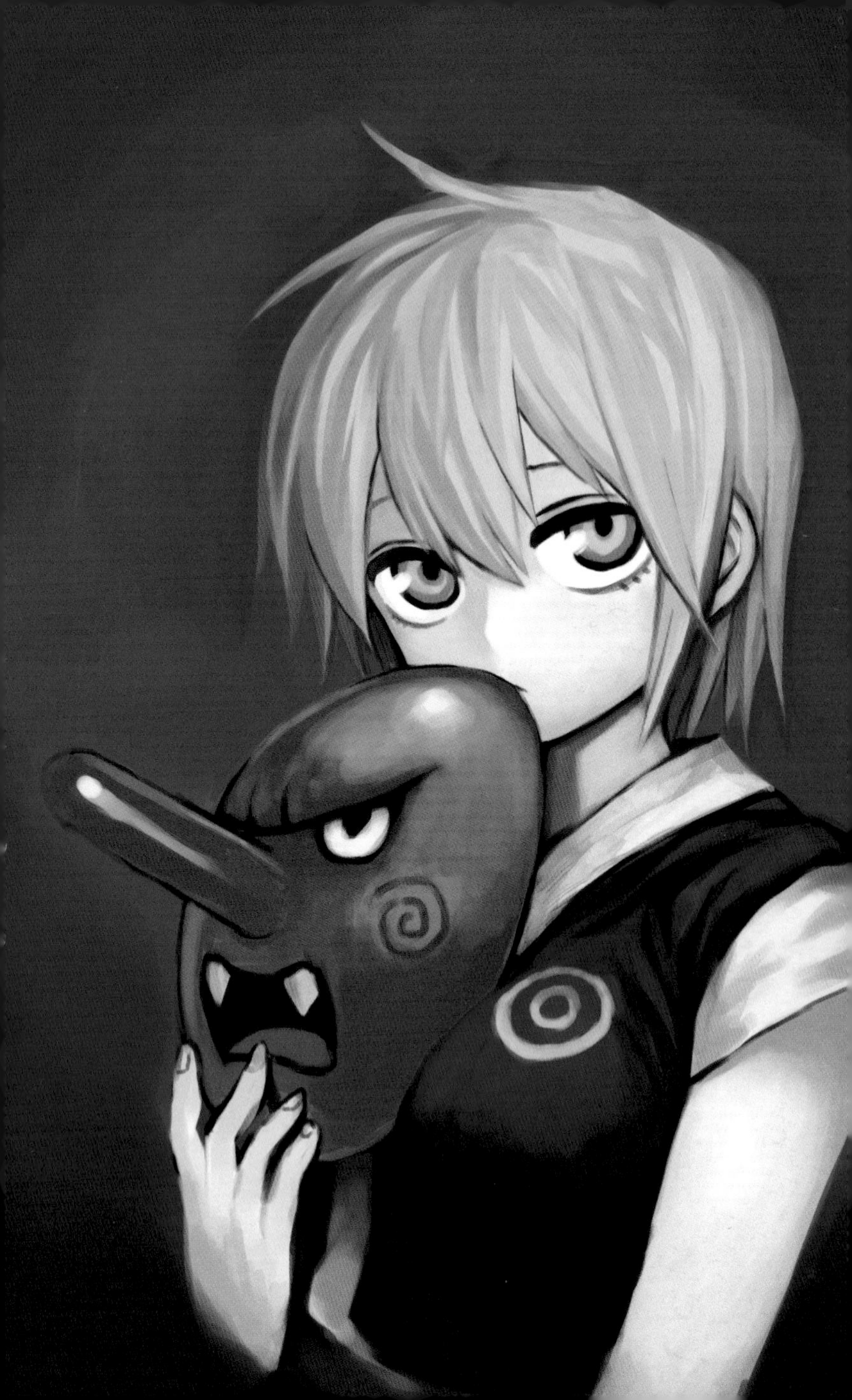

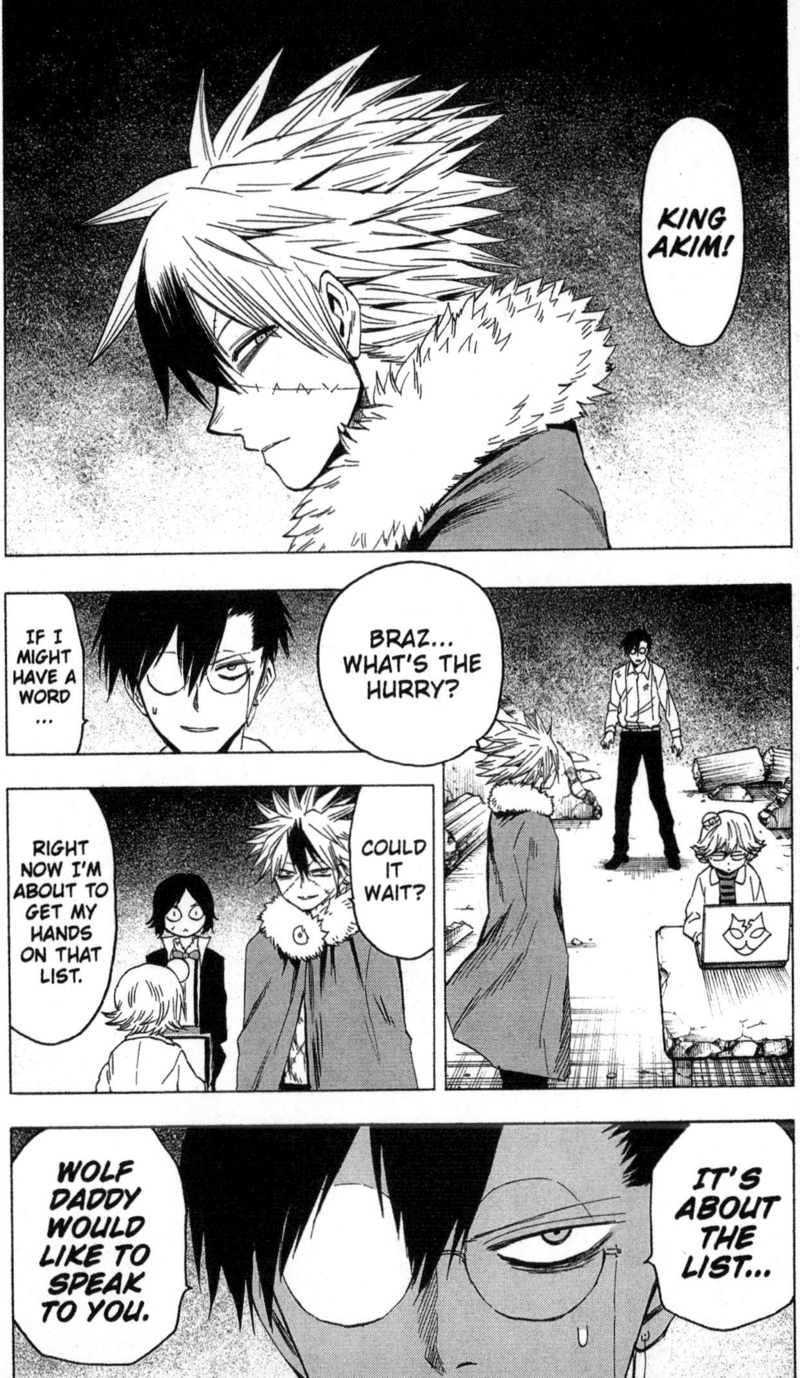
KING AKIM!
BRAZ... WHAT'S THE HURRY?
IF I MIGHT HAVE A WORD...
COULD IT WAIT?
RIGHT NOW I'M ABOUT TO GET MY HANDS ON THAT LIST.
IT'S ABOUT THE LIST...
WOLF DADDY WOULD LIKE TO SPEAK TO YOU.

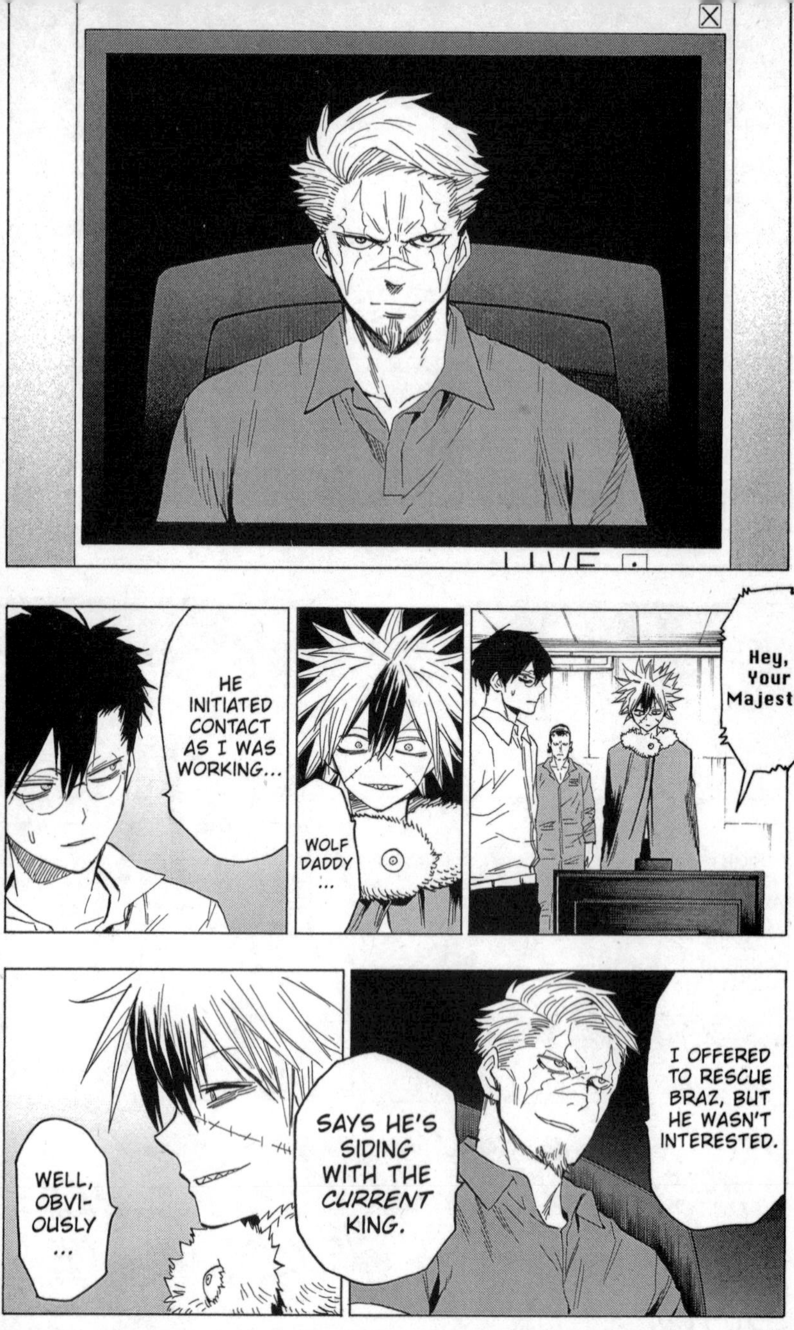
Hey, Your Majesty.
WOLF DADDY ...
HE INITIATED CONTACT AS I WAS WORKING...
I OFFERED TO RESCUE BRAZ, BUT HE WASN'T INTERESTED.
SAYS HE'S SIDING WITH THE *CURRENT* KING.
WELL, OBVI-OUSLY ...

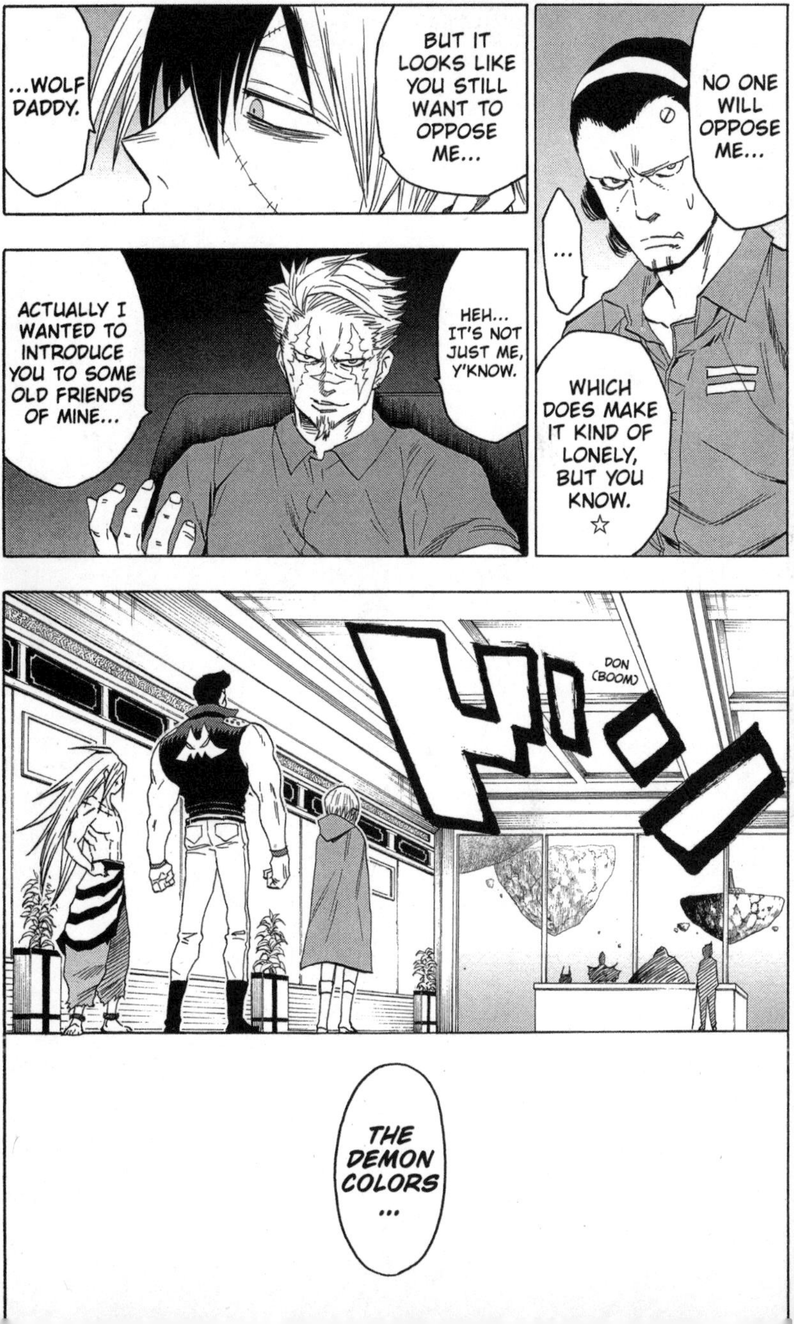
NO ONE WILL OPPOSE ME...
...
WHICH DOES MAKE IT KIND OF LONELY, BUT YOU KNOW. ☆
BUT IT LOOKS LIKE YOU STILL WANT TO OPPOSE ME...
...WOLF DADDY.
HEH... IT'S NOT JUST ME, Y'KNOW.
ACTUALLY I WANTED TO INTRODUCE YOU TO SOME OLD FRIENDS OF MINE...
DON (BOOM)
THE DEMON COLORS ...

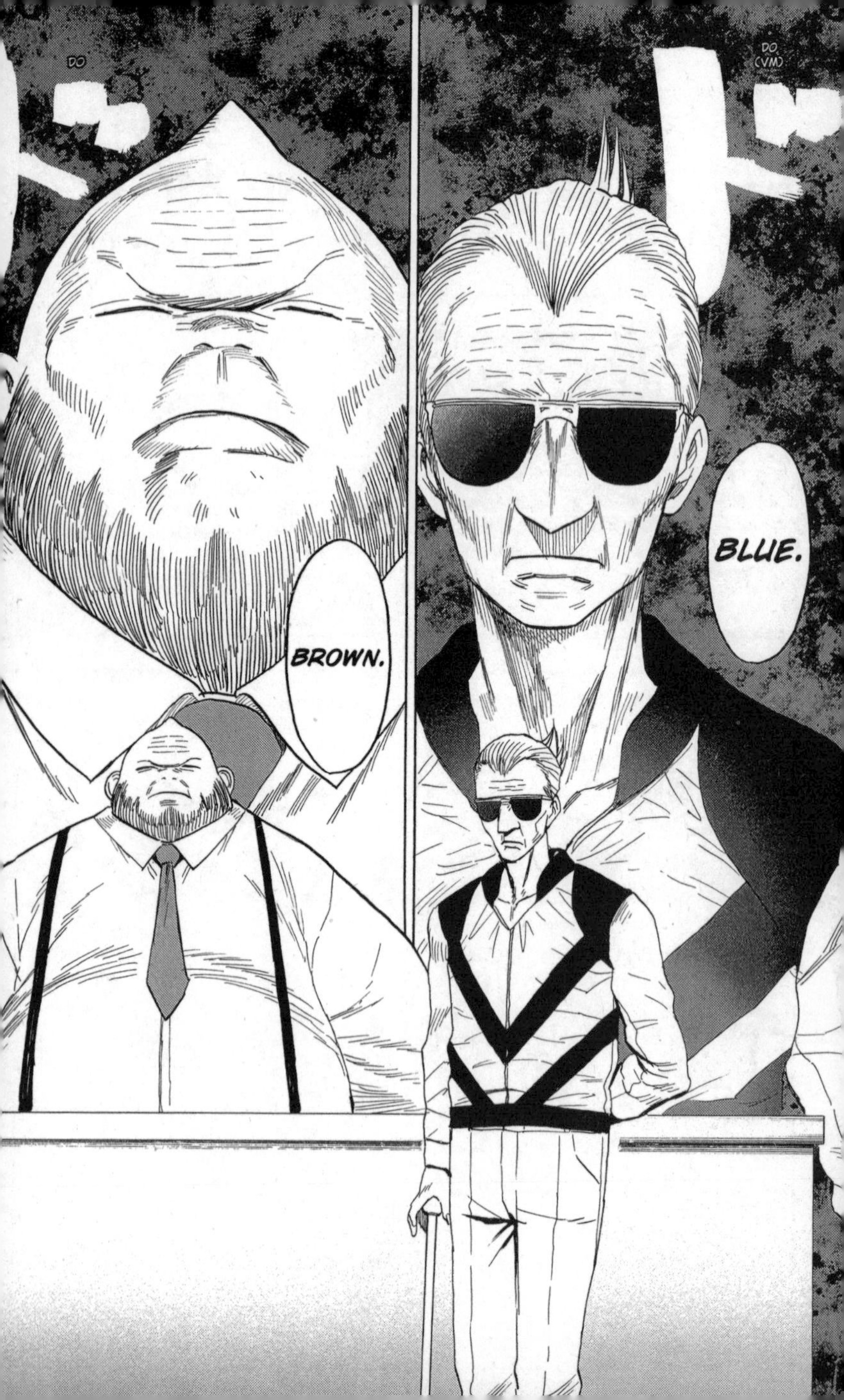
DO (VM)
BLUE.
DO
BROWN.

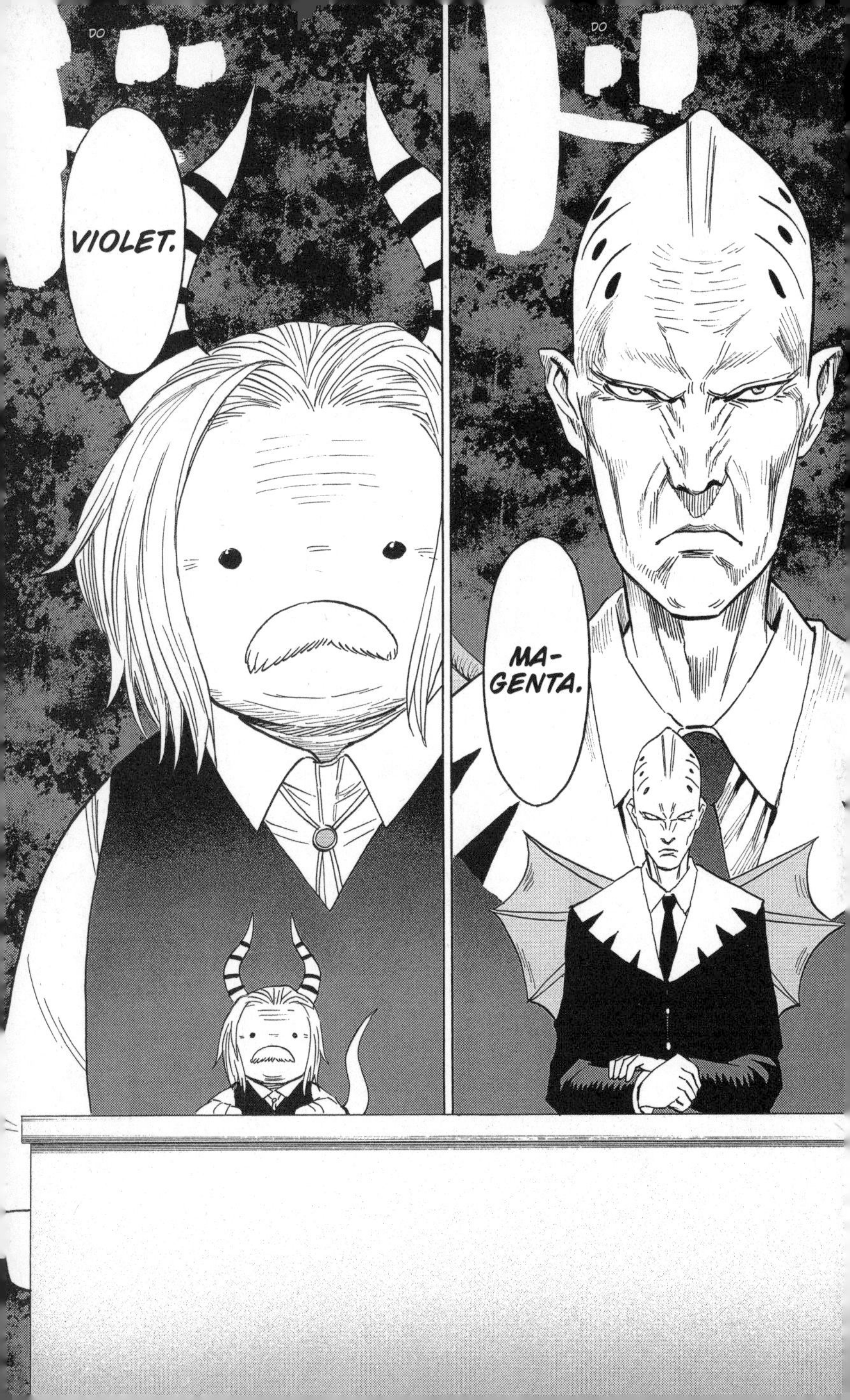
DO
MA-GENTA.
DO
VIOLET.

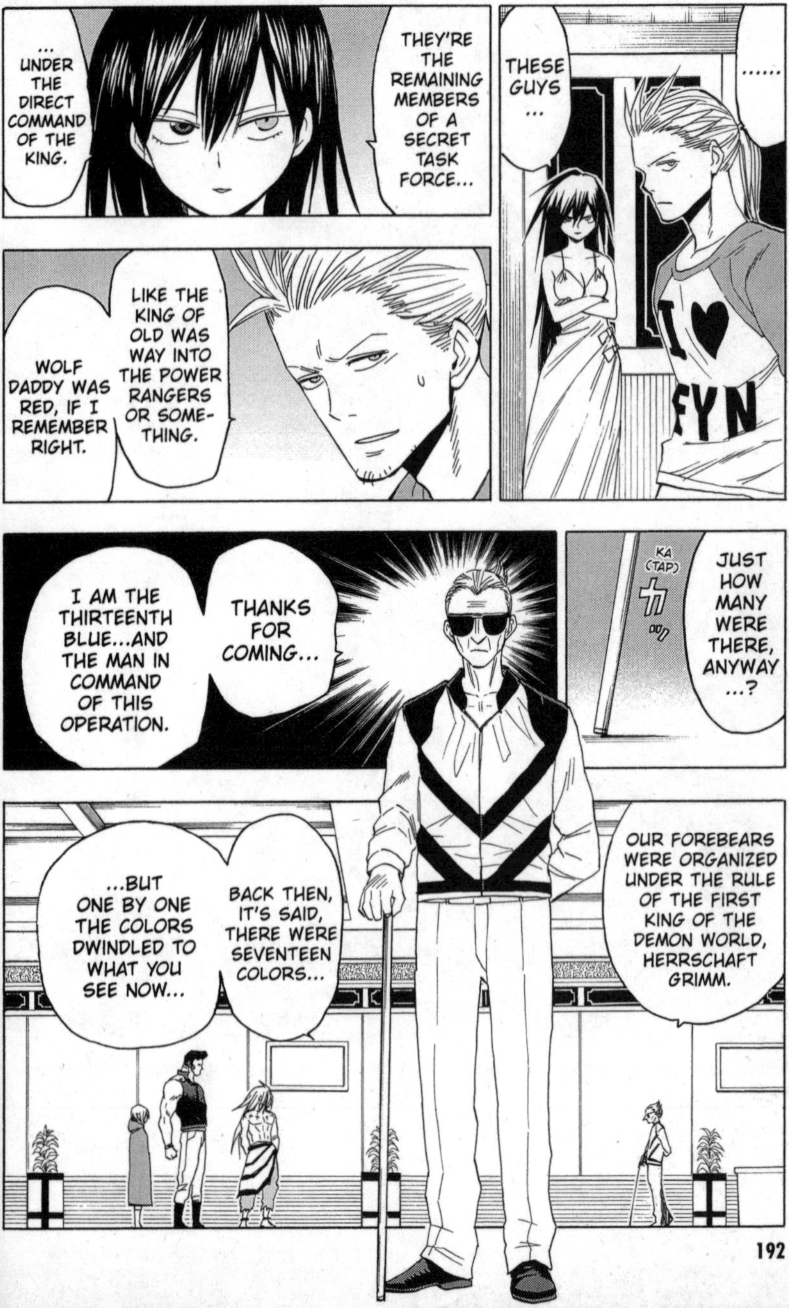
......
THESE GUYS...
THEY'RE THE REMAINING MEMBERS OF A SECRET TASK FORCE...
...UNDER THE DIRECT COMMAND OF THE KING.
LIKE THE KING OF OLD WAS WAY INTO THE POWER RANGERS OR SOMETHING.
WOLF DADDY WAS RED, IF I REMEMBER RIGHT.
JUST HOW MANY WERE THERE, ANYWAY...?
KA (TAP)
カッ
THANKS FOR COMING...
I AM THE THIRTEENTH BLUE...AND THE MAN IN COMMAND OF THIS OPERATION.
OUR FOREBEARS WERE ORGANIZED UNDER THE RULE OF THE FIRST KING OF THE DEMON WORLD, HERRSCHAFT GRIMM.
BACK THEN, IT'S SAID, THERE WERE SEVENTEEN COLORS...
...BUT ONE BY ONE THE COLORS DWINDLED TO WHAT YOU SEE NOW...
FYN

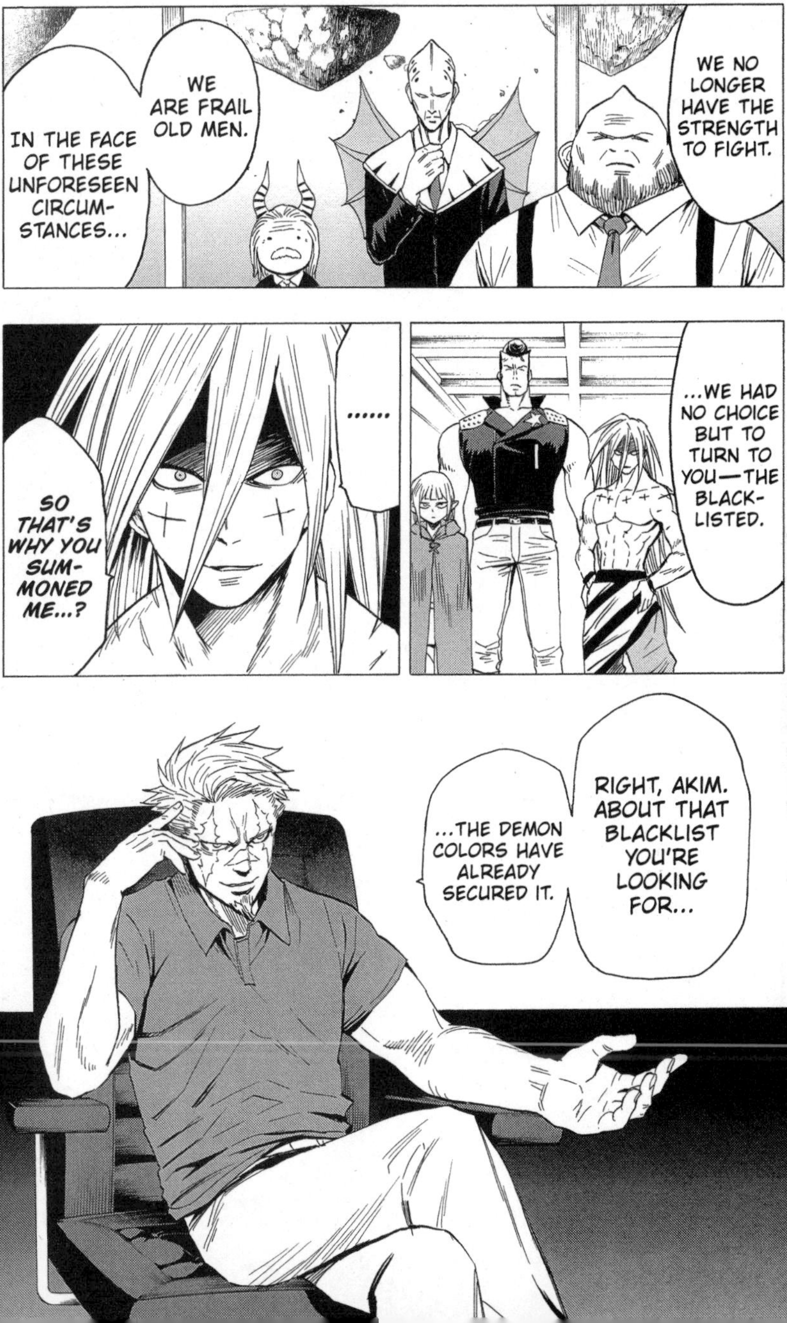
WE NO LONGER HAVE THE STRENGTH TO FIGHT.
WE ARE FRAIL OLD MEN.
IN THE FACE OF THESE UNFORESEEN CIRCUM-STANCES...
...WE HAD NO CHOICE BUT TO TURN TO YOU—THE BLACK-LISTED.
......
SO THAT'S WHY YOU SUM-MONED ME...?
RIGHT, AKIM. ABOUT THAT BLACKLIST YOU'RE LOOKING FOR...
...THE DEMON COLORS HAVE ALREADY SECURED IT.

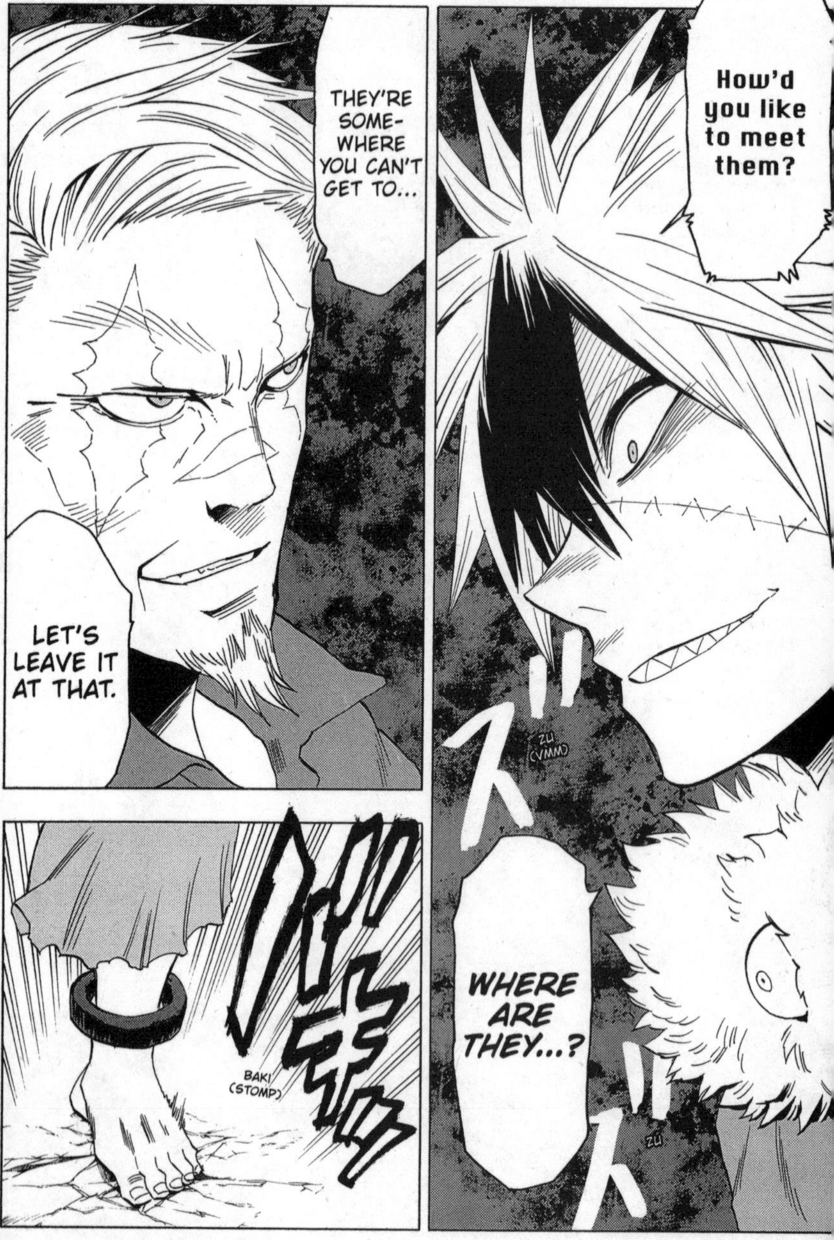
How'd you like to meet them?
ZU (VMM)
WHERE ARE THEY...?
ZU
THEY'RE SOME-WHERE YOU CAN'T GET TO...
LET'S LEAVE IT AT THAT.
BAKI (STOMP)

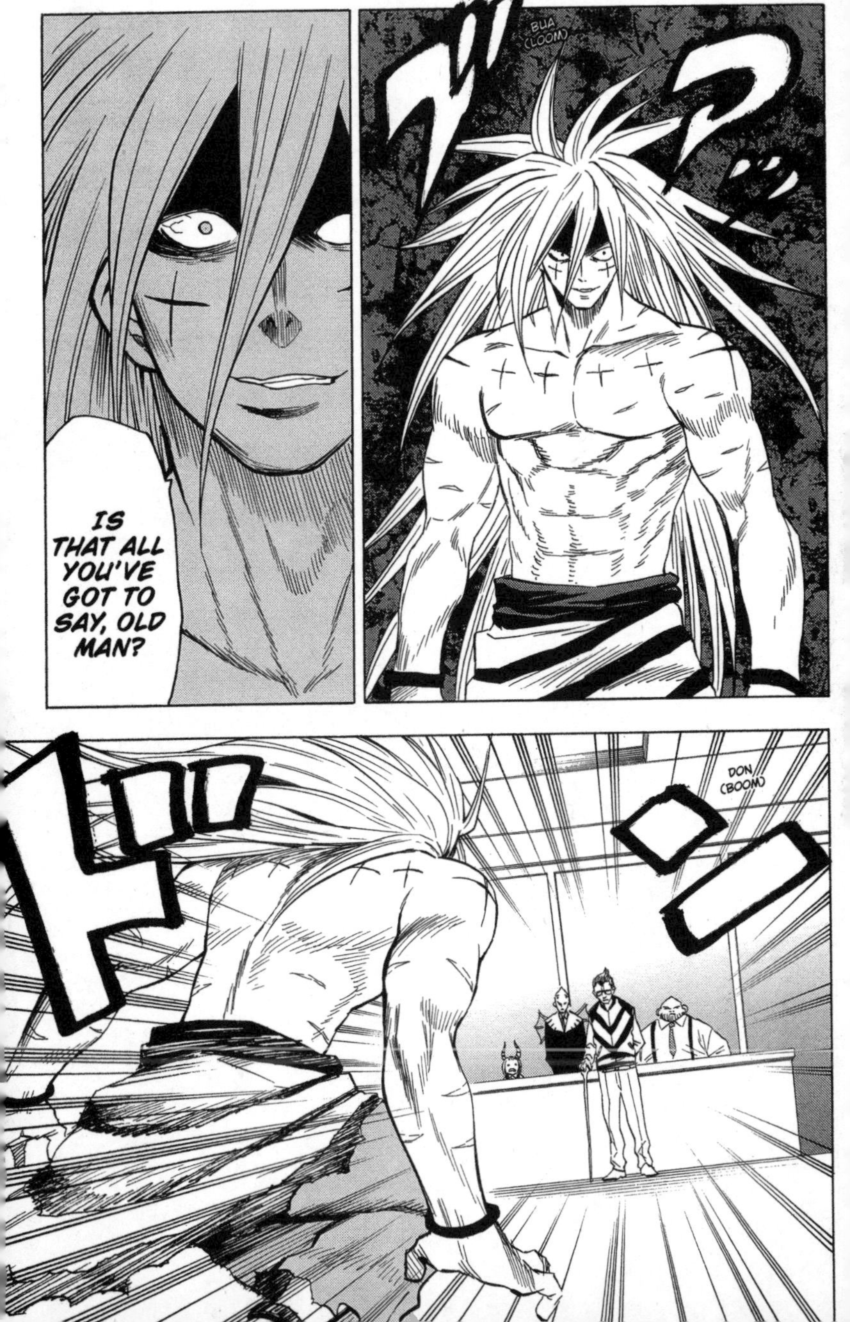
BUA (LOOM)
IS THAT ALL YOU'VE GOT TO SAY, OLD MAN?
DON (BOOM)

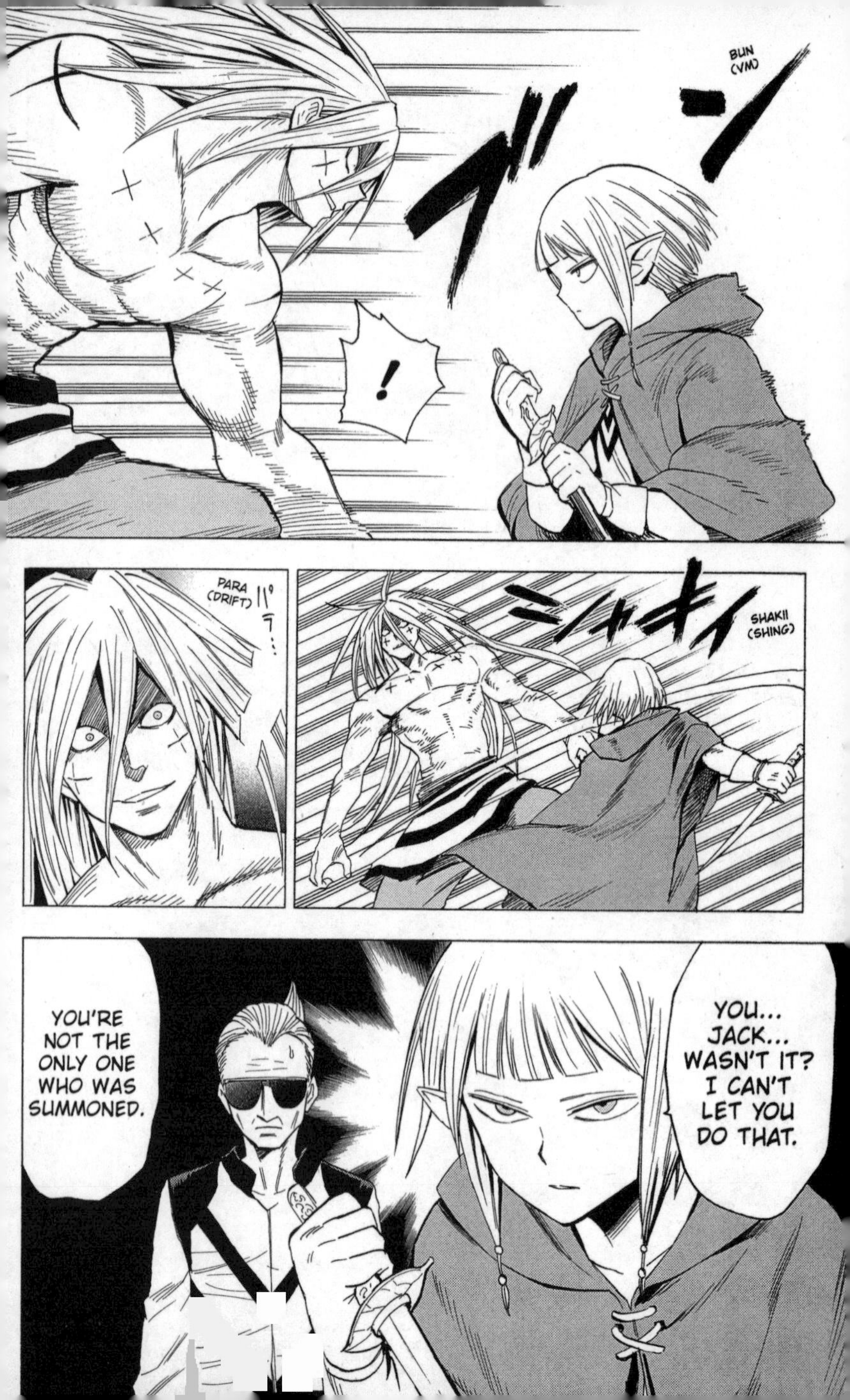
BUN (VM)
!
SHAKII (SHING)
PARA (DRIFT)
YOU... JACK... WASN'T IT? I CAN'T LET YOU DO THAT.
YOU'RE NOT THE ONLY ONE WHO WAS SUMMONED.

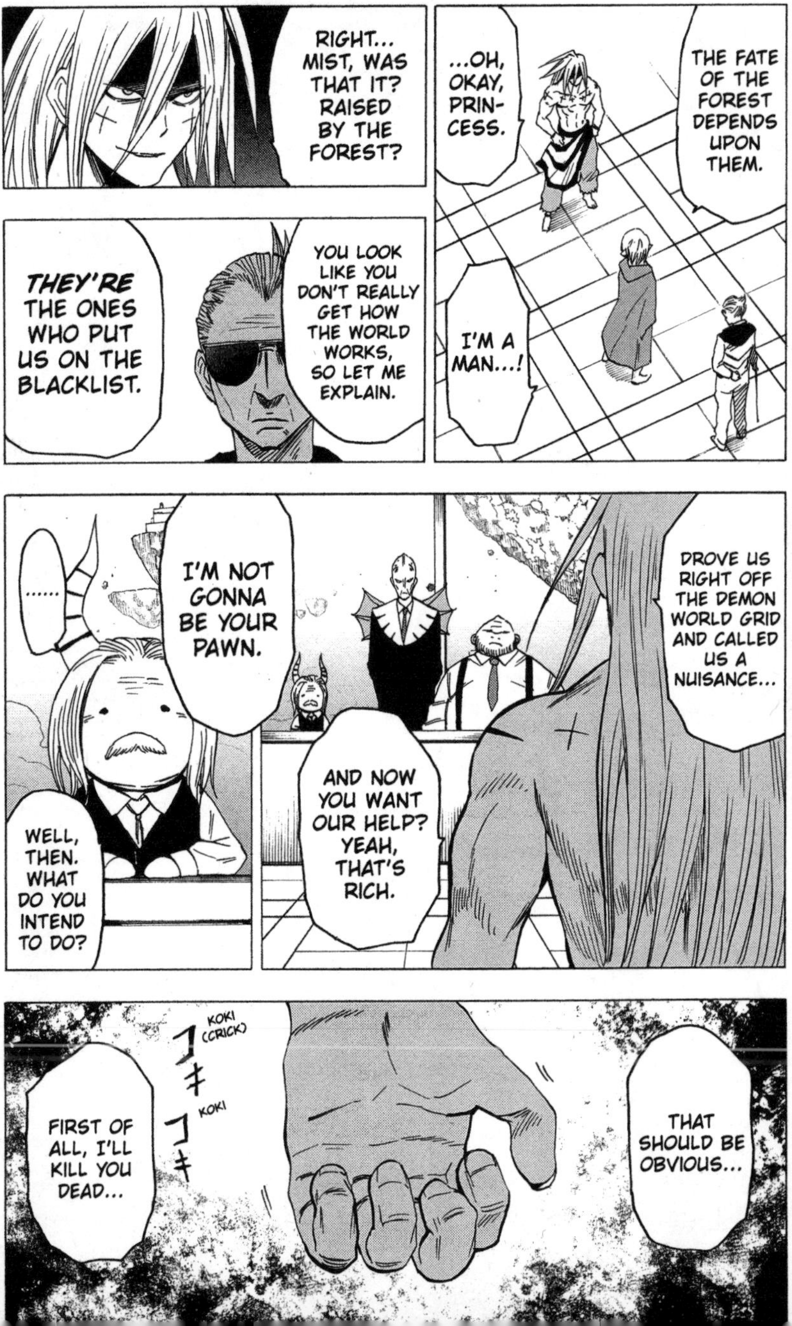
THE FATE OF THE FOREST DEPENDS UPON THEM.
...OH, OKAY, PRIN-CESS.
I'M A MAN...!
RIGHT... MIST, WAS THAT IT? RAISED BY THE FOREST?
YOU LOOK LIKE YOU DON'T REALLY GET HOW THE WORLD WORKS, SO LET ME EXPLAIN.
THEY'RE THE ONES WHO PUT US ON THE BLACKLIST.
DROVE US RIGHT OFF THE DEMON WORLD GRID AND CALLED US A NUISANCE...
AND NOW YOU WANT OUR HELP? YEAH, THAT'S RICH.
I'M NOT GONNA BE YOUR PAWN.
......
WELL, THEN. WHAT DO YOU INTEND TO DO?
THAT SHOULD BE OBVIOUS...
コキ
KOKI (CRICK)
コキ
KOKI
FIRST OF ALL, I'LL KILL YOU DEAD...

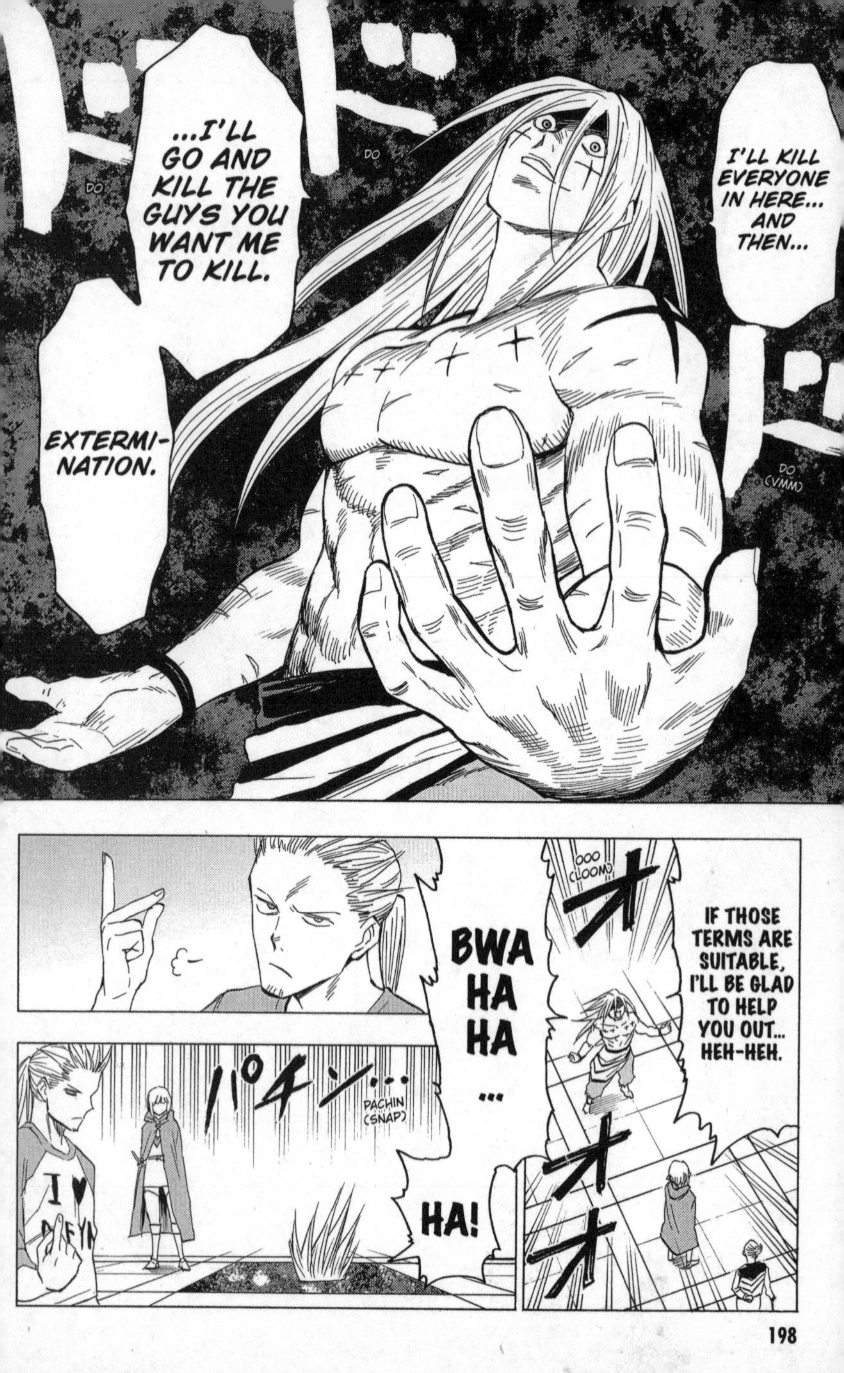
I'LL KILL EVERYONE IN HERE... AND THEN...
DO (VMM)
DO
...I'LL GO AND KILL THE GUYS YOU WANT ME TO KILL.
DO
EXTERMI-NATION.
IF THOSE TERMS ARE SUITABLE, I'LL BE GLAD TO HELP YOU OUT... HEH-HEH.
OOO (LOOM)
BWA HA HA ...
HA!
PACHIN (SNAP)

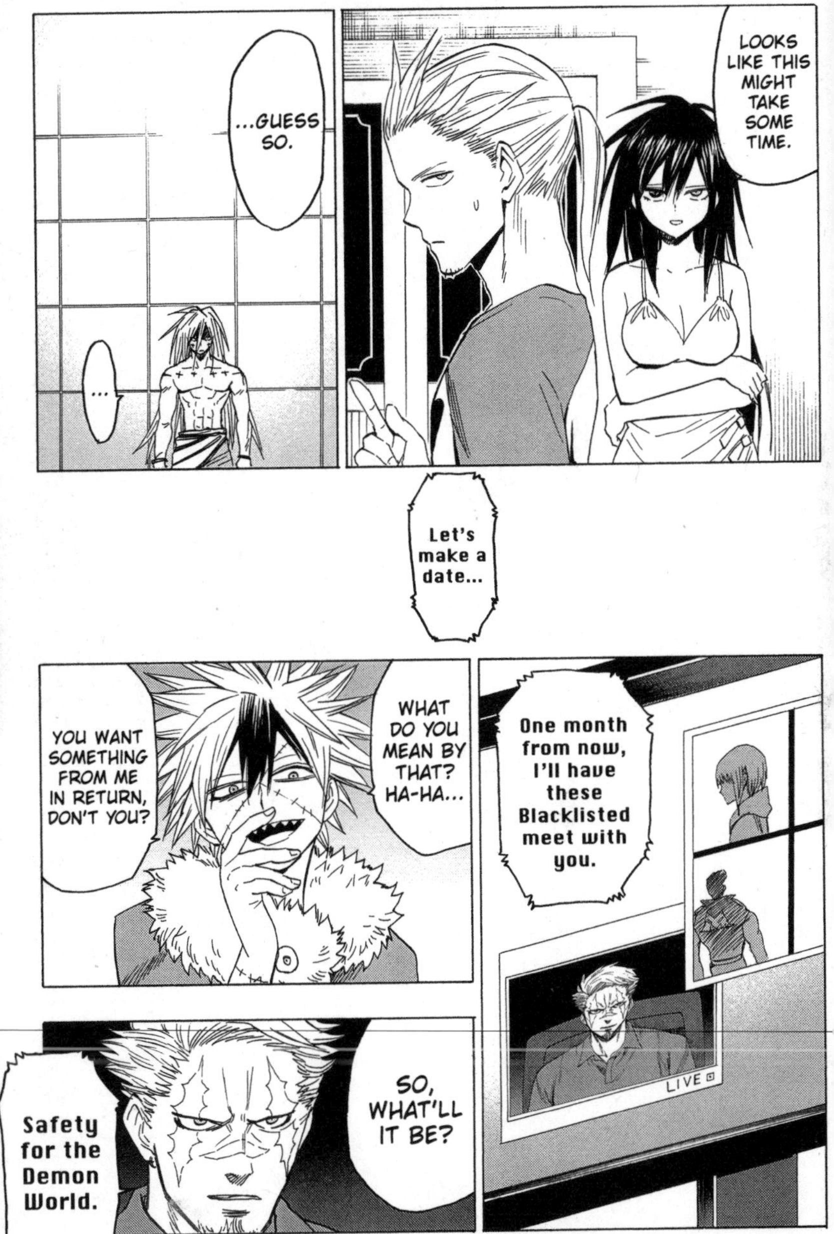
LOOKS LIKE THIS MIGHT TAKE SOME TIME.
...GUESS SO.
...
Let's make a date...
One month from now, I'll have these Blacklisted meet with you.
LIVE
WHAT DO YOU MEAN BY THAT? HA-HA...
YOU WANT SOMETHING FROM ME IN RETURN, DON'T YOU?
SO, WHAT'LL IT BE?
Safety for the Demon World.

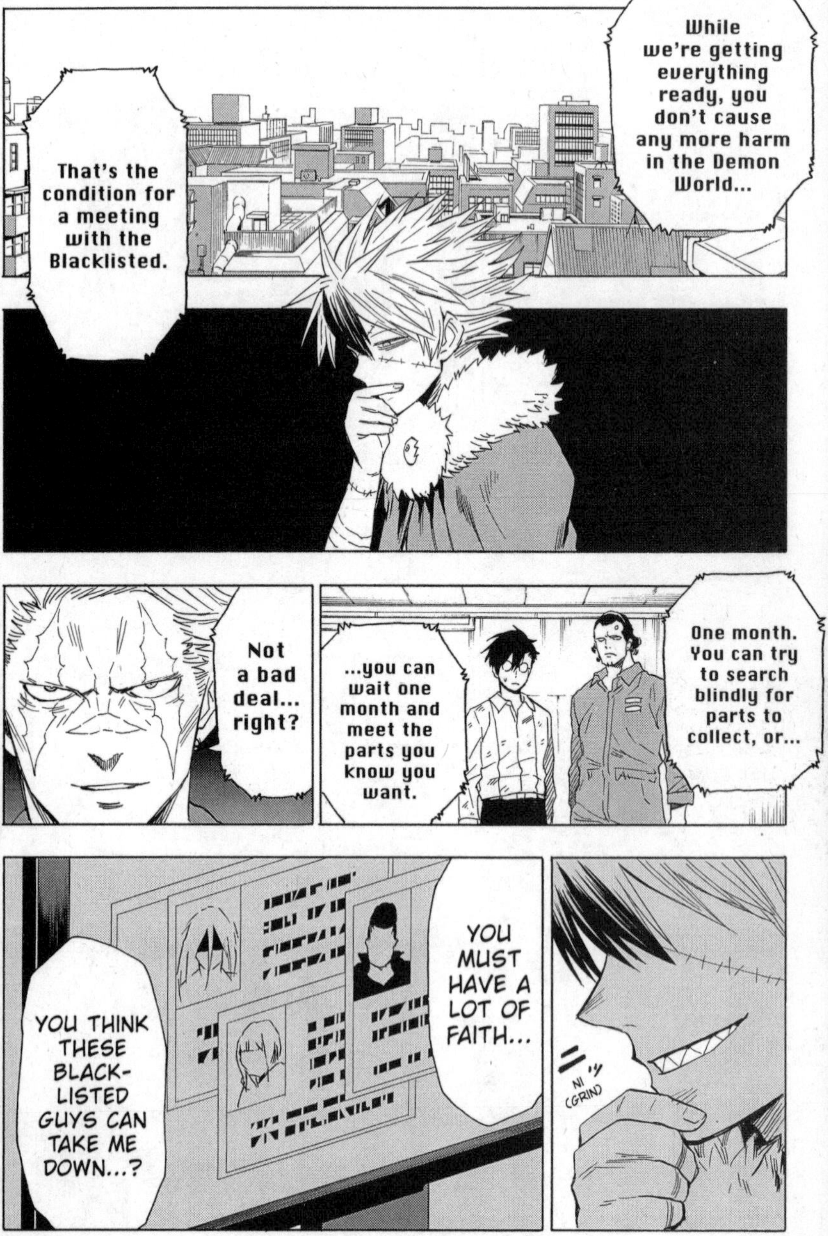
While we're getting everything ready, you don't cause any more harm in the Demon World...
That's the condition for a meeting with the Blacklisted.
One month. You can try to search blindly for parts to collect, or...
...you can wait one month and meet the parts you know you want.
Not a bad deal... right?
NI (GRIN)
YOU MUST HAVE A LOT OF FAITH...
YOU THINK THESE BLACK-LISTED GUYS CAN TAKE ME DOWN...?

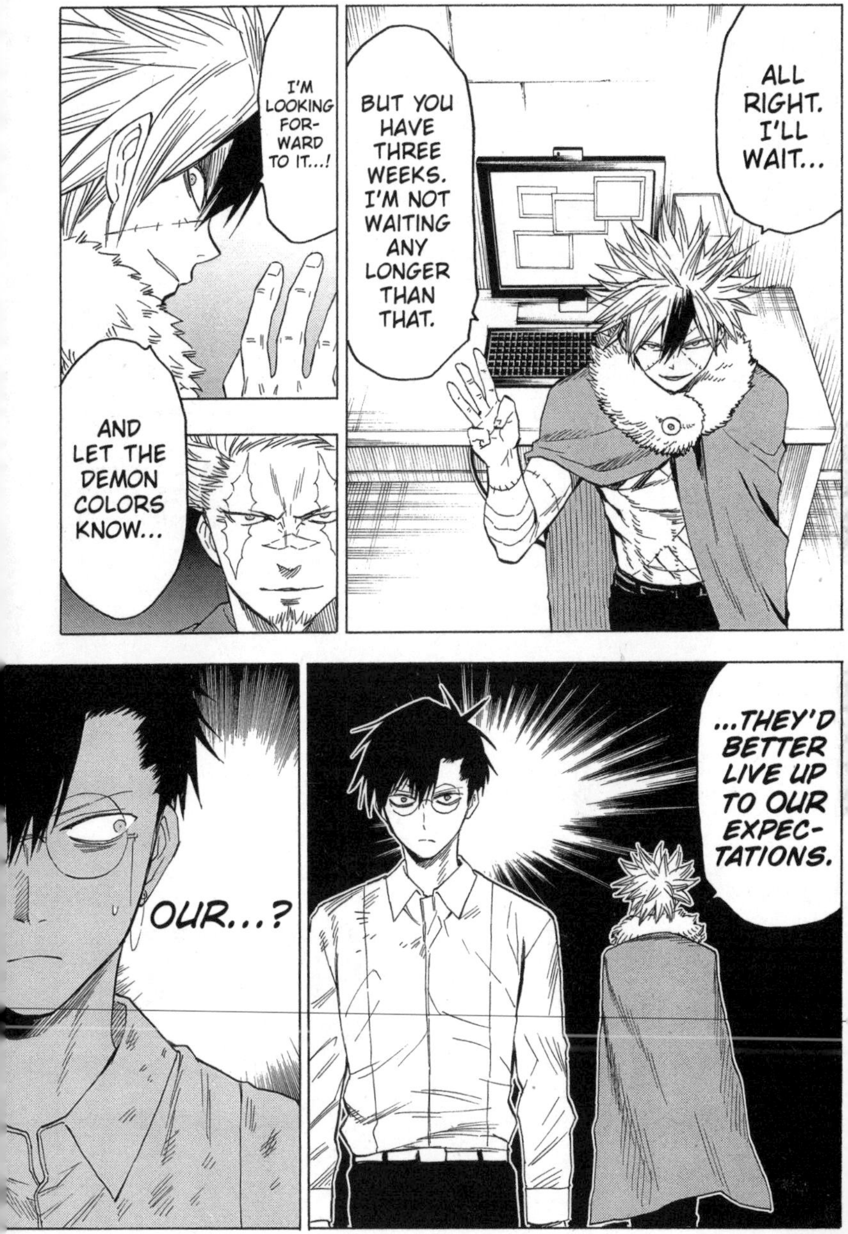
ALL RIGHT. I'LL WAIT...
BUT YOU HAVE THREE WEEKS. I'M NOT WAITING ANY LONGER THAN THAT.
I'M LOOKING FOR-WARD TO IT...!
AND LET THE DEMON COLORS KNOW...
...THEY'D BETTER LIVE UP TO OUR EXPEC-TATIONS.
OUR...?

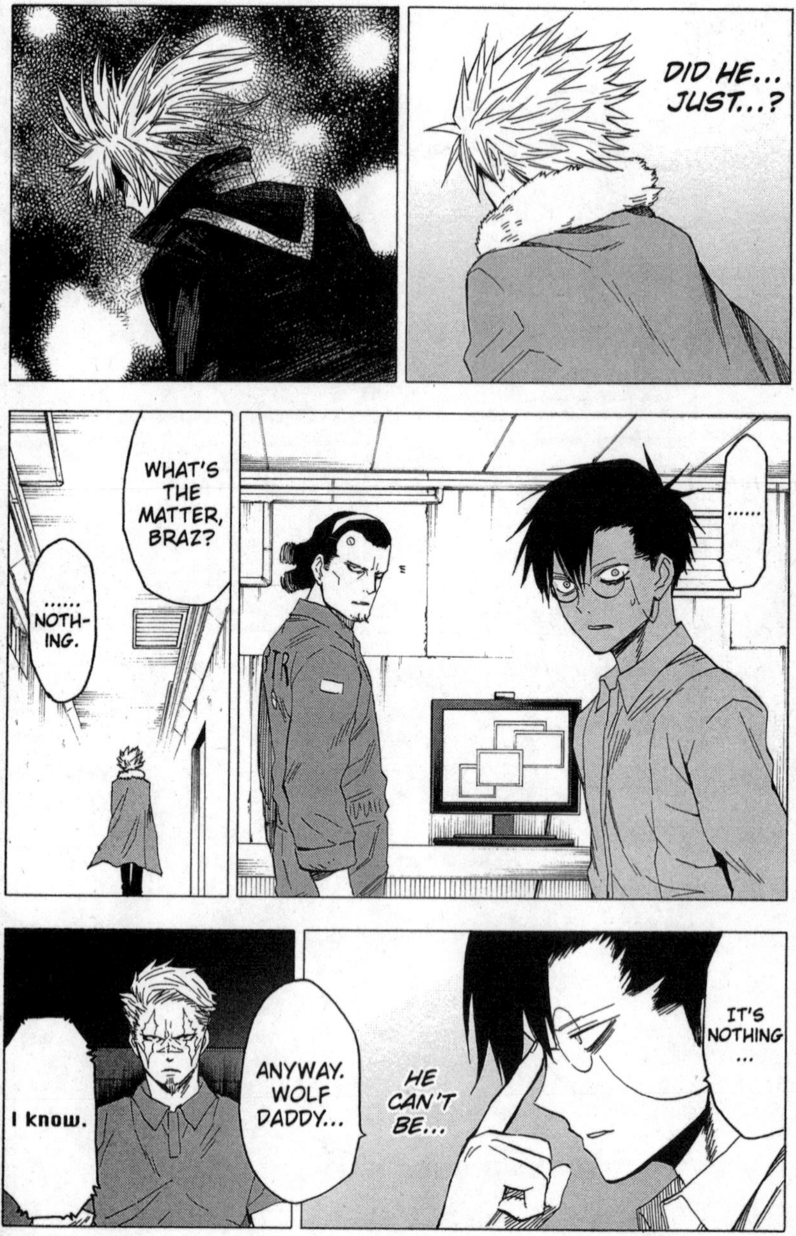
DID HE... JUST...?
......
WHAT'S THE MATTER, BRAZ?
...... NOTHING.
IT'S NOTHING ...
HE CAN'T BE...
ANYWAY. WOLF DADDY...
I know.

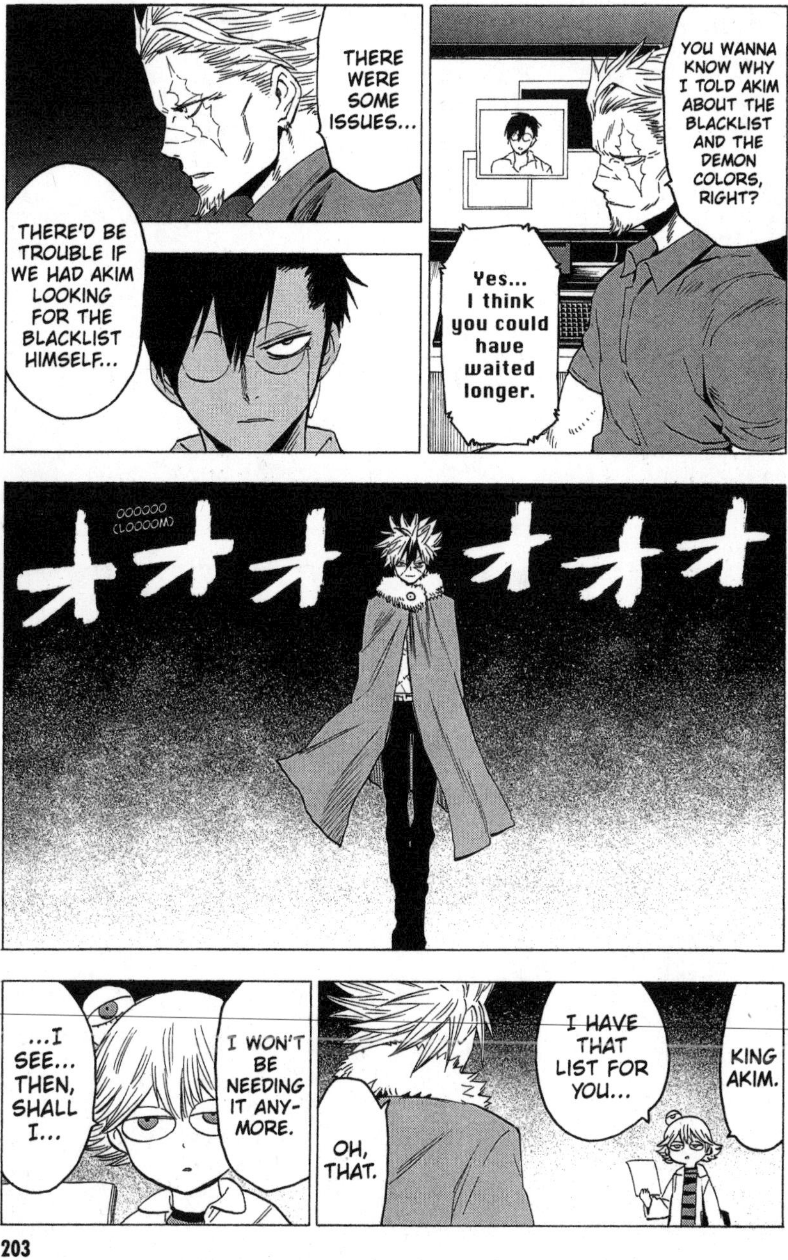
YOU WANNA KNOW WHY I TOLD AKIM ABOUT THE BLACKLIST AND THE DEMON COLORS, RIGHT?
Yes... I think you could have waited longer.
THERE WERE SOME ISSUES...
THERE'D BE TROUBLE IF WE HAD AKIM LOOKING FOR THE BLACKLIST HIMSELF...
OOOOOO (LOOOOM)
KING AKIM.
I HAVE THAT LIST FOR YOU...
OH, THAT.
I WON'T BE NEEDING IT ANY-MORE.
...I SEE... THEN, SHALL I...

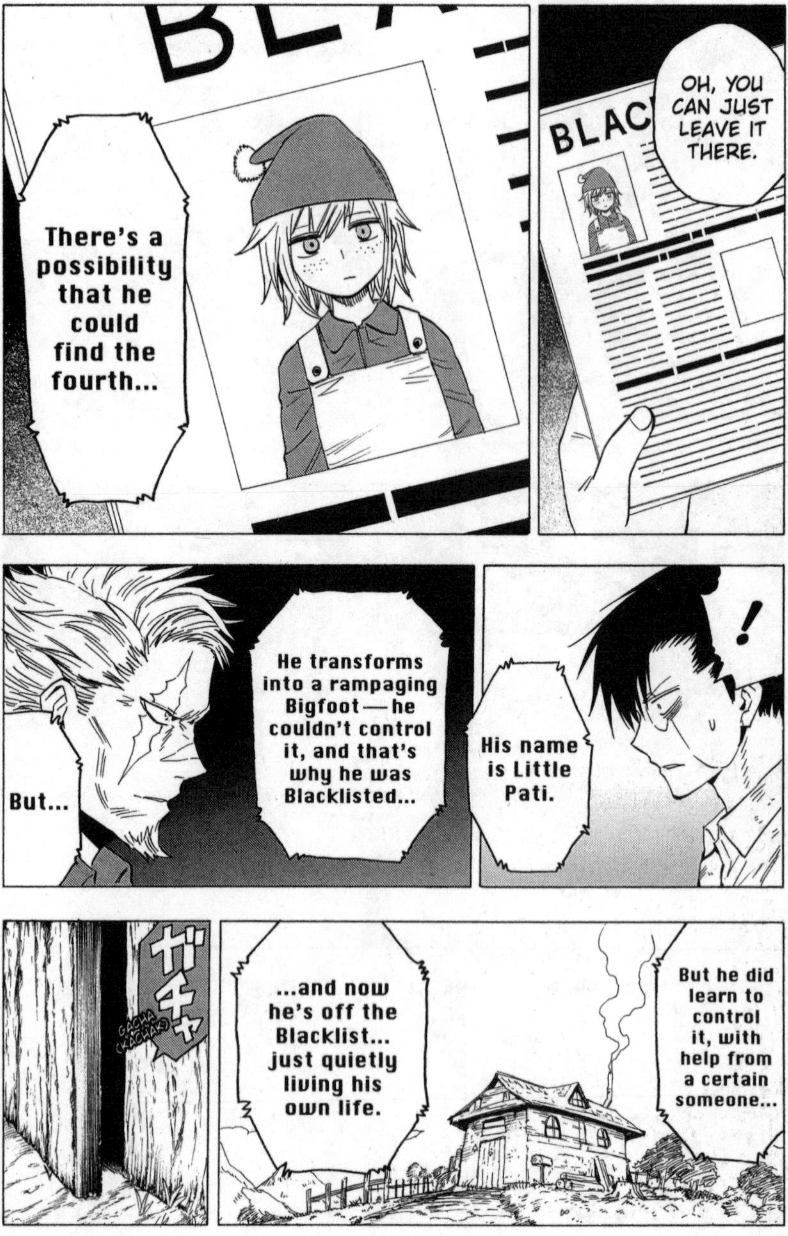
OH, YOU CAN JUST LEAVE IT THERE.
There's a possibility that he could find the fourth...
His name is Little Pati.
He transforms into a rampaging Bigfoot—he couldn't control it, and that's why he was Blacklisted...
But...
But he did learn to control it, with help from a certain someone...
...and now he's off the Blacklist... just quietly living his own life.
ガチャ
GACHA (KACHAK!)

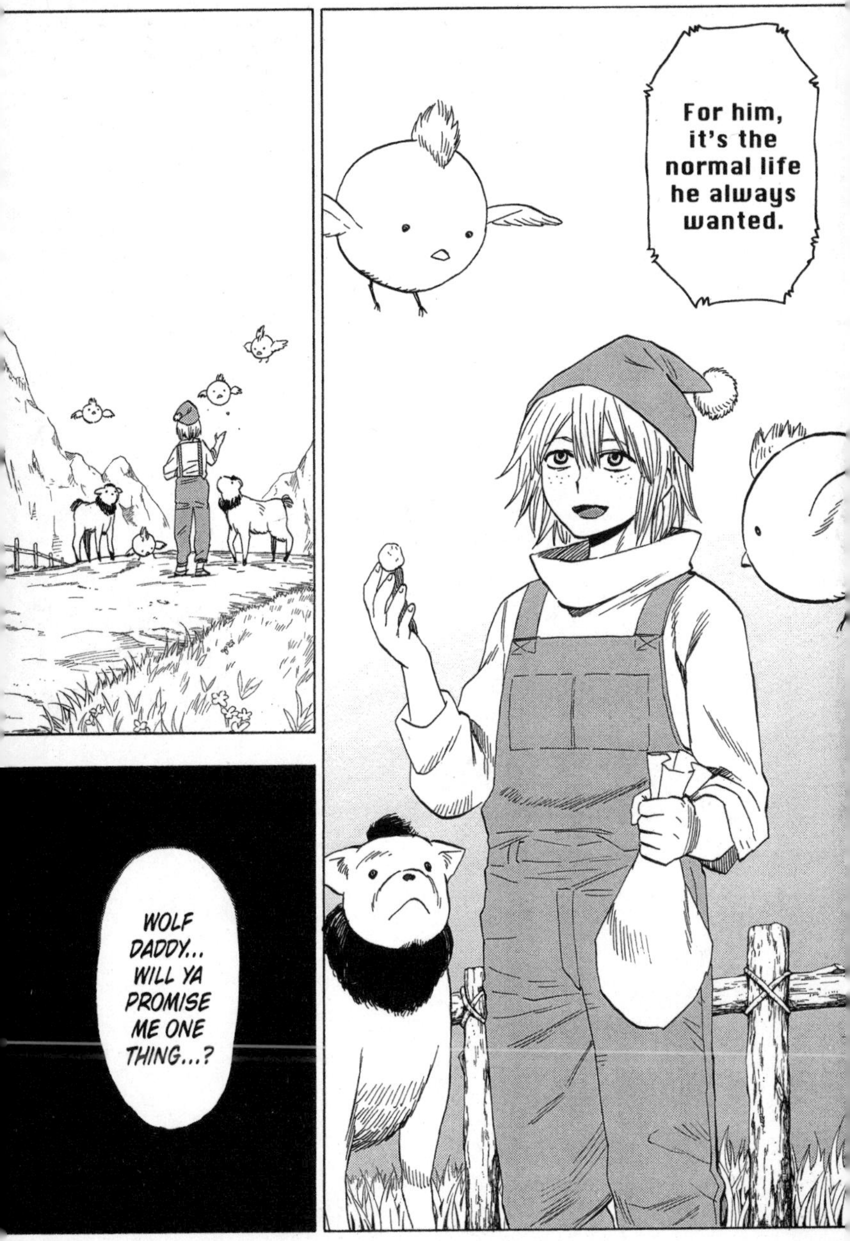
For him, it's the normal life he always wanted.
WOLF DADDY... WILL YA PROMISE ME ONE THING...?

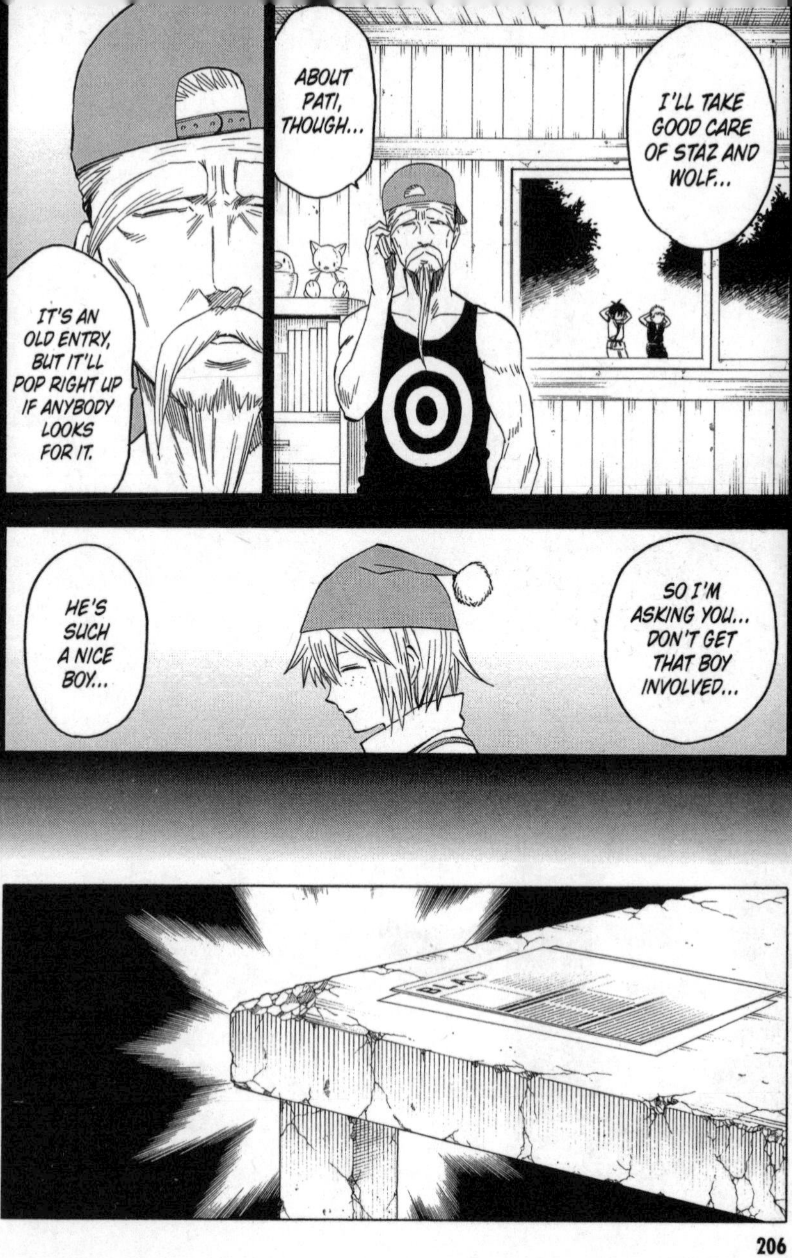
I'LL TAKE GOOD CARE OF STAZ AND WOLF...
ABOUT PATI, THOUGH...
IT'S AN OLD ENTRY, BUT IT'LL POP RIGHT UP IF ANYBODY LOOKS FOR IT.
SO I'M ASKING YOU... DON'T GET THAT BOY INVOLVED...
HE'S SUCH A NICE BOY...

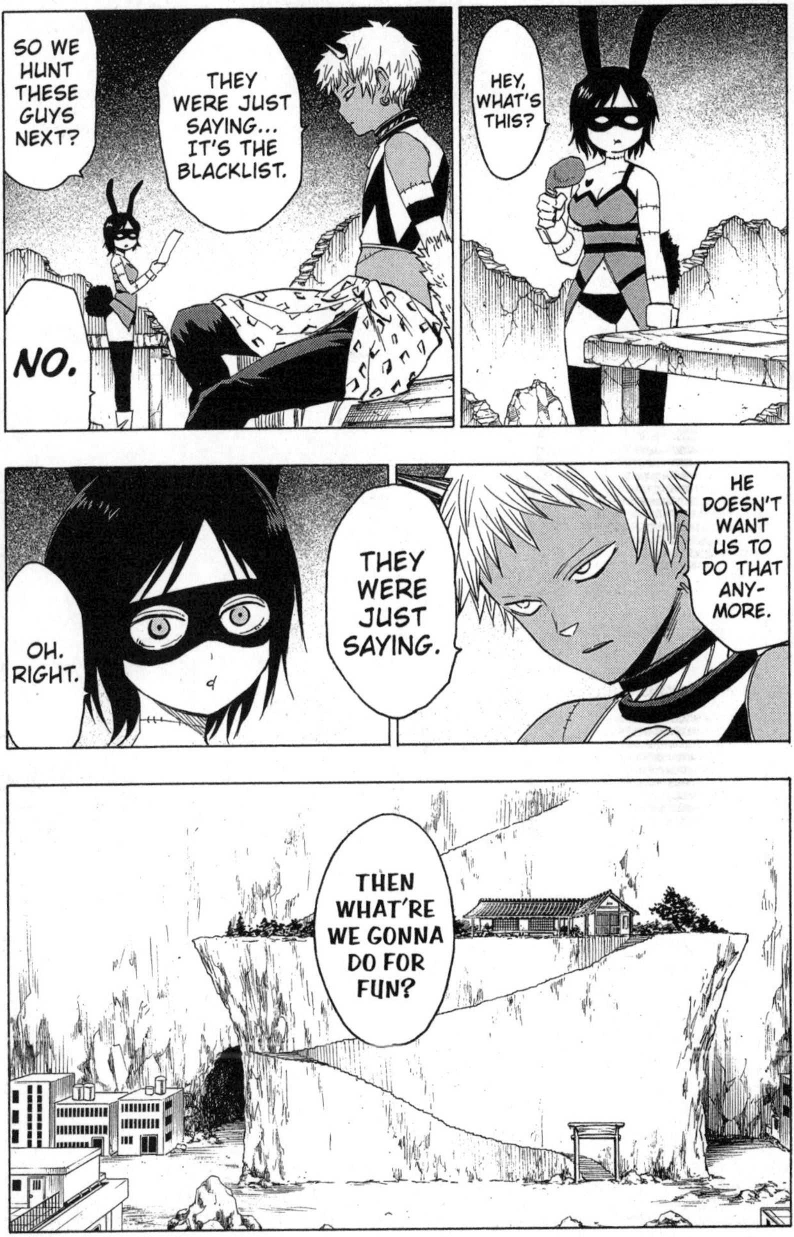
HEY, WHAT'S THIS?
THEY WERE JUST SAYING... IT'S THE BLACKLIST.
SO WE HUNT THESE GUYS NEXT?
NO.
HE DOESN'T WANT US TO DO THAT ANY-MORE.
THEY WERE JUST SAYING.
OH. RIGHT.
THEN WHAT'RE WE GONNA DO FOR FUN?

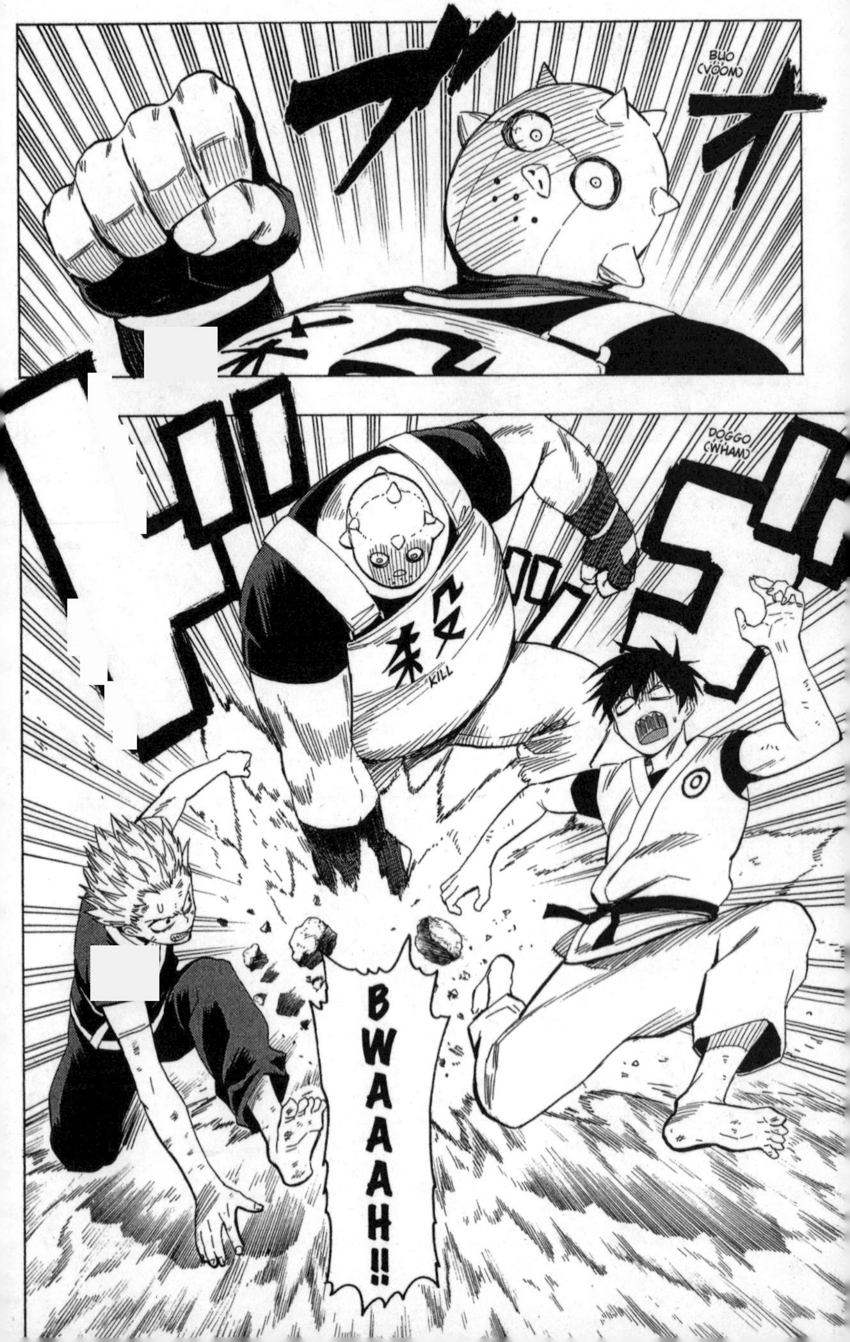
BUO
(VOOM)
DOGGO
(WHAM)
KILL
BWAAAAH!!

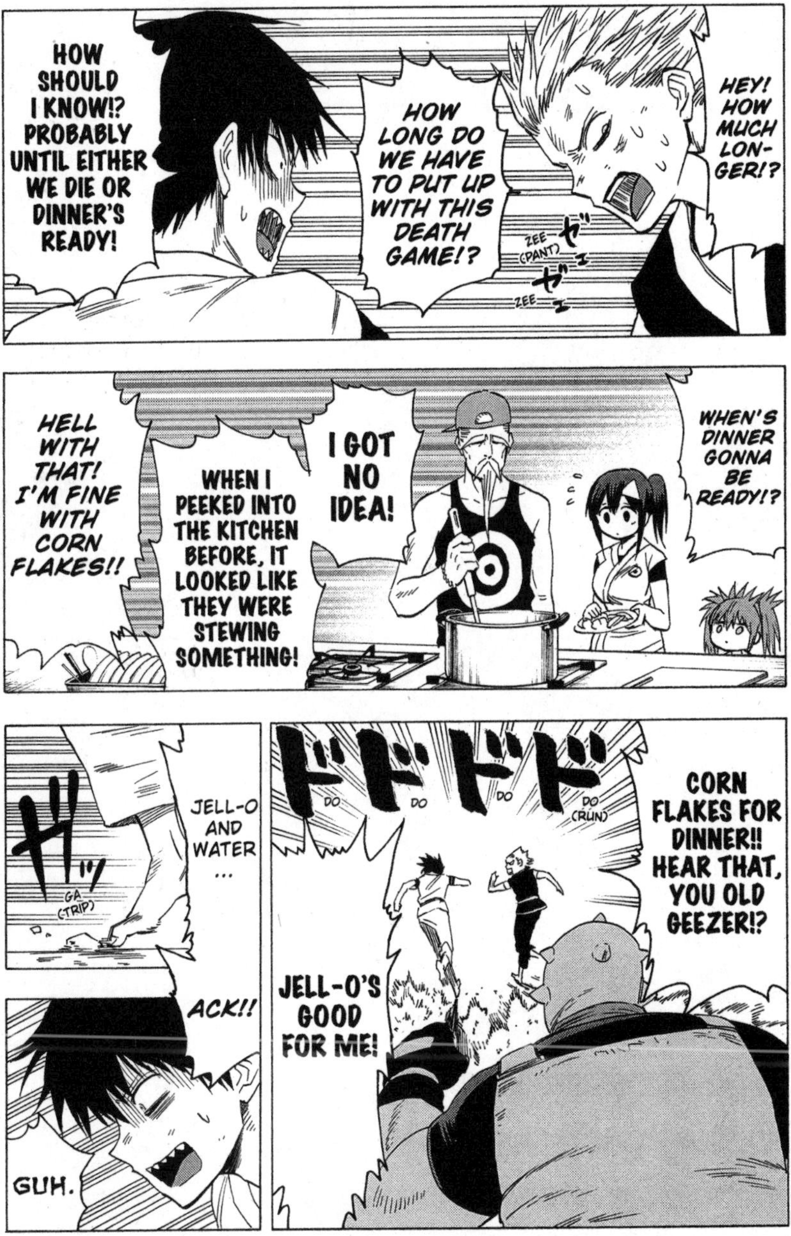
HEY! HOW MUCH LON-GER!?
HOW LONG DO WE HAVE TO PUT UP WITH THIS DEATH GAME!?
ゼェ ZEE (PANT)
ゼェ ZEE
HOW SHOULD I KNOW!? PROBABLY UNTIL EITHER WE DIE OR DINNER'S READY!
WHEN'S DINNER GONNA BE READY!?
I GOT NO IDEA!
WHEN I PEEKED INTO THE KITCHEN BEFORE, IT LOOKED LIKE THEY WERE STEWING SOMETHING!
HELL WITH THAT! I'M FINE WITH CORN FLAKES!!
ドドドド
DO DO DO DO (RUN)
CORN FLAKES FOR DINNER!! HEAR THAT, YOU OLD GEEZER!?
JELL-O'S GOOD FOR ME!
JELL-O AND WATER...
ガッ
GA (TRIP)
ACK!!
GUH.

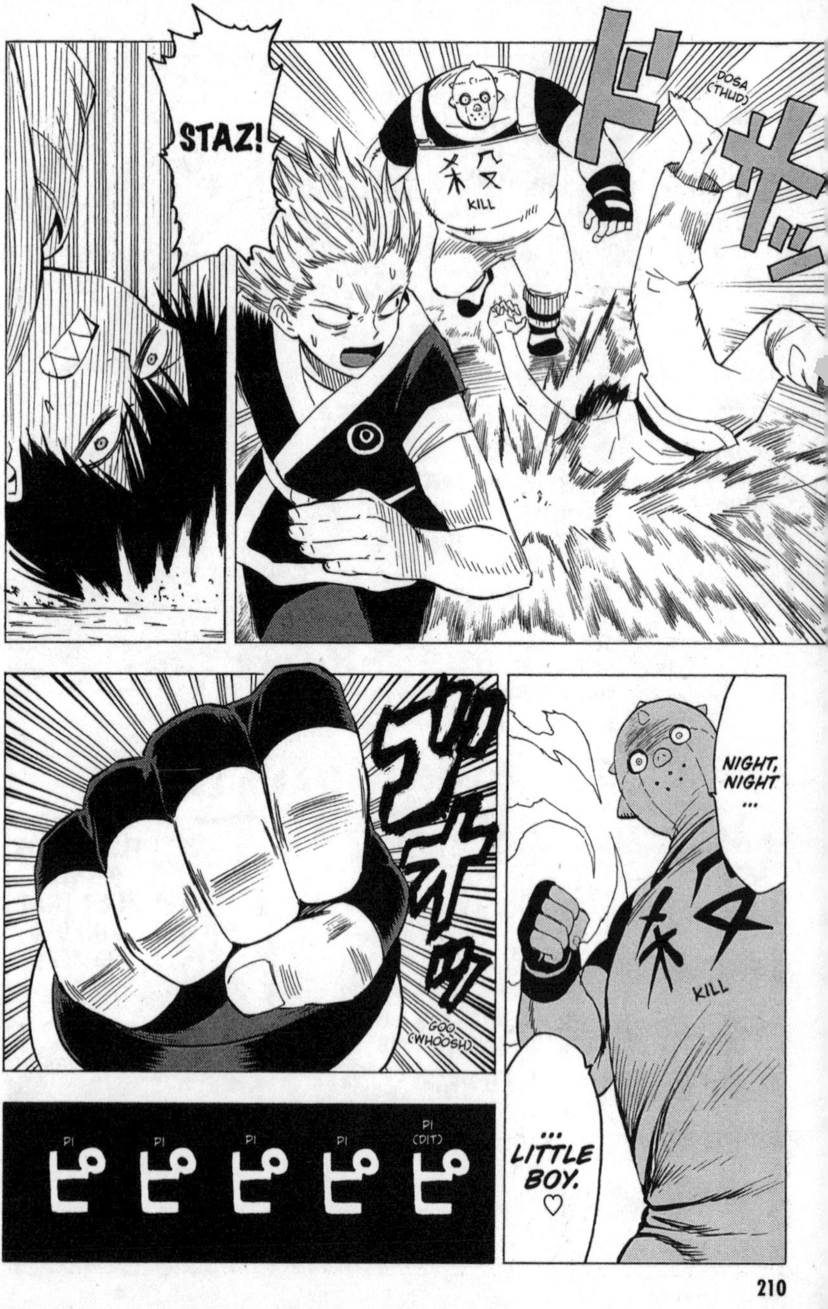
DOSA (THUD)
KILL
STAZ!
NIGHT, NIGHT ...
KILL
... LITTLE BOY. ♡
GOO (WHOOSH)
PI PI PI PI PI (DIT)

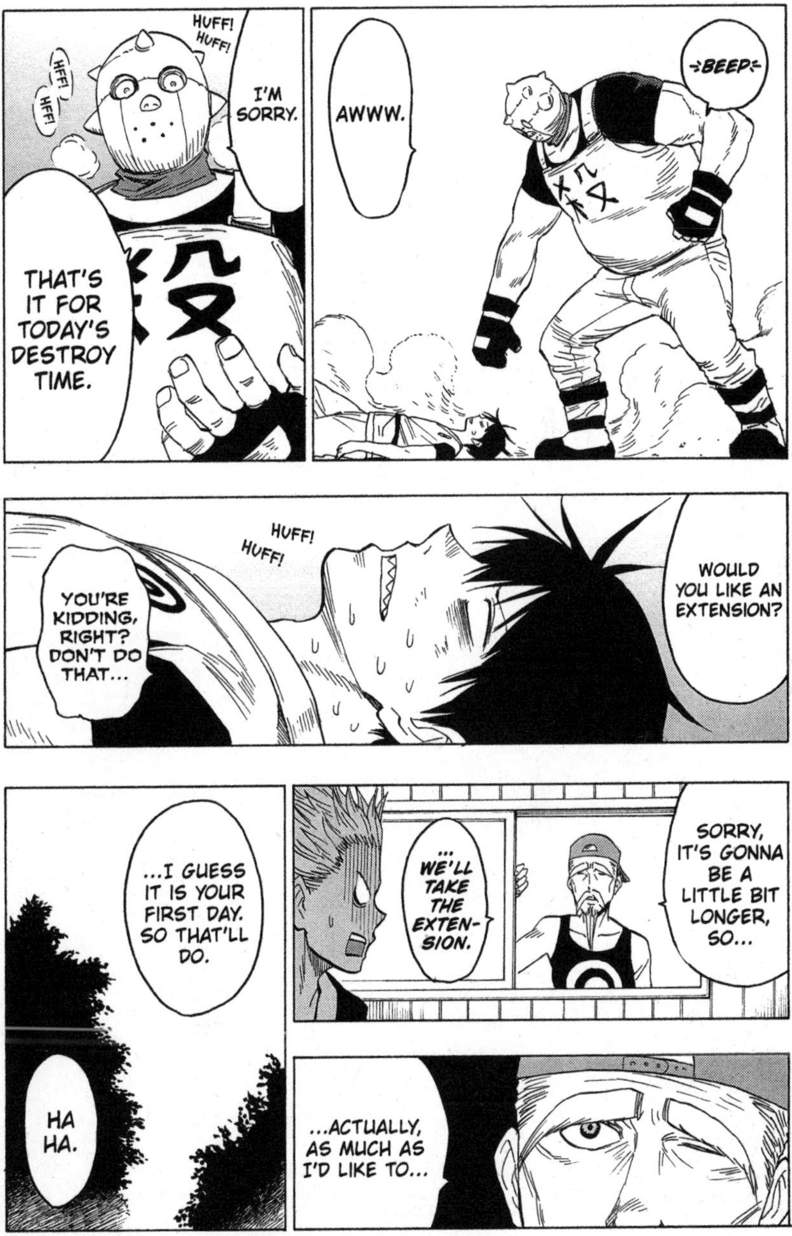
BEEP
AWWW.
HUFF! HUFF!
I'M SORRY.
HFF! HFF!
THAT'S IT FOR TODAY'S DESTROY TIME.
WOULD YOU LIKE AN EXTENSION?
HUFF! HUFF!
YOU'RE KIDDING, RIGHT? DON'T DO THAT...
SORRY, IT'S GONNA BE A LITTLE BIT LONGER, SO...
...WE'LL TAKE THE EXTEN-SION.
...ACTUALLY, AS MUCH AS I'D LIKE TO...
...I GUESS IT IS YOUR FIRST DAY. SO THAT'LL DO.
HA HA.

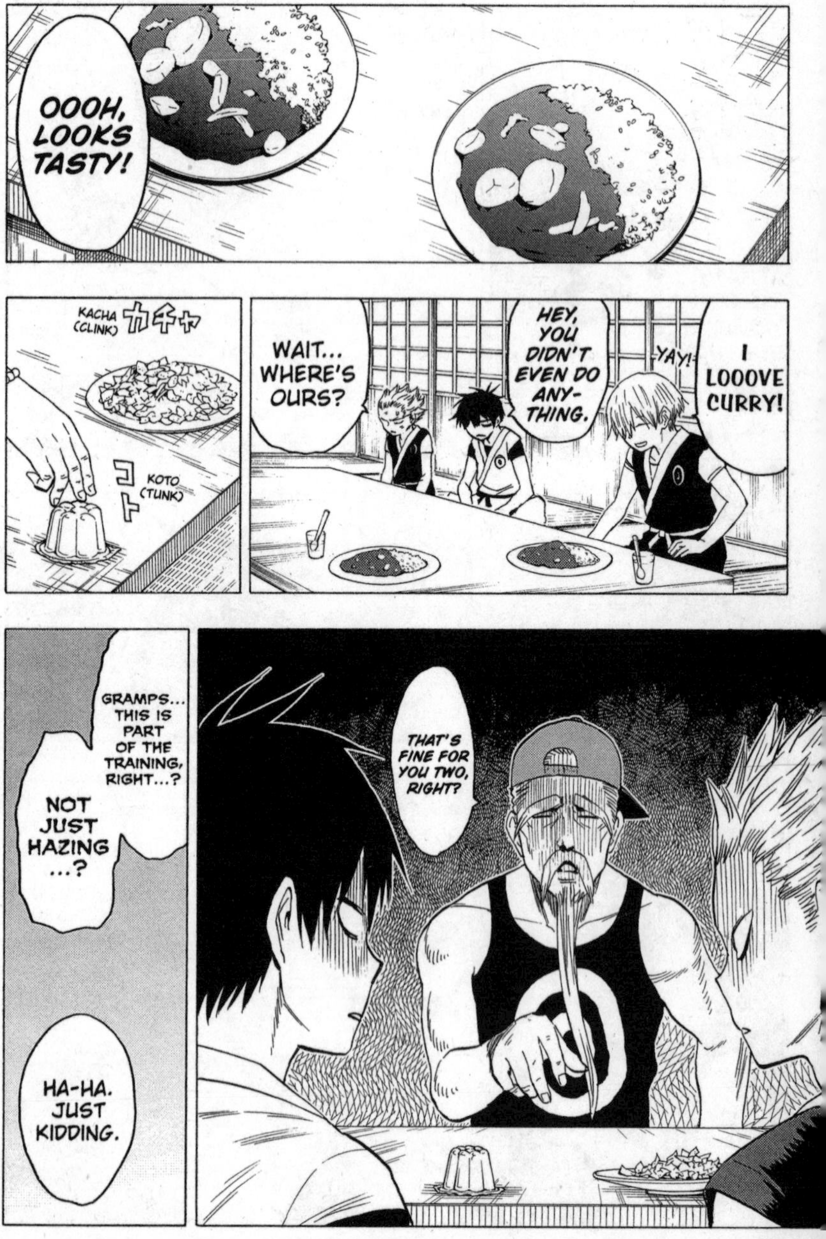
OOOH, LOOKS TASTY!
I LOOOVE CURRY!
YAY!
HEY, YOU DIDN'T EVEN DO ANY-THING.
WAIT... WHERE'S OURS?
KACHA (CLINK) カチャ
KOTO (TUNK) コト
THAT'S FINE FOR YOU TWO, RIGHT?
GRAMPS... THIS IS PART OF THE TRAINING, RIGHT...?
NOT JUST HAZING ...?
HA-HA. JUST KIDDING.

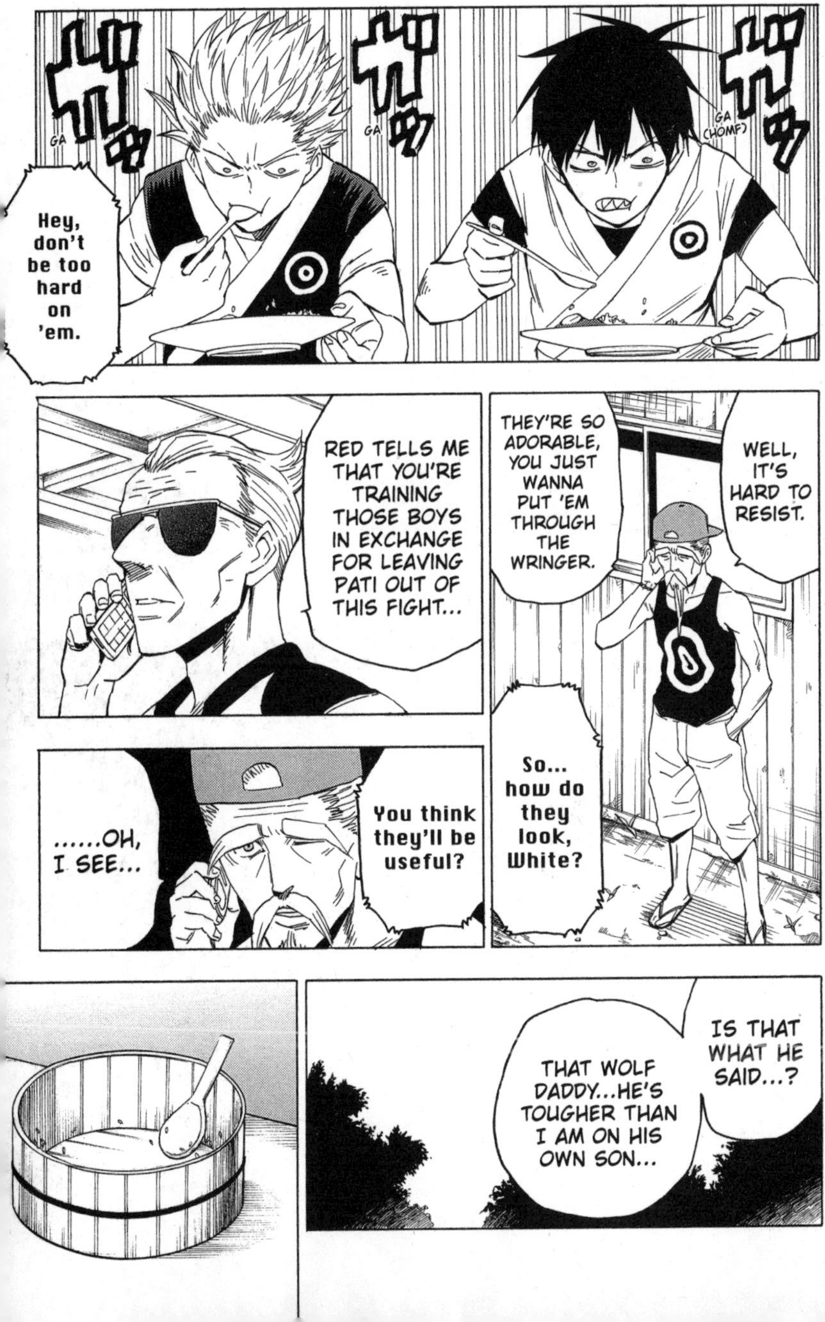
GA (HOMF)
GA
GA
Hey, don't be too hard on 'em.
WELL, IT'S HARD TO RESIST.
THEY'RE SO ADORABLE, YOU JUST WANNA PUT 'EM THROUGH THE WRINGER.
So... how do they look, White?
RED TELLS ME THAT YOU'RE TRAINING THOSE BOYS IN EXCHANGE FOR LEAVING PATI OUT OF THIS FIGHT...
You think they'll be useful?
......OH, I SEE...
IS THAT WHAT HE SAID...?
THAT WOLF DADDY...HE'S TOUGHER THAN I AM ON HIS OWN SON...

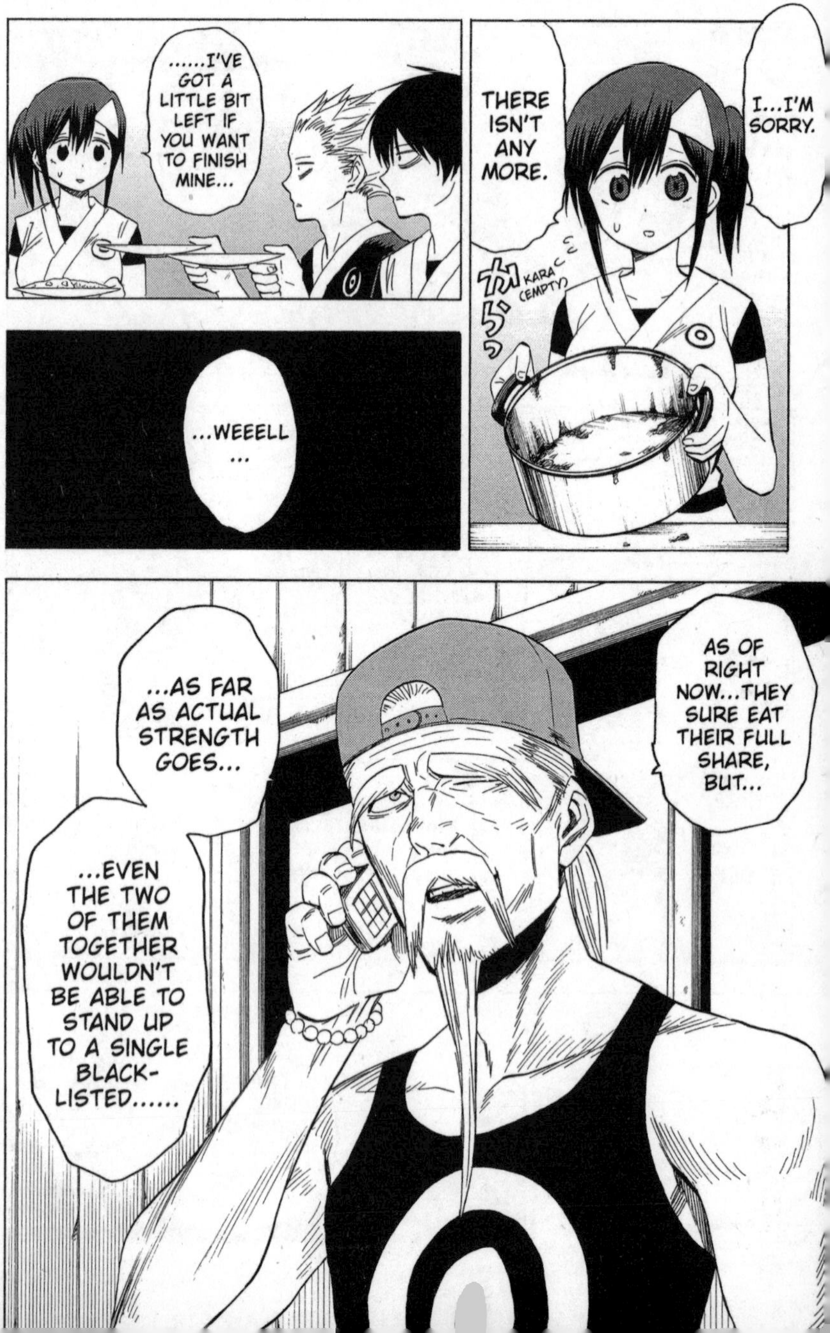
I...I'M SORRY.
THERE ISN'T ANY MORE.
から
KARA (EMPTY)
......I'VE GOT A LITTLE BIT LEFT IF YOU WANT TO FINISH MINE...
...WEEELL ...
AS OF RIGHT NOW...THEY SURE EAT THEIR FULL SHARE, BUT...
...AS FAR AS ACTUAL STRENGTH GOES...
...EVEN THE TWO OF THEM TOGETHER WOULDN'T BE ABLE TO STAND UP TO A SINGLE BLACK-LISTED......

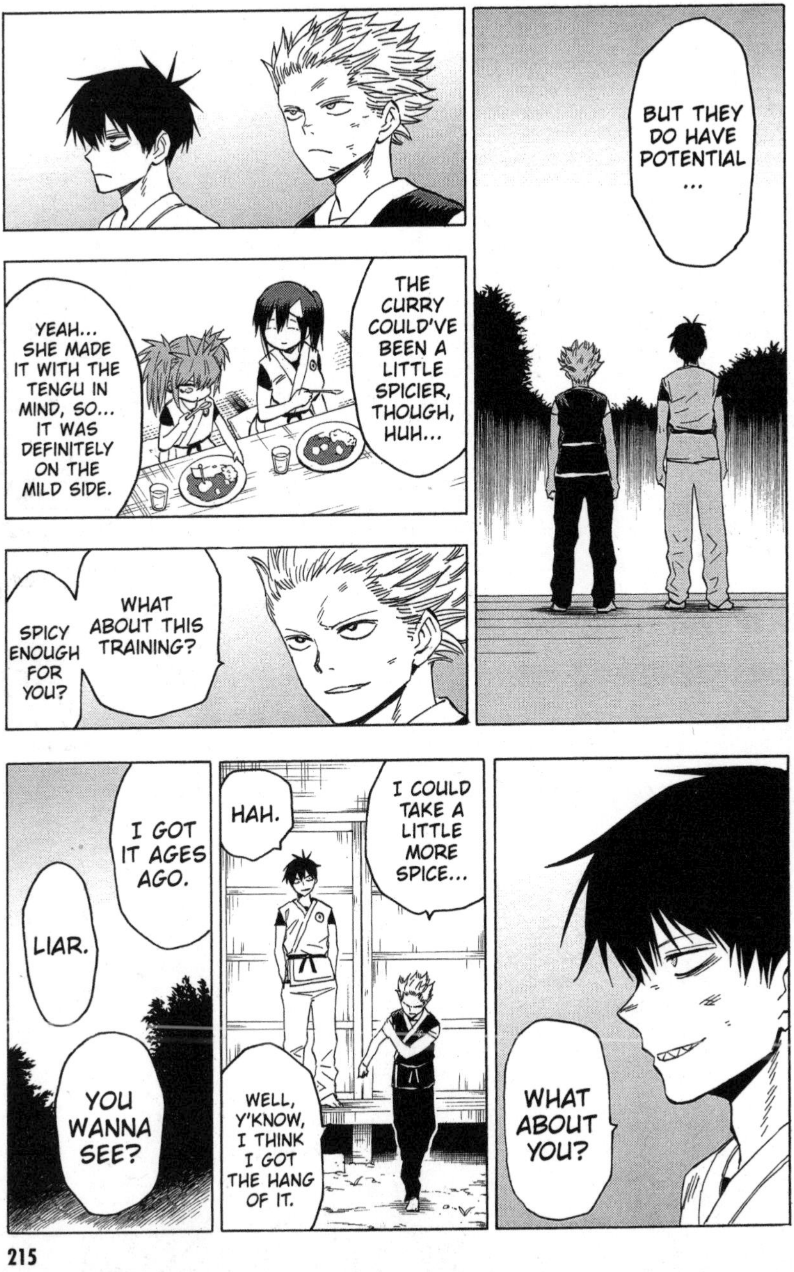
BUT THEY DO HAVE POTENTIAL ...
THE CURRY COULD'VE BEEN A LITTLE SPICIER, THOUGH, HUH...
YEAH... SHE MADE IT WITH THE TENGU IN MIND, SO... IT WAS DEFINITELY ON THE MILD SIDE.
WHAT ABOUT THIS TRAINING?
SPICY ENOUGH FOR YOU?
WHAT ABOUT YOU?
I COULD TAKE A LITTLE MORE SPICE...
HAH.
WELL, Y'KNOW, I THINK I GOT THE HANG OF IT.
I GOT IT AGES AGO.
LIAR.
YOU WANNA SEE?

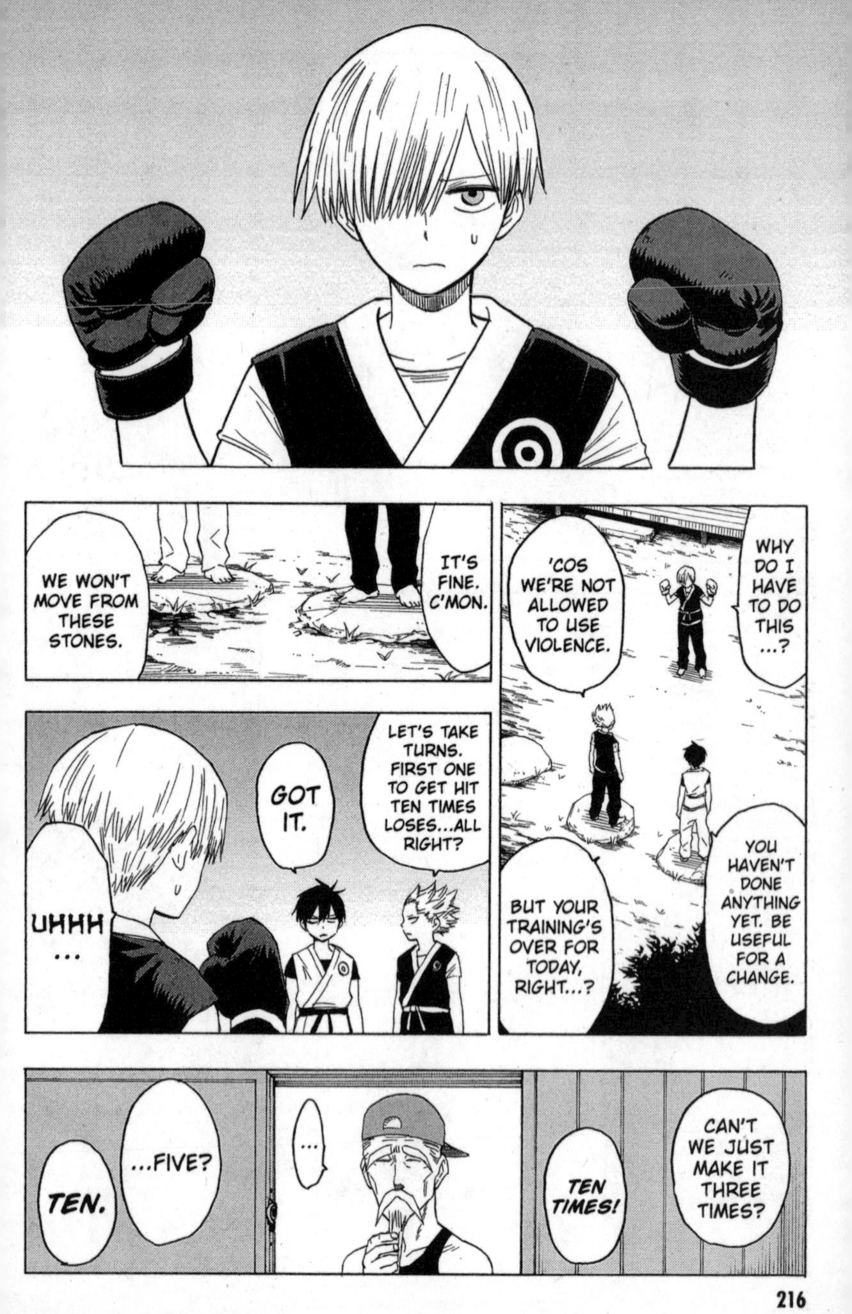
WHY DO I HAVE TO DO THIS ...?
'COS WE'RE NOT ALLOWED TO USE VIOLENCE.
YOU HAVEN'T DONE ANYTHING YET. BE USEFUL FOR A CHANGE.
BUT YOUR TRAINING'S OVER FOR TODAY, RIGHT...?
IT'S FINE. C'MON.
WE WON'T MOVE FROM THESE STONES.
LET'S TAKE TURNS. FIRST ONE TO GET HIT TEN TIMES LOSES...ALL RIGHT?
GOT IT.
UHHH ...
CAN'T WE JUST MAKE IT THREE TIMES?
TEN TIMES!
...
...FIVE?
TEN.

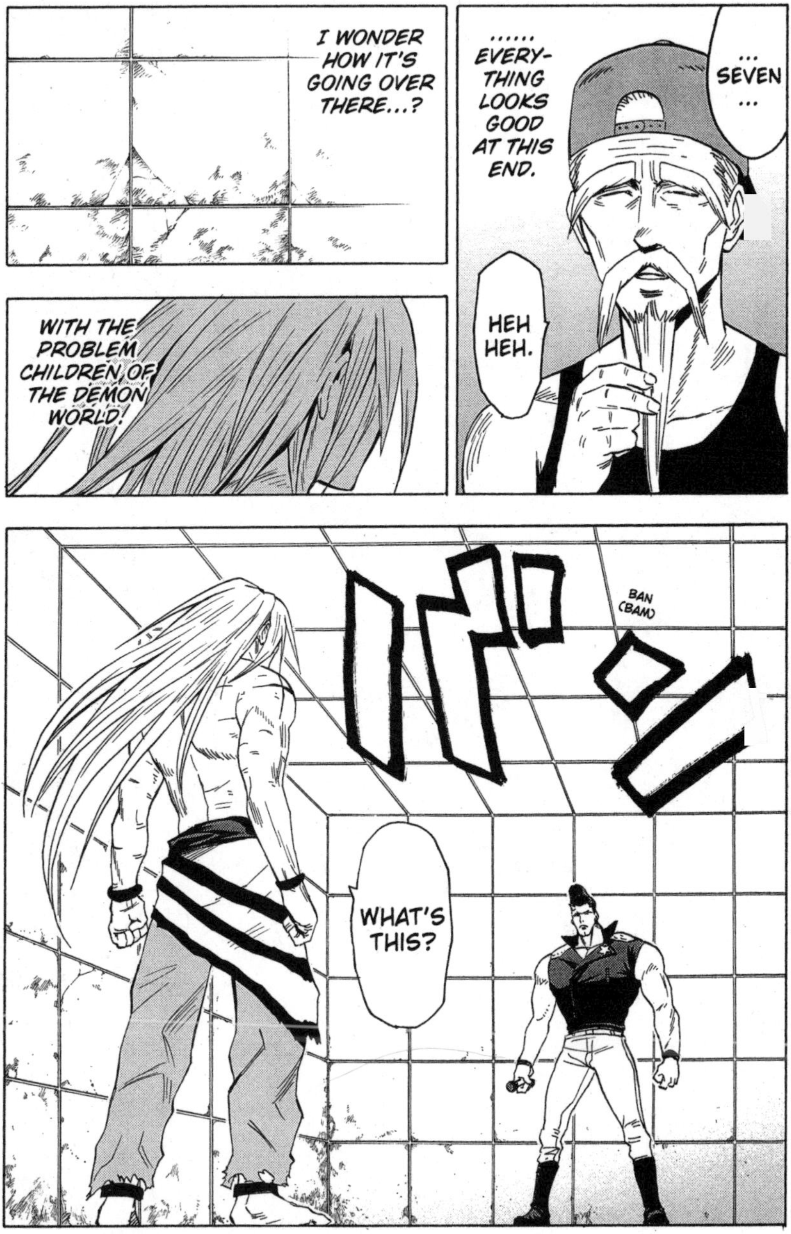
... SEVEN ...
...... EVERY-THING LOOKS GOOD AT THIS END.
HEH HEH.
I WONDER HOW IT'S GOING OVER THERE...?
WITH THE PROBLEM CHILDREN OF THE DEMON WORLD!
BAN (BAM)
WHAT'S THIS?

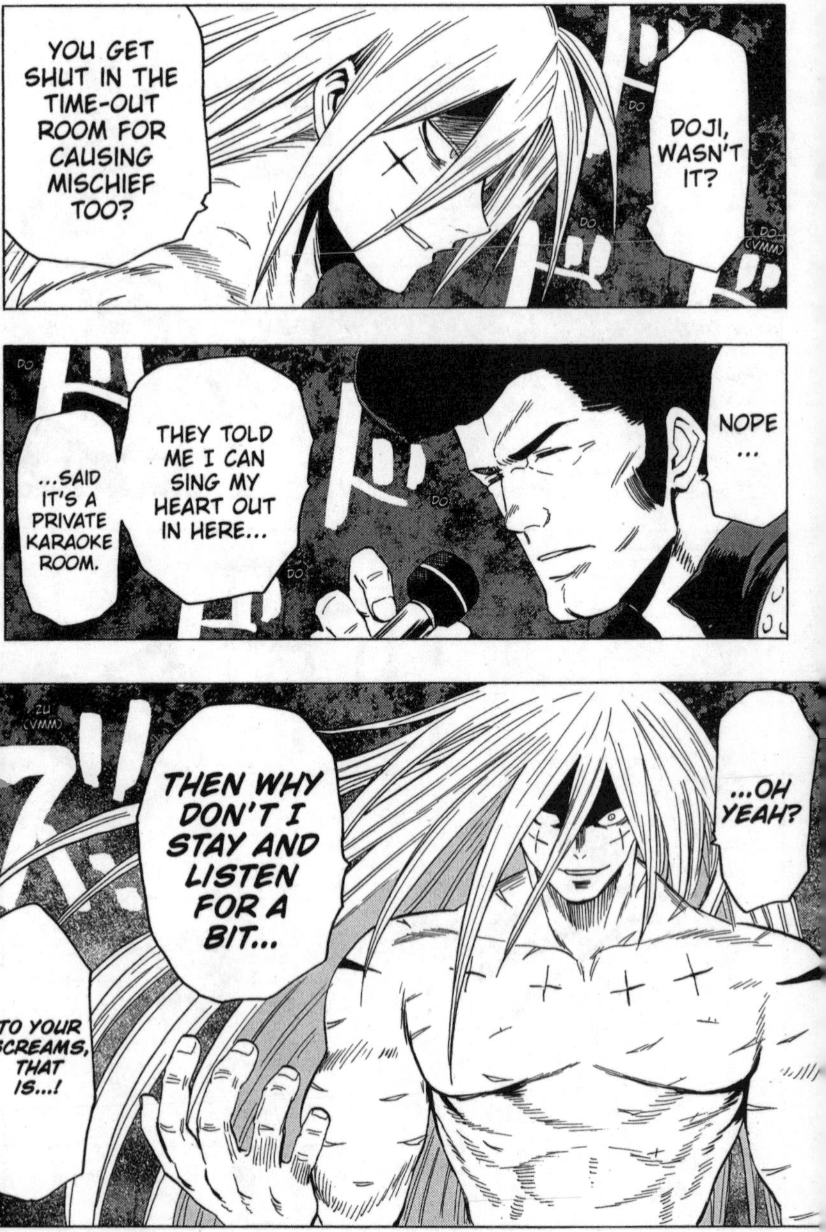
DOJI, WASN'T IT?
YOU GET SHUT IN THE TIME-OUT ROOM FOR CAUSING MISCHIEF TOO?
DO
DO
DO (VMM)
NOPE ...
THEY TOLD ME I CAN SING MY HEART OUT IN HERE...
...SAID IT'S A PRIVATE KARAOKE ROOM.
DO
DO
DO
...OH YEAH?
THEN WHY DON'T I STAY AND LISTEN FOR A BIT...
TO YOUR SCREAMS, THAT IS...!
ZU (VMM)

♠ To Be Continued ♠

BLOOD LAD

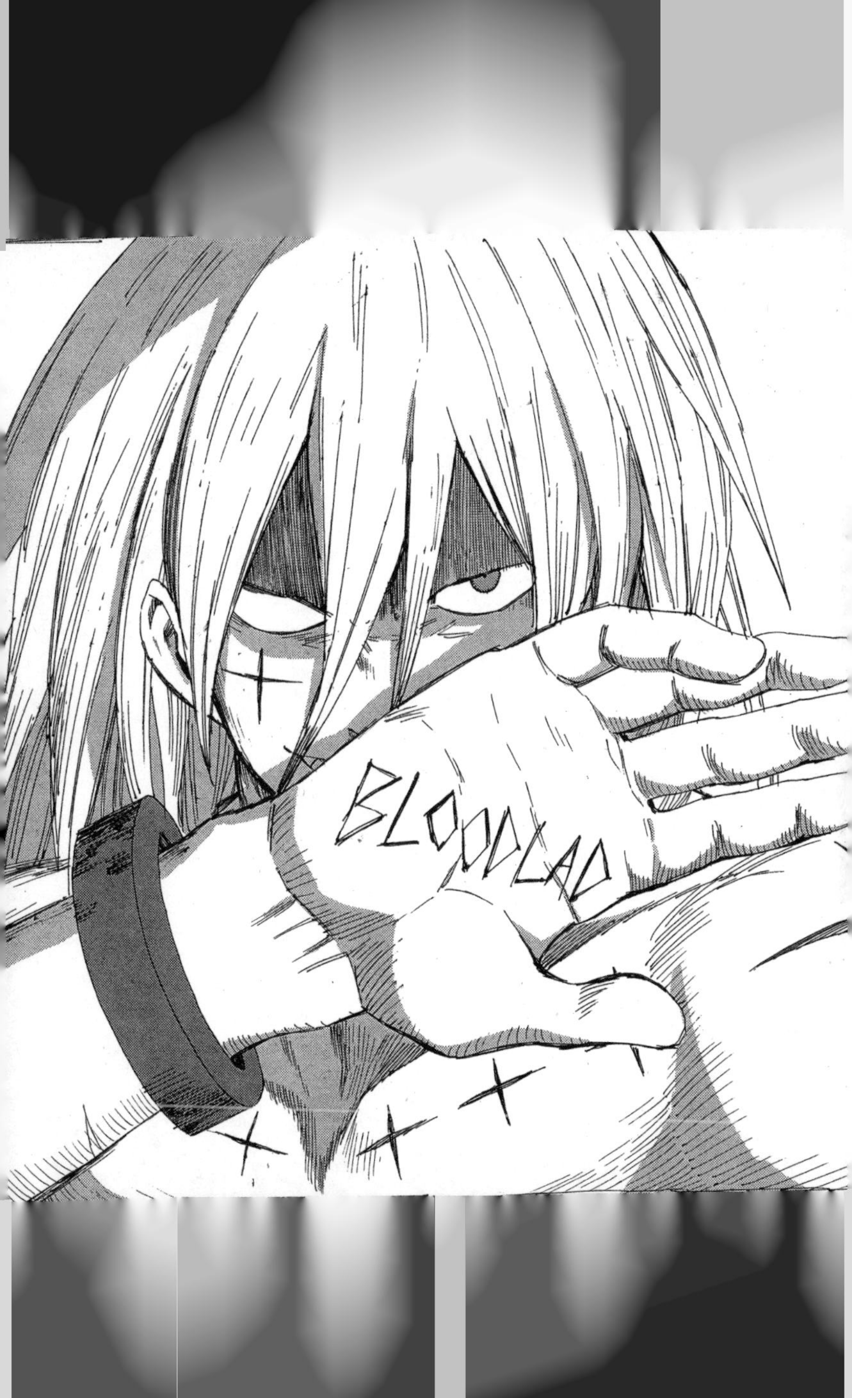
BLOODLAD

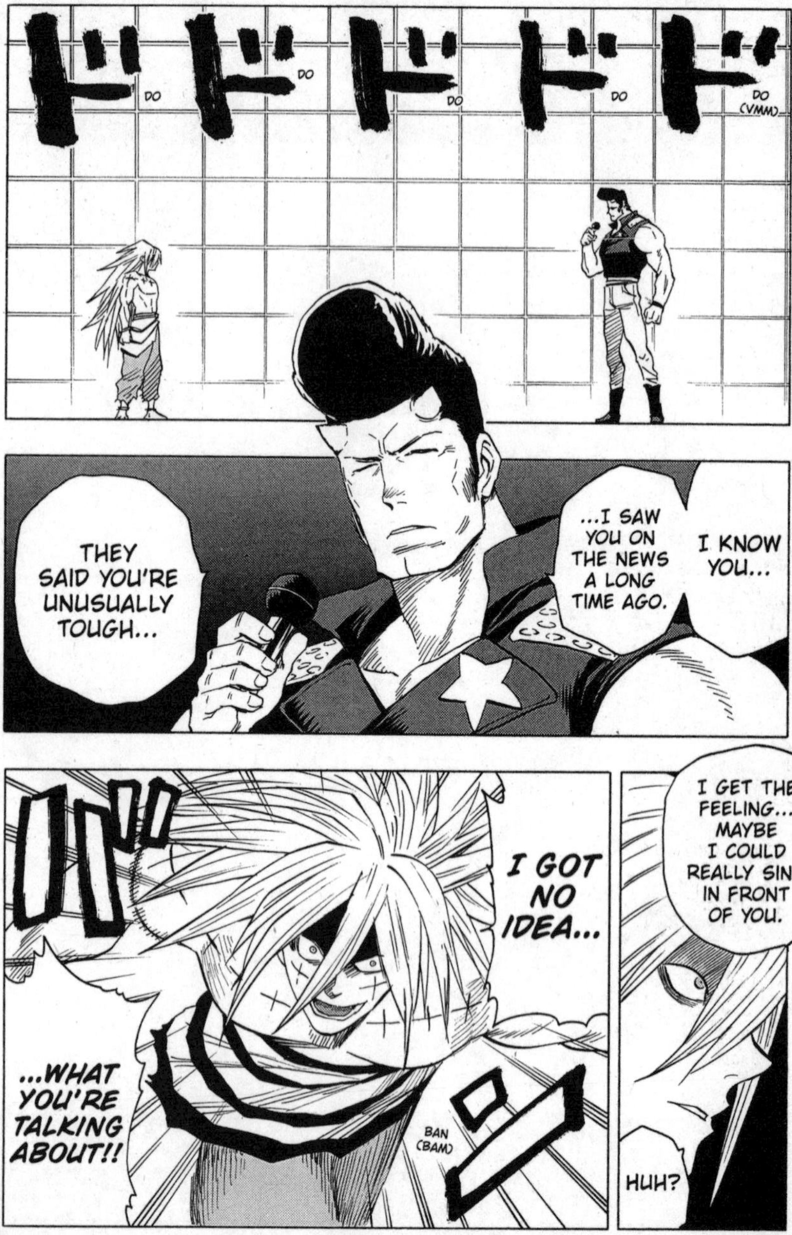

ドドドドド
DO (VMM)
DO
DO
DO
DO
I KNOW YOU...
...I SAW YOU ON THE NEWS A LONG TIME AGO.
THEY SAID YOU'RE UNUSUALLY TOUGH...
I GET THE FEELING... MAYBE I COULD REALLY SING IN FRONT OF YOU.
HUH?
I GOT NO IDEA...
...WHAT YOU'RE TALKING ABOUT!!
BAN (BAM)

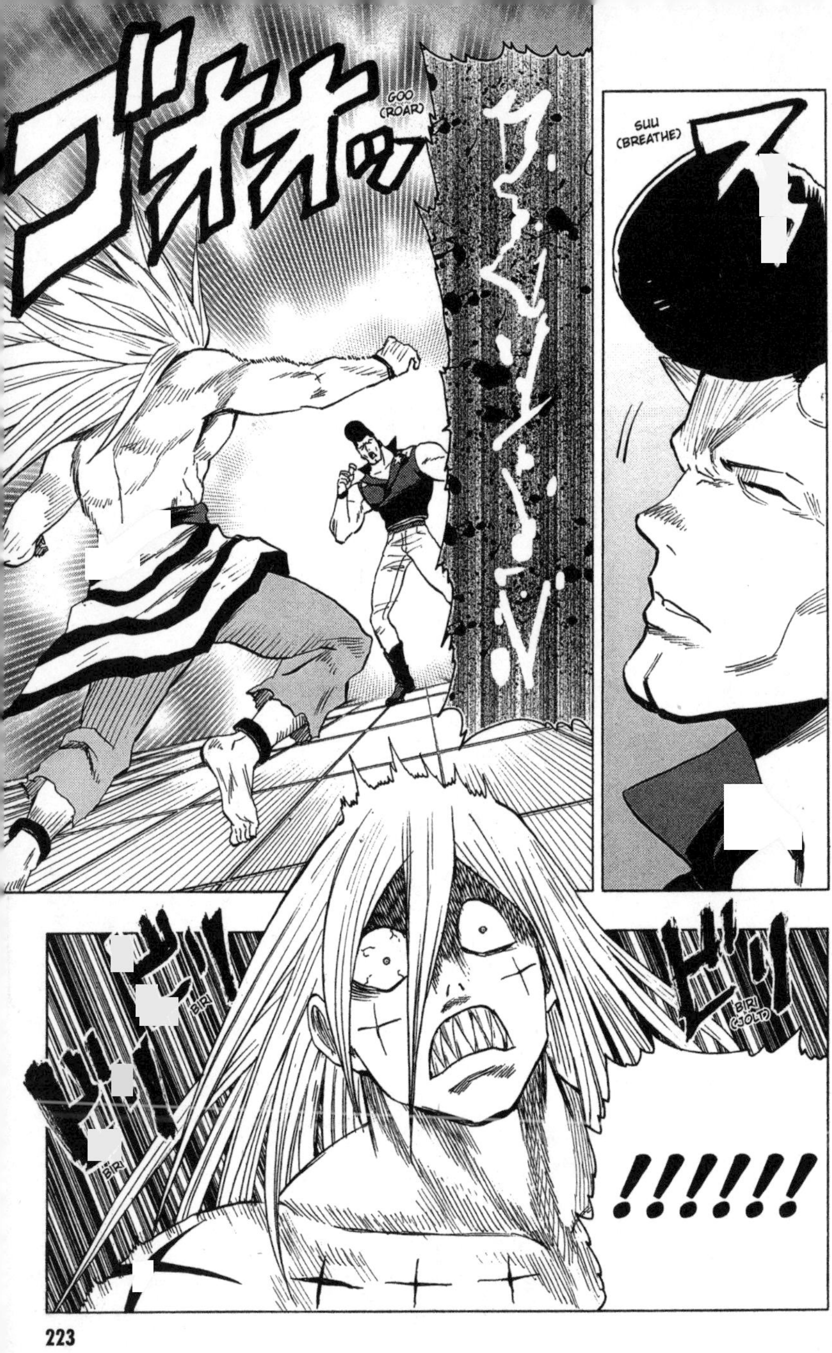
SUU (BREATHE)
GOO (ROAR)
BIRI (JOLT)
!!!!!!
BIRI
BIRI

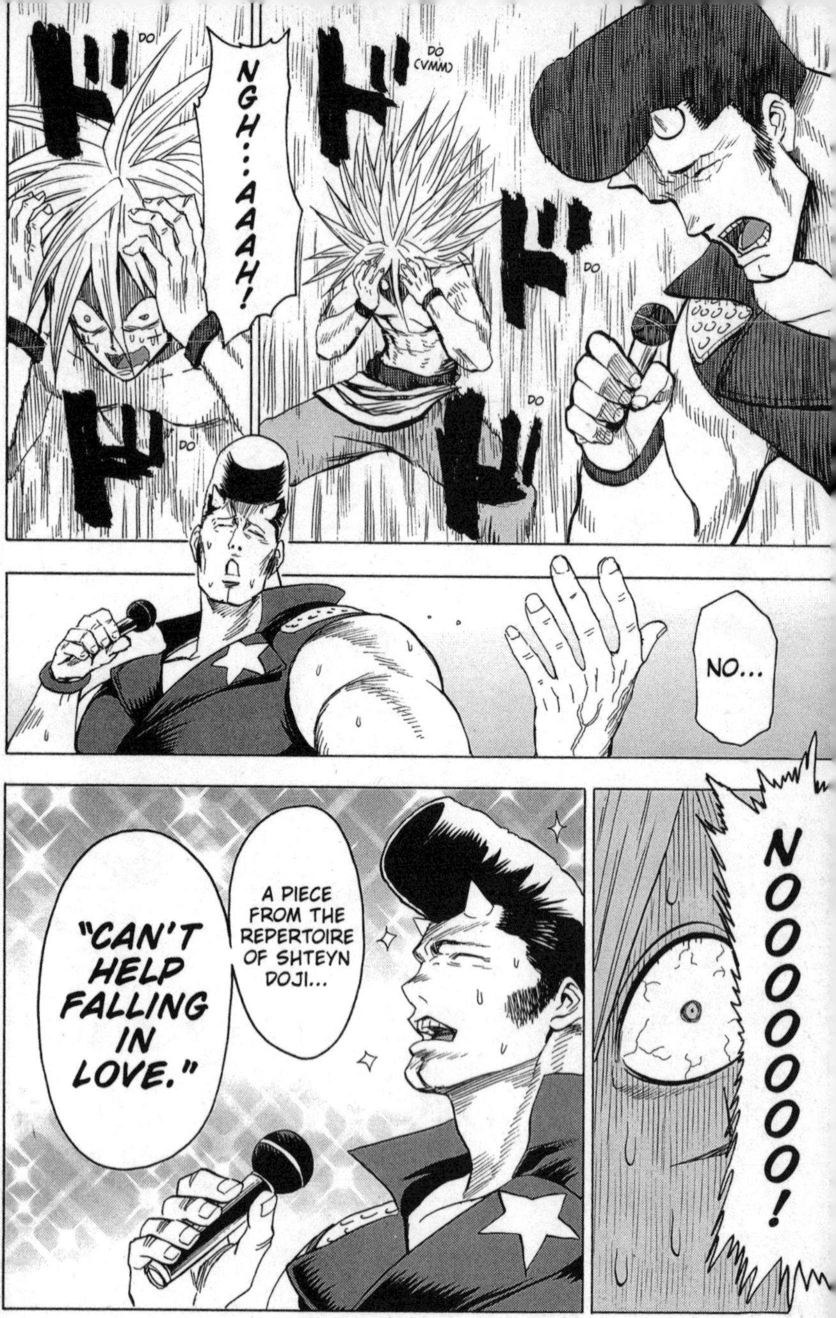
DO
(VMM)
NGH...AAAAH!
DO
DO
DO
DO
NO...
NOOOOOOO!
A PIECE FROM THE REPERTOIRE OF SHTEYN DOJI...
"CAN'T HELP FALLING IN LOVE."

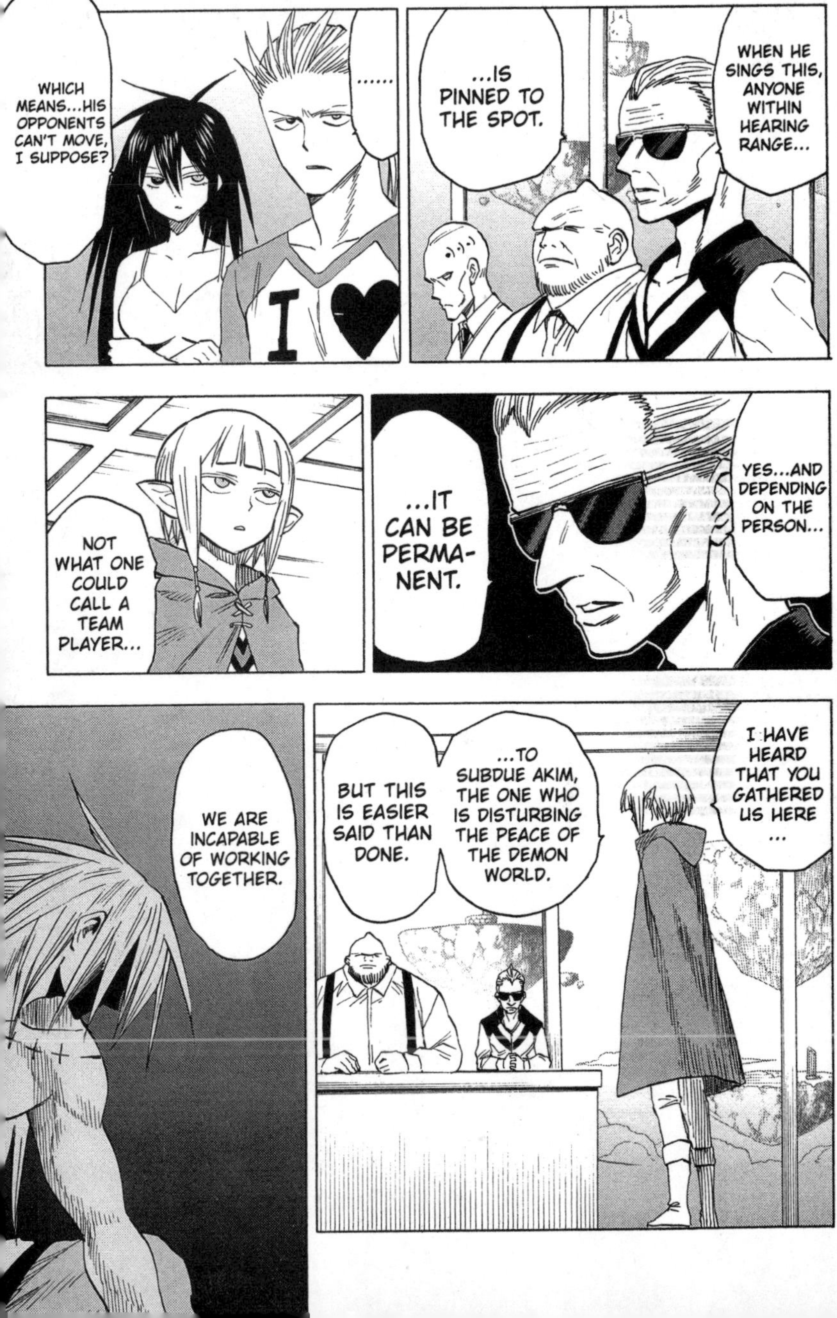
WHEN HE SINGS THIS, ANYONE WITHIN HEARING RANGE...
...IS PINNED TO THE SPOT.
......
WHICH MEANS...HIS OPPONENTS CAN'T MOVE, I SUPPOSE?
YES...AND DEPENDING ON THE PERSON...
...IT CAN BE PERMA-NENT.
NOT WHAT ONE COULD CALL A TEAM PLAYER...
I HAVE HEARD THAT YOU GATHERED US HERE ...
...TO SUBDUE AKIM, THE ONE WHO IS DISTURBING THE PEACE OF THE DEMON WORLD.
BUT THIS IS EASIER SAID THAN DONE.
WE ARE INCAPABLE OF WORKING TOGETHER.

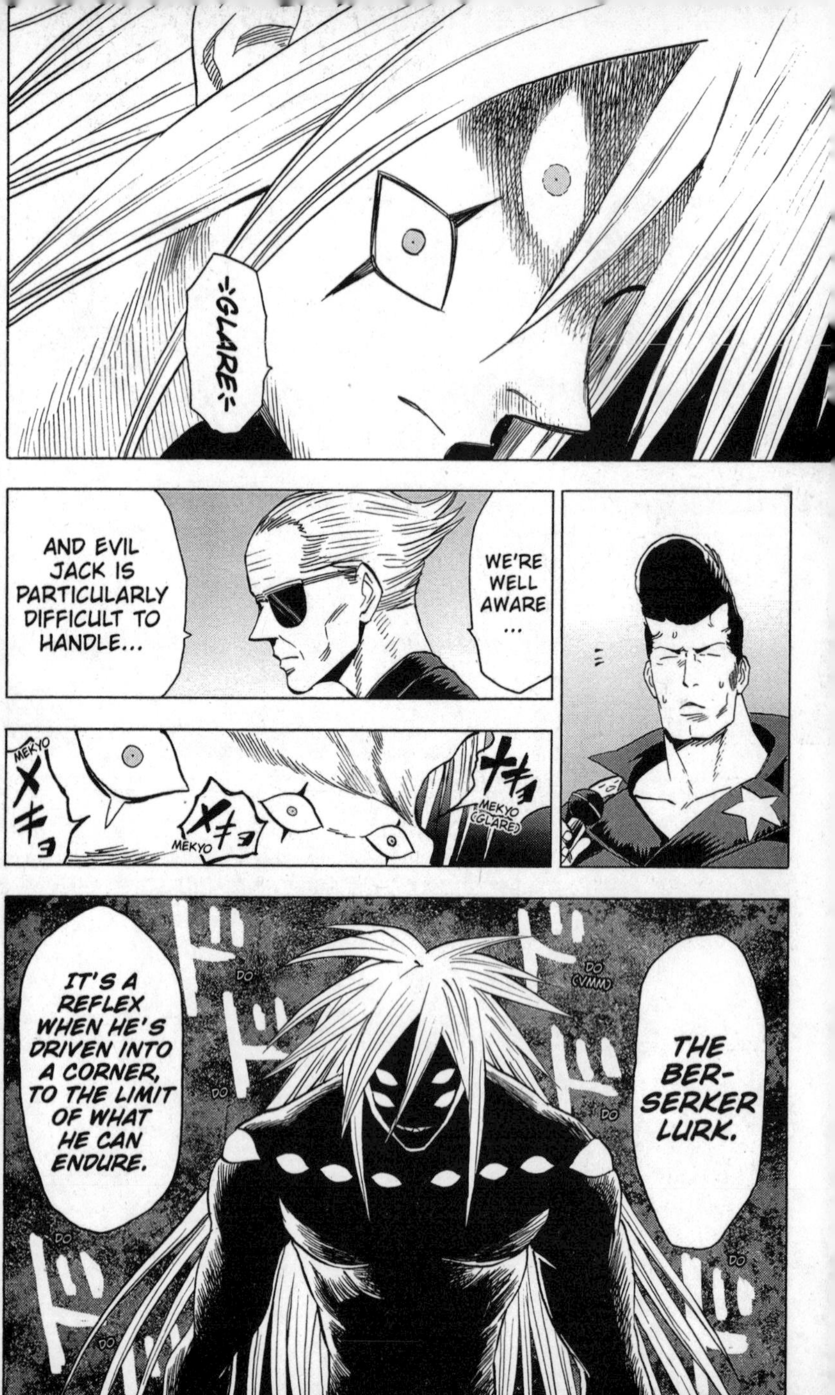
GLARE
WE'RE WELL AWARE...
AND EVIL JACK IS PARTICULARLY DIFFICULT TO HANDLE...
MEKYO (GLARE)
MEKYO
MEKYO
DO (VMM)
THE BER-SERKER LURK.
IT'S A REFLEX WHEN HE'S DRIVEN INTO A CORNER, TO THE LIMIT OF WHAT HE CAN ENDURE.
DO
DO
DO
DO
DO

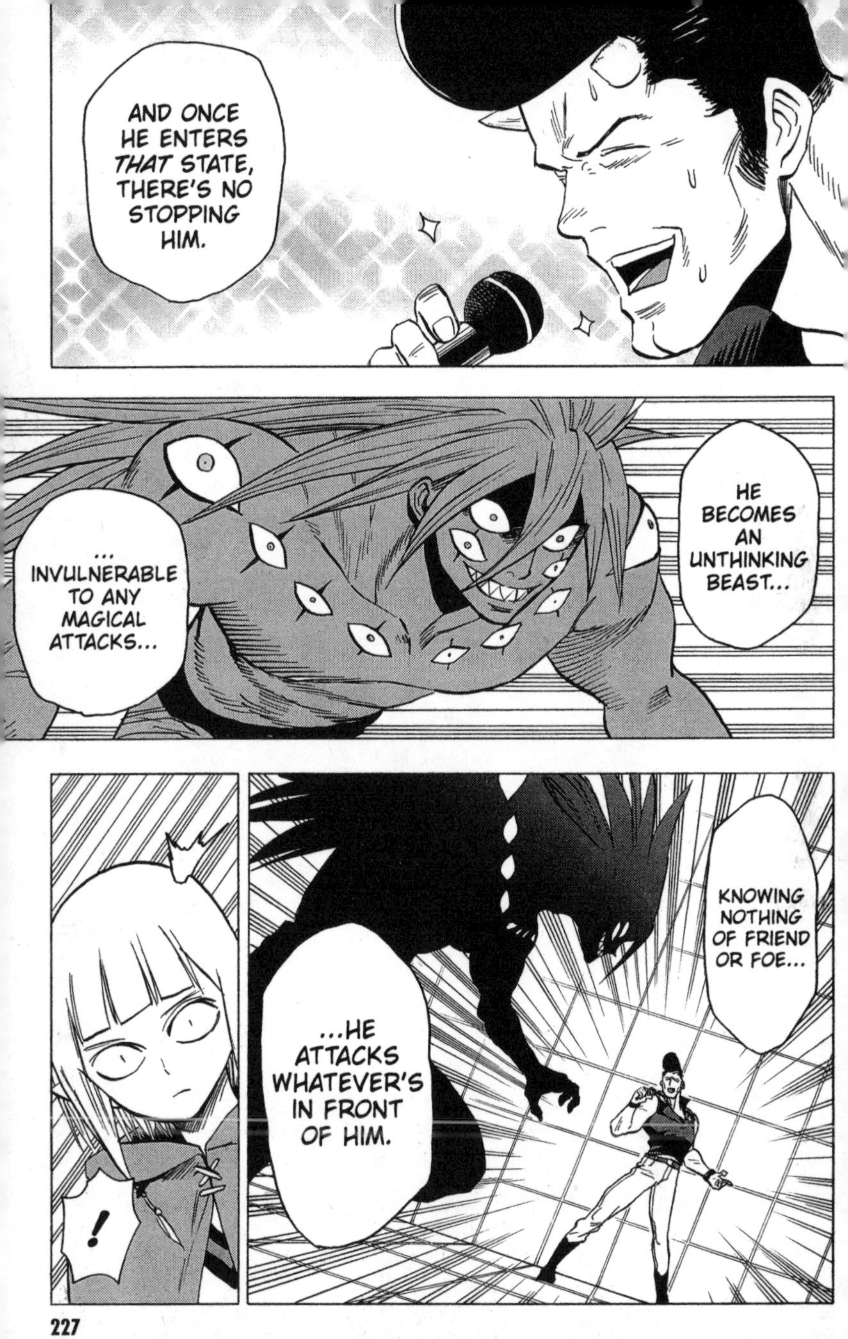
AND ONCE HE ENTERS *THAT* STATE, THERE'S NO STOPPING HIM.
HE BECOMES AN UNTHINKING BEAST...
...INVULNERABLE TO ANY MAGICAL ATTACKS...
KNOWING NOTHING OF FRIEND OR FOE...
...HE ATTACKS WHATEVER'S IN FRONT OF HIM.
!

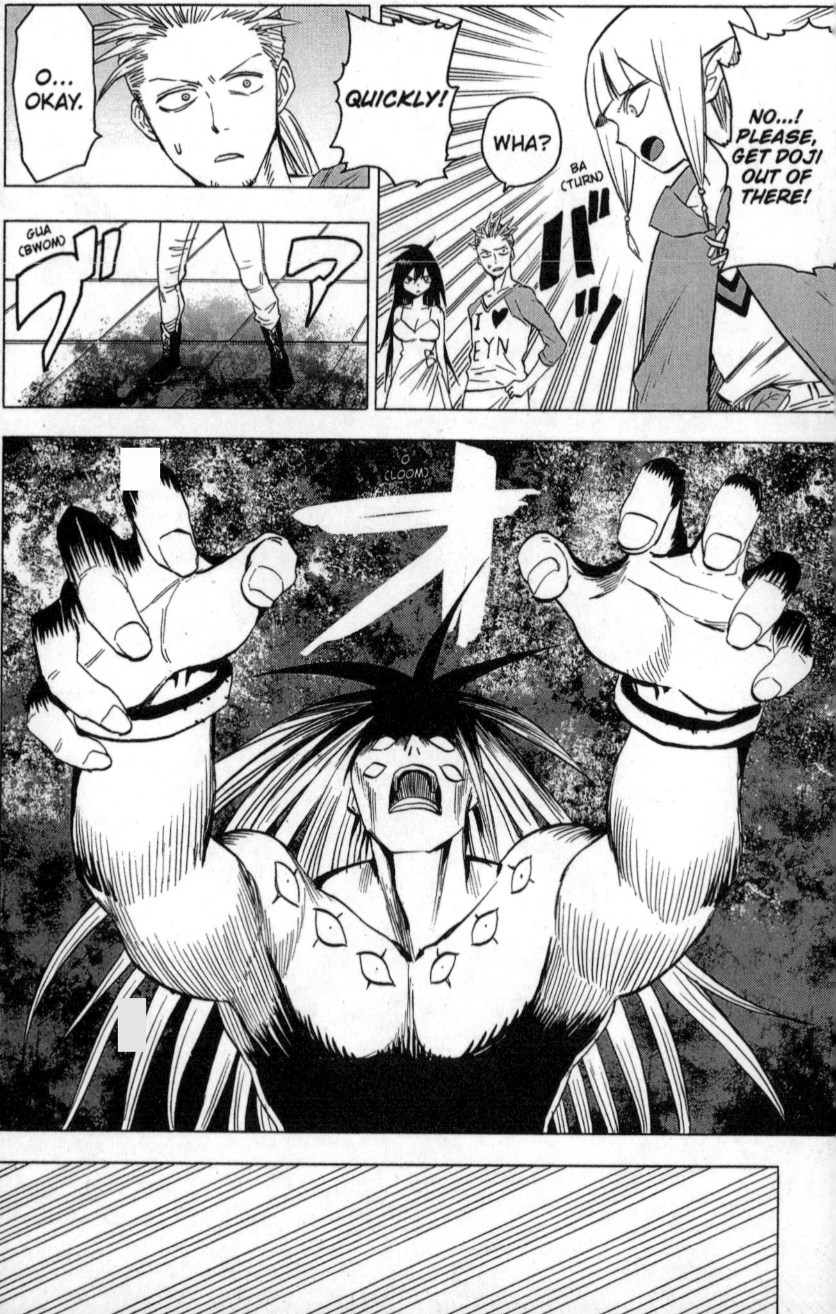
NO...! PLEASE, GET DOJI OUT OF THERE!
WHA?
BA (TURN)
QUICKLY!
O... OKAY.
GUA (BWOM)
O (LOOM)

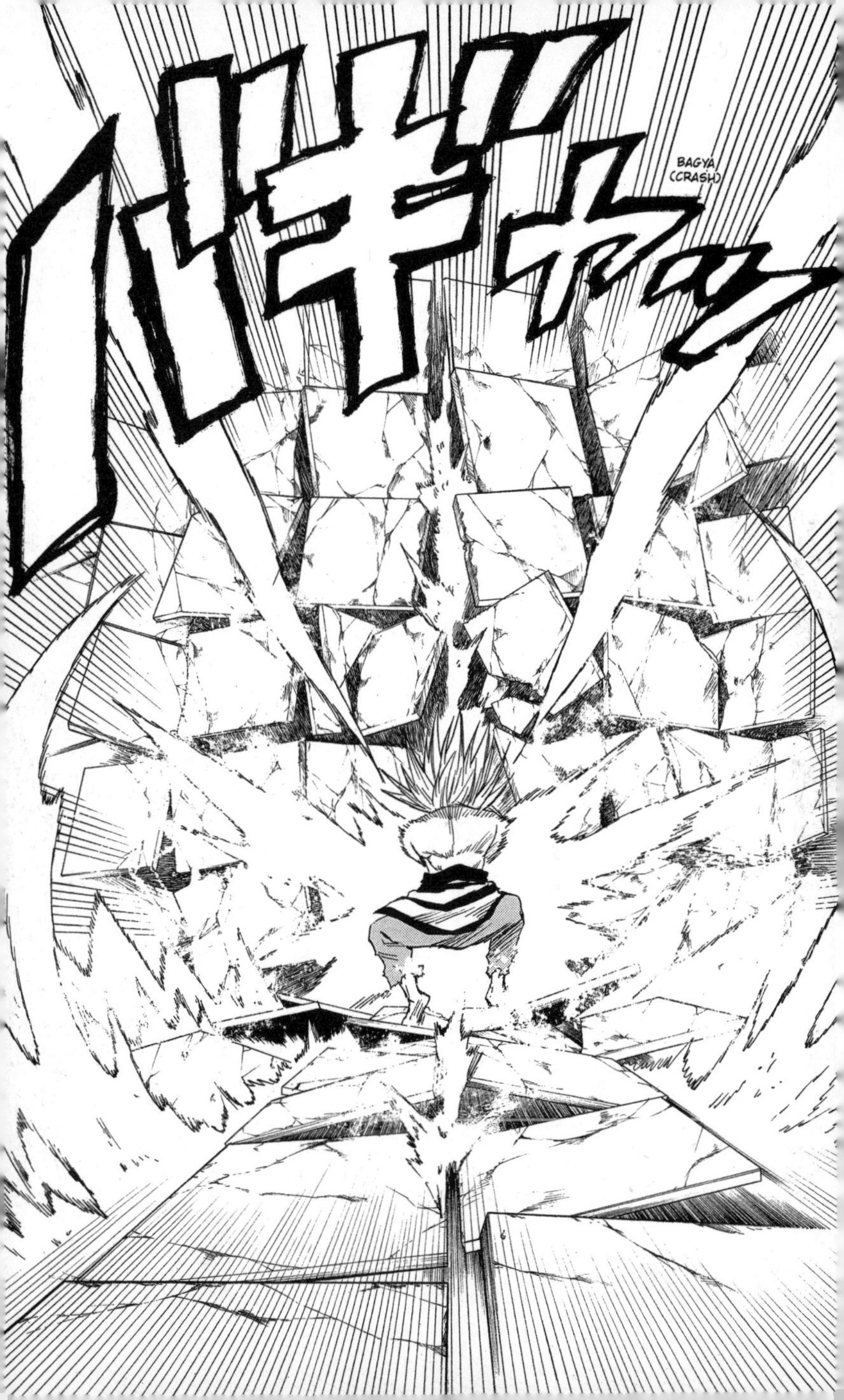
バギャ
BAGYA
(CRASH)

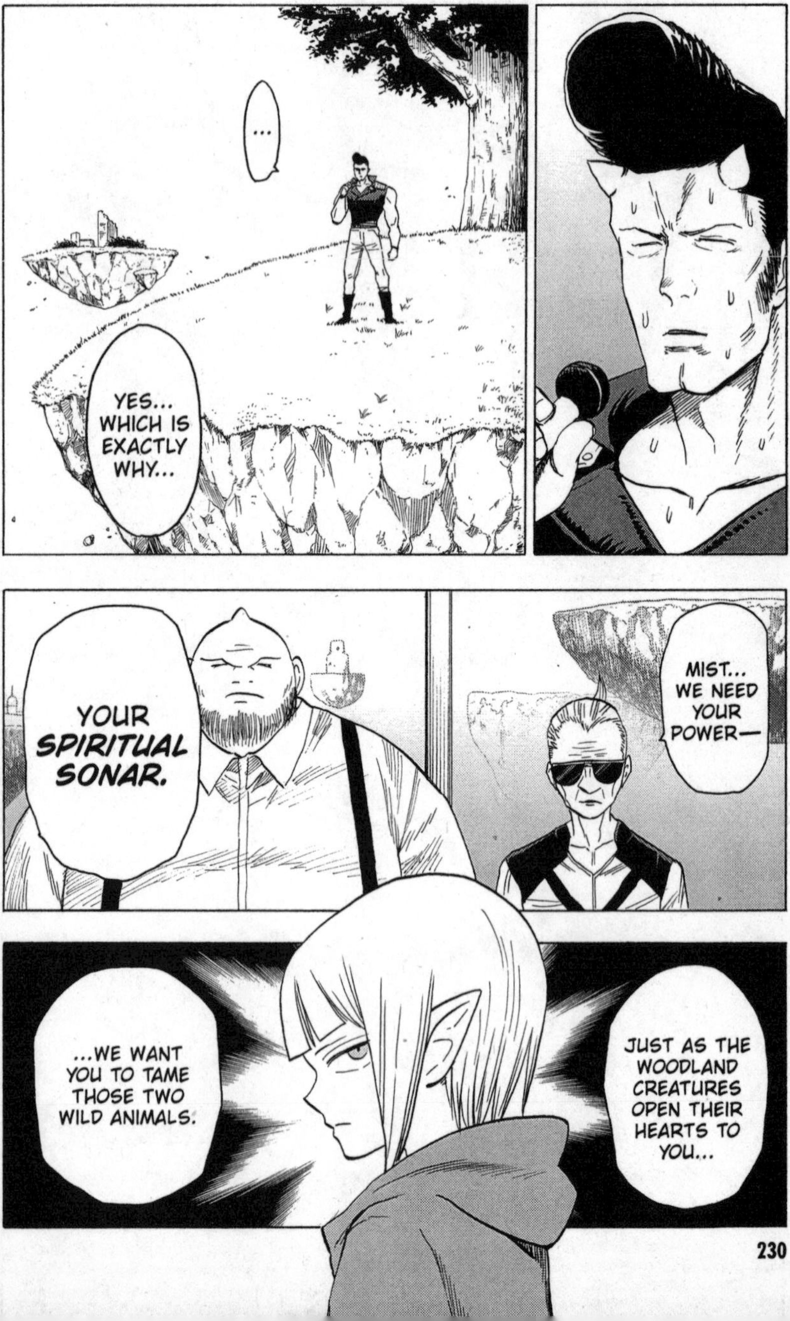
...
YES... WHICH IS EXACTLY WHY...
MIST... WE NEED YOUR POWER—
YOUR SPIRITUAL SONAR.
JUST AS THE WOODLAND CREATURES OPEN THEIR HEARTS TO YOU...
...WE WANT YOU TO TAME THOSE TWO WILD ANIMALS.

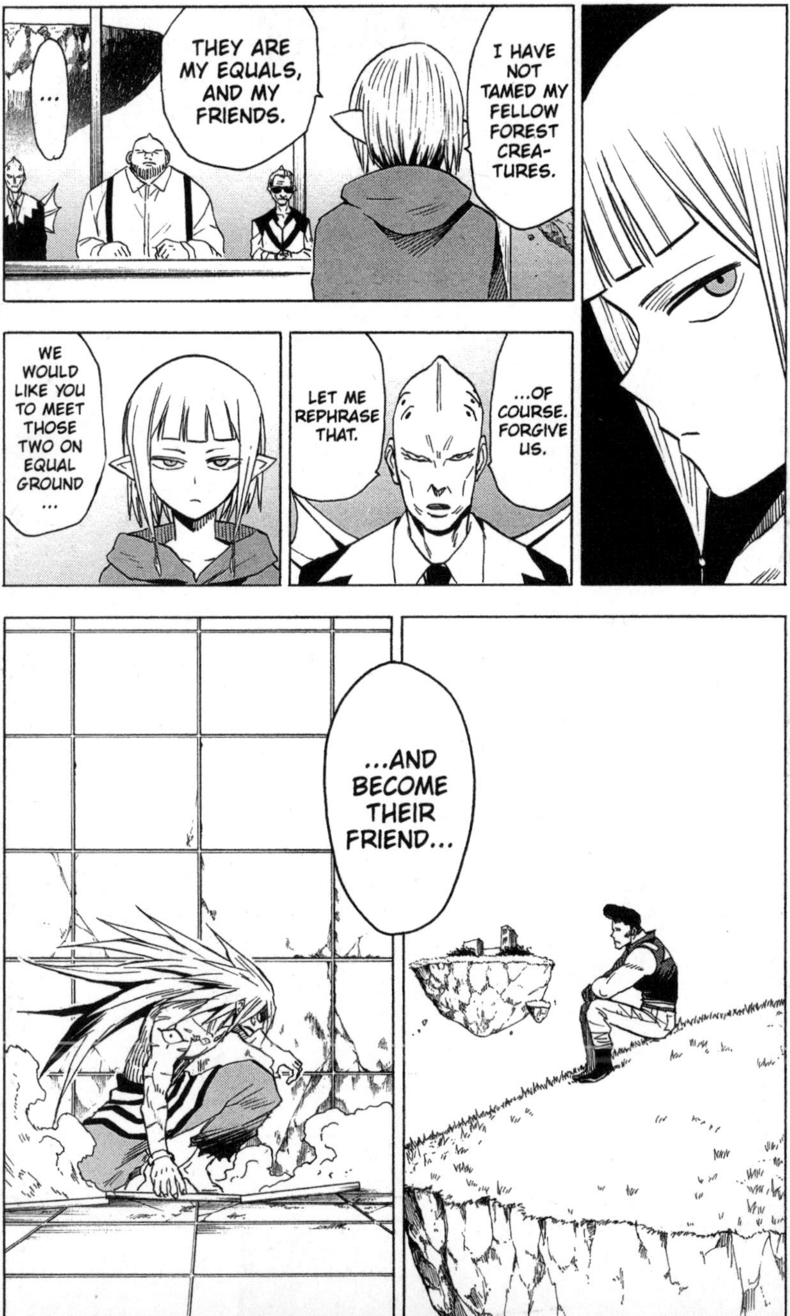
I HAVE NOT TAMED MY FELLOW FOREST CREA- TURES.
THEY ARE MY EQUALS, AND MY FRIENDS.
...
...OF COURSE. FORGIVE US.
LET ME REPHRASE THAT.
WE WOULD LIKE YOU TO MEET THOSE TWO ON EQUAL GROUND ...
...AND BECOME THEIR FRIEND...

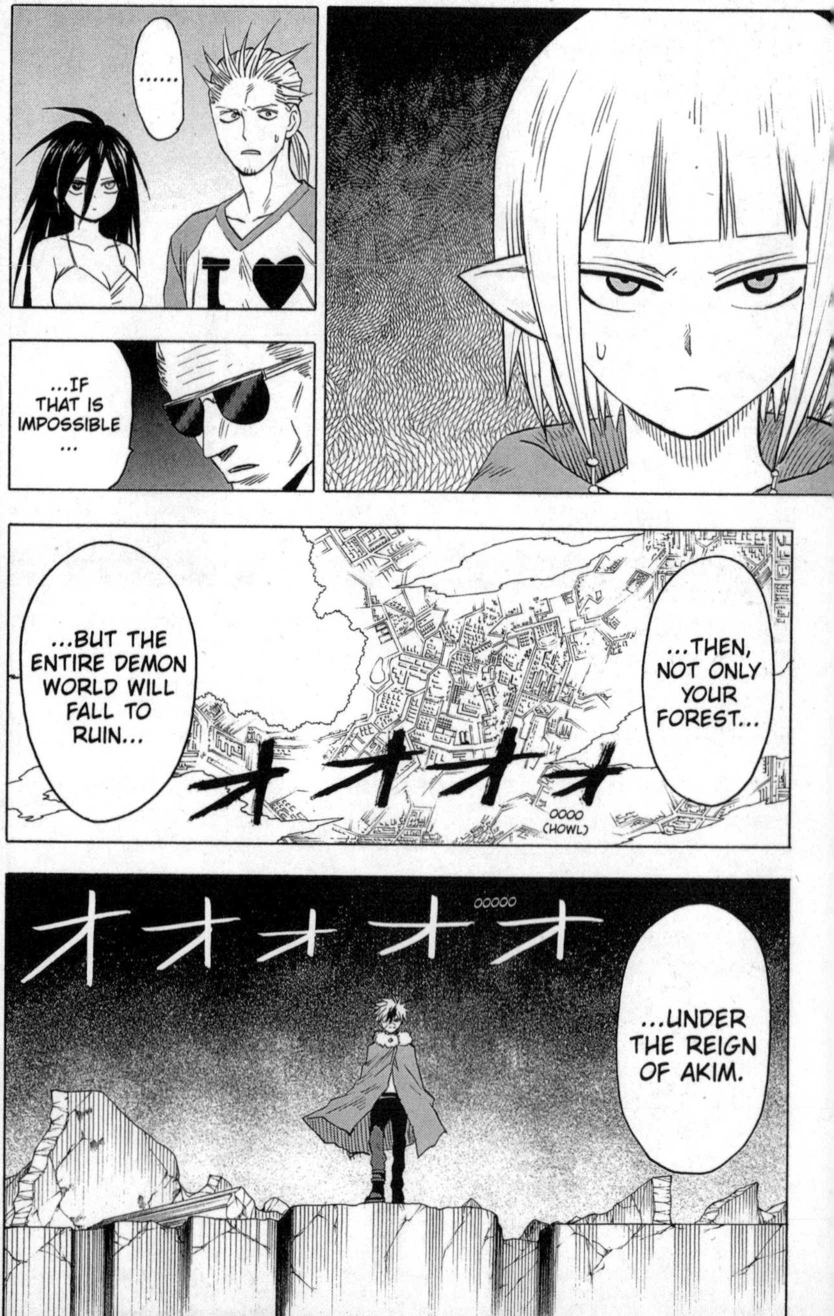
......
...IF THAT IS IMPOSSIBLE...
...THEN, NOT ONLY YOUR FOREST...
オオオオ
OOOO (HOWL)
...BUT THE ENTIRE DEMON WORLD WILL FALL TO RUIN...
オオオオオ
OOOOO
...UNDER THE REIGN OF AKIM.

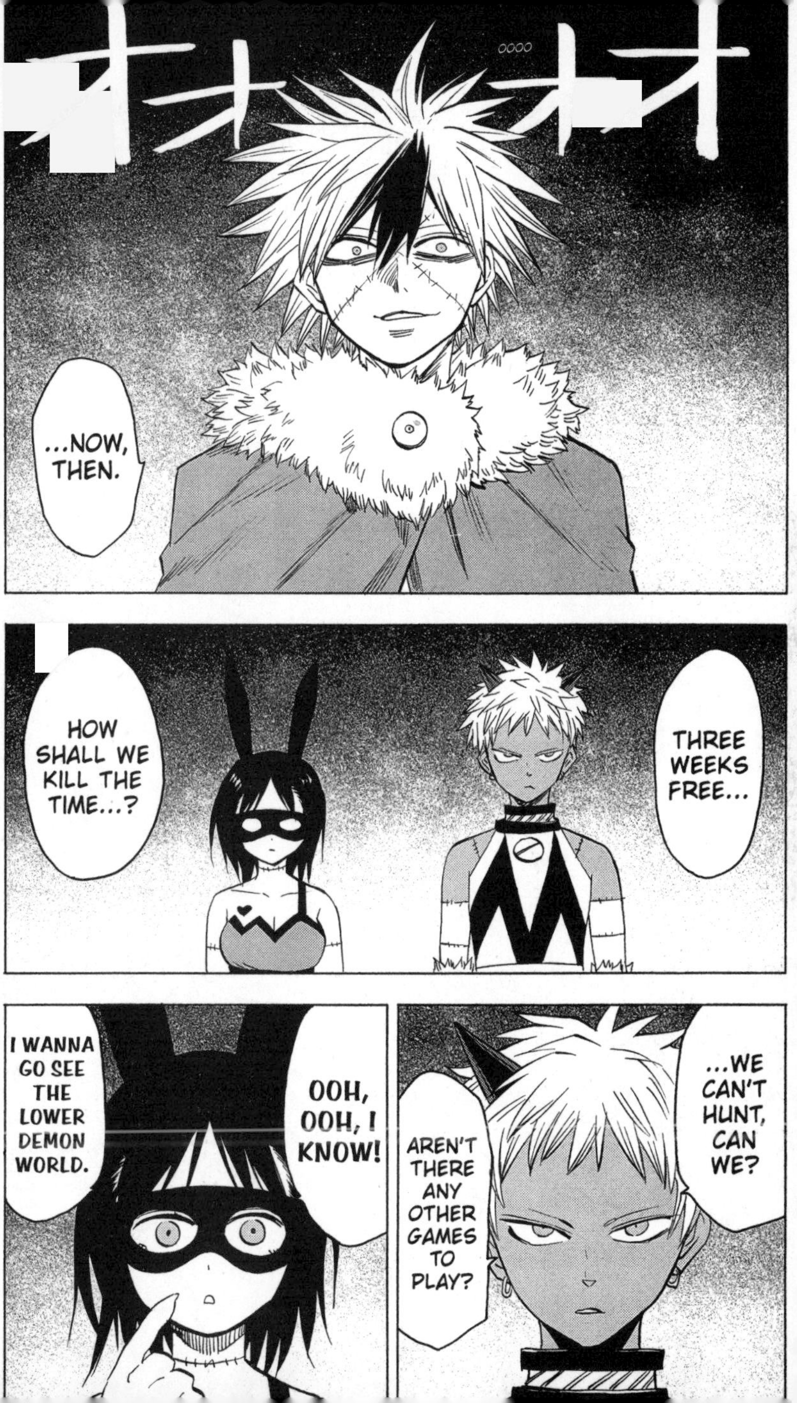
oooo
...NOW, THEN.
THREE WEEKS FREE...
HOW SHALL WE KILL THE TIME...?
...WE CAN'T HUNT, CAN WE?
AREN'T THERE ANY OTHER GAMES TO PLAY?
OOH, OOH, I KNOW!
I WANNA GO SEE THE LOWER DEMON WORLD.

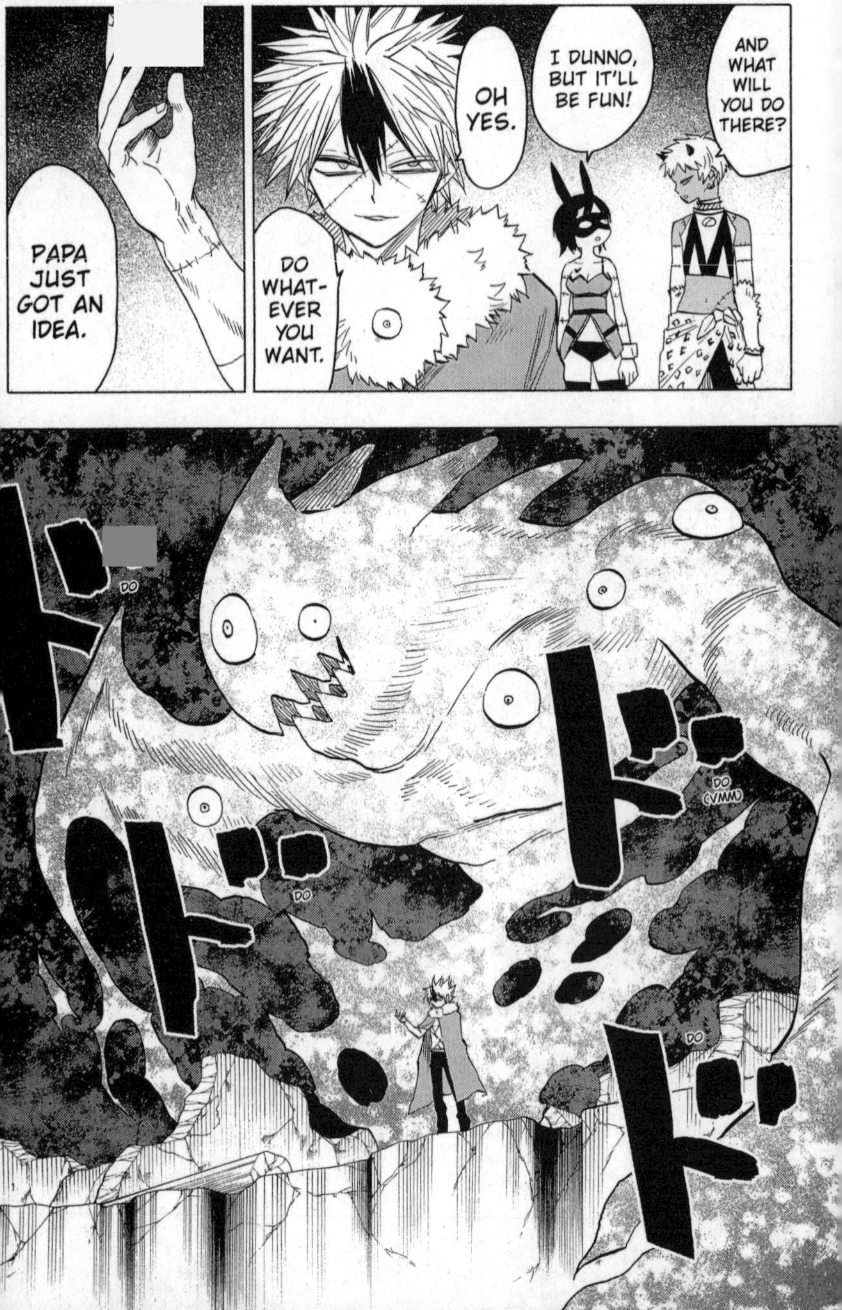
AND WHAT WILL YOU DO THERE?
I DUNNO, BUT IT'LL BE FUN!
OH YES.
DO WHAT-EVER YOU WANT.
PAPA JUST GOT AN IDEA.
DO
DO (VMM)
DO
DO

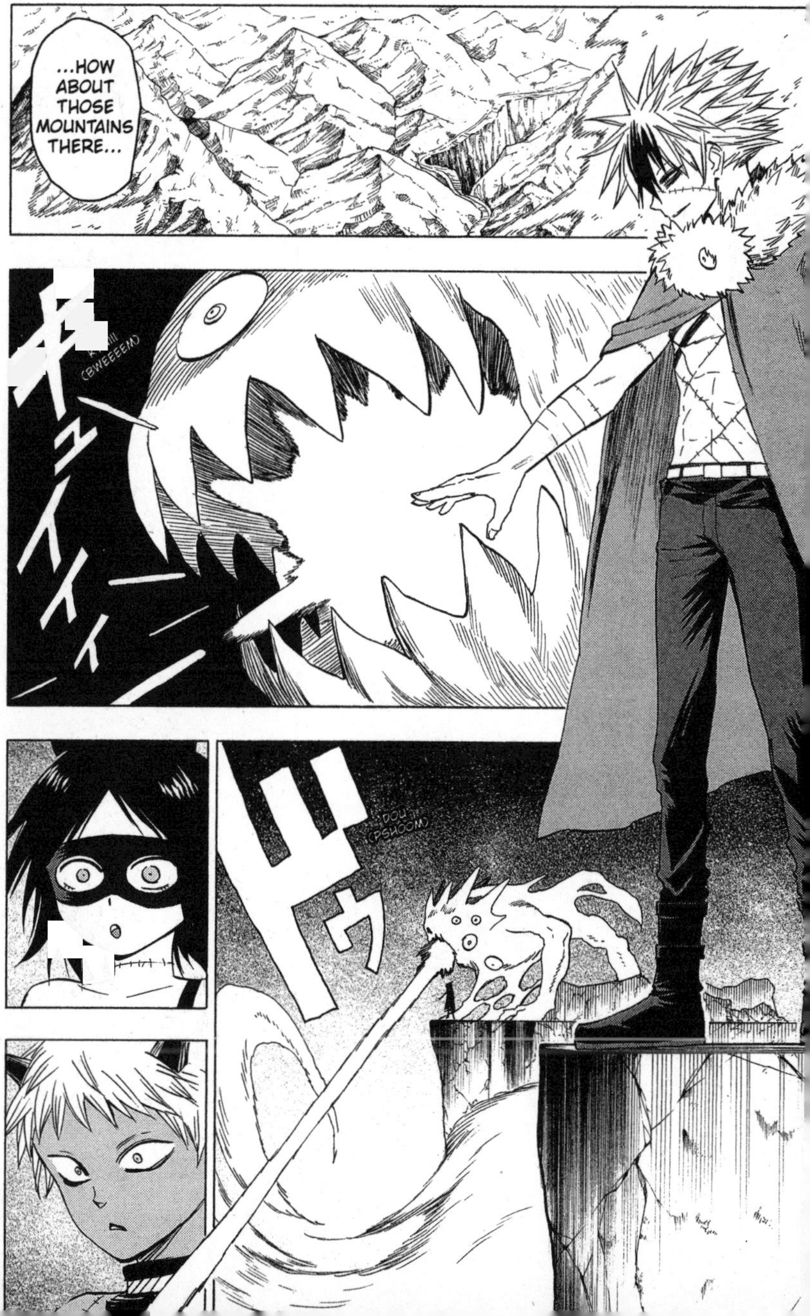
...HOW ABOUT THOSE MOUNTAINS THERE...
(BWEEEEM)
ドウ
DOU
(PSHOOM)

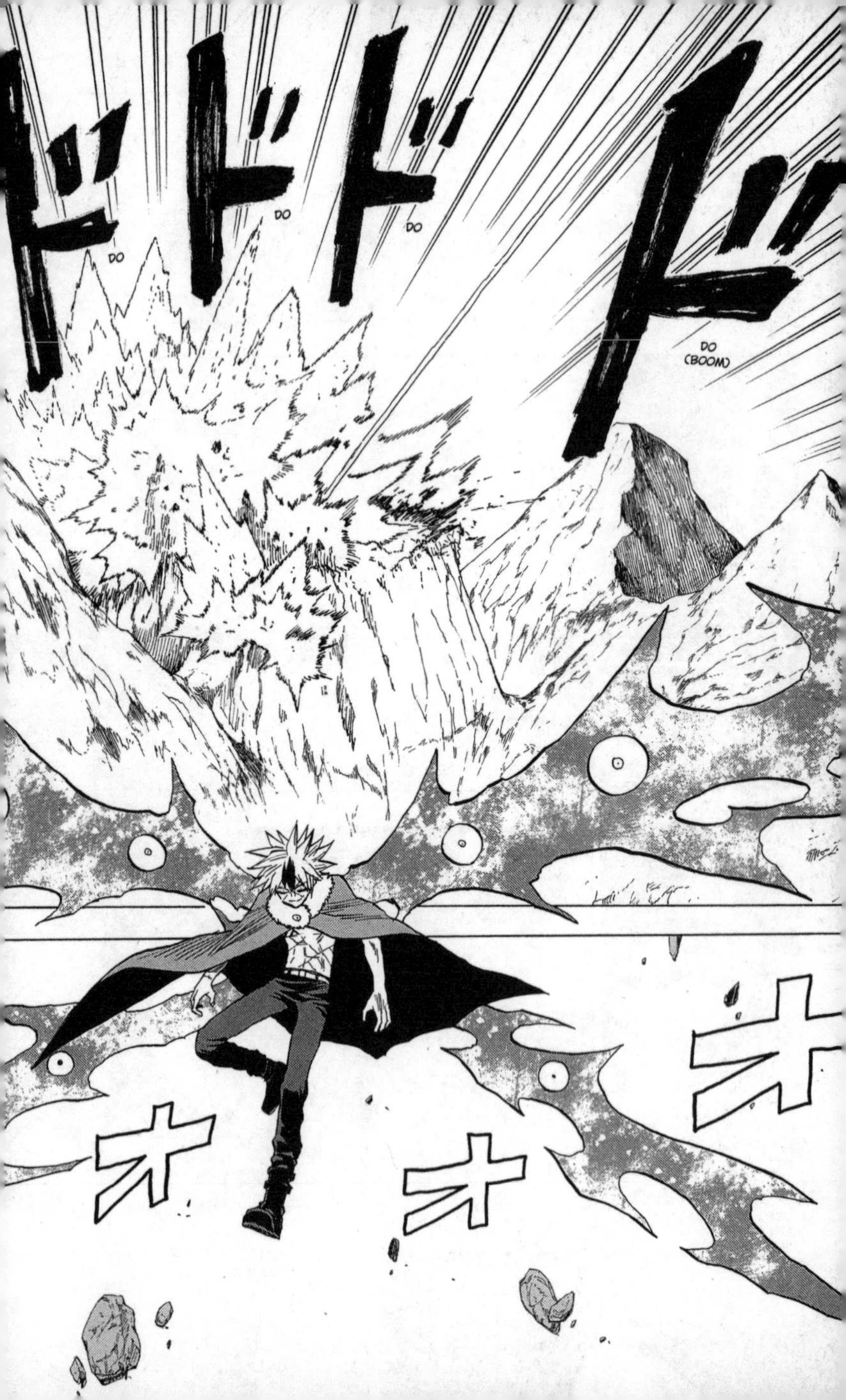
ドドドド
DO (BOOM)
DO
DO
DO
オオオ

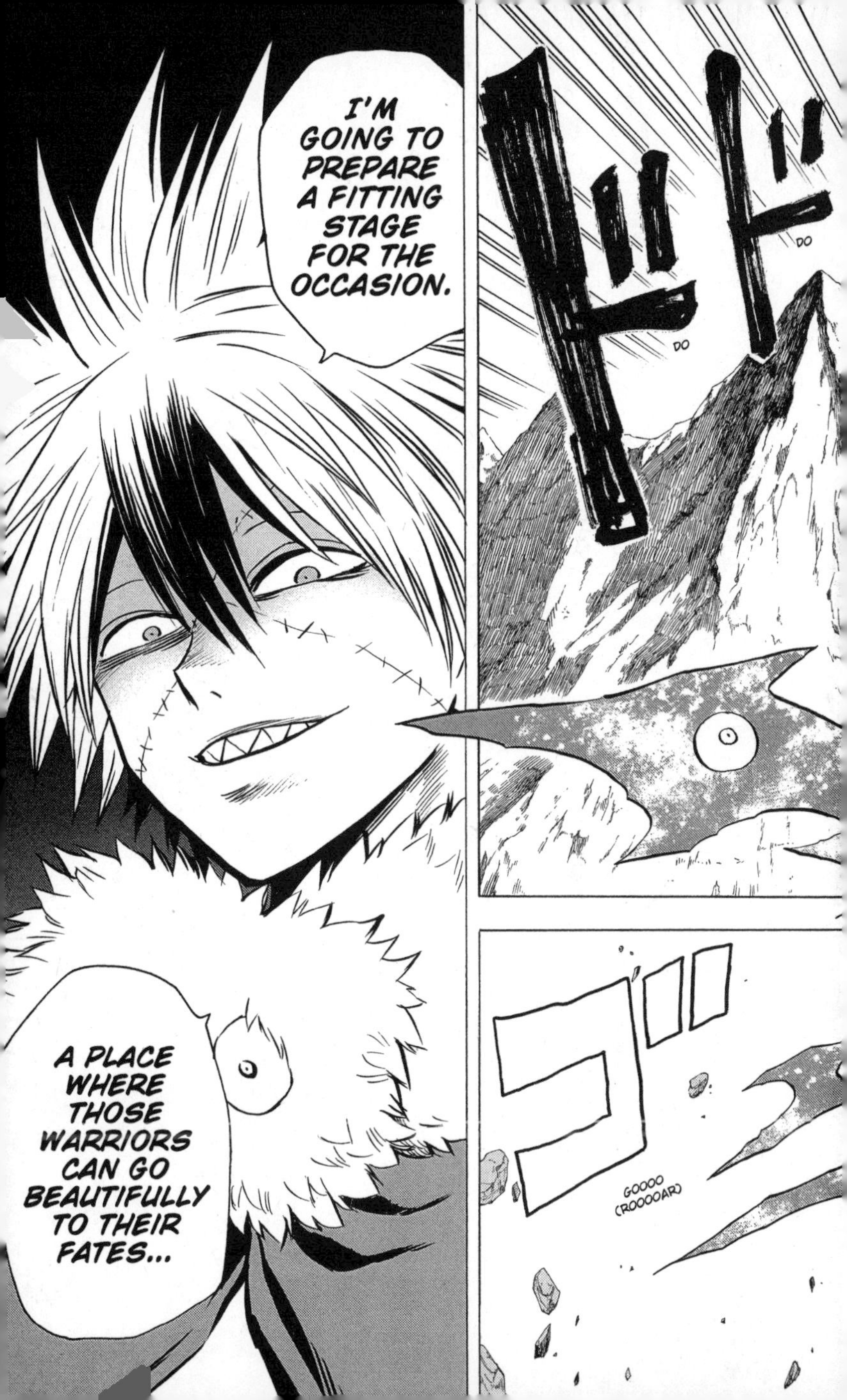
DO
DO
GOOOO (ROOOOAR)
I'M GOING TO PREPARE A FITTING STAGE FOR THE OCCASION.
A PLACE WHERE THOSE WARRIORS CAN GO BEAUTIFULLY TO THEIR FATES...

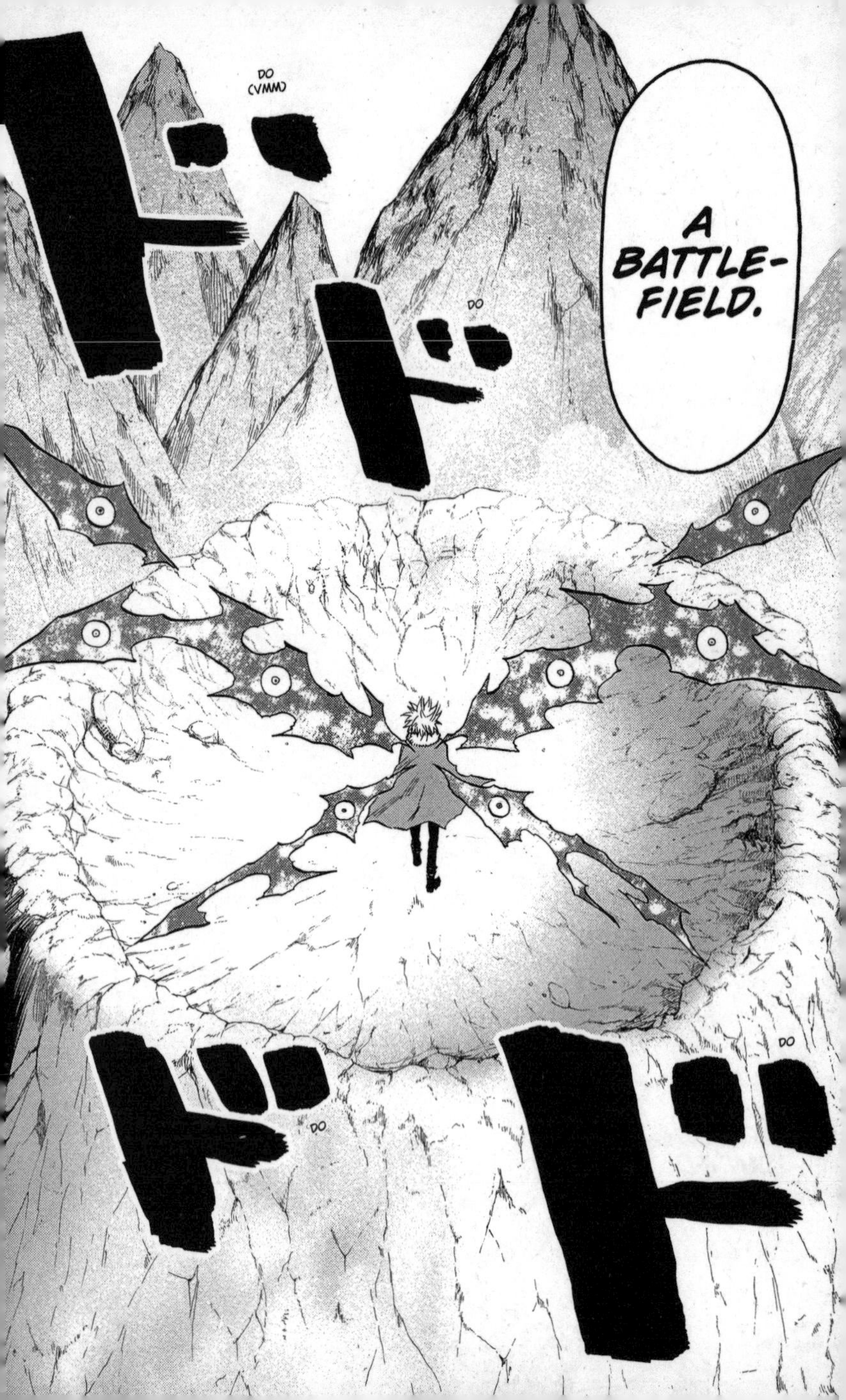
A BATTLE-FIELD.
DO
DO (VMM)
DO
DO

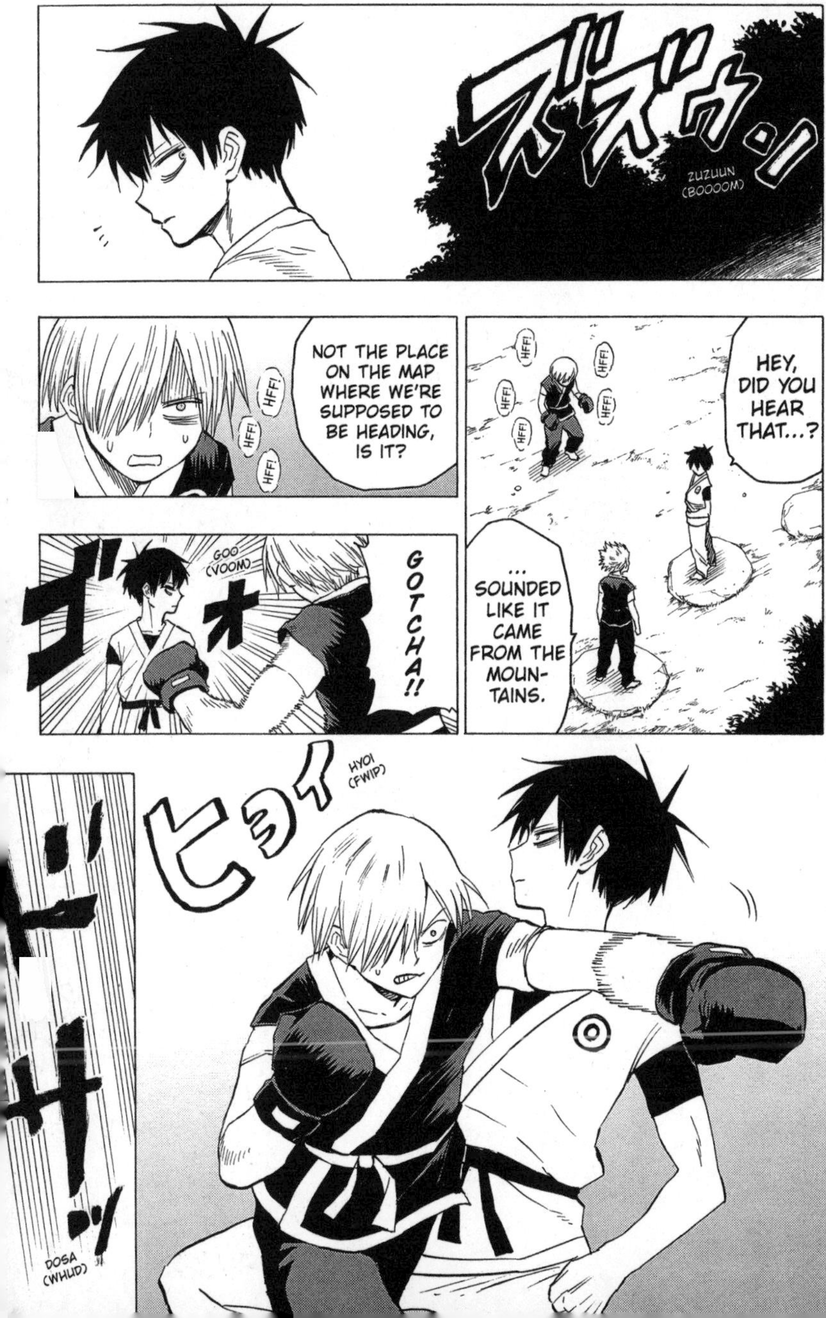
ZUZUUN (BOOOOM)
HEY, DID YOU HEAR THAT...?
HFF!
HFF!
HFF!
HFF!
HFF!
... SOUNDED LIKE IT CAME FROM THE MOUN-TAINS.
NOT THE PLACE ON THE MAP WHERE WE'RE SUPPOSED TO BE HEADING, IS IT?
HFF!
HFF!
HFF!
GOTCHA!!
GOO (VOOM)
HYOI (FWIP)
DOSA (WHUD)

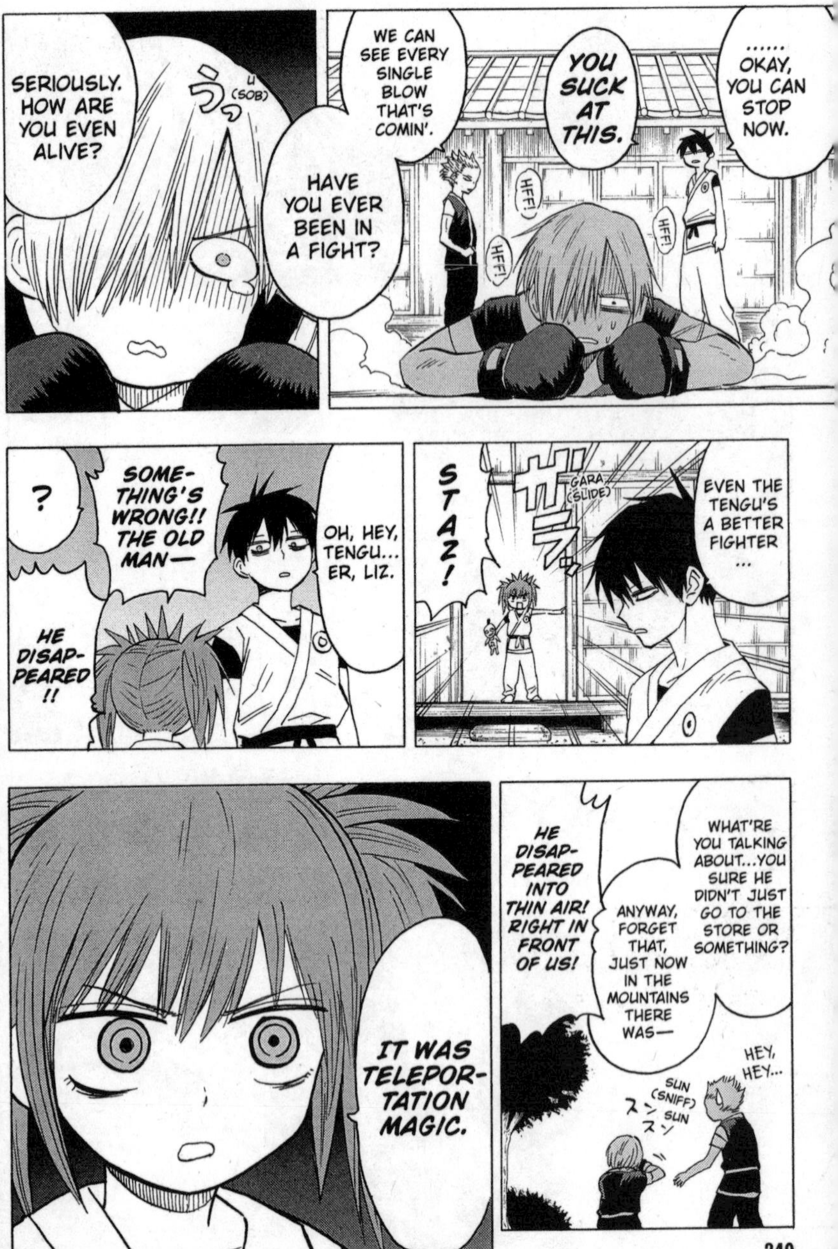
...... OKAY, YOU CAN STOP NOW.
YOU SUCK AT THIS.
WE CAN SEE EVERY SINGLE BLOW THAT'S COMIN'.
HAVE YOU EVER BEEN IN A FIGHT?
HFF!
HFF!
HFF!
U (SOB)
SERIOUSLY. HOW ARE YOU EVEN ALIVE?
EVEN THE TENGU'S A BETTER FIGHTER ...
GARA (SLIDE)
STAZ!
OH, HEY, TENGU... ER, LIZ.
SOME-THING'S WRONG!! THE OLD MAN—
?
HE DISAP-PEARED !!
WHAT'RE YOU TALKING ABOUT...YOU SURE HE DIDN'T JUST GO TO THE STORE OR SOMETHING?
HE DISAP-PEARED INTO THIN AIR! RIGHT IN FRONT OF US!
ANYWAY, FORGET THAT, JUST NOW IN THE MOUNTAINS THERE WAS—
HEY, HEY...
SUN (SNIFF) SUN
IT WAS TELEPOR-TATION MAGIC.

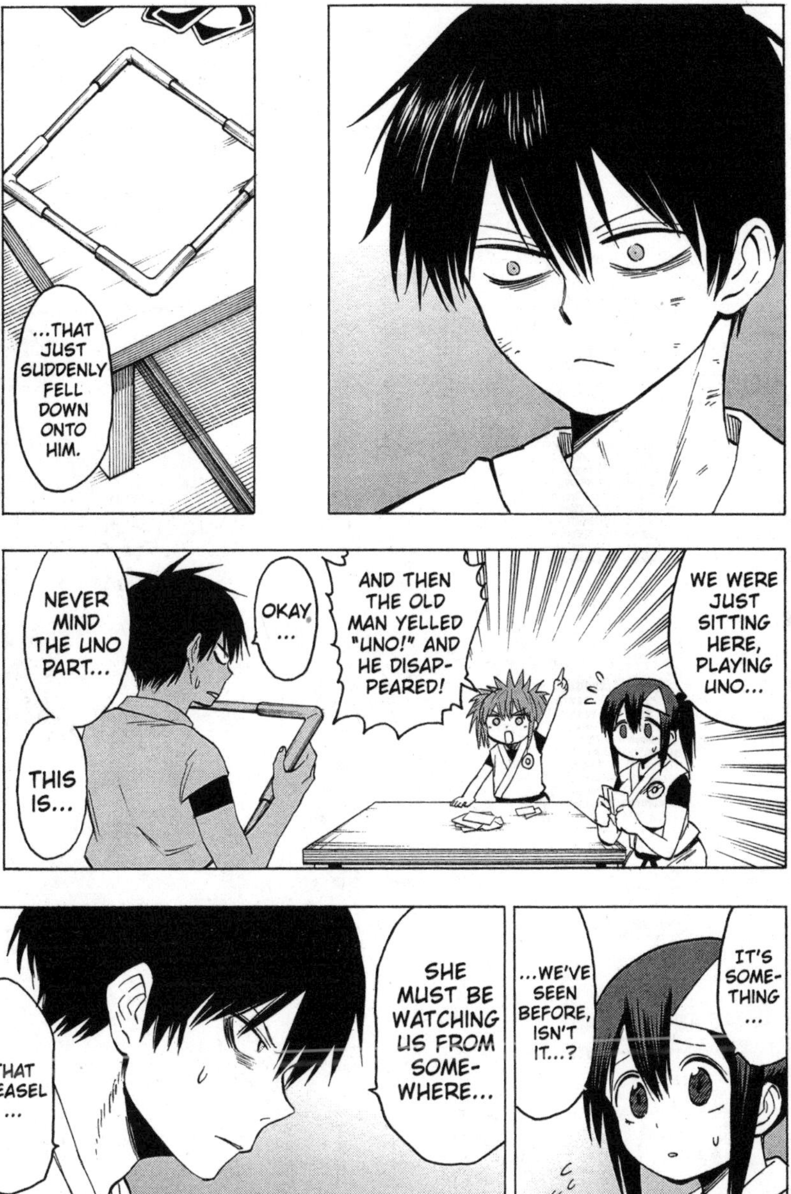
...THAT JUST SUDDENLY FELL DOWN ONTO HIM.
WE WERE JUST SITTING HERE, PLAYING UNO...
AND THEN THE OLD MAN YELLED "UNO!" AND HE DISAPPEARED!
OKAY...
NEVER MIND THE UNO PART...
THIS IS...
IT'S SOMETHING...
...WE'VE SEEN BEFORE, ISN'T IT...?
SHE MUST BE WATCHING US FROM SOMEWHERE...
THAT WEASEL...

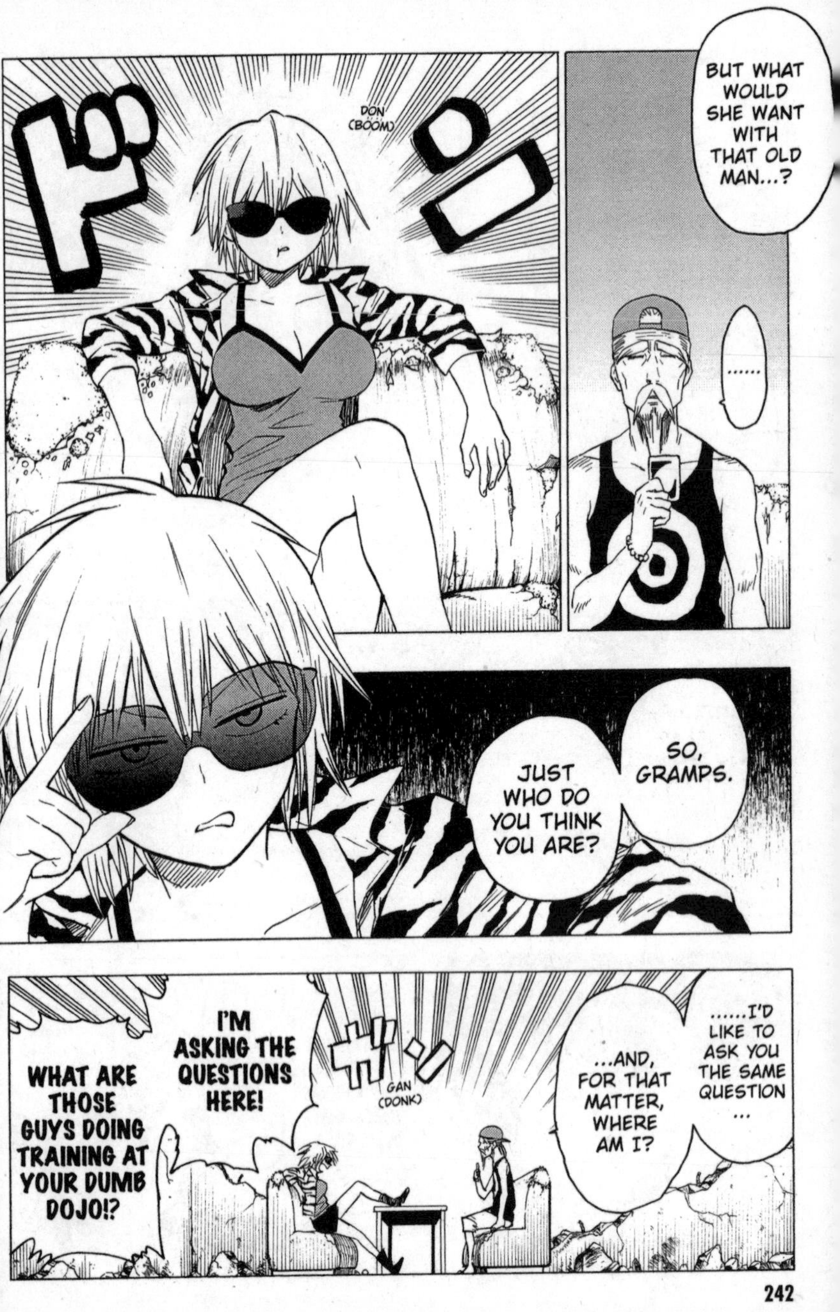
BUT WHAT WOULD SHE WANT WITH THAT OLD MAN...?
......
DON (BOOM)
SO, GRAMPS.
JUST WHO DO YOU THINK YOU ARE?
......I'D LIKE TO ASK YOU THE SAME QUESTION ...
...AND, FOR THAT MATTER, WHERE AM I?
GAN (DONK)
I'M ASKING THE QUESTIONS HERE!
WHAT ARE THOSE GUYS DOING TRAINING AT YOUR DUMB DOJO!?

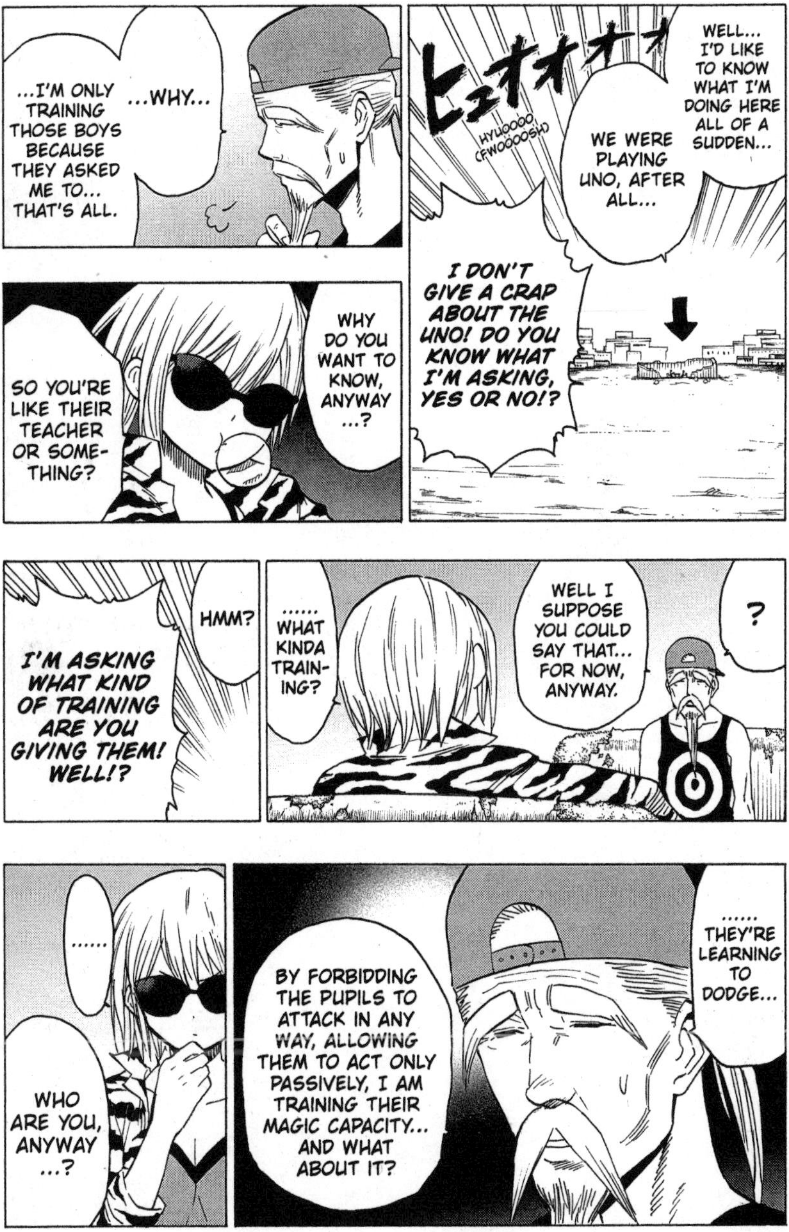

WELL... I'D LIKE TO KNOW WHAT I'M DOING HERE ALL OF A SUDDEN...
WE WERE PLAYING UNO, AFTER ALL...
ヒュオオオオ
HYUOOOO (FWOOOOSH)
I DON'T GIVE A CRAP ABOUT THE UNO! DO YOU KNOW WHAT I'M ASKING, YES OR NO!?
...WHY...
...I'M ONLY TRAINING THOSE BOYS BECAUSE THEY ASKED ME TO... THAT'S ALL.
WHY DO YOU WANT TO KNOW, ANYWAY...?
SO YOU'RE LIKE THEIR TEACHER OR SOMETHING?
?
WELL I SUPPOSE YOU COULD SAY THAT... FOR NOW, ANYWAY.
......WHAT KINDA TRAINING?
HMM?
I'M ASKING WHAT KIND OF TRAINING ARE YOU GIVING THEM! WELL!?
......THEY'RE LEARNING TO DODGE...
BY FORBIDDING THE PUPILS TO ATTACK IN ANY WAY, ALLOWING THEM TO ACT ONLY PASSIVELY, I AM TRAINING THEIR MAGIC CAPACITY... AND WHAT ABOUT IT?
......
WHO ARE YOU, ANYWAY...?

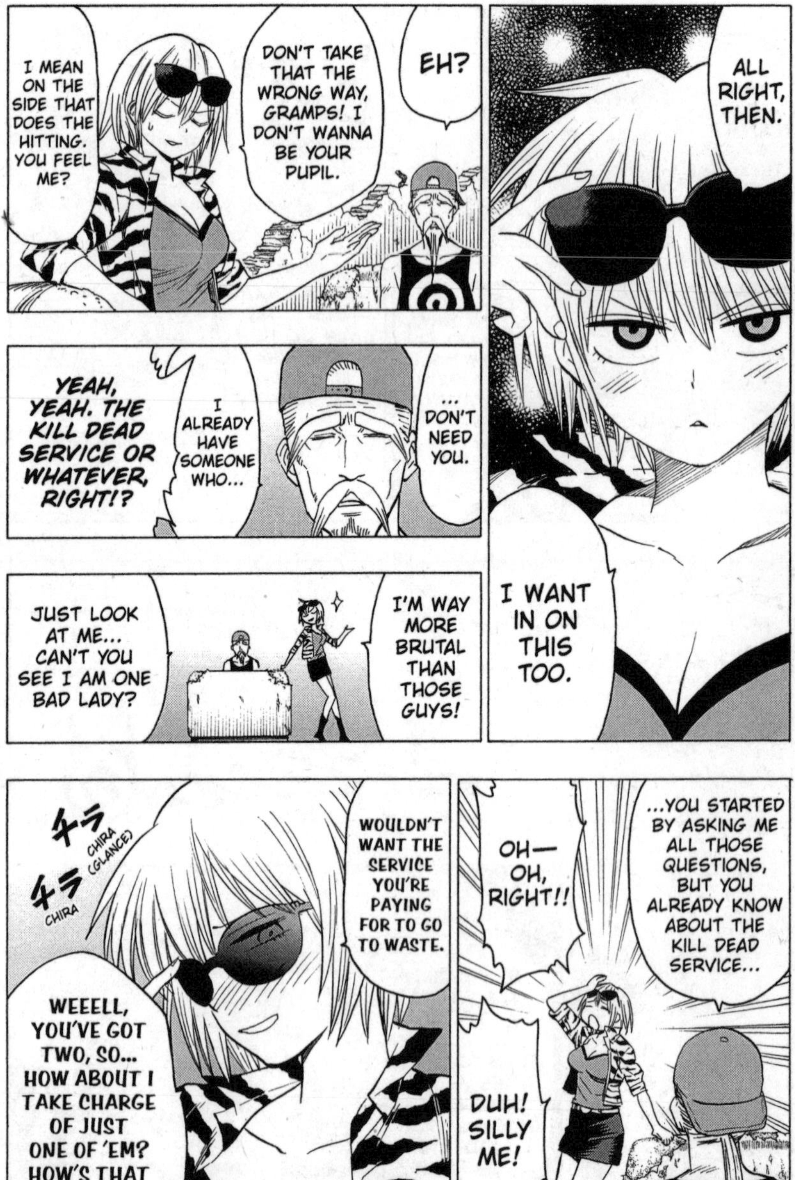
ALL RIGHT, THEN.
I WANT IN ON THIS TOO.
EH?
DON'T TAKE THAT THE WRONG WAY, GRAMPS! I DON'T WANNA BE YOUR PUPIL.
I MEAN ON THE SIDE THAT DOES THE HITTING. YOU FEEL ME?
... DON'T NEED YOU.
I ALREADY HAVE SOMEONE WHO...
YEAH, YEAH. THE KILL DEAD SERVICE OR WHATEVER, RIGHT!?
I'M WAY MORE BRUTAL THAN THOSE GUYS!
JUST LOOK AT ME... CAN'T YOU SEE I AM ONE BAD LADY?
...YOU STARTED BY ASKING ME ALL THOSE QUESTIONS, BUT YOU ALREADY KNOW ABOUT THE KILL DEAD SERVICE...
OH— OH, RIGHT!!
DUH! SILLY ME!
WOULDN'T WANT THE SERVICE YOU'RE PAYING FOR TO GO TO WASTE.
チラ
CHIRA (GLANCE)
チラ
CHIRA
WEEELL, YOU'VE GOT TWO, SO... HOW ABOUT I TAKE CHARGE OF JUST ONE OF 'EM? HOW'S THAT SOUND?

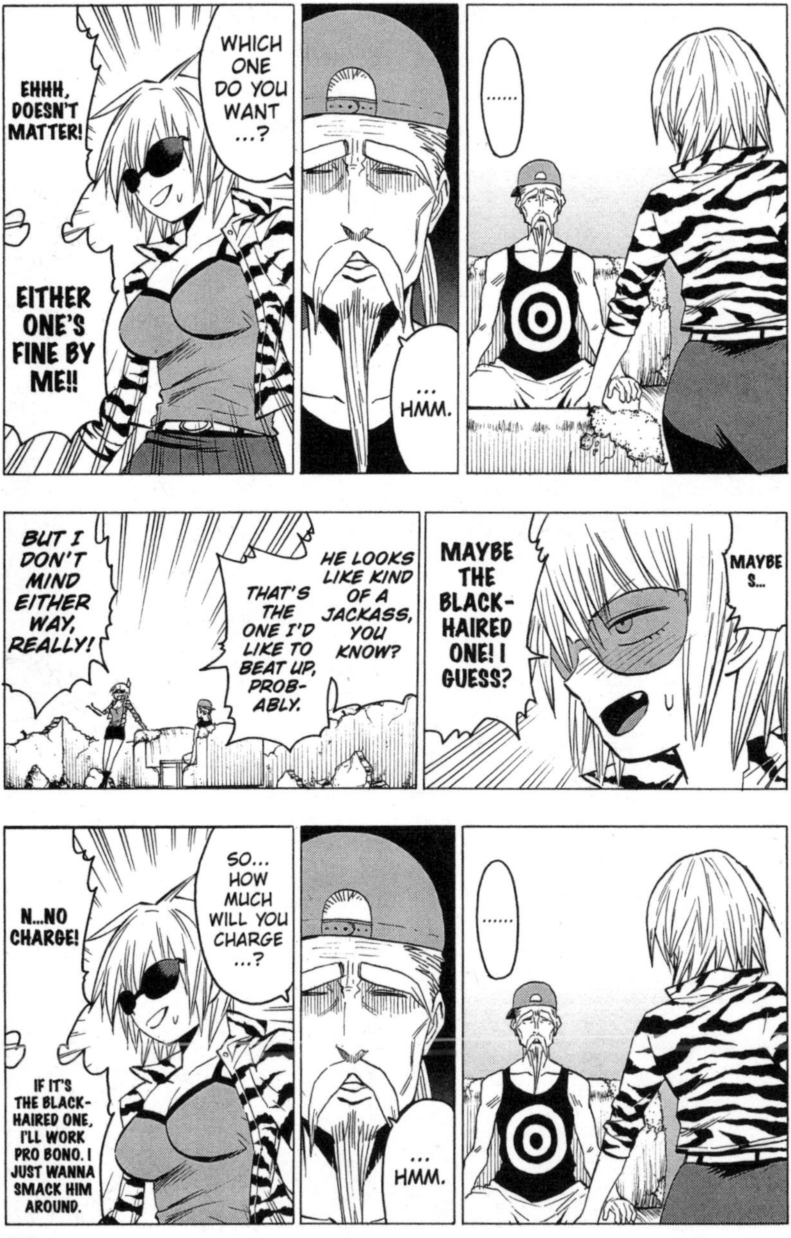
......
... HMM.
WHICH ONE DO YOU WANT ...?
EHHH, DOESN'T MATTER!
EITHER ONE'S FINE BY ME!!
MAYBE S...
MAYBE THE BLACK-HAIRED ONE! I GUESS?
HE LOOKS LIKE KIND OF A JACKASS, YOU KNOW?
THAT'S THE ONE I'D LIKE TO BEAT UP, PROBABLY.
BUT I DON'T MIND EITHER WAY, REALLY!
......
... HMM.
SO... HOW MUCH WILL YOU CHARGE ...?
N...NO CHARGE!
IF IT'S THE BLACK-HAIRED ONE, I'LL WORK PRO BONO. I JUST WANNA SMACK HIM AROUND.

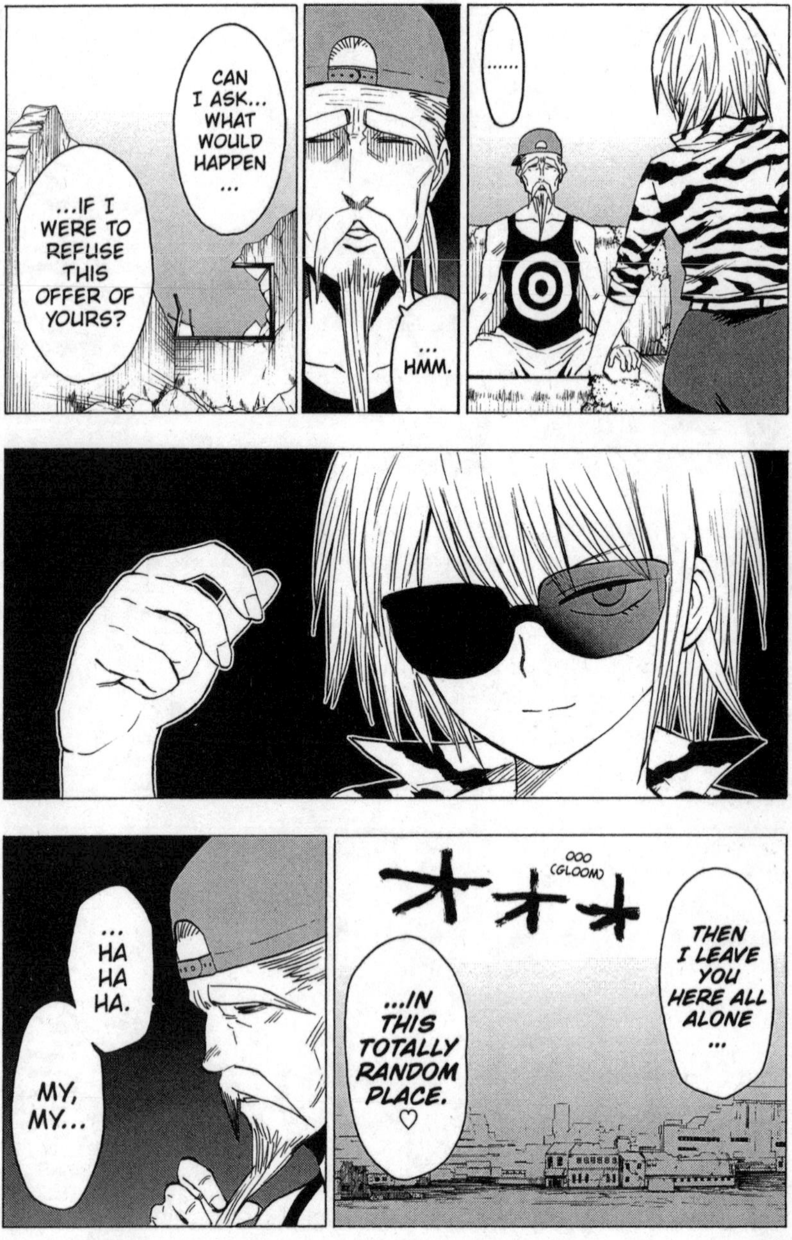
......
... HMM.
CAN I ASK... WHAT WOULD HAPPEN ...
...IF I WERE TO REFUSE THIS OFFER OF YOURS?
OOO (GLOOM)
THEN I LEAVE YOU HERE ALL ALONE ...
...IN THIS TOTALLY RANDOM PLACE. ♡
... HA HA HA.
MY, MY...

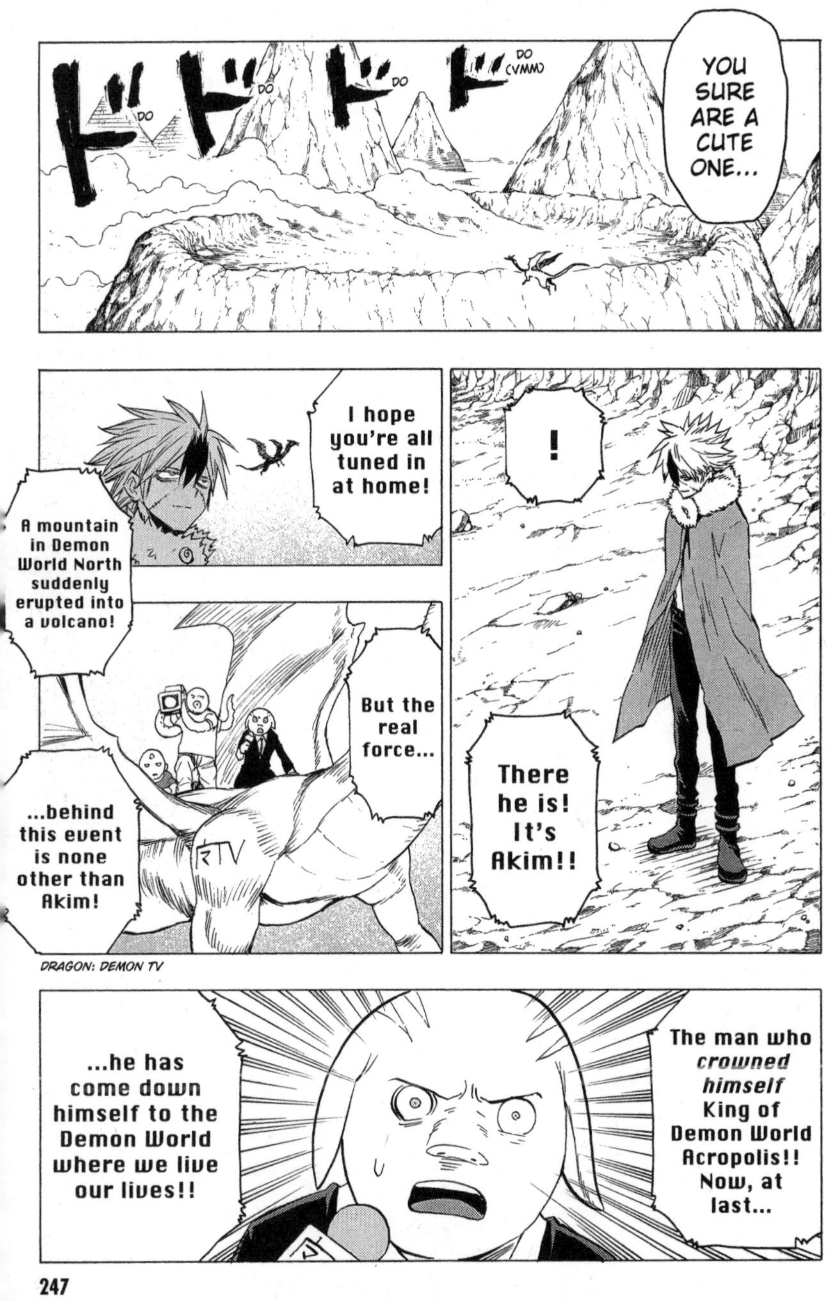
YOU SURE ARE A CUTE ONE...
DO DO DO DO (VMM)
!
There he is! It's Akim!!
I hope you're all tuned in at home!
A mountain in Demon World North suddenly erupted into a volcano!
But the real force...
...behind this event is none other than Akim!
DRAGON: DEMON TV
The man who *crowned himself* King of Demon World Acropolis!! Now, at last...
...he has come down himself to the Demon World where we live our lives!!

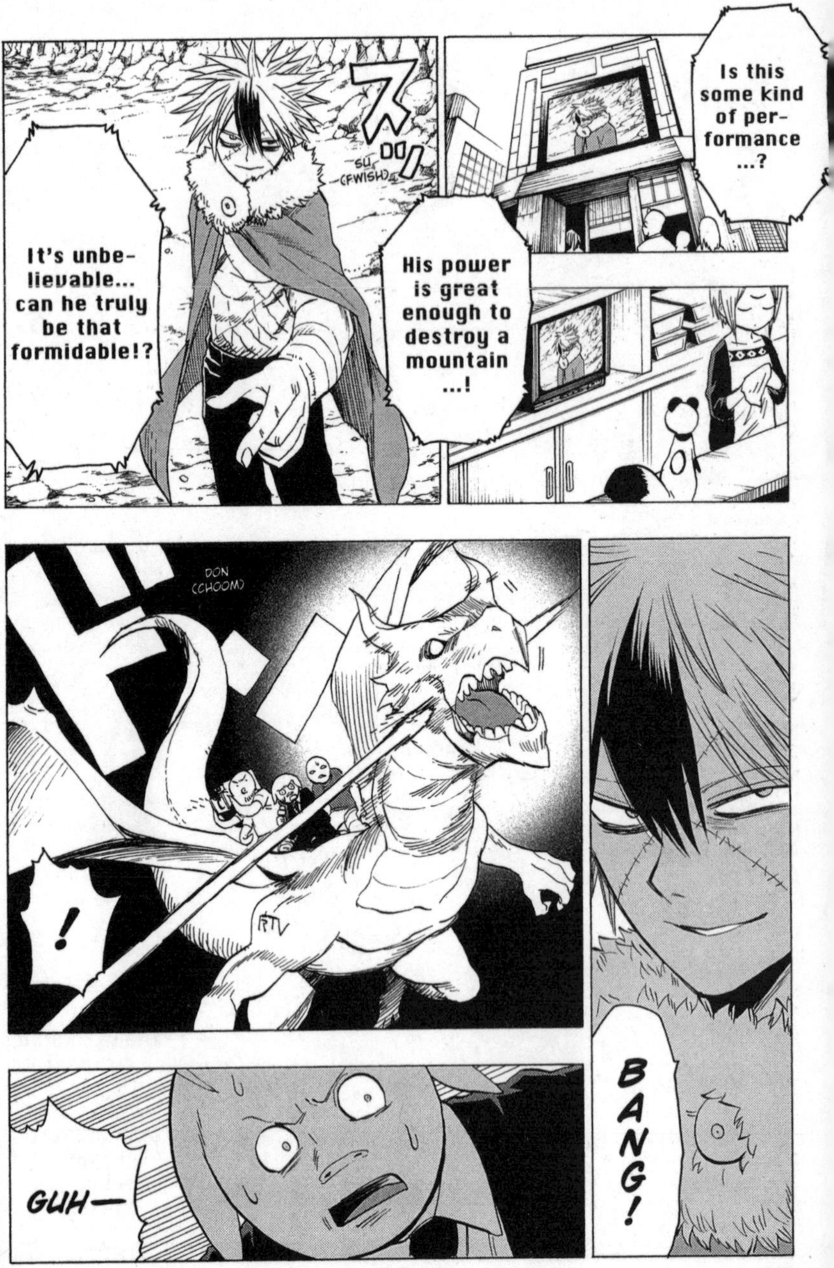
Is this some kind of per-formance ...?
His power is great enough to destroy a mountain ...!
SU (FWISH)
It's unbe-lievable... can he truly be that formidable!?
BANG!
DON (CHOOM)
!
GUH—

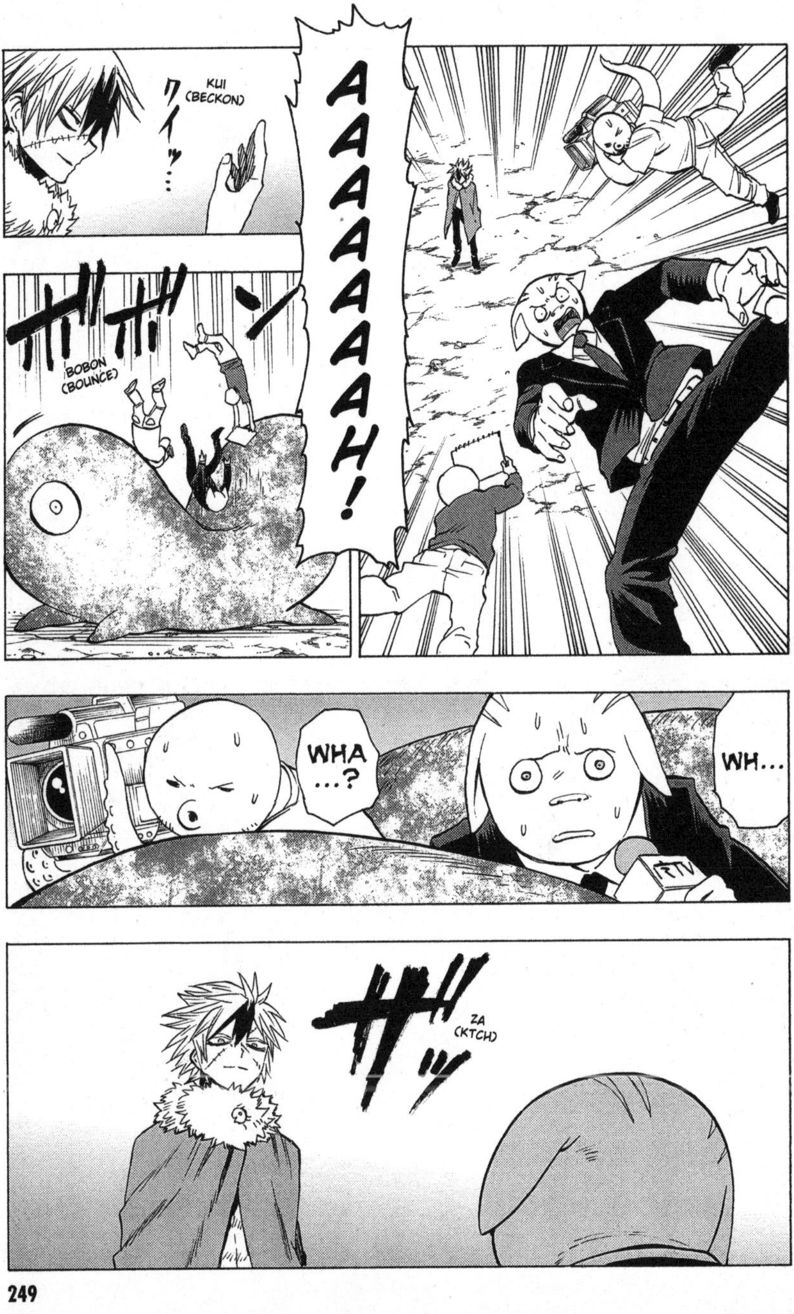
AAAAAAAH!
KUI (BECKON)
BOBON (BOUNCE)
WH...
WHA ...?
ZA (KTCH)

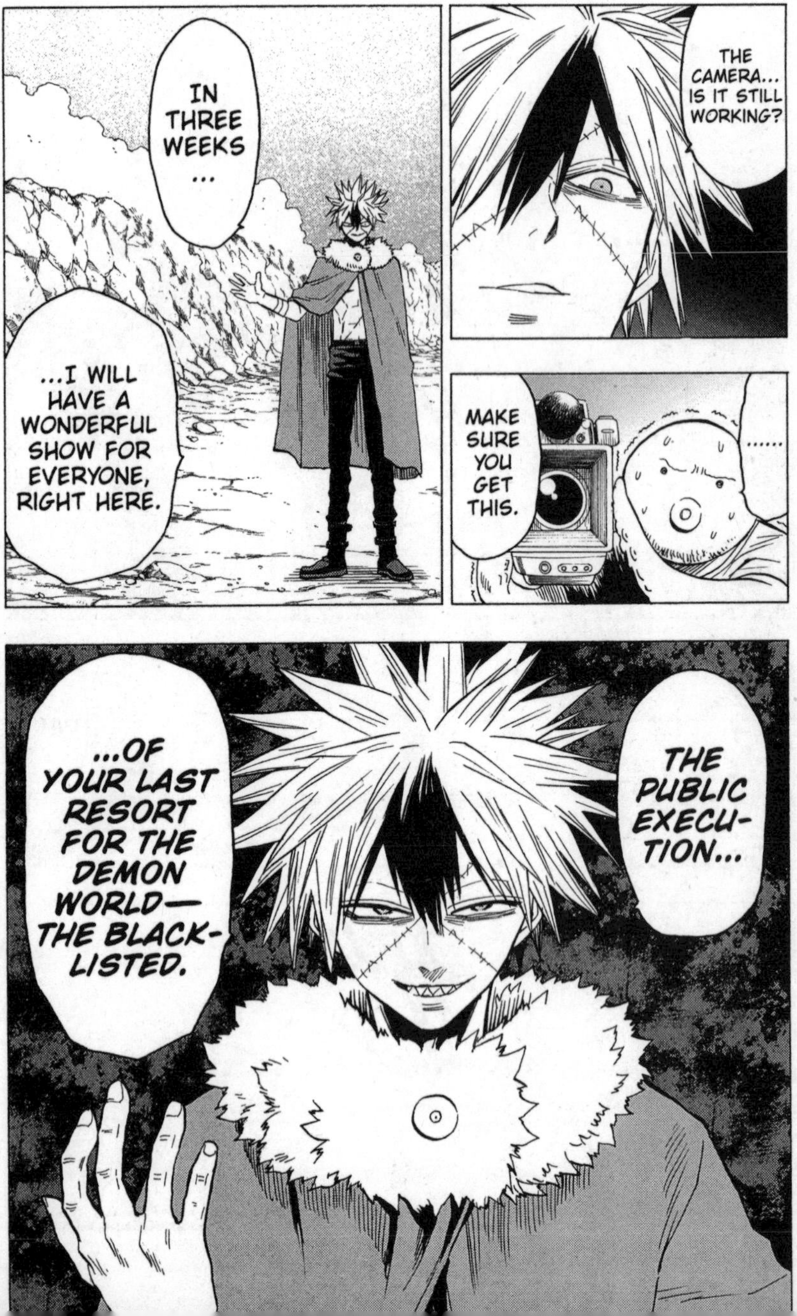
THE CAMERA... IS IT STILL WORKING?
......
MAKE SURE YOU GET THIS.
IN THREE WEEKS ...
...I WILL HAVE A WONDERFUL SHOW FOR EVERYONE, RIGHT HERE.
THE PUBLIC EXECU-TION...
...OF YOUR LAST RESORT FOR THE DEMON WORLD—THE BLACK-LISTED.

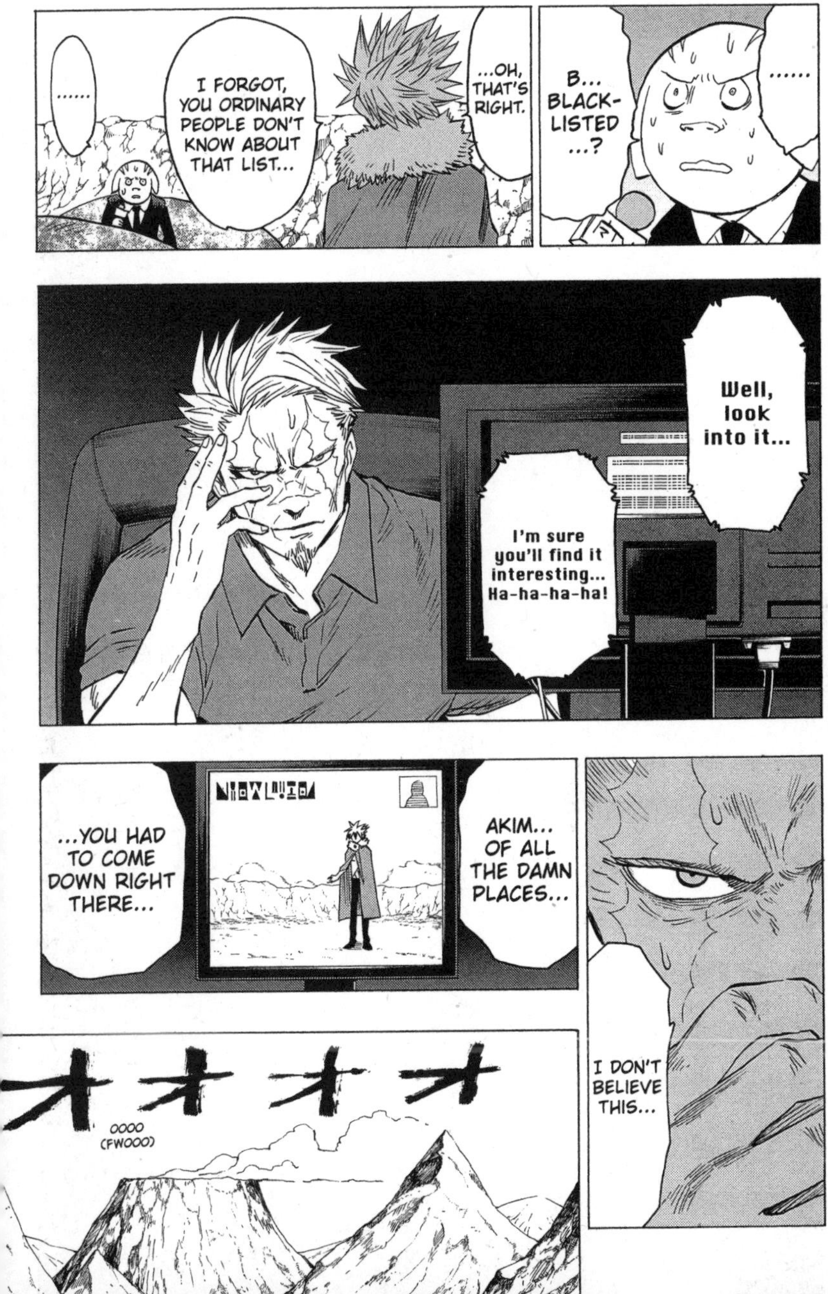
......
B... BLACK-LISTED ...?
...OH, THAT'S RIGHT.
I FORGOT, YOU ORDINARY PEOPLE DON'T KNOW ABOUT THAT LIST...
......
Well, look into it...
I'm sure you'll find it interesting... Ha-ha-ha-ha!
I DON'T BELIEVE THIS...
AKIM... OF ALL THE DAMN PLACES...
...YOU HAD TO COME DOWN RIGHT THERE...
オオオオ
OOOO (FWOOO)

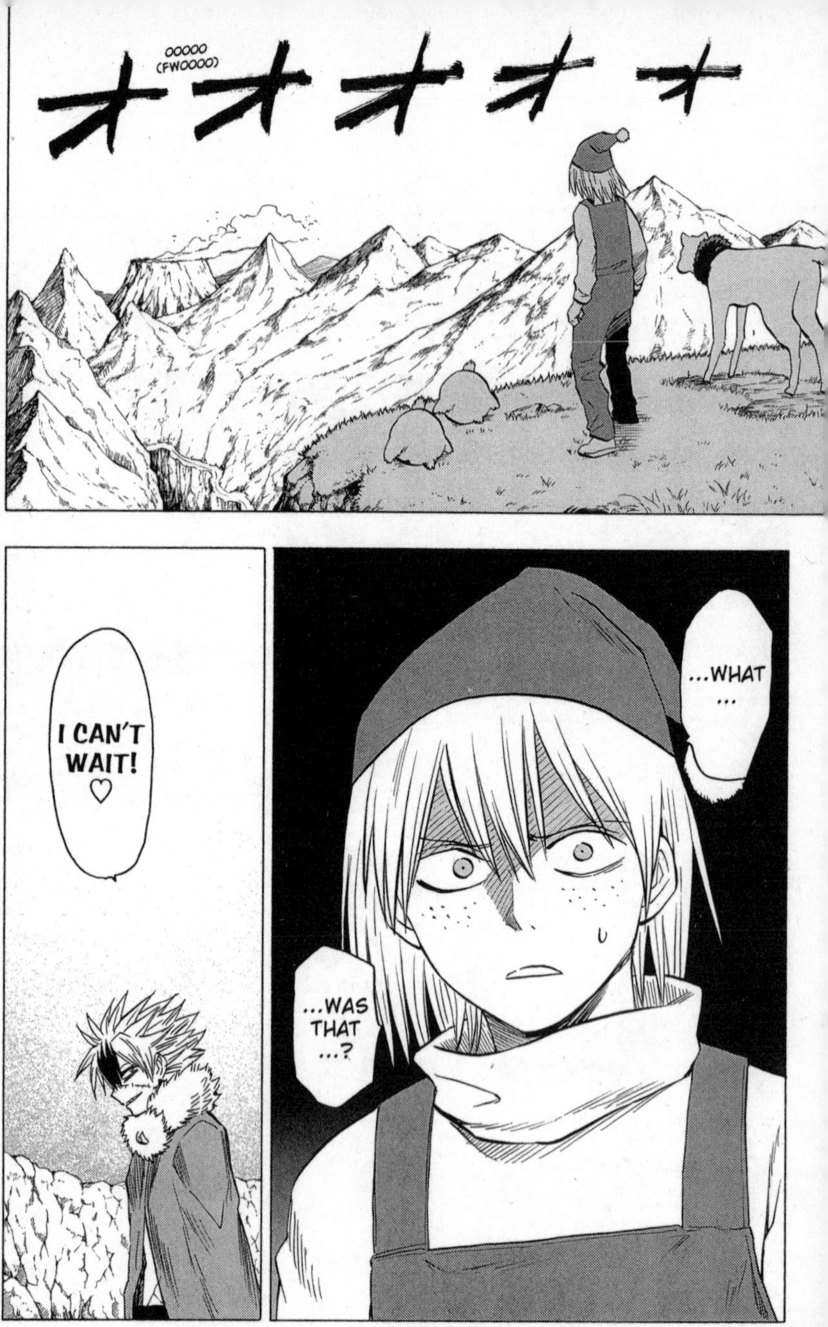
OOOOO (FWOOOO)
...WHAT ...
...WAS THAT ...?
I CAN'T WAIT! ♡

♠ To Be Continued ♠

BLOOD LAD

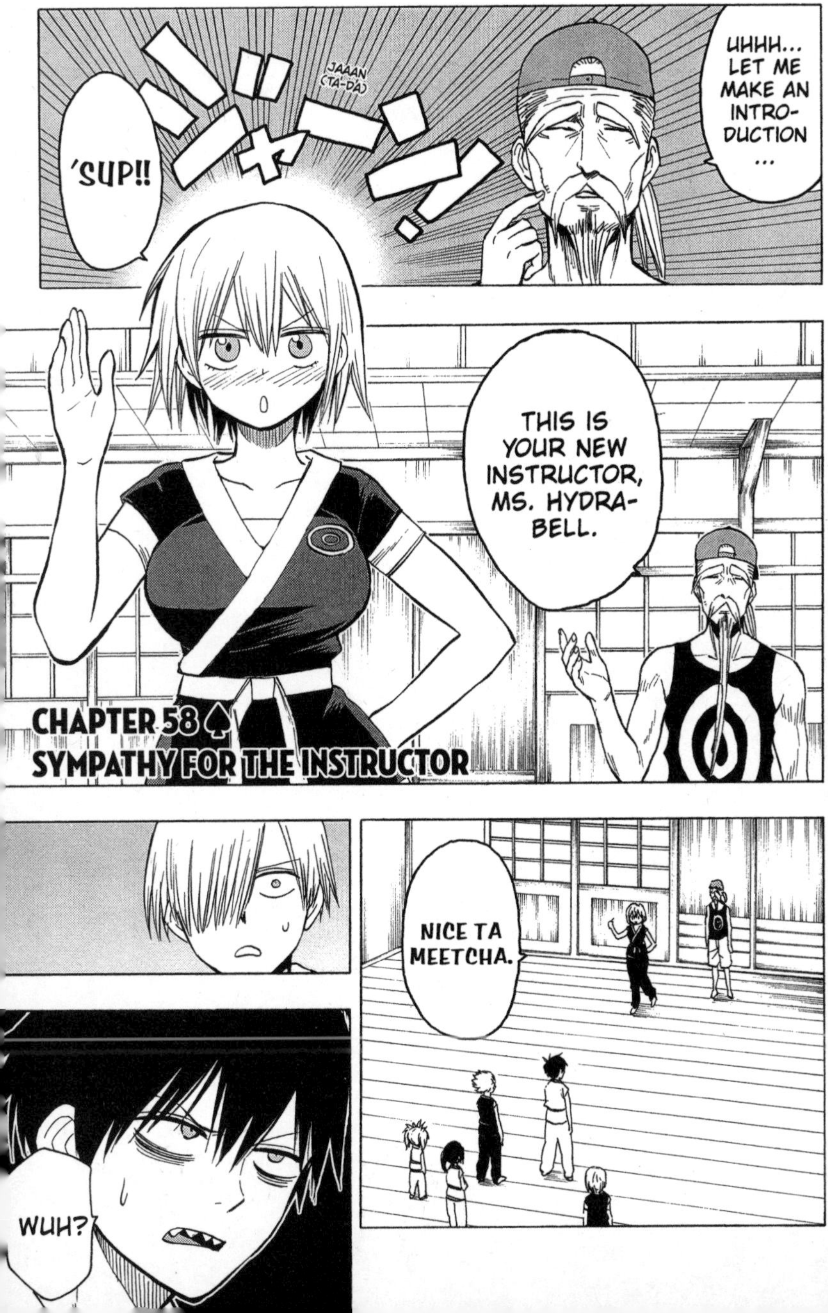
UHHH... LET ME MAKE AN INTRODUCTION ...
JAAAN (TA-DA)
'SUP!!
THIS IS YOUR NEW INSTRUCTOR, MS. HYDRABELL.
CHAPTER 58
SYMPATHY FOR THE INSTRUCTOR
NICE TA MEETCHA.
WUH?

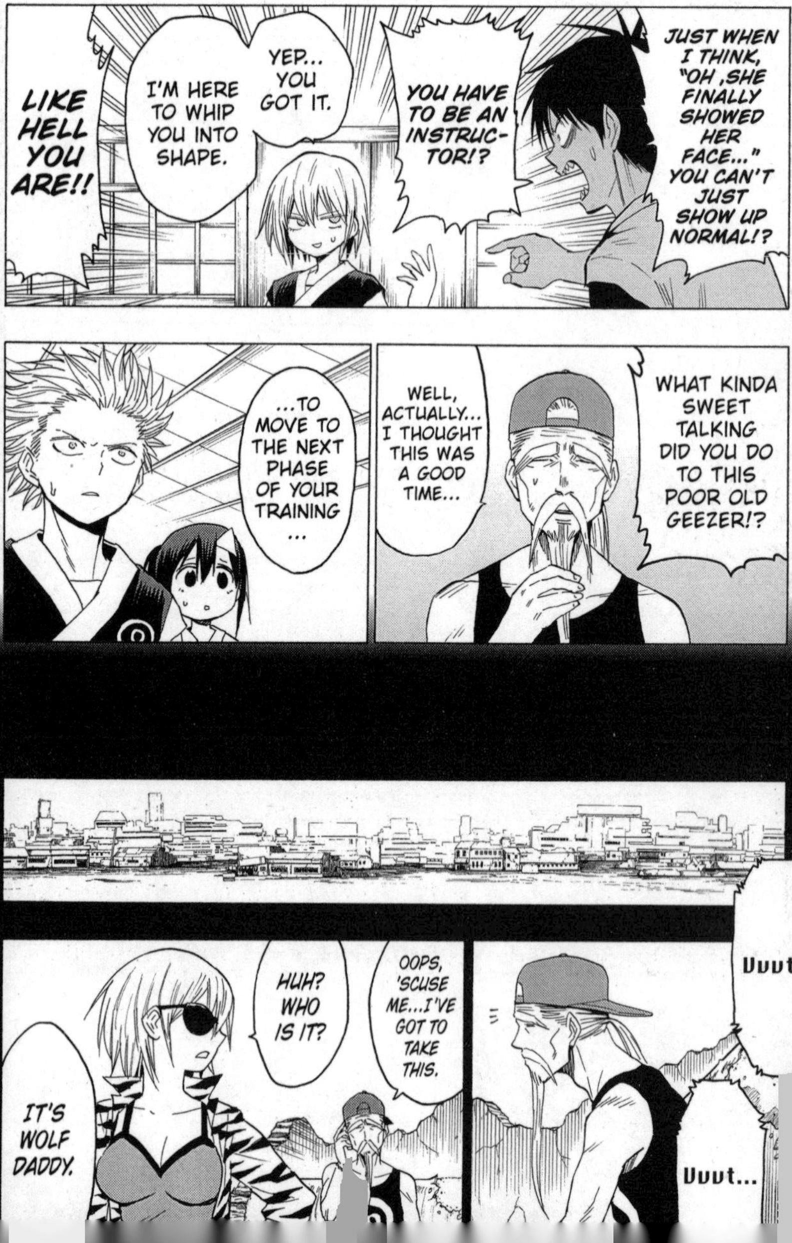
JUST WHEN I THINK, "OH ,SHE FINALLY SHOWED HER FACE..." YOU CAN'T JUST SHOW UP NORMAL!?
YOU HAVE TO BE AN INSTRUC-TOR!?
YEP... YOU GOT IT.
I'M HERE TO WHIP YOU INTO SHAPE.
LIKE HELL YOU ARE!!
WHAT KINDA SWEET TALKING DID YOU DO TO THIS POOR OLD GEEZER!?
WELL, ACTUALLY... I THOUGHT THIS WAS A GOOD TIME...
...TO MOVE TO THE NEXT PHASE OF YOUR TRAINING ...
Vvvt...
Vvvt...
OOPS, 'SCUSE ME...I'VE GOT TO TAKE THIS.
HUH? WHO IS IT?
IT'S WOLF DADDY.

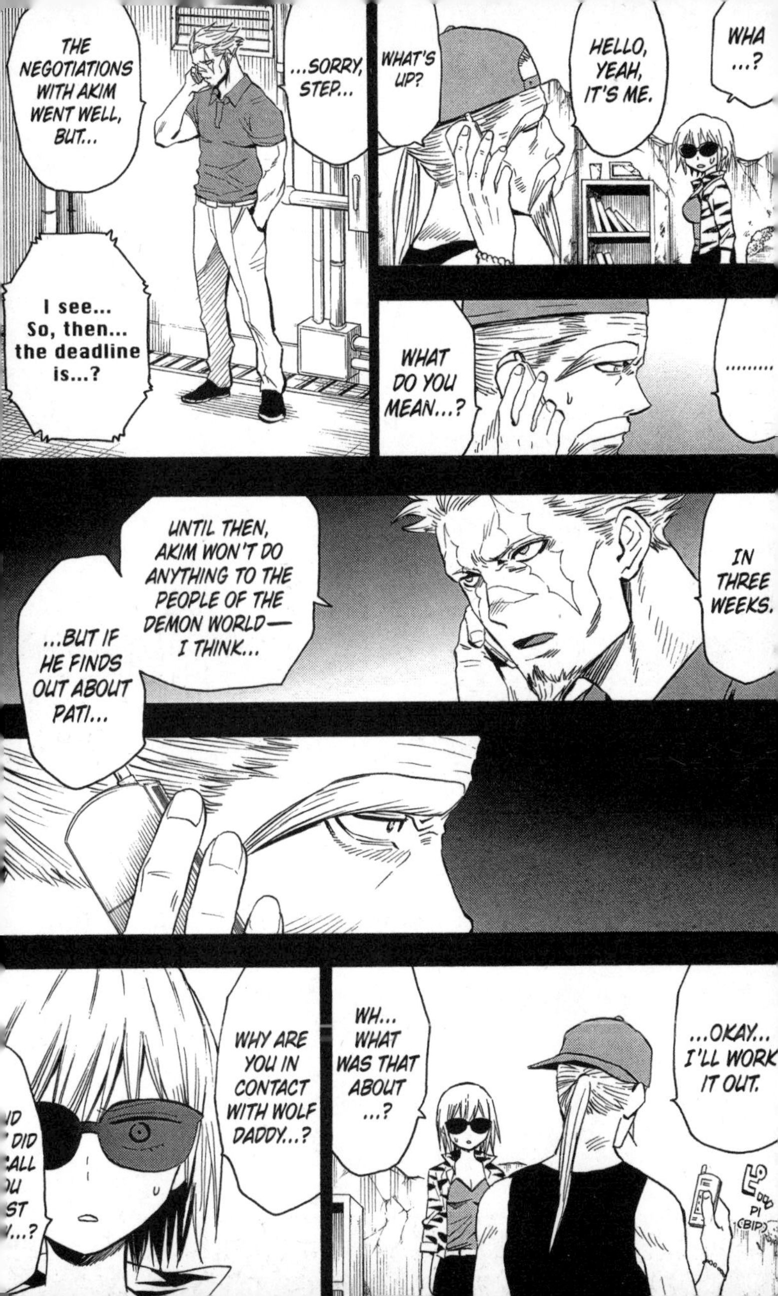
WHA ...?
HELLO, YEAH, IT'S ME.
WHAT'S UP?
....
WHAT DO YOU MEAN...?
...SORRY, STEP...
THE NEGOTIATIONS WITH AKIM WENT WELL, BUT...
I see... So, then... the deadline is...?
IN THREE WEEKS.
UNTIL THEN, AKIM WON'T DO ANYTHING TO THE PEOPLE OF THE DEMON WORLD— I THINK...
...BUT IF HE FINDS OUT ABOUT PATI...
...OKAY... I'LL WORK IT OUT.
PI (BIP)
WH... WHAT WAS THAT ABOUT ...?
WHY ARE YOU IN CONTACT WITH WOLF DADDY...?

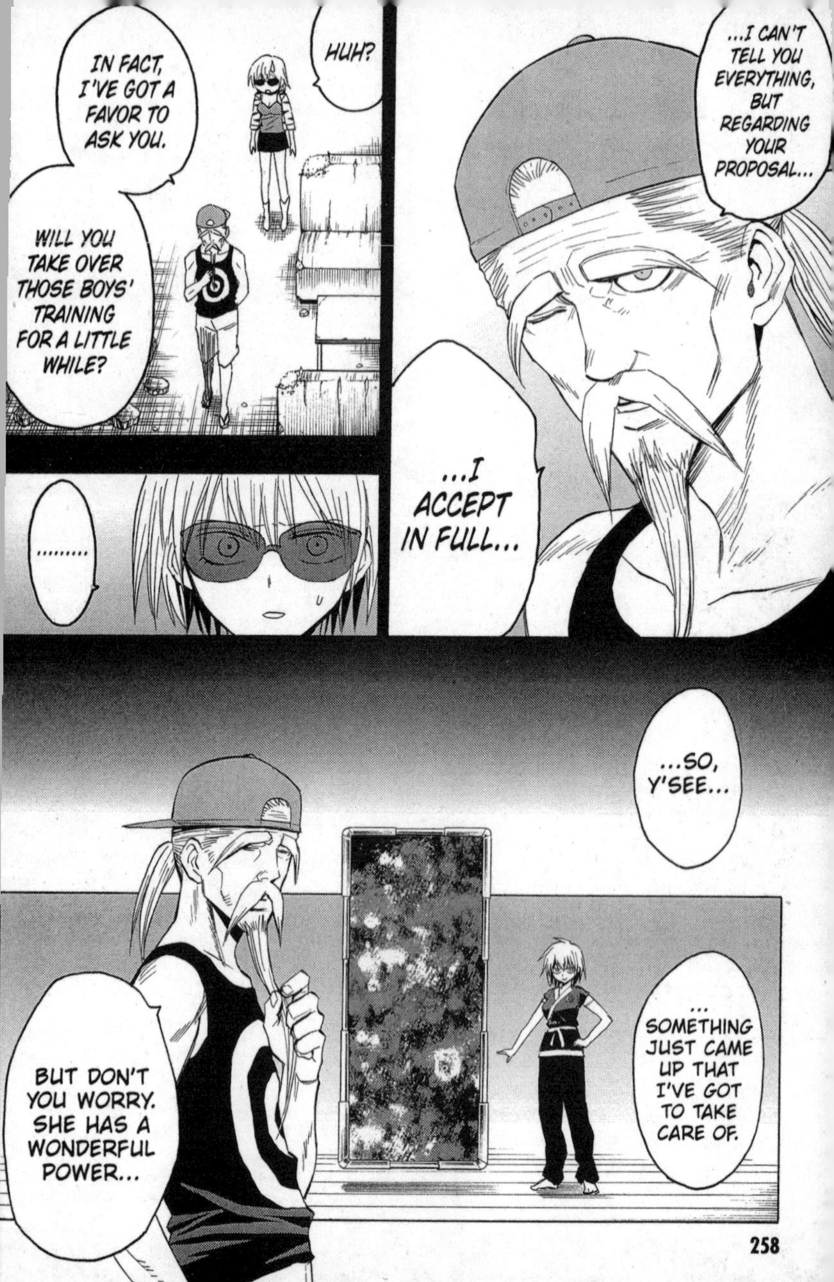
...I CAN'T TELL YOU EVERYTHING, BUT REGARDING YOUR PROPOSAL...
...I ACCEPT IN FULL...
HUH?
IN FACT, I'VE GOT A FAVOR TO ASK YOU.
WILL YOU TAKE OVER THOSE BOYS' TRAINING FOR A LITTLE WHILE?
....
...SO, Y'SEE...
...SOMETHING JUST CAME UP THAT I'VE GOT TO TAKE CARE OF.
BUT DON'T YOU WORRY. SHE HAS A WONDERFUL POWER...

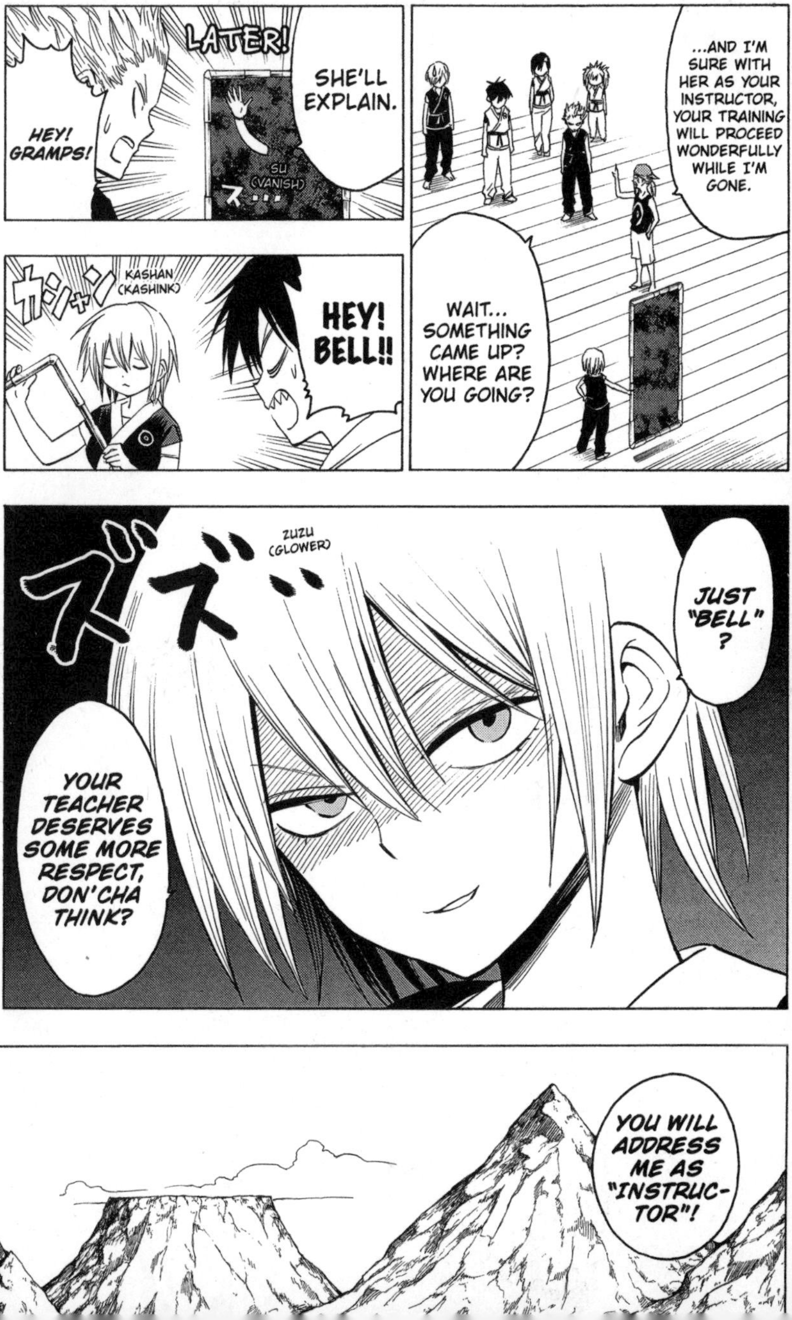
...AND I'M SURE WITH HER AS YOUR INSTRUCTOR, YOUR TRAINING WILL PROCEED WONDERFULLY WHILE I'M GONE.
WAIT... SOMETHING CAME UP? WHERE ARE YOU GOING?
SHE'LL EXPLAIN.
LATER!
SU (VANISH)
HEY! GRAMPS!
HEY! BELL!!
KASHAN (KASHINK)
JUST "BELL"?
ZUZU (GLOWER)
YOUR TEACHER DESERVES SOME MORE RESPECT, DON'CHA THINK?
YOU WILL ADDRESS ME AS "INSTRUC-TOR"!

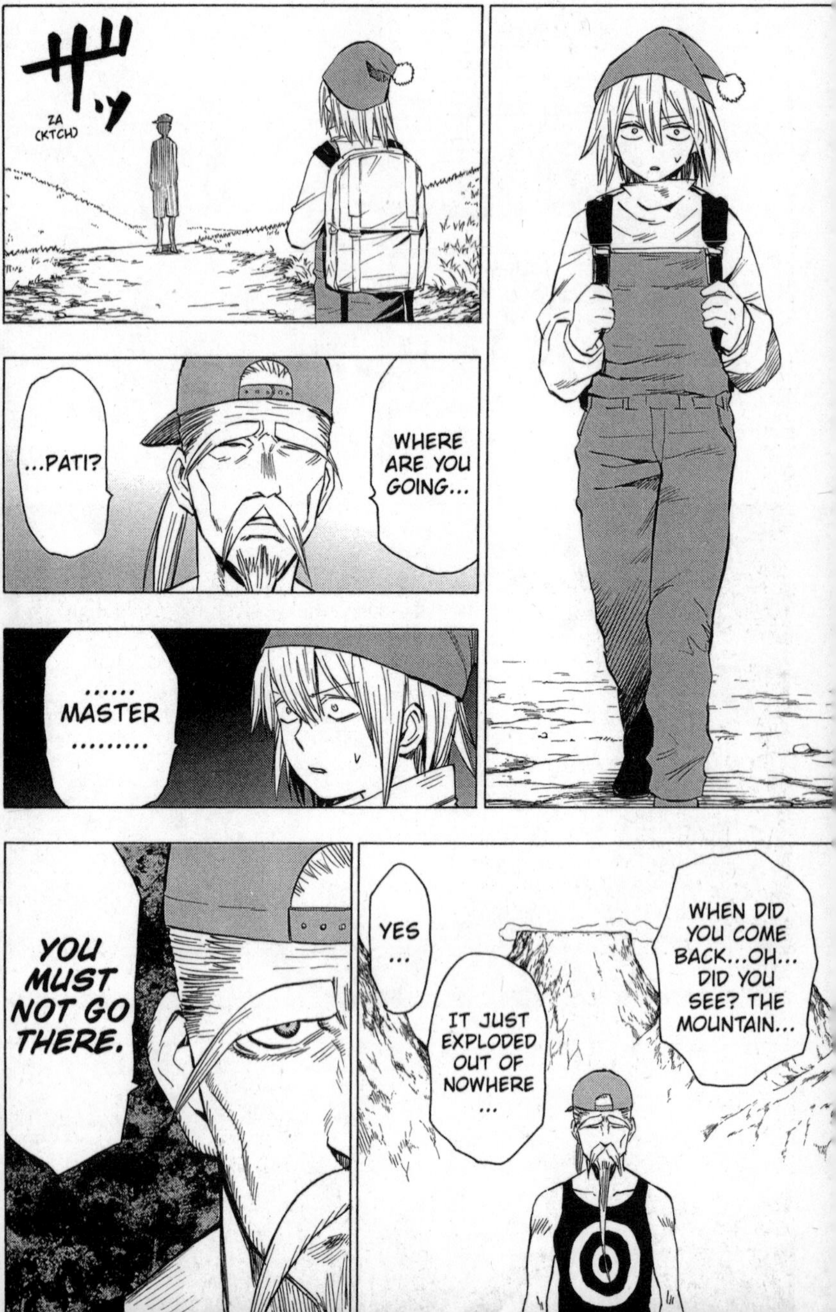
ZA
(KTCH)
WHERE ARE YOU GOING...
...PATI?
...... MASTER ....
WHEN DID YOU COME BACK...OH... DID YOU SEE? THE MOUNTAIN...
YES ...
IT JUST EXPLODED OUT OF NOWHERE ...
YOU MUST NOT GO THERE.

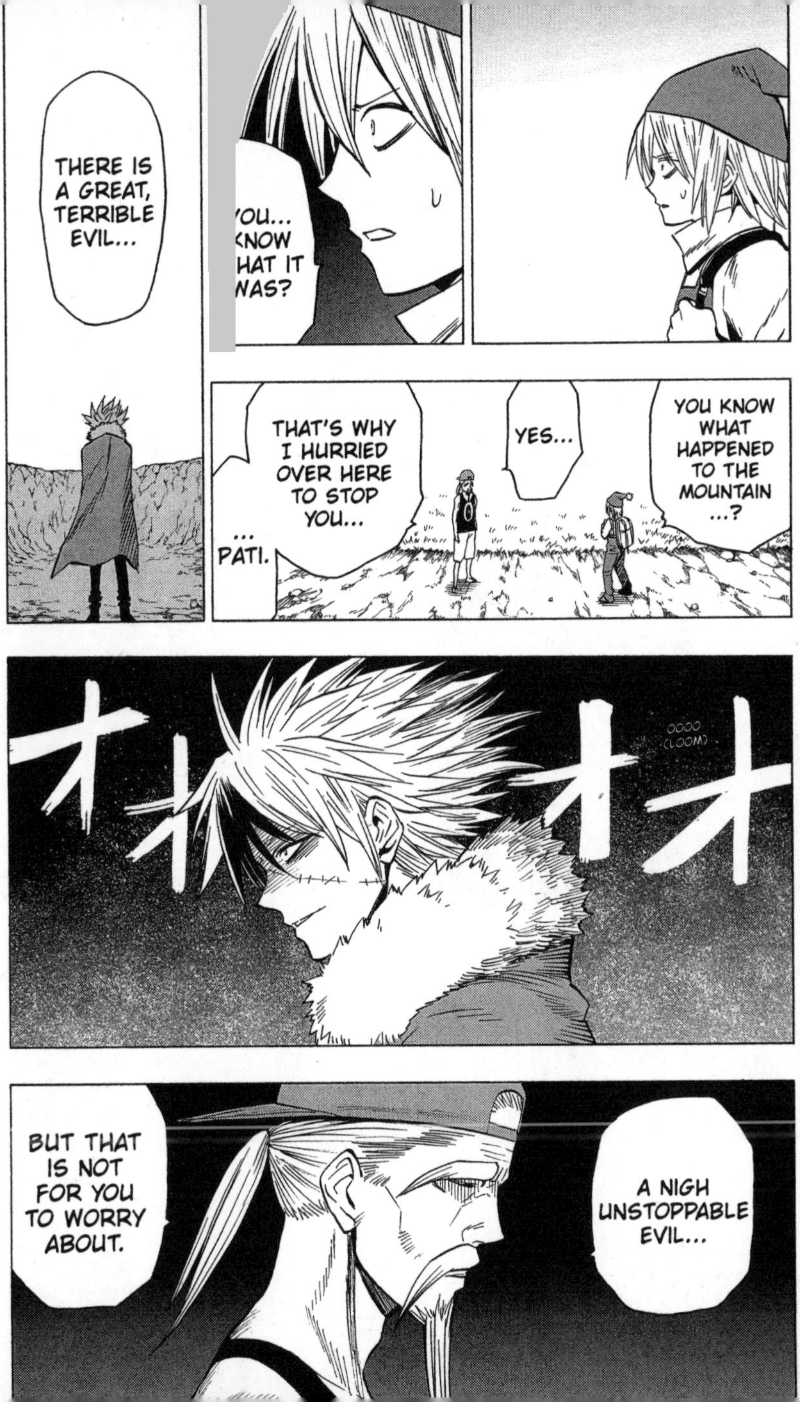
YOU... KNOW WHAT IT WAS?
YOU KNOW WHAT HAPPENED TO THE MOUNTAIN ...?
YES...
THAT'S WHY I HURRIED OVER HERE TO STOP YOU...
... PATI.
THERE IS A GREAT, TERRIBLE EVIL...
OOOO (LOOM)
A NIGH UNSTOPPABLE EVIL...
BUT THAT IS NOT FOR YOU TO WORRY ABOUT.

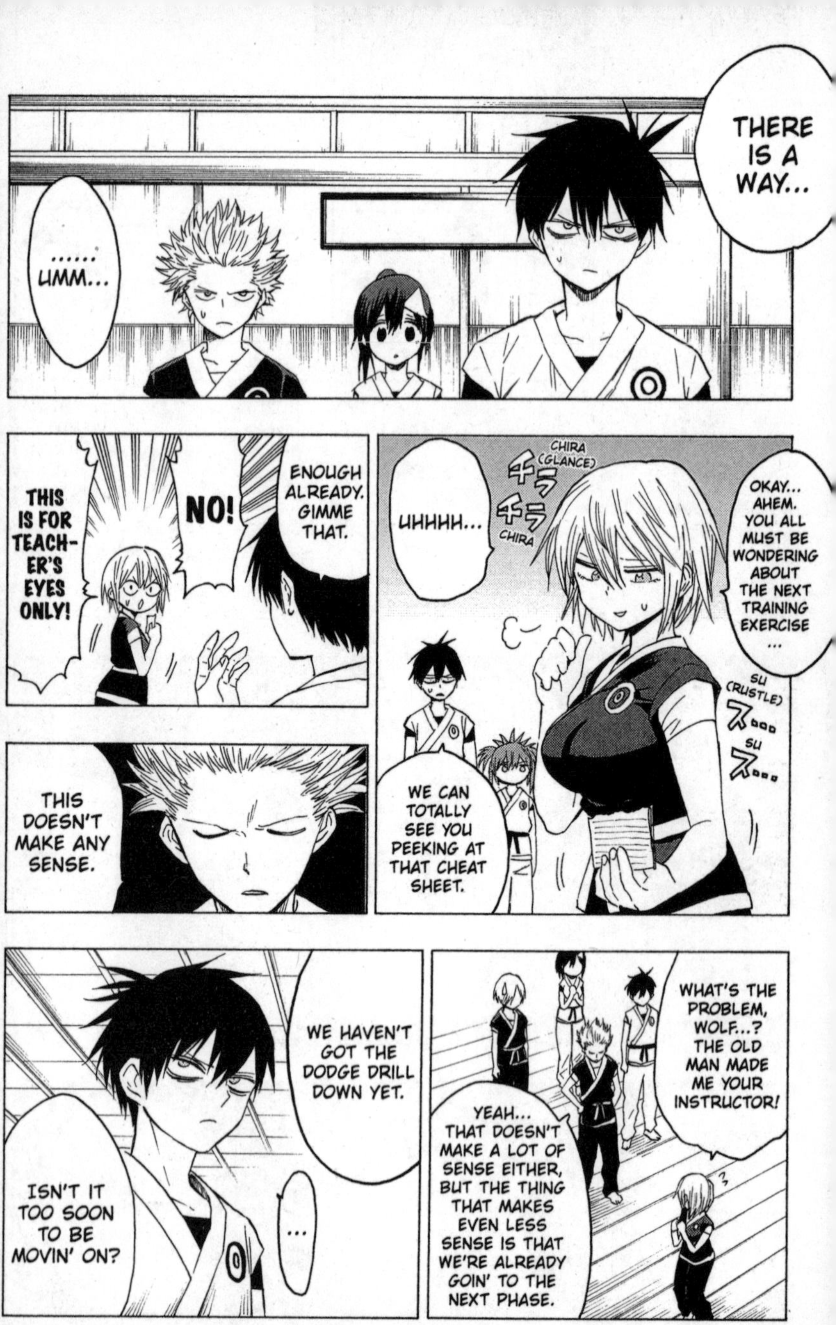
THERE IS A WAY...
......UMM...
OKAY... AHEM. YOU ALL MUST BE WONDERING ABOUT THE NEXT TRAINING EXERCISE...
チラ CHIRA (GLANCE)
チラ CHIRA
ス... SU (RUSTLE)
ス... SU
UHHHH...
WE CAN TOTALLY SEE YOU PEEKING AT THAT CHEAT SHEET.
ENOUGH ALREADY. GIMME THAT.
NO!
THIS IS FOR TEACHER'S EYES ONLY!
THIS DOESN'T MAKE ANY SENSE.
WHAT'S THE PROBLEM, WOLF...? THE OLD MAN MADE ME YOUR INSTRUCTOR!
YEAH... THAT DOESN'T MAKE A LOT OF SENSE EITHER, BUT THE THING THAT MAKES EVEN LESS SENSE IS THAT WE'RE ALREADY GOIN' TO THE NEXT PHASE.
WE HAVEN'T GOT THE DODGE DRILL DOWN YET.
...
ISN'T IT TOO SOON TO BE MOVIN' ON?

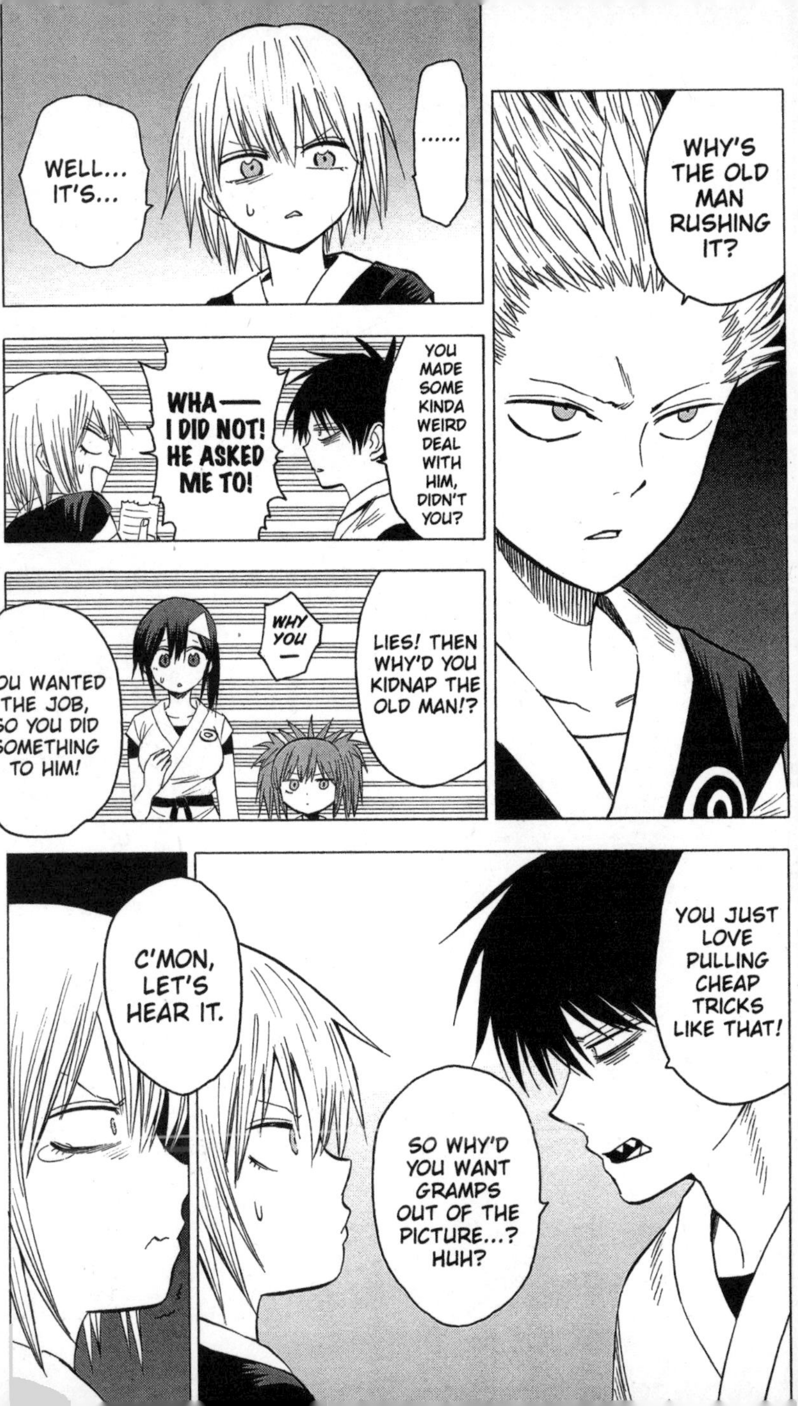

WHY'S THE OLD MAN RUSHING IT?
......
WELL... IT'S...
YOU MADE SOME KINDA WEIRD DEAL WITH HIM, DIDN'T YOU?
WHA— I DID NOT! HE ASKED ME TO!
LIES! THEN WHY'D YOU KIDNAP THE OLD MAN!?
WHY YOU—
YOU WANTED THE JOB, SO YOU DID SOMETHING TO HIM!
YOU JUST LOVE PULLING CHEAP TRICKS LIKE THAT!
SO WHY'D YOU WANT GRAMPS OUT OF THE PICTURE...? HUH?
C'MON, LET'S HEAR IT.

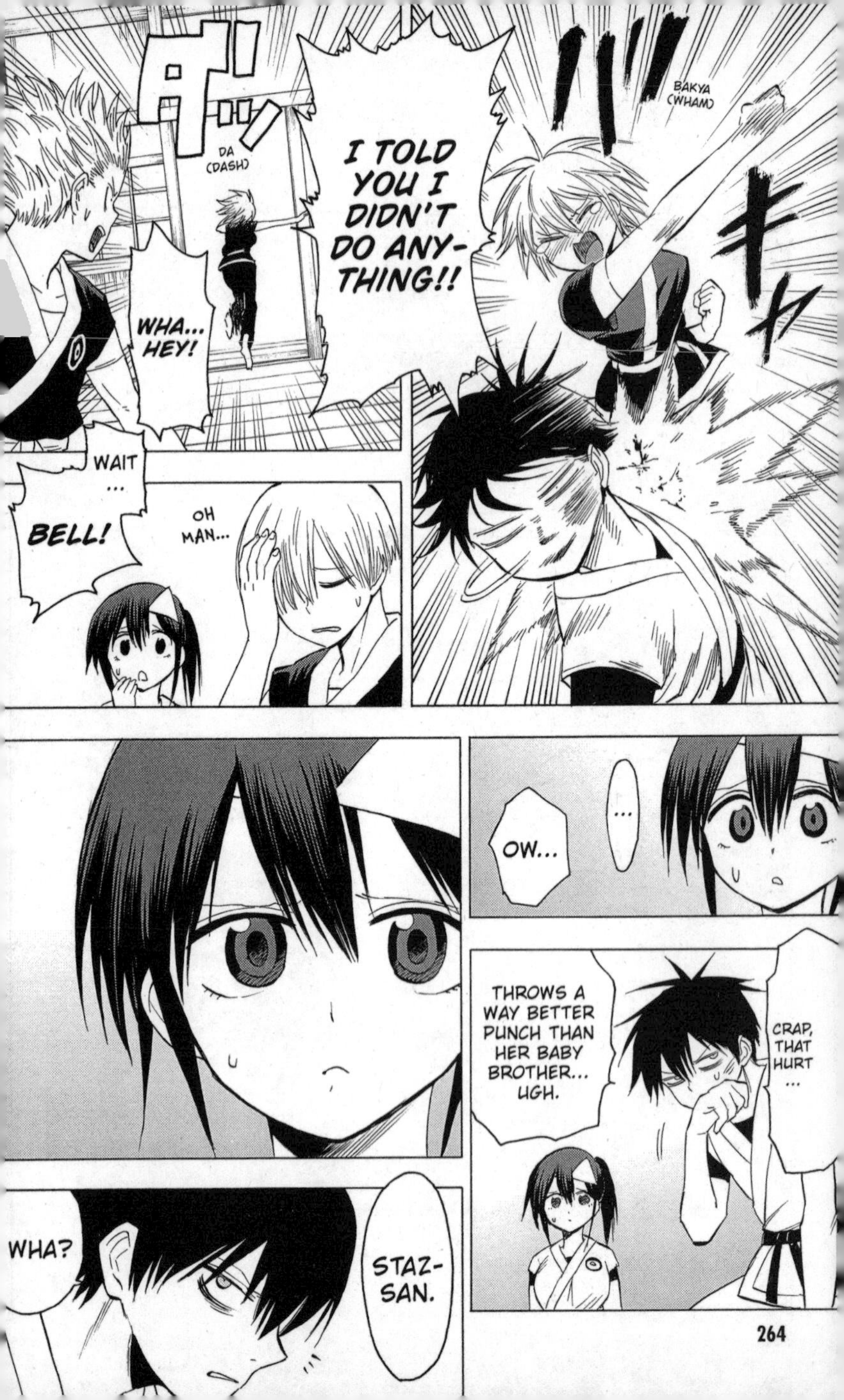
I TOLD YOU I DIDN'T DO ANY-THING!!
BAKYA (WHAM)
DA (DASH)
WHA... HEY!
WAIT... BELL!
OH MAN...
...
OW...
CRAP, THAT HURT...
THROWS A WAY BETTER PUNCH THAN HER BABY BROTHER... UGH.
STAZ-SAN.
WHA?

HUH?

POKO
(BINK)

......

YOU DON'T HAVE NEARLY ENOUGH TRAINING...!

...YOU DON'T......

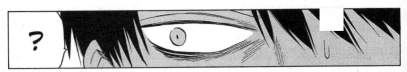

?

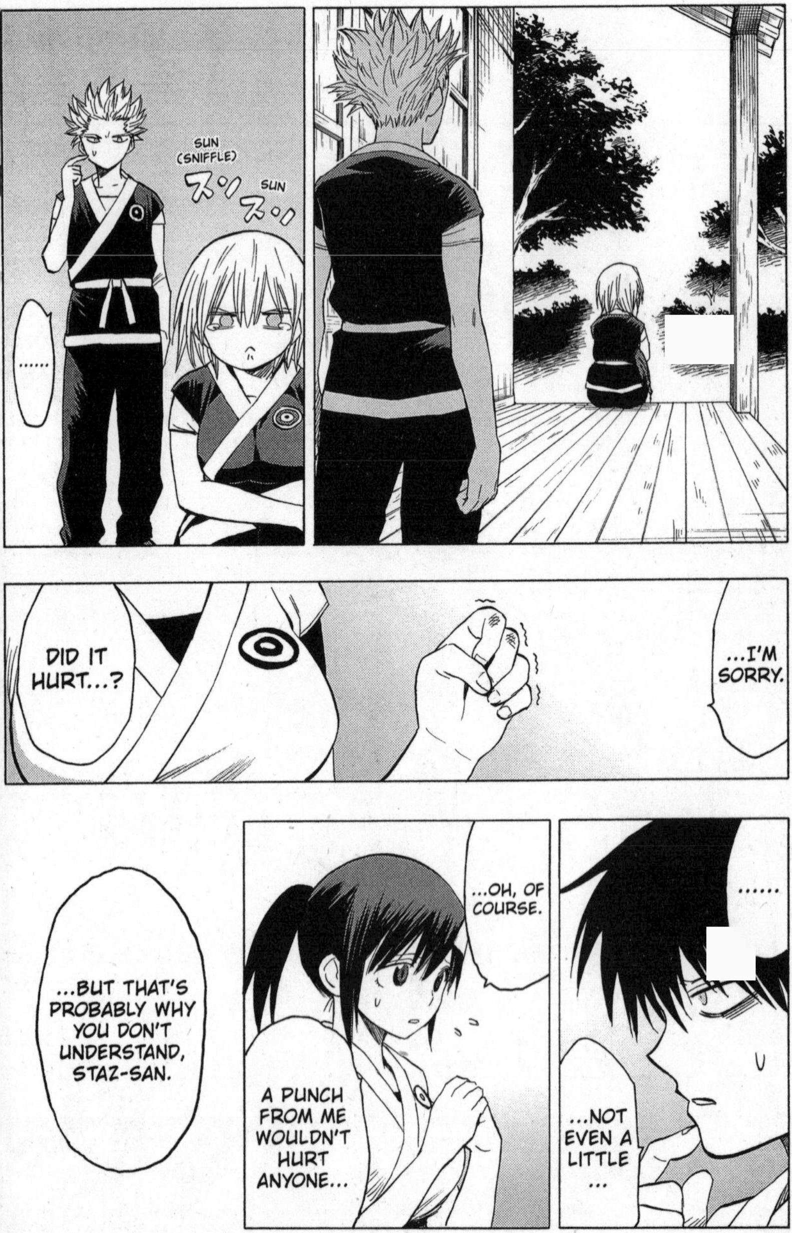

SUN (SNIFFLE)
SUN
......
...I'M SORRY.
DID IT HURT...?
......
...NOT EVEN A LITTLE ...
...OH, OF COURSE.
A PUNCH FROM ME WOULDN'T HURT ANYONE...
...BUT THAT'S PROBABLY WHY YOU DON'T UNDERSTAND, STAZ-SAN.

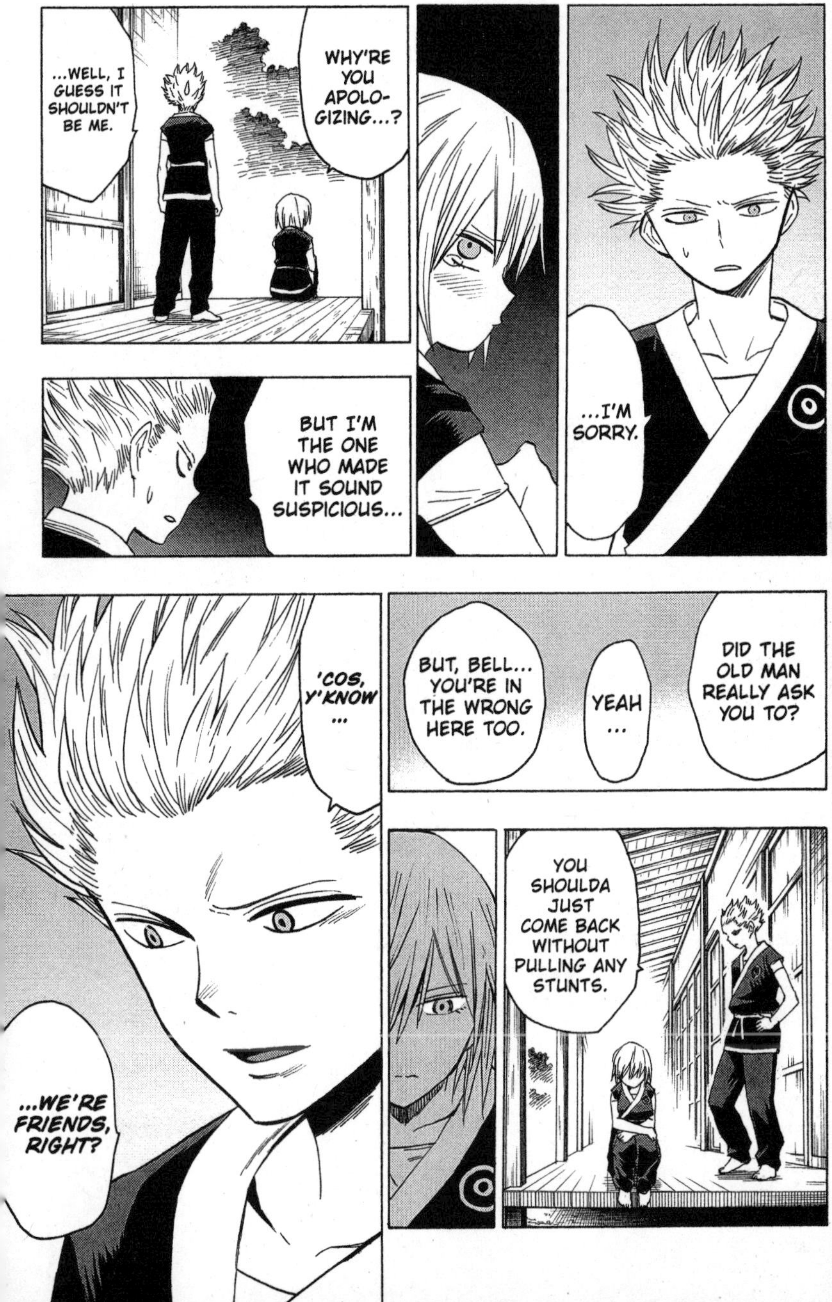
...I'M SORRY.
WHY'RE YOU APOLOGIZING...?
...WELL, I GUESS IT SHOULDN'T BE ME.
BUT I'M THE ONE WHO MADE IT SOUND SUSPICIOUS...
DID THE OLD MAN REALLY ASK YOU TO?
YEAH ...
BUT, BELL... YOU'RE IN THE WRONG HERE TOO.
YOU SHOULDA JUST COME BACK WITHOUT PULLING ANY STUNTS.
'COS, Y'KNOW ...
...WE'RE FRIENDS, RIGHT?

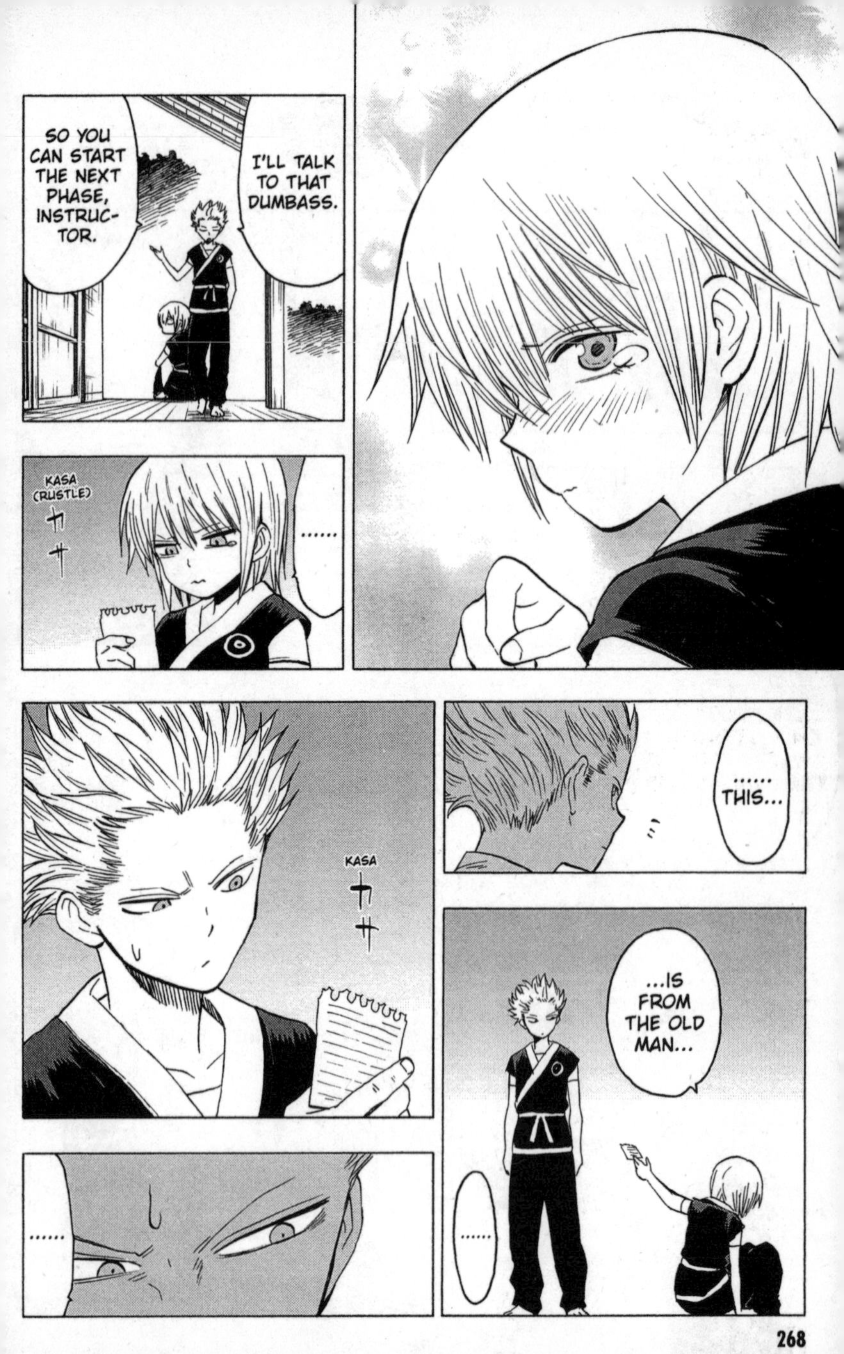
I'LL TALK TO THAT DUMBASS.
SO YOU CAN START THE NEXT PHASE, INSTRUCTOR.
......
KASA (RUSTLE)
...... THIS...
...IS FROM THE OLD MAN...
......
KASA
......

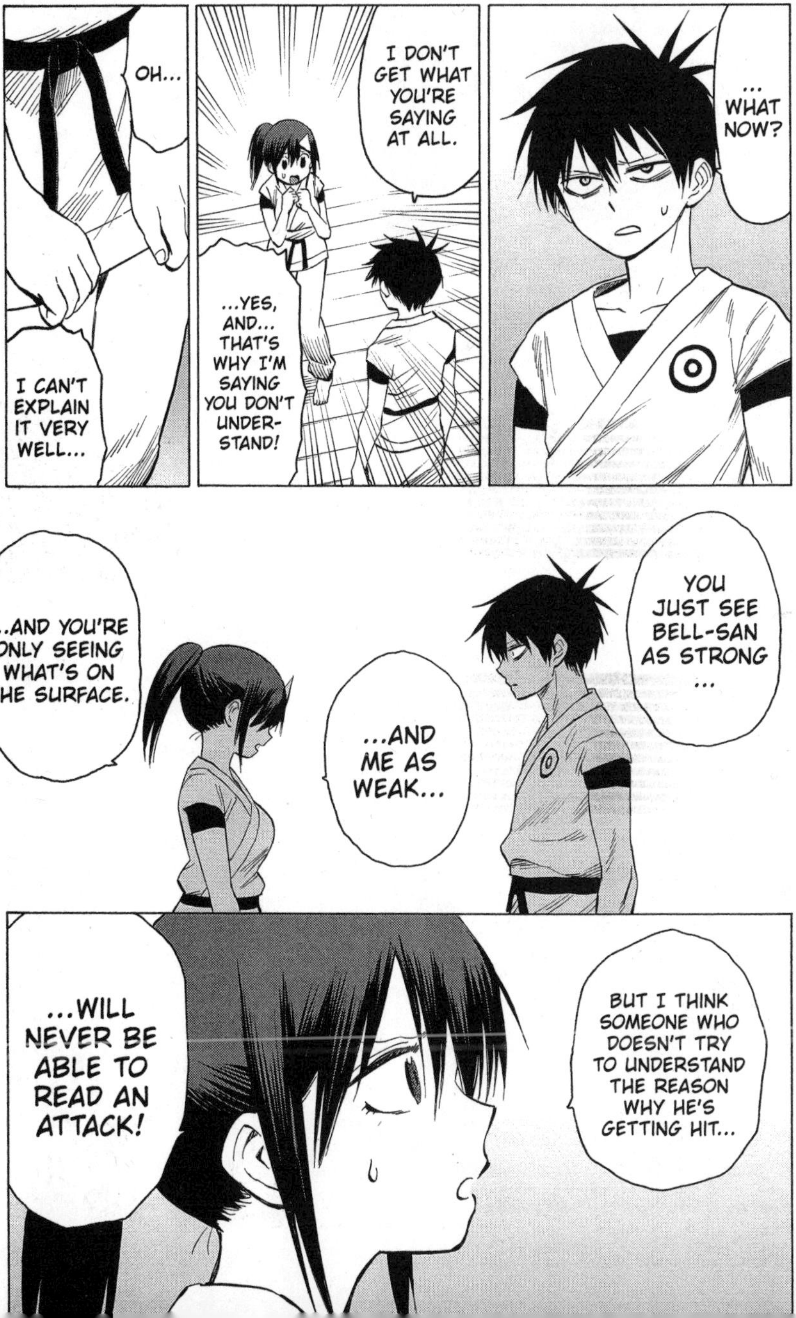
... WHAT NOW?
I DON'T GET WHAT YOU'RE SAYING AT ALL.
...YES, AND... THAT'S WHY I'M SAYING YOU DON'T UNDER-STAND!
OH...
I CAN'T EXPLAIN IT VERY WELL...
YOU JUST SEE BELL-SAN AS STRONG ...
...AND ME AS WEAK...
...AND YOU'RE ONLY SEEING WHAT'S ON THE SURFACE.
BUT I THINK SOMEONE WHO DOESN'T TRY TO UNDERSTAND THE REASON WHY HE'S GETTING HIT...
...WILL NEVER BE ABLE TO READ AN ATTACK!

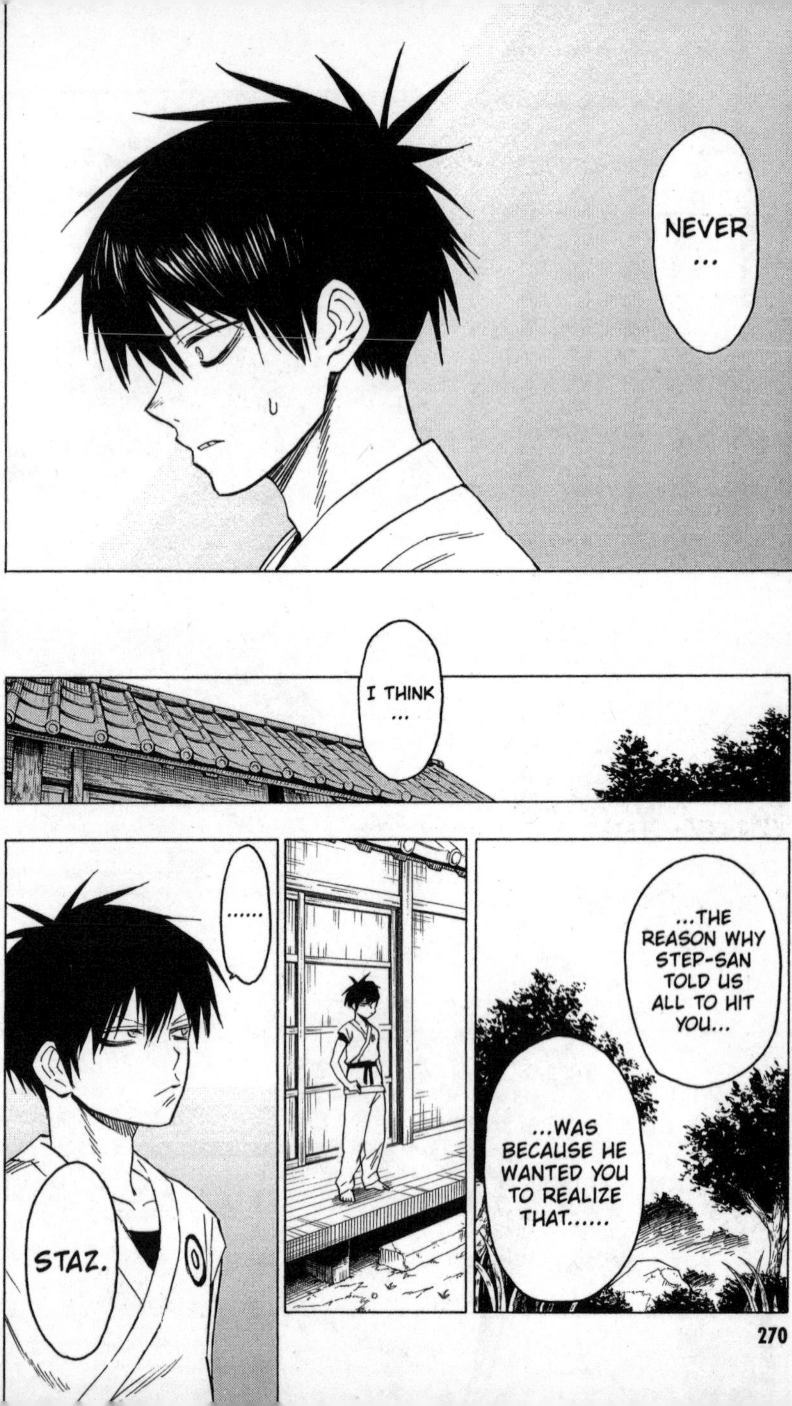
NEVER ...
I THINK ...
...THE REASON WHY STEP-SAN TOLD US ALL TO HIT YOU...
...WAS BECAUSE HE WANTED YOU TO REALIZE THAT......
......
STAZ.

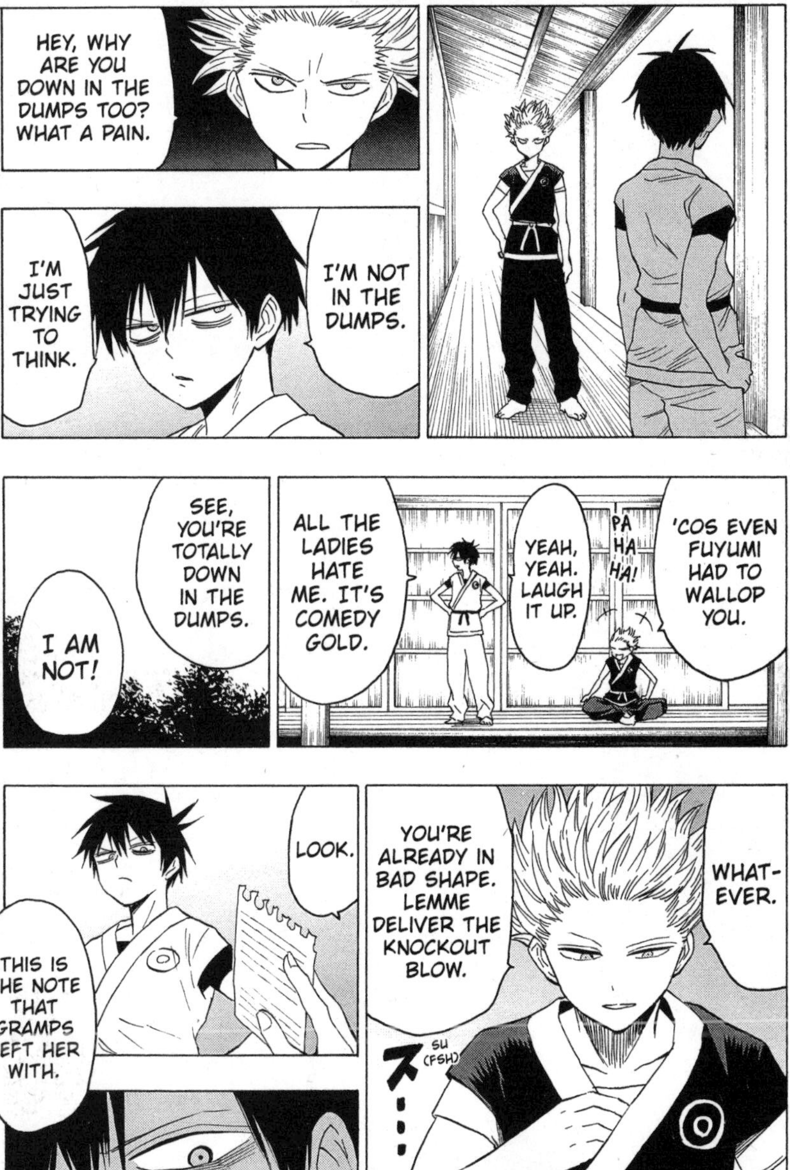
HEY, WHY ARE YOU DOWN IN THE DUMPS TOO? WHAT A PAIN.
I'M NOT IN THE DUMPS.
I'M JUST TRYING TO THINK.
'COS EVEN FUYUMI HAD TO WALLOP YOU.
PA HA HA!
YEAH, YEAH. LAUGH IT UP.
ALL THE LADIES HATE ME. IT'S COMEDY GOLD.
SEE, YOU'RE TOTALLY DOWN IN THE DUMPS.
I AM NOT!
WHAT-EVER.
YOU'RE ALREADY IN BAD SHAPE. LEMME DELIVER THE KNOCKOUT BLOW.
SU (FSH)
LOOK.
THIS IS THE NOTE THAT GRAMPS LEFT HER WITH.

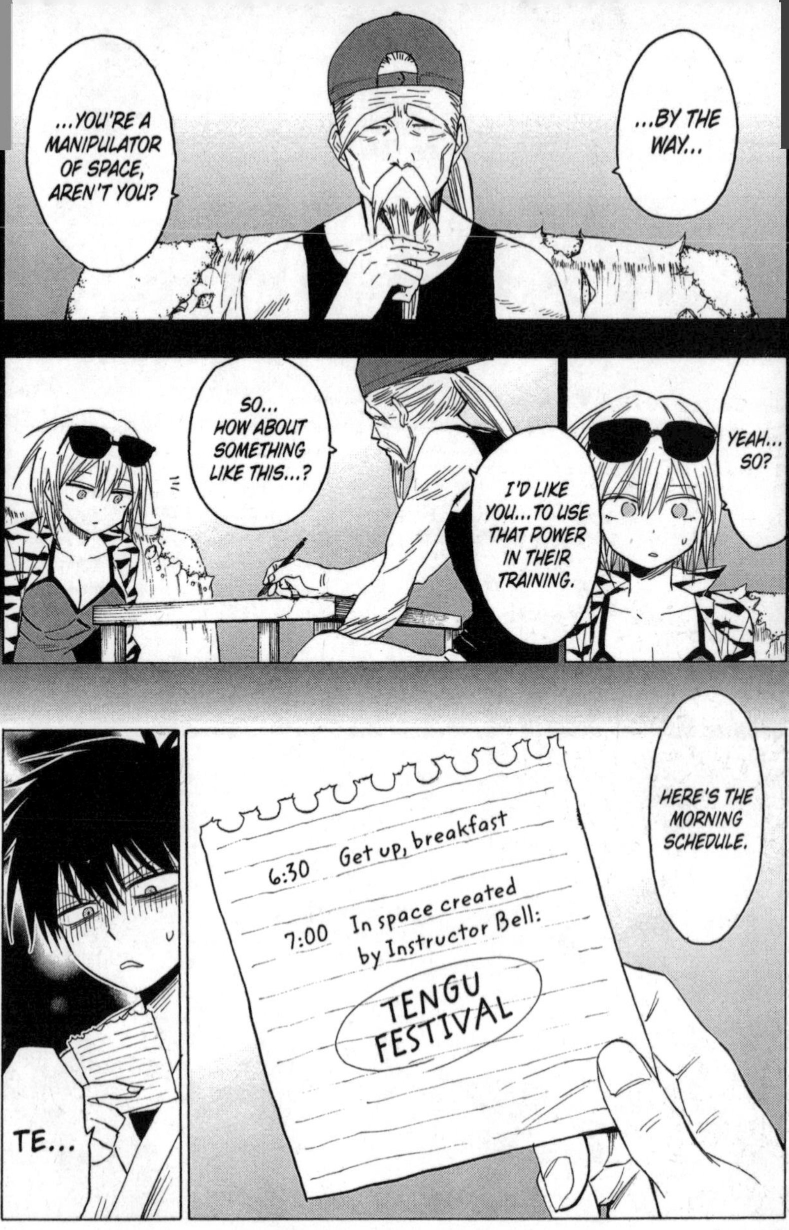
...BY THE WAY...
...YOU'RE A MANIPULATOR OF SPACE, AREN'T YOU?
YEAH... SO?
I'D LIKE YOU...TO USE THAT POWER IN THEIR TRAINING.
SO... HOW ABOUT SOMETHING LIKE THIS...?
HERE'S THE MORNING SCHEDULE.
6:30 Get up, breakfast
7:00 In space created by Instructor Bell:
TENGU FESTIVAL
TE...

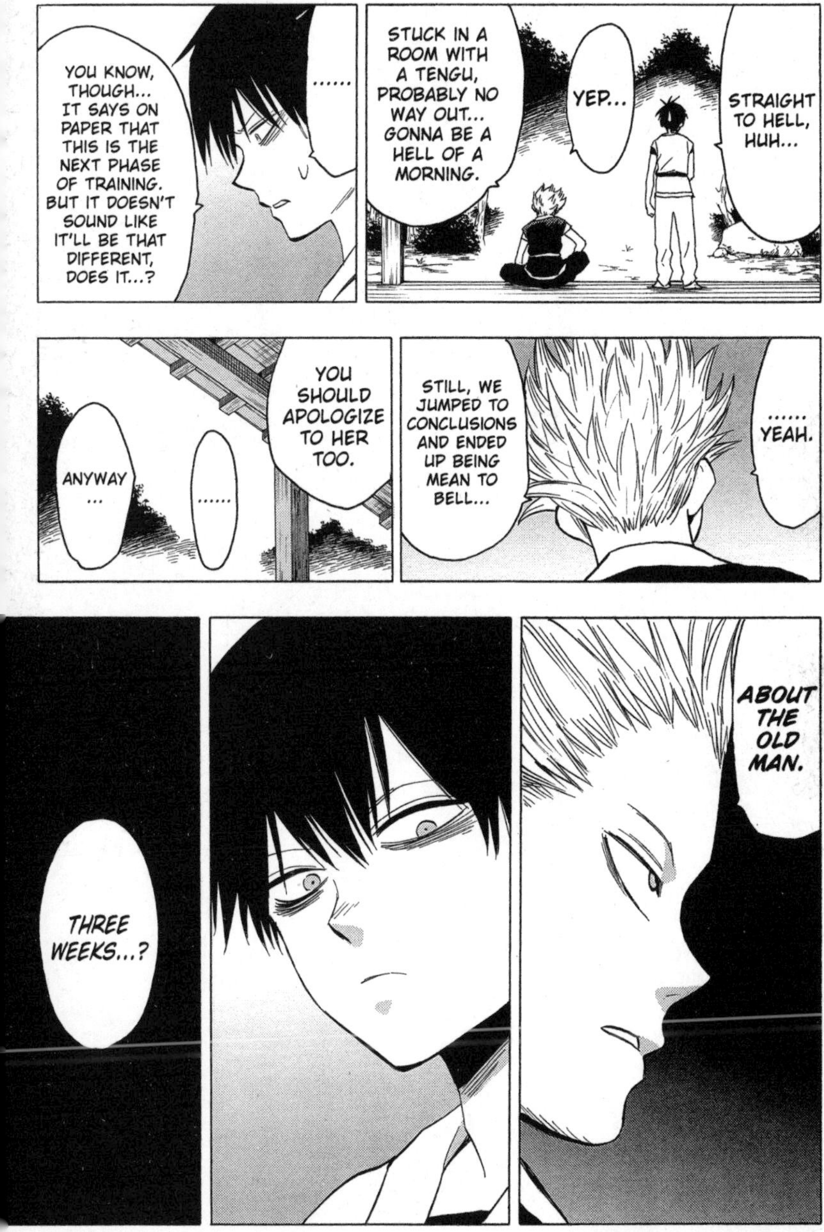
STRAIGHT TO HELL, HUH...
YEP...
STUCK IN A ROOM WITH A TENGU, PROBABLY NO WAY OUT... GONNA BE A HELL OF A MORNING.
......
YOU KNOW, THOUGH... IT SAYS ON PAPER THAT THIS IS THE NEXT PHASE OF TRAINING. BUT IT DOESN'T SOUND LIKE IT'LL BE THAT DIFFERENT, DOES IT...?
...... YEAH.
STILL, WE JUMPED TO CONCLUSIONS AND ENDED UP BEING MEAN TO BELL...
YOU SHOULD APOLOGIZE TO HER TOO.
......
ANYWAY ...
ABOUT THE OLD MAN.
THREE WEEKS...?

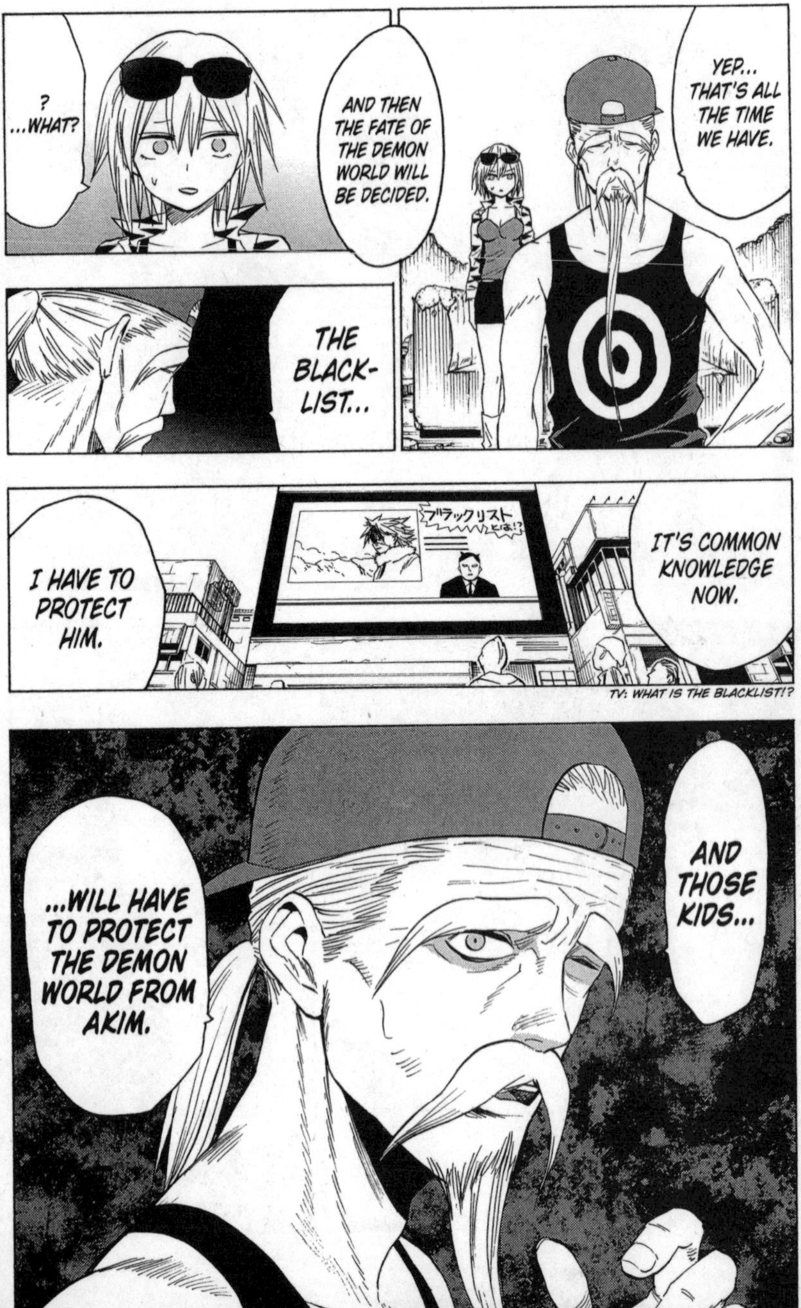
YEP... THAT'S ALL THE TIME WE HAVE.
AND THEN THE FATE OF THE DEMON WORLD WILL BE DECIDED.
? ...WHAT?
THE BLACK-LIST...
IT'S COMMON KNOWLEDGE NOW.
ブラックリストとは!?
I HAVE TO PROTECT HIM.
TV: WHAT IS THE BLACKLIST!?
AND THOSE KIDS...
...WILL HAVE TO PROTECT THE DEMON WORLD FROM AKIM.

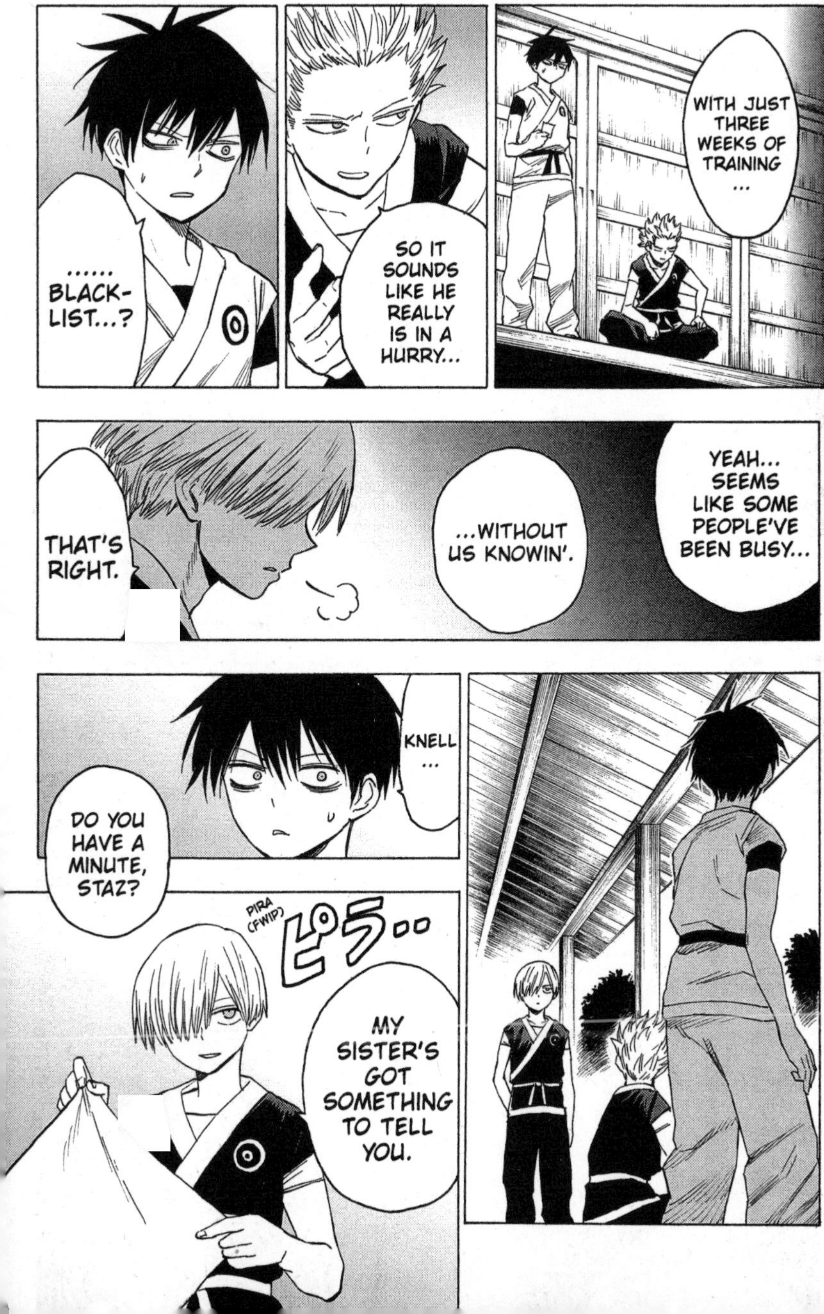
WITH JUST THREE WEEKS OF TRAINING ...
SO IT SOUNDS LIKE HE REALLY IS IN A HURRY...
...... BLACK-LIST...?
YEAH... SEEMS LIKE SOME PEOPLE'VE BEEN BUSY...
...WITHOUT US KNOWIN'.
THAT'S RIGHT.
KNELL ...
DO YOU HAVE A MINUTE, STAZ?
PIRA (FWIP)
MY SISTER'S GOT SOMETHING TO TELL YOU.

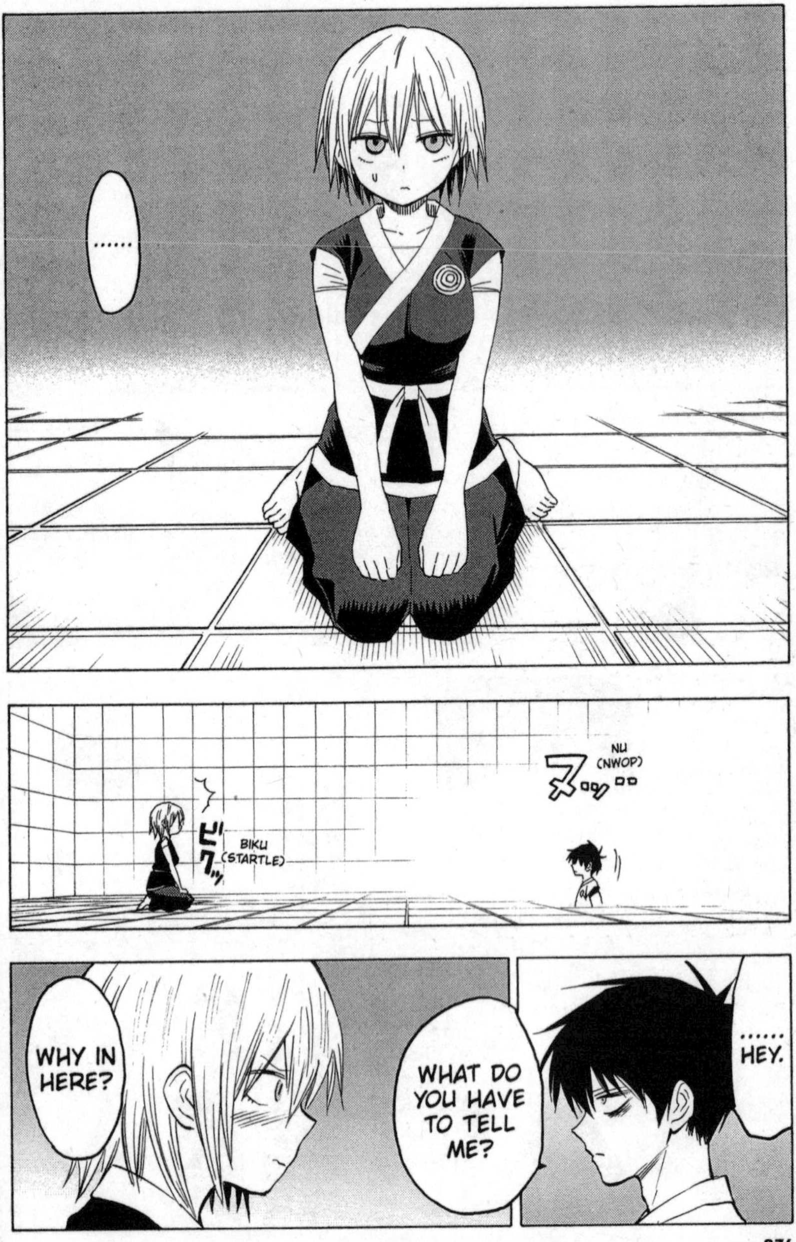
......
NU (NWOP)
BIKU (STARTLE)
......
HEY.
WHAT DO YOU HAVE TO TELL ME?
WHY IN HERE?

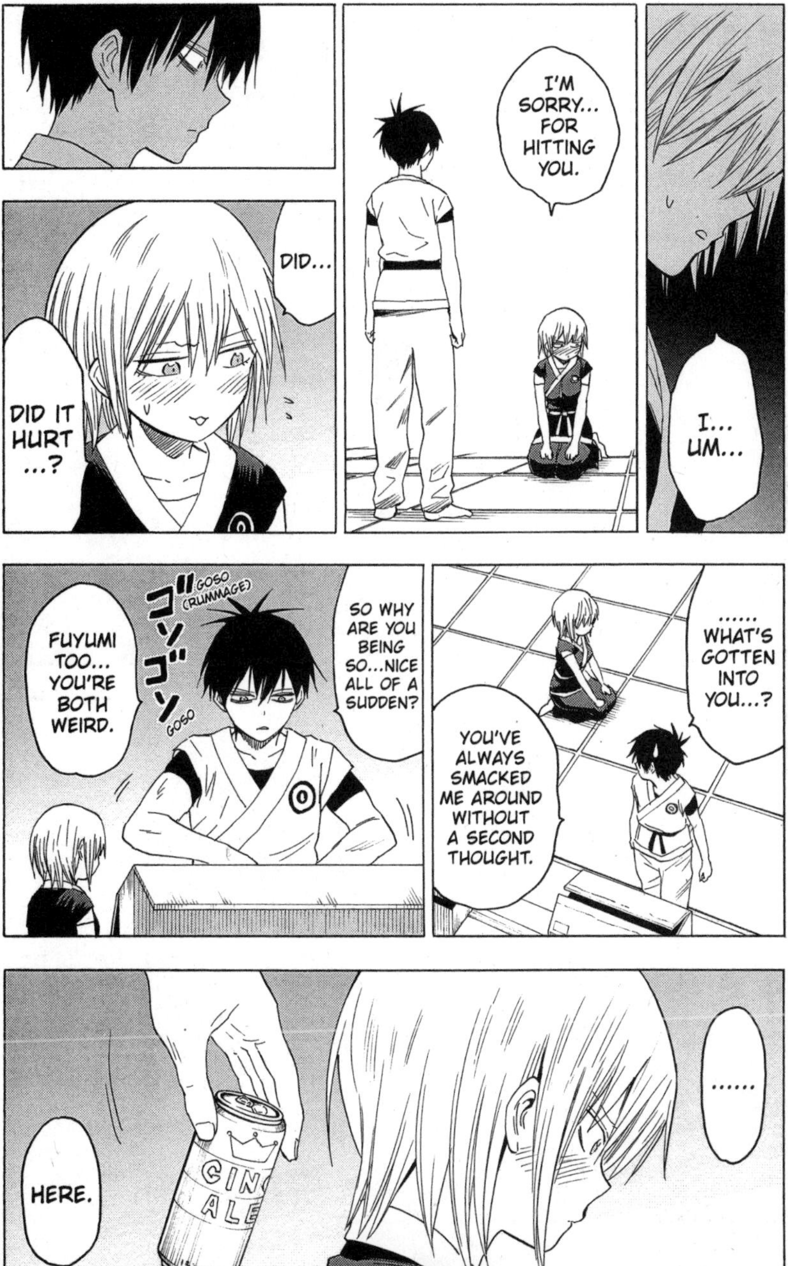
I... UM...
I'M SORRY... FOR HITTING YOU.
DID...
DID IT HURT ...?
...... WHAT'S GOTTEN INTO YOU...?
YOU'VE ALWAYS SMACKED ME AROUND WITHOUT A SECOND THOUGHT.
SO WHY ARE YOU BEING SO...NICE ALL OF A SUDDEN?
GOSO (RUMMAGE)
GOSO
FUYUMI TOO... YOU'RE BOTH WEIRD.
......
HERE.

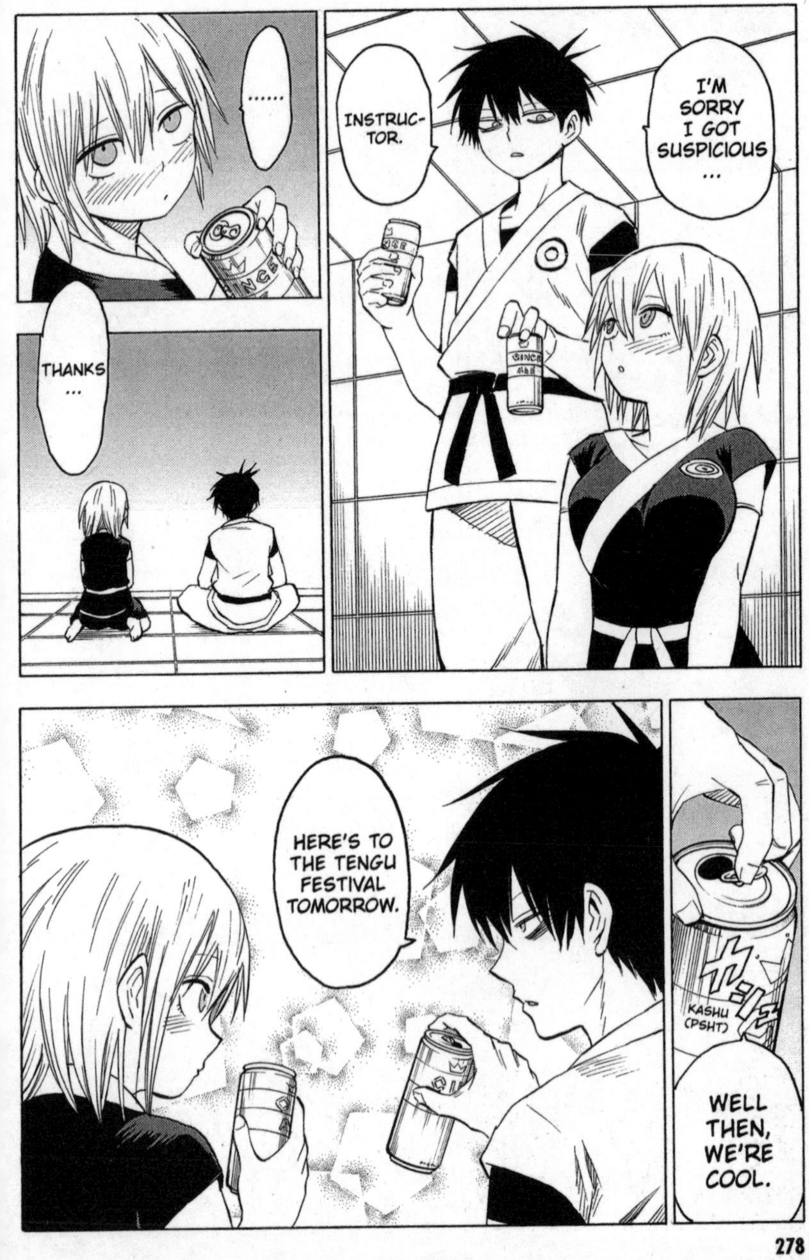
I'M SORRY I GOT SUSPICIOUS ...
INSTRUCTOR.
......
THANKS ...
KASHU (PSHT)
WELL THEN, WE'RE COOL.
HERE'S TO THE TENGU FESTIVAL TOMORROW.

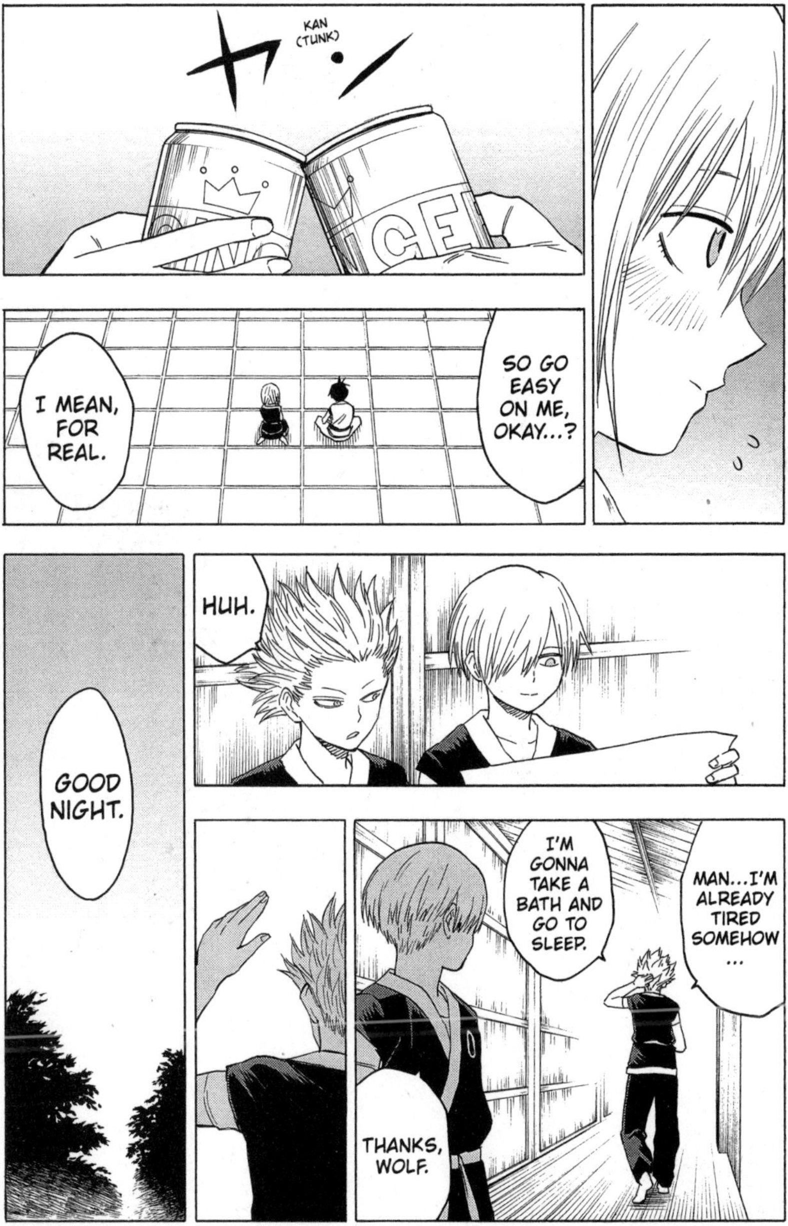
KAN
(TUNK)
SO GO EASY ON ME, OKAY...?
I MEAN, FOR REAL.
HUH.
MAN...I'M ALREADY TIRED SOMEHOW ...
I'M GONNA TAKE A BATH AND GO TO SLEEP.
THANKS, WOLF.
GOOD NIGHT.

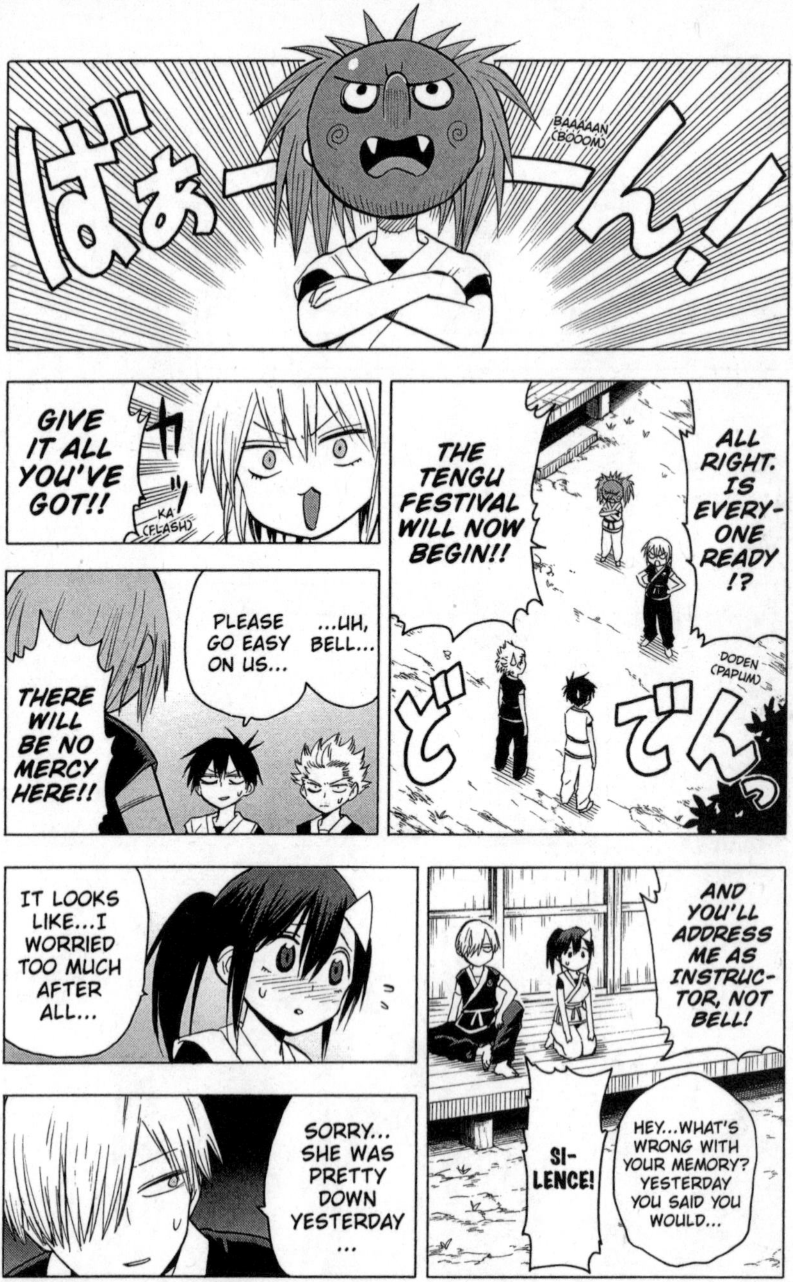
ばぁーん!
BAAAAAN (BOOOM)
ALL RIGHT. IS EVERYONE READY!?
THE TENGU FESTIVAL WILL NOW BEGIN!!
どでんっ
DODEN (PAPUM)
GIVE IT ALL YOU'VE GOT!!
KA (FLASH)
...UH, BELL...
PLEASE GO EASY ON US...
THERE WILL BE NO MERCY HERE!!
AND YOU'LL ADDRESS ME AS INSTRUCTOR, NOT BELL!
HEY...WHAT'S WRONG WITH YOUR MEMORY? YESTERDAY YOU SAID YOU WOULD...
SI-LENCE!
IT LOOKS LIKE...I WORRIED TOO MUCH AFTER ALL...
SORRY... SHE WAS PRETTY DOWN YESTERDAY ...

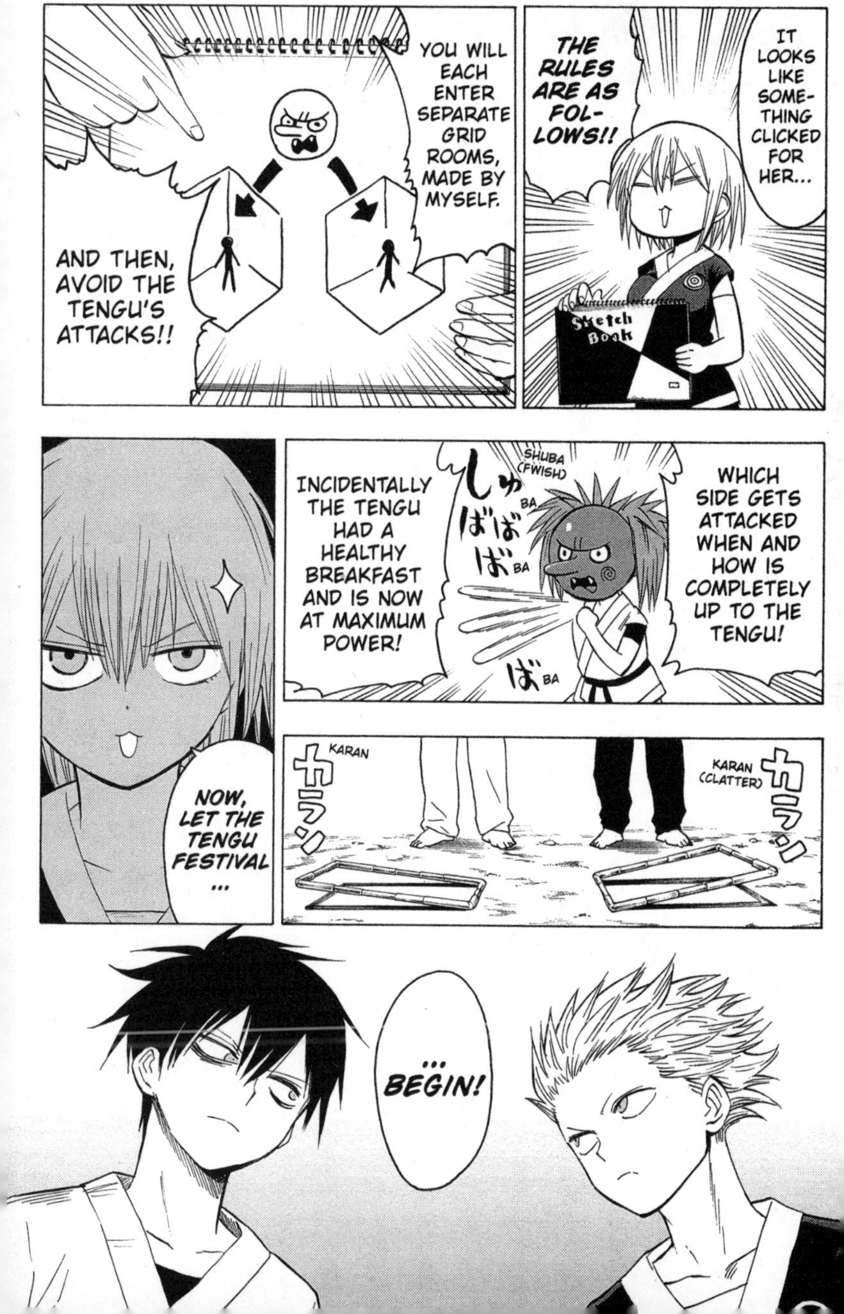
IT LOOKS LIKE SOMETHING CLICKED FOR HER...
THE RULES ARE AS FOLLOWS!!
Sketch Book
YOU WILL EACH ENTER SEPARATE GRID ROOMS, MADE BY MYSELF.
AND THEN, AVOID THE TENGU'S ATTACKS!!
WHICH SIDE GETS ATTACKED WHEN AND HOW IS COMPLETELY UP TO THE TENGU!
しゅばばばば
SHUBA (FWISH) BA BA BA
INCIDENTALLY THE TENGU HAD A HEALTHY BREAKFAST AND IS NOW AT MAXIMUM POWER!
カラン
KARAN (CLATTER)
カラン
KARAN
NOW, LET THE TENGU FESTIVAL ...
... BEGIN!

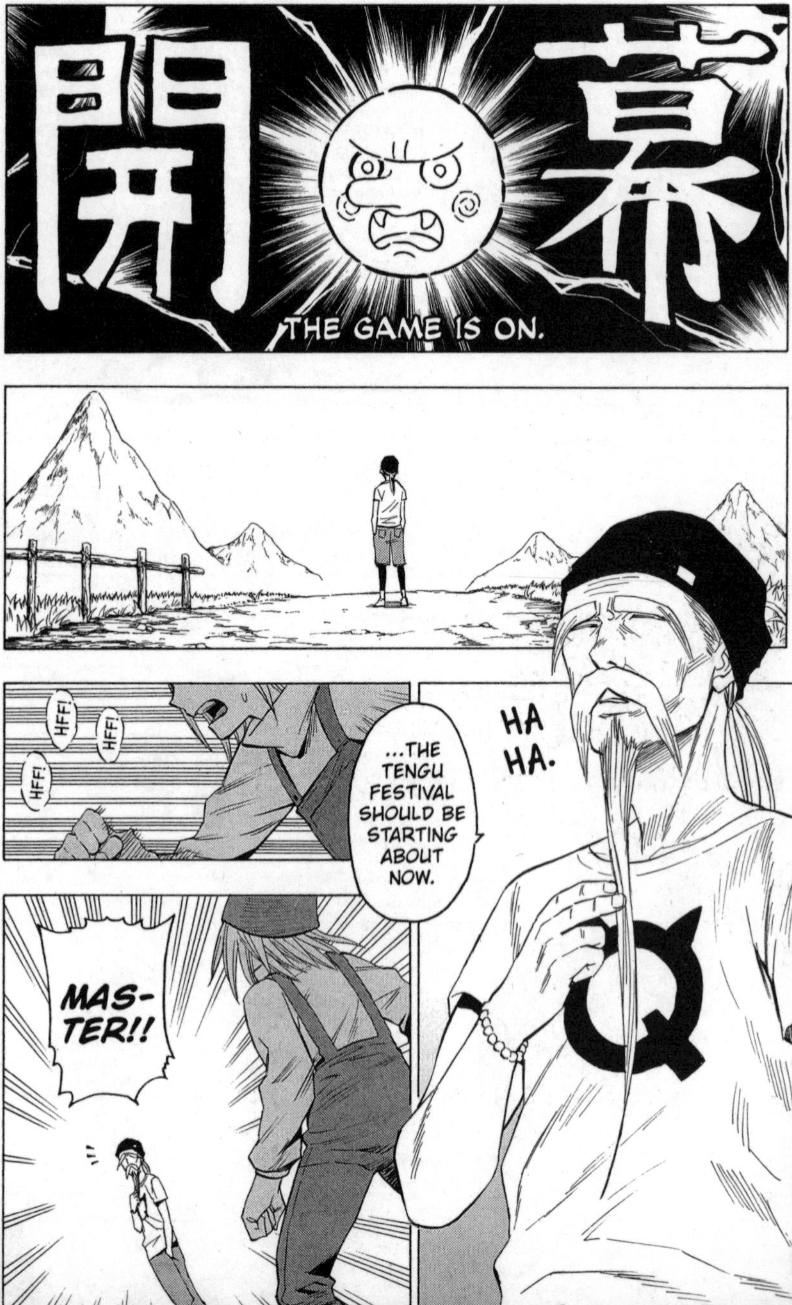
開幕
THE GAME IS ON.
HA HA.
...THE TENGU FESTIVAL SHOULD BE STARTING ABOUT NOW.
HFF!
HFF!
HFF!
MAS-TER!!
!!

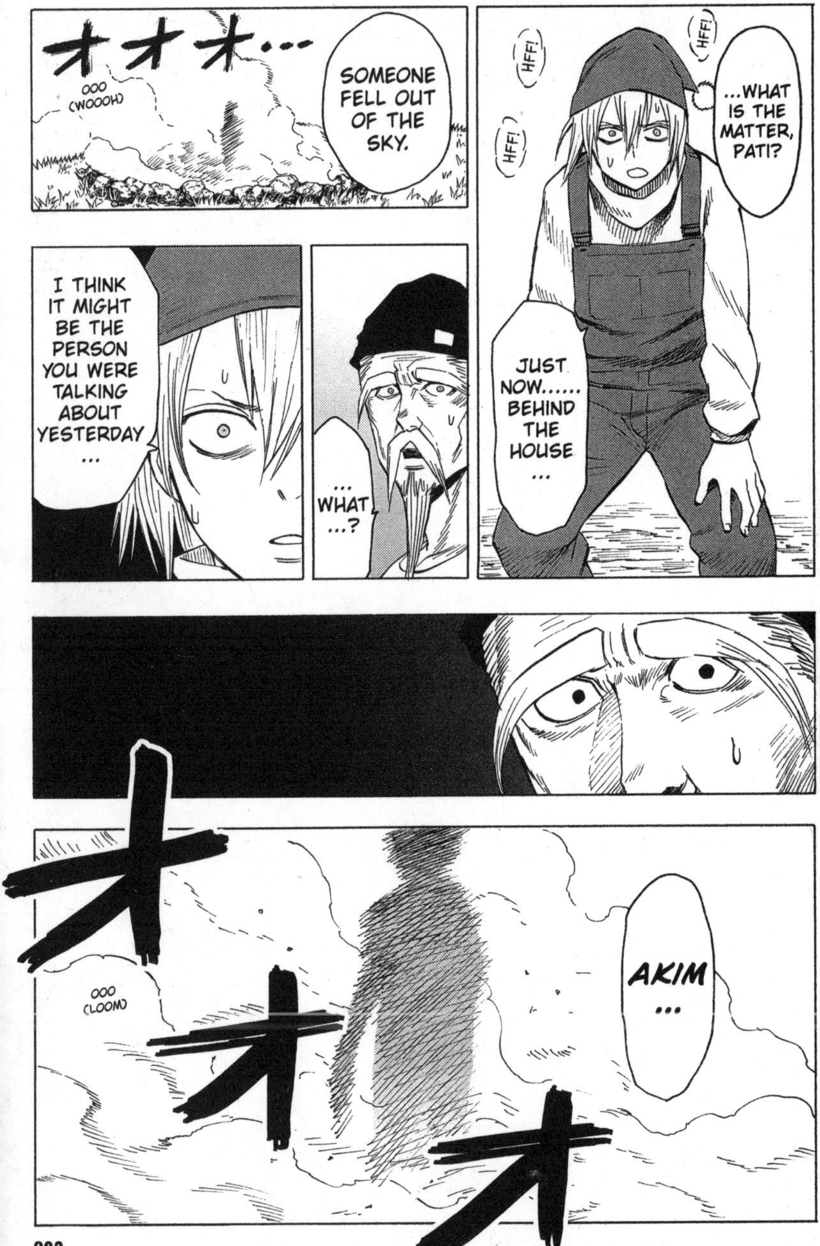
(HFF!)
(HFF!)
(HFF!)
...WHAT IS THE MATTER, PATI?
JUST NOW...... BEHIND THE HOUSE ...
オオオ...
OOO (WOOOH)
SOMEONE FELL OUT OF THE SKY.
... WHAT ...?
I THINK IT MIGHT BE THE PERSON YOU WERE TALKING ABOUT YESTERDAY ...
AKIM ...
オオオ
OOO (LOOM)

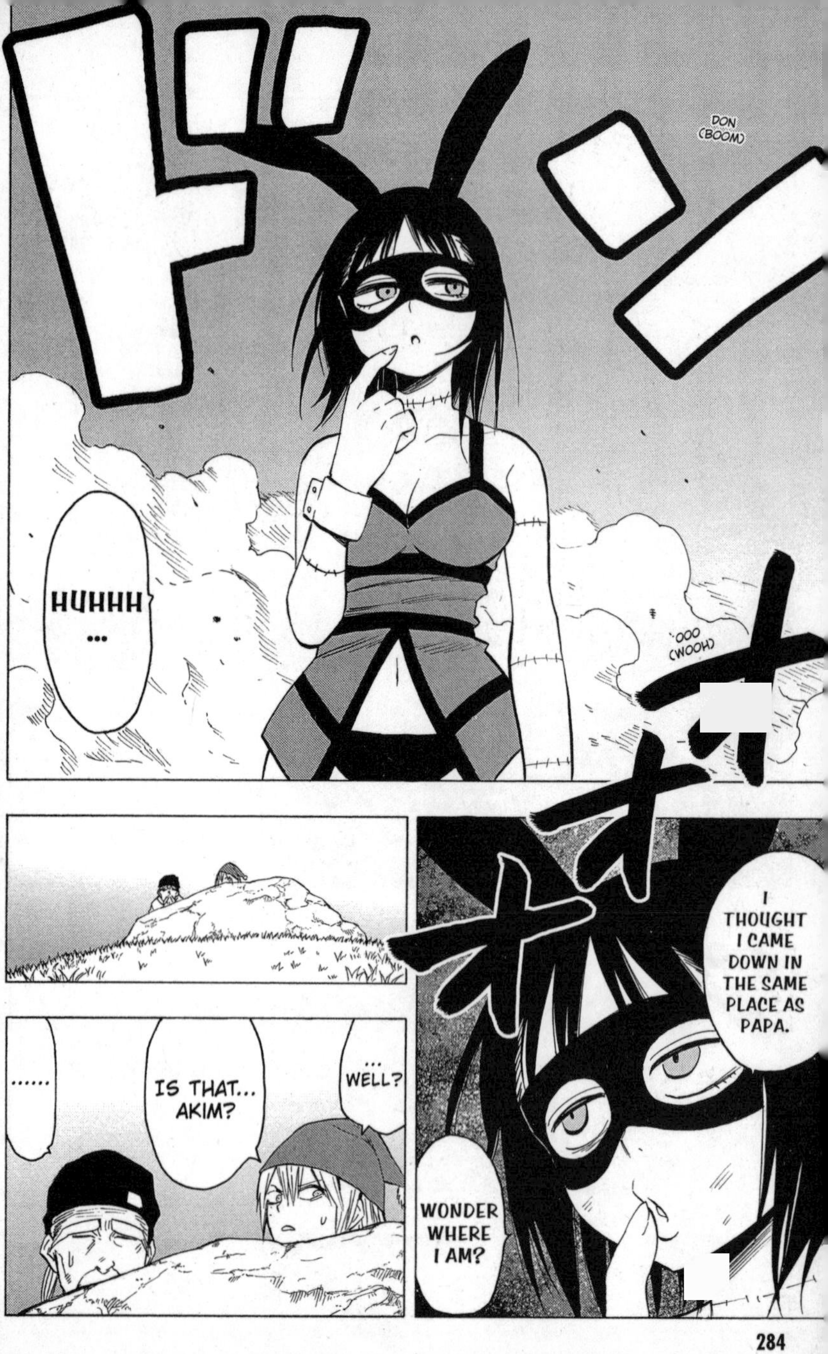
DON (BOOM)
OOO (WOOH)
HUHHH ...
I THOUGHT I CAME DOWN IN THE SAME PLACE AS PAPA.
WONDER WHERE I AM?
... WELL?
IS THAT... AKIM?
......

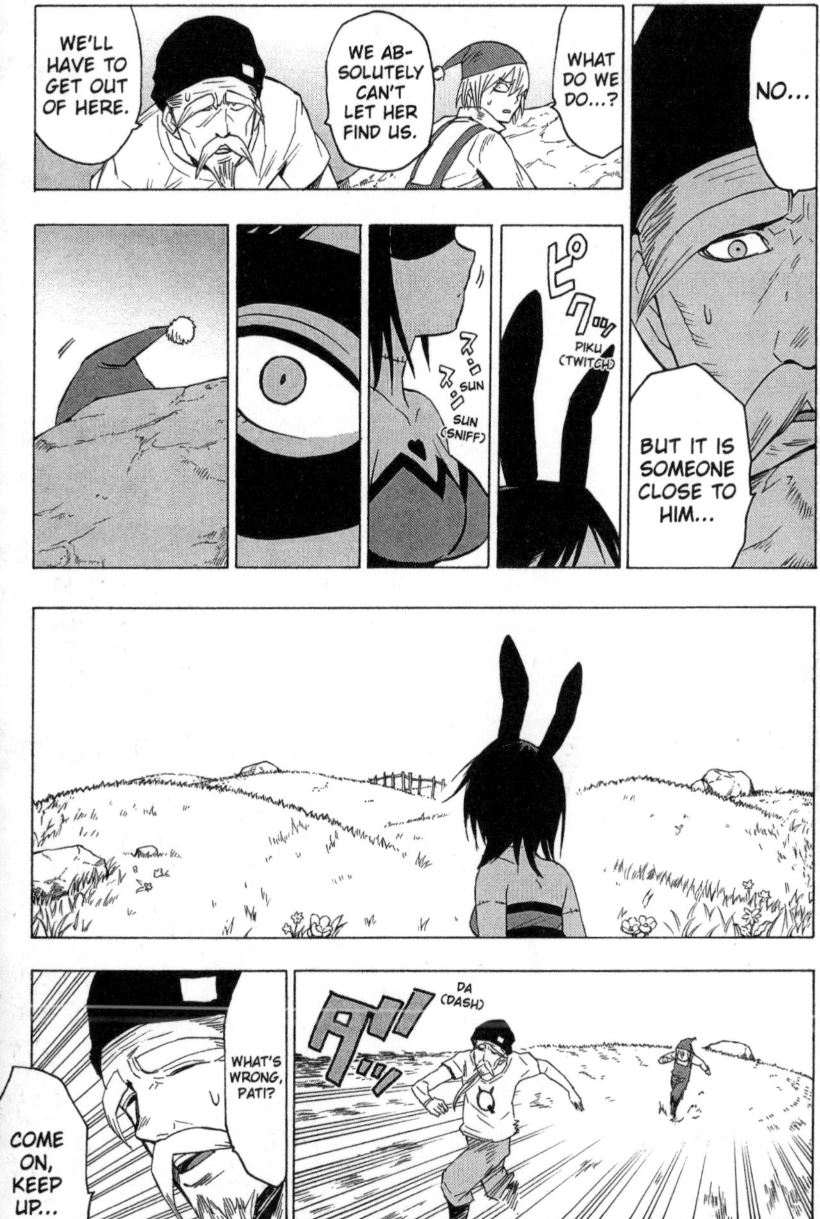
NO...
BUT IT IS SOMEONE CLOSE TO HIM...
WHAT DO WE DO...?
WE AB-SOLUTELY CAN'T LET HER FIND US.
WE'LL HAVE TO GET OUT OF HERE.
PIKU (TWITCH)
SUN SUN (SNIFF)
DA (DASH)
WHAT'S WRONG, PATI?
COME ON, KEEP UP...

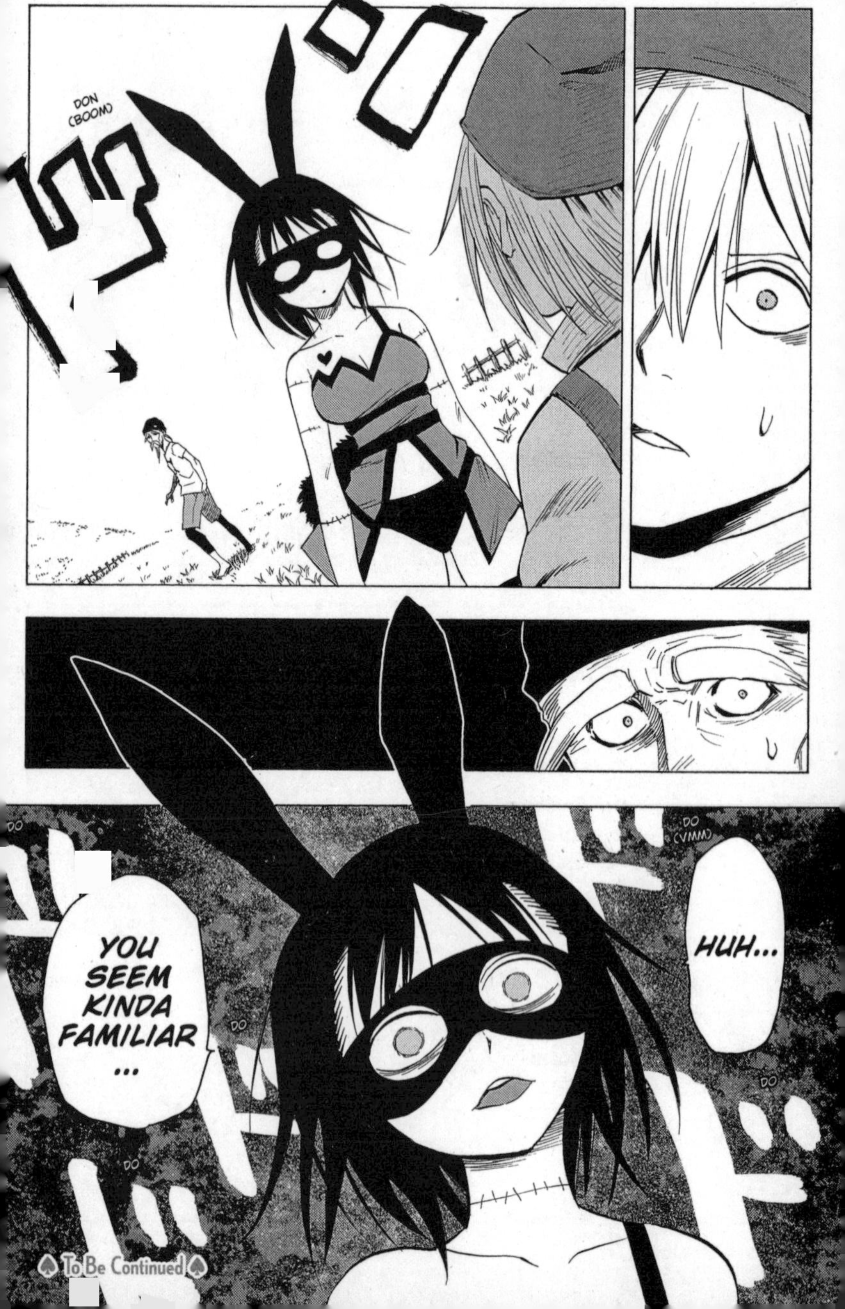
DON (BOOM)
DO (VMM)
HUH...
DO
YOU SEEM KINDA FAMILIAR ...
DO
DO
DO
To Be Continued

BLOOD LAD

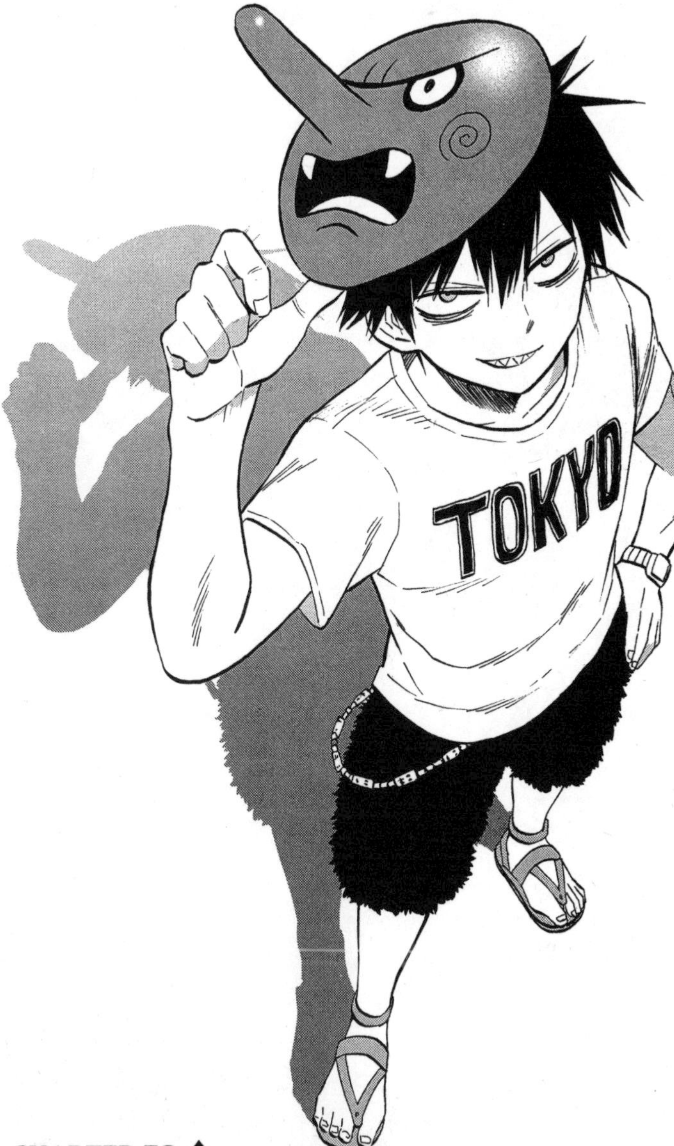
TOKYO

CHAPTER 59 ♠
THE TENGU FESTIVAL BEGINS!

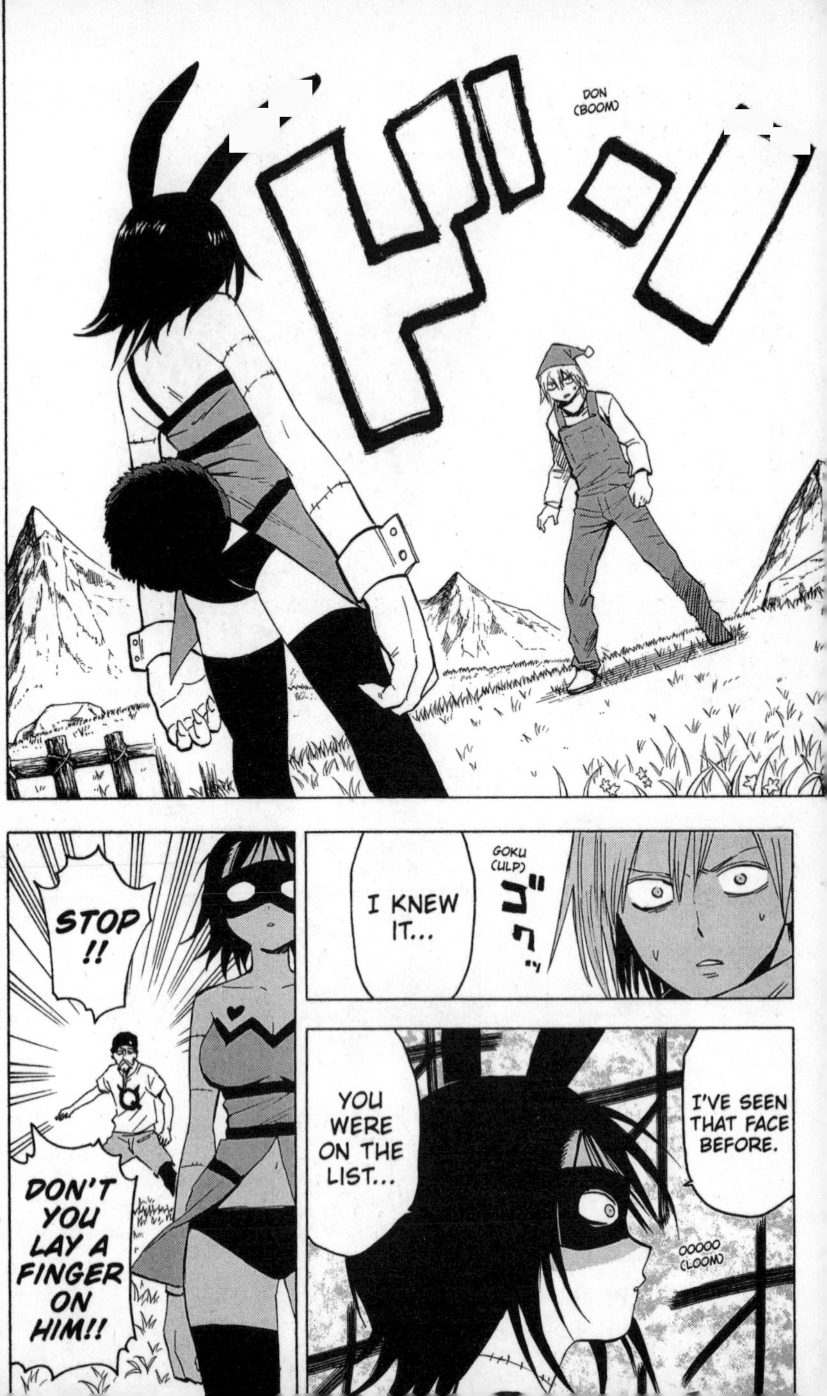
DON
(BOOM)
GOKU
(ULP)
I KNEW IT...
I'VE SEEN THAT FACE BEFORE.
YOU WERE ON THE LIST...
OOOOO
(LOOM)
STOP!!
DON'T YOU LAY A FINGER ON HIM!!

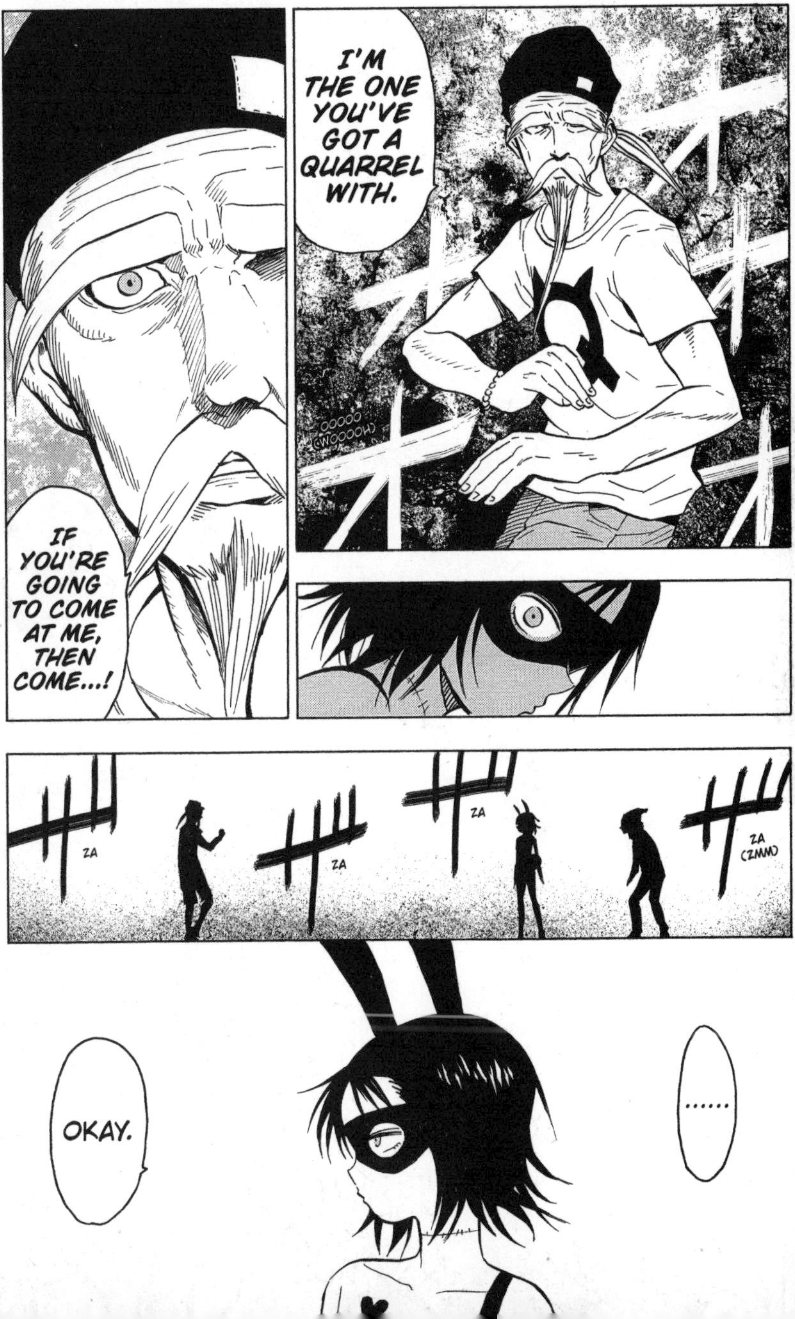
I'M THE ONE YOU'VE GOT A QUARREL WITH.
OOOOO
(WOOOOH)
IF YOU'RE GOING TO COME AT ME, THEN COME...!
ZA
(ZMM)
ZA
ZA
ZA
......
OKAY.

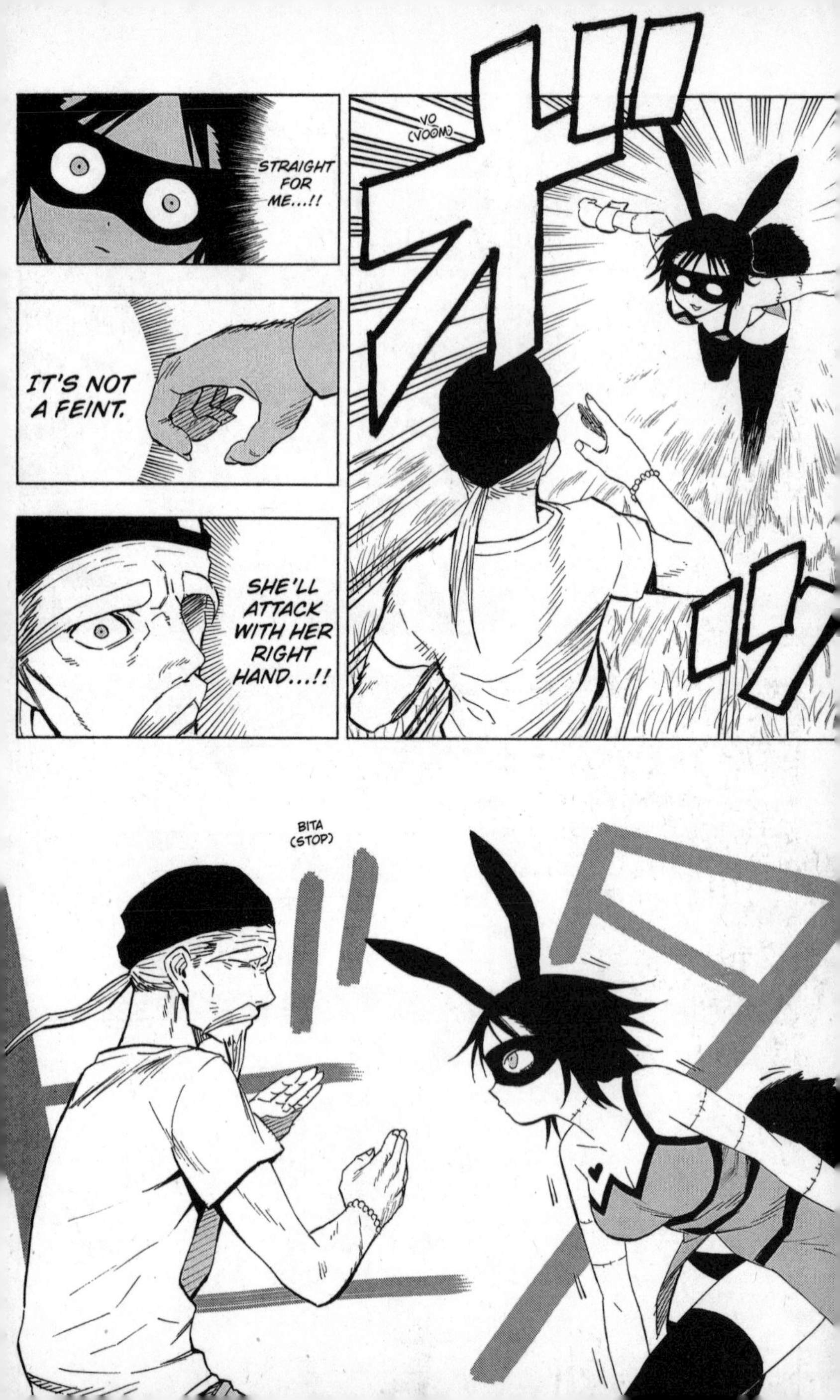
VO (VOOM)
STRAIGHT FOR ME...!!
IT'S NOT A FEINT.
SHE'LL ATTACK WITH HER RIGHT HAND...!!
BITA (STOP)

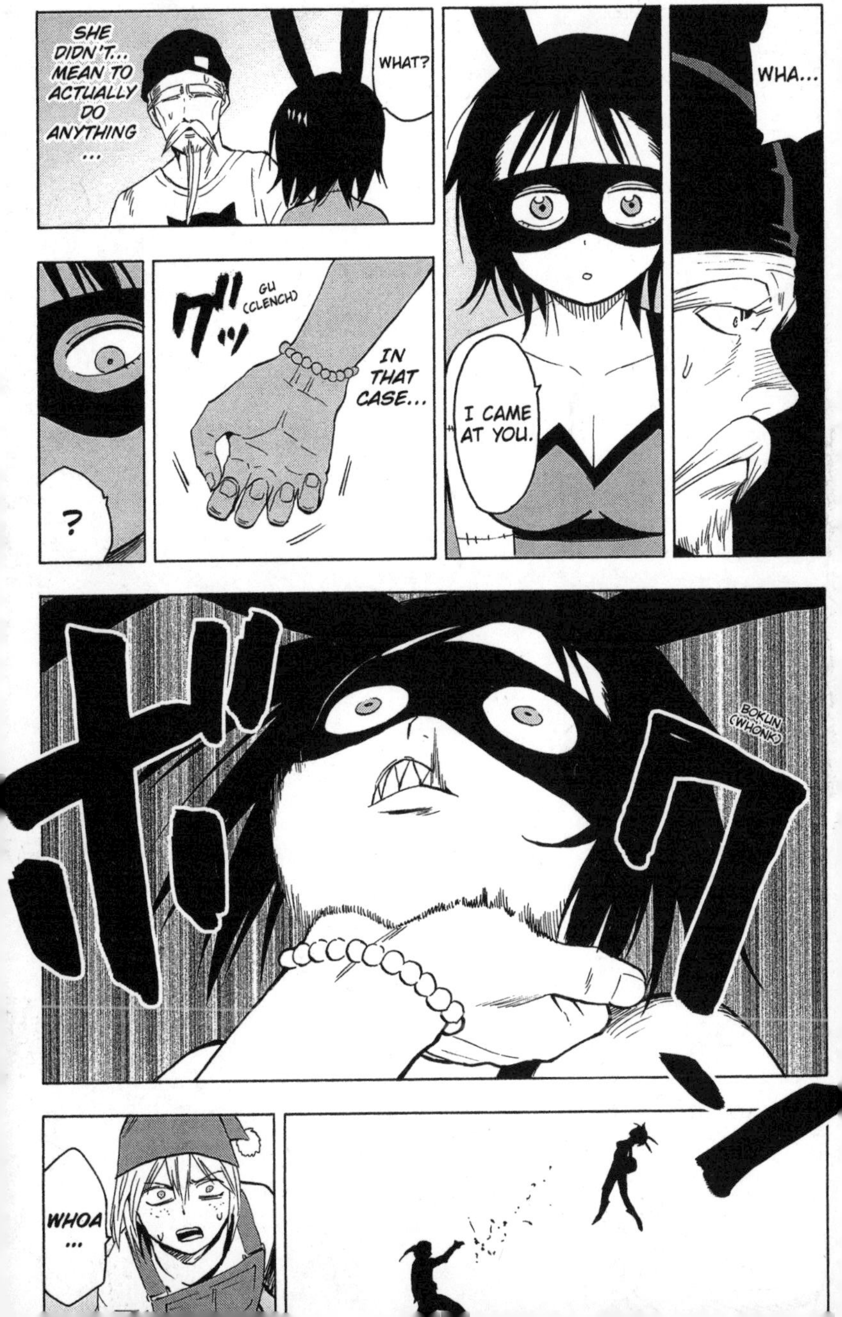
WHA...
I CAME AT YOU.
WHAT?
SHE DIDN'T... MEAN TO ACTUALLY DO ANYTHING...
GU (CLENCH)
IN THAT CASE...
?
BOKUN (WHONK)
WHOA...

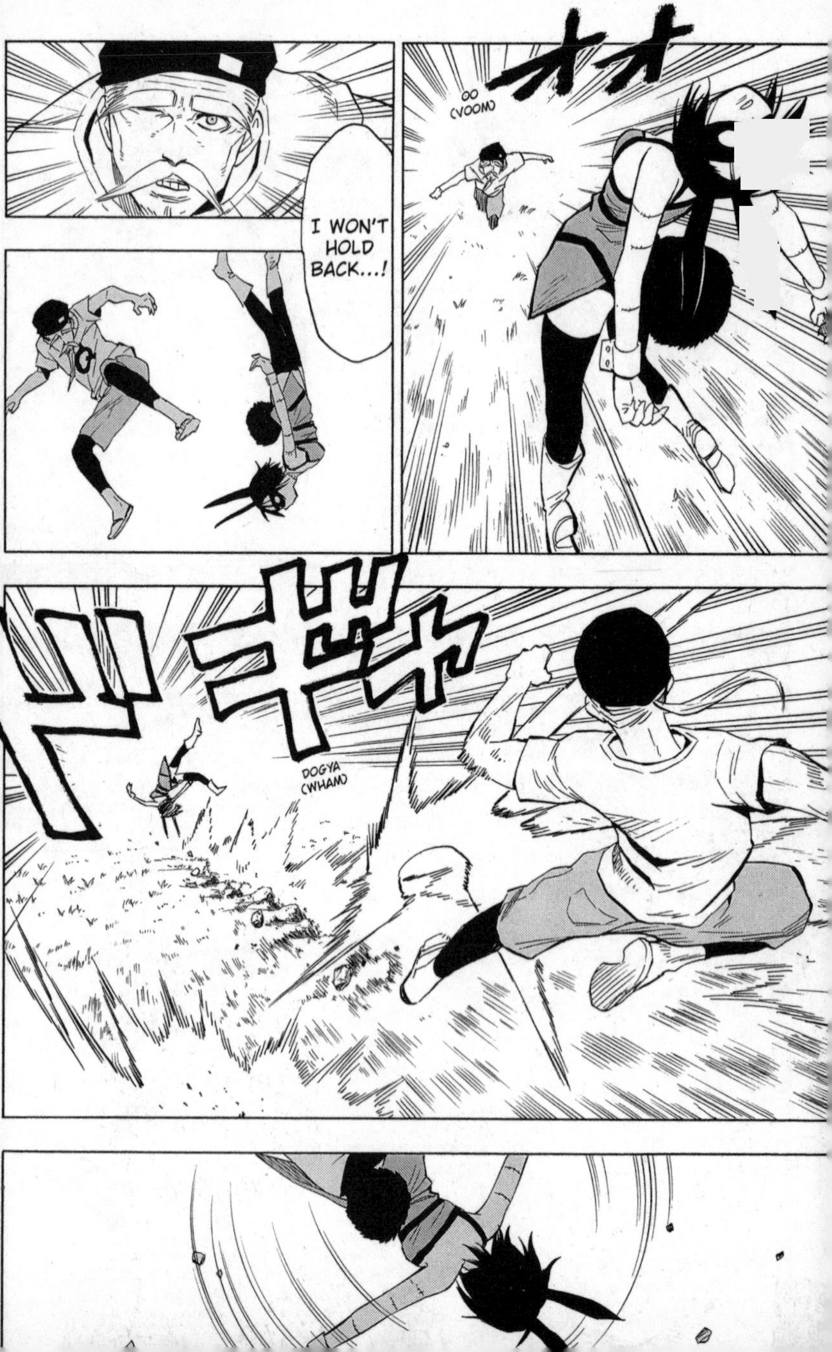
オオ
OO (VOOM)
I WON'T HOLD BACK...!
ドギャ
DOGYA (WHAM)

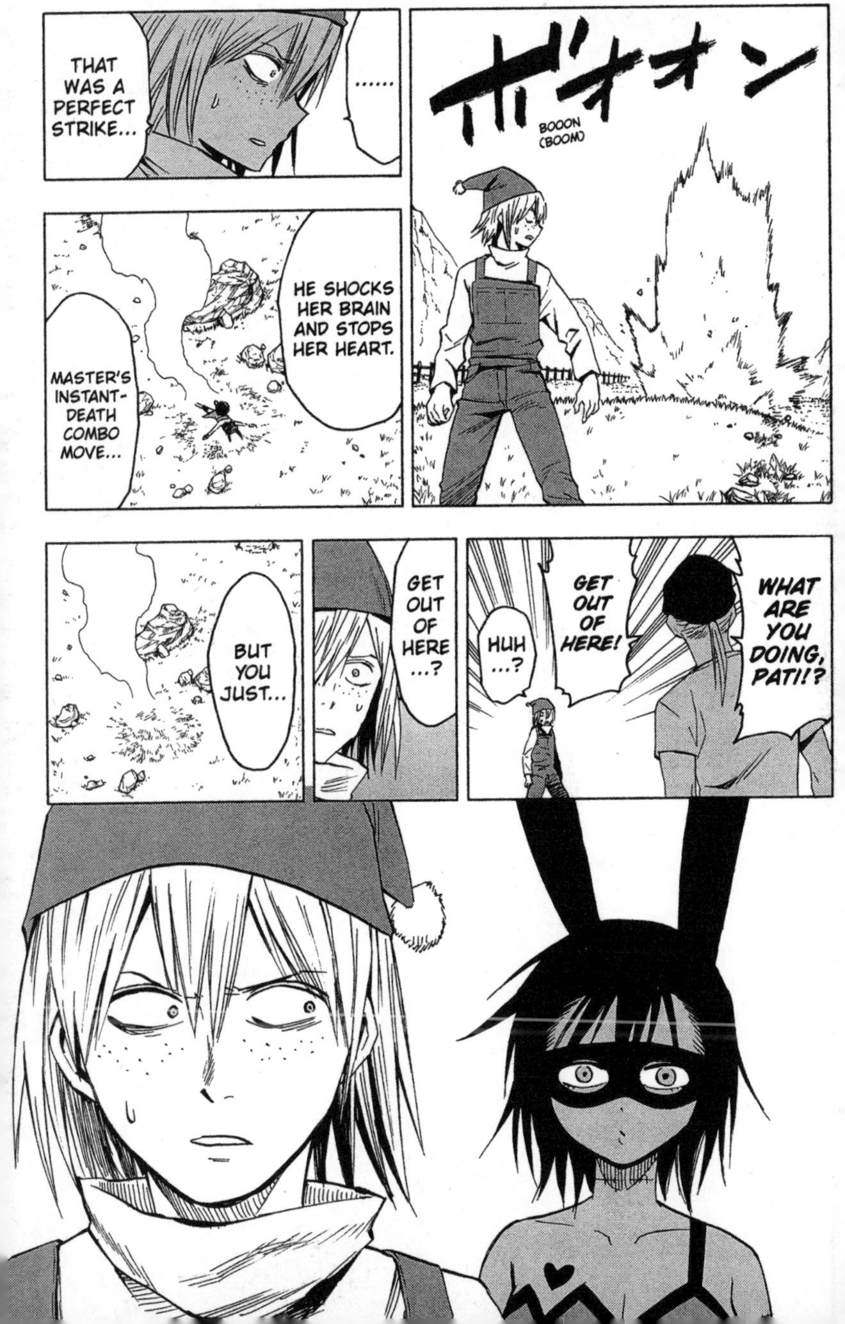
ボオオン
BOOON (BOOM)
......
THAT WAS A PERFECT STRIKE...
HE SHOCKS HER BRAIN AND STOPS HER HEART.
MASTER'S INSTANT-DEATH COMBO MOVE...
WHAT ARE YOU DOING, PAT!!?
GET OUT OF HERE!
HUH ...?
GET OUT OF HERE ...?
BUT YOU JUST...

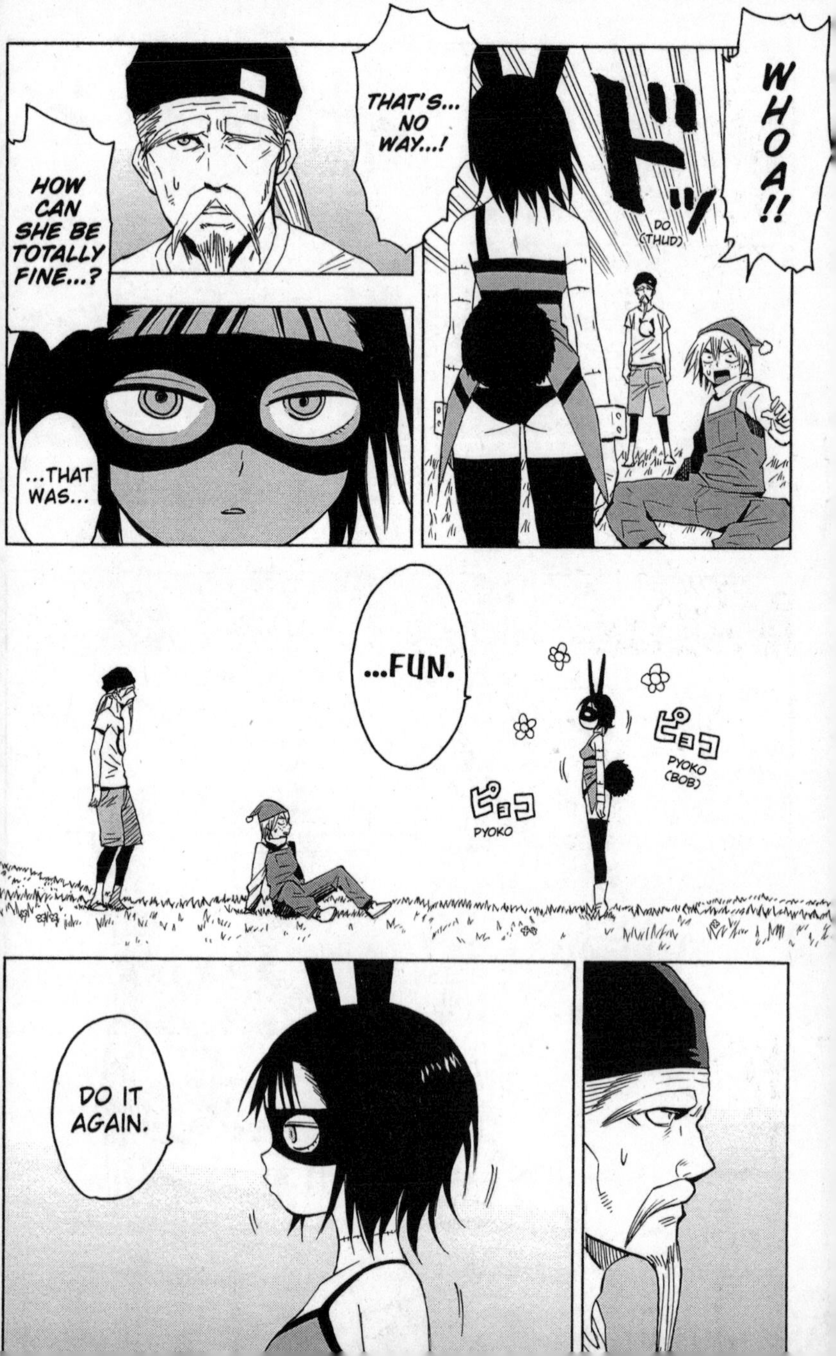
WHOA!!
ドッ
DO
(THUD)
THAT'S... NO WAY...!
HOW CAN SHE BE TOTALLY FINE...?
...THAT WAS...
...FUN.
ピョコ
PYOKO
(BOB)
ピョコ
PYOKO
DO IT AGAIN.

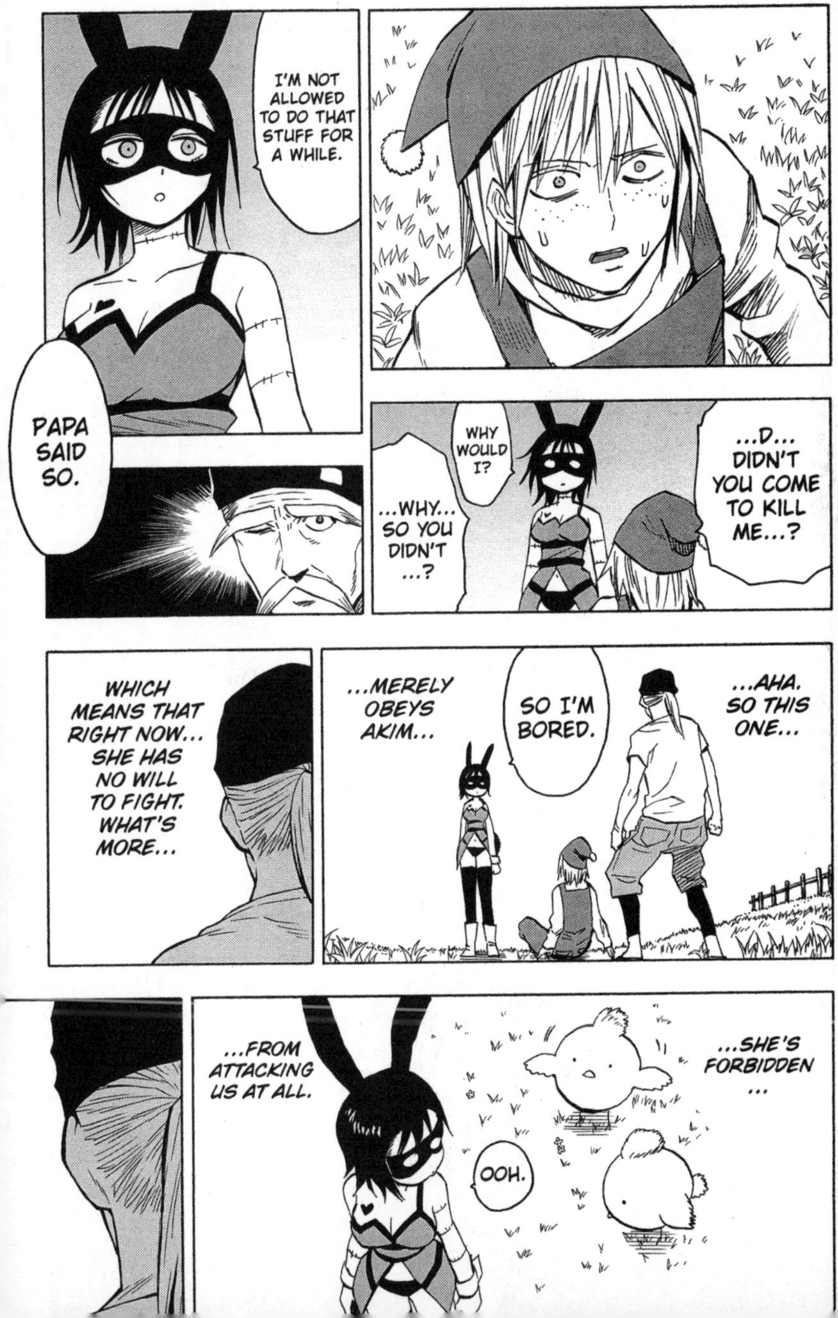
...D... DIDN'T YOU COME TO KILL ME...?
WHY WOULD I?
...WHY... SO YOU DIDN'T ...?
I'M NOT ALLOWED TO DO THAT STUFF FOR A WHILE.
PAPA SAID SO.
...AHA. SO THIS ONE...
SO I'M BORED.
...MERELY OBEYS AKIM...
WHICH MEANS THAT RIGHT NOW... SHE HAS NO WILL TO FIGHT. WHAT'S MORE...
...SHE'S FORBIDDEN ...
OOH.
...FROM ATTACKING US AT ALL.

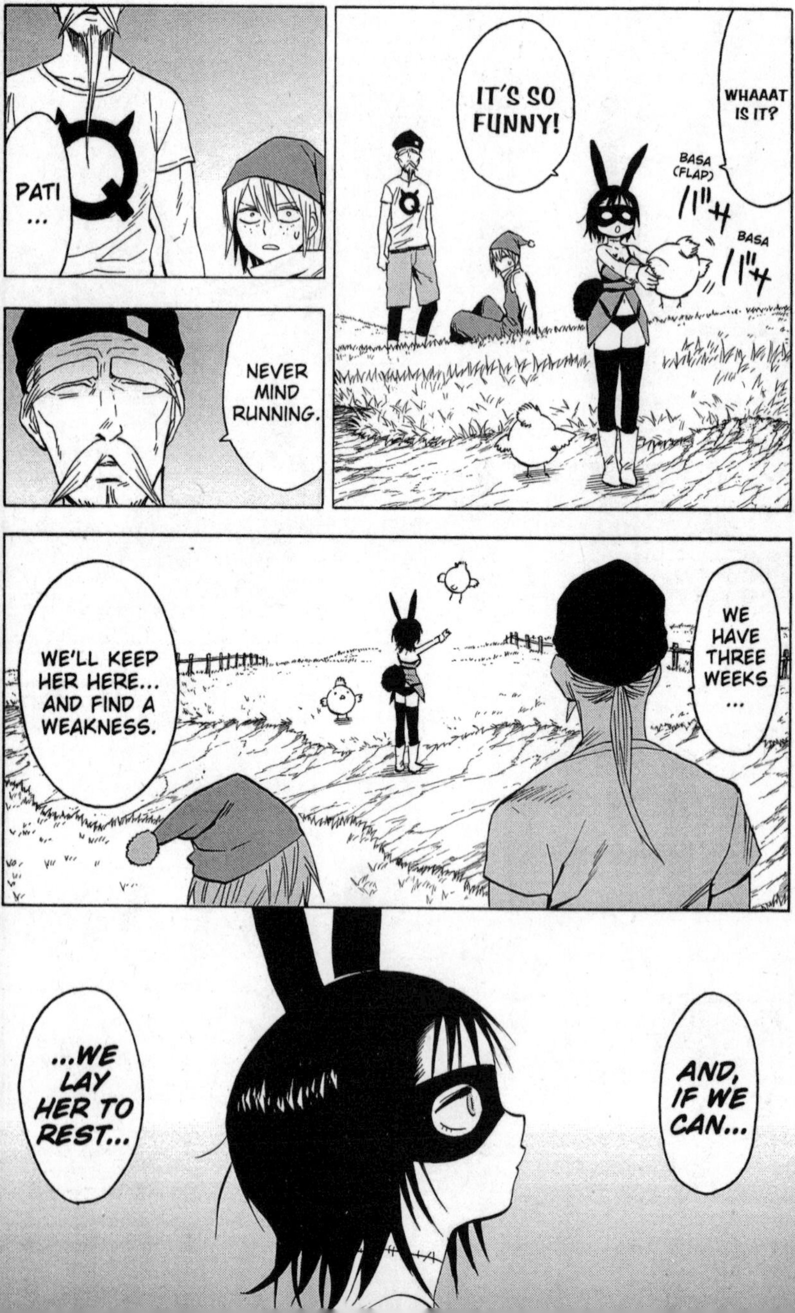
WHAAAT IS IT?
IT'S SO FUNNY!
BASA (FLAP)
バサ
BASA
バサ
PATI ...
NEVER MIND RUNNING.
WE HAVE THREE WEEKS ...
WE'LL KEEP HER HERE... AND FIND A WEAKNESS.
AND, IF WE CAN...
...WE LAY HER TO REST...

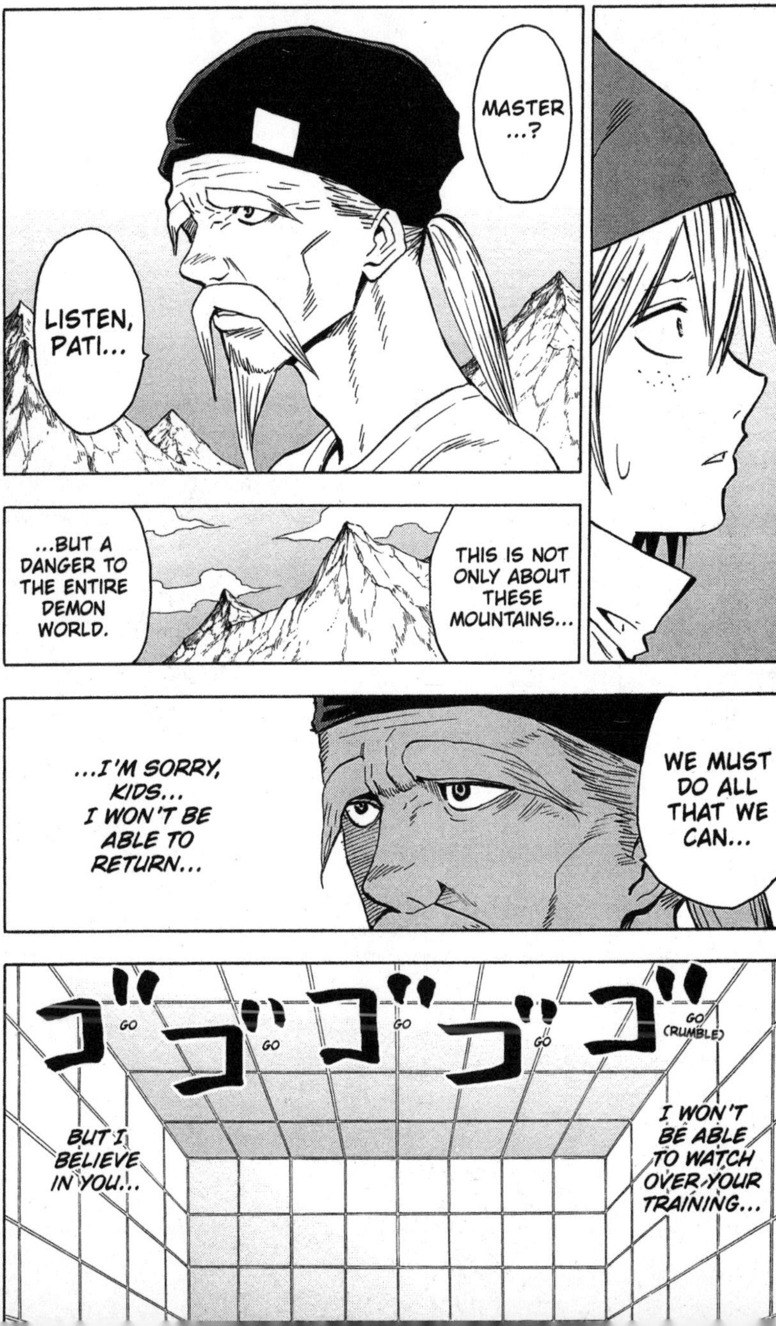
MASTER ...?
LISTEN, PATI...
THIS IS NOT ONLY ABOUT THESE MOUNTAINS...
...BUT A DANGER TO THE ENTIRE DEMON WORLD.
WE MUST DO ALL THAT WE CAN...
...I'M SORRY, KIDS... I WON'T BE ABLE TO RETURN...
ゴゴゴゴゴ
GO GO GO GO GO (RUMBLE)
I WON'T BE ABLE TO WATCH OVER YOUR TRAINING...
BUT I BELIEVE IN YOU...

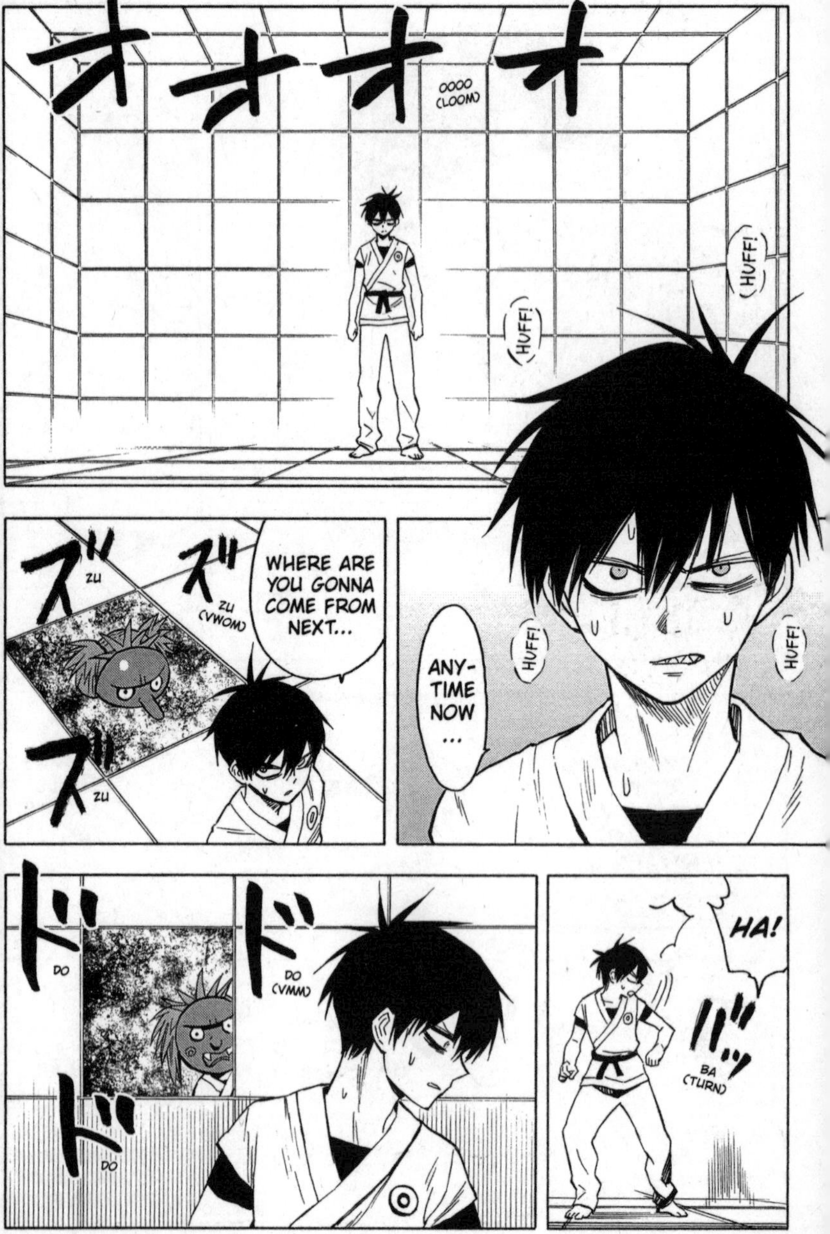

オオオオ
OOOO (LOOM)
(HUFF!)
(HUFF!)
(HUFF!)
(HUFF!)
ANY-TIME NOW ...
ズズズ
ZU ZU (VWOM) ZU
WHERE ARE YOU GONNA COME FROM NEXT...
HA!
バッ
BA (TURN)
ドドド
DO DO (VMM) DO

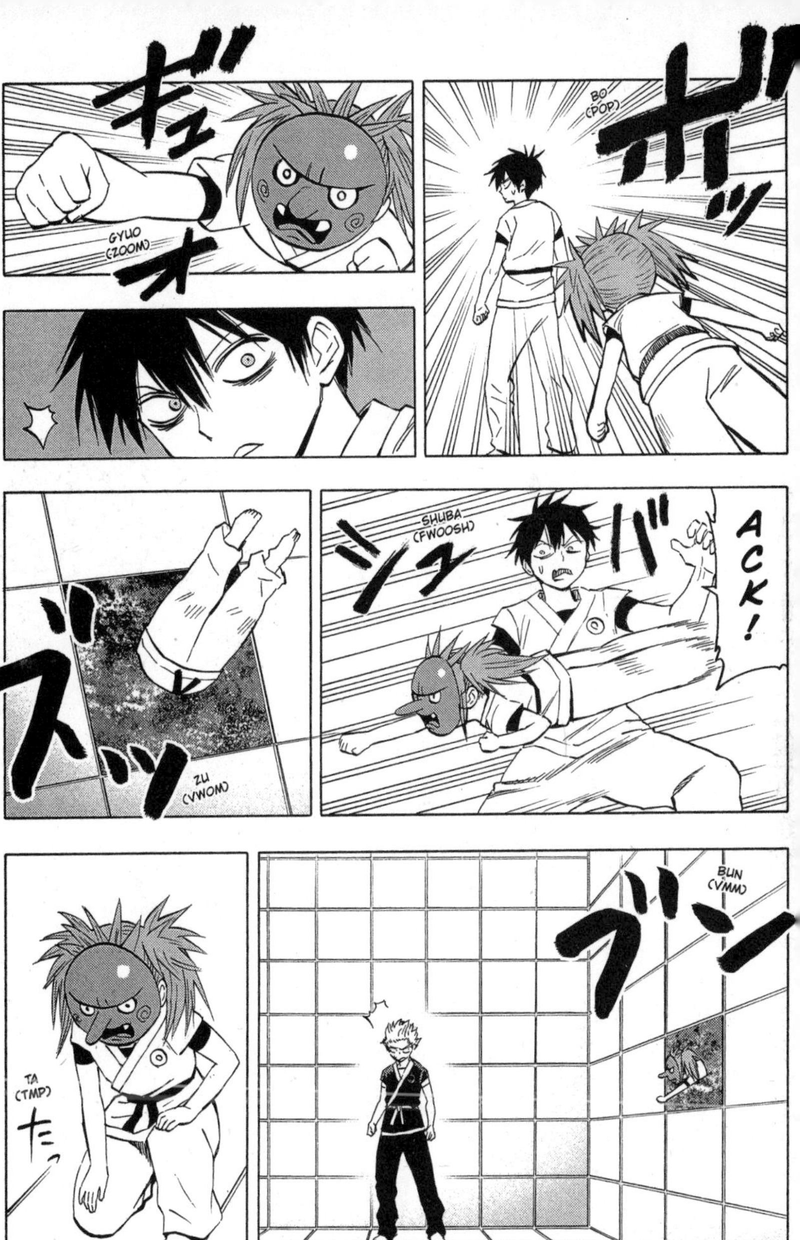
ボッ
BO
(POP)
ギュオ
GYUO
(ZOOM)
シュバ
SHUBA
(FWOOSH)
ACK!
ズッ
ZU
(VWOM)
ブン
BUN
(VMM)
たっ
TA
(TMP)

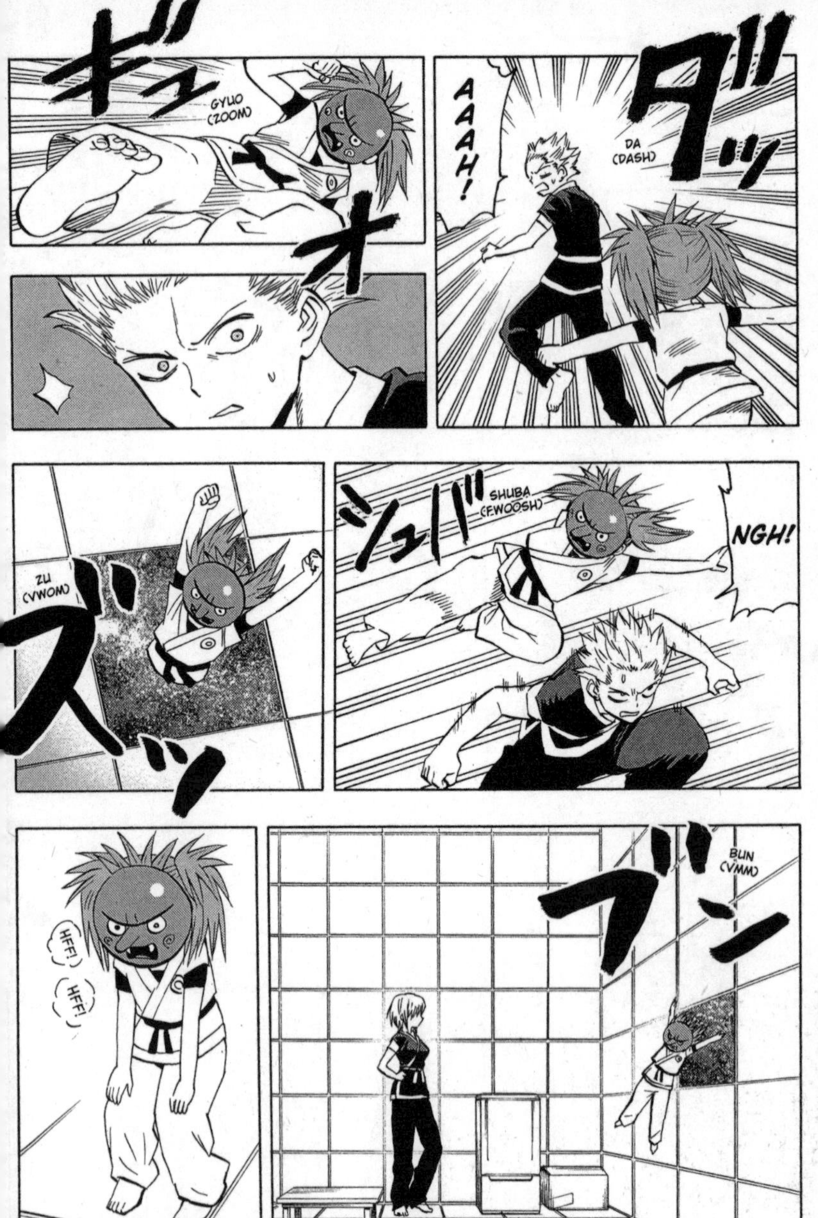
DA
(DASH)
AAAAH!
GYUO
(ZOOM)
NGH!
SHUBA
(FWOOSH)
ZU
(VWOM)
BUN
(VMM)
HFF!
HFF!

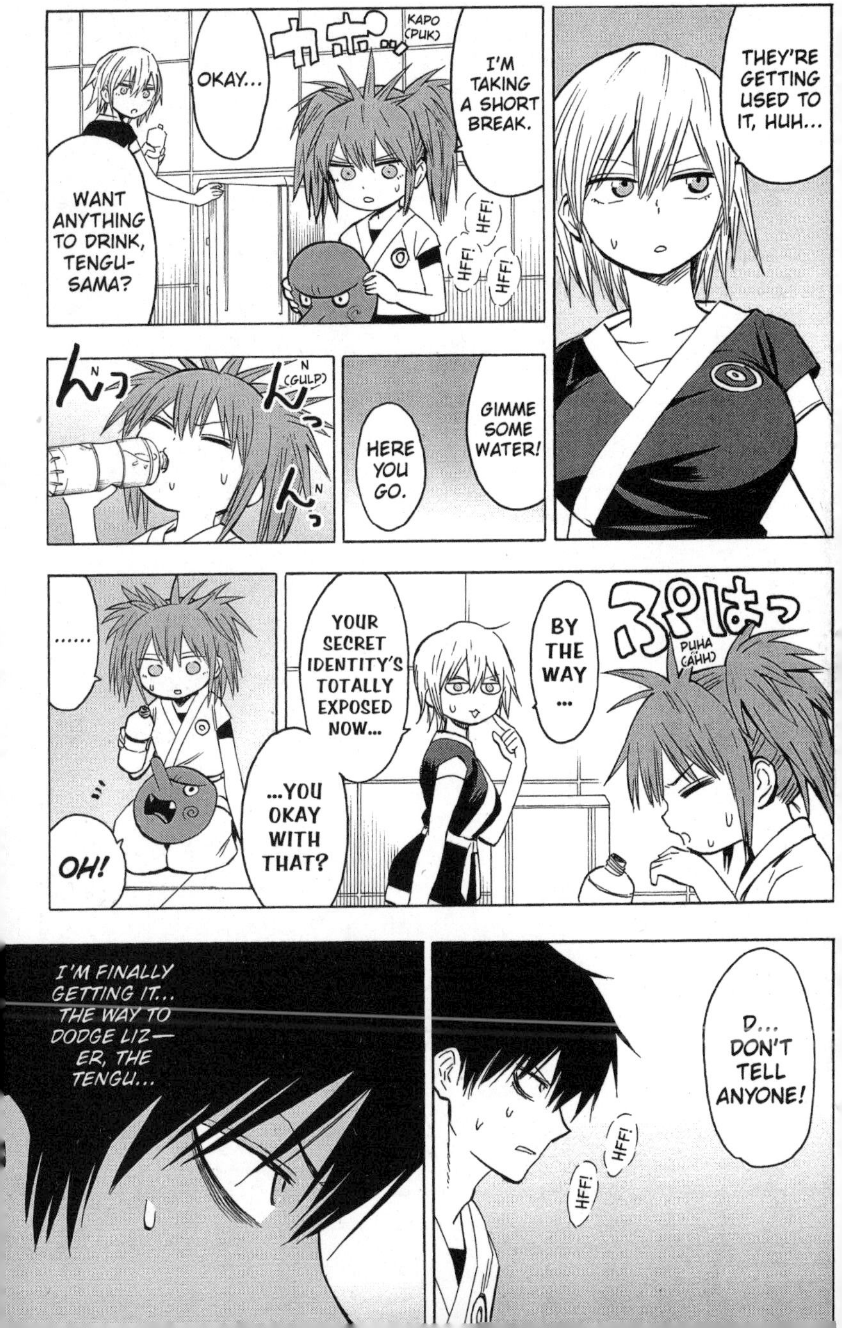
THEY'RE GETTING USED TO IT, HUH...
KAPO (PUK)
I'M TAKING A SHORT BREAK.
OKAY...
WANT ANYTHING TO DRINK, TENGU-SAMA?
HFF! HFF! HFF!
GIMME SOME WATER!
HERE YOU GO.
N (GULP)
N
N
ぷはっ
PUHA (AHH)
BY THE WAY...
YOUR SECRET IDENTITY'S TOTALLY EXPOSED NOW...
...YOU OKAY WITH THAT?
......
OH!
D... DON'T TELL ANYONE!
HFF! HFF!
I'M FINALLY GETTING IT... THE WAY TO DODGE LIZ-ER, THE TENGU...

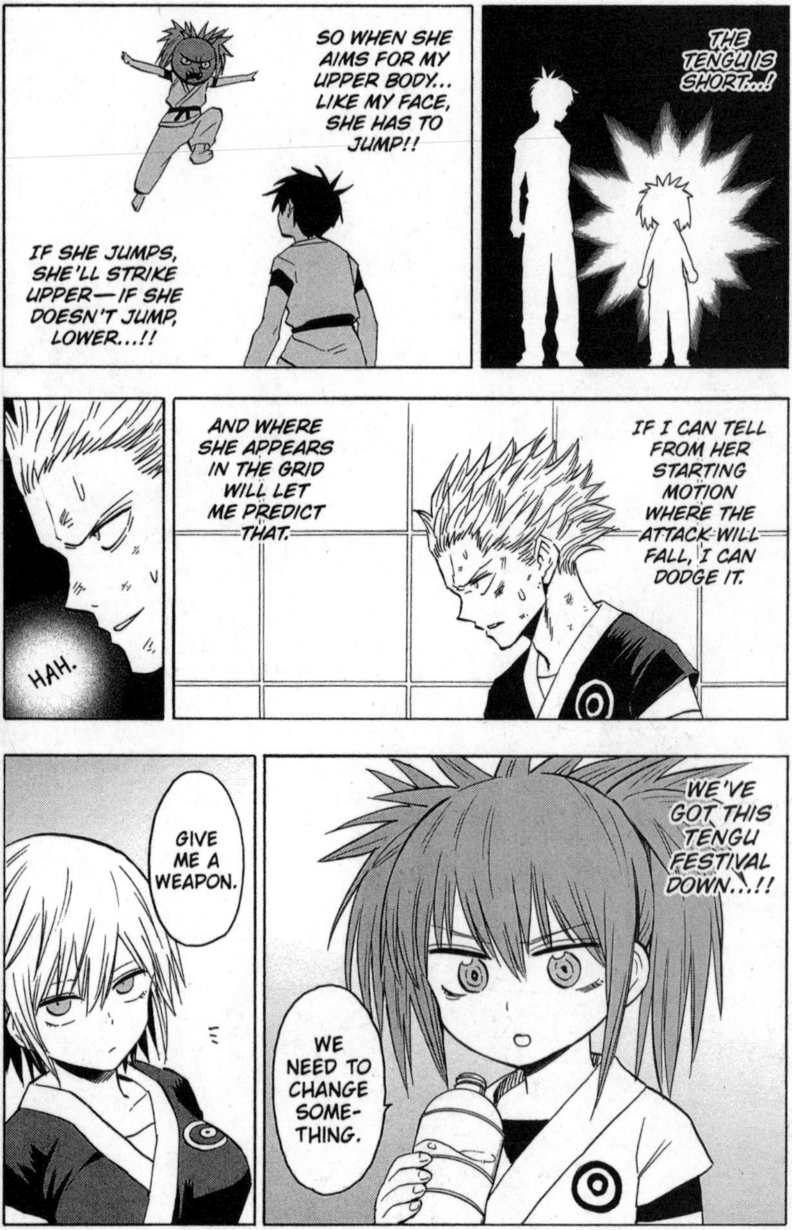
THE TENGU IS SHORT...!
SO WHEN SHE AIMS FOR MY UPPER BODY... LIKE MY FACE, SHE HAS TO JUMP!!
IF SHE JUMPS, SHE'LL STRIKE UPPER—IF SHE DOESN'T JUMP, LOWER...!!
IF I CAN TELL FROM HER STARTING MOTION WHERE THE ATTACK WILL FALL, I CAN DODGE IT.
AND WHERE SHE APPEARS IN THE GRID WILL LET ME PREDICT THAT.
HAH.
WE'VE GOT THIS TENGU FESTIVAL DOWN...!!
WE NEED TO CHANGE SOME-THING.
GIVE ME A WEAPON.

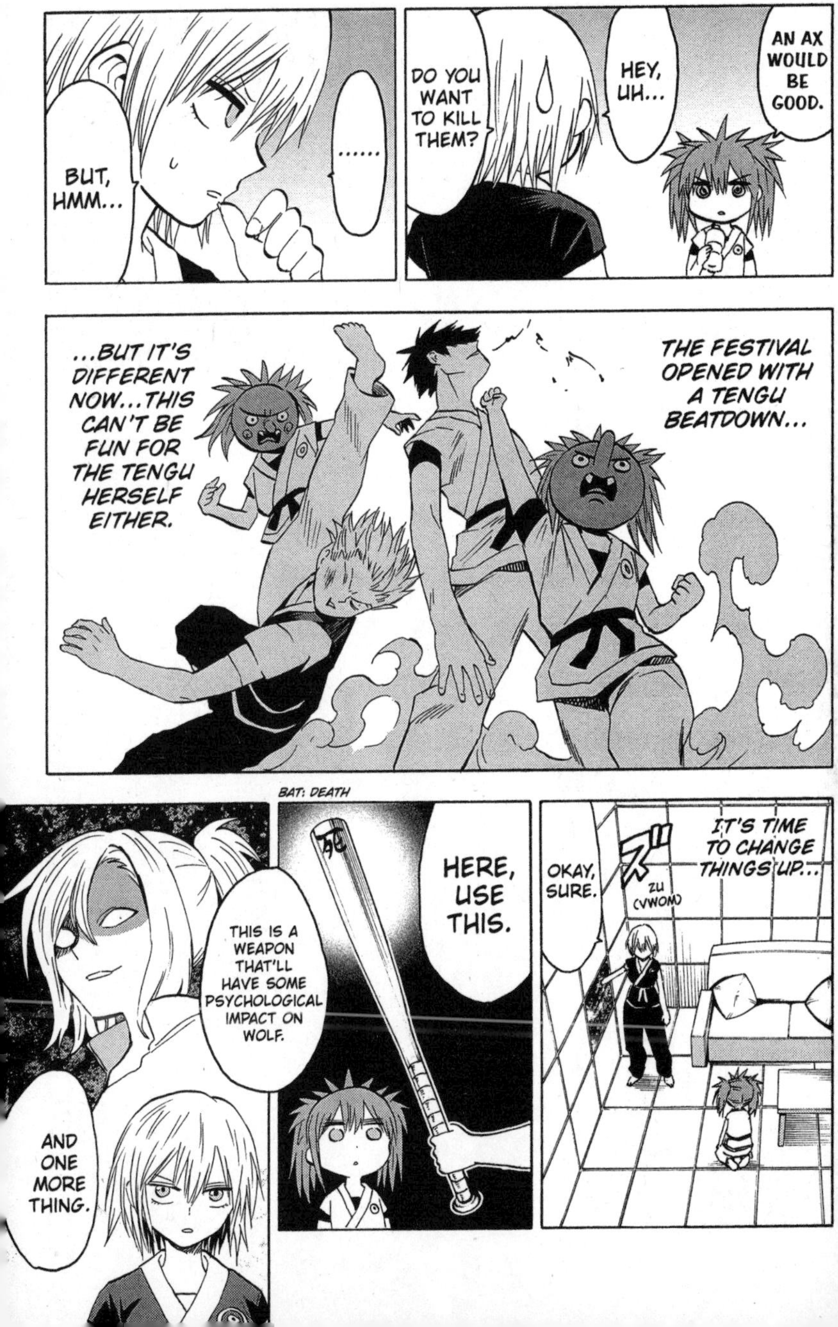
AN AX WOULD BE GOOD.
HEY, UH...
DO YOU WANT TO KILL THEM?
......
BUT, HMM...
THE FESTIVAL OPENED WITH A TENGU BEATDOWN...
...BUT IT'S DIFFERENT NOW...THIS CAN'T BE FUN FOR THE TENGU HERSELF EITHER.
IT'S TIME TO CHANGE THINGS UP...
ズ
ZU (VWOM)
OKAY, SURE.
HERE, USE THIS.
死
BAT: DEATH
THIS IS A WEAPON THAT'LL HAVE SOME PSYCHOLOGICAL IMPACT ON WOLF.
AND ONE MORE THING.

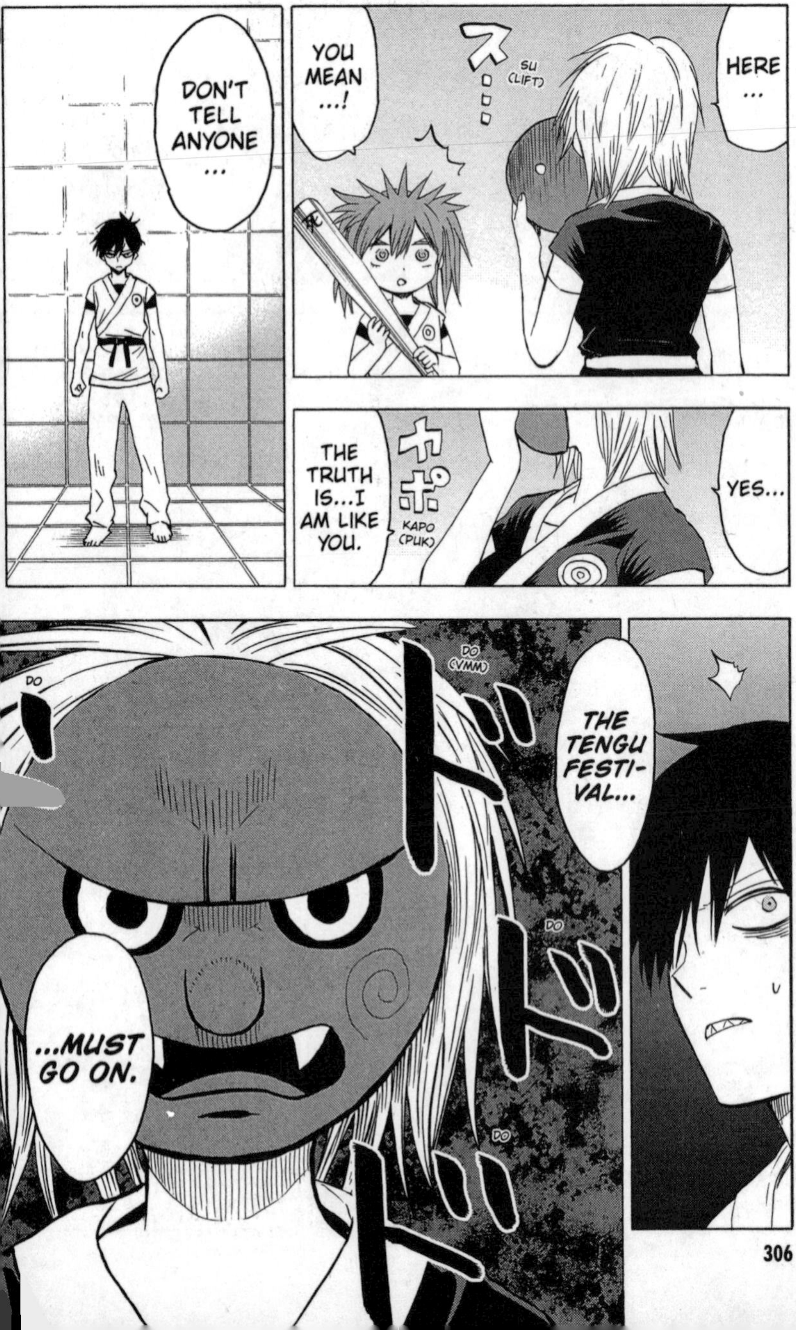
HERE...
SU (LIFT)
YOU MEAN...!
YES...
KAPO (PUK)
THE TRUTH IS...I AM LIKE YOU.
DON'T TELL ANYONE...
THE TENGU FESTIVAL...
DO (VMM)
DO
DO
DO
...MUST GO ON.

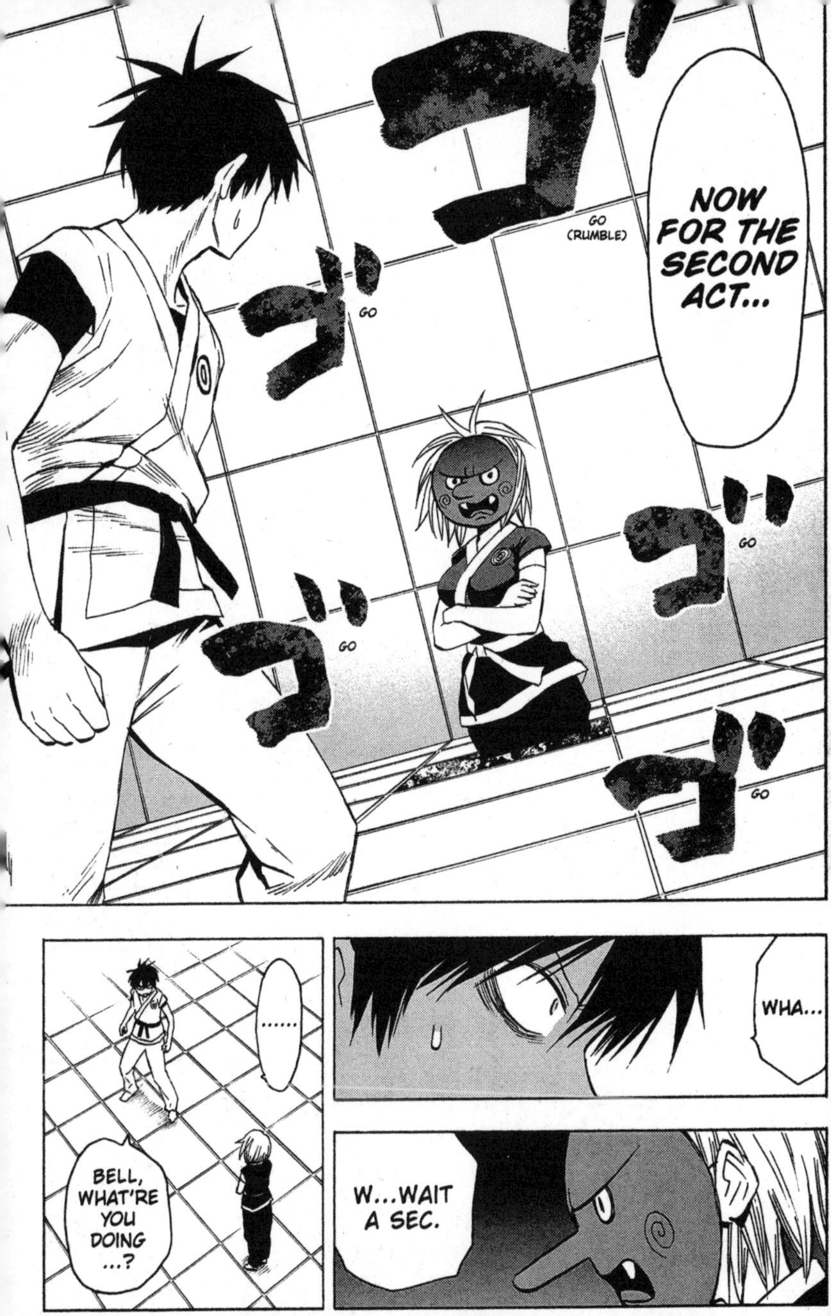
NOW FOR THE SECOND ACT...
GO (RUMBLE)
GO
GO
GO
GO
WHA...
W...WAIT A SEC.
......
BELL, WHAT'RE YOU DOING ...?

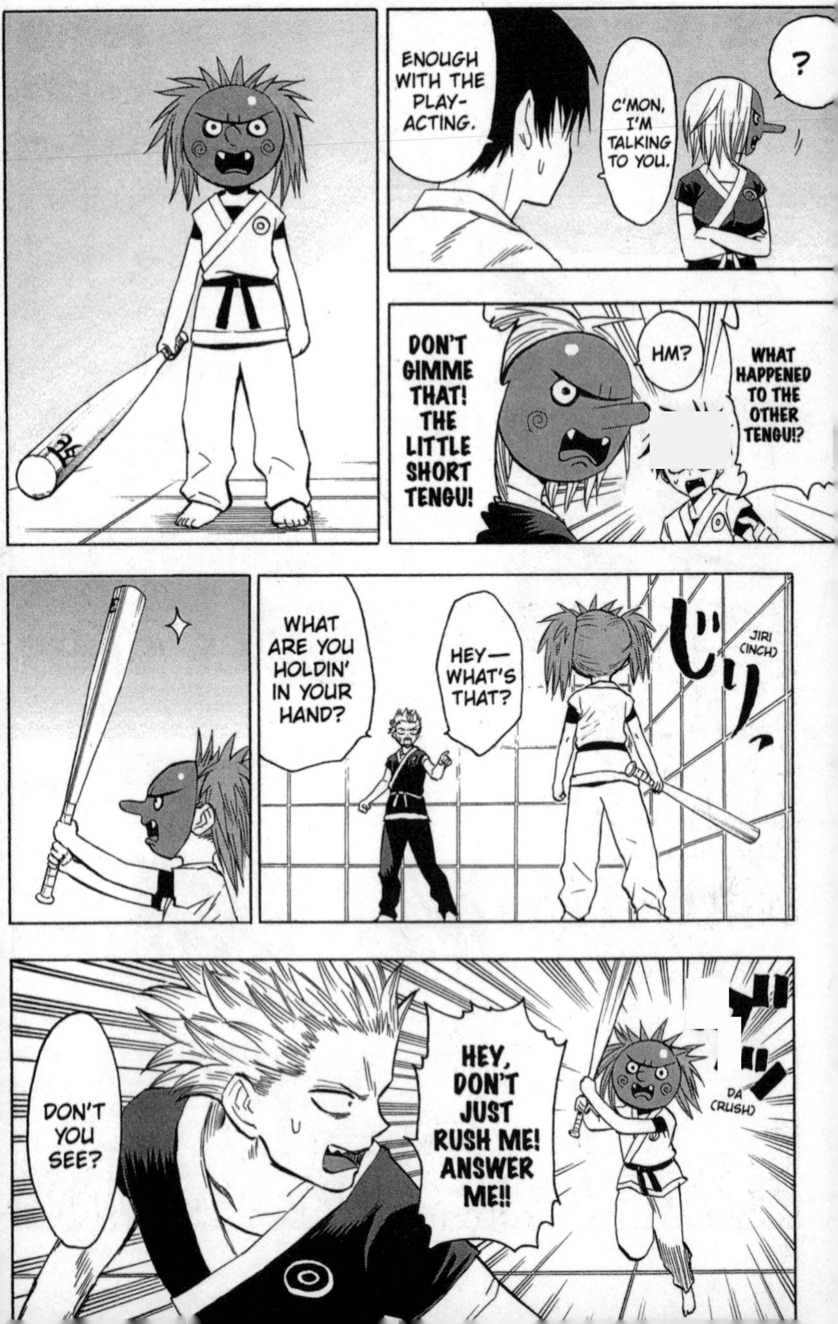
?
C'MON, I'M TALKING TO YOU.
ENOUGH WITH THE PLAY-ACTING.
WHAT HAPPENED TO THE OTHER TENGU!?
HM?
DON'T GIMME THAT! THE LITTLE SHORT TENGU!
JIRI (INCH)
HEY— WHAT'S THAT?
WHAT ARE YOU HOLDIN' IN YOUR HAND?
DA (RUSH)
HEY, DON'T JUST RUSH ME! ANSWER ME!!
DON'T YOU SEE?

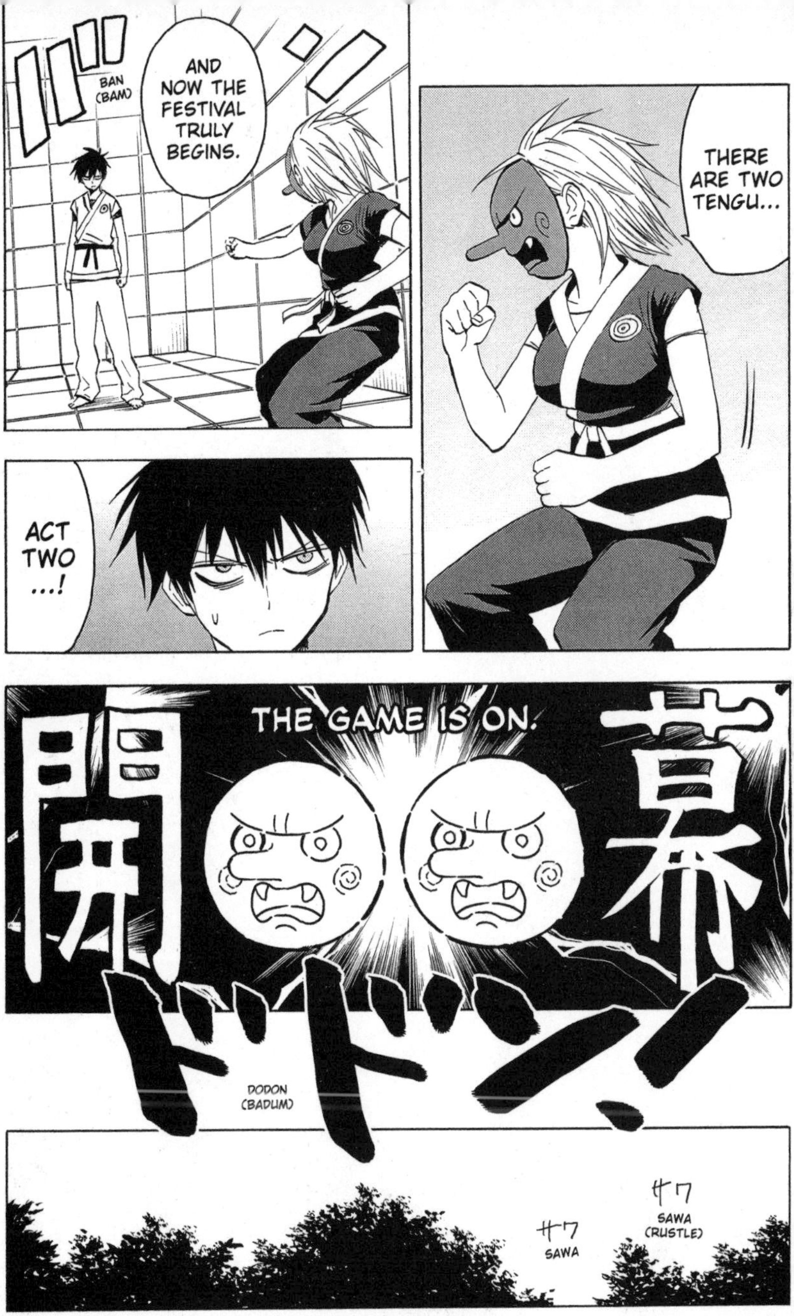

THERE ARE TWO TENGU...
AND NOW THE FESTIVAL TRULY BEGINS.
BAN (BAM)
ACT TWO ...!
開幕
THE GAME IS ON.
ドドン
DODON (BADUM)
サワ
SAWA (RUSTLE)
サワ
SAWA

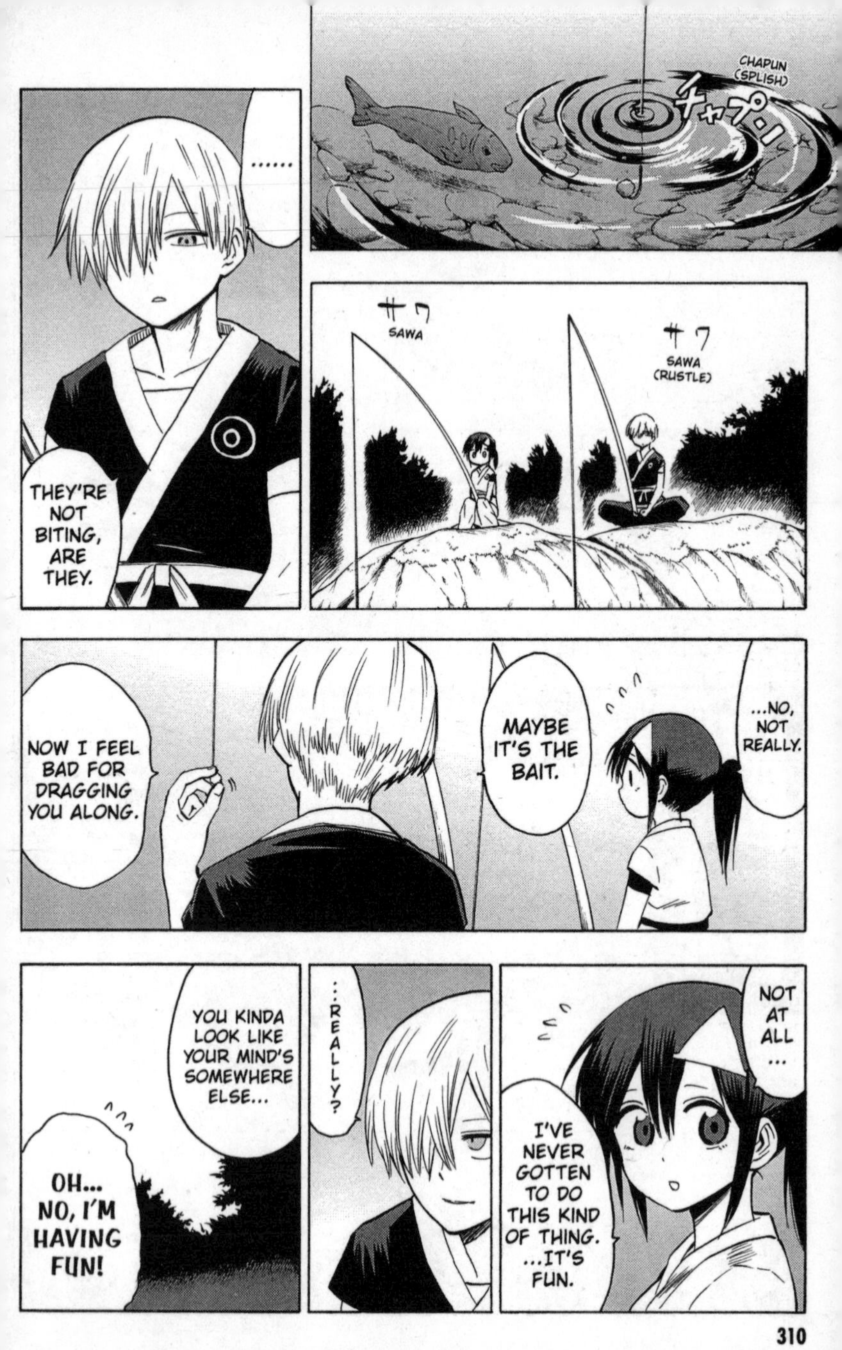
CHAPUN (SPLISH)
サワ
SAWA
サワ
SAWA (RUSTLE)
......
THEY'RE NOT BITING, ARE THEY.
...NO, NOT REALLY.
MAYBE IT'S THE BAIT.
NOW I FEEL BAD FOR DRAGGING YOU ALONG.
NOT AT ALL...
I'VE NEVER GOTTEN TO DO THIS KIND OF THING. ...IT'S FUN.
...REALLY?
YOU KINDA LOOK LIKE YOUR MIND'S SOMEWHERE ELSE...
OH... NO, I'M HAVING FUN!

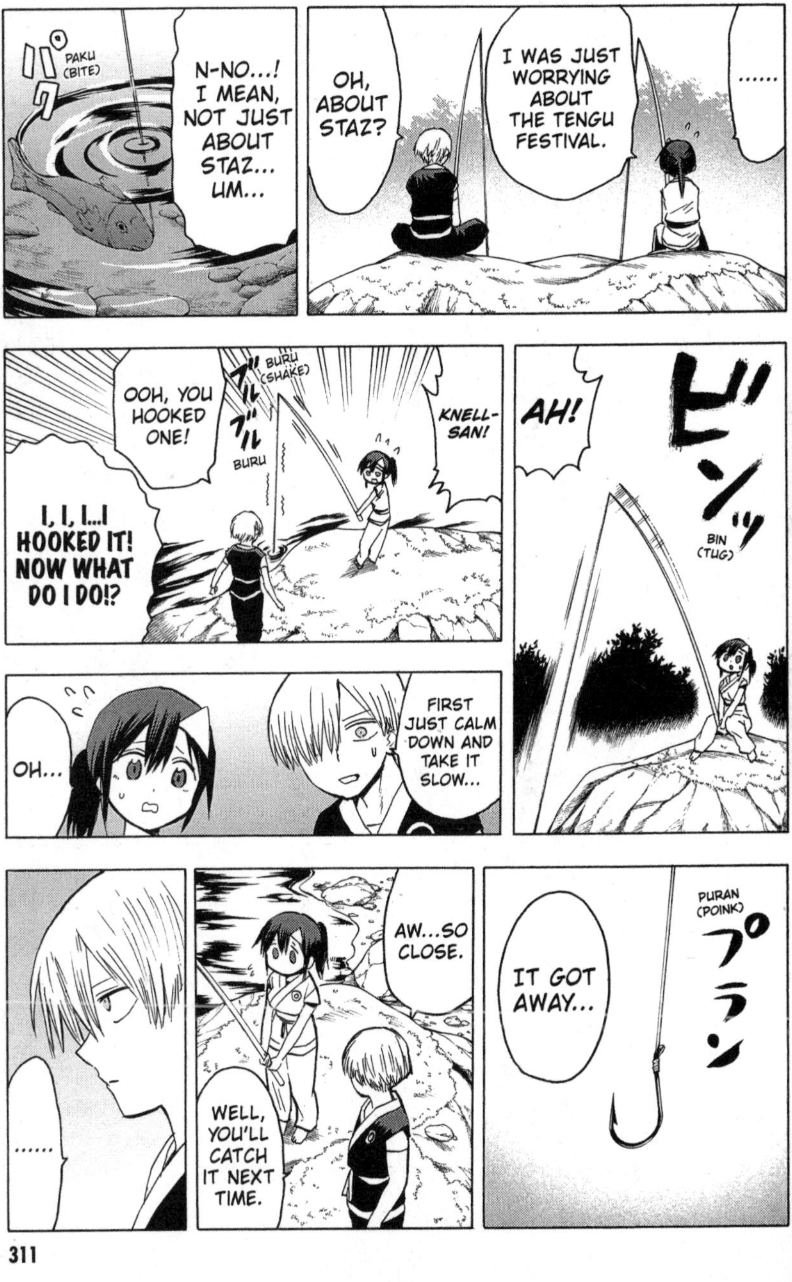
......
I WAS JUST WORRYING ABOUT THE TENGU FESTIVAL.
OH, ABOUT STAZ?
N-NO...! I MEAN, NOT JUST ABOUT STAZ... UM...
PAKU (BITE)
BIN (TUG)
AH!
KNELL-SAN!
BURU (SHAKE)
OOH, YOU HOOKED ONE!
BURU
I, I, I...I HOOKED IT! NOW WHAT DO I DO!?
FIRST JUST CALM DOWN AND TAKE IT SLOW...
OH...
PURAN (POINK)
IT GOT AWAY...
AW...SO CLOSE.
WELL, YOU'LL CATCH IT NEXT TIME.
......

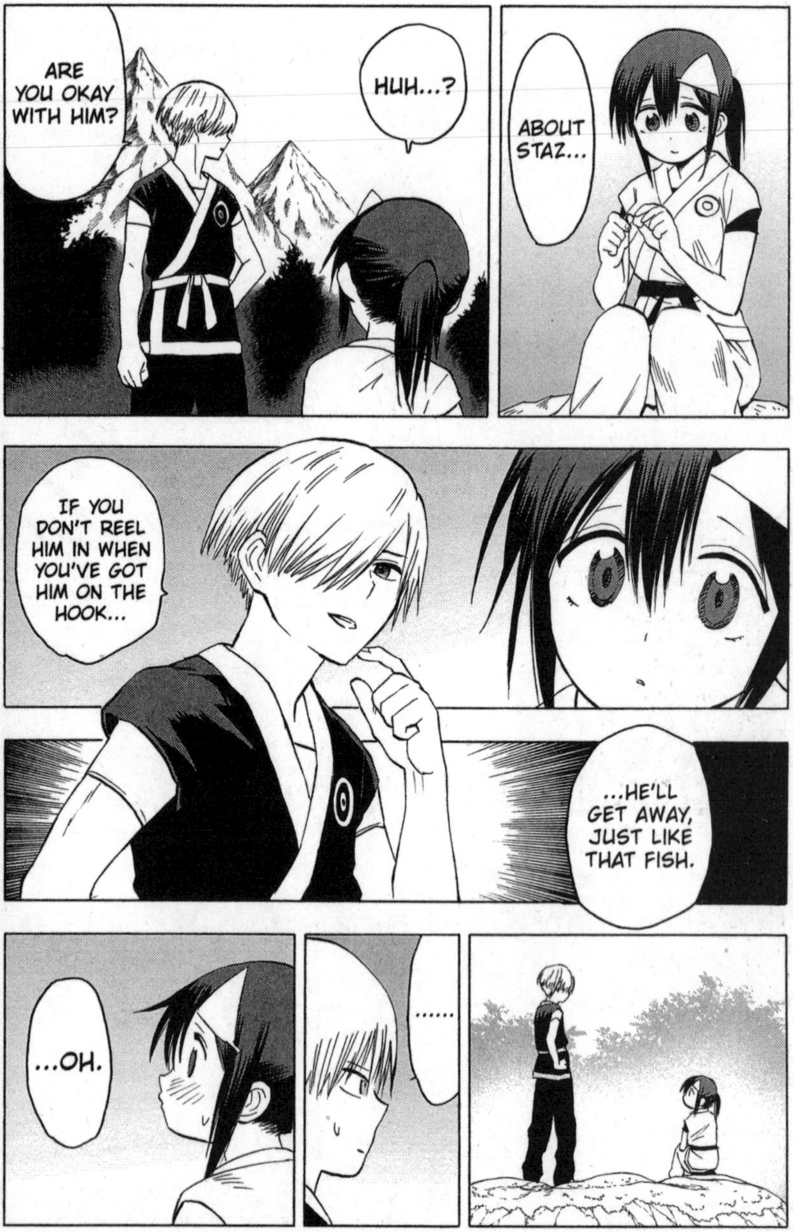
ABOUT STAZ...
HUH...?
ARE YOU OKAY WITH HIM?
IF YOU DON'T REEL HIM IN WHEN YOU'VE GOT HIM ON THE HOOK...
...HE'LL GET AWAY, JUST LIKE THAT FISH.
......
...OH.

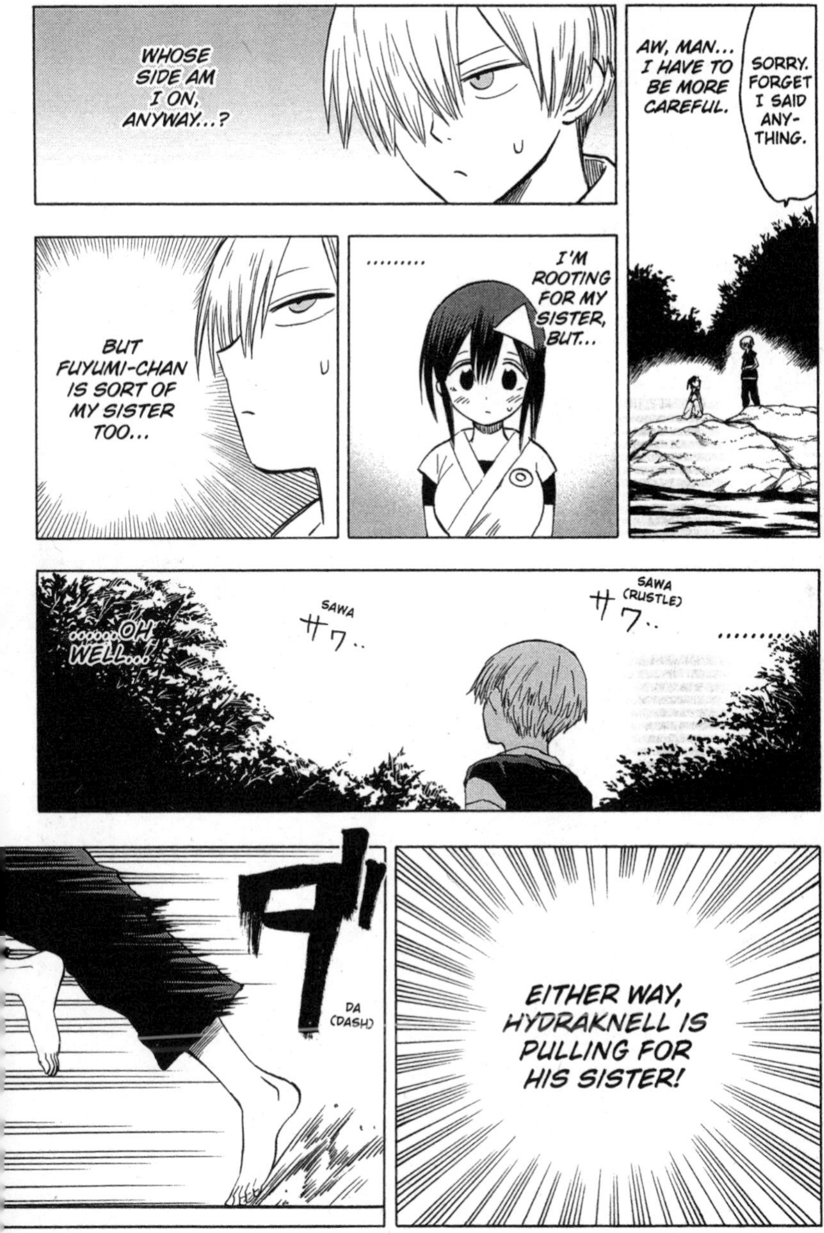

SORRY. FORGET I SAID ANYTHING.
AW, MAN... I HAVE TO BE MORE CAREFUL.
WHOSE SIDE AM I ON, ANYWAY...?
I'M ROOTING FOR MY SISTER, BUT...
....
BUT FUYUMI-CHAN IS SORT OF MY SISTER TOO...
....
SAWA (RUSTLE)
サワ..
SAWA
サワ..
......OH WELL...!
EITHER WAY, HYDRAKNELL IS PULLING FOR HIS SISTER!
ダ
DA (DASH)

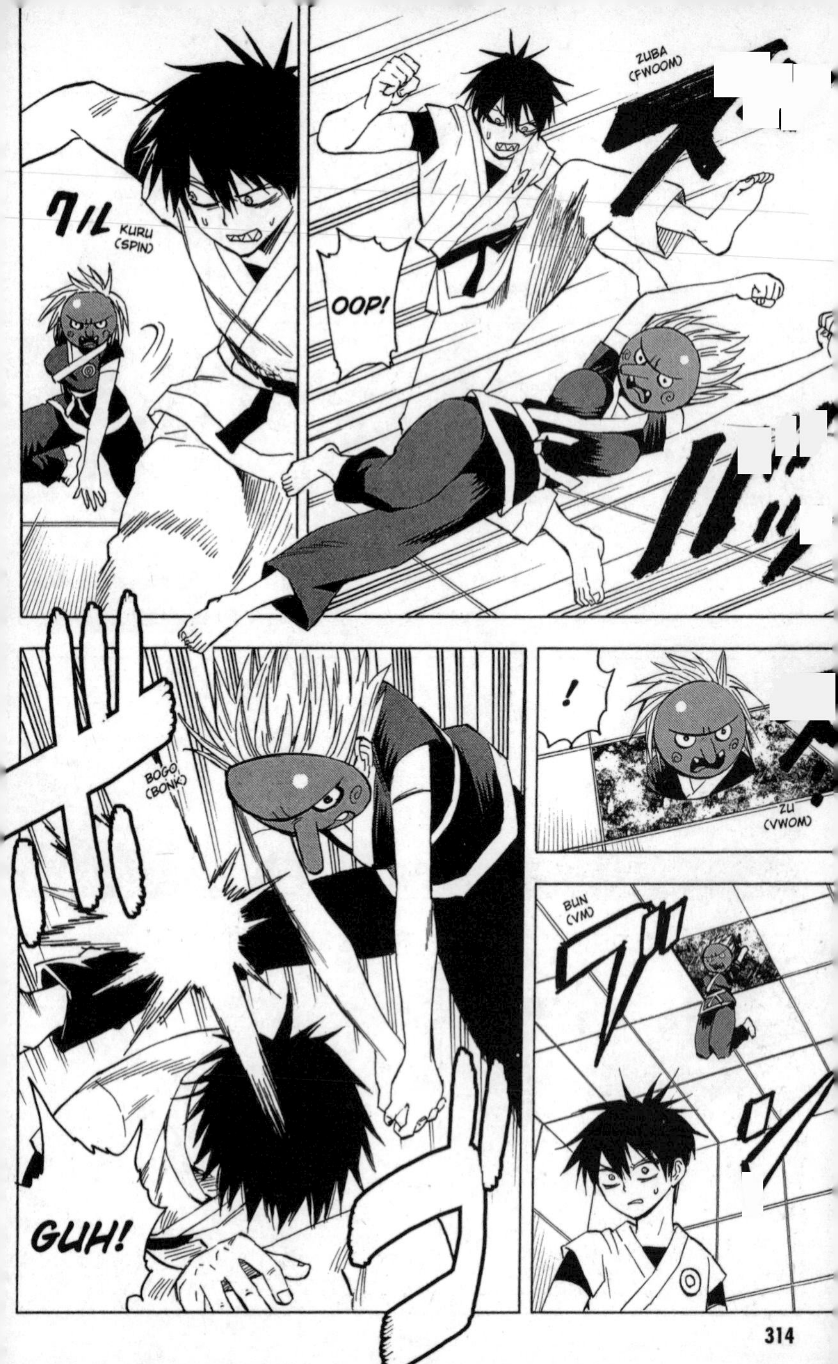
ZUBA
(FWOOM)
OOP!
KURU
(SPIN)
!
ZU
(VWOM)
BUN
(VM)
BOGO
(BONK)
GUH!

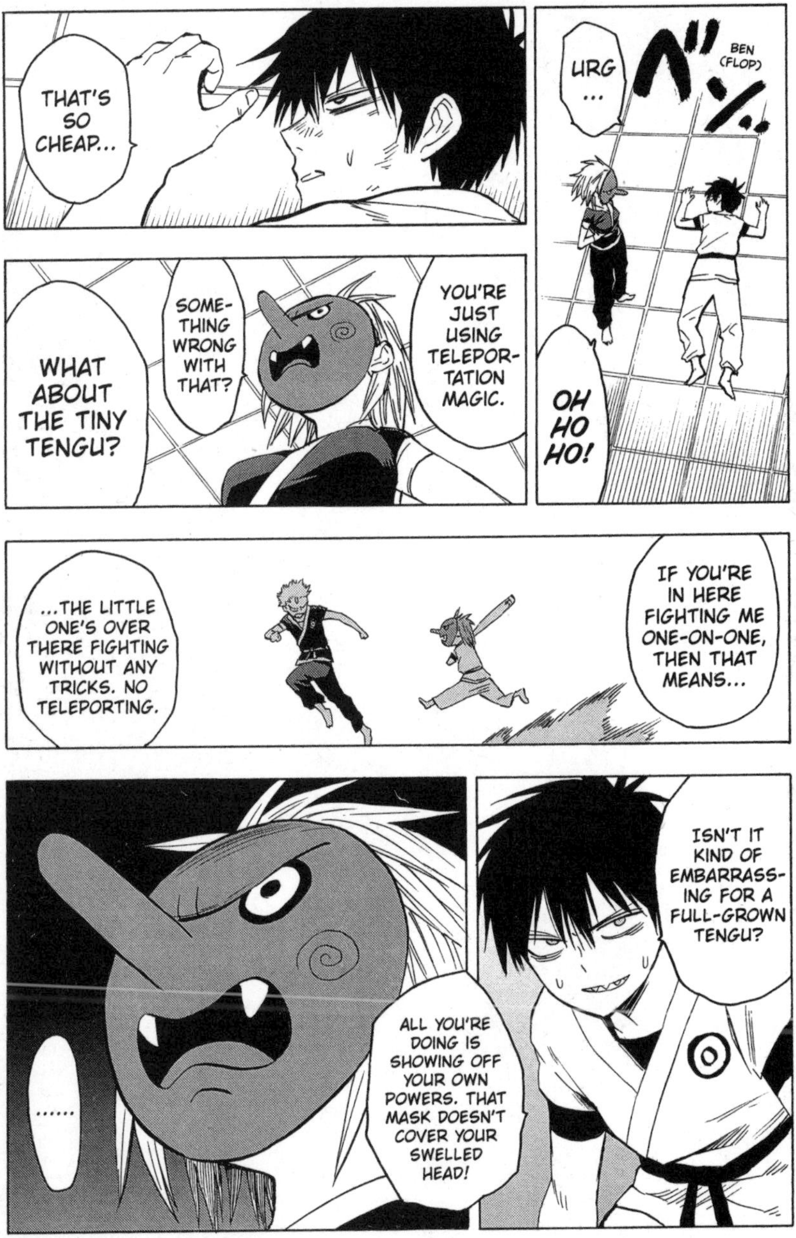
URG...
ベ゙ン
BEN (FLOP)
OH HO HO!
THAT'S SO CHEAP...
YOU'RE JUST USING TELEPORTATION MAGIC.
SOMETHING WRONG WITH THAT?
WHAT ABOUT THE TINY TENGU?
IF YOU'RE IN HERE FIGHTING ME ONE-ON-ONE, THEN THAT MEANS...
...THE LITTLE ONE'S OVER THERE FIGHTING WITHOUT ANY TRICKS. NO TELEPORTING.
ISN'T IT KIND OF EMBARRASSING FOR A FULL-GROWN TENGU?
ALL YOU'RE DOING IS SHOWING OFF YOUR OWN POWERS. THAT MASK DOESN'T COVER YOUR SWELLED HEAD!
......

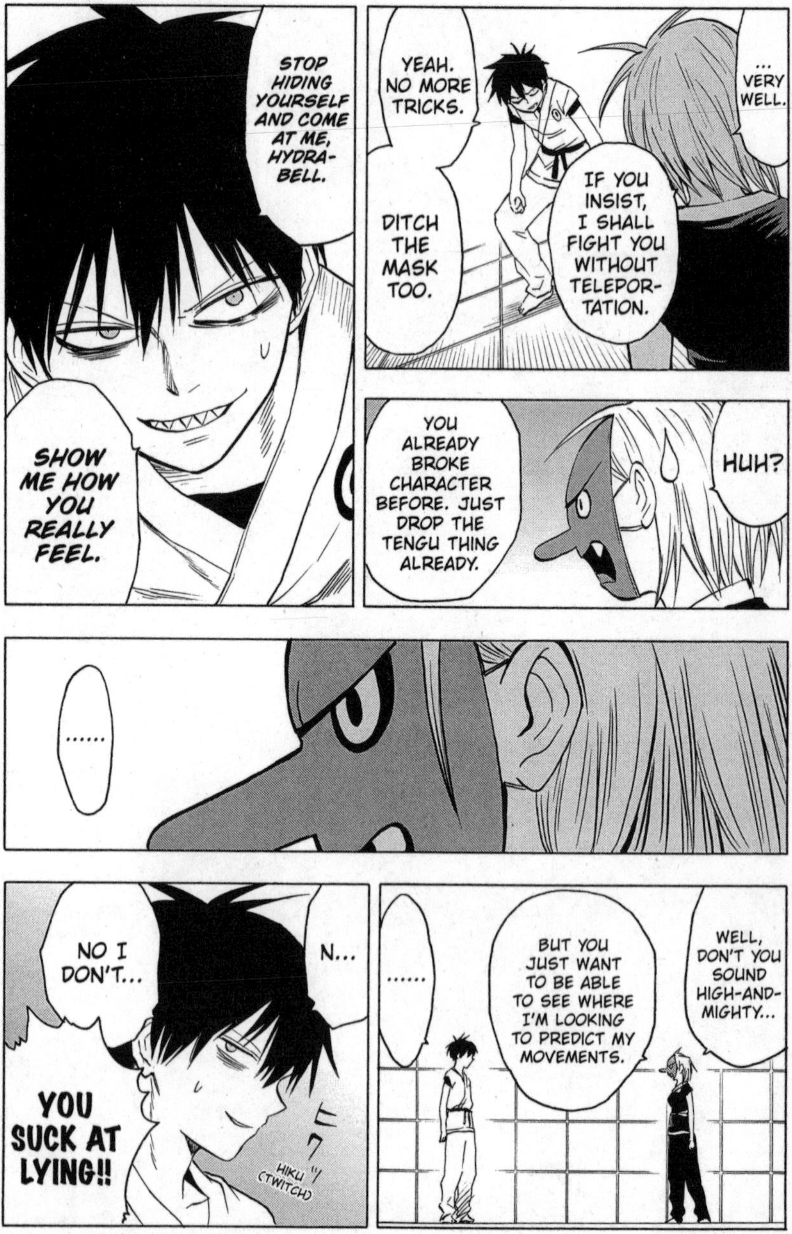

... VERY WELL.
IF YOU INSIST, I SHALL FIGHT YOU WITHOUT TELEPORTATION.
YEAH. NO MORE TRICKS.
DITCH THE MASK TOO.
HUH?
YOU ALREADY BROKE CHARACTER BEFORE. JUST DROP THE TENGU THING ALREADY.
STOP HIDING YOURSELF AND COME AT ME, HYDRABELL.
SHOW ME HOW YOU REALLY FEEL.
......
WELL, DON'T YOU SOUND HIGH-AND-MIGHTY...
BUT YOU JUST WANT TO BE ABLE TO SEE WHERE I'M LOOKING TO PREDICT MY MOVEMENTS.
......
N...
NO I DON'T...
YOU SUCK AT LYING!!
HIKU (TWITCH)

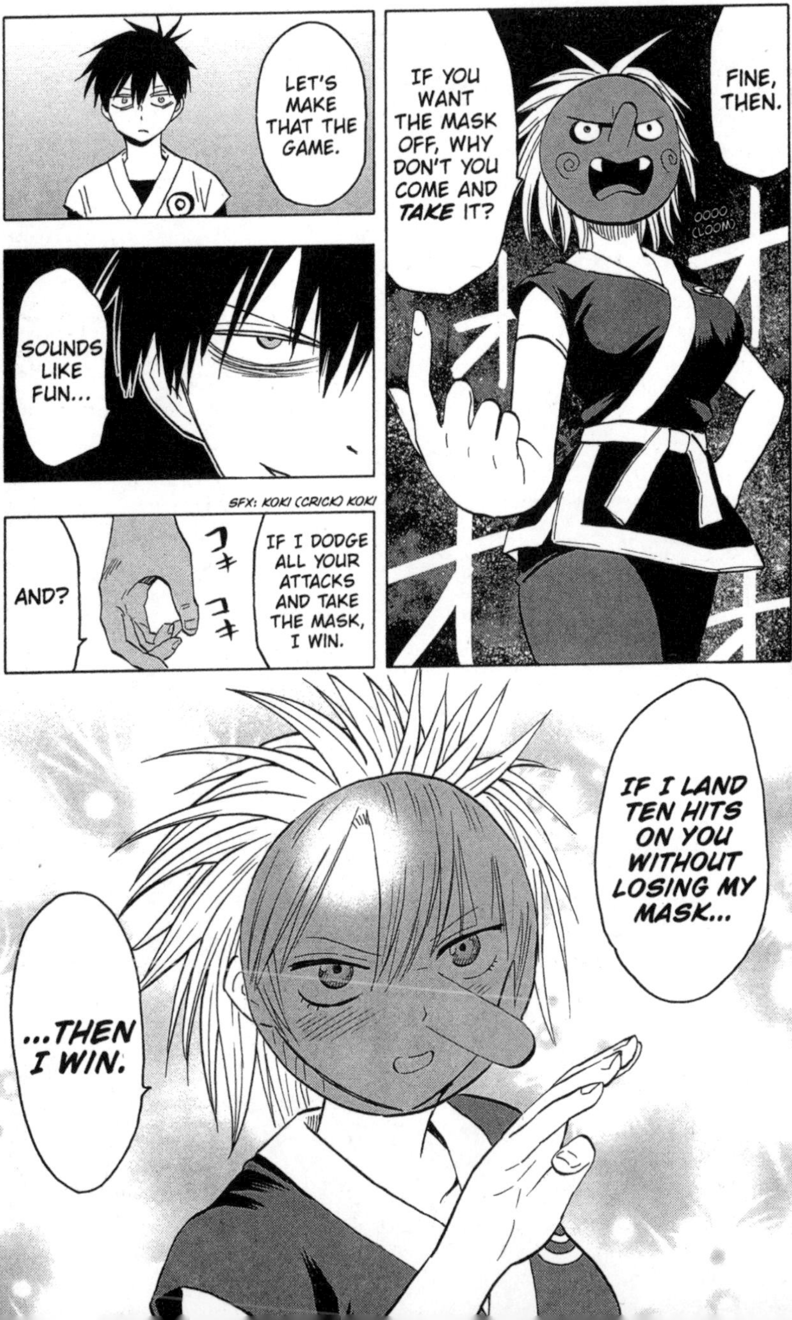
FINE, THEN.
IF YOU WANT THE MASK OFF, WHY DON'T YOU COME AND *TAKE* IT?
OOOO (LOOM)
LET'S MAKE THAT THE GAME.
SOUNDS LIKE FUN...
SFX: KOKI (CRICK) KOKI
IF I DODGE ALL YOUR ATTACKS AND TAKE THE MASK, I WIN.
コキ
コキ
AND?
IF I LAND TEN HITS ON YOU WITHOUT LOSING MY MASK...
...THEN I WIN.

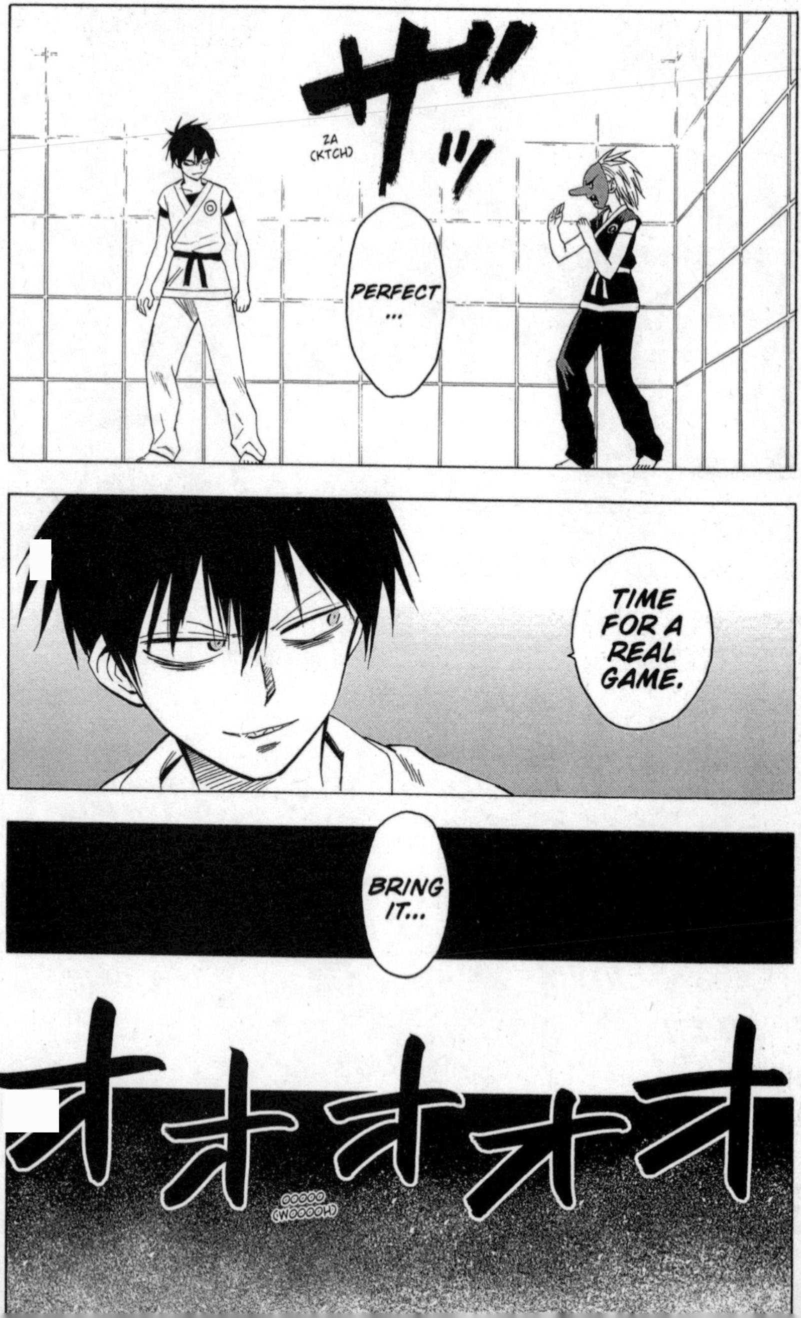
ザッ
ZA (KTCH)
PERFECT ...
TIME FOR A REAL GAME.
BRING IT...
オオオオオ
OOOOO (WOOOOH)

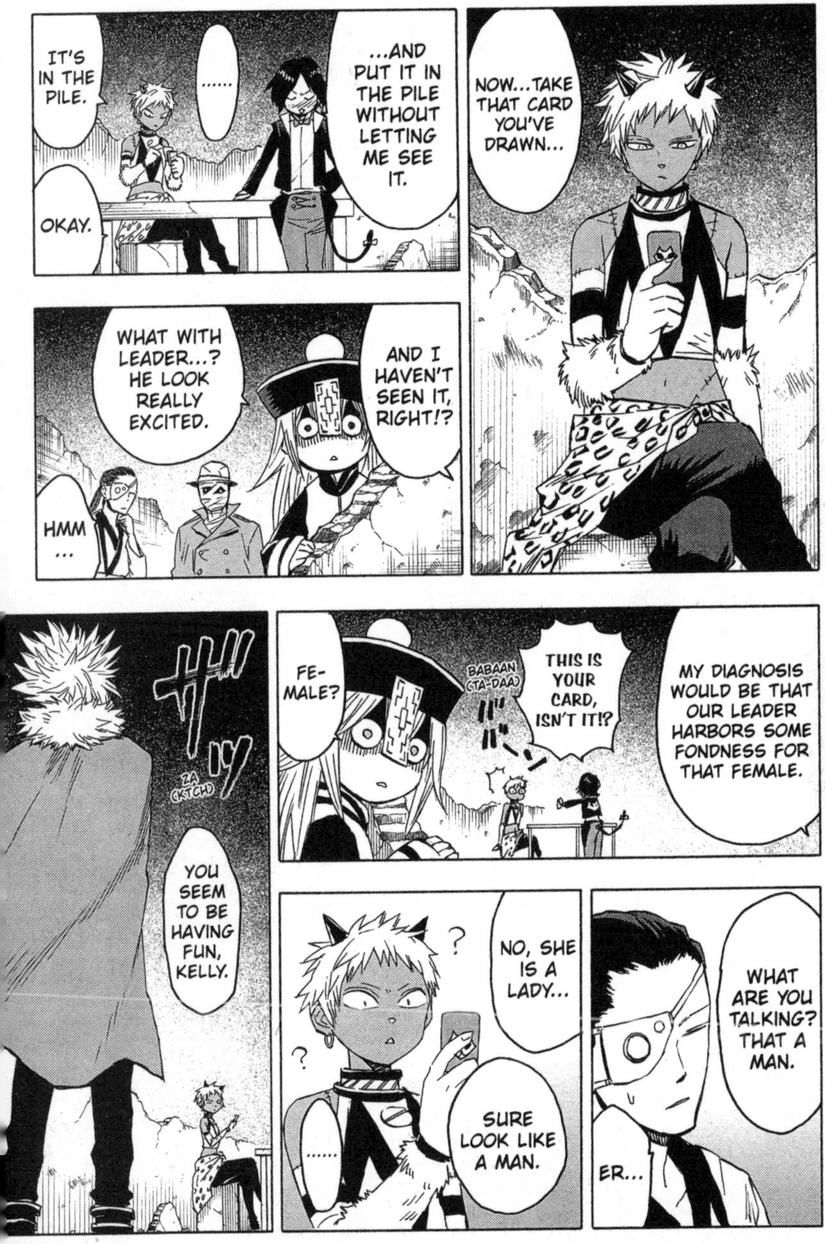
NOW...TAKE THAT CARD YOU'VE DRAWN...
...AND PUT IT IN THE PILE WITHOUT LETTING ME SEE IT.
......
IT'S IN THE PILE.
OKAY.
AND I HAVEN'T SEEN IT, RIGHT!?
WHAT WITH LEADER...? HE LOOK REALLY EXCITED.
HMM...
MY DIAGNOSIS WOULD BE THAT OUR LEADER HARBORS SOME FONDNESS FOR THAT FEMALE.
THIS IS YOUR CARD, ISN'T IT!?
BABAAN (TA-DAA)
FE-MALE?
WHAT ARE YOU TALKING? THAT A MAN.
ER...
NO, SHE IS A LADY...
SURE LOOK LIKE A MAN.
......
ZA (KTCH)
YOU SEEM TO BE HAVING FUN, KELLY.

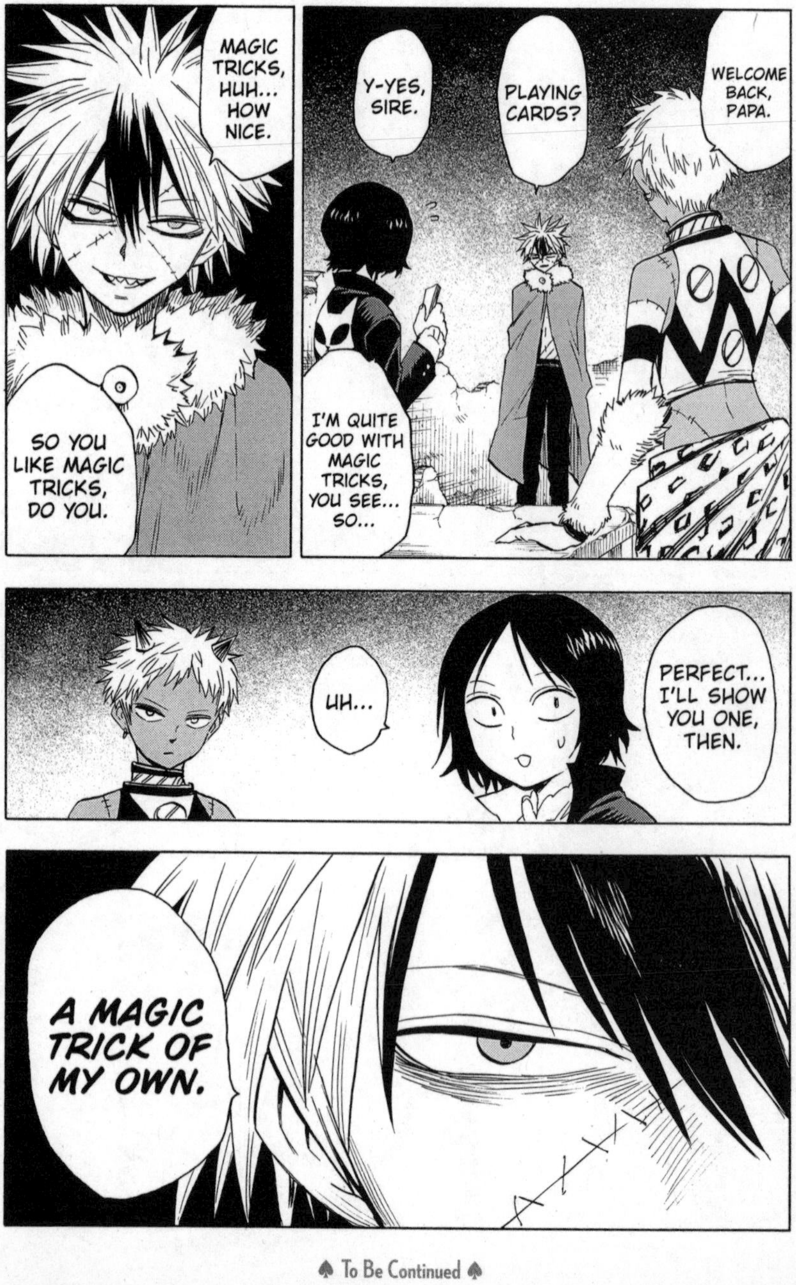

WELCOME BACK, PAPA.
PLAYING CARDS?
Y-YES, SIRE.
I'M QUITE GOOD WITH MAGIC TRICKS, YOU SEE... SO...
MAGIC TRICKS, HUH... HOW NICE.
SO YOU LIKE MAGIC TRICKS, DO YOU.
PERFECT... I'LL SHOW YOU ONE, THEN.
UH...
A MAGIC TRICK OF MY OWN.

♠ To Be Continued ♠

BLOOD LAD

CHAPTER 60 ♠ TOP SECRET

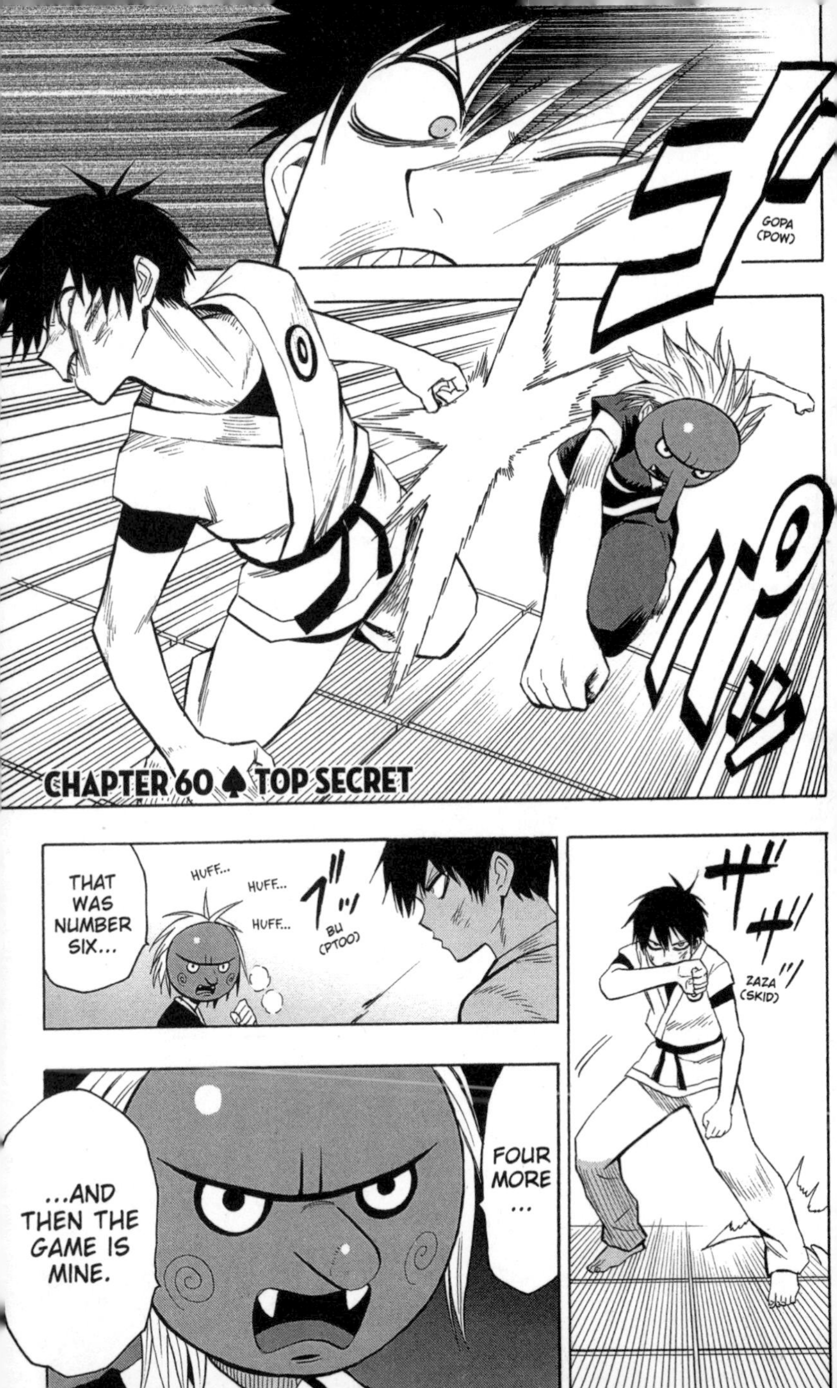
GOPA (POW)
ZAZA (SKID)
HUFF... HUFF... HUFF...
BU (PTOO)
THAT WAS NUMBER SIX...
FOUR MORE...
...AND THEN THE GAME IS MINE.

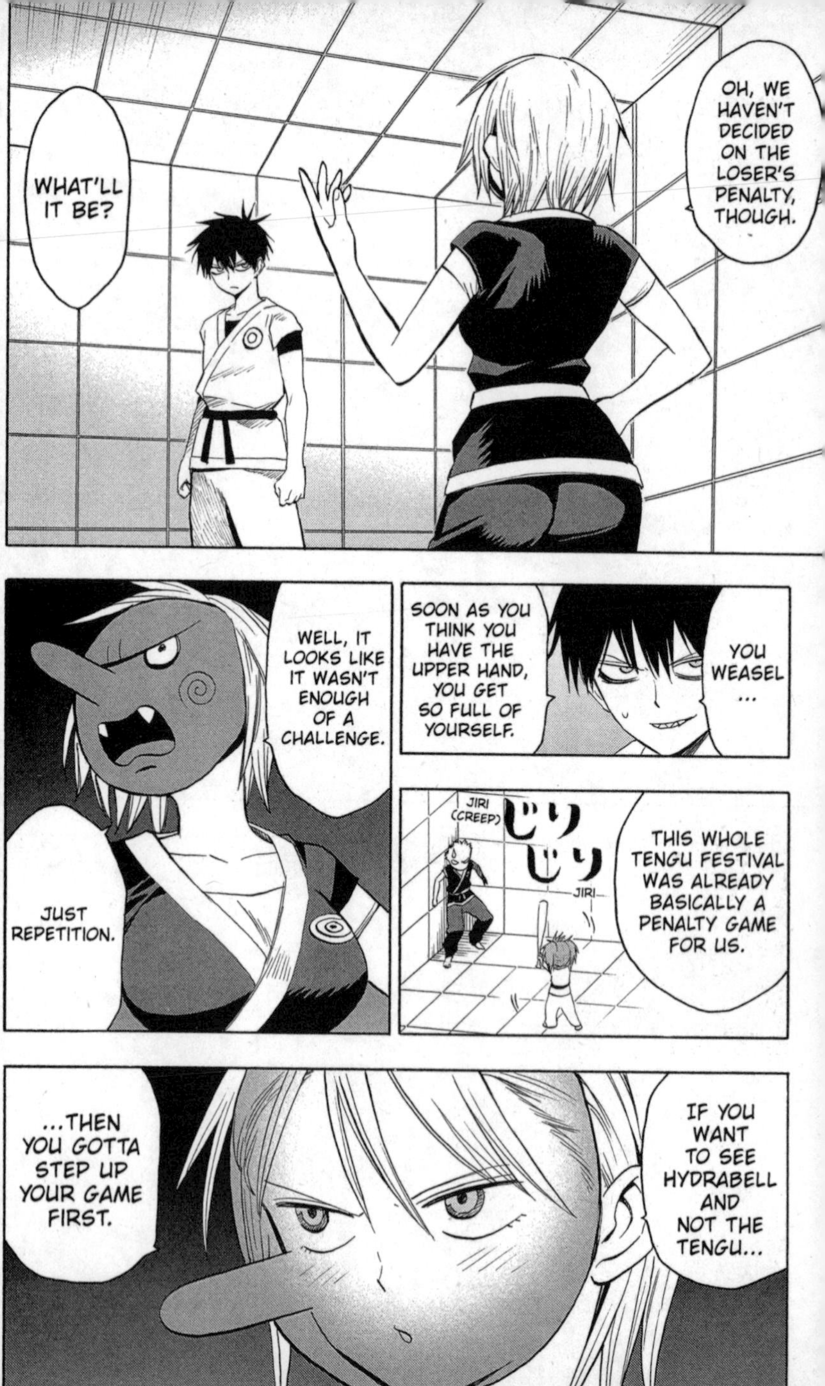
OH, WE HAVEN'T DECIDED ON THE LOSER'S PENALTY, THOUGH.
WHAT'LL IT BE?
YOU WEASEL...
SOON AS YOU THINK YOU HAVE THE UPPER HAND, YOU GET SO FULL OF YOURSELF.
じり じり
JIRI (CREEP)
JIRI
THIS WHOLE TENGU FESTIVAL WAS ALREADY BASICALLY A PENALTY GAME FOR US.
WELL, IT LOOKS LIKE IT WASN'T ENOUGH OF A CHALLENGE.
JUST REPETITION.
IF YOU WANT TO SEE HYDRABELL AND NOT THE TENGU...
...THEN YOU GOTTA STEP UP YOUR GAME FIRST.

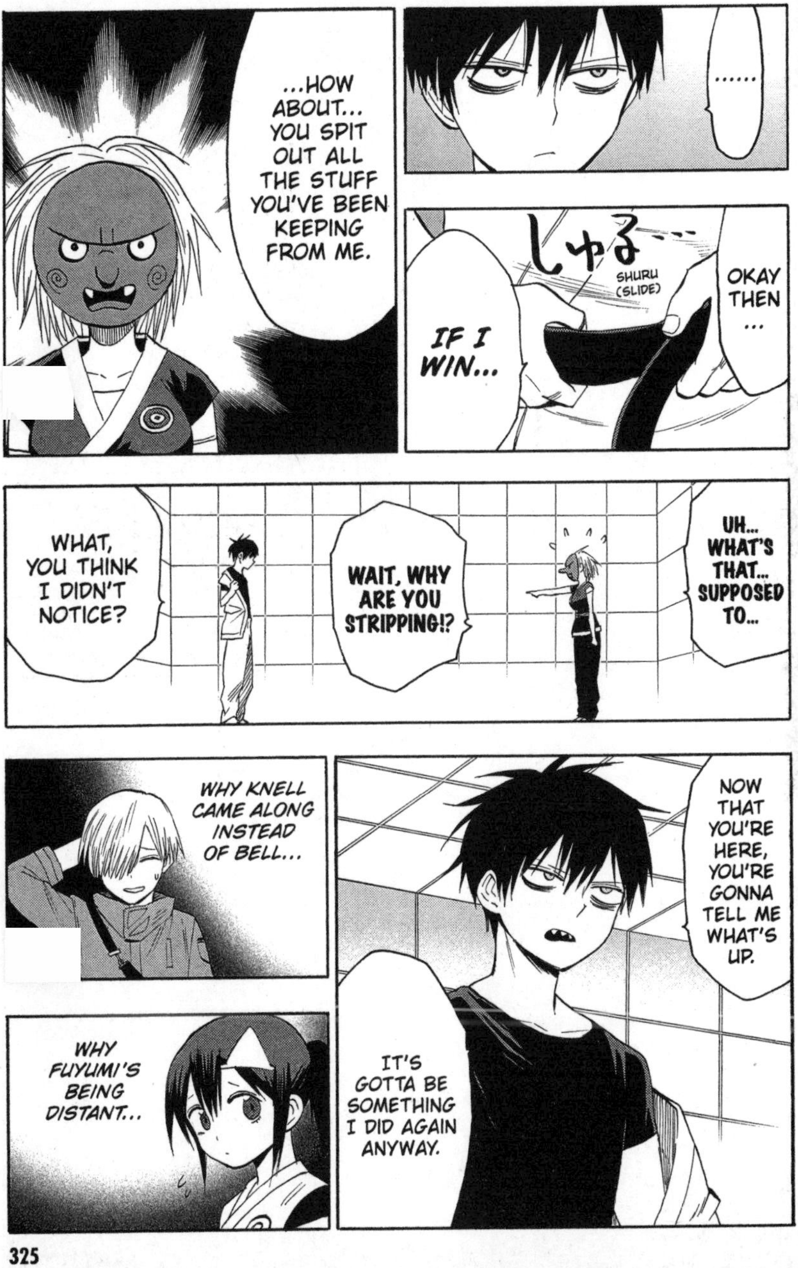
......
OKAY THEN ...
しゅる
SHURU (SLIDE)
IF I WIN...
...HOW ABOUT... YOU SPIT OUT ALL THE STUFF YOU'VE BEEN KEEPING FROM ME.
UH... WHAT'S THAT... SUPPOSED TO...
WAIT, WHY ARE YOU STRIPPING!?
WHAT, YOU THINK I DIDN'T NOTICE?
NOW THAT YOU'RE HERE, YOU'RE GONNA TELL ME WHAT'S UP.
IT'S GOTTA BE SOMETHING I DID AGAIN ANYWAY.
WHY KNELL CAME ALONG INSTEAD OF BELL...
WHY FUYUMI'S BEING DISTANT...

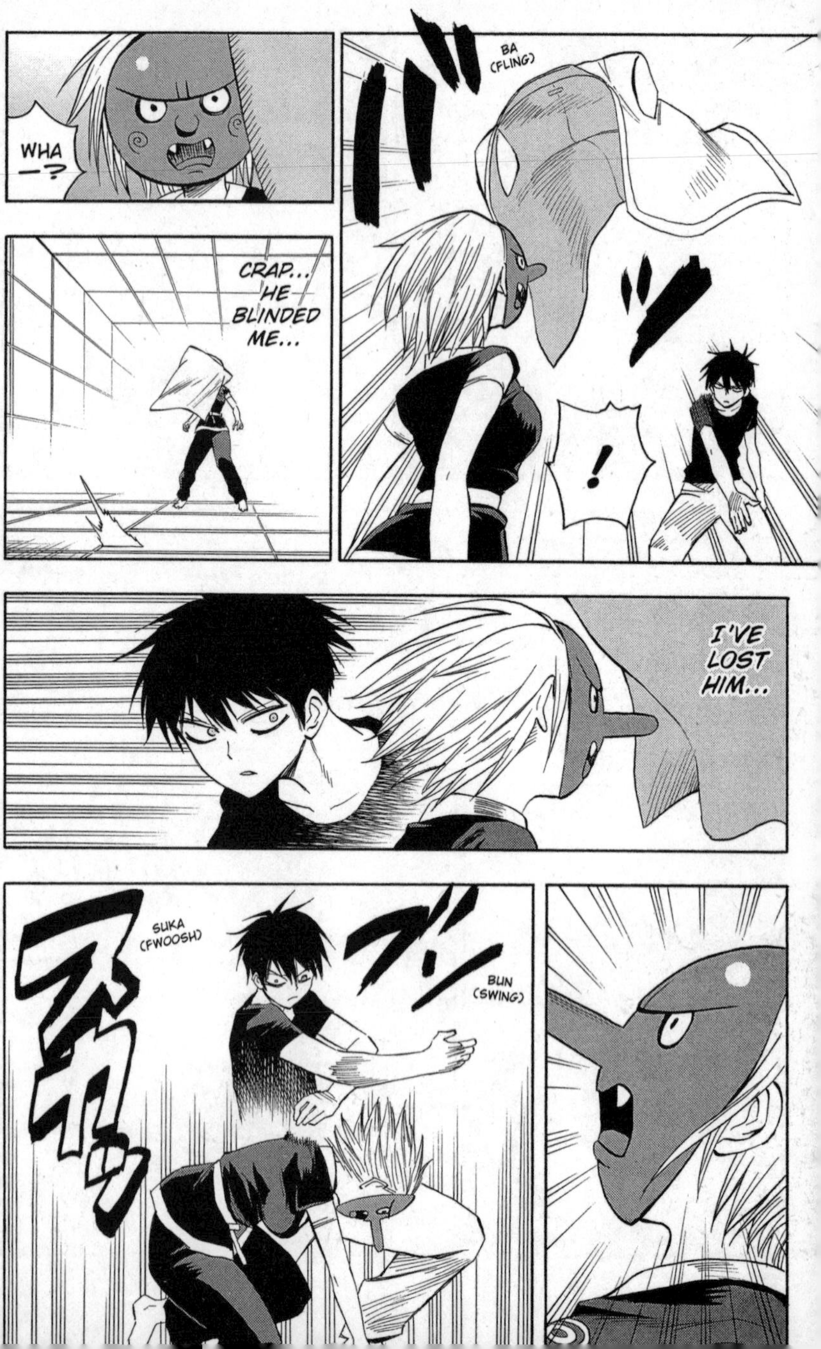

BA (FLING)
!
WHA—?
CRAP... HE BLINDED ME...
I'VE LOST HIM...
BUN (SWING)
SUKA (FWOOSH)

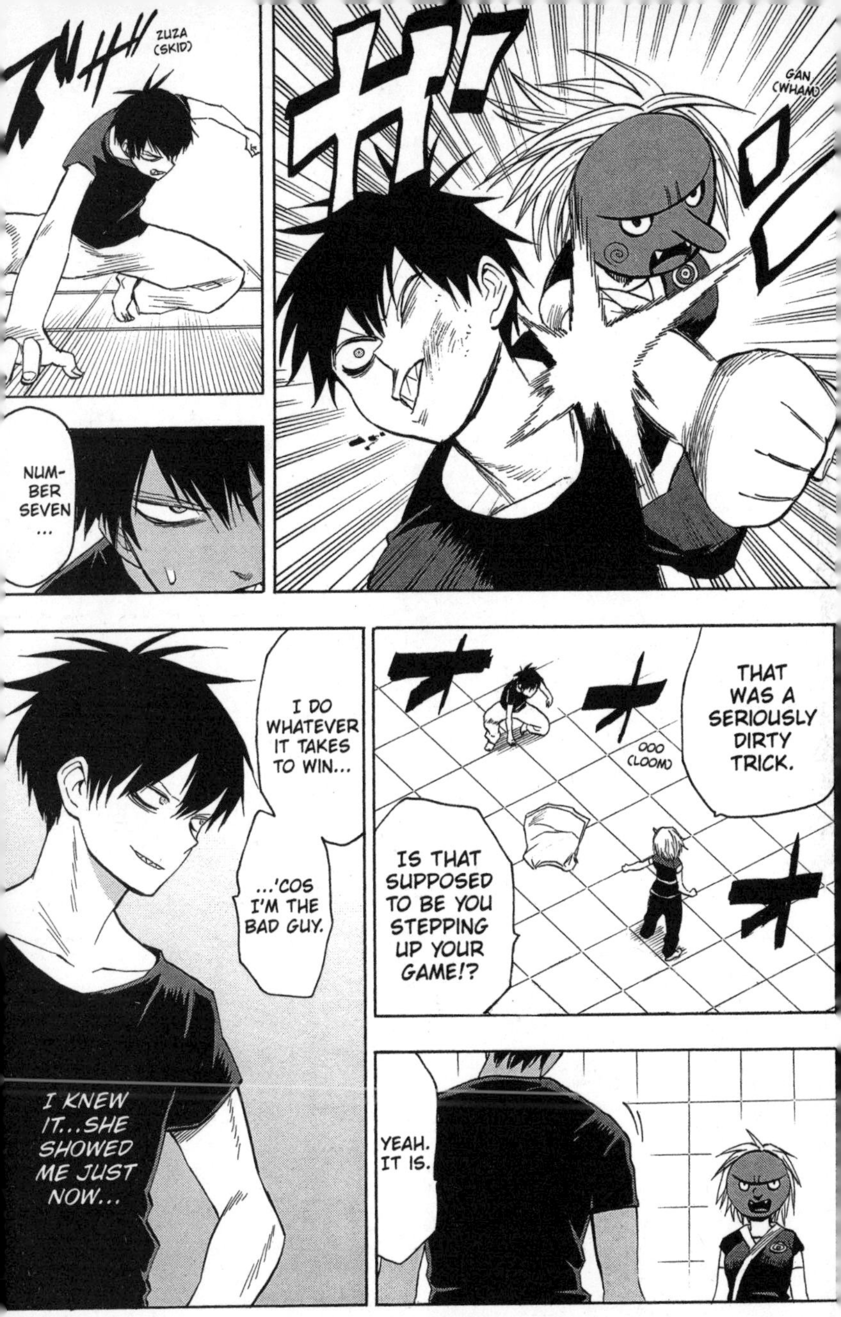
GAN (WHAM)
ZUZA (SKID)
NUMBER SEVEN...
THAT WAS A SERIOUSLY DIRTY TRICK.
OOO (LOOM)
IS THAT SUPPOSED TO BE YOU STEPPING UP YOUR GAME!?
YEAH. IT IS.
I DO WHATEVER IT TAKES TO WIN...
...'COS I'M THE BAD GUY.
I KNEW IT...SHE SHOWED ME JUST NOW...

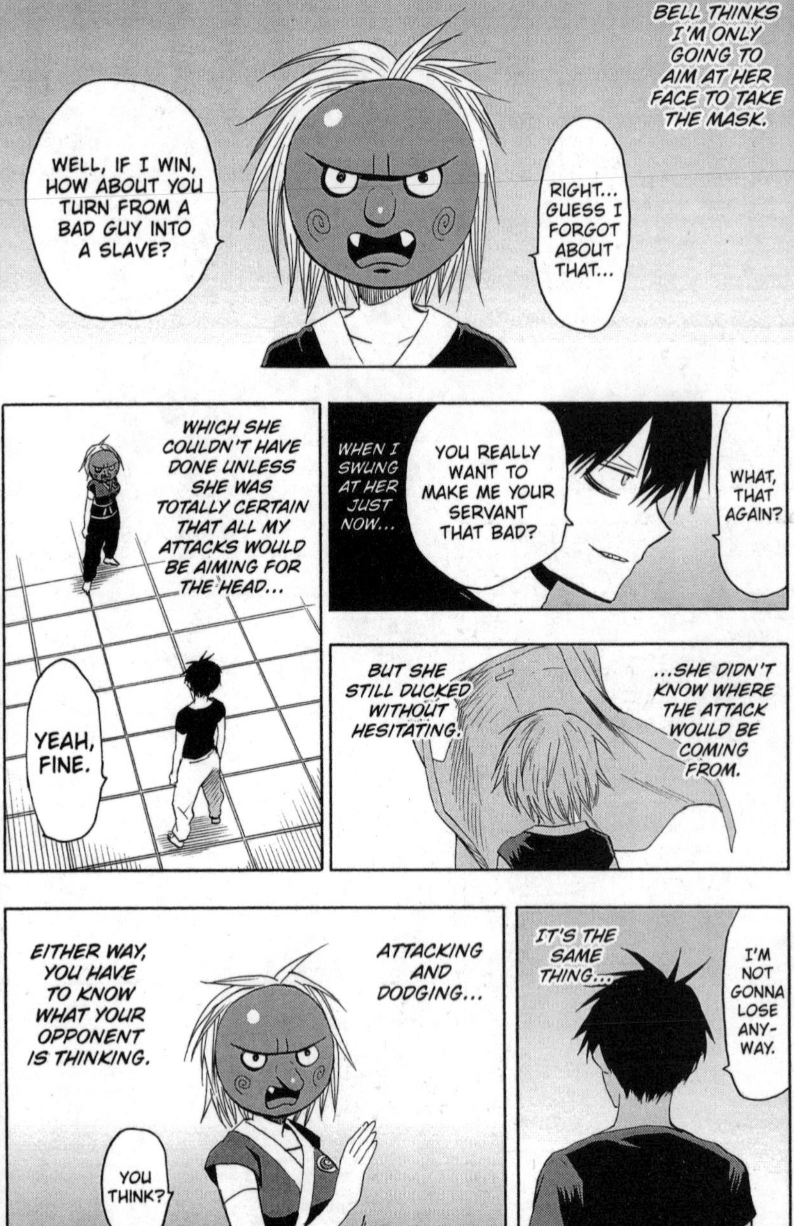
BELL THINKS I'M ONLY GOING TO AIM AT HER FACE TO TAKE THE MASK.
RIGHT... GUESS I FORGOT ABOUT THAT...
WELL, IF I WIN, HOW ABOUT YOU TURN FROM A BAD GUY INTO A SLAVE?
WHAT, THAT AGAIN?
YOU REALLY WANT TO MAKE ME YOUR SERVANT THAT BAD?
WHEN I SWUNG AT HER JUST NOW...
...SHE DIDN'T KNOW WHERE THE ATTACK WOULD BE COMING FROM.
BUT SHE STILL DUCKED WITHOUT HESITATING.
WHICH SHE COULDN'T HAVE DONE UNLESS SHE WAS TOTALLY CERTAIN THAT ALL MY ATTACKS WOULD BE AIMING FOR THE HEAD...
YEAH, FINE.
I'M NOT GONNA LOSE ANY-WAY.
IT'S THE SAME THING...
ATTACKING AND DODGING...
EITHER WAY, YOU HAVE TO KNOW WHAT YOUR OPPONENT IS THINKING.
YOU THINK?

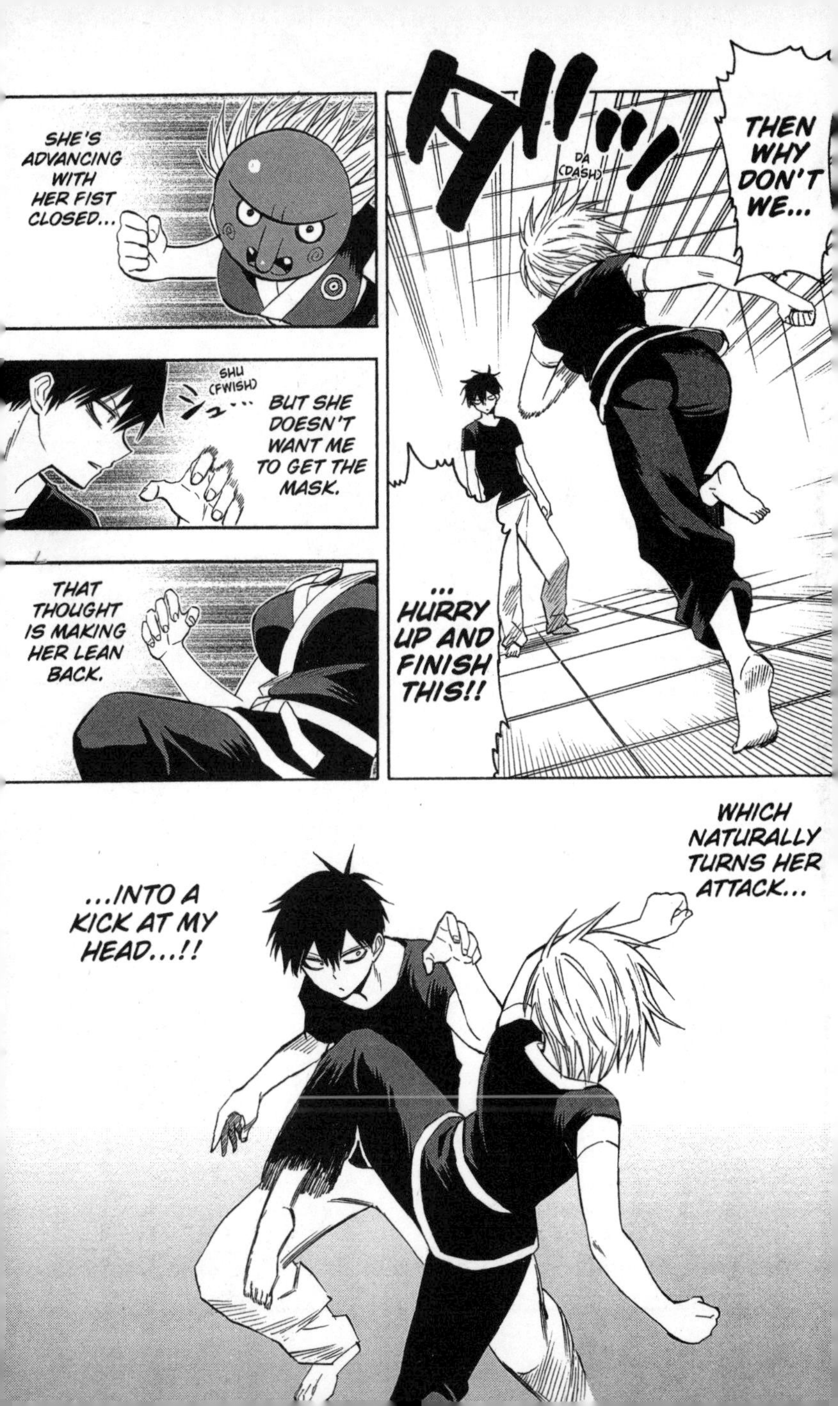

タッ
DA (DASH)
THEN WHY DON'T WE...
...HURRY UP AND FINISH THIS!!
SHE'S ADVANCING WITH HER FIST CLOSED...
シュ
SHU (FWISH)
BUT SHE DOESN'T WANT ME TO GET THE MASK.
THAT THOUGHT IS MAKING HER LEAN BACK.
WHICH NATURALLY TURNS HER ATTACK...
...INTO A KICK AT MY HEAD...!!

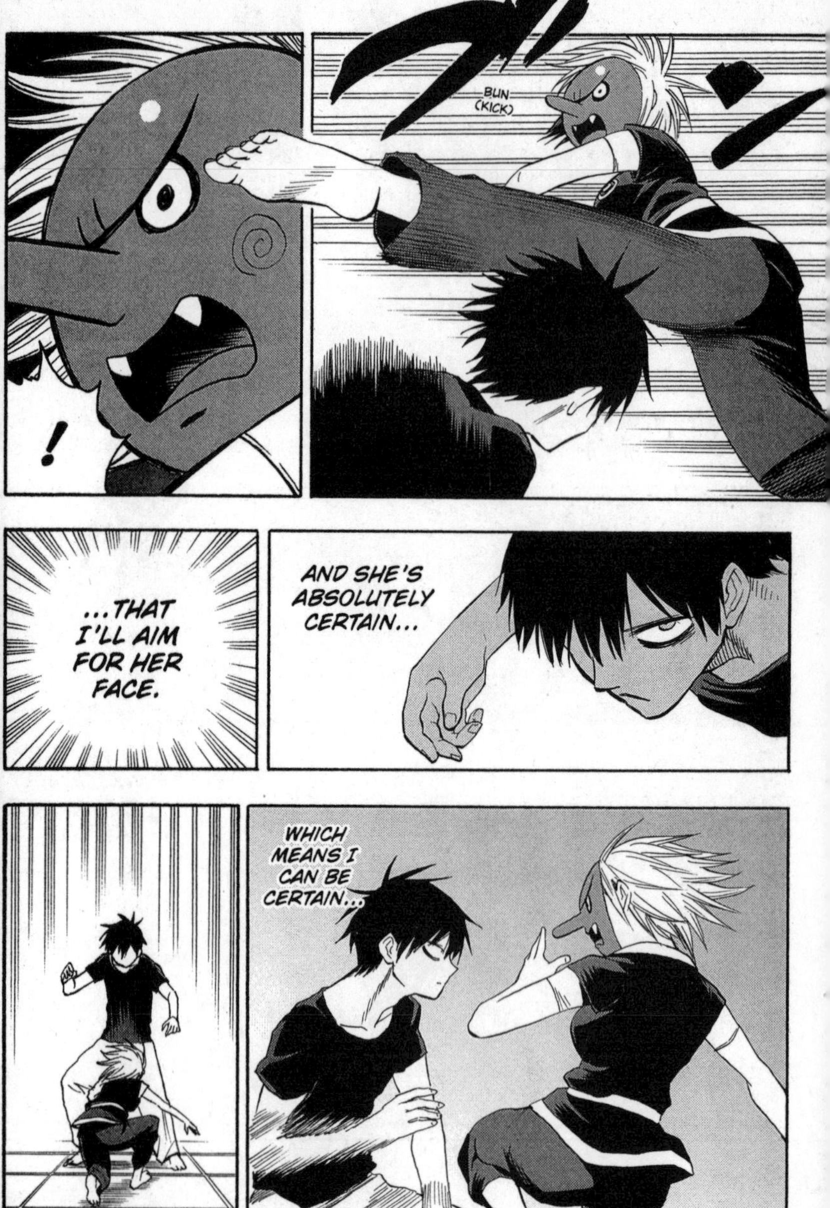
BUN (KICK)
!
AND SHE'S ABSOLUTELY CERTAIN...
...THAT I'LL AIM FOR HER FACE.
WHICH MEANS I CAN BE CERTAIN...

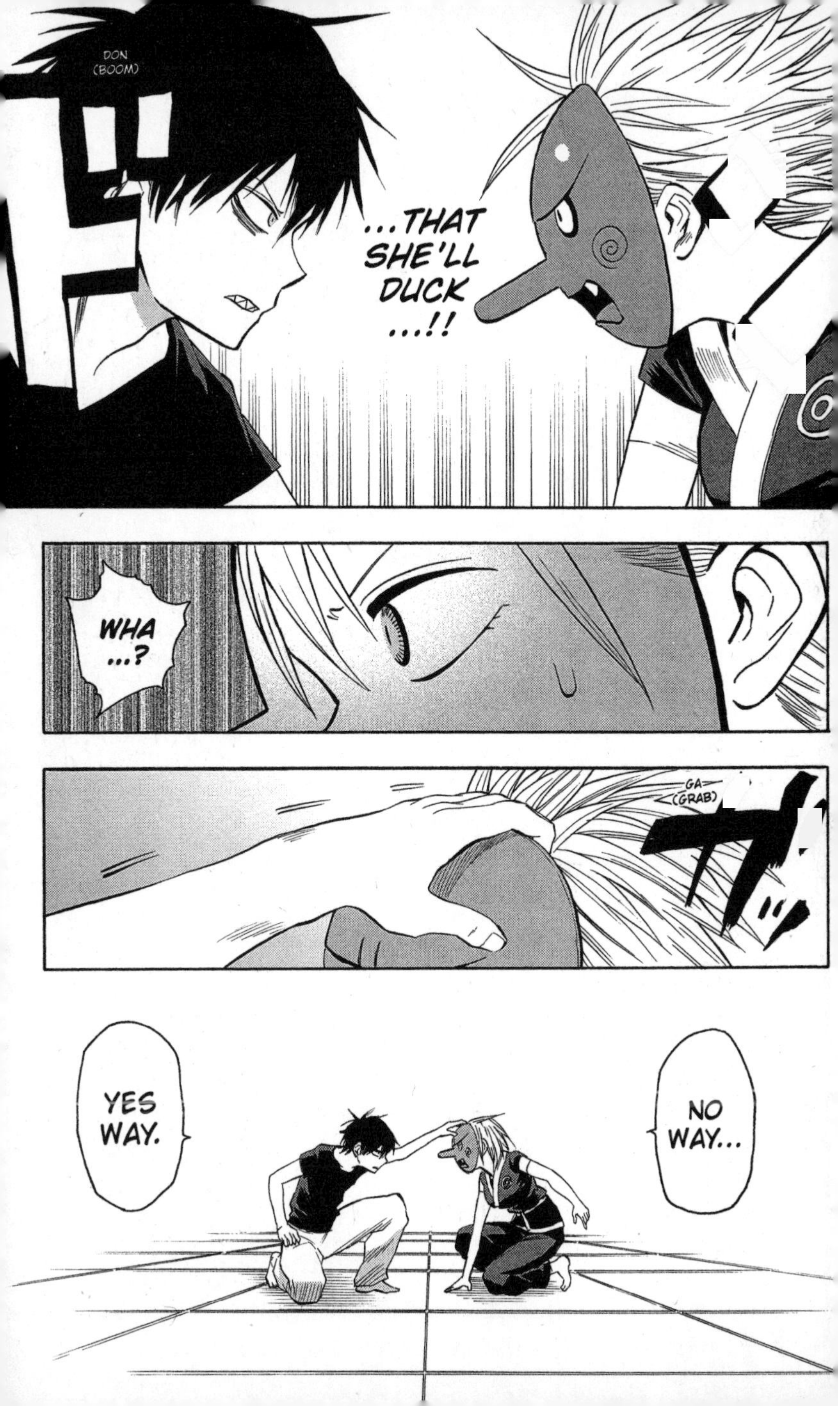
...THAT SHE'LL DUCK ...!!
DON (BOOM)
WHA ...?
GA (GRAB)
NO WAY...
YES WAY.

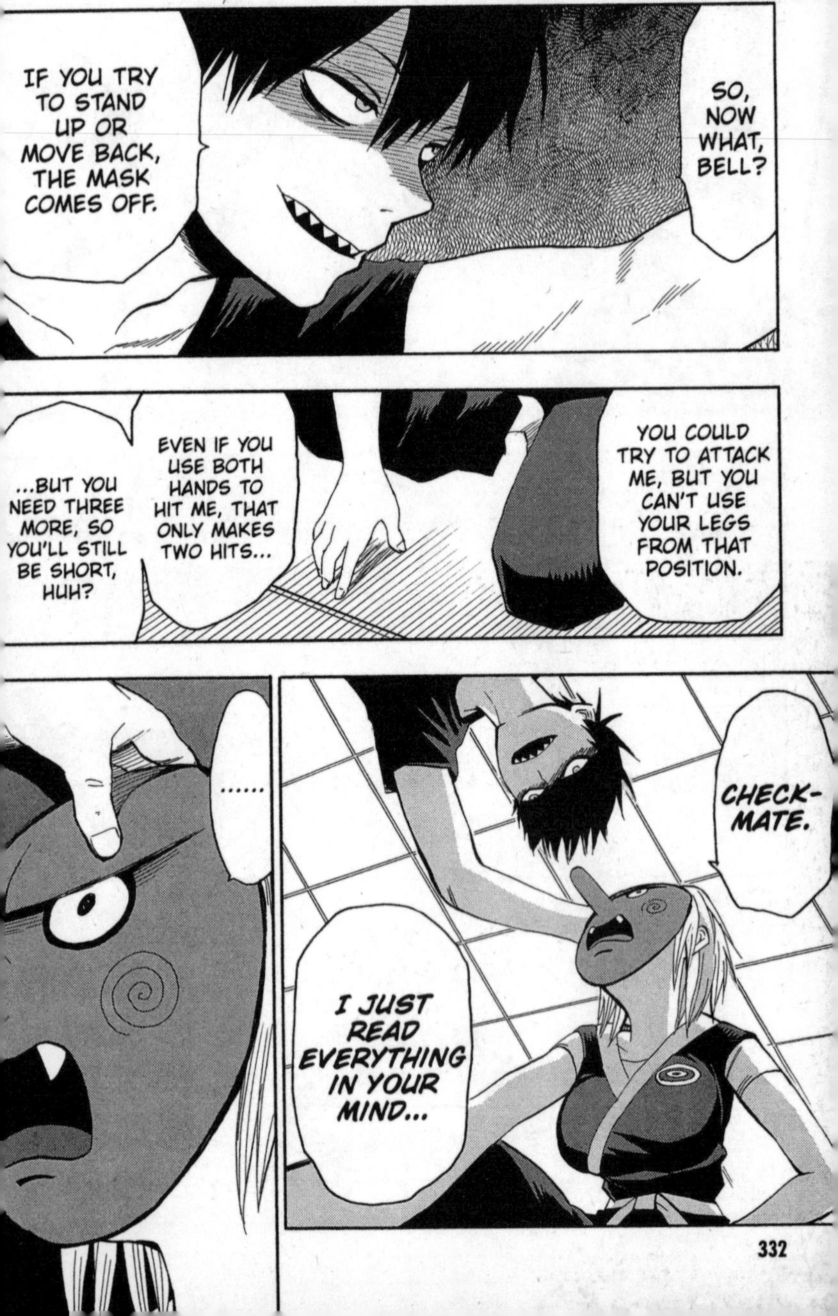
SO, NOW WHAT, BELL?
IF YOU TRY TO STAND UP OR MOVE BACK, THE MASK COMES OFF.
YOU COULD TRY TO ATTACK ME, BUT YOU CAN'T USE YOUR LEGS FROM THAT POSITION.
EVEN IF YOU USE BOTH HANDS TO HIT ME, THAT ONLY MAKES TWO HITS...
...BUT YOU NEED THREE MORE, SO YOU'LL STILL BE SHORT, HUH?
CHECK-MATE.
I JUST READ EVERYTHING IN YOUR MIND...
......

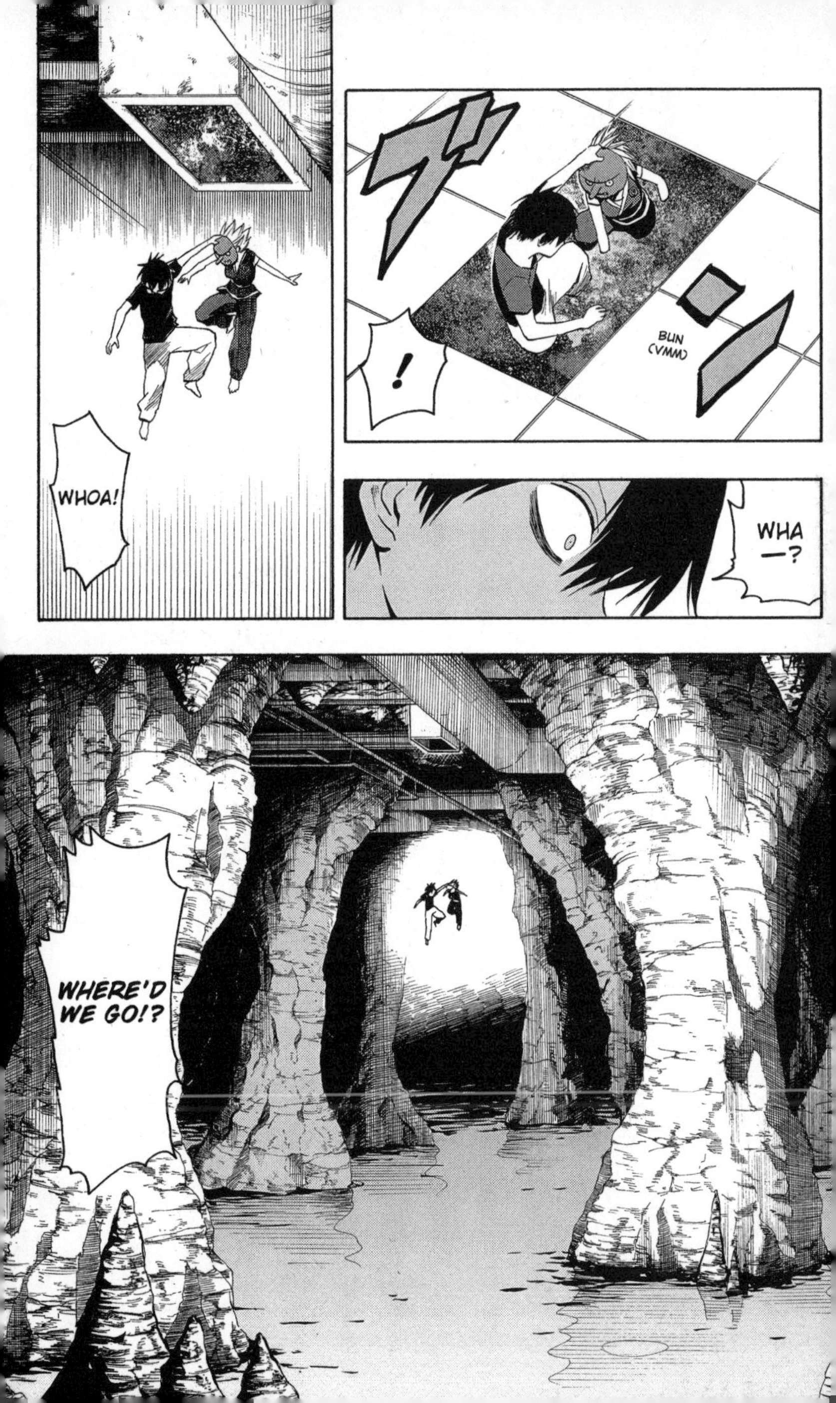

ブン
BUN
(VMM)
!
WHA—?
WHOA!
WHERE'D WE GO!?

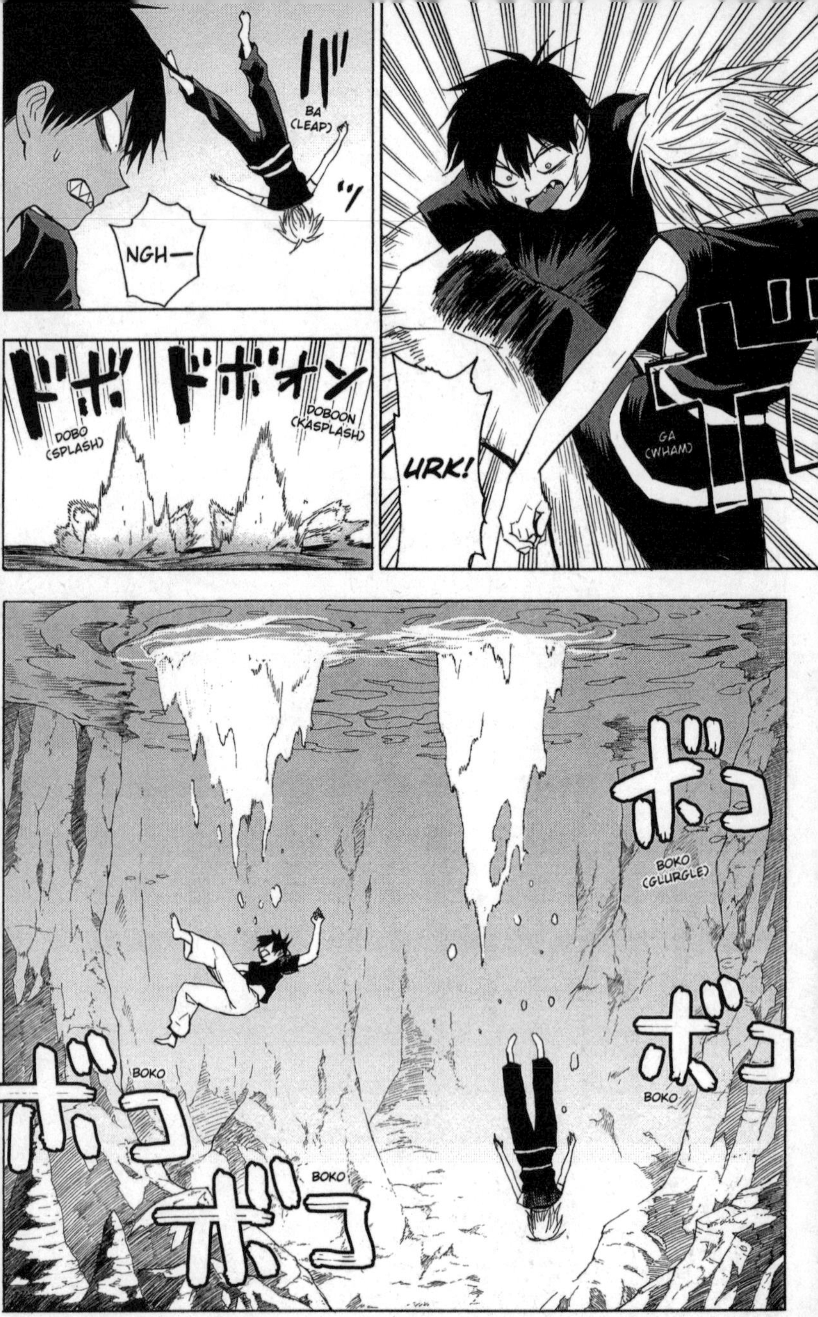

URK!
GA (WHAM)
BA (LEAP)
NGH—
ドボ ドボオン
DOBO (SPLASH)
DOBOON (KASPLASH)
BOKO (GLURGLE)
BOKO
BOKO
BOKO

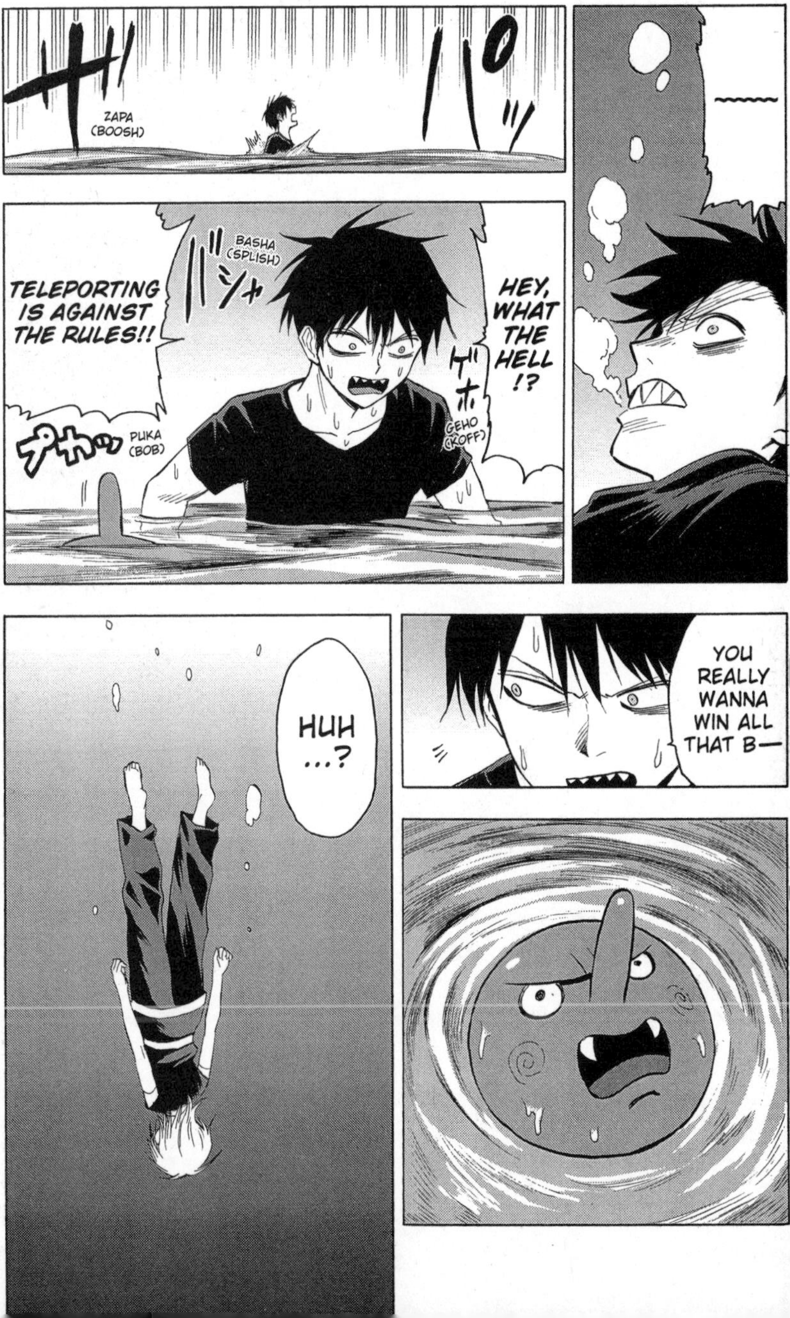
ZAPA (BOOSH)
BASHA (SPLISH)
HEY, WHAT THE HELL !?
GEHO (KOFF)
TELEPORTING IS AGAINST THE RULES!!
PUKA (BOB)
YOU REALLY WANNA WIN ALL THAT B—
HUH ...?

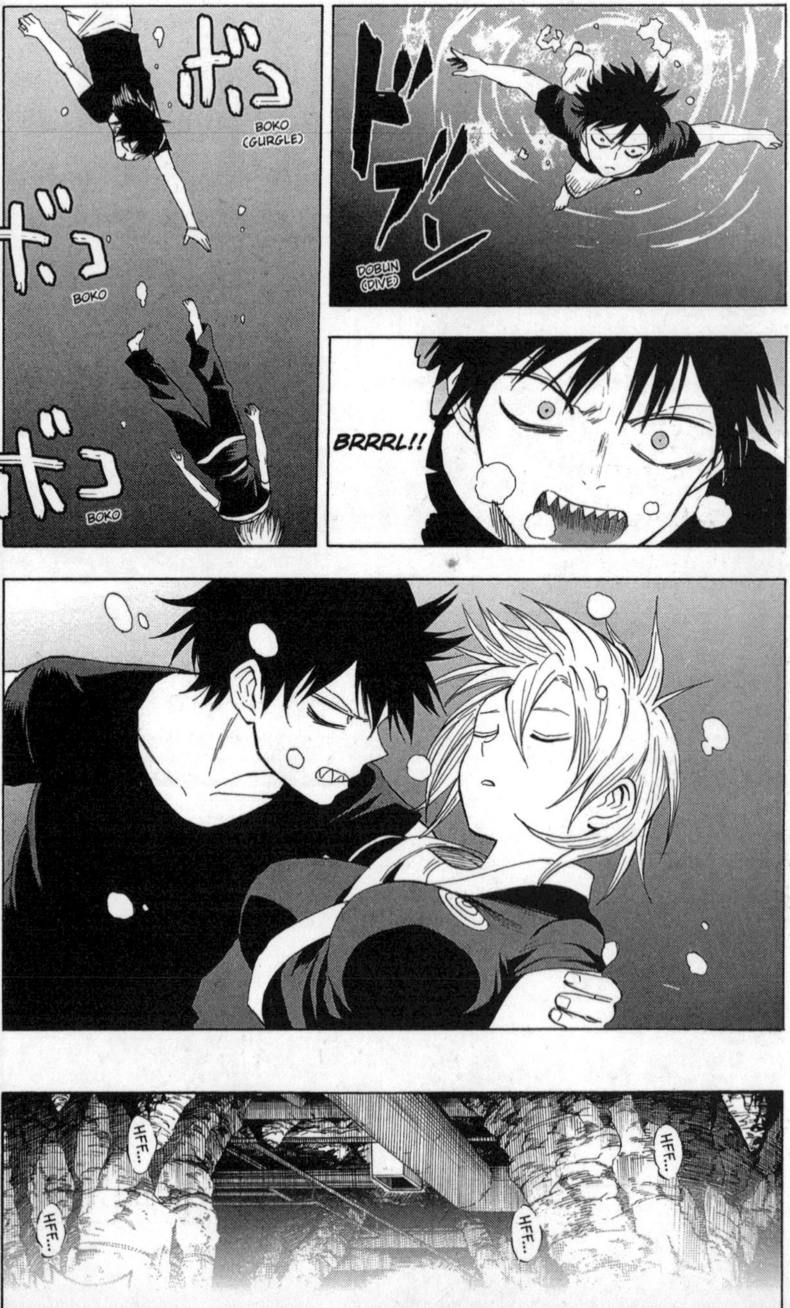
ドブン
DOBUN (DIVE)
BRRRL!!
ぼこ
BOKO (GURGLE)
ぼこ
BOKO
ボコ
BOKO
HFF...
HFF...
HFF...
HFF...

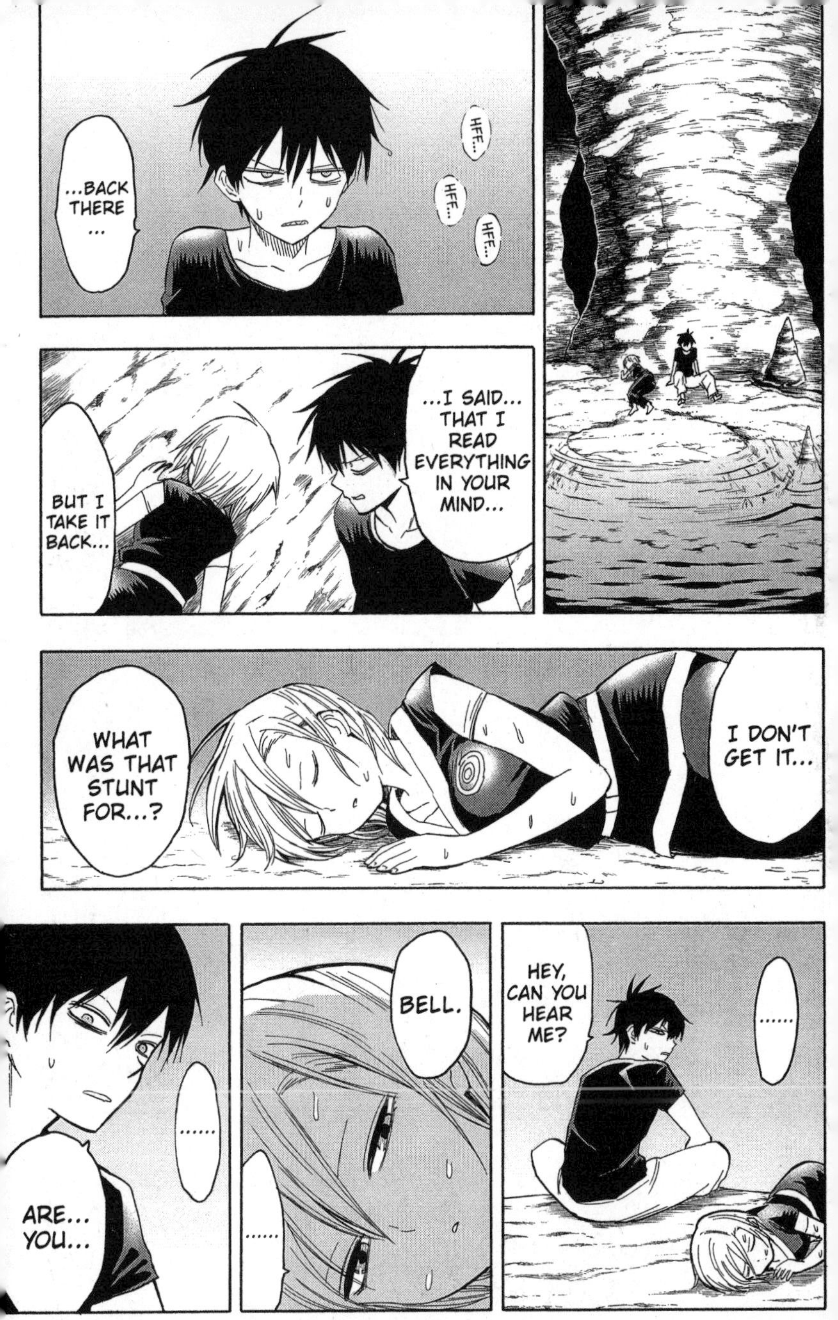
HFF...
HFF...
HFF...
...BACK THERE ...
...I SAID... THAT I READ EVERYTHING IN YOUR MIND...
BUT I TAKE IT BACK...
I DON'T GET IT...
WHAT WAS THAT STUNT FOR...?
......
HEY, CAN YOU HEAR ME?
BELL.
......
......
ARE... YOU...

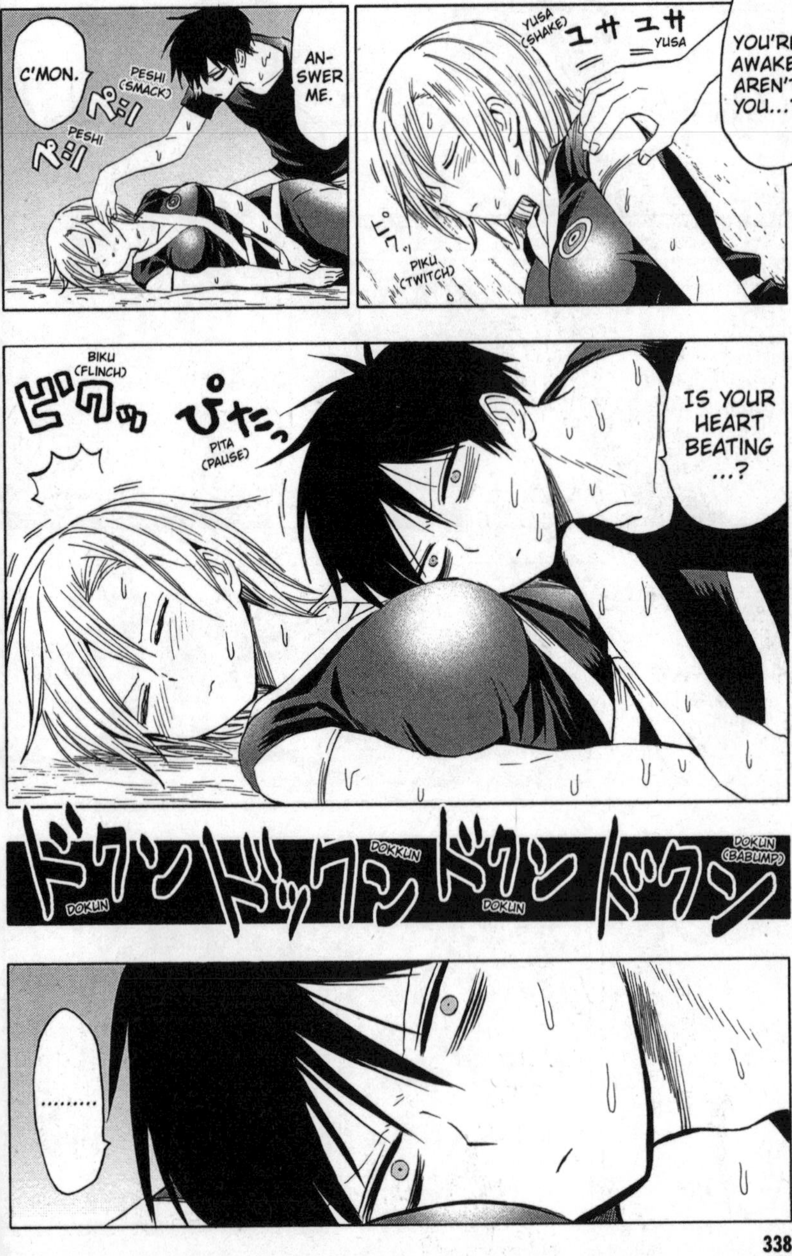
YUSA (SHAKE)
ユサ ユサ
YUSA
YOU'RE AWAKE, AREN'T YOU...?
PIKU (TWITCH)
AN-SWER ME.
C'MON.
PESHI (SMACK)
PESHI
IS YOUR HEART BEATING ...?
PITA (PAUSE)
BIKU (FLINCH)
DOKUN (BABUMP)
DOKUN
DOKKUN
DOKUN
....

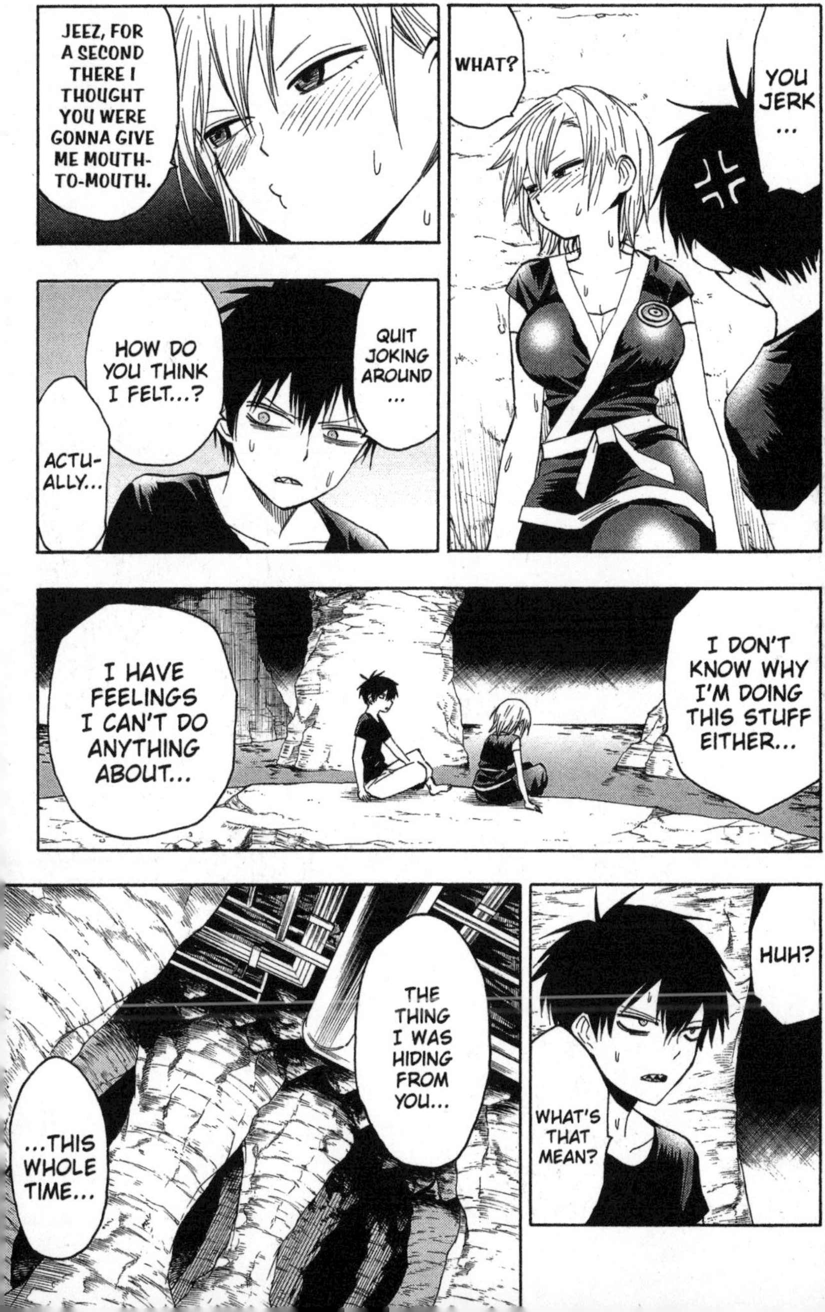
YOU JERK...
WHAT?
JEEZ, FOR A SECOND THERE I THOUGHT YOU WERE GONNA GIVE ME MOUTH-TO-MOUTH.
QUIT JOKING AROUND...
HOW DO YOU THINK I FELT...?
ACTU-ALLY...
I DON'T KNOW WHY I'M DOING THIS STUFF EITHER...
I HAVE FEELINGS I CAN'T DO ANYTHING ABOUT...
HUH?
WHAT'S THAT MEAN?
THE THING I WAS HIDING FROM YOU...
...THIS WHOLE TIME...

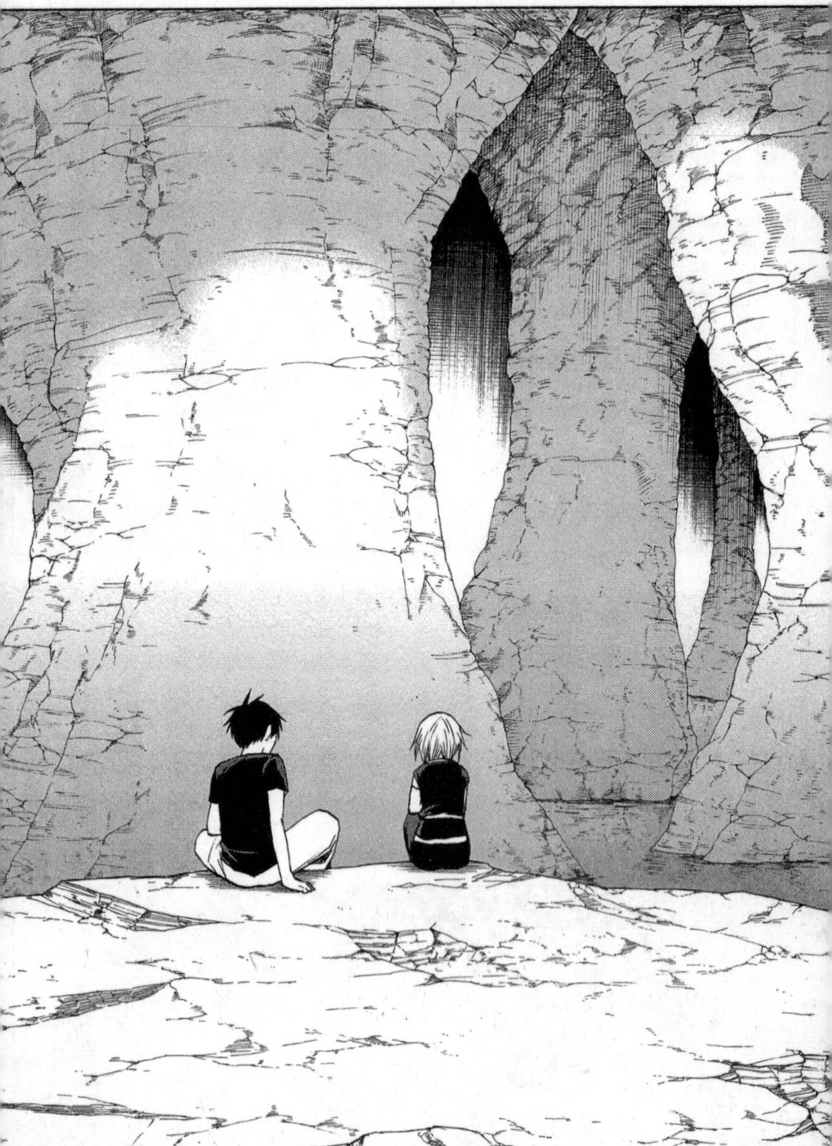

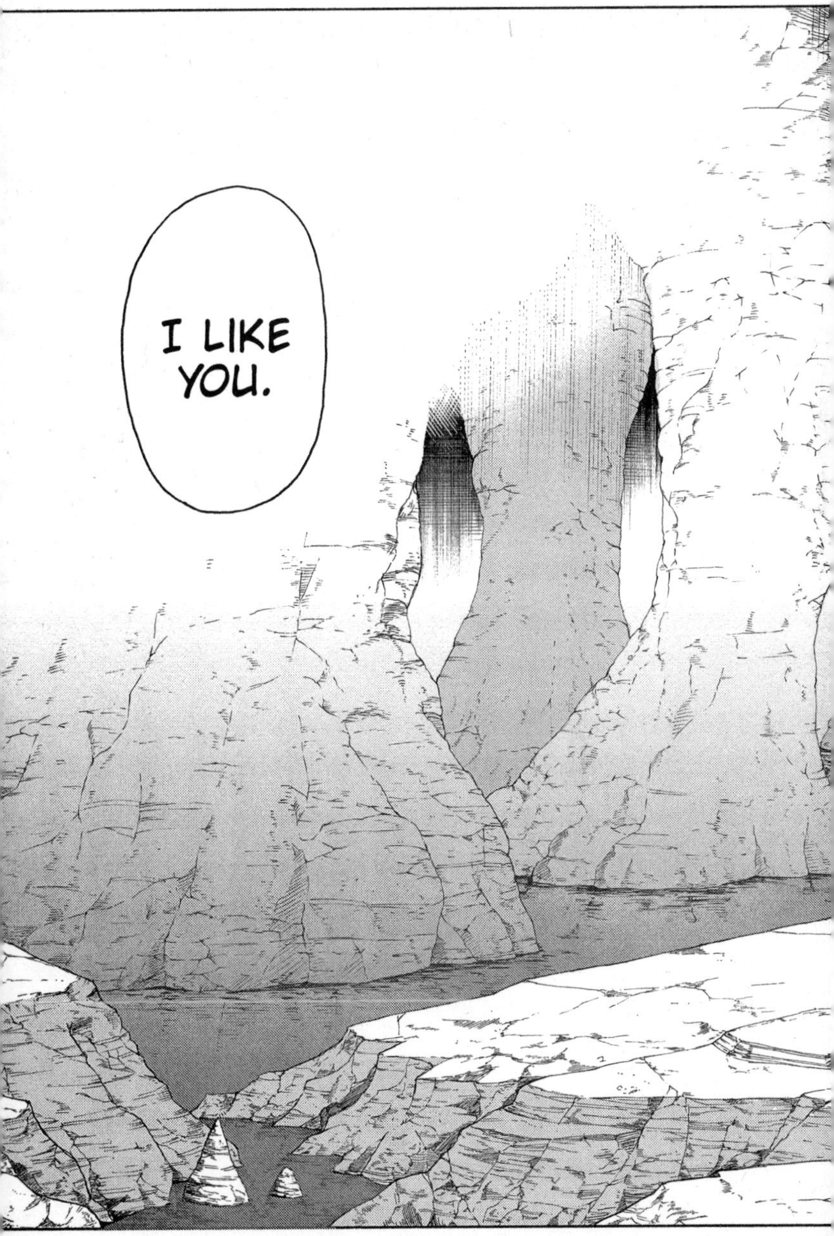
I LIKE YOU.

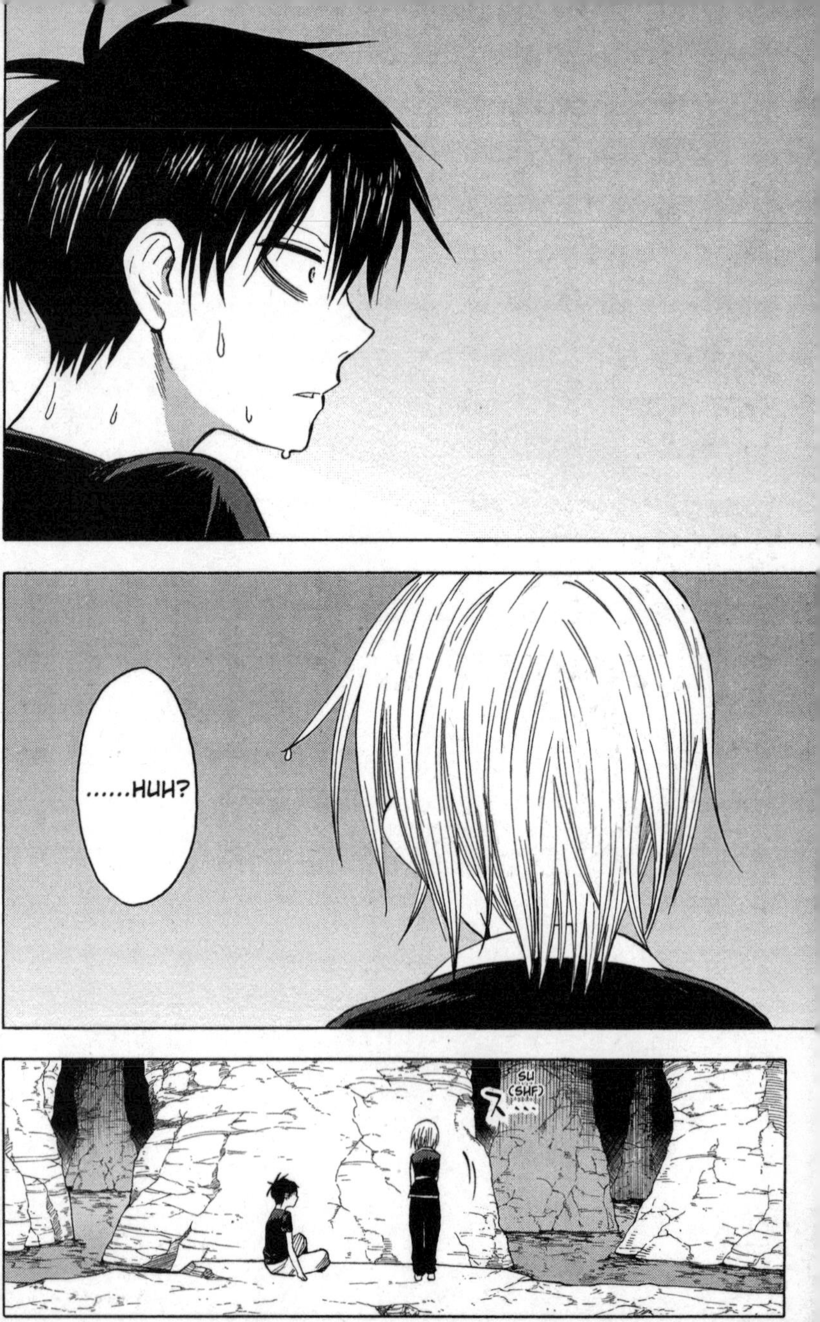
......HUH?
ス...
SU (SHF)

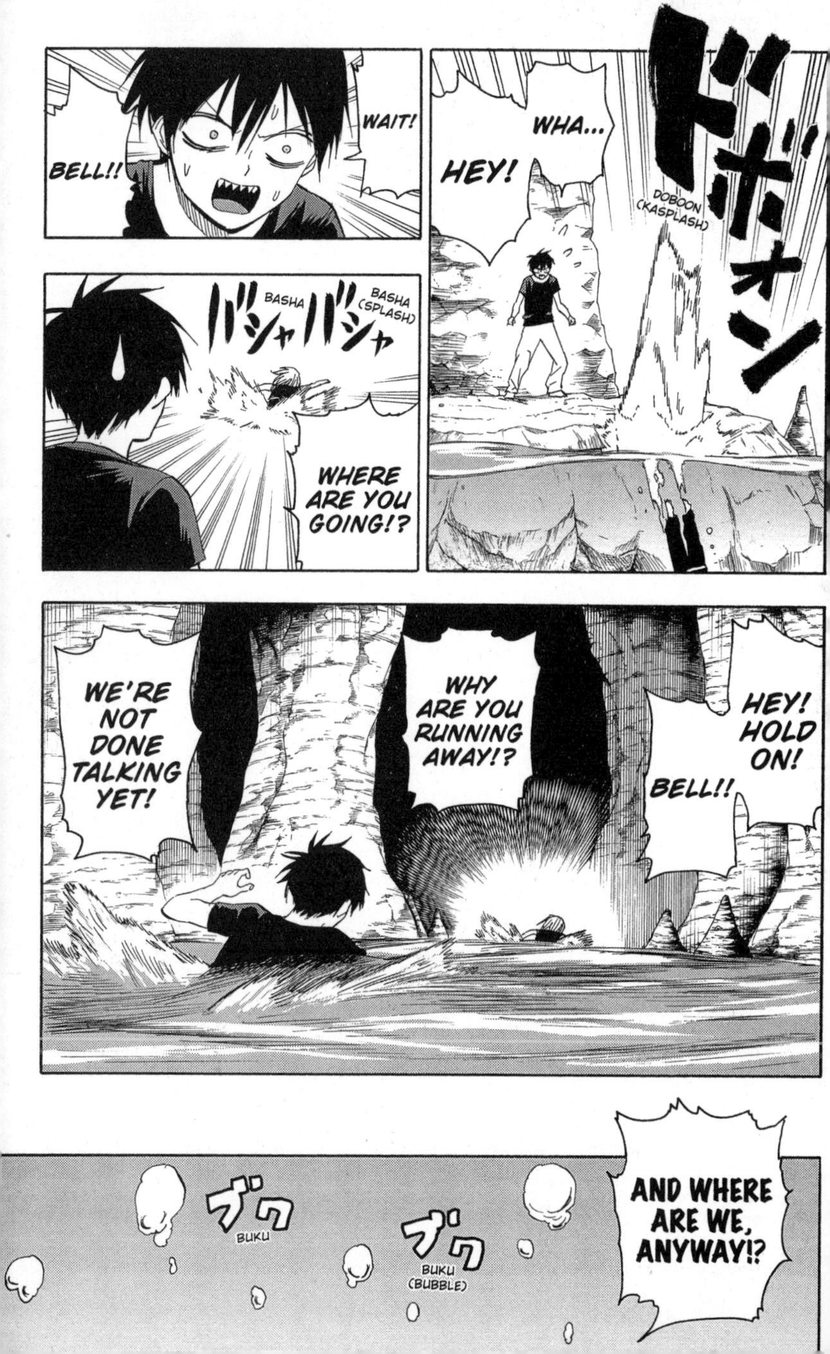
ドボォン
DOBOON (KASPLASH)
WHA...
HEY!
WAIT!
BELL!!
バシャバシャ
BASHA BASHA (SPLASH)
WHERE ARE YOU GOING!?
HEY! HOLD ON!
BELL!!
WHY ARE YOU RUNNING AWAY!?
WE'RE NOT DONE TALKING YET!
AND WHERE ARE WE, ANYWAY!?
ブク
BUKU (BUBBLE)
ブク
BUKU

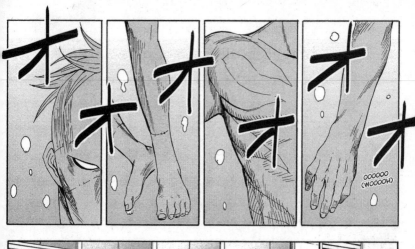

OOOOOO
(WOOOOH)

EACH PART
IS OVER
10,000
ORGAN...

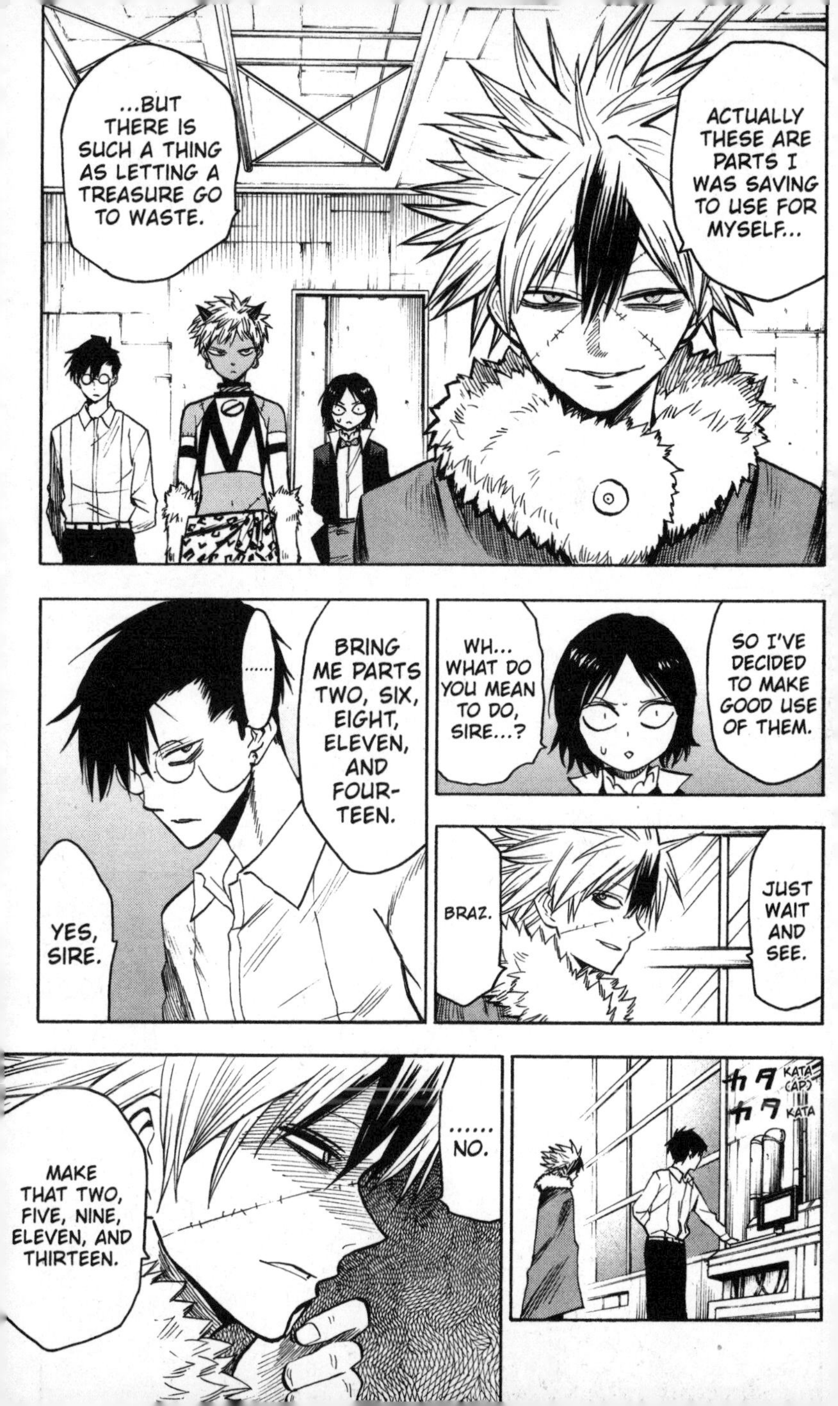
ACTUALLY THESE ARE PARTS I WAS SAVING TO USE FOR MYSELF...
...BUT THERE IS SUCH A THING AS LETTING A TREASURE GO TO WASTE.
SO I'VE DECIDED TO MAKE GOOD USE OF THEM.
WH... WHAT DO YOU MEAN TO DO, SIRE...?
JUST WAIT AND SEE.
BRAZ.
......
BRING ME PARTS TWO, SIX, EIGHT, ELEVEN, AND FOUR-TEEN.
YES, SIRE.
カタ KATA
カタ KATA
...... NO.
MAKE THAT TWO, FIVE, NINE, ELEVEN, AND THIRTEEN.

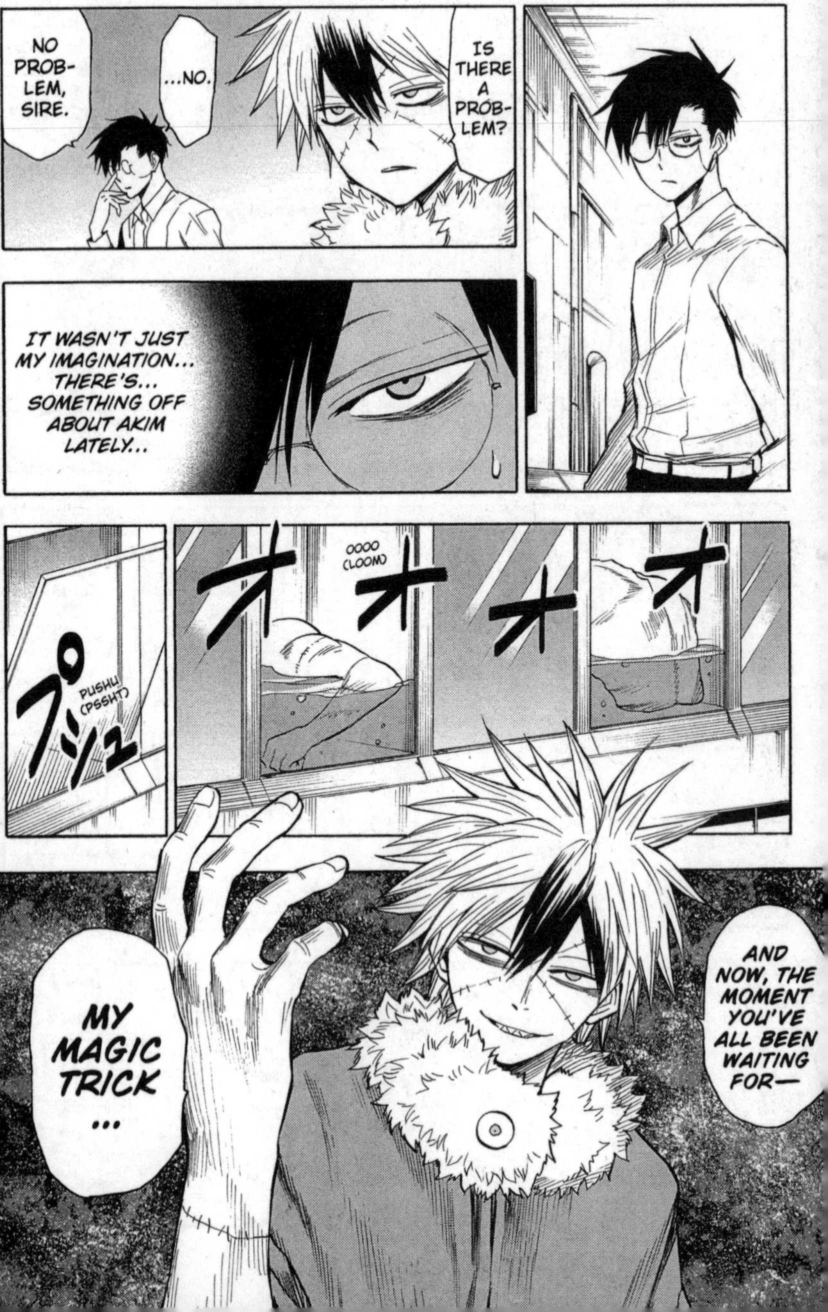
IS THERE A PROB-LEM?
...NO.
NO PROB-LEM, SIRE.
IT WASN'T JUST MY IMAGINATION... THERE'S... SOMETHING OFF ABOUT AKIM LATELY...
オオオ
OOOO (LOOM)
プシュ
PUSHU (PSSHT)
AND NOW, THE MOMENT YOU'VE ALL BEEN WAITING FOR—
MY MAGIC TRICK ...

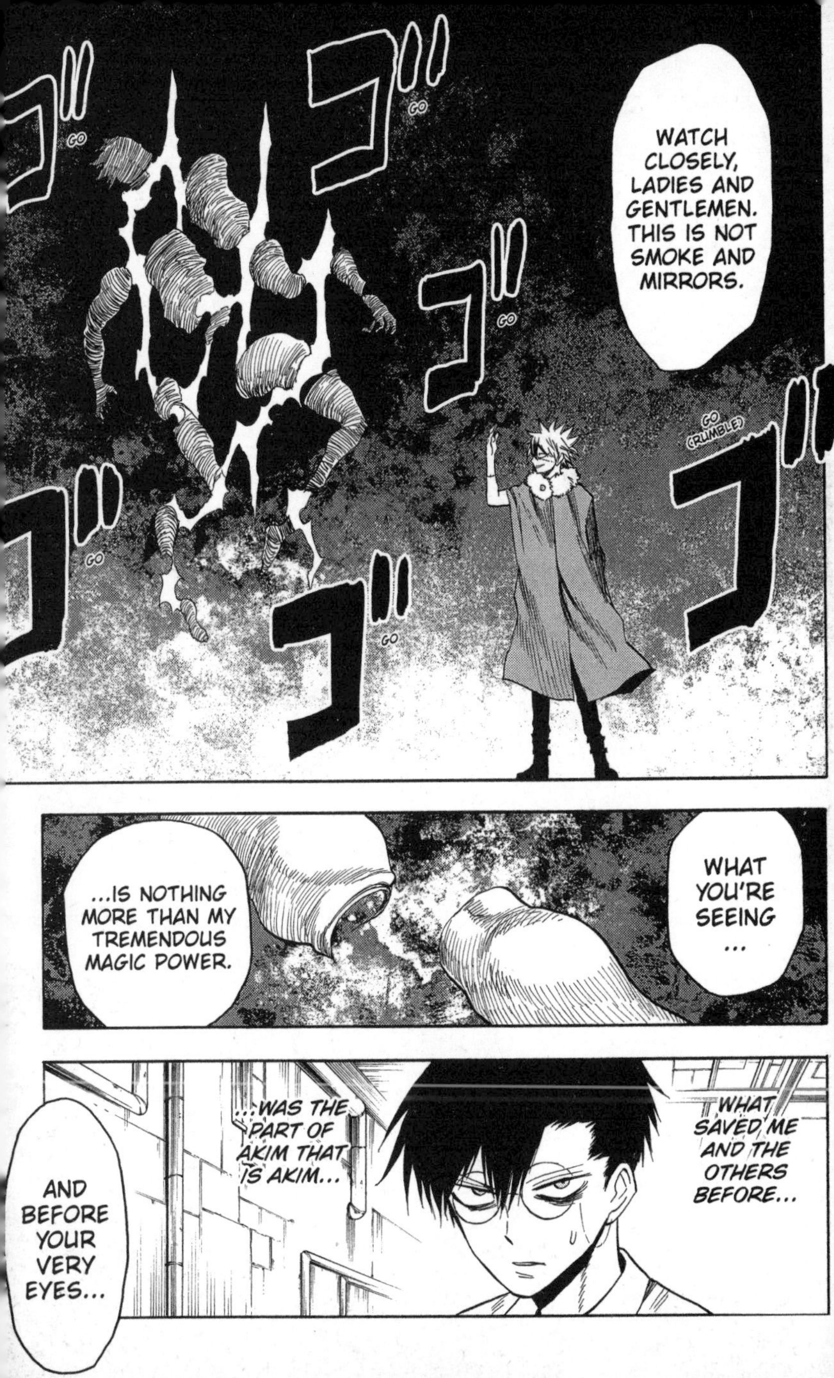
WATCH CLOSELY, LADIES AND GENTLEMEN. THIS IS NOT SMOKE AND MIRRORS.
GO (RUMBLE)
GO
GO
GO
GO
GO
WHAT YOU'RE SEEING...
...IS NOTHING MORE THAN MY TREMENDOUS MAGIC POWER.
WHAT SAVED ME AND THE OTHERS BEFORE...
...WAS THE PART OF AKIM THAT IS AKIM...
AND BEFORE YOUR VERY EYES...

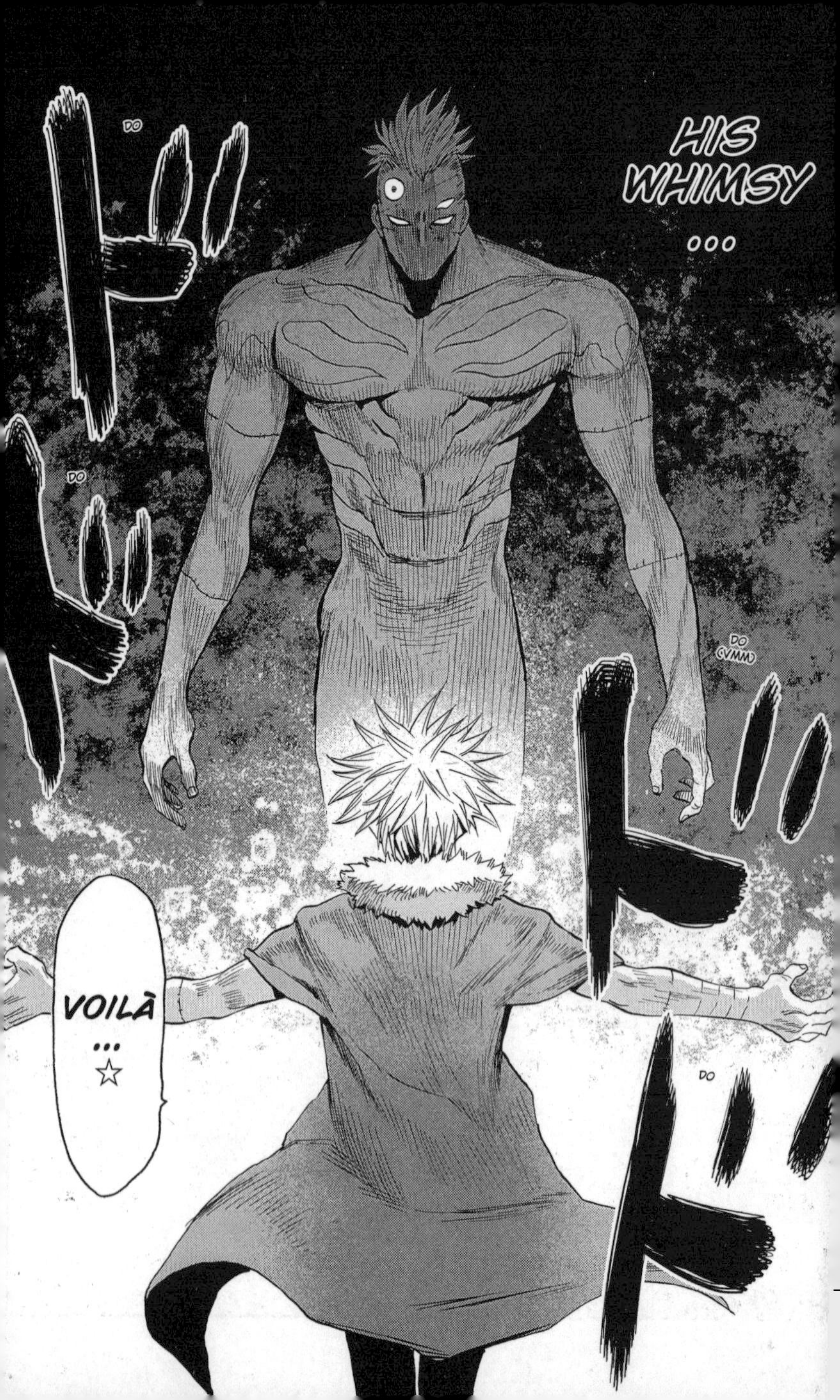
HIS WHIMSY
...
DO
DO
DO
DO (VMM)
VOILÀ ... ☆
DO

...NO LONGER HAS THAT...

THIS AKIM...

AMBER.

THAT'LL BE YOUR NAME.

ズン

ZUN
(THUD)

...HMM, LET'S SEE...
....

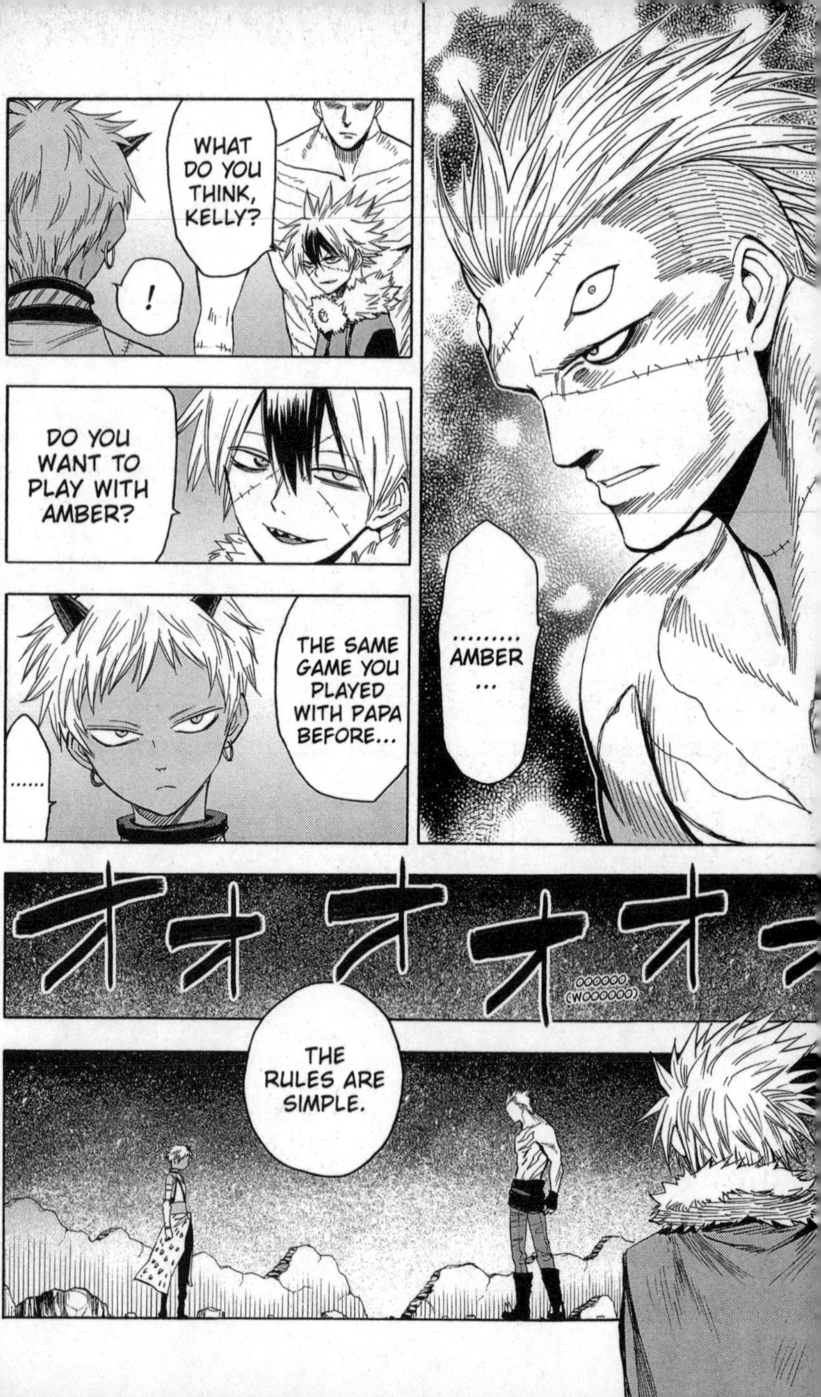
....
AMBER
...
WHAT DO YOU THINK, KELLY?
!
DO YOU WANT TO PLAY WITH AMBER?
THE SAME GAME YOU PLAYED WITH PAPA BEFORE...
......
オオオオオ
OOOOOO
(WOOOOOO)
THE RULES ARE SIMPLE.

TAKE ONE OF YOUR OPPONENT'S PARTS, ANY PART.
THE FIRST ONE TO TAKE SOMETHING WINS...
...UP UNTIL NOW...
...THE ALTER EGOS THAT AKIM MADE WERE FILLED WITH MAGIC FROM "AKIM."
BUT THIS ONE...
UNDER-STOOD.

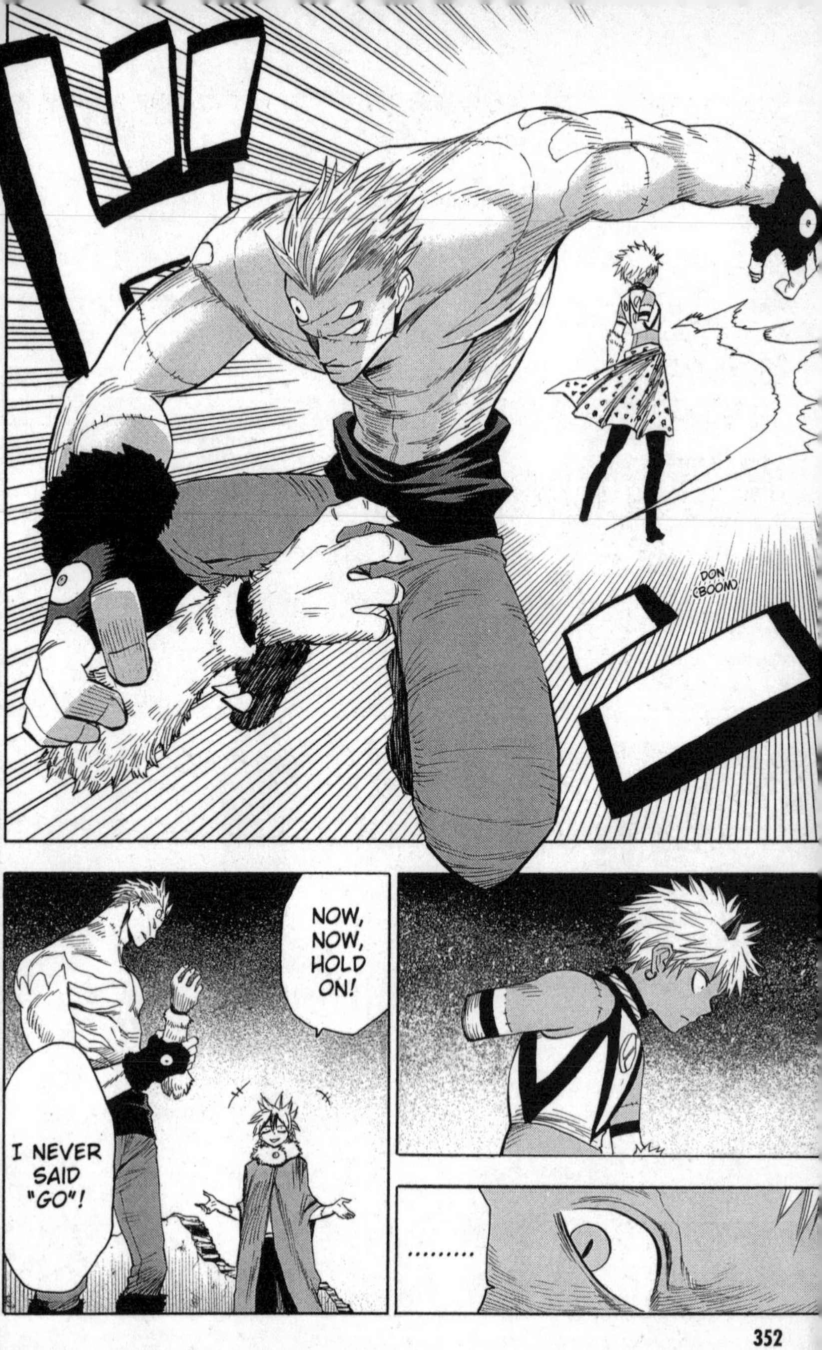
DON (BOOM)
....
NOW, NOW, HOLD ON!
I NEVER SAID "GO"!

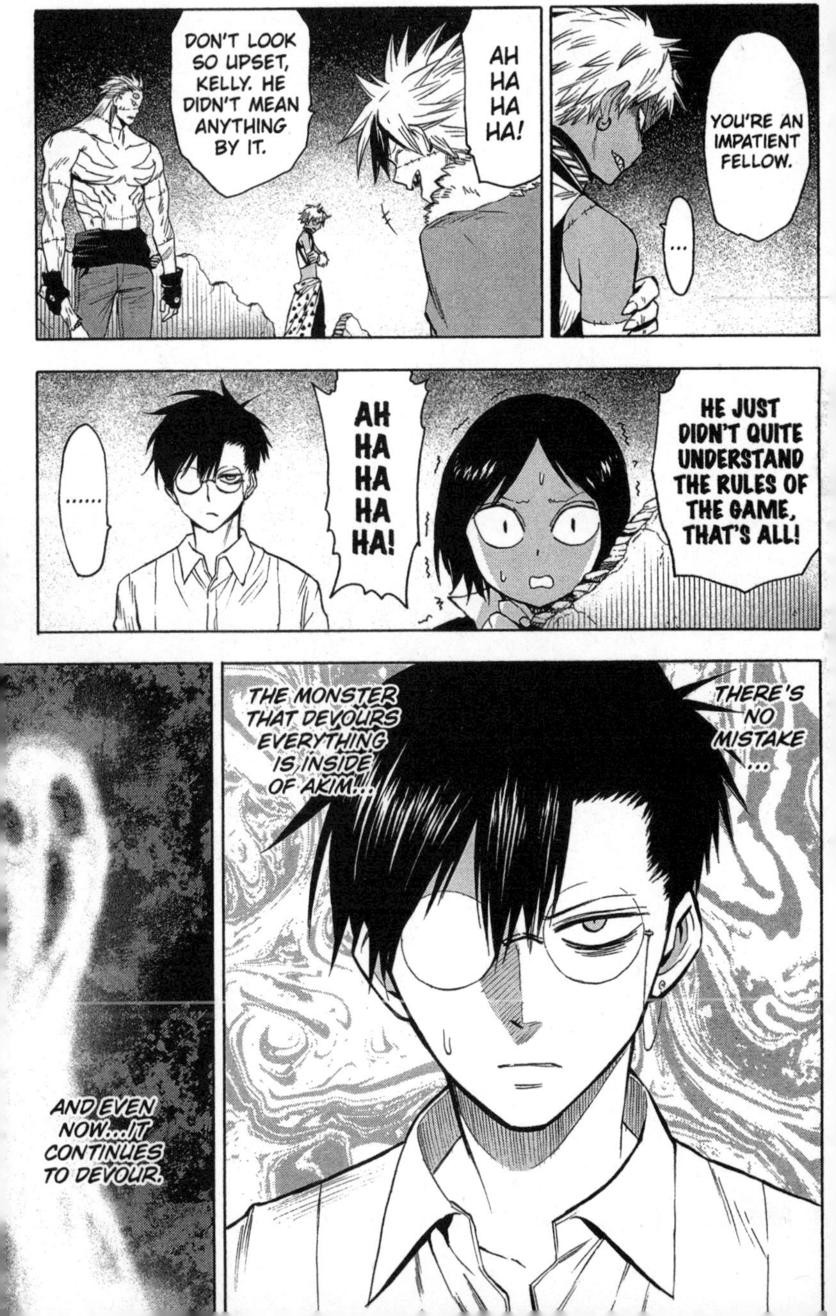
YOU'RE AN IMPATIENT FELLOW.
...
AH HA HA HA!
DON'T LOOK SO UPSET, KELLY. HE DIDN'T MEAN ANYTHING BY IT.
HE JUST DIDN'T QUITE UNDERSTAND THE RULES OF THE GAME, THAT'S ALL!
AH HA HA HA HA HA!
......
THERE'S NO MISTAKE...
THE MONSTER THAT DEVOURS EVERYTHING IS INSIDE OF AKIM...
AND EVEN NOW...IT CONTINUES TO DEVOUR.

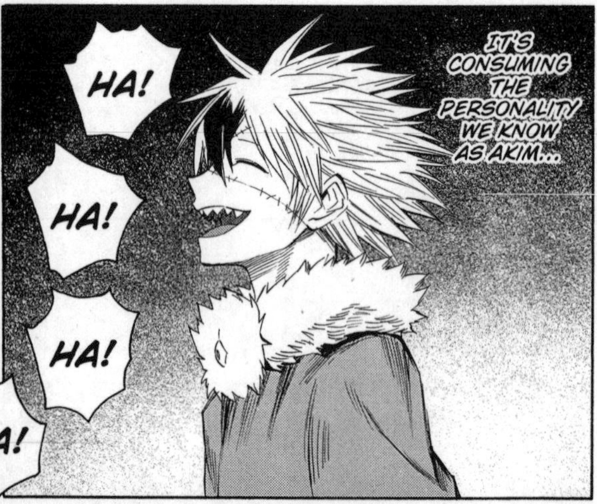
IT'S CONSUMING THE PERSONALITY WE KNOW AS AKIM...
HA!
HA!
HA!
HA!

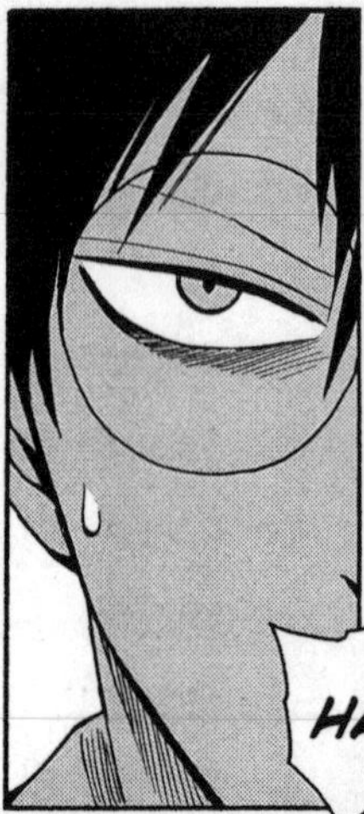

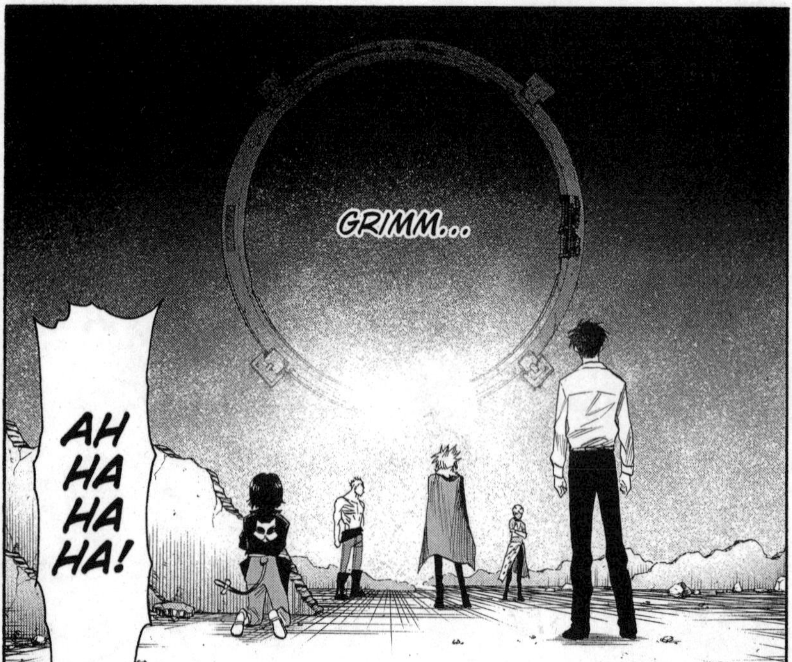
GRIMM...
AH HA HA HA!

♠ To Be Continued ♠

To Be

Continued

BLOOD LAD

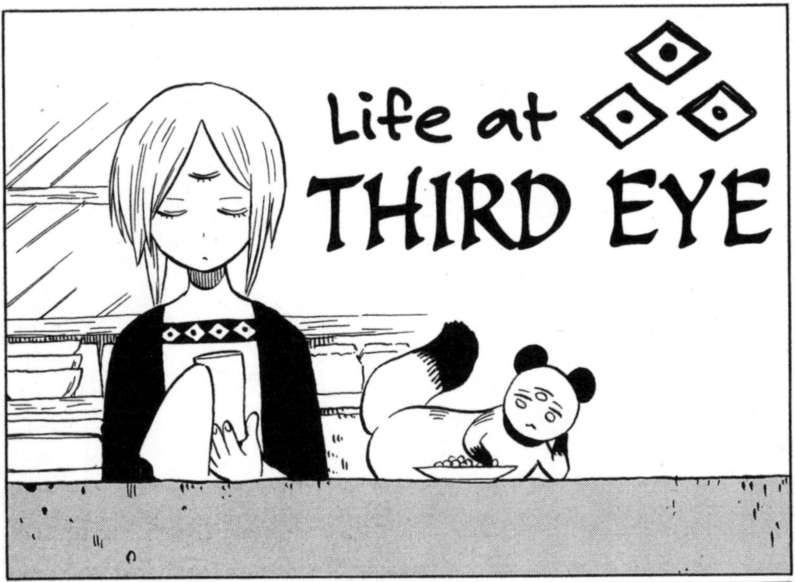
Life at
THIRD EYE

CHILLIN'

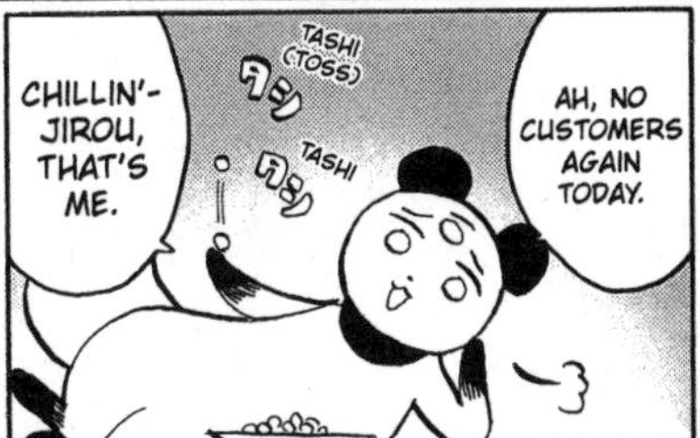
AH, NO CUSTOMERS AGAIN TODAY.
TASHI (TOSS)
タシ
TASHI
タシ
CHILLIN'-JIROU, THAT'S ME.

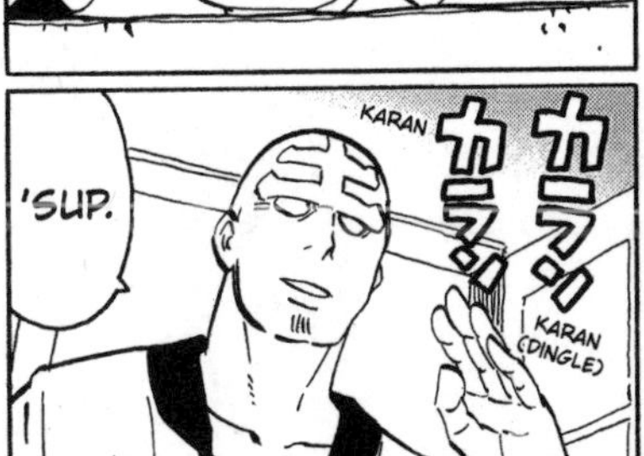
カラッ
KARAN
カラッ
KARAN (DINGLE)
'SUP.

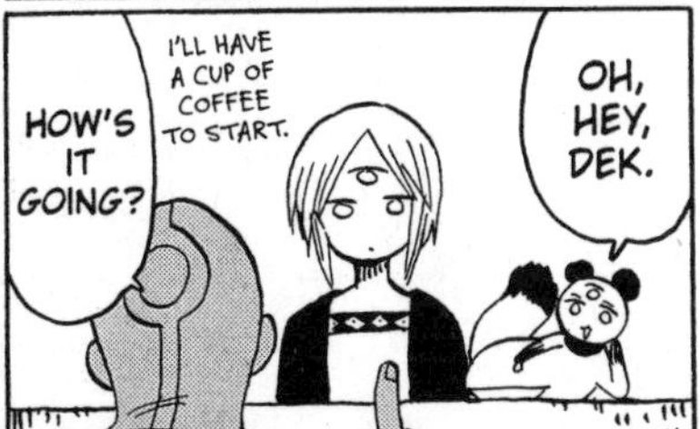
OH, HEY, DEK.
I'LL HAVE A CUP OF COFFEE TO START.
HOW'S IT GOING?

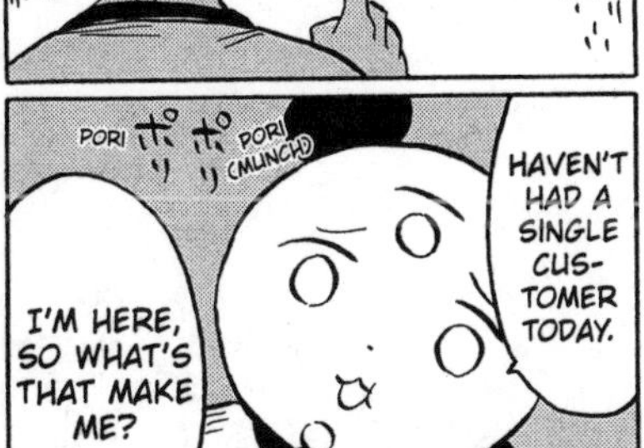
PORI (MUNCH)
ポリ
ポリ
PORI
HAVEN'T HAD A SINGLE CUS-TOMER TODAY.
I'M HERE, SO WHAT'S THAT MAKE ME?

BEDSIDE

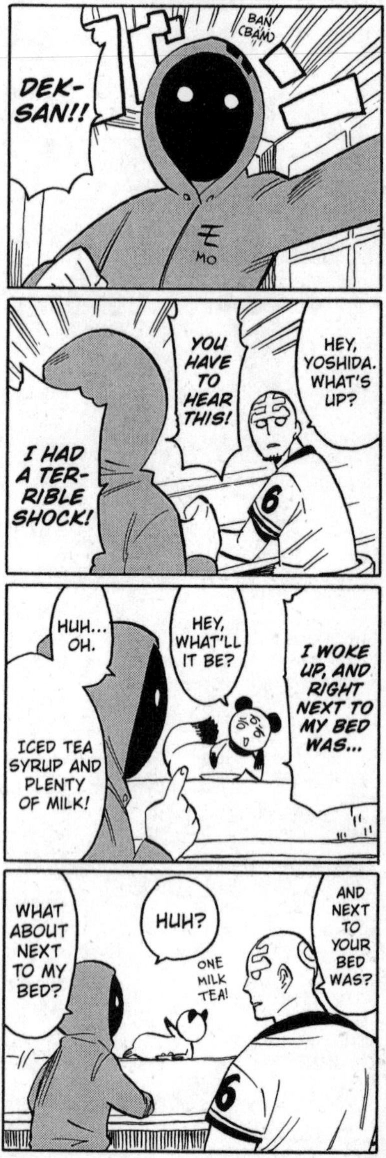
BAN (BAM)
DEK-SAN!!
HEY, YOSHIDA. WHAT'S UP?
YOU HAVE TO HEAR THIS!
I HAD A TER-RIBLE SHOCK!
I WOKE UP, AND RIGHT NEXT TO MY BED WAS...
HEY, WHAT'LL IT BE?
HUH... OH.
ICED TEA SYRUP AND PLENTY OF MILK!
AND NEXT TO YOUR BED WAS?
HUH?
ONE MILK TEA!
WHAT ABOUT NEXT TO MY BED?

ARM

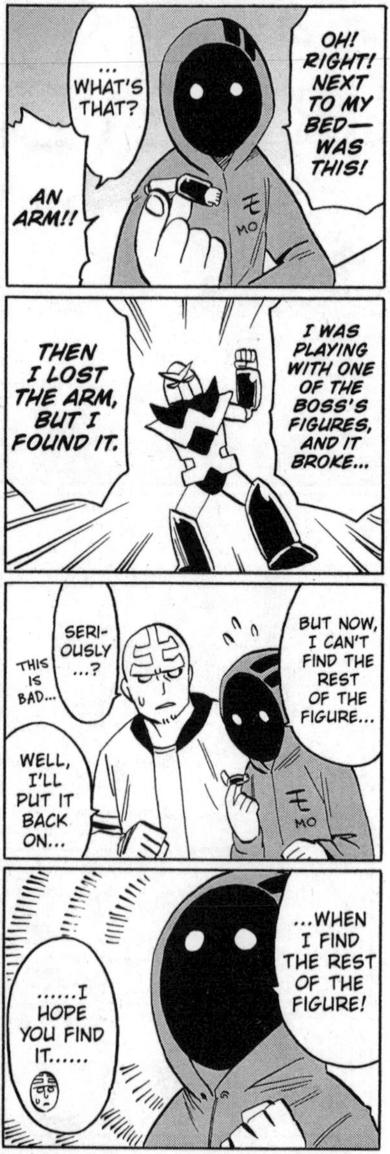
OH! RIGHT! NEXT TO MY BED— WAS THIS!
... WHAT'S THAT?
AN ARM!!
I WAS PLAYING WITH ONE OF THE BOSS'S FIGURES, AND IT BROKE...
THEN I LOST THE ARM, BUT I FOUND IT.
BUT NOW, I CAN'T FIND THE REST OF THE FIGURE...
SERI-OUSLY ...?
THIS IS BAD...
WELL, I'LL PUT IT BACK ON...
...WHEN I FIND THE REST OF THE FIGURE!
......I HOPE YOU FIND IT......

HE FORGOT

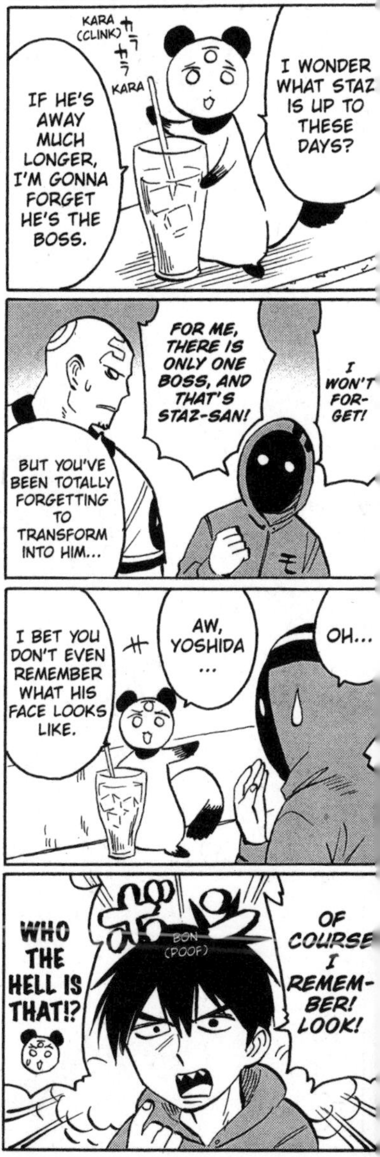
I WONDER WHAT STAZ IS UP TO THESE DAYS?
KARA (CLINK)
KARA
IF HE'S AWAY MUCH LONGER, I'M GONNA FORGET HE'S THE BOSS.
I WON'T FOR-GET!
FOR ME, THERE IS ONLY ONE BOSS, AND THAT'S STAZ-SAN!
BUT YOU'VE BEEN TOTALLY FORGETTING TO TRANSFORM INTO HIM...
OH...
AW, YOSHIDA ...
I BET YOU DON'T EVEN REMEMBER WHAT HIS FACE LOOKS LIKE.
OF COURSE I REMEM-BER! LOOK!
BON (POOF)
WHO THE HELL IS THAT!?

HIDDEN TALENT

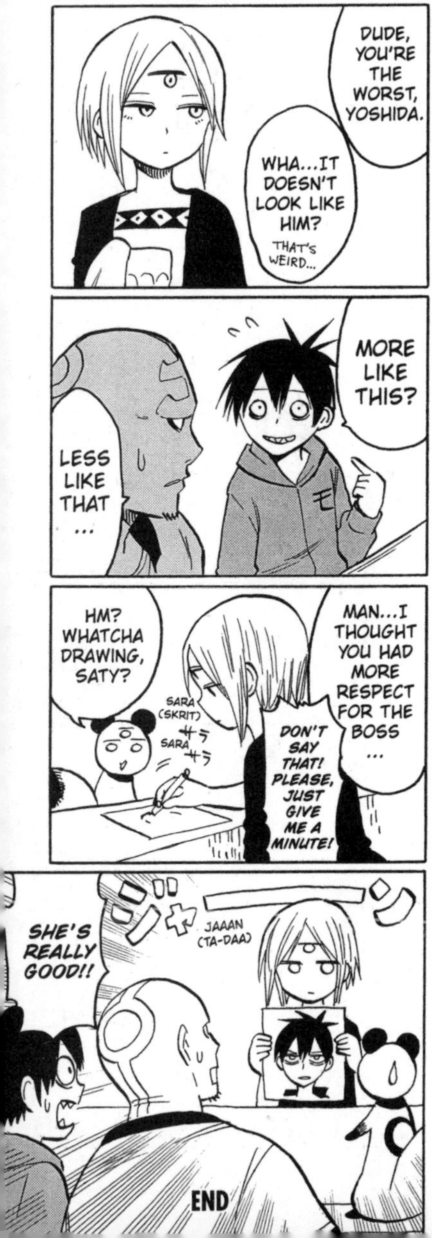
DUDE, YOU'RE THE WORST, YOSHIDA.
WHA...IT DOESN'T LOOK LIKE HIM?
THAT'S WEIRD...
MORE LIKE THIS?
LESS LIKE THAT ...
MAN...I THOUGHT YOU HAD MORE RESPECT FOR THE BOSS ...
DON'T SAY THAT! PLEASE, JUST GIVE ME A MINUTE!
HM? WHATCHA DRAWING, SATY?
SARA (SKRIT)
SARA
JAAAN (TA-DAA)
SHE'S REALLY GOOD!!
END

BLOOD LAD 12

These images appeared under the jacket of the original edition of *Blood Lad*!

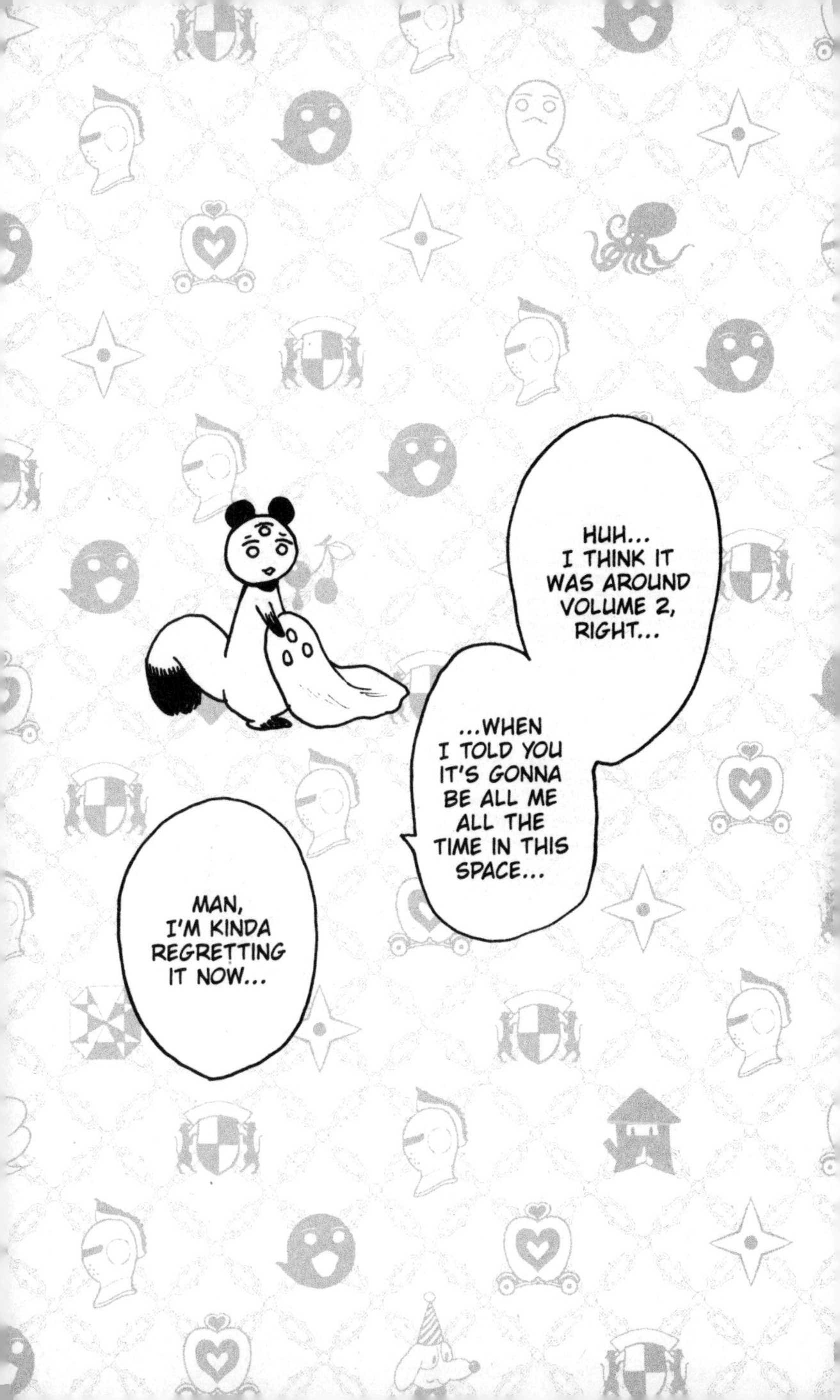
HUH... I THINK IT WAS AROUND VOLUME 2, RIGHT...
...WHEN I TOLD YOU IT'S GONNA BE ALL ME ALL THE TIME IN THIS SPACE...
MAN, I'M KINDA REGRETTING IT NOW...

BLOOD LAD ❻

YUUKI KODAMA

Translation: Melissa Tanaka

Lettering: Alexis Eckerman

BLOOD LAD Volumes 11 and 12 © Yuuki KODAMA 2014. Edited by KADOKAWA SHOTEN. First published in Japan in 2014 by KADOKAWA CORPORATION, Tokyo. English translation rights arranged with KADOKAWA CORPORATION, Tokyo, through TUTTLE-MORI AGENCY, INC., Tokyo.

Translation © 2015 by Hachette Book Group, Inc.

Yen Press
Hachette Book Group
1290 Avenue of the Americas
New York, NY 10104

www.HachetteBookGroup.com
www.YenPress.com

Yen Press is an imprint of Hachette Book Group, Inc.
The Yen Press name and logo are trademarks of Hachette Book Group, Inc.

The publisher is not responsible for websites (or their content) that are not owned by the publisher.

First Yen Press Edition: May 2015

ISBN: 978-0-316-34206-3

10 9 8 7 6 5 4 3 2 1

BVG

Printed in the United States of America